UNDERSTANDING AND USING ENGLISH

FIFTH EDITION

*Newman P. Birk
and Genevieve B. Birk*

The Odyssey Press
A Division of
The Bobbs-Merrill Company, Inc.
Indianapolis and New York

ACKNOWLEDGMENTS

The authors are grateful to the following writers, publishers, and literary agents for permission to use the materials listed below.

Appleton-Century-Crofts: passage from *Why Men Fight* by Bertrand Russell.

Edward Arnold, Ltd.: passages from *The Human Situation* by W. Macneile Dixon.

The Atlantic Monthly Company: "The Business of a Biographer" by Catherine Drinker Bowen.

Beacon Press: passage from *Notes of a Native Son* by James Baldwin.

Brandt & Brandt: passage from *Nineteen Eighty-Four* by George Orwell.

Columbia University Press: "Skunk" from *The Columbia Encyclopedia*, Second Edition.

Coward-McCann: passages from "Memphitis, the Skunk" in *Down to Earth* by Alan Devoe, and *Lord of the Flies* by William Golding.

Thomas Y. Crowell Company: "Epic" from *The Reader's Encyclopedia*, edited by William Rose Benét.

Doubleday & Company: passages from "Little White Girl" in *The Southern Album* by Sara Haardt, and *The Theatre of the Absurd* by Martin Esslin.

E. P. Dutton: passage from *Clea* by Lawrence Durrell.

Henry Pratt Fairchild: passage from *Economics for the Millions*.

Funk & Wagnalls Company: definition of *finish* from the *Standard College Dictionary*, Text Edition.

Harcourt, Brace and Company: passages from *Orlando* by Virginia Woolf, *The Autobiography of Lincoln Steffens*, *Boston Adventure* by Jean Stafford, *The Collected Essays of George Orwell*, *Microbe Hunters* by Paul de Kruif, *Idle Men* by Stuart Chase, *Language in Action* by S. I. Hayakawa, *Sartoris* by William Faulkner, *All the King's Men* by Robert Penn Warren, and "Noon Wine" in *Pale Horse, Pale Rider* by Katherine Anne Porter.

Harper & Brothers: passages from *The Mind in the Making* by James Harvey Robinson, *Devils, Drugs, and Doctors* by Howard W. Haggard, *Only Yesterday* by Frederick L. Allen, *The Second Tree from the Corner* by E. B. White, *Man in the Modern World* by Julian Huxley, and *Call to Greatness* by Adlai Stevenson.

Harper and Row: passage from *Profiles in Courage* by John F. Kennedy, and excerpt from p. 31 in *Kennedy* by Theodore C. Sorensen. Copyright © 1965 by Theodore C. Sorensen.

Harvard University Press: passage from *The Uses of the University* by Clark Kerr.

Granville Hicks: passage from *I Like America*.

Henry Holt and Company: passages from *Proposed Roads to Freedom* by Bertrand Russell, and *Psychology* by William James.

Holt, Rinehart and Winston: passage from *The Sane Society* by Erich Fromm.

Houghton Mifflin Company: passages from *Kit Carson* by Stanley Vestal, *Looking Backward* by Edward Bellamy, *Patterns of Culture* by Ruth Benedict, *Mein Kampf* by Adolf Hitler (trans. Ralph Manheim), *Silent Spring* by Rachel Carson, and *The Politics of Hope* by Arthur M. Schlesinger, Jr.

Alfred A. Knopf, Inc.: passages from "Marriage à la Mode" in *The Garden Party* by Katherine Mansfield, "A Cup of Tea" and "Widowed" in *The Short Stories of Katherine Mansfield, Lady Chatterley's Lover* by D. H. Lawrence, *Portrait of Jennie* by Robert Nathan, and *Buddenbrooks* by Thomas Mann.

J. B. Lippincott Company: passage from *Thunder on the Left* by Christopher Morley.

Little, Brown & Company: passages from *Teacher in America* by Jacques Barzun, and *Ship of Fools* by Katherine Anne Porter.

Andrew Nelson Lytle: passage from "Mister McGregor."

Elsie McKeogh: passage from "Prelude to Reunion" by Oliver LaFarge.

The Macmillan Company: passages from *The Renaissance* by Walter Pater, and *Public Opinion* by Walter Lippmann.

The Nation: passage from "The Riddles of Franklin Roosevelt" by Raymond Swing.

National Council of Teachers of English: "What If an Educator Had Written 'The Lord's Prayer'?" by Thomas R. Dodge in *English Journal,* January, 1971. Copyright © 1971 by the National Council of Teachers of English. Reprinted by permission of the publisher and Thomas R. Dodge.

W. W. Norton & Company: passages from *Mysticism and Logic* by Bertrand Russell and *The Mature Mind* by H. A. Overstreet.

Harold Ober Associates: passage from "The Bear" by William Faulkner.

Oxford University Press: passages from *The Sea Around Us* by Rachel L. Carson, *Dictionary of Modern English Usage* by H. W. Fowler, and *Uses of the Past* by Herbert J. Muller.

Thomas Clark Pollock: "Spelling Report" by Thomas Clark Pollock in *College English,* November, 1954.

G. P. Putnam's Sons: passage from *The Art of Writing* by Sir Arthur Quiller-Couch.

Random House: passages from "Speech of Acceptance" in *Major Campaign Speeches* and from *Putting First Things First* by Adlai Stevenson, *Intruder in the Dust* and *The Sound and the Fury* by William Faulkner.

The Reader's Digest: passage from "Slow Motion Picture of High-Speed Death" by E. A. Walz III and C. B. Wall in *The Reader's Digest,* February, 1957, copyright, 1957, by The Reader's Digest Association, Inc., reprinted with permission.

Susan Lawsine Ries: "Racing for the Moon: America's Project Apollo."

Rinehart & Company: passages from *The Naked and the Dead* by Norman Mailer and *Selected Works of Stephen Vincent Benét.*

St. Martin's Press: passages from *The Human Situation* by Macneile Dixon.

Saturday Review: passage from "Nixon after the Honeymoon" by Henry Brandon. Copyright 1970 Saturday Review, Inc.

Charles Scribner's Sons: passages from "Pulvis et Umbra," "Aes Triplex" in *Virginibus Puerisque,* "Requiem," and *Essays on Literature,* all by Robert Louis Stevenson; passages from "In Another Country" in *Men without Women,* "Snows of Kilimanjaro" and "The Three-Day Blow" in *Short Stories of Ernest Hemingway,* and *Farewell to Arms,* all by

Ernest Hemingway; passages from *The Enjoyment of Poetry* by Max Eastman, *Of Time and the River* by Thomas Wolfe, and *The Fortunes of Oliver Horn* by F. H. Smith.

Simon and Schuster: passage from *Peace of Mind* by Joshua Loth Liebman.

James Thurber: passages from *Let Your Mind Alone!* and *Ladies' and Gentlemen's Guide to Modern English Usage.*

Time: passage from "Let's Wait" by the Editors of *Time.*

Vanguard Press: passage from *The Victim* by Saul Bellow.

The Viking Press: passages from "Arrangement in Black and White" by Dorothy Parker in *The Portable Dorothy Parker;* "The Harness" and "The Chrysanthemums" in *The Long Valley, The Grapes of Wrath,* and *Cannery Row,* all by John Steinbeck; "Clay" and "The Dead" in *Dubliners* and *A Portrait of the Artist as a Young Man* by James Joyce; *Candle in the Dark* by Irwin Edman, "The Philosopher" in *Winesburg, Ohio* by Sherwood Anderson.

Carl B. Wall: passage from "Slow Motion Picture of High-Speed Death" by E. A. Walz III and C. B. Wall in *The Reader's Digest,* February, 1957.

The World Publishing Company: definition of *base* in *Webster's New World Dictionary,* College Edition, copyright, 1964, by The World Publishing Company.

Yale University Press: passages from *Modern Democracy* and *New Liberties for Old* by Carl Becker and *On Understanding Science* by James B. Conant.

TO THE TEACHER

A basic purpose of *Understanding and Using English* has always been to make the study of English freshly interesting and significant to the college student. In keeping with this purpose, many of the changes in the fifth edition, ranging from comments on tone and usage to new illustrative material, are designed to recognize change in society and to make the book contemporary. Unchanged, however, are the principle of giving the student numerous examples to help him experience directly the effects of language and the qualities of style, and the principle of indicating that although usage is not constant, there is still such a thing as preferred or appropriate usage.

Instructors familiar with the fourth edition of *Understanding and Using English* will see that the development of Part One, *Using English Effectively*, is in a number of ways similar: the early chapters move from the uses of language and the concept of appropriateness to sentences, then style, paragraphs, and the whole composition. Interrupting this order is Chapter 3, "The Practice of Writing"; this chapter, which might be anywhere in the first two parts of the book, is put here because it is intended to guide students as they prepare to write their first papers, and so is likely to be assigned near the beginning of the term. With two exceptions, chapters in Part One need not be assigned in the order in which they appear. The exceptions are that Chapter 4, "The Structure of Sentences," and Chapter 5, "The Sense of Style," do belong in sequence because matters of structure discussed in Chapter 4 are further developed in "The Sense of Style"; and the detailed analysis of the essay in Chapter 7 involves material in Chapters 1, 2, 4, 5, and 6. Sections of the last chapter in Part One—"Everyday Uses of English"—can be assigned in any order when the instructor thinks his students might profit from practical advice about such matters as reading for study, taking notes, and writing examinations.

Part Two, *Understanding Kinds of Prose,* is considerably different from a roughly corresponding part in the fourth edition. The chapter on literature in general, and the chapters on the short story, poetry, drama, and novel are omitted. Five chapters on the types of writing many instructors want their students to do—on informative, evaluative, persuasive, and descriptive writing, and on autobiography, simple narrative, and personal essay—are expanded and accompanied by topics for writing. Whereas Chapter 3, "The Practice of Writing," mentioned above, is a view of the process and the problems of composition and is not limited to one type of writing, these five chapters in Part Two (which need not be read in sequence) may be assigned any time, in preparation for *particular* kinds of papers. With the revised concept of the purpose of Part Two—to provide guidance for the writing of various types of nonfiction prose—it has seemed logical to include in it Chapter 14 on the research paper.

Part Three, a Handbook, seems to have different uses for different classes: sometimes teachers assign large sections of it for review; sometimes they simply ask students to use it for reference in writing or correcting papers. Articles in Part Three are self-contained, with occasional references to other articles in which terms are defined; the student who has difficulty with, for example, connectives, can read the article on connectives without reading preceding material. Revisions in Part Three are mainly of two kinds. They bring up to date certain parts like the section on the dictionary and an expanded glossary of usage, and they amplify other articles to make the Handbook a more complete guide in technical problems that students may encounter, possibly now and possibly in later courses in writing. To give one example, added material on quotation marks with other marks of punctuation may be of little use to a student in his freshman English course, but it is there if, perhaps later, he is doing narrative writing. Some additions to Part Three are meant for students who will keep their copies of *Understanding and Using English.*

G. B. B.

CONTENTS

PART 3
UNDERSTANDING CONVENTIONS: A HANDBOOK OF GRAMMAR, RHETORIC, MECHANICS, AND USAGE

Section 3.   STYLE AND RHETORIC: SUMMARY AND REVIEW

Section 4.   PUNCTUATION

PART 1

Using
English Effectively

Chapter 1

THE USES
OF LANGUAGE

We live in a world of words, and we are affected, perhaps more than we realize, by the words we use, read, and hear. News, much of it alarming, rolls from busy presses; books multiply; shouts and slogans fill the air and sometimes threaten to drown the voices of reason and excellence that we need to hear. Ill-considered words by a government spokesman produce a wave of excitement in Washington and in the country, and occasionally a flurried explanation of what the speaker really intended to say. A single word in a broadcast by Radio Hanoi—"*will* hold talks" instead of "*could* hold talks"—sent a flutter of hope through the capitals of the world. From words and their effects we have nowhere to hide, even if we chose to do so.

Language is a vital shaping force in the personal, social, academic, and professional lives of students. Every time they read or listen, they are using English; knowledge about facts, ideas, values, and human experience comes to them largely through the spoken and written word. Every time they speak or write—in the classroom, in meetings, in the campus newspaper, to friends— they are using English; by means of words they persuade others, impress them, inform them, share experiences with them, get along with them. The language students use shows their education, their information, their manners, their temper, their taste, their tact, their judgment, their sense of humor, and their attitude toward themselves and toward others. Their skill in understanding and using English is of the greatest significance in their intellectual growth, in the friends they make, in the kind of person they marry, in the position they achieve and hold.

Some students of language believe that if man could use language and scientific knowledge with full understanding, all or nearly all human problems could be solved. According to this view, wars and other clashes between nations and groups are often caused by an ignorance of the true relationships between words and things; individual misunderstandings are largely the result of a similar ignorance and of the consequent failure to interpret or communicate effectively; and even personal and psychological ills can be cured by a language therapy that consists in part of putting freely into words one's deepest fears, desires, and inner conflicts, and so being led to analyze them consciously and rationally and to perceive their real meaning.

Writers who express this view have made significant contributions to the understanding of language. Although they seem to us to make some extravagant claims and to place undue reliance on the power of science and of scientific thinking to solve all types of human problems, we believe they are right in insisting that the language men think in, use, and hear, profoundly influences their beliefs and behavior. We are concerned in this chapter with an analysis of principles that will lead to a more perceptive and hence more effective use of language and to a better informed response to the language of others. We shall deal first with the functions of language, then with various aspects of meaning, and then with more complex aspects of meaning.

The most important function of language is to communicate meaning. However, there are other uses; one of these, sometimes very important, is thinking in words to solve problems or to arrive at beliefs. For example, although Miss X, a college freshman, feels that she should take part in the class discussions in her English course, something seems to prevent her doing so. In considering her problem she could think, "The reason I don't talk in class is that I have an inferiority complex." If she thinks in this language, it will seem that both logic and science (the inferiority complex) are against her, and she may sit passively in class for the rest of the year, silent and resigned to her "inferiority complex." If, on the other hand, she thinks, "I've simply been making excuses; the fact is that I'm somewhat shy and need to overcome my shyness," then the language she uses—"excuses" instead of the authoritative-sounding "reason," a curable "shyness" instead of an intimidating "complex"—will encourage her to overcome her shyness. Another example, one that involves a crucial decision: In what words did President Truman and his advisers think when they decided to use the atomic bomb against Japan in World War II? They could have thought, "Shall we bring the war to a quick end and save the lives of thousands of American soldiers?" Or they could have thought, "What will be the effect on the men, women, and children of the bombed city, and what will be the effect on other nations when they see the use the United States has made of atomic power?" This example is over-simplified, of course, but it may suggest how the words men think in can affect their decisions and their actions. Much of the bitter disagreement about the war in Vietnam stemmed from the different words in which people thought: on the one hand, for instance, "We are honoring our commitments and are defending our own security against Communism"; and, on the other hand, "How long must this senseless slaughter go on in a war no one can win?"

Some other noncommunicative uses of language can be mentioned and passed over rapidly. When one writes lists or notes for himself, or very personal diaries, when he sings to himself, talks to himself, or swears at a chair that he has run into in the dark, he uses words not for communication but simply for his own convenience and satisfaction. About such use of language little helpful or enlightening comment can be made—except perhaps that of the moralist on the language addressed to the chair.

In this book we are primarily concerned with the most important use of language—the communication of various kinds of meaning from one mind to another. The power to communicate meaning through language, to build up in this way an ever-increasing store of knowledge, and to pass that accumulated knowledge on to succeeding generations is one of the most significant and distinctively human capacities. Without language, the literature, philosophy, technical knowledge, and complex social order that we often take for granted would be nonexistent; civilization as we know it would be impossible; and man would be an inarticulate savage. Man has far to go before he is truly civilized; but perhaps his best hope is developing the ability to communicate with his fellow men.

I. WORDS AND MEANING

A. The Meaning of Words and the Importance of Context

In the sentence "The horse won the race," the word *horse* has a reasonably definite meaning for all of us. We all know that it refers to a quadruped about five feet high at the shoulder and that the animal has a mane and tail, and hooves instead of feet. But why does the word *horse* have this meaning? One obvious answer, of course, is that we have been brought up among English-speaking people. It just happens that people in our society apply the word *horse* to the animal. How and why that first happened is beyond our present inquiry; we are concerned with the question: how did the English word *horse* come to have its meaning for *us?* The answer lies in our past experiences with the word and with the animal it refers to. Since *horse* is a common word and horses are fairly common things, we probably had our first experience with the word early. Perhaps we saw the animal, and our parents told us it was called a horse; perhaps we saw or heard the word, and someone used other words to explain its meaning. Later on we read or heard the word frequently, and perhaps we saw animals—horses or pictures of horses—and applied the word to them. At any rate we established a relationship between the word *horse* and an actual animal of a particular kind, so that the word came to call to mind the animal, and the animal came to call to mind the word: the word *horse* had come to have a general meaning for us.

In brief, we can say that we learned the general meaning of the word from hearing it in various contexts. When we came across the word *horse* in our primer, the context was the other words with which the word was used. If there was a picture of a horse in the primer, that too was a part of the context, for it helped us to understand what *horse* means. When we saw an actual horse by the roadside and someone told us that it was called *horse,* the whole experience of seeing the horse and hearing the word was the context for us. The **context,** then, is the surrounding words or circumstances that help to make clear to us just what a word (locution) refers to. (*Locution* is a convenient term used to refer to a word or to a group of related words. A locution therefore may be a single word, a phrase, a clause, or an entire sentence.) Because of the general idea we had developed of the meaning of the word *horse* from meeting it in various contexts we were able, on seeing the word in the sentence "The horse won the race," to assume that it referred to a quadruped about five feet high at the shoulder, with a mane and a tail, and hooves instead of feet.

After the general conventional meaning of a word has become established, the context serves to make clear the more definite or particular meaning of the word when it is used to refer to a particular "horse." The words *won the race* give us a more definite idea of what *horse* means in our illustrative sentence. We assume that the horse is a race horse; if we read on and find out what kind of race it was and perhaps what color the horse was, the context will then give us a still more particular idea of the animal itself, the referent.

Of course, *horse* does not always mean animal horse. This word, like many other common words, has a variety of meanings that have also been established by our experience with it in other contexts; we determine which meaning is appropriate from the context in which the word occurs. What, for example, does the word *horse* refer to in the following sentences?

> On the merry-go-round the children preferred to ride on the *horses* and the lions. [The referent is the imitation horses.]
> The carpenter sawed the board on the *horse*. [The referent is a wooden frame.]
> That woman is a *horse*. [Here the referent is a quality hard to define accurately, perhaps that of being large-boned and awkward.]

These examples show that *horse* is used to refer not only to various particular animal horses but also to non-animate things and even to ideas ("large-boned," "awkward"). They show also how the context helps us to identify the particular meaning intended.

Let us take a more complicated example of the way context determines meaning: the sentence "Put out the light, and then put out the light." This sentence, though grammatically well-constructed, does not by itself make sense, does not convey any clear and definite meaning. Since the individual words have a good many different meanings, the reader cannot tell which one is appropriate here. *Put out* and *light* are particularly puzzling. Notice some of the meanings these words have:

> To *put out* the cat [place him outside]
> To *put out* effort [expend effort]
> To *put out* a baseball player [cause an "out" in baseball]
> To be *put out* by what someone does to you [inconvenienced or exasperated]
> To *put out* the light [extinguish it]

> A *light* burden [not heavy]
> A *light* color [not dark]
> To see the *light* [the truth]
> To see the *light* [the illumination]
> To be in a *light* mood [gay, carefree]
> To *light* a fire [cause the fuel to blaze]
> The speed of *light* [light rays]
> *Light*headed [dizzy, unstable, fickle]

Put out the light, and then put out the light, like the single word *horse,* will not have a clear and exact meaning until we place it in a larger context, a passage from Shakespeare's play *Othello.* In fact, to get the full meaning of the quoted sentence, it would be necessary to know the whole play. A synopsis of the play and the quoting of a passage from it, however, may provide sufficient context to transform an ambiguous sentence into a poignantly meaningful expression. Othello, a just and admirable man, is tricked by his subordinate, Iago, into believing that his wife, Desdemona, is guilty of infidelity. Although he loves Desdemona so deeply that she is the "light" of his life, of his happiness, Othello convinces himself that the "cause" of justice, virtue, honor, demands that "she must die, else she'll betray more men." The following lines are spoken by him as he is about to extinguish the light, a candle or lamp, and then to smother Desdemona. He extinguishes the candle because he fears that his resolution will fail if the light enables him to see her:

> It is the cause, it is the cause, my soul:
> Let me not name it to you, you chaste stars!
> It is the cause. Yet I'll not shed her blood,
> Nor scar that whiter skin of hers than snow
> And smooth as monumental alabaster.

> Yet she must die, else she'll betray more men.
> *Put out the light, and then put out the light:*
> If I quench thee, thou flaming minister,
> I can again thy former light restore,
> Should I repent me: but once put out thy light,
> Thou cunning'st pattern of excelling nature,
> I know not where is that Promethean heat
> That can thy light relume. When I have pluck'd the rose,
> I cannot give it vital growth again;
> It needs must wither . . .

After this soliloquy Othello accuses Desdemona, refuses to believe her protestations of innocence, and kills her, only to learn soon afterward of Iago's trickery and her constancy. Othello then kills himself because he has in truth "put out the light, and then put out the light."

The line spoken by Othello illustrates the force and significance of the surrounding words—the **verbal context**—in establishing the particular meaning of words and even of sentences. Not only words and sentences, but also paragraphs and even larger units of expression often depend upon verbal context for their full meaning.

Besides the verbal context, there is also the context of circumstances. Often the meaning of a locution is clarified by the nonverbal circumstances in which the locution is used. For instance, a man with a smoke-blackened face runs out of a house and shouts "Fire!" or an officer shouts "Fire!" to a group of soldiers armed with rifles. The different meaning of the word *fire* in each case is established by the **context of circumstances**—that is, by the time, place, and conditions in which the locution is used.

Locutions taken out of the context of their own time are subject to misinterpretation. For example, in 1801 Thomas Jefferson in his *First Inaugural Address* spoke approvingly of the national policy of "entangling alliances with none." Because of the great respect for the wisdom of Jefferson, this phrase has frequently been quoted to support an isolationist policy in world affairs. If we compare the situation at the time that Jefferson recommended the avoidance of "entangling alliances" with the present world situation more than a century and a half later, we readily see that the two situations (circumstances) are very different. Jefferson might well advocate a different policy to fit the changed context of circumstances, and to quote him as opposing "entangling alliances" such as NATO or the United Nations is to misinterpret his statement of policy by taking it out of context.

One of the first rules for understanding language—and for using it properly—is: Determine what the locution means in its full context. The full context may be the verbal context, or the context of circumstances, or both. To take locutions or even larger units out of their context may distort their meaning. When context changes, meaning changes.

B. The Two Kinds of Meaning: Attitudinal and Factual

The meaning that language communicates is infinitely various; it can be simple, as in a comment on the weather or a warning about an approaching automobile; or it can be extremely complex, as in a play by Shakespeare or a book on relativity.

If we use *knowledge* in its broadest sense (i.e., anything a mind is aware of) we can say that every meaning that language communicates is knowledge. The kind of meaning conveyed will then depend upon the kind of knowledge communicated; hence the discussion of kinds of meaning needs to be prefaced by considering the two basic kinds of knowledge: inside knowledge and outside knowledge.

What one knows about what is going on in his own mind or what he learns or conjectures about what is going on inside the minds of others is **inside knowledge;** what he knows about the world outside is **outside knowledge.** The distinction between the two kinds of knowledge is a very important one. Some concrete examples will help to make it clear.

If I tell you I am sad, I communicate inside knowledge or meaning; if I say there is a red truck in the driveway, I communicate outside knowledge. In the first statement I am talking about something that only I can know about at first hand, the actual *feeling* of sadness that is *inside* me. In the comment about the red truck I am talking about objects in the outside world—the truck and the driveway; by looking at the truck you too can have first-hand knowledge of it, by which you can check my statement. If you tell me that what I called a truck is really a station wagon, I can look again and see that I should have said station wagon. If I say, "I am sad because I don't own the beautiful red station wagon in the driveway," I communicate outside information about the ownership and color and location of the station wagon, and I also communicate my inside knowledge about the station wagon when I call it beautiful and say that I feel sad about not owning it. Notice that the presence of the red station wagon is a matter of fact (i.e., is true or false), and that whether the station wagon is beautiful or not is a matter of taste or opinion. Most of the time, as in the example just above, language communicates both outside and inside knowledge, fact and attitude.

Meaning that conveys knowledge (facts and ideas about facts) concerning the outside world is **factual meaning.** Meaning that conveys knowledge (feelings, attitudes, value judgments, beliefs) of the subjective, inside world is **attitudinal meaning.**

Attitudinal meaning includes all forms of inside, first-person knowledge. If I look into my own consciousness I find there at different times all kinds of states of mind that are parts of inside knowledge—emotions, moods, desires, fears, wishes, sympathies, hopes, likes and dislikes, tastes, judgments, doubts, beliefs. Will and conscience are also parts of inside knowledge, for I can *feel* my will tell me to do something and feel my conscience tell me not to do it. Some things shock me, some sadden me, some delight me. . . . When I put into words any of these bits of inside knowledge, they become the attitudinal meaning that I communicate.

Verbal communication usually involves three things—the communicator, the subject of the communication, and the audience (the hearer or reader). Hence *we may define attitudinal meaning most briefly and exactly as the attitude or feeling of the communicator* (1) *toward himself,* (2) *toward his subject, and* (3) *toward his audience.* To clarify this definition let us suppose that a student were to say to a friend, "My paper was easily the best in the class. I just dashed it off, of course. It's too bad you are so slow and stupid that you can't write as well as I do." The friend might well object to the speaker's "attitude": he might say that the speaker was conceited (attitude toward himself), was too proud of his paper (attitude toward his subject), and was condescending toward his hearer (attitude toward his audience). If the speaker had said, "When the professor told me that my paper was the best in the class, I was ashamed because I had just dashed it off and I knew you had worked hard and long on yours," he would have expressed a different attitude toward himself, his subject, and his hearer.

Factual meaning communicates facts and ideas about the world outside. It consists of what one knows or conjectures about the world that the senses —sight, hearing, taste, etc.—report to us. This "world," as we are using the word, is very large indeed—not only the literal world but all the objects and material forces in the universe. When we speak of a **fact** we mean any bit of knowledge about this world that can come through the senses; and when we speak of an **idea,** we mean a generalization arrived at on the basis of such facts. That an apple falls from a tree is a fact, and the statement of the law of gravity is the expression of an idea based on this fact, on other similar facts, and on reasoning about such facts. Since facts, in our special sense of the word,[1] are statements about information that comes through the senses, a statement of fact can presumably be checked and verified by the senses of other people besides the person making the statement. That horses generally have five legs might thus be in intention a statement of fact, but it would be a false statement because it is an inaccurate observation about objects in the outside world. Ideas too can be verified, though with less certainty than facts; for complex ideas like the structure of the atom or the concept of evolution involve a great many facts and a great deal of reasoning on these facts. The general statements arrived at by such a combination of facts and reasoning may be called hypotheses or laws, depending on how well they are substantiated.

---

[1] In everyday usage, the statement "I feel sad" is a fact; but *fact* in our more limited use of the word must be a statement of outside knowledge. "I feel sad," since it expresses inside knowledge, would not fit our definition of *fact.*

We can say that statements of factual meaning are true or false; or, if they deal with matters hard to verify, probably true or probably false; but when we deal with attitudinal statements, the words true or false are difficult to apply—how can we test or verify, for example, someone's statement that to him a garbage-littered street is beautiful? We need to look now at the relationship between the two kinds of meaning and the intention of the communicator.

C. Intention and Meaning: The Three Parts of Meaning

On the basis of strict logic, intention would be classified as a part of attitudinal meaning, for just what a communicator's intention or purpose is, is a matter of inside knowledge. Though an audience can, and often should, conjecture about it, only the communicator can really know his purpose at first hand. It is wise to remember that our ideas about a speaker's intention are at best only conjecture. Well-intentioned but blunt and untactful people are often misunderstood because of their linguistic inability to communicate their good intentions; and glib and plausible people sometimes skillfully conceal selfish intentions. Reaching the soundest possible judgment (i.e., the most probable conjecture) about the intentions of others and using language in such a way as to make clear one's own good will and honest intention are both important in the effective use of language.

Intention may be defined as the effect the communicator wishes to produce on his audience. For example, the intention of communicator *C* may be to get audience *A* to move out of the path of a speeding car, or to sympathize with him because of his unhappiness; the intention of a politician may be to persuade the citizens to vote for him; the intention behind the weather report or behind a mathematics text is to inform the reader about coming weather or about mathematics. Although intention, in some communication, may be complex and changing, we can say that in general a communicator has one of **four primary intentions:** (1) he wants simply to communicate factual knowledge as clearly as he can (i.e., *to inform*); (2) he wants to communicate factual knowledge *and* to pass judgment (i.e., *to evaluate* or criticize); (3) he wants to communicate (or to appear to communicate) factual knowledge *and* to influence the attitudes or ideas or actions of the audience (i.e., *to persuade* or convince); or (4) he wants *to communicate experience*—to enable others to share his feelings, attitudes, states of mind, or at any rate to cause others to experience certain feelings, attitudes, states of mind.[2] Poets, novelists, short-story

---

2 Joshua Whatmough in *Language: A Modern Synthesis*, 1956, pp. 88 ff., lists four uses of language: the *informative,* used in the setting forth of the facts of the situation; the *dynamic,* used in the formation and organization of opinion; the *emotive,* used to move others to action; and the *aesthetic,* "manifested chiefly but not solely in poetry and other deliberately cultivated styles." In our terminology the *dynamic* and the *emotive* categories would be included under the use of language to persuade or convince, and the *aesthetic*

writers—all artists who use the medium of language—usually have the primary intention of communicating experience, interpreting human life and human values, rather than informing or persuading. Language used primarily to entertain or amuse or supply escape from daily routine can also be said to have the communication of experience as its chief aim, for escaping or being amused or entertained is a kind of experience.

At times—in very casual conversation, for example—a communicator may hardly know what his intention is and may have trouble stating it if asked to do so. Thus he may communicate without conscious awareness of his intention. At other times, however, he may be sharply aware and may select his language carefully to realize that intention. A pleasure-loving college student who has exceeded his allowance and is writing home for more money is likely to be very much aware of his intention, and his parents, when they read of high costs and hard studying, may also be aware. A part of linguistic wisdom is to be aware—and sometimes wary—of the intentions of others.

Because intention is so important in the use of language, we shall disregard here the logic that would make it a subordinate part of attitudinal meaning, and we shall speak therefore of two *kinds* of meaning, attitudinal and factual, but of the three *parts* of meaning. The **three parts of meaning** are: factual meaning (facts and ideas about facts), attitude, and intention. Which of these parts of meaning is most significant will vary with the communication.

In primarily informative writing the factual meaning is, of course, most important, though intention and attitude are still present. In a chemistry text, for instance, the writer is chiefly concerned with supplying facts and ideas about the outside world, and the wise reader concentrates on absorbing and understanding the factual knowledge presented. Here the general intention is obvious: the writer wishes to inform. The attitude may be described as impersonal and unemotional; the writer takes his subject seriously, or he wouldn't be writing a book about it, but he is not primarily concerned with using language to convey his feelings about himself, or his subject, or his reader. He has used language successfully if he has presented the facts clearly to the particular type of reader he is writing for.

But in many kinds of communication, intention and attitude are more im-

---

is similar to, though not identical with, what we have called the communication of experience. Students of language are not in agreement on the labels they apply to the various uses of language or on the relative importance they attribute to those uses; despite these differences in terminology and emphasis, however, they appear to be in general agreement on the actual uses or functions of language. In the discussion of large abstract subjects of this sort, different approaches and different emphases require changes in terminology, since the use of familiar terms in unfamiliar ways would be misleading. Our terminology is not intended to be definitive here or in similar circumstances elsewhere; we have simply made the divisions and chosen the labels that are most useful for our purposes. Of course we have tried to use standard terms when we have been able to use also their standard meanings.

portant than facts. A common fallacy is the belief that communicating facts and ideas about the outside world is always the main function of language. Actually there are many uses of language—literary, social, and political—in which factual meaning is secondary, and in which intention and attitude are of primary importance. If the reader will examine his own use of language for one day he will see that a good part of the time he is not concerned primarily with communicating facts and ideas. He gets up on a cold rainy day and says "Good morning" to everyone he meets; he says "Good-by" (originally a kind of blessing meaning "God be with you") to people whom he has no desire to bless. When he is introduced to someone, he may say, "How do you do," even though he does not care how the person does; or he may say, less properly, "Pleased to meet you," though he would have chosen to avoid the introduction. When he writes an angry letter to a laundry that has lost three of his shirts, he begins it "Dear Sir" and ends with "Very truly yours." A large part of his light conversation deals with the weather, in which perhaps neither he nor his companion is interested. All these polite conventional uses of language are primarily intention or attitude, and people unconsciously accept them as such. To a casual "How are you?" a man with a toothache may well say, "Fine, thanks."

Language is also used to establish or to maintain friendly relations. When we joke, or tell stories, or chat in a friendly way about trivial matters, we are frequently more interested in letting people know that we like them and in causing them to like us than we are in exchanging factual knowledge. People sometimes talk merely because they find silence embarrassing or because they feel that they will be considered unfriendly if they are silent.

Another common use of language in which factual meaning is not of primary importance is the expressing and sharing of our feelings and beliefs, our response to experience. Bacon wrote that communicating with friends doubles joys and cuts grief in half; language is the main medium through which this communication and sharing occur. We may enjoy talking to people who have the same political or social or philosophical ideas as ours, not because we are gaining new facts or ideas but because we enjoy agreeing with someone—or, better, having someone agree with us.

That language is frequently, perhaps most commonly, used for purposes other than communicating factual information seems hard to deny, yet many "practical" people take a severe view when they read literature. Assuming that all writing deals with the facts and ideas of outside knowledge, they miss the attitudinal meaning—the conveying of experience and of human values—with which literature is chiefly concerned. Such people think that when they have a synopsis of a story they have the "meaning of the story" and believe that a sentence summary of a poem is the essence of the poem. But the short-story writer, novelist, essayist, dramatist, or poet is not primarily concerned with facts and ideas; outside knowledge is frequently only a small part of the whole meaning he wishes to convey, just as it is likely to be a small part of a love letter or an intimate conversation. Men don't live by facts and ideas alone. They think and know, and much of their language deals with thought and knowledge, but they also feel and respond. Mathematicians and engineers and atomic scientists fall in love and have friends and quarrel among themselves, and they use language to express their emotions and attitudes.

What has been said thus far about the importance of intention and attitude should not, however, lead us to underestimate the very great significance of factual meaning in language. Men have to inform one another, to educate one another, to convince one another by facts and by logic; and when language is used for these purposes, factual information is the most important part of the meaning. The point to bear in mind is not that fact is unimportant, but that intention and attitude are much more important than many people realize when they use the word *meaning*.

D. Words and the Two Kinds of Meaning: Charged Words

Early in this chapter we arrived at some generalizations about the way single words take on and convey meaning and about the importance of context. We were then chiefly concerned with factual meaning, though we also touched on attitudinal meaning in discussing the passage from *Othello*. In this section we shall consider the way individual words function in conveying, often simultaneously, *both* kinds of meaning, but our chief stress will be on attitudinal meaning because interpreting that kind of meaning presents more problems.

It seems appropriate here to issue a warning that applies particularly to this section and, in some measure, to the whole book. Most generalizations about language are part truths and so will hold good only part of the time; they must be applied flexibly. We have said, for instance, that single words often convey both kinds of meaning at the same time. Although this statement is true for many words, it is not true for all. For example, some single words—*roses, garbage, moonlight*—clearly convey both attitudinal and factual meaning; they refer to outside objects (factual meaning), and the naming of each object produces a different feeling (attitudinal meaning)—there is, indeed, a kind of emotional shock (further attitudinal meaning) produced by the proximity of garbage to roses. Other words, though, resist such analysis—are structure words, useful in tying the sentence together but not easily analyzable in terms of either kind of meaning: for instance, the words *the* and *but* and *not* in this sentence.

The factual meaning of a word, as we have said earlier, communicates outside knowledge by referring to an object, an act, or an idea about the outside world, and the particular factual meaning of the word is fixed by the context in which the word occurs. The word *house,* for example, in the context *my house is small* refers to a particular physical structure, an object; the word *dancing* in *they were dancing a waltz* refers in this context to a particular physical action. When used in context, words that refer to tangible objects or to physical actions like dancing usually convey clear factual meaning and seldom cause misunderstandings.[3] Words that refer to ideas about facts, particularly when the facts or the ideas about them are complex, do cause misunderstandings. It may be hard to define and agree on the exact factual meaning of such words as *corporation* and *armed forces,* for example, because *corporation* refers to a complicated idea or concept, and *armed forces* is a general word that covers a great many particular facts and so may be open to dispute. Factual meaning becomes even more difficult to separate and interpret when words have a vague factual meaning and a very strong attitudinal meaning. Examples of such words are *liberty, Americanism, Communism, extremism.* Since words of this sort involve special problems, we shall discuss them more fully later. Although the factual meaning of words can lead to serious misunderstandings, men have less trouble in communicating factual knowledge than in communicating feelings, attitudes, and values.

The attitudinal meaning of words is determined by context in much the same way that the factual meaning is. Early in this chapter we saw that our whole past experience with a word (*horse,* for instance) in different contexts tends to fix for us a certain set of general factual meanings for the word (animal horse, carpenter's horse, merry-go-round horse). In the context, "The *horse* won the race," we can tell that animal horse is referred to. Since words usually have attitudinal as well as factual meanings, when the factual meaning of a word varies in different contexts, the attitudinal meaning varies with it. In the phrases, *race horse, horse meat, horse play,* the factual meaning of the word *horse* changes, and as the referent (thing referred to) changes, our response (attitude) also changes: we may feel admiration for the beauty and speed of a race horse, feel distaste for horse meat, feel impatience with horse play. Other words work the same way: *machine* and *grafter,* for example, produce different feelings in us as they refer in different contexts to sewing machine or political machine, to a grafter of trees or a dishonest receiver of money:

> She sewed the shirt on the *machine.*
> Votes were bought by the political *machine.*
>
> He is a skillful *grafter* of trees.
> He is a politician and a *grafter.*

As we think about the examples given, it becomes evident that the attitudinal meaning of a word, like the factual meaning, is usually dependent upon (1) the general conventional meanings of the word and (2) the context

---

[3] Even the word *house,* though, can be ambiguous if a point of law is involved. There are laws about how distant a house must be from the edge of the owner's property; suppose an attached garage is too near—is the garage properly a part of the house?

in which the word is used. When we listen or read, our minds select the particular factual meaning indicated by the context, and respond emotionally to
that meaning. In this process we find what things or ideas words refer to, and
we also feel a series of emotional *charges* (attractions or repulsions), as we
think of the referents of the words. These charges are the attitudinal meaning
of the passage. Language that gives us a number of strong charges can be
called **charged language,** and words that give strong charges can be called
charged words. We shall first discuss the types of charged words and later consider the characteristics and devices of charged language.

E. Types of Charged Words

Words differ in the amount of charge and in the way they get the charge
they carry. Some words, because of the way we have generally used them and
because of our emotions about the things they customarily refer to, seem to
carry an unusual amount of emotional meaning *independent* of context and
of referent. The word as word is already charged, "precharged" by our previous associations with it: just hearing or seeing it produces an emotion in us.
This tends to block discriminating thought about what the word refers to in
a particular context and makes us respond only to the charge of feeling that
the word carries for us. Such precharged words cause us to prejudge referents.
During World War I, for example, some people objected to the playing of
Beethoven's symphonies because Beethoven was a "German." These people
were reacting to the precharged word *German,* and it blocked their thinking
about the music of a composer who deserves the respect of all civilized men.

Other charged words are more lightly precharged. They carry with them
a cluster of suggestions or *connotations,* favorable or unfavorable, which are
not strong enough to block all thought about the factual meaning, but which
are likely to color our feeling about the referent. In the statements "She is a
thin girl" and "She is a slender girl," *thin* and *slender* differ in their connotation or attitudinal meaning: most people will respond less favorably to the
idea of a "thin" girl; the response will be still less favorable if she is described
as "skinny." Such lightly charged words are, of course, common in everyday
speech and writing. To refer to an automobile as a *jalopy,* or to a very indus-
trious student as a *grind,* or to one's college as *alma mater* is to use lightly
charged, connotative words.

Still other charged words get their charge, light or heavy, not simply from
our store of past associations and our feeling about the word, but from the
feeling aroused in us by the word's referent, its factual meaning, as we think
of it in a particular context. The same word may have strong emotional
meaning in one context and little emotional meaning in another; or it may
carry a positive charge in one context and a negative charge when another
context calls to mind a different referent. In the sentences "A fire crackled
cheerfully on the hearth" and "A fire is raging through the South End," the

word *fire* is very differently charged by the image of the referent that the surrounding words bring to mind. The charge carried by the second *light* in the line from *Othello* (Put out the light, and then put out the light) comes from the feeling aroused by a referent that has been established by context. *Light* in this passage is a "context-charged" word; in another context— "moonlight and roses"—the word has a different charge or attitudinal meaning.

With the understanding that charged words vary a great deal in the origin and the intensity of the emotional meaning they carry, we can proceed to consider some common types of charged words. Our categories are not mutually exclusive: these words work in so many subtle and different ways that they defy consistent logical analysis. As a result, a word that belongs in one category on the basis of one principle of analysis may belong in another category when another principle is used. Most of the words we shall discuss are precharged rather than context-charged; and, though people differ in their responses to these words, most of them are quite heavily charged for many people.

Home, mother, God, father, love, bride, sea, and *sky* are some of the **charged words of everyday living.** For nearly everyone, the words themselves seem to be loaded with a power to produce an immediate emotional response of some sort; the word *God* produces an emotional response even in professed atheists, and the word *father* produces a response in orphans. These charged words of everyday living get their particular power from the fact that we hear and see them frequently in contexts that involve our feelings; consequently we build up strong emotional associations around them. Such words are, of course, powerful conductors of attitudinal meaning and are important in all communication that has even the secondary aim of expressing or evoking feeling.

For many people *home* suggests comfort, warmth, security. Undertakers have this in mind when they call their establishments funeral *homes*. Robert Louis Stevenson makes a poetic use of charged words of everyday living— *home, sailor, sea, hunter, hill*—in the last two lines of his epitaph; and in particular he communicates his feeling about death by his use and repetition of the word *home*.

REQUIEM

Under the wide and starry sky,
Dig the grave and let me lie.
Glad did I live and gladly die,
    And I laid me down with a will.

This be the verse you grave for me:
Here he lies where he longed to be;
Home is the sailor, home from sea,
    And the hunter home from the hill.

Another type of charged words is **taboo words**—for example, profanity and four-letter words about which many people have built up inhibitions. In recent years the use of such words has considerably increased, in novels, in the theater, and in campus riots and other demonstrations; but some of the old taboos still cling and give the words a special power of emphasis or shock. The power to shock is, indeed, frequently the reason for using the words.

A good many **proper names** also belong in the category of charged words. Earlier in this chapter we considered the persuasive force of statements made by Thomas Jefferson. Much of this persuasive force can be attributed to the name *Thomas Jefferson,* and to the favorable emotional associations that Americans have with that name. Proper names that are charged with meaning, like charged words dealing with everyday living, may be charged positively or negatively. For many Americans, for example, the names Washington, Jefferson, Lincoln, have a positive charge, and the names Castro, Hitler, and Stalin may have a negative charge. We may feel a favorable response to anything associated with the first group and an unfavorable response to anything associated with the second. The proper place-name *Vietnam* has become charged, unfavorably, for many people. It is natural enough to respond to proper names; sometimes, however, the response may be harmful, for our emotions may be so moved as to prevent our analyzing a factual meaning that is overshadowed by the feeling the proper names evoke.

Abstract words may also be charged. They differ from concrete words in that they frequently do not have the same clear and definite factual meaning for different audiences. Abstract words generally name qualities *(intelligence, honor),* concepts *(evolution, scientific method),* and conditions *(poverty, insanity).* Concrete words generally refer to things that exist in the physical world and can be perceived by the senses: *chair, apple, light bulb, rose bush.* Concrete words when used even in brief contexts usually communicate a definite enough factual meaning to enable us to understand one another. When a man tells his son to "feed the dog," the meaning of these words is certainly clear enough for everyday purposes; if the son is obedient, the dog gets fed and the father's factual communication has been successful.

But some abstract words—particularly words dealing with beliefs or values—cause trouble. If the same father tells his son, "The American way of life is being threatened by communism," or, "Your generation has no values," the factual meaning is much less clear and definite. If the son is intelligent and also inconsiderate, he may ask his father what he means by such abstract terms as *American way of life* and *communism,* or by *values.* It would have been easy for the father to make completely clear what dog was to receive what food (i.e., to define his words *dog* and *food),* but when he tries to define the value-words his son has asked about, he has a different and difficult problem. Quite possibly the son will challenge his definition, "But what you call communism isn't communism; communism means . . . ." Then he will give his own definition of the term. An hour or so later each may still be insisting that communism "means" this or that, and still later the father and son may go to bed, each sure that his definition was "the correct" definition, and each puzzled and depressed by the "wrong-headedness" of the other.

This unhappy father and his unhappy son have been dealing with **charged abstract words.** Such words stand for ideas and beliefs about which men have strong convictions. Like precharged concrete words, they tend to evoke a strong emotional response, positive or negative, whenever they are used, a response so strong that the factual meaning of the referent may be obscured or disregarded. The following list of abstract words that are emotion-ally-precharged for many people will supply examples and will also give the reflective reader a chance to consider which are most charged for him and why.

> Communist, integration, extremism, moderation, fascist, socialistic, progressive, liberal, totalitarian, undemocratic, Republican, Democrat, capitalist, labor, reac-tionary, un-American, radical, freedom, liberty, free enterprise, regimentation, collectivism, foreigners, religion, science, virtue, decency, Protestant, Catholic, Jew, moral, sin, immorality, faith, atheist, morality, truth, beauty, success, happiness, Christian, sex, justice, peace, war, loyalty, sportsmanship, security, aggression, ac-tivism, Establishment, relevance, Law and Order

It is hard to overestimate the almost magical influence that these words and others like them have on the private and public concerns of men. Such words are woven into the fabric of human living; when men talk or write or read or think about subjects like government, economics, sociology, history, philosophy, religion, ethics, law, literature, art, current events—even lan-guage itself—they cannot escape abstract words, for abstract words must be used in dealing with such subjects; and it is, or at least seems to be, inevitable that some of these words will (1) have a different factual meaning (i.e., refer to different facts and ideas) for different people, and (2) become charged posi-tively or negatively with emotion—will, in short, be *charged abstract words.*

Because such words have great emotional power it is difficult to write about them. Each reader of this book, for example, probably feels that *some* of the terms in the list above do have a clear and definite meaning. Suppose we try the word *communist.* Those who hate communists are quite sure that they know, and that every intelligent person should know, just what a com-munist is. But some of those whom they label "communists" indignantly deny the label. They may say they are not communists, they are "progressives" or "Marxists" or "liberals"; or, they simply object to a war which they sin-cerely think is not a war against communism. Other terms on the list produce similar results. Probably few people would say that they are opposed to law or to order; but the phrase "Law and Order," used as a slogan in the Nixon presidential campaign in 1968 and in other campaigns since then, has come to mean to some observers that the rights of citizens and groups of citizens to meet and protest are to be dangerously subordinated to the interest of the police and the courts in maintaining order at any cost. Because Albert Einstein did not believe in a "personal God" and defined "religion" as devotion to some suprapersonal cause, some people would say that he was an "atheist" and had no "religion." Russians sometimes say that they have "freedom" (meaning freedom from want, assured employment) and that we do not; Americans sometimes reply that Russians do not have freedom (meaning free choice of occupation, civil liberties, etc.) but that we do.

In the illustrations given, one person or group is asserting something about an abstract term that is denied by another group. Each feels that the other is not telling the "truth." In each case we can say either that the term means different things to different people (i.e., that the factual meaning is different), or that one-half of the people mentioned are actually engaging in deliberate falsehood. Since many differences of this sort occur every day between people who seem honest, intelligent, and well intentioned, it seems that it often is the unfixed meaning of the abstractions used, and not deliberate falsehood, that produces the conflict. In fact it often happens that each person in a disagreement feels so sure he is telling the "truth" that he accuses the other person of "distorting the truth"; and the accused person is frequently stung by the "injustice" of the accusation and the "dishonesty" of his accuser.

Charged words of race and nationality, a special kind of charged abstract words, work in the same deceptive way, but more subtly. Sometimes they give a certain amount of accurate, factual information; sometimes they give little or none. When we are told that a man is an Italian, for example, we have little or no sure information about him, for the only statement that we can make with certainty about all Italians is that they live in Italy or that some of their ancestors lived in Italy. There are no physical traits common to all Italians—some are blond and others are dark, some are short and others are tall; and there are no traits of personality or intellect that all Italians share— some are educated and some are not, some are quick to anger and others are slow, some speak Italian and others do not. The word *Italian* is applied to people (Dante, Marconi, Al Capone, Mussolini, Garibaldi, Michelangelo) who perhaps have little in common except the fact that they or their ancestors were born in Italy.

What has been said of the word *Italian* is also true of *German, Irishman, American, Frenchman,* and numerous other words of nationality. In every case the word tells us nothing certain about the man except that he or his ancestors were or are natives or naturalized citizens of a particular country. The word *Jew* actually tells us less than any of the words mentioned above, for there is nothing that distinguishes all people called Jews, neither nationality nor, as was originally the case, a common religion.

Some words of race and nationality do convey a certain amount of factual meaning. *Negro, Japanese, Chinese, American Indian* are likely to give some information about the physical appearance of the human being to whom they are applied. To say, for example, that Ralph Bunche, former United States diplomat and Undersecretary of the United Nations, is a Negro is to make a statement with some factual meaning; from that statement we gain a general idea of his skin color and hair. But even when words of race or nationality do have some factual meaning, they often focus interest on what is least significant about a human being. Certainly skin color and hair are not the most important considerations if one is trying to evaluate Dr. Bunche as a person.

Charged words of race and nationality are deceptive because to many people they seem to give more information than they actually do. Often they are precharged words that cause us to prejudge the referent. Words like *Negro* and *Japanese* that give a limited amount of information about physical characteristics frequently misguide because they lead people to jump from physical characteristics to judgments of character and personality. To argue from physical traits to character traits is to use the kind of poor logic found in such generalizations as "All blondes are unreliable," or "All red-haired people are hot tempered." Because labels of race and nationality are misleading, we use language well if whenever possible we tear off the precharged label and look directly at the referent, the individual to whom the label refers.

A subclass of charged words of race and nationality consists of names considered insulting by those to whom they are applied. In a period of urban disturbance in the late nineteen-sixties, *Newsweek* magazine reported that police in Washington, D. C., kept an updated list of words to be avoided, among them *spic, wop, kike, chink, burrhead, dago, nigger, polack, bohunk, limey, frog,* and *kraut.* Black policemen were further advised to avoid, when they were dealing with non-Negro groups, the terms *whitey* and *honky.* All such words, even though used thoughtlessly, without conscious malice, have the power to injure and to inflame.

Charged words of personal attitude serve to express directly our tastes or distastes, our approval or disapproval. Examples of such words are *good, bad, interesting, dull, beautiful, ugly, disgusting, attractive.* When a word or an expression passes judgment on a subject and does not give us any outside knowledge, it is an expression of personal attitude, and if it expresses strong feeling, it is a charged word of personal attitude; it tells us how the communicator feels but conveys no outside knowledge of the subject itself. If A and B both read the same book and A calls it interesting and B calls it dull, neither has given information about the book itself; instead each has simply expressed his feeling (attitude) toward it. Points to notice about the use of charged words of personal attitude are that both A and B are likely to believe that they have given information about the subject itself, and that an unwary audience is likely to think so too. Unless we distinguish clearly between fact and opinion, we are likely to deceive ourselves or to be deceived by others.

Sometimes, though, we use words like *good, bad, interesting, dull* to convey more than mere personal feeling; we mean them to express not only our individual judgment or attitude but the judgment that would be expressed by any group of people competent to voice an opinion. The statements that Einstein was a great scientist, for example, and that Shakespeare was a great poet are value judgments, but they deserve to be given more weight than mere expressions of personal attitude; they represent a consensus of informed and competent opinion. Most people respect such more or less authoritative judgments even if they personally do not agree with them, and they indicate their respect by remarks like, "I think Shakespeare is dull, but people say he's a great writer." The habit of expressing our personal judgments so that it is clear that we know they are mere personal judgments is a good one. If one prefaces such statements by "I think" or "it seems to me," he sounds less dogmatic and he makes possible a rational discussion of subjects that are matters of taste or attitude.

Charged scale words and charged words of multiple standards are subclasses of charged words of personal attitude but they are so important in any use of language that they deserve special consideration. Examples of such words are:

tall, short; high, low; far, near; heavy, light; young, old; dark, light; fat, thin; long, short; strong, weak; many, few; much, little (scale words);

and

good, bad; pleasing, unpleasing; valuable, worthless; moral, immoral; real, unreal; beautiful, ugly; true, false (words of multiple standards).

The words on this list do not have fixed and definite meanings; they take on meaning in the light of some standard in the mind of the communicator and in the mind of the audience. When we speak of a *tall* man, for example, we have in mind the usual height of men; when of a *tall* building, the usual height of buildings. If people have in mind the same or a similar standard, the words serve their purpose, but both scale words and the words of multiple standards can produce pointless arguments and frustrating misunderstandings. Two people who agree that the distance to town is two miles will waste time arguing about whether it is a "long walk" or not; what constitutes a "long walk" is a matter of opinion or of the standard one chooses. Similarly it is a waste of time to argue in heated and general terms about whether a play or a movie is *good* without reference to the particular standards that the speakers have in mind as they use the word *good*. A movie may be good by one standard and bad by another. Intelligent and fruitful discussion calls for agreement on facts and on standards. Such discussion makes possible areas of agreement and defines points of difference.

Sometimes the words listed above apply to outside knowledge, sometimes to inside knowledge, sometimes to both. The paired words labeled *scale words* refer to outside knowledge and have meaning in relation to measurable physical standards like height, distance, weight, age, etc. When the factual meaning of these scale words is uncertain, we can generally clarify it by stating how high in feet, how heavy in pounds, etc.

The paired words labeled *words of multiple standards* are more complex in meaning than the earlier scale words, for they are related to different kinds of standards, and may refer to several such standards at the same time. For example, the word *good* in the expression *good English,* can mean *good* in the sense of effective or efficient, *good* in the sense of artistically pleasing, *good* in the sense of morally approvable, and *good* in all three ways at the same time. What is true of *good,* also holds good for *true.* (Notice how often we use these two words; the other words on the multiple standard list are also used very frequently, and all such words influence our beliefs, tastes, and values.) The word *true* is used in the general sense of accurate and reliable; it may refer to something that is in accord with outside knowledge and reason (scientific or factual truth); it may mean in accord with certain values and beliefs (moral or religious or philosophical truth); it may mean in accord with human inner experience and taste (artistic or inner truth as when we speak of the truth in fiction—in a novel, for instance); and it may even mean a combination of all these kinds of truth. *Good* and *true* and *beautiful* are perhaps the most significant and the most confusing words in our language; like other charged words of multiple standards, they can be used for good ends, or for ends that are neither beautiful nor good nor true.

A final category of charged words is **charged words of fact-and-value.** We have seen that many words or expressions convey inside and outside knowledge simultaneously. If we say that a girl is slender (a lightly charged word), we indicate something about her physical form and at the same time we suggest our own favorable or admiring attitude. If we call a man a villain or rascal (these are heavily charged words), we imply that he has performed unjust or unkind acts and at the same time we communicate our disapproval. Reporters, in presenting items of news, are expected to avoid words like *rascal* and *villain* and to limit themselves to statements of verifiable fact, such as that the man has been adjudged guilty in court of bigamy, desertion of his first wife, cruelty to his children, and assault on his second "wife" with a dangerous weapon. Though charged words of fact-and-value are often useful, they should not be taken at face value unless they are substantiated by reporter-like facts. In interpreting unfavorably charged words, it is well to bear in mind the legal presumption that a man is innocent until he is proved guilty. Fairminded writers and speakers generally supply facts that support the favorable or unfavorable implications of the fact-and-value words they use. When such facts are lacking, an audience is justified in questioning the reliability of the implied judgment and also the trustworthiness of the communicator.

Charged words, abstract or concrete, may be used to convey different kinds of meaning and to serve different intentions. Sometimes the user may be innocent of any concealed intention and may think he is simply stating a "fact." For him the words have, or seem to have, clear factual meaning, and he is simply trying to convey that meaning. The father and son, mentioned earlier in the chapter, belong in this category, and their whole frustrating debate grew out of their honest intentions and their ignorance of the characteristics of charged words. In daily life a good many misunderstandings are produced in this way. The college student who in good faith describes a girl as a "beauty" and even more concretely as a "good dancer" and arranges for a friend to take her dancing may be trusting too much in the factual meaning that these charged words have *for him.* His friend may have a disappointing evening because the girl is "too thin to be beautiful" and "too tall to be a good dancer." *Beauty* and *good dancer* mean different things to different people.[4]

Charged words may also be used deliberately to influence people's feelings and judgments. Newspapers and periodicals frequently use them for this purpose in their editorial columns and cartoons, in captions under photographs, and even in headlines. Words in cartoons have a particularly forceful charge, for along with the words—*Republican Party* or *Democratic Party,* for example—the cartoonist gives the image that he would like us to associate with the word or to accept as its meaning. Illustrated advertisements work in a similar way, and of course advertisers in general are more interested in influencing the reader than in informing him. Many syndicated columnists, editorial writers, and news commentators are masters of charged words and other techniques of charged language. By such means they exercise tremendous persuasive power over their audiences, and cause many uninformed people to approve, almost mechanically, what the communicator approves and to condemn what he condemns. Students are invited to examine objectively the use of charged words by their favorite columnist, editorial writer, or news commentator. Most students will not need to be invited to examine critically the speeches and writings of those writers and commentators with whom they strongly disagree.

It is wise to be on guard against heavily charged words; they are often the tools or weapons of unscrupulous people who use them to obscure facts in a fog of synthetic emotion and to becloud the real issues. But users of charged words are not necessarily mercenary or subversive or hypocritical propagandists. Charged words often serve the essential function of giving forceful expression to honest feeling and belief; they can arouse men and unite them and sustain them.

4 These two expressions illustrate the fact that it is hard to place words in definite categories. Here, for example, *beauty* can be called a charged abstract word and also a charged word of personal attitude. In the phrase "good dancer," *dancer* is a fairly concrete word, but *good,* like *beauty,* is a charged abstract word that conveys personal attitude.

F. Summary

Let us restate the main points covered thus far in this chapter.

Words take on their general conventional meaning for us as a result of our encountering them in different contexts that serve to relate the word *(horse)* to its referent (the animal itself). The specific meaning of a word any time it is used is determined by the context, either verbal or circumstantial or both, in which the word occurs, and by our knowledge of the conventionally accepted or general meanings of the word. The device of quoting words outside the context that gives them particular meaning is misleading and sometimes dishonest.

Though language has many functions, its most important function is the communication of meaning from one mind to another. There are two kinds of knowledge, inside and outside, and two kinds of meaning, attitudinal and factual. Attitudinal meaning communicates inside knowledge (what one knows about what is going on in his own mind, or what he learns or conjectures about what is inside the minds of others); and factual meaning communicates outside knowledge (facts, and ideas about facts that refer to the physical world, the world of the senses). Outside knowledge and factual meaning can be verified and agreed upon; inside knowledge and attitudinal meaning relate to matters of taste, or feelings, or values for which there is often no generally established and agreed-upon standard.

The most useful definitions for the two kinds of meaning are: Attitudinal meaning is the attitude or feeling of the communicator (1) toward himself, (2) toward his subject, and (3) toward his audience; factual meaning is the part of meaning that communicates facts, and ideas based on facts about the outside world.

Intention shapes meaning. It may be defined as the effect which the communicator wishes to produce on his audience. The four primary intentions are (1) to inform, (2) to evaluate, (3) to persuade, and (4) to communicate experience. Because of its importance in the analysis of meaning, intention is here considered one of the three parts of meaning—namely, factual meaning (facts and ideas about facts), attitudinal meaning, and, of course, intention. The significance of these three parts of meaning varies in different communications, but intention and attitude are often more important than is generally recognized.

When we examine the meaning of individual words, we see that many words convey, often simultaneously, both factual and attitudinal meaning. In general, the factual meaning of words is easier to fix and interpret than the attitudinal meaning; this is especially true when words refer to concrete objects or actions.

Words that carry strong charges (i.e., strong attitudinal meaning) are called charged words, and language that gives a number of strong charges is charged language. Some charged words, precharged by our previous experience with them, seem to carry strong emotional meaning independent of context and referent; connotative words are lightly precharged words; and words that gain all or most of their meaning not so much from previous association as from use in a particular context may be called context-charged words. Some common types of charged words are: charged words of everyday living, taboo words, charged proper names, charged abstract words (particularly words dealing with controversial beliefs and values), charged words of race and nationality, charged words of personal attitude, charged scale words and charged words of multiple standards, charged words of fact-and-value.

Charged words may be used to convey different kinds of meaning and to serve different intentions; they may be used unconsciously and impulsively or consciously and purposefully; they may express honest feeling or sham feeling. It is wise to be on guard against charged words because of their great emotional force and their power to obscure facts and to prevent objective and rational judgments; on the other hand, charged words and charged language are necessary forcefully to express honest emotions and sincere convictions.

II. SELECTION, SLANTING, AND
CHARGED LANGUAGE

In the first section of this chapter we focused on the way single words acquire and convey meaning and the kinds of meaning they convey. In this section we shall consider the way groups of words work together in larger contexts. Since words, singly or in groups, serve as symbols to convey knowledge, it is desirable here to consider a principle that underlies all knowledge and all use of words.

A. The Principle of Selection

Before it is expressed in words, our knowledge, both inside and outside, is influenced by the principle of selection. What we know or observe depends on what we notice; that is, what we select, consciously or unconsciously, as worthy of notice or attention. As we observe, the principle of selection determines which facts we take in.

Suppose, for example, that three people, a lumberjack, an artist, and a tree surgeon are examining a large tree in a forest. Since the tree itself is a complicated object, the number of particulars or facts about it that one could observe would be very great indeed. Which of these facts a particular observer will notice will be a matter of selection, a selection determined by his interests and purposes. A lumberjack might be interested in the best way to cut the tree down, cut it up, and transport it to the lumber mill. His interest would then determine his principle of selection in observing and thinking about the tree. The artist might consider painting a picture of the tree, and his purpose would furnish his principle of selection. The tree surgeon's professional interest in the physical health of the tree might establish a principle of selection for him. If each man were now required to write an exhaustive, detailed report on everything he observed about the tree, the facts supplied by each would differ, for each would report those facts that his particular principle of selection led him to notice.[5]

The principle of selection holds not only for the specific facts that people observe but also for the facts they remember. A student suddenly embarrassed may remember nothing of the next ten minutes of class but may have a vivid memory of the sensation of the blood mounting, as he blushed, up his face and into his ears. In both noticing and remembering, the principle of selection applies, and it is influenced not only by our special interest and point of view but by our whole mental state at the moment.

The principle of selection then serves as a kind of sieve or screen through which our knowledge passes before it becomes our knowledge. Since we can't notice everything about a complicated object or situation or action or state of our own consciousness, what we do notice is determined by whatever principle of selection is operating for us at the time we gain the knowledge.

It is important to remember that what is true of the way the principle of selection works for us is true also of the way it works for others. Even before we or other people put knowledge into words to express meaning, that knowledge has been screened or selected. Before an historian or an economist writes a book, or before a reporter writes a news article, the facts that each is to present have been sifted through the screen of a principle of selection. Before one person passes on knowledge to another, that knowledge has already been selected and shaped, intentionally or unintentionally, by the mind of the communicator.

B. The Principle of Slanting

When we put our knowledge into words, a second process of selection, the process of slanting, takes place. Just as there is something, a rather mysterious principle of selection, which chooses for us what we will notice, and what will then become our knowledge, there is also a principle which operates, with or without our awareness, to select certain facts and feelings from our store of

---

[5] Of course all three observers would probably report a good many facts in common— the height of the tree, for example, and the size of the trunk. The point we wish to make is that each observer would give us a different impression of the tree because of the different principle of selection that guided his observation.

knowledge, and to choose the words and the emphasis that we shall use to communicate our meaning.[6] **Slanting** may be defined as the process of selecting (1) knowledge—factual and attitudinal; (2) words; and (3) emphasis, to achieve the intention of the communicator. Slanting is present in some degree in all communication: one may *slant for* (favorable slanting), *slant against* (unfavorable slanting), or *slant both ways* (balanced slanting).

The favorable or unfavorable or balanced slanting of the subject matter is determined, as we have said, by the intention of the communicator: he selects the knowledge, the words, and the emphasis, and he adapts them to fit his intention and to achieve his purpose. Sometimes he slants his material consciously and deliberately; sometimes, especially in spontaneous or impulsive uses of language, he is unaware that he is making a choice, and after he has spoken, he may be surprised at what he has said. In such spontaneous utterances, slanting still occurs and is still controlled by intention, but the intention operates on a subconscious rather than a conscious level.

A lawyer engaged in presenting his concluding argument to a jury is likely to be sharply aware of his intention and very careful of the way he slants facts and words to achieve that intention, but the same lawyer in answer to a casual question about his golf game might without conscious awareness of intention or of slanting give a long and ecstatic account of how he sank a thirty-foot putt on the ninth green. In this account his unconscious intention (perhaps in this case his desire to have his audience admire his golfing skill) would determine what facts he selected and how he expressed himself. We can say, then, that although both intention and slanting are present in verbal communication, the communicator's awareness of them is subject to wide variation, and they may do their work at different mental levels. In the next three sections we shall examine separately each of the three basic devices of slanting; later we shall go on to consider ways in which these devices work together to produce charged language.

C. Slanting by Use of Emphasis

Slanting by use of the devices of emphasis is unavoidable,[7] for emphasis is simply the giving of stress to subject matter, and so indicating what is im-

---

6 Notice that the "principle of selection" is at work as we *take in* knowledge, and that slanting occurs as we *express* our knowledge in words.

7 When emphasis is present—and we can think of no instance in the use of language in which it is not—it necessarily influences the meaning by playing a part in the favorable, unfavorable, or balanced slant of the communicator. We are likely to emphasize by voice stress, even when we answer *yes* or *no* to simple questions. For a more detailed treatment of emphasis see the section in Chapter 5.

portant and what is less important. In speech, for example, if we say that Socrates was *a wise old man,* we can give several slightly different meanings, one by stressing *wise,* another by stressing *old,* another by giving equal stress to *wise* and *old,* and still another by giving chief stress to *man.* Each different stress gives a different slant (favorable or unfavorable or balanced) to the statement because it conveys a different attitude toward Socrates or a different judgment of him. Connectives and word order also slant by the emphasis they give: consider the difference in slanting or emphasis produced by *old but wise, old and wise, wise but old.* In writing, we cannot indicate subtle stresses on words as clearly as in speech, but we can achieve our emphasis and so can slant by the use of more complex patterns of word order, by choice of connectives, by underlining heavily stressed words, and by marks of punctuation that indicate short or long pauses and so give light or heavy emphasis. Question marks, quotation marks, and exclamation points can also contribute to slanting.[8] It is impossible either in speech or in writing to put two facts together without giving some slight emphasis or slant. For example, if we have in mind only two facts about a man, his awkwardness and his strength, we subtly slant those facts favorably or unfavorably in whatever way we choose to join them:

More Favorable Slanting	*Less Favorable Slanting*
He is awkward and strong.	He is strong and awkward.
He is awkward but strong.	He is strong but awkward.
Although he is somewhat awkward, he is very strong.	He may be strong, but he's very awkward.

With more facts and in longer passages it is possible to maintain a delicate balance by alternating favorable and unfavorable emphasis and so producing a balanced effect.

All communication, then, is in some degree slanted by the *emphasis* of the communicator.

D. Slanting by Selection of Facts

To illustrate the technique of slanting by selection of facts, we shall examine three passages of informative writing that achieve different effects simply by the selection and emphasis of material. Each passage is made up of true statements or facts about a dog, yet the reader is given three different impressions. The first passage is an example of objective writing or balanced slanting, the second is slanted unfavorably, and the third is slanted favorably.

---

[8] Consider the slanting achieved by punctuation in the following sentences: He called the Senator an honest man? *He* called the Senator an honest man? He called the Senator an honest man! He said one more such "honest" senator would corrupt the state.

A. Balanced presentation

Our dog, Toddy, sold to us as a cocker, produces various reactions in various people. Those who come to the back door she usually growls and barks at (a milkman has said that he is afraid of her); those who come to the front door, she whines at and paws; also she tries to lick people's faces unless we have forestalled her by putting a newspaper in her mouth. (Some of our friends encourage these actions; others discourage them. Mrs. Firmly, one friend, slaps the dog with a newspaper and says, "I know how hard dogs are to train.") Toddy knows and responds to a number of words and phrases, and guests sometimes remark that she is a "very intelligent dog." She has fleas in the summer, and she sheds, at times copiously, the year round. Her blonde hairs are conspicuous when they are on people's clothing or on rugs or furniture. Her color and her large brown eyes frequently produce favorable comment. An expert on cockers would say that her ears are too short and set too high and that she is at least six pounds too heavy.

The passage above is made up of facts, verifiable facts,[9] deliberately selected and emphasized to produce a *balanced* impression. Of course not all the facts about the dog have been given—to supply *all* the facts on any subject, even such a comparatively simple one, would be an almost impossible task. Both favorable and unfavorable facts are used, however, and an effort has been made to alternate favorable and unfavorable details so that neither will receive greater emphasis by position, proportion, or grammatical structure.

B. Facts slanted *against*

That dog put her paws on my white dress as soon as I came in the door, and she made so much noise that it was two minutes before she had quieted down enough for us to talk and hear each other. Then the gas man came and she did a great deal of barking. And her hairs are on the rug and on the furniture. If you wear a dark dress they stick to it like lint. When Mrs. Firmly came in, she actually hit the dog with a newspaper to make it stay down, and she made some remark about training dogs. I wish the Birks would take the hint or get rid of that noisy, short-eared, overweight "cocker" of theirs.

This unfavorably slanted version is based on the same facts, but now these facts have been selected and given a new emphasis. The speaker, using her selected facts to give her impression of the dog, is quite possibly unaware of her negative slanting.

Now for a favorably slanted version:

9 *Verifiable facts* are facts that can be checked and agreed upon and proved to be true by people who wish to verify them. That a particular theme received a failing grade is a verifiable fact; one needs merely to see the theme with the grade on it. That the instructor should have failed the theme is not, strictly speaking, a verifiable fact, but a matter of opinion. Possibly student and teacher will not agree on this matter of opinion. That women on the average live longer than men is a verifiable fact; that they live better is a matter of opinion, a value judgment.

C. Facts slanted *for*

What a lively and responsive dog! When I walked in the door, there she was with a newspaper in her mouth, whining and standing on her hind legs and wagging her tail all at the same time. And what an intelligent dog. If you suggest going for a walk, she will get her collar from the kitchen and hand it to you, and she brings Mrs. Birk's slippers whenever Mrs. Birk says she is "tired" or mentions slippers. At a command she catches balls, rolls over, "speaks," or stands on her hind feet and twirls around. She sits up and balances a piece of bread on her nose until she is told to take it; then she tosses it up and catches it. If you are eating something, she sits up in front of you and "begs" with those big dark brown eyes set in that light, buff-colored face of hers. When I got up to go and told her I was leaving, she rolled her eyes at me and sat up like a squirrel. She certainly is a lively and an intelligent dog.

Speaker C, like Speaker B, is selecting from the "facts" summarized in balanced version A and is emphasizing his facts to communicate his impression.

All three passages are examples of *reporting* (i.e., consist of verifiable facts), yet they give three very different impressions of the same dog because of the different ways the speakers slanted the facts. Some people say that figures don't lie, and many people believe that if they have the "facts," they have the "truth." Yet if we carefully examine the ways of thought and language, we see that any knowledge that comes to us through words has been subjected to the double screening of the principle of selection and the slanting of language. Since a communicator usually cannot know all the facts and figures, he can give us only the ones he knows; and when he puts his knowledge into words, he necessarily slants by the emphasis he gives it. Because it is easy to give a biased impression in this way even without intending to do so, responsible communicators make an effort to supply a representative sampling of favorable and unfavorable details and to give a reasonably balanced slanting, particularly when they are evaluating something or are simply trying to give reliable information.

Wise listeners and readers realize that the double screening produced by the principle of selection and by slanting takes place even when people honestly try to report the facts as they know them. (Speakers B and C, for instance, probably thought of themselves as simply giving information about a dog and were not deliberately trying to mislead.) Wise listeners and readers know too that deliberate manipulators of language, by mere selection and emphasis, can make their slanted facts appear to support almost any cause.

In arriving at opinions and values we cannot always be sure that the facts that sift into our minds through language are representative and relevant and true. We need to remember that much of our information about politics, government, business, and foreign affairs comes to us selected and slanted. More than we realize, our opinions on these matters may depend on what newspaper we read or what news commentator we listen to. Worthwhile opinions call for knowledge of reliable facts and reasonable arguments for and against—and such opinions include beliefs about morality and truth as well as about public affairs. Because complex subjects involve knowing and dealing with many facts on both sides, reliable judgments are at best difficult to arrive at. If we want to be fair-minded, we must be willing to subject our opinions to continual testing by new knowledge, and must realize that after all they *are* opinions, more or less trustworthy. Their trustworthiness will depend on the representativeness of our facts, on the quality of our reasoning, and on the standard of values that we choose to apply.

We shall not give here a passage illustrating the unscrupulous slanting of facts. Such a passage would also include irrelevant facts and false statements presented as facts, along with various subtle distortions of fact. Yet to the uninformed reader the passage would be indistinguishable from a passage intended to give a fair account. If two passages (B and C) of casual and unintentional slanting of facts about a dog can give such contradictory impressions of a simple subject, the reader can imagine what a skilled and designing manipulation of facts and statistics could do to mislead an uninformed reader about a really complex subject. An example of such manipulation might be the account of the United States that Soviet propaganda has supplied to the average Russian. Such propaganda, however, would go beyond the mere slanting of the facts: it would clothe the selected facts in charged words and would make use of the many other devices of slanting that appear in charged language.

E. Slanting by Use of Charged Words

In the passages describing the dog Toddy, we were illustrating the technique of slanting by the selection and emphasis of facts. Though the facts selected had to be expressed in words, the words chosen were as factual as possible, and it was the selection and emphasis of facts and not of words that was mainly responsible for the two distinctly different impressions of the dog. In the passages below we are demonstrating another way of slanting —slanting by the use of charged words. This time the accounts are very similar in the facts they contain; the different impressions of the subject, Corlyn, are produced not by different facts but by the subtle selecting of charged words.

The passages were written by a clever student who was told to choose as his subject a person in action, and to write two descriptions, each using the "same facts." The assignment required that one description be slanted positively and the other negatively, so that the first would make the reader favorably inclined toward the person and the action, and the second would make him unfavorably inclined.

Here is the favorably charged description. Read it carefully and form your opinion of the person before you go on to read the second description.

CORLYN

Corlyn paused at the entrance to the room and glanced about. A well-cut black dress draped subtly about her slender form. Her long blonde hair gave her chiseled features the simple frame they required. She smiled an engaging smile as she accepted a cigarette from her escort. As he lit it for her she looked over the flame and into his eyes. Corlyn had that rare talent of making every male feel that he was the one man in the world.

She took his arm and they descended the steps into the room. She walked with an effortless grace and spoke with equal ease. They each took a cup of coffee and joined a group of friends near the fire. The flickering light danced across her face and lent an ethereal quality to her beauty. The good conversation, the crackling logs, and the stimulating coffee gave her a feeling of internal warmth. Her eyes danced with each leap of the flames.

Taken by itself this passage might seem just a description of an attractive girl. The favorable slanting by use of charged words has been done so skillfully that it is inconspicuous. Now we turn to the unfavorably slanted description of the "same" girl engaged in the "same" actions:

CORLYN

Corlyn halted at the entrance to the room and looked around. A plain black dress hung on her thin frame. Her stringy bleached hair accentuated her harsh features. She smiled an inane smile as she took a cigarette from her escort. As he lit it for her she stared over the lighter and into his eyes. Corlyn had a habit of making every male feel that he was the last man on earth.

She grasped his arm and they walked down the steps and into the room. Her pace was fast and ungainly, as was her speech. They each reached for some coffee and broke into a group of acquaintances near the fire. The flickering light played across her face and revealed every flaw. The loud talk, the fire, and the coffee she had gulped down made her feel hot. Her eyes grew more red with each leap of the flames.

When the reader compares these two descriptions, he can see how charged words influence the reader's attitude. One needs to read the two descriptions several times to appreciate all the subtle differences between them. Words, some rather heavily charged, others innocent-looking but lightly charged, work together to carry to the reader a judgment of a person and a situation. If the reader had seen only the first description of Corlyn, he might well have thought that he had formed his "own judgment on the basis of the facts." And the examples just given only begin to suggest the techniques that may be used in heavily charged language.

F. Slanting and Charged Language

Thus far we have dealt with one device or technique of slanting at a time. When slanting of facts, or words, or emphasis, or any combination of the three *significantly influences* feelings toward, or judgments about, a subject, the language used is charged language.

The way of determining whether or not a communication is charged is to ask: Does this communication strongly affect my emotions or attitudes or judgments? Does it express strong emotions, attitudes, or judgments of the communicator? Does it significantly affect the emotions, attitudes, or judgments of most people? If an expression strongly affects me, it is charged for me; if it expresses the strong feeling of the communicator, it is charged for him; and if it significantly affects most people, it is charged for them and can be said to be generally charged.

Of course communications vary in the amount of charge they carry and in their effect on different people; what is very favorably charged for one person may have little or no charge, or may even be adversely charged, for others. It is sometimes hard to distinguish between charged and uncharged expression. But it is safe to say that whenever we wish to convey any kind of inner knowledge—feelings, attitudes, judgments, values—we are obliged to convey that attitudinal meaning through the medium of charged language; and when we wish to understand the inside knowledge of others, we have to interpret the charged language that they choose, or are obliged, to use. Charged language, then, is the natural and necessary medium for communicating charged or attitudinal meaning. At times we have difficulty in living with it, but we should have even greater difficulty in living without it.

Some of the difficulties in living with charged language are caused by its use in dishonest propaganda, in some editorials, in many political speeches, in most advertising, in certain kinds of effusive salesmanship, and in blatantly insincere, or exaggerated, or sentimental expressions of emotion. Other difficulties are caused by the misunderstandings that charged language produces. A charged phrase misinterpreted in a love letter; a charged word spoken in haste or in anger; an acrimonious argument about religion or politics or athletics or fraternities; the frustrating uncertainty produced by the effort to understand the complex attitudinal meaning in a poem or a play or a short story—these troubles, all growing out of the use of charged language, may give us the feeling that Robert Louis Stevenson expressed when he said, "The battle goes sore against us to the going down of the sun."

But however charged language is abused and whatever misunderstandings it may cause, we still have to live with it—and even by it. It shapes our attitudes and values even without our conscious knowledge; it gives purpose to, and guides, our actions; through it we establish and maintain relations with other people and by means of it we exert our greatest influence on them. Without charged language, life would be but half life. The relatively uncharged language of bare factual statement, though it serves its informative purpose well and is much less open to abuse and to misunderstanding, can describe only the bare land of factual knowledge; to communicate knowledge of the turbulencies and the calms and the deep currents of the sea of inner experience we must use charged language.

G. The Heavily Charged Language of Persuasion or Prejudice

In the passages about the dog Toddy and the girl Corlyn we have already examined specimens of charged language. Besides being slanted by emphasis, the Toddy passages were charged by selection of fact, the Corlyn passages by charged words.

Heavily charged language makes use of the same basic devices, but it uses them with great force and combines them in all sorts of ways. The person who uses heavily charged language generally is, or wishes to appear to be, in a state of strong emotion. He is attacking something or defending something, recommending some course of action or communicating values and beliefs. He is engaged in a struggle in which words are weapons or tools; sometimes, like a man in a fight, he may be ready to use any implement, any false reasoning or distortion that will serve his purpose. He is likely to use various types of charged words and the devices of slanting that we have discussed; he may present personal opinion as fact, and cite "facts" whether they are true or not and whether they are relevant or not; he may engage in name-calling directed against his opponents, and may use innuendo, irony, ridicule, and charged figures of speech. He may produce his effect consciously or unconsciously, by overstatement or by understatement. (Consider the effect of Jonathan Swift's understatement, "Last week I saw a woman flayed and you will hardly believe how much it altered her appearance for the worse.") In recent years we have seen many examples of heavily charged language in civil rights demonstrations, campus protests, and discussions of the war in Indochina.

Charged language used to persuade or convince gains some of its most telling effects not so much from particular words and phrases as from the whole positive or negative drift or slant of the passage. Such drift is frequently produced by the **"right-on-our-side"** technique. The communicator is trying to lead his audience to share, and to identify itself with, the attitude he takes or appears to take. He does this by presenting two opposing sides. On one side (the communicator's, which he slants favorably as "our side") are admirable people motivated by high principles and striving to do good; on the other side are undesirable and even hateful people bent on doing harm. The audience is intended to be sympathetic with "our side" and to identify itself emotionally with "our" cause. This "right-on-our-side" technique is a common method of slanting, found very often in persuasive writing or speaking.

Excerpts from a speech by Vice President Spiro T. Agnew, as reported by United Press International in February 1970 will illustrate some of the techniques of heavily charged language. Mr. Agnew reportedly told a cheering audience in St. Louis, Missouri, that the Democrats might very well seek their leaders among the young deserters who have fled to Canada and Sweden but that "we Republicans shall look elsewhere." He added:

As for these deserters, malcontents, radicals, incendiaries, the civil and uncivil disobedients among our young, SDS, PLP, Weatherman I and Weatherman II, the revolutionary action movement, Yippies, Hippies, Yahoos, Black Panthers, Lions and Tigers alike—I would swap the whole damn zoo for a single platoon of the kind of young Americans I saw in Vietnam. . . .

The Democratic Party sits teetering on the edge of political and financial ruin— dragged there by the blunders and excesses of its current leaders. . . . For all our Republican attacks on Roosevelt, Truman, Acheson, Kennedy and Johnson, there were assuredly a more impressive and formidable array of political adversaries than the present crop of complainers. The old lions and wolves of the Democratic Party are gone or in retirement; and in their place we find only tabby cats and lap dogs. . . .

The rank-and-file Democrat in this country . . . has had a bellyful of politicians who fawn over young radicals who have no manners and less sense; he is fed up with the limousine liberals running his party; he is fed up with the whole gang. And to these Democrats who have had enough of this kind of leadership, I say, come on over to our side; there's lots of room in the inn.

A critical reader of this passage might underline examples of name-calling; might note that some of the most powerfully charged expressions involve figures of speech: *whole damn zoo, sits teetering, dragged there, crop of complainers, tabby cats and lap dogs, bellyful of politicians, limousine liberals, whole gang, room in the inn;* and might note the several ways of making "our side" appear the "right" side.

H. The Charged Language of Evaluation

One of the functions of language is to pass judgment on something or to evaluate its worth. Common examples of such evaluative or critical communication are editorials on national and international affairs, news commentary that reports and interprets, and reviews of films, plays, television programs, and books. Good critical writing supplies both information and informed judgments. In imparting judgments, however, critics necessarily use the charged language of attitudinal meaning; one may get very different impressions of the same subject from writers who are simply attempting to evaluate honestly.

The following excerpts from two reviews[10] of the same book will illustrate. A good critic gives us not necessarily the truth, but truth as it appears to him, after he has exercised his best judgment.

A. THE RIDDLES OF FRANKLIN ROOSEVELT

John Gunther calls his new Roosevelt book both a "profile" and a "summary." It also is a compilation to about a third of its length, composed in the now established Gunther technique, of an impressive assortment of details, some of facts important and trivial, some of ideas deliberately artless and penetrating. Thus the Roosevelt

---

[10] Raymond Swing, "The Riddles of Franklin Roosevelt," *The Nation,* June 3, 1950; the editors of *Time,* "Let's Wait," *Time,* June 5, 1950.

story has been accorded the treatment of the notable "Inside" works that have given Mr. Gunther a unique place in political journalism. It need not be debated whether this treatment assures a satisfactory biography; it does not. Mr. Roosevelt was both too complex and too paradoxical to be illuminated by a catalogue of his contradictions and questions about his qualities. He needs the synthesis of a great interpretative biography, operating like a shaft of light that reveals unity formed out of disunity and harmony underlying discord. Mr. Gunther has not undertaken to write this biography. It is not his method or his art. He is a compiler, as was Mr. Sandburg writing about Lincoln. He does not go in for the portraiture that grows out of selection, that is, the suppression of detail. He must note everything, stop and conjecture about everything, delight in everything, and both marvel and cavil.

All this makes a book that is informative, entertaining, and in this case also important, and because Mr. Gunther is an indefatigable gatherer of detail, a book that is fresh even in the familiar field of Rooseveltiana. But Mr. Gunther has not departed from his established formula. He writes about F. D. R. as he writes about a continent. But since F. D. R. was not a continent, it is clear that Mr. Gunther does not write about him *because* he understands him and feels compelled to share his understanding. He is searching, and we share his search.

B. LET'S WAIT

Journalist John Gunther has made a career of breezing through countries, even whole continents, and persuading his readers that he is giving them inside stuff. His "Inside" (Europe, Latin America, Asia, U.S.A.) books have considerable popular virtues: they can be read in a hammock, they seldom induce thought, and they almost never leave a deep residue of conviction or concern. Writing with ebullience and wide-eyed surprise, he projects men and events just far enough beyond the daily-news level to satisfy those who dislike being serious but are plagued by the need to seem informed.

In *Roosevelt in Retrospect*, Gunther has brought these talents to bear on the complex personality of Franklin Delano Roosevelt. In spite of his avowed aim of getting at his subject's "root qualities and basic sources of power," Gunther has conspicuously failed to "pin something of his great substance against the wall of time." Getting inside a man is something quite different from getting into a continent or a country; it takes more than visas. What Gunther has achieved is a lively journalistic profile pieced together with materials largely lifted from the mushrooming literature on F. D. R. and loosely held together by Gunther's own surface researches.

Writing "as objectively as possible," Gunther is obviously too dazzled by the Roosevelt glitter to do a balanced job.

A comparison of statements made about particular topics will highlight some of the techniques of charged language used in the reviews. For example, on the subject of Mr. Gunther's "Inside" books:

In A	In B
the notable "Inside" works that have given Mr. Gunther a unique place in political journalism.	His "Inside" . . . books have considerable popular virtues: they can be read in a hammock, they seldom induce thought, . . .

On the parallel between this book and the "Inside" books:

In A	In B
He writes about F. D. R. as he writes about a continent.	Getting inside a man is something quite different from getting into a continent or a country; it takes more than visas.
He is searching and we share his search.	

On Mr. Gunther's method:

In A	In B
the now established Gunther technique	breezing through countries, even whole continents, and persuading his readers that he is giving them inside stuff
an impressive assortment of details	
He is a compiler, as was Mr. Sandburg writing about Lincoln.	pieced together with materials largely lifted from the mushrooming literature on F. D. R. and loosely held together by Gunther's own surface researches
an indefatigable gatherer of detail	

On the value of the book:

In A	In B
Mr. Gunther has not undertaken to write this [great interpretative] biography. It is not his method or his art.	Gunther has conspicuously failed to "pin something of his great substance against the wall of time."
a book that is informative, entertaining, and in this case also important, . . . a book that is fresh even in the familiar field of Rooseveltiana	a lively journalistic profile pieced together with materials largely lifted from the mushrooming literature on F. D. R.

On Mr. Gunther's attitude toward his subjects:

In A	In B
deliberately artless and penetrating	wide-eyed surprise
delight in everything, and both marvel and cavil	obviously too dazzled

Passage B, with its conspicuous use of irony and ridicule, is much more heavily charged and slanted than passage A. Passage A illustrates the inconspicuously charged language that many readers do not think of as charged at all.

I. Summary

The purpose of this section on the principle of selection, slanting, and charged language has been to give the reader an understanding of certain principles and devices and to let him see and feel for himself the effects that they can produce. As the reader reviews this section, he will find it useful to keep the following points in mind:

1. All knowledge that we gain from the language of others has been processed and molded by the operations of (*a*) the principle of selection and (*b*) the principle of slanting. *As* we gain first-hand knowledge, and *before* we put it into words, our interests and purposes supply a principle of selection that determines what things we will notice and remember, and so shapes the raw materials of our knowledge. *When* we put these raw materials into words, we select from and modify them (i.e., slant them) to suit our intention by the way we choose facts, words, and emphasis.

2. Slanting may be defined as the selection of (*a*) knowledge (factual and attitudinal), (*b*) words, and (*c*) emphasis to achieve the conscious or unconscious intention of the communicator. The impression produced is determined by the way the communicator slants to achieve his intention: one may slant for (favorable slanting), slant against (unfavorable slanting), or slant both ways (balanced slanting). Responsible communicators make an effort to be fair and to aim at balanced slanting, particularly when their primary intention is to inform or to evaluate.

3. Charged language is a product of slanting; it may be defined as the slanting of knowledge or words or emphasis in a way that significantly influences feelings toward, or judgments of, a subject. Although charged language is more subject to misuse and misinterpretation than factual language, it is essential for expressing attitudinal meaning.

4. Heavily charged language makes forceful use of the devices of charged language and combines them in various ways. It is often (though not always) used insincerely to express exaggerated emotions and prejudiced attitudes or to work on the emotions and prejudices of the audience. Some of the devices frequently used in heavily charged language are: irrelevant or untrue facts, charged proper names and other charged words and expressions, charged comparisons, name-calling, innuendo, ridicule, the false appearance of logical reasoning, the "right-on-our-side" technique.

5. Often, the use of heavily charged language should act as a warning signal to an audience, especially if the communicator makes extreme use of charged words and if he appeals to prejudices. On the other hand, any communicator who wants to express sincere attitudes and convictions must use slanting and charged language to do so, and heavily charged language may be fully justified under circumstances that require the forceful communication of strong feeling and deep conviction.

6. In this section the reader has had an opportunity to examine and to feel some of the effects of slanting and charged language: in the Toddy passages, the slanting of verifiable facts by selection and emphasis; in the Corlyn passages, slanting by emphasis and the use of charged words; in the excerpts from Mr. Agnew's speech, an example of deliberately and heavily charged persuasive language; and in the reviews of *Roosevelt in Retrospect*, two consciously charged, but we think sincere, efforts to evaluate the same book.

III. THE RESPONSIBLE USE OF LANGUAGE

Much has been written about the devaluation or debasing of language in contemporary life; and here and there in the preceding pages we have touched on this problem of devaluation, particularly in connection with heavily charged language. Although such language is not necessarily dishonest, too often—in politics and in advertising, for example—words are used to obscure rather than to communicate meaning. The result may be the "credibility gap" much talked of in recent years, and it may be a profound skepticism about language in general. The American public has become only too familiar with a kind of doubletalk in which words have lost sensible, intelligible meanings. An instance is the frequently quoted statement of the American Army major who, viewing the rubble of a provincial Vietnamese city, said that it was necessary to destroy the town to save it. Martin Esslin, an authority on the Theater of the Absurd, has pointed out that when absurd drama shows the breakdown of communication and the degeneration of dialogue into random nonsensical talk, the drama represents the sort of divorce that has in fact occurred between reality and language.

The purpose of this brief section is to suggest a standard by which language, used with integrity, may be a more authentic means of communication than it sometimes is now.

The word *good,* as we noted in considering words of multiple standards, can mean effective for a purpose, or artistically pleasing, or morally good. This statement has relevance for our own use of language and for our judgment of the use of language by others: really good language is good in all three ways—it is effective in achieving the communicator's intention; it is satisfying in expression; and it is morally good in that it tells as much truth as the communicator can justly and reasonably convey under the circumstances. In later chapters we shall discuss skill and artistry in expression; here we shall discuss the responsible use of language in communicating and interpreting factual and attitudinal meaning. Words are, in effect, deeds, and the use of language is a kind of action. Some words, like the order "Fire" given to armed men, are commands to action; and most words ultimately, directly or indirectly, produce action. Ethical standards that apply to actions apply with equal force to words, and we are as responsible for what we say as for what we do.

There are circumstances that may require partial truth, shading of truth, withholding of truth, or even direct falsehood. Politicians under some circumstances may have to deal in the part-truths of partisan politics; a host's tact and kindness may call for the shading of truth when he says he enjoyed the evening to a guest who has stayed too long; a doctor may properly withhold from a critically injured accident victim the shocking knowledge that her husband has been killed in the accident; a statesman may in some situations conclude that denial of a truth or the practicing of downright falsehood is the lesser of two evils. All of these circumstances constitute somewhat exceptional moral choices. Though they are exceptions to the general rule that truth is the end of language, they do not contradict the principle that requires the responsible user of language to tell as much truth as he can under the circumstances.

The communicator is obliged, too, to communicate his truth with awareness of its probable effect, with thoughtful restraint, and with consideration for the feelings of other people. Truth can hurt. People are hurt worst, not by falsehoods, but by personal and stinging truths spoken impulsively or angrily or maliciously. We all know from painful experience that the truth hurts, and that it hurts most when it points to a standard we cannot possibly attain or to an action or to a defect that we regret and suffer for, but cannot rectify.

One of the uses of language, it is true, is to let off emotional steam; everyone has the right to say silly things now and then, to use words to express high spirits, or friendly banter, or pent up feelings, to luxuriate in exaggerated and picturesque speech; but we need to choose the time and the place and the audience; and we need to remember that steam burns can be painful. There is the truth of first thought with its sometimes hasty or impulsive or unjust judgments, and there is the better truth of second thought and reasonable, considered judgments. The truth of first thought, of spontaneous utterance, is often lively and colorful—and sometimes very revealing; conversation devoid of it would be too conscious and calculated, particularly conversation between close friends; but some truths of first thought, such as spiteful or cutting comment, malicious gossip, snap judgments based on prejudice, and witty but damaging remarks on other people, are better left unsaid even in private talk. Humane consideration for the feeling of others, in speech and in action, is perhaps the best evidence of responsibility.

In any kind of serious and open discussion, the responsible communicator presents the best truth that his knowledge and reason and feelings can lead him to. Even then there may be a problem: what seems true to him may seem false to well-qualified people who arrive at other opinions and beliefs. In such cases he can present his views as the truth-for-him without insisting that there must be only one true side of complex and many-sided truth.

Thus far we have been saying that the use of language in speech and writing constitutes a kind of moral action, that the end or purpose of the responsible communicator (with the exceptions that we have mentioned) is expressing some kind of truth. Skill in interpreting the communication of others is also a requisite for the responsible use of language. The general standard for interpreting a communication is set by the basic intent of the communicator—whether he wishes to inform, to evaluate, to persuade, or to communicate experience; for each intention aims at a different kind of truth and needs to be judged by a different standard. We shall deal with interpreting the language of others in the next two sections.

A. A Critical View of Language

The principle of selection, as we have said, is operative for all knowledge before it becomes knowledge, and knowledge communicated through language is necessarily subjected to favorable, unfavorable, or balanced slanting. Awareness of these facts should cause us to be alert and analytical, but should not make us chronically suspicious.

Often, particularly in the communication of factual knowledge, slanting has little or no significant influence on the meaning. In much scientific writing, for example, the communicator is simply trying to convey facts and ideas clearly; he makes a conscientious effort to slant both ways by including all the relevant facts and ideas, even those which do not support his theory; he uses a technical and standardized language that carries little attitudinal meaning, and he emphasizes in order to show logical connections rather than to appeal to the reader's feelings. But slanting becomes increasingly important in meaning as the emotional or attitudinal element increases and as purpose shifts from the informative presentation of facts and ideas to the communication of attitudes and beliefs and experiences.

Since intention determines slanting, an analysis of the way a communicator slants will often reveal his intention and will help in evaluating what he has to say. Heavy use of slanting is not necessarily suspect in all kinds of communication, but one-sided slanting often indicates that the communicator is either unconsciously prejudiced and off balance, or that he is purposefully playing on the emotions of the gullible reader to serve his own ends.

On the other hand, it is good to remember that opinions different from our own may be held by someone who sincerely has something to say and must use strong language to express his strong feeling. If we have no sound reason for questioning his sincerity, we will gain most from a sympathetic reading in which we try to see the subject through his eyes and with emotions similar to his, however much his point of view may differ from our own. Only after we have seen, and felt, and understood the whole of the communicator's message will we be in a position to reach a fair and sound judgment of his intention or his meaning.

B. An Approach to Critical Reading

We are suggesting here, not a single standard for judging different kinds of writing aimed at different effects, but a critical attitude, a state of mind.

It is the willingness to look steadily at a communication and judge it first *objectively,* according to the success of the writer in achieving his purpose, and then *personally,* according to our beliefs and values. Critical reading is an intellectual process in which, first, the reader suspends judgment and tries by analysis to gain a clear understanding of the material; second, he determines in the light of his analysis just what the writer's purpose was and with what skill the writer has accomplished that purpose; and third, he arrives at his personal evaluation, determining the worth and truth of the communication *for him.*

The preliminary step, gaining an impartial understanding of the communication, calls for some method of analysis. The method recommended here is suggested by Rudyard Kipling:

> I keep six honest serving men
> (They taught me all I know):—
> Their names are What and Why and When
> And How and Where and Who.

These six serving men supply us with the questions we need to answer in order to understand a piece of writing. For some types of communication some of the questions may be irrelevant or inappropriate, but the general method intelligently adapted can be applied with profit to all types of writing.

Since it is sometimes easier to answer one question first, sometimes another, the more detailed suggestions given below do not necessarily represent the sequence of steps in the analysis. Usually it is best to start with the question that we can answer with most certainty.

1. **When** and **where.** Knowing just when and where a communication appeared may help us judge its reliability and the intention of the writer. An article on the effects of alcohol published in a medical journal in 1972 would obviously be more authoritative and trustworthy than a tract published by the Prohibition Party in 1918.

2. **How.** An analysis of how a communication is written can do much to reveal the character of the writer and to afford a surer knowledge of his purpose. The reader should give particular consideration to: choice of language; sentence structure, rhythm, alliteration, and other aspects of style; use of the techniques of slanting and charging; the way the writer reasons if reasoning is involved; the attitude of the writer toward his reader, his subject, and himself; the use of general statements and substantiating particulars.

3. **What.** The "what," the factual meaning of the communication, is, of course, always important. The reader should as far as possible reduce what is said to factual, uncharged language. He is then in a better position to make an unprejudiced judgment of the subject matter. This kind of factual restatement is particularly useful in examining writing that aims to persuade or to convince the reader.

4. Who. The more we know about the background, knowledge, experience, and reputation of a writer, the more we are helped in judging what he says. If we have no information about him, we can often deduce a great deal from the "how" and "what" of his writing. Is he an educated man? Does he have special knowledge of his subject? Does he seem to be presenting his material fairly? Is his use of English fair, good, or excellent? What attitude does he take toward his reader and himself? What seems to be his position or profession?

5. Why. Sometimes the "why," the intention, is apparent on the face of the communication, as it is in a mathematics text; sometimes it is subtly concealed under charged language and specious logic, as it usually is in propaganda and advertising. A careful reader will always be alert to the concealed intention, which often is to be discovered only by close examination of inconspicuous slanting or use of lightly charged words. After he has completed his six-point analysis, he should reconsider in the light of the other five points his interpretation of the "why." He needs to be sure he has interpreted the why (intention) correctly; if he fails here, his later judgments will have little validity.

6. To whom. The audience for whom a piece of writing is intended may determine to a considerable extent the "how," and to some extent the "what" and "why." Very often the reader may profitably add to Kipling's six serving men one more—*To Whom?* That is, for what audience, or what kind of audience, was this communication written?

In applying the whole method of analysis described here, it is essential that the reader suspend judgment, be scrupulously fair in analyzing each point, and make an honest effort to follow as exactly as possible the "what" (the full meaning) of the communicator. He must resist the very strong temptation (1) to twist the words of the communicator to fit his own meaning for them, (2) to close his mind to views that are different from his own, and (3) to accept or reject facts and judgments and attitudes before he has made a fair effort to follow and to understand the whole piece of writing.

After the reader has completed his analysis, he is ready to decide how well the communicator has used the means at his disposal—organization, facts, and language—to achieve his purpose. In this *objective* judgment he is not interested in the truth or value of the communication; he is simply considering the writer's success in achieving his end, whatever that end may be. One can, for example, admire Hitler's skill as a propagandist, even though one condemns the purpose for which Hitler was using language; one can admire the skill or craftsmanship of a poet or short-story writer even though the particular type of poem or short story is not pleasing to one's taste.

Thus far the reader has been primarily concerned with understanding the communication and then with answering two questions about it: "What is the writer trying to do?" and "How well has he achieved his purpose?" The final question is, "What is my evaluation of the whole piece of writing?" Now the reader can fairly let his taste, his code of morality, and his view of truth come into play. He can say, "Hitler was a skillful propagandist, but I have read *Mein Kampf* and have thought about it, and I am convinced that he was wrong on these points: . . ." He can say, "I have given this poem or short story a fair reading and I understand what the writer is trying to do and how he has done it [or I honestly don't understand]; I regard it as good literature [or as poor literature] for these reasons: . . ." This final step, the *personal* evaluation, is usually almost automatic. Executing it is like deciding whether we like a house after we have lived in it for some time. We know all the facts about it; evaluating is now simply a matter of balancing merits and defects, and then expressing our judgment accurately.

A final note: there is some danger that the approach to critical reading presented here may sound much more formidable and more time-consuming than it actually is; the reader may simply throw up his hands and say, "If I have to go through all that to reach a critical evaluation, I'll just keep my prejudices." But if he will suspend judgment about this method of reading and will give it a fair trial, he will find that learning to evaluate critically is comparable to learning to play a good game of bridge or chess—and is perhaps less difficult. Bridge players who pause for only a moment and then play a difficult hand rapidly and skillfully, chess players who can look at the board and plan twelve moves ahead, achieve with ease and assurance feats of analysis beyond the comprehension of the novice. The practiced reader analyzes and judges what he reads with similar speed and assurance and with a greater sense of reward.

CHAPTER REVIEW

Review for Section I, pages 5–26

If your reading of this section has been adequate you should:

1. be able to define accurately and explain clearly the following terms:

locution	charged words
context	connotative words
referent	charged words of everyday living
fact	charged abstract words
idea	charged words of personal attitude
intention	charged words of fact-and-value

2. be able to distinguish between and give apt examples to clarify the meaning of the following terms:

verbal context and context of circumstances
inside and outside knowledge
factual meaning, attitudinal meaning, intention
charged scale words and charged words of multiple standards

3. be able to clarify and expand, with the use of concrete examples whenever possible, any statement in the section summary on pages 25–26.

Review for Section II, pages 26–39
   If your reading of this section has been adequate you should:
   1. be able to define accurately and explain clearly each of the following
terms:

the principle of selection   reporting
slanting   the "right-on-our-side" technique
charged language

2. be able to distinguish between and illustrate:

slanting and the principle of selection
verifiable fact and opinion (or value judgment)
slanting for, slanting against, and balanced slanting
conscious and unconscious intention

3. be able to explain clearly to someone unfamiliar with the subject:

the effect of the principle of selection and of slanting on the knowledge that
comes to us through language
   the three basic devices of slanting (give brief but clear examples of each)
   why charged language is difficult to live with and difficult to live without
   an intelligent attitude to take toward the use of heavily charged language
   the likelihood of communicating knowledge without slanting it in some way
   the basic devices of slanting illustrated in: (*a*) the Toddy passages, (*b*) the Corlyn
passages, (*c*) the Agnew speech, (*d*) the two book reviews
   how one may determine whether a communication is charged or not

4. be able to clarify and expand, with the use of concrete examples whenever possible, any statement in the section summary on pages 38–39.

Review for Section III, pages 40–45
   If your reading of this section has been adequate you should:
   1. be able to explain and comment on:

the responsible use of language
the process of critical reading

2. be able to give full and critical answers to the following questions:

What is the relative importance of slanting in factual communication and in
attitudinal communication?

What general principles should guide the responsible user of language?
Do you agree with the principles stated?

EXERCISES

Exercises for Section I, pages 5–26

I. During the war in Vietnam, some Americans of draft age were involved
in antiwar demonstrations, were burning draft cards, and were leaving this
country for Canada to avoid the draft. Below are some of the terms that were
applied to these young men. What attitude appears to be expressed by each of
the terms? Which seem to you the most favorably charged, which the most unfavorably charged, and which the most nearly factual or neutral?

draft dissenters	draft dodgers
draft resisters	draft evaders
conscientious objectors	deserters
protesters	peaceniks
traitors	escapists
pacifists	yellow-bellies
peace lovers	demonstrators for peace
activists	rebels
patriots	communists
radicals	delinquents

II. Senator Smathers of Florida, campaigning in 1950 against Senator
Claude Pepper, is said to have told rural audiences:

Are you aware that Claude Pepper is known all over Washington as a shameless
extrovert? Not only that, but this man is reliably reported to practice nepotism with
his sister-in-law, and he has a sister who was once a thespian in wicked New York.
Worst of all, it is an established fact that Mr. Pepper, before his marriage, practiced
celibacy.

What is the factual meaning of the senator's statement? What kind of response
did he apparently intend his listeners to have? How would you describe the
technique of conveying attitudinal, as opposed to factual, meaning?

III. To see how words with vague or very complex factual meaning are
commonly used, examine the following newspaper headlines. What is the
factual meaning, the referent, of each of the italicized words or abbreviations?

U.S. says tires fail safety tests
U.S. walks on moon again
U.S. takes firm stand in Paris talks
U.S. bans bio-war
Science studies rocks

Army to tell of massacres
U.S. to probe Panther deaths
U.S. endorses troop withdrawal from Laos

IV. Richard M. Weaver, in a book called *The Ethics of Rhetoric,* published in 1957, made a study of words which at that time seemed to have the greatest power to arouse favorable and unfavorable responses in Americans. Among the "god terms," those that carried the greatest blessing, Mr. Weaver included *American, progress* and *progressive, science, modern, efficient,* and *democracy.* The principal "devil term," he thought, was *Communist,* followed by the opposites of the "god terms": *un-American, unprogressive, unscientific,* etc. He also observed that *aggressor* was rapidly becoming a potent devil term, one that carried very strong condemnation.

What seems to you to be the force of these words at the present time? If any of them have declined in their power to influence feelings and attitudes, to what would you attribute the decline? What do you think are the four or five most powerful god terms and devil terms operating in American society and politics today?

V. A, making an important long-distance call, is interrupted by B. A thinks of three ways of conveying to B that he does not want to be disturbed: (1) "Excuse me, please; this is a very important long-distance call"; (2) "Hello, be with you in a minute"; (3) "Shut the door and be quiet." Consider the difference in factual meaning, attitude, and intention of these three communications. If you were the speaker, which expression would you use, and why? Is one of the expressions "better English" than the other two?

VI. "The board is on the fence." What different meanings can this sentence have, and what determines its meaning?

VII. In the sentences below, substitute for each italicized locution an expression with a similar factual meaning but a less favorable connotation. Examples:

She *placed a moist cloth* on his forehead. [slapped a wet rag]
He *talked steadily* for half an hour. [droned on]

1. He *strode* onto the platform and *smiled* at the audience.
2. The woman *reproved* her *carefree* daughter for the *untidiness* of the girl's room.
3. The *policeman* had a *large, strong neck.*
4. He *left college* because he *had difficulty with* English, mathematics, and biology.
5. The army *withdrew to a strategic position.*
6. He read the *description on the jacket* of the book.
7. He is a *high-ranking officer* in the Navy and a *strict disciplinarian.*
8. He *closed* the door, *tossed* the book on the table, and *called* to his wife.
9. He is an *affectionate* parent who *treats his children with indulgence.*

10. She is an *unmarried woman* of fifty who is always ready to *give information* about her neighbors and who *takes an interest in everything they do.*

11. He *frankly admitted* that he had *misrepresented the facts,* and he *asked for considerate treatment.*

12. The Mayor spoke *forthrightly.* He *stated the facts* without *attempting to conceal his honest indignation.*

VIII. In the discussion of scale words and words of multiple standards, particular attention was given to the words *true* and *good.*

A. In each of the sentences below, consider what the word *true* means and what questions you would raise or what tests or standards you would apply to decide whether in your opinion the statement is true.

B. Follow a similar procedure with the word *good* as it is used in the contexts provided (i.e., what does *good* mean in each case and what tests or standards would you apply in judging a can opener, manners, a movie, etc?).

C. Try to summarize what you have learned about the way these two words work.

1. It is *true* that lead is heavier than aluminum.
2. It is *true* that the average American eats more food than the average Chinese.
3. It is *true* that Hemingway is a better novelist than Ayn Rand.
4. It is *true* that Lincoln delivered an address at Gettysburg.
5. It is *true* that Christianity and Judaism are better religions than Islam (i.e., Mohammedanism).
6. It is *true* that kindness is better than cruelty.

1. A *good* can opener
2. *Good* manners
3. A *good* western movie
4. A *good* movie
5. *Good* rock or *good* classical music
6. A *good* political speech made by a presidential candidate
7. A *good* businessman
8. A *good* competitor in sports
9. A *good* news commentator or columnist
10. A *good* person or human being

IX. In the light of what you have learned about language, comment on the use of language in the following statements.

1. I'm telling you the truth. He's the meanest man in the world.
2. I don't care if he was born in this country and has a good reputation in town. You can't trust a Russian.
3. Tests show that clothes wash 60% whiter with Bubblo, the Magic Soap.
4. He must be a communist. He has a lot of radical literature around his house.
5. How do I know his parents are ignorant Polacks? Why, I've met them, and they can't even speak good English.

6. I don't believe in national health insurance because it's undemocratic.

7. The book was so dull, I went to sleep before I was half through it.

8. What do you mean, saying a fourteen-story building is tall? Why, in New York we have buildings . . . .

Exercises for Section II, pages 26–39

I. When Dr. John W. Gardner became Secretary of Health, Education, and Welfare, he said, "We are all faced with a series of great opportunities— brilliantly disguised as insoluble problems." What techniques of slanting do you find in this statement?

II. Vice President Spiro Agnew, criticizing the October 1969 Vietnam Moratorium, created a stir of both approval and disapproval with the statement below. Comment on Mr. Agnew's use of language.

A spirit of national masochism prevails, encouraged by an effete corps of impudent snobs who characterize themselves as intellectuals.

III. Jot down the facts that you would include in the description of your English classroom if you were describing it for:

1. A person who planned to paint it
2. A teacher who was considering holding the class there
3. A janitor whom you want to reprove for his care of the building
4. A friend whom you want to persuade to apply for admission to your college

IV. The following passage is a collection of verifiable facts about a college professor. Read the passage, and then see the questions below.

Professor Bestworst, a man of sixty, teaches a course in English. The twenty-five students in the course average two and a half hours of study a day, and three of the students who received a grade of C spent an average of four hours a day. The two A students spent respectively an hour and a half and three hours. Professor Bestworst starts the class exactly at the beginning of the hour. Usually he also stops exactly on the hour, but four times he talked over, once for ten minutes. He announced at the beginning of the term that students could expect ten-minute unannounced quizzes at the beginning of the hour on the assignment for that day, and he gave eight such quizzes, one on the day before Christmas vacation. He graded all the quizzes, wrote detailed comments on a number of them, and returned them. Students never complain that they cannot hear Professor Bestworst, and the secretary whose office is next to his classroom says that she overhears him quite clearly. She says also that she hears frequent laughter from the students. Miss Languish, a C student in the class, says that the course is dull and is unreasonably hard, and Miss Beaver, a B student, says that it is the best course in the college and that she would like to take it again. One student in the class estimated that Professor Bestworst said "I think" or "I believe" or "it seems to me" an average of thirty times each class hour; another student said that the professor was undogmatic and did not require students to agree with him. Girls in the class who scrutinize Professor Bestworst's dress comment favorably on his ties but notice that he often wears the same suit for two weeks and that on winter days he sometimes lectures with his galoshes on.

1. What general conclusions about the professor and his course do you think it would be fair to draw?

2. What might be said by a student who liked the professor very much? By one who was hostile toward the professor?

3. With the facts as a basis, write two passages of charged language, one favorable and the other unfavorable, about Professor Bestworst.

V. Write three descriptions (each about 150 words) of a person or place that you know. Selecting from the same basic facts, but using any devices of charging and slanting you wish to use, try in the first account to create a favorable impression of the subject and in the second an unfavorable impression. In the third account, write an impartial or balanced report of the same person or place. This third account should consist entirely of verifiable facts. Make it at least as long as the other two, and try, by means of verifiable detail, to make it as interesting to the reader as the charged and slanted versions.

VI. We have summarized on page 39 the principal techniques of charging and slanting. Jot down notes for an analysis of these techniques in the two passages quoted below.

1. The following paragraph is taken from Volume II, Chapter 2, of Hitler's *Mein Kampf*, published in 1926.

Since nationality or rather race does not happen to lie in language but in the blood, we would only be justified in speaking of a Germanization if by such a process we succeeded in transforming the blood of the subjected people. But this is impossible. Unless a blood mixture brings about a change, which, however, means the lowering of the level of the higher race. The final result of such a process would consequently be the destruction of precisely those qualities which had formerly made the conquering people capable of victory. Especially the cultural force would vanish through a mating with the lesser race, even if the resulting mongrels spoke the language of the earlier, higher race a thousand times over. For a time, a certain struggle will take place between the different mentalities, and it may be that the steadily sinking people, in a last quiver of life, so to speak, will bring to light surprising cultural values. But these are only individual elements belonging to the higher race, or perhaps bastards in whom, after the first crossing, the better blood still predominates and tries to struggle through; but never final products of a mixture. In them a culturally backward movement will always manifest itself.

2. This passage is the first paragraph in *The Crisis,* a history-making book written by Thomas Paine in 1776.

These are the times that try men's souls. The summer soldier and the sunshine patriot will in this crisis shrink from the service of his country; but he that stands it NOW deserves the love and thanks of man and woman. Tyranny, like hell, is not easily conquered; yet we have this consolation with us, that the harder the conflict, the more glorious the triumph. What we obtain too cheap, we esteem too lightly: 'tis dearness only that gives everything its value. Heaven knows how to put a proper price upon its goods; and it would be strange indeed if so celestial an article as

FREEDOM should not be highly rated. Britain, with an army to enforce her tyranny, has declared that she has a right (*not only to*) TAX but "to BIND *us in* ALL CASES WHATSOEVER,*" and if being *bound in that manner* is not slavery, then is there not such a thing as slavery upon earth. Even the expression is impious, for so unlimited a power can belong only to GOD.

VII. Bring to class three examples of charged language that you have read in newspapers or magazines or have heard on radio or television. Be prepared to discuss the intention of the writer or speaker in each case, and to analyze the particular techniques he has used to accomplish his intention.

VIII. In the late nineteen-sixties, when opposition to the war in Vietnam was mounting, a number of statements were made to counter the opposition and to support pursuit of the war. Below are some of these statements. Like the demands for ending the war, they may well express sincere convictions, but their authors are using charged language. What words and combinations of words seem to you to be strongly charged? Which statements best illustrate the right-on-our-side technique?

This war is, and always has been, a crusade for freedom, democracy, and self-determination for South Vietnam.

We cannot stand by while Vietnam and all Southeast Asia fall victim to aggression.

We are in Vietnam, and we must stay there, to honor our treaty obligations.

By defending South Vietnam the United States defends its own vital security.

You can't just turn the country over to the Commies.

We have a moral commitment to the peace-loving people of Vietnam.

We have a duty to the brave men who have already died for this cause.

A defeat in Vietnam would make the U.S. look like a paper tiger.

The enemy is China. Our aim is to restrain militant Chinese Communism.

We want peace but only peace with honor.

Withdrawal from Vietnam would place the United States in mortal danger and could lead to catastrophe for all mankind.

We are seeking to prevent World War III.

Criticism of the war should be halted; it gives aid and comfort to the enemy.

We cannot abandon our pledges and our allies.

It would be an unthinkable blow to our prestige to withdraw.

I am not going to be the first President to preside over an American defeat.

Besides fighting for the Vietnamese, we are fighting for ourselves and for international stability.

This peace march [October 15, 1969] is playing into the hands of people whose business it is to kill American fighting men.

A shameful retreat in Vietnam would destroy the United States as a world leader.

Exercises for Section III, pages 40–45

The following passages are taken out of their context and are presented without any of the information the reader usually has about the author and the date and occasion of the communication. Since the passages are given without the clues that usually help shape judgment, the analysis and the evaluation of them present a particular problem and challenge. The order of analysis will not be the same for each passage; the following questions, however, should be applied to each, and answered in all possible detail:

1. What is the factual meaning of the passage? (The *What*)
2. Are there any clues as to the *When* and *Where*? Is the writing modern? Do any allusions date it or place it? Do you think it is part of a speech, a report, a letter, a story, a textbook, or an essay? Under what circumstances was this communication probably made?
3. What can you say about the style and use of language? About the tone? (The *How*)
4. What seems to be the author's intention? (The *Why*)
5. For what kind of audience was this intended? To what kind of audience would it appeal? (*To Whom*)
6. What conclusions can you draw about the writer of the passage? (The *Who*)
7. What, after your analysis, is your personal reaction to this piece of writing? Do you like it, dislike it? Why?

(1)

Now, let me talk briefly about this younger generation. I have not and do not condemn this generation of young Americans. Like Edmund Burke, I would not know how to "draw up an indictment against a whole people." They are our sons and daughters. They contain in their numbers many gifted, idealistic and courageous young men and women.

But they also list in their numbers an arrogant few who march under the flags and portraits of dictators, who intimidate and harass university professors, who use gutter obscenities to shout down speakers with whom they disagree, who openly profess their belief in the efficacy of violence in a democratic society.

The preceding generation had its own breed of losers—and our generation dealt with them through our courts, our laws and our system. The challenge now is for the new generation to put their own house in order.

(2)

Mississippi and its citizens are being treated with utmost and unjustified contempt by national political leaders, by national television and news media, by sarcastic, martini-sipping pseudo-intellectuals of every breed.

The opinion of these people does not matter a tinker's dam except that they are somehow accepted as the new gospel by those of influence, whose past testaments have destroyed nearly every worthwhile attribute and heritage in American political, social and economic life.

(3)

Wear your learning like your watch, in a private pocket; and do not pull it out and strike it, merely to show that you have one. If you are asked what o'clock it is, tell it, but do not proclaim it hourly and unasked, like the watchman.

(4)

Let us reflect in another way, and we shall see that there is great reason to hope that death is a good, for one of two things: either death is a state of nothingness and utter unconsciousness, or, as men say, there is a change and migration of the soul from this world to another. Now if you suppose that there is no consciousness, but a sleep like the sleep of him who is undisturbed even by the sight of dreams, death will be an unspeakable gain. For if a person were to select the night in which his sleep was undisturbed even by dreams, and were to compare with this the other days and nights of his life, and then were to tell us how many days and nights he had passed in the course of his life better and more pleasantly than this one, I think that any man, I will not say a private man, but even the great king will not find many such days or nights, when compared with the others. Now if death is like this, I say that to die is gain; for eternity is then only a single night. But if death is the journey to another place, and there, as men say, all the dead are, what good, O my friends and judges, can be greater than this? If indeed when the pilgrim arrives in the world below, he is delivered from the professors of justice in this world, and finds the true judges who are said to give judgment there, . . . that pilgrimage will be worth making. What would not a man give if he might converse with Orpheus and Musæus and Hesiod and Homer? Nay, if this be true, let me die again and again. I, too, shall have a wonderful interest in a place where I can converse with Palamedes, and Ajax the son of Telamon, and other heroes of old, who have suffered death through an unjust judgment; and there will be no small pleasure, as I think, in comparing my own suffering with theirs. Above all, I shall be able to continue my search into true and false knowledge; as in this world, so also in that; I shall find out who is wise, and who pretends to be wise, and is not.

(5)

Society is commonly too cheap. We meet at very short intervals, not having had time to acquire any new value for each other. We meet at meals three times a-day, and give each other a new taste of that old musty cheese that we are. We have had to agree on a certain set of rules, called etiquette and politeness, to make this frequent meeting tolerable and that we need not come to open war. We meet at the post office, and at the sociable, and about the fireside every night; we live thick and are in each other's way, and stumble over one another, and I think that we thus lose some respect for one another. Certainly less frequency would suffice for all important and hearty communications. Consider the girls in a factory—never alone, hardly in their dreams. It would be better if there were but one inhabitant to a square mile, as where I live. The value of a man is not in his skin, that we should touch him.

(6)

But when men have realized that time has upset many fighting faiths, they may come to believe even more than they believe the very foundation of their own conduct that the ultimate good desired is better reached by free trade in ideas—that the best test of truth is the power of the thought to get itself accepted in the competition of the market, and that truth is the only ground on which their wishes safely can be carried out. That at any rate is the theory of our Constitution. It is an experiment, as all life is an experiment. Every year if not every day we have to wager our salvation upon some prophecy based upon imperfect knowledge. While that experiment is part of our system, I think that we should be eternally vigilant against attempts to check the expression of opinions that we loathe and believe to be fraught with death, unless they so imminently threaten immediate interference with the lawful and pressing purposes of the law that an immediate check is required to save the country.

(7)

The statesmen of both of the groups of nations now arrayed against one another have said, in terms that could not be misinterpreted, that it was no part of the purpose they had in mind to crush their antagonists. But the implications of these assurances may not be equally clear to all—may not be the same on both sides of the water. I think it will be serviceable if I attempt to set forth what we understand them to be.

They imply, first of all, that it must be a peace without victory. It is not pleasant to say this. I beg that I may be permitted to put my own interpretation upon it and that it may be understood that no other interpretation was in my thought. I am seeking only to face realities and to face them without soft concealments. Victory would mean peace forced upon the loser, a victor's terms imposed upon the vanquished. It would be accepted in humiliation, under duress, at an intolerable sacrifice, and would leave a sting, a resentment, a bitter memory upon which terms of peace would rest, not permanently, but only as upon quicksand. Only a peace between equals can last.

(8)

Sometimes a war is entered upon, because the enemy is too strong, and sometimes because he is too weak. Sometimes our neighbors want the things which we have, or have the things which we want; and we both fight, till they take ours or give us theirs. It is a very justifiable cause of a war to invade a country after the people have been wasted by famine, destroyed by pestilence, or embroiled by factions among themselves. It is justifiable to enter into war against our nearest ally, when one of his towns lies convenient for us, or a territory of land, that would render our dominions round and complete. If a prince sends forces into a nation, where the people are poor and ignorant, he may lawfully put half of them to death, and make slaves of the rest, in order to civilize and reduce them from their barbarous way of living. It is a very kingly, honourable, and frequent practice, when one prince desires the assistance of another to secure him against an invasion, that the assistant, when he hath driven out the invader, should seize on the dominions himself, and kill, imprison or banish the prince he came to relieve. . . . For these reasons, the trade of a soldier is held the most honourable of all others; because a soldier is . . . hired to kill in cold blood as many of his own species, who have never offended him, as possibly he can.

(9)

By *genteelism* is here to be understood the substituting, for the ordinary natural word that first suggests itself to the mind, of a synonym that is thought to be less soiled by the lips of the common herd, less familiar, less plebeian, less vulgar, less improper, less apt to come unhandsomely betwixt the wind and our nobility. The truly genteel do not offer *beer,* but *ale;* invite one to *step,* not *come,* this way; take in not *lodgers,* but *paying guests;* send their boys not to *school,* but to *college;* never *help,* but *assist,* each other to potatoes; keep *stomachs* and *domestics* instead of *bellies* and *servants;* and have quite forgotten that they could ever have been guilty of *toothpowder* and *napkins* and *underclothing,* of *before* and *except* and *about,* where nothing now will do for them but *dentifrice, serviette, lingerie, ere, save, anent.*

(10)

We meet in an hour of grief and challenge. Dag Hammarskjöld is dead. But the United Nations lives on. His tragedy is deep in our hearts, but the task for which he died is at the top of our agenda. A noble servant of peace is gone. But the quest for peace lies before us.

The problem is not the death of one man; the problem is the life of this organization. It will either grow to meet the challenges of our age, or it will be gone with the wind, without influence, without force, without respect. Were we to let it die, to enfeeble its vigor, to cripple its powers, we would condemn the future.

For in the development of this organization rests the only true alternative to war, and war appeals no longer as a rational alternative. Unconditional war can no longer lead to unconditional victory. It can no longer serve to settle disputes. It can no longer be of concern to great powers alone. For nuclear disaster, spread by winds and waters and fear, could well engulf the great and the small, the rich and the poor, the committed and the uncommitted alike. Mankind must put an end to war or war will put an end to mankind.

(11)

The worst of our youngsters are growing up to become booted, sideburned, ducktailed, unwashed, leather-jacketed slobs whose favorite sport is ravaging little girls and stomping polio victims to death; the best of our youth are coming into maturity for all the world like young people fresh from a dizzying roller-coaster ride with everything blurred, nothing clear, with no positive standards, with everything in doubt.

(12)

With the media bombarding us daily with millions of words, we have to have a critical method, some kind of intellectual method, by means of which to decide whom and what to believe and to what degree.

My own work in semantics has been dedicated to this end. It was developed out of my interest in Nazi propaganda in the 1930s. And one of the things that alarms me is the tremendous similarity between the tactics of the Hitler youth and "brownshirts" and the resemblance to the New Left. There is a similar desire not to let anyone speak who disagrees with them.

One of the very difficult and surprising things of the present time is that there are so many young men and women who have adopted this as a technique in disrupting the intellectual lives of the rest of you.

So what we need among other things is a critical and intellectual method, and don't forget this method is never cultivated by screaming and shouting and hollering and interrupting speakers.*

* The sources of the twelve passages are: (1) Spiro T. Agnew, Speech before the Alabama Chamber of Commerce, November 20, 1969. (2) Editorial in the Clarksdale (Mississippi) *Press Register,* July, 1964. (3) Lord Chesterfield to his son, 1748. (4) Socrates, speech at his trial, 399 B.C. (from the Jowett translation of Plato's *Apology*). (5) Henry David Thoreau, *Walden,* 1854. (6) Oliver Wendell Holmes, dissenting opinion on the Abrams case, 1919. (7) Woodrow Wilson, Address to the Senate, January 22, 1917. (8) Jonathan Swift, *Gulliver's Travels,* 1726. (9) H. W. Fowler, *Modern English Usage,* 1926. (10) John F. Kennedy, Address to the United Nations, September 25, 1961. (11) Max Rafferty, candidate for the United States Senate from California, June 1968. (12) S. I. Hayakawa, president of San Francisco State University, in a speech at Northeastern University, January 1970.

Chapter 2

APPROPRIATE ENGLISH

To the question *What is good English?* a number of answers may be given. Some of them are: Good English is correct English. It is clear. It is economical. It is interesting. In later chapters of this book we shall discuss these and other qualities which good English is likely to have. At present, it may be useful to consider briefly some limitations of these criteria for good English.

The skillful speaker and writer is familiar with the conventions of his language and knows that in order to communicate effectively he usually must follow standard practice in certain matters of grammar and usage. There are, however, at least two objections to the view that good English is merely correct English. One objection is that judgments differ on what constitutes correctness: one textbook or one teacher may stress "rules" like "Avoid slang," "Do not write incomplete sentences"; and another text or teacher may cite, as examples of good writing, sentences that contain slang or that lack either a subject or a predicate. A second objection is that, although dogmatic rules for "correct" writing may be helpful in training some young people to write acceptably, they are not, by themselves, adequate guides for the mature student. Since they emphasize avoidance of error, they may encourage the mistaken view that language is fixed rather than flexible, hedged with *don'ts* rather than rich in alternatives. In order to use English freely and effectively the college student needs to understand the nature of language and the principles that underlie the rules. He will then be in a position to exercise judgment in following conventional rules or departing from them. He will see, too, that many important uses of English do not involve questions of correctness, but are matters of intelligent choice. Aware of alternatives, he will learn to choose, among different ways of expressing an idea, the way best suited to the circumstances and to his purpose in speaking or writing.

Clarity, economy, and interest also have limitations as criteria of good English. Although effective expression is usually clear, there are occasions on which speakers and writers need to be *un*clear; for example, diplomats, politicians, and statesmen may wish to respond obscurely to questions about classified information or about their future plans. Calvin Coolidge was justifiably proud of his answer, "I do not choose to run," when reporters asked him whether he would seek reelection. The ambiguous word *choose* exactly served his purpose of appearing to give a direct answer and yet not really committing himself; like later aspirants, he seemed to be a reluctant candidate, but still was in the race. Economy in language—making each word carry as much meaning as possible—is likely to be a trait of good English. But repetition of words and details may create an atmosphere that is part of the writer's attitudinal meaning. Skillful speakers, too, may not want to be economical: Franklin Roosevelt is said to have talked at length about trivial matters when he wanted to avoid being asked a question; and in certain social situations most people are willing to talk quite uneconomically to fill a strained silence. A communication must, of course, be interesting to attract and hold the attention of others; but interest depends on audience and circumstances. A professor lecturing on business law to a group of law students will probably not use the same devices for interest as the writer of a popular magazine article on the same subject; the writer of a statistical report will not try to be interesting in the common sense of the word "interesting." In a special sense, one may be "interested" in a communication as a curiosity—because it is outrageously unconventional, tasteless, or dull. To say that good English is interesting is, therefore, to establish an elusive standard.

Perhaps the most reliable generalization one can make about good English is: good English is effective English. It achieves the speaker's or writer's purpose; and in order to do so, it must be appropriate to the material he wants to communicate (or conceal), to the time and place, to the audience aimed at, and to the impression of himself he wants to give.

I. VARIETIES OF ENGLISH

Different degrees of education and different social circumstances produce varieties of English—that is, differences in construction, pronunciation, and vocabulary. There is no difference in factual meaning between *He took his sister to a movie* and *He done taken his sister to a movie,* but we recognize the first sentence as standard English and the second as nonstandard English. We shall use the terms *formal English, informal English,* and *colloquial English* for three kinds of standard English.

The lines between the varieties of usage are not distinct: thousands of words, as well as the conventional sentence structure of English are common to all of them, and many sentences are not clearly characteristic of one kind of English rather than another. Also, the varieties are not static: since good usage at a particular time is determined by the practice of educated people of that time, expressions once considered nonstandard have, through general usage by educated people, been accepted as part of standard English; and other expressions once in good standing—double negatives like "He doesn't fear nothing," for example—are now regarded as nonstandard because they are no longer used by educated people. The varieties, then, are not settled and not mutually exclusive; but, in spite of their shifting and overlapping, it is possible to point out certain characteristics that distinguish them.

A. Nonstandard English

Nonstandard English, the English used by people with little or no education, is nearly always spoken, seldom written except in fiction that reproduces this type of speech. Although it has numerous words in common with standard usage, it is characterized by the misuse of words, the use of nonstandard words, and the corruption of what is now considered correct or conventional grammatical form. Examples of nonstandard English are:

They *was* tired after they *clum* the hill.
He said he *didn't have no* interest in *this here* election.
He didn't *graduate high school* because he *hadn't wrote* his English papers.
Our senator *seen* his duty and *done* it *noble.*

Another characteristic of nonstandard English is its limited vocabulary. People of little education seldom use, seldom know, words that express subtle or complex meanings. Although it is possible to express almost any idea in nonstandard language, many words may be needed to define or clarify the idea, because the definitive, more formal word is not known: "Doc says there ain't nothing wrong with her. I mean she's sick but she ain't. It's in her mind." With the formal word, one could say, "Her illness is psychosomatic."

Slang is an important part of nonstandard English, and, indeed, of language in general. In the area of slang and shoptalk, nonstandard and standard English overlap. Shoptalk is the talk, often consisting of verbal short cuts, used by people in the same occupation. *Gym, math, ec, soc, dorm, cat lab,* for instance, have been used by generations of college students. Some slang and shop talk, particularly when they name something new in a culture, trade, or profession, may eventually become an accepted part of standard usage; *close-up* and *fade-out* from the movie industry, and *squeeze play* from baseball and bridge are old examples; more recent examples are *hippie, loan shark, hot line*. Recently, too, space travel has made familiar a specialized shoptalk: *LM* (lunar module), *EVA* (extra-vehicular activity). Much slang is, however, by its very nature faddish and short-lived. It aims at an ever-changing novelty and picturesqueness, chiefly through incongruous figures of speech. The virtue of slang as part of language is this novelty and freshness—when it is new. Its weaknesses are that it so quickly becomes stale; that it is often unintelligible to a general audience; and that it conveys a poor impression of the user, who appears to lack the power of individual expression, since he relies heavily on stereotypes. Some slang is used in the informal talk of educated people and in informal writing. It becomes objectionable when it is overused, or used inappropriately in situations that require more formal language.

A slightly different category of nonstandard English is the nonstandard dialect or idiom of particular cultural groups. Many teachers have observed, for example, that ghetto children communicate easily with one another; but because the children use words in special senses, or words that do not have standard meanings, they cannot make themselves clear to outsiders. Other culture groups also have their vernacular, much of which is incomprehensible to those who do not use it. Some expressions, on the other hand, spread from the subculture into the larger culture and become part of current slang; examples are *pot* (marijuana), *dig* (understand), *pad* (room, lodgings), and *trip* (experience with psychedelic drugs).

Since college students will be speaking to and writing for educated groups, they will, of course, need a command of English well above the nonstandard in order to express complex ideas in a way that merits attention and respect. Except in narratives that represent uncultivated speech, nonstandard English is out of place in college writing.

B. Standard English: Formal, Informal, Colloquial

Formal English is the English, more often written than spoken, used by highly educated people in formal situations. One finds examples of formal English in scholarly articles and theses, in formal lectures and public addresses, in some technical and scientific writing, in some textbooks, sermons, essays, novels, and poetry. Among the characteristics of formal English are: long sentences, often in parallel and balanced construction, often with modifiers interrupting the normal sentence order; periodic sentences—sentences with the meaning suspended till the end; triads—three parallel phrases or clauses; and allusions—brief references to literature or history which only a well-educated audience would understand. Formal English is likely to be impersonal rather than personal in its style; the writer usually is concerned with communicating his subject rather than his feeling toward it. Contractions *can't, won't, shouldn't,* etc.) and colloquial expressions are avoided in formal style, and those who use this English tend to be conservative, in general, about grammar and usage. An important characteristic of formal English is a wide and exact vocabulary, frequently specialized or technical.

College students, in most of their communication, will not be using formal English, but they may hear formal English in lectures and read it in texts, critical articles, and literature. They will also, in their formal papers and reports and in their later communication with professional groups, need to use as well as understand this kind of English.

Informal English, the English most commonly written and spoken by educated people, ranges from the rather formal informality of most newspaper editorials to the greater informality of magazine articles addressed to general readers and of serious discussions among friends. Lectures for unspecialized audiences, informal essays, business letters, and most current novels, short stories, and plays are written in informal English. In vocabulary and sentence style, informal English is less formal and elaborate than formal English; its sentences are likely to be shorter and to have more of the rhythms and uncomplicated constructions of speech. It is more often personal than impersonal: the speaker or writer includes himself and his feelings and attitudes in his communication. Allusions in informal English are usually to widely-understood current affairs rather than to the historical and literary events of which formal English assumes understanding. Because informal English is the language that most educated people will be using in most of their activities in life, it is the English at which students should aim in most of their writing.

Written informal English is generally tighter in its sentence structure and more precise in expression than spoken informal English, since the writer has the opportunity to revise his sentences and substitute careful phrasing for the hastily selected spoken words. Spoken informal English, in informal situations, merges into the third level of standard usage.

Colloquial is defined in *Webster's Seventh New Collegiate Dictionary* as "used in or characteristic of familiar and informal conversation." Colloquial English is conversational English, more often spoken than written, which has the short sentences and the casual constructions and vocabulary of the everyday, relaxed speech of educated people. Abundant use of contractions, as in informal talk, incomplete sentences, some use of slang, and the use of colloquial expressions like *let's don't, rarely ever, can't seem to* are frequent characteristics of this conversational English. Formal structures are often simplified: "I'm sure she'll be there" instead of the more formal "I am sure *that* she will be there." Colloquial English is personal and familiar in tone.

The diagram below shows the overlapping of the three types of standard usage:

English used by highly educated people addressing an audience of their peers. It is found often in poetry and other serious literature, in formal essays, scholarly articles, lectures, sermons, and formal public addresses.

High informal English, used in many newspaper editorials, novels, stories, essays, semiformal lectures, and in most business correspondence.

FORMAL

I
N
F
R
M
A
L

English words and constructions common to all categories.[1]

More informal, familiar English, blending into colloquial.

COLLOQUIAL

Conversational English, more often spoken than written. It may include some slang and shop talk. It is written in fiction which reproduces informal speech, in some sports writing, and in intimate personal letters in which one writes as he would talk.

The following examples will clarify the generalizations made about the types of standard English, and will further show the gradations from formal to colloquial usage. The first passage, written by a twentieth-century historian, illustrates many of the traits of formal English:

To have faith in the dignity and worth of the individual man as an end in himself, to believe that it is better to be governed by persuasion than by coercion, to believe that fraternal good will is more worthy than a selfish and contentious spirit, to believe that in the long run all values are inseparable from the love of truth and the disinterested search for it, to believe that knowledge and the power it confers should be used to promote the welfare and happiness of all men rather than to serve

---

[1] Nonstandard English, not represented in this diagram, also uses many words and constructions that belong to the common body of English, as well as many nonstandard words and constructions.

the interests of those individuals and classes whom fortune and intelligence endow with temporary advantage—these are the values which are affirmed by the traditional democratic ideology. . . . The case for democracy is that it accepts the rational and humane values as ends, and proposes as the means of realizing them the minimum of coercion and the maximum of voluntary assent. We may well abandon the cosmological temple in which the democratic ideology originally enshrined these values without renouncing the faith it was designed to celebrate. The essence of that faith is belief in the capacity of man, as a rational and humane creature, to achieve the good life by rational and humane means. The chief virtue of democracy, and the sole reason for cherishing it, is that with all its faults it still provides the most favorable conditions for achieving that end by those means.—CARL L. BECKER, *New Liberties for Old*

Sentence length in this passage ranges from twenty-five to a hundred and twenty words. The most conspicuously formal construction is the long periodic first sentence; the main idea, suspended until the end, is preceded by five parallel phrases: *To have faith . . . to believe . . . to believe . . . to believe . . . to believe . . . these are the values. . . .* Distinctively formal words in the consistently formal vocabulary are *coercion, contentious, cosmological, enshrined.*

The following paragraph, by a modern philosopher, is a less formal example of formal English:

But if men forget that the future will some day be a present, they forget, too, that the present is already here, and that even in a dark time some of the brightness for which they long is open to the responsive senses, the welcoming heart, and the liberated mind. The moments as they pass even now have their tang and character. They may yield even now the contagious joy of feeling and perception. Here are the familiar flowers, the music we love, the poetry by which we are moved. Here are the books and companions, the ideas and the relaxations, the gaieties and the co-operative tasks of our familiar world. These things may be threatened, they may be precarious, they may be ours only by the grace of God, or of geographical or economic accident. But undeniably, beckoningly, along with the portents and alarms, here they are. Here, in all tragic times, they always have been, affording challenge and delight to the senses, solace and nourishment for the affections, and friendly stimulus to the understanding.—IRWIN EDMAN, *Candle in the Dark*

Because the writer of this passage uses *our* and *we* and creates for the reader emotional associations with the material, the style is more personal than that of the first illustration. The passage is formal, however, in the general level of writing, the studied exactness of the vocabulary, the balanced sentences, and the numerous triads or triple constructions, one example of which is *to the responsive senses, the welcoming heart, and the liberated mind.* The next-to-last sentence, *But undeniably, beckoningly . . . here they are,* is a comparatively short periodic sentence. The last sentence, *Here, in all tragic times, they always have been.* . . . shows the use of introductory modifiers, more characteristic of formal English than of the less formal levels.

The paragraph below, about a very early period in the history of the earth, might be classified as high informal English:

During all this time the continents had no life. There was little to induce living things to come ashore, forsaking their all-providing, all-embracing mother sea. The lands must have been bleak and hostile beyond the power of words to describe. Imagine a whole continent of naked rock, across which no covering mantle of green had been drawn—a continent without soil, for there were no plants to aid in its formation and bind it to the rocks with their roots. Imagine a land of stone, a silent land, except for the sound of the rains and winds that swept across it. For there was no living voice, and no living thing moved over the surface of the rocks. —RACHEL L. CARSON, *The Sea Around Us*

Vocabulary and sentence structure, both excellent, are less formal than in the passages quoted earlier. Although the writing is informative and generally impersonal, a certain personal feeling is created by the sentence rhythms and by involving the reader in the material ("Imagine a whole continent. . . .").

The following example of informal English, part of an account of a boy's breaking in a new colt, is personal, autobiographical writing. The vocabulary is precise and the sentences are carefully constructed, but the passage, particularly toward the end, has a movement and tone suggestive of spoken English.

She was a cream-colored mare with a black forelock, mane, and tail and a black stripe along the middle of her back. Tall, slender, high-spirited, I thought then—I think now—that she was the most beautiful of horses. Colonel Carter had bred and reared her with me and my uses in mind. She was a careful cross of a mustang mare and a thoroughbred stallion, with the stamina of the wild horse and the speed and grace of the racer. And she had a sense of fun. As Colonel Carter got down out of his buggy and went up to her, she snorted, reared, flung her head high in the air, and, coming down beside him, tucked her nose affectionately under his arm. . . . I fed, I led, I cleaned her, gently, as if she were made of glass; she was playful and willing, a delight. When Colonel Carter came home with my father for supper, he questioned me.

"You should not have worked her today," he said. "She has come all the way from Stockton and must be tired. Yes, yes, she would not show her fatigue; too fine for that, and too young to be wise. You have got to think for her, consider her as you would your sisters."

Sisters! I thought; I had never considered my sisters. I did not say that, but Colonel Carter laughed and nodded to my sisters. It was just as if he had read my thought. But he went on to draw on my imagination a centaur; the colt as a horse's body—me, a boy, as the head and brains of one united creature. I liked that. I would be that. I and the colt: a centaur.—LINCOLN STEFFENS, *The Autobiography of Lincoln Steffens*

In the passage below, another example of good informal English, most of the sentences are short and simply constructed, and most of them begin with the subject and verb. Expressions like "You count your words," "The poor fellow," "As for us," and the allusions to matters of common knowledge—"giving the world a Cadillac," "caught in the brier patch of English usage," "Simonize our grandmother"—contribute to the informality of the style.

A publisher in Chicago has sent us a pocket calculating machine by which we may test our writing to see whether it is intelligible. The calculator was developed by General Motors, who, not satisfied with giving the world a Cadillac, now dream of bringing perfect understanding to men. The machine (it is simply a celluloid card with a dial) is called the Reading Ease Calculator and shows four grades of "reading ease"—Very Easy, Easy, Hard, and Very Hard. You count your words and syllables, set the dial, and an indicator lets you know whether anybody is going to understand what you have written. An instruction book came with it, and after mastering the simple rules we lost no time in running a test on the instruction book itself, to see how *that* writer was doing. The poor fellow! His leading essay, the one on the front cover, tested Very Hard.

Our next step was to study the first phrase on the face of the calculator: "How to test Reading-Ease of written matter." There is, of course, no such thing as reading ease of written matter. There is the ease with which matter can be read, but that is a condition of the reader, not of the matter. Thus the inventors and distributors of this calculator get off to a poor start, with a Very Hard instruction book and a slovenly phrase. Already they have one foot caught in the brier patch of English usage.

Not only did the author of the instruction book score badly on the front cover, but inside the book he used the word "personalize" in an essay on how to improve one's writing. A man who likes the word "personalize" is entitled to his choice, but we wonder whether he should be in the business of giving advice to writers. "Whenever possible," he wrote, "personalize your writing by directing it to the reader." As for us, we would as lief Simonize our grandmother as personalize our writing.[2]

Finally, the following passage, written to represent the language of a sixteen-year-old boy, is one type of colloquial English:

I was thinking about Sheila Coe. She's Kerry's girl. They fight but they get along. She's awfully pretty and she can swim like a fool. Once Kerry sent me over with her tennis racket and we had quite a conversation. She was fine. And she didn't pull any of this big sister stuff, either, the way some girls will with a fellow's kid brother.

And when the canoe came along, by the edge of the lake, I thought for a moment it was her. I thought maybe she was looking for Kerry and maybe she'd stop and maybe she'd feel like talking to me again. I don't know why I thought that—I didn't have any reason. Then I saw it was just the Sharon kid, with a new kind of bob that made her look grown-up, and I felt sore. She didn't have any business out on the

<hr/>

[2] From "Calculating Machine," *The Second Tree from the Corner*, copyright, 1951, by E. B. White, published by Harper & Row.

lake at her age. She was just a Sophomore in High, the same as me.—STEPHEN VINCENT BENÉT, "Too Early Spring"

II. THE USER'S CHOICE

If Charles Meade, a student, receives a formal invitation, conventions of etiquette and language demand that he make a formal reply: "Mr. Charles Meade accepts with pleasure [or, regrets that he is unable to accept] the kind invitation of President Miles Weston to a dinner for the Senior Class at the Sheraton Hotel on Tuesday, April the twentieth, at eight o'clock." Variation from the prescribed formal language would be inappropriate and would not achieve his purpose of making the proper polite response. Another student, James Mangle, who receives the same invitation and replies: "Dear Prexy, Thanks for your invitation. I'm sorry I can't make it. Have a dinner date with my roommate's beautiful sister. . . ." is using language inappropriately and blunderingly. If, however, James Mangle had received a hastily written note from a close friend who was inviting him to a party Friday night, he might suitably have made his informal reply; a formal reply under these circumstances would, of course, be ludicrous.

In other situations, too, one's usage may be prescribed by prevailing conventions. Formal English would doubtless be inappropriate in an informal meeting to discuss dormitory rules. Colloquial English or very informal English is out of place in a formal term paper. In his less formal writing, though, the student often has some choice of levels. Choosing the one that will be most effective in the whole situation requires an awareness of the different kinds of expression and of the different effects they are likely to produce.

Consider the choice involved in the following expressions of the same idea:

He's nuts.
He's insane.
He's schizophrenic.

He pounded it out on the keys.
He played some lively music.
He played a gavotte.

We put on the feed bag at six.
We eat at six.
We dine at six.

He always lays down for his beauty sleep at ten.
He always hits the sack at ten.
He always goes to bed at ten.
He habitually retires at ten.

Probably, and particularly if the communication is written, the colloquial and slang expressions will be rejected as inappropriate; certainly the use of *lays* in the last example will be. But how will one choose between *insane* and *schizophrenic, some lively music* and *a gavotte, eat* and *dine, always goes to bed* and *habitually retires?* To a considerable extent, the choice will be determined by the formality of the subject, the audience, and the circumstances. It should be noted, though, that *schizophrenic* is more exact than *insane* (as *insane* is more exact than *nuts, batty, crazy,* etc.); for one who knows the word, it defines the insanity; it carries precise information. The same is true of *gavotte;* the word is more accurate than *some lively music.* For an audience that would understand them, then, there might be an advantage in using these more exact, more formal words. On the other hand, there is no difference in exactness between *eat* and *dine, goes to bed* and *retires;* also, the simple informal expressions seem more appropriate than the formal ones for simple statements about habits of eating and going to bed; in most circumstances they would be the right expressions to choose.

Some students err in trying to write too formally; they strive for elegance and impressiveness by substituting formal expressions for informal ones that have the same meaning and that are more appropriate for the material. Formal words used unnecessarily in an informal context are "heavy words"; they have too much bulk or weight for the situation; the result of using them is strained, pretentious, "heavy" writing. The following sentences are examples of this undesirable heaviness in the expression of comparatively slight ideas:

I endeavored to peruse the volume. [I tried to read the book.]
I anticipate the termination of the current semester. [I anticipate, or look forward to, the end of this semester.]
I requested her permission to view the kittens. [I asked her to let me see the kittens.]
I decided to wend my way to my place of residence. [I decided to go home.]

Writers of such pompous absurdities need to be told to say what they have to say as simply and directly as possible. Usually they are happy to learn that they can relax and write more naturally.

Many students, on the other hand, relax too much. They need to raise the level of usage in their writing, not by straining for elegance, and not by trying to ornament their prose with long or heavy words, but by using accurately words that have precise meanings and that are appropriate to the subjects they are discussing. In the following sentences taken from students' examinations, lack of adequate vocabulary, as well as an unsure sense of language, probably accounts for the lapses in expression:

He gave *a bunch of figures on the amount of the soil washing away.* [statistics on soil erosion]

Primitive tribes believed in *a God that had the shape like a man*. [an anthropomorphic God]

The essays were all stimulating, though the one by John Dewey was *rough*. [difficult, or complex, or abstract—something which says more exactly what the writer means]

After an analysis of immigrations to the United States, the author *got going on the bad ideas of race*. [discussed misunderstandings about race]

Hamlet was disturbed and unbalanced when he found that his father had been *bumped off*. [murdered]

The reader will note that one objection to these sentences is that their usage is not consistent. A more serious objection to some of them is that the expression is fuzzy and unclear; "got going on the bad ideas of race," for example, leaves the writer's meaning in doubt. A final objection is that the loose informality is not appropriate in an academic discussion of such subjects as Dewey, Hamlet, and anthropology.

A particular problem of appropriateness, for students and their teachers, rises from the fact that a number of expressions that not long ago were regarded as nonstandard English are now either recognized as standard spoken English, or considered to be in transition from nonstandard to standard usage. Examples are the use of *who* for *whom* in sentences in which the pronoun comes at the beginning of a sentence or clause, in the place normally occupied by the subject ("*Who* is he searching for?"), and the use of *like* as a conjunction ("It looks *like* winter has come."). Since these constructions seldom appear in formal written English, since many careful users of English object to them, and since college students are being trained to communicate easily with educated groups, most teachers will expect their students to use the formal constructions in writing, except in dialogue: "*Whom* is he searching for?" "It looks *as though* winter has come."[3]

In general, then, the college student should develop an awareness of the varieties of usage so that he will be able to choose the one best suited to the occasion. His usage will not always be the same. Students preparing for the professions will, perhaps more than others, realize that a competent doctor, lawyer, teacher, sociologist, or psychologist must be able to use more than one kind of language. He must talk with and write for his colleagues in a way they will respect, and he must also communicate skillfully with people who do not have his training and vocabulary. The student can best prepare for such multiple use of language by practicing good informal English, by learning to express himself simply, clearly, and graphically, and by developing an ability to use formal words and constructions for an audience that understands and expects them.

---

3 Other expressions of this kind are discussed in the Glossary of Usage, page 486.

III. APPROPRIATE TONE

Tone is clearly important in speech and conversation—we frequently say we don't like someone's tone—and it is equally, though less obviously, important in many kinds of writing. Tone is the *manner of verbal expression* that a speaker or writer adopts. Good tone, like good manners, is a product of a sympathetic and imaginative understanding of the needs and feelings of other people. Tone is also like manners in that it is a reflection of personality; it is the part of meaning that gives the audience an impression of the personality of the communicator and of his attitudes toward them and toward himself. For example, one's tone may be serious or facetious, hostile or friendly, condescending or respectful or obsequious, sarcastic or sentimental, ironic or literal, formal or informal, impersonal or personal, assertive or questioning, authoritative or modest, frank or reserved or secretive, sincere or insincere, enthusiastic or indifferent. The expression of all such attitudes is part of tone, and the tone is appropriate or inappropriate as the attitudes are suited or unsuited to the audience, the material, and the personality of the speaker or writer.

It is difficult to generalize about appropriate tone in days when the militant, strident tone of criticism or protest is common, when the angry "language of confrontation" often replaces the language of moderation and reason. We believe, nevertheless, that the principles discussed here are applicable to most of the college student's spoken and written communication.

In speech, tone is conveyed not only by words but by the whole impact the communicator makes on his audience—his voice, his facial expressions, his gestures, the stresses and pauses in his speech. The writer has the more difficult task of conveying his attitudes and something of his personality without these aids. Also, the speaker has the advantage of being able to watch the responses of his audience and to adapt his tone as he goes along. The best that the writer can do is to keep his reader constantly in mind and to try to adjust his language and tone to the needs and feelings of that imagined reader.

Some things generally to be avoided in both speech and writing are: talking down to the audience—stating or laboring the obvious and so implying that their information is very limited; talking over the heads of the audience—employing words or allusions or foreign phrases beyond their comprehension, in a display of one's superior knowledge; expressing false enthusiasm or Pollyanna-like cheerfulness; using humor,[4] back-slapping familiarity, sarcasm, or exaggeration not suited to the audience or the subject; making dogmatic, aggressive, or conceited pronouncements.

---

[4] Humor well used is, of course, a delight; appropriate wit and humor can be invaluable in establishing a friendly tone and a feeling of shared experience between the speaker or writer and his audience.

The opening sentence of a student theme illustrates some of these faults in tone: "No one can tell me that the lipstick girls use doesn't clog their digestive tracts and ruin their stomachs!" Whatever one may think of this thesis, the expression of it—that is, the tone—is not effective: the writer's attitude toward the audience seems to be combative, his language is extravagant and emotional, and he seems to be aggressive and too sure of himself. A different phrasing, like "I have sometimes wondered if the lipstick girls use and swallow may not do them some physical harm," would have produced a less dogmatic and more reasonable tone, and a better reader-writer relationship.

A communicator's usage is, of course, another important part of his tone, since it reveals a great deal about him, his attitude toward his subject matter, and his assumptions about his audience. In particular, both the use of inappropriately heavy language and the overuse of slang or inappropriately informal language are aspects of tone. Heavy words suggest a stuffy, pompous person or an affected person trying too hard to impress others with his vocabulary. Too colloquial language suggests a casual or careless person, not enough concerned with his material and his audience to work for better expression.

A golden rule in writing is "Write for others as you would have them write for you." The writer who fails to organize his material, or to explain unfamiliar technical terms, or to revise unclear sentences, is making unfair demands on his readers, asking them to do the work of clarifying that he should have done. Such deficiencies indicate, or appear to indicate, a lack of consideration for the reader, and so are matters of tone.

Tone in speech or writing is like tact in human relations—most effective when least conspicuous. When tone is thoroughly appropriate to the audience and the material, it is a significant though hardly noticed part of meaning; it simultaneously conveys the communicator's attitudes and reveals him as he is—or at least as he would like to be thought to be: unaffected, courteous, unconceited, and reasonable.

CHAPTER REVIEW

If your reading of this chapter has been adequate, you should be able to explain the following terms, and to give clear, full answers to the questions below.

good English	slang
formal English	shoptalk
informal English	"heavy words"
colloquial English	tone
nonstandard English	

1. What are the characteristics of each of the varieties of English?
2. What are the advantages of formal English? Of informal English?
3. In what kind of writing is colloquial English likely to be appropriate?
4. What are the advantages and disadvantages of slang?
5. Can you think of circumstances in which a speaker would be justified in using nonstandard English?
6. How can one determine appropriate usage?
7. What kinds of tone should generally be avoided in speech and writing?

EXERCISES

I. The passages below are statements on the death of President Kennedy. The first, an excerpt from the remarks made in the Senate by Democratic Leader Mike Mansfield, is high informal English; the second, spoken by the assistant clerk of Superior Criminal Court, South Boston, is colloquial English with some nonstandard expression. In what respects is the second passage more effective English than the first?

This is the profile of the man who walked among us not long ago on the floor of the Senate. This is the profile of the man who emerged to reawaken the nation to its finest meaning. This is the man who struck new sparks of hope in a world dark with unspeakable fears.

His death . . . has fused the many faces of courage into a single profile of courage set in the enduring frame of faith and reason. This is what we have of him now. It is so little to have and yet so much.

Oh, I remember when he used to come marching down this street in a parade and boy, he had that walk, and no hat, and "my name is Jack Kennedy, I'm a candidate for Congress," and, girls used to flock around him—young, young, personality second to none—God we'll miss him.

And we'll miss that "vigah," and that "New Frontier" talk, too—that'll all go out, and nobody will say it any more, because he was an original. He was like the late President Roosevelt, and him saying, "my f-r-i-e-n-d-s," and you don't hear anybody say that any more, do you? And you ain't gonna hear anyone say "vigah" any more, either.

II. The three passages below present similar ideas in formal, informal, and nonstandard English. Point out in each passage the specific traits of style and language which are characteristic of the three kinds of English.

What a monstrous specter is this man, the disease of the agglutinated dust, lifting alternate feet or lying drugged with slumber; killing, feeding, growing, bringing forth small copies of himself; grown upon with hair like grass, fitted with eyes that move and glitter in his face; a thing to set children screaming;—and yet looked at nearlier, known as his fellows know him, how surprising are his attributes! Poor soul,

here for so little, cast among so many hardships, filled with desires so incommensu-
rate and so inconsistent, savagely surrounded, savagely descended, irremediably condemned to prey upon his fellow lives: who should have blamed him had he been of a
piece with his destiny and a being merely barbarous? And we look and behold him
instead filled with imperfect virtues: infinitely childish, often admirably valiant,
often touchingly kind; sitting down, amidst his momentary life, to debate of right
and wrong and the attributes of the deity; rising up to do battle for an egg or die
for an idea; singling out his friends and his mate with cordial affection; bringing
forth in pain, rearing with long-suffering solicitude, his young. To touch the heart of
his mystery, we find in him one thought, strange to the point of lunacy: the thought
of duty; the thought of something owing to himself, to his neighbor, to his God; an
ideal of decency, to which he would rise if it were possible; a limit of shame, below
which, if it be possible, he will not stoop.—ROBERT LOUIS STEVENSON, *Pulvis et Umbra*

In fact, I'm amazed at how much goodness there is in people even in a system that
puts a premium on badness. It's striking to see how generous we can be when our
imaginations are touched by a great emergency, a flood, say, or a fire. It's encourag-
ing to see how much sheer heroism there is, how people will forget their own skins
and risk their lives for others. I know plenty of dishonest people, but I know few
who seem to enjoy their dishonesty, and even they might have been all right if
they'd been caught young enough.

If people are as good as this when it pays to be bad, what mightn't we expect
of them if the incentive to disloyalty and dishonesty could be taken away? I have
known a man to go out of his way to help me when I was in trouble, and then try
to cheat me out of three cents on an order of groceries. I'd trust that man in a
cooperative society, and I'd trust myself, though I've done my share of dishonest
things.—GRANVILLE HICKS, *I Like America*

"This here ol' man jus' lived a life an' jus' died out of it. I don't know whether he
was good or bad, but that don't matter much. He was alive, an' that's what matters.
An' now he's dead, an' that don't matter. Heard a fella tell a poem one time, an'
he says, 'All that lives is holy.' Got to thinkin', an' purty soon it means more than
the words says."—JOHN STEINBECK, *The Grapes of Wrath*

III. The two paragraphs below deal with similar situations. How would
you classify the language in each, and for what reasons?

I can smell death. It's a gift, I reckon, one of them no-count gifts like good conversation that don't do you no good no more. Once Cousin John Mebane come to see
us, and as he leaned over to pat me on the head—he was polite and hog-friendly to
everybody, chillun and poverty-wropped kin especial—I said, "Cousin John, what
makes you smell so funny?" Ma all but took the hide off'n me; but four days later
they was dressen him in his shroud. Then I didn't know what it was I'd smelled, but
by this time I'd got better acquainted with the meanen.—ANDREW NELSON LYTLE,
"Mister McGregor"

She wept bitterly when the hour came to bid little Johann farewell. He put his
arms about her and embraced her. Then, with his hands behind his back, resting

his weight on one leg while the other poised on the tip of the toes, he watched her out of sight; his face wore the same brooding, introspective look with which he had stood at his father's death-bed, and his grandmother's bier, witnessed the breaking-up of the great household, and shared in so many events of the same kind, though of lesser outward significance. The departure of old Ida belonged to the same category as other events with which he was already familiar: breakings-up, closings, endings, disintegrations—he had seen them all. Such events did not disturb him—they had never disturbed him. But he would lift his head, with the curling light-brown hair, inflate one delicate nostril, and it was as if he cautiously sniffed the air about him, expecting to perceive that odour, that strange and yet familiar odour which, at his grandmother's bier, not all the scent of the flowers had been able to disguise.—THOMAS MANN, *Buddenbrooks*

IV. Comment on the usage and the tone in the following sentences, suggesting revisions when either usage or tone seems inappropriate. In judging appropriateness, you will need to consider such things as: the probable situation in which the statement occurs; whether it is spoken or written; whether language or tone inappropriate in one situation might be satisfactory in another.

1. What's the idea, Officer, saying I was doing seventy? Your speedometer's wrong.
2. Obviously the faculty has an utter and sinister disregard for the inalienable rights of we students!
3. Do like I do. Adopt a stoical attitude toward such misadventure and you'll perk right up.
4. Anyone can see there's no point in studying a foreign language.
5. *I* don't have to call on *my* friends to arrange dates for me.
6. I deem it advantageous to take math along with chem.
7. I tell ya, Gertie, men are all alike; they's none of them won't hand ya that line.
8. When we penetrate to the final entities, the startling fact of spatial existence discloses itself.
9. Upon his admission to the institution of his choice, he entertained hopes of affiliating himself with a fraternal organization.
10. However, because of his misdemeanors, he was, before initiation, kicked out.
11. Of course I don't know anything about the subject, but I would greatly appreciate it, nevertheless, if I might be permitted to voice my very humble opinion.
12. Good fences make good neighbors.
13. In *my* day, young ladies were modest and well mannered.
14. *I* never say nasty things about other people.
15. The President announced the plan of building a new dormitory as soon as funds are available.
16. Prexy says they're going to build a new dorm when they get the money.
17. Prexy announced the plan of erecting a new dorm as soon as the cash is available.
18. The night closed down, black, cavernous, deep in palpable loneliness. I've got the jitters, he thought.

19. Listen, Prof, maybe I messed up the English exam; O.K., but I knew it cold. I think I rate another try.

20. What a lovely dress, dear. With your figure, that fullness around the hips is good.

21. I just don't know why it is that people confide in me.

22. Although I made extensive preparation for the examination, the moment I entered the classroom I clutched.

V. Good writing generally has a consistent level of usage. Sometimes, though, a skillful writer gets effects he wants by a deft mixing of levels. The paragraph below is a mixture of high informal and low informal usage. In what words and constructions is it most formal? Where is it most informal? What do you think is gained by the variation in usage?

How would you describe the tone of the passage and where is it most evident? What makes the paragraph interesting?

It is now, apparently, Hollywood's considered opinion that there is too big a separation between screen and audience, and that once this gap is bridged, the industry will be revitalized. (The lion, leaping, must land in your lap; the kiss, delivered, must be delivered where it belongs, on the lips of the person who paid his money at the box office.) This simple-minded notion that art is a matter of tactuality is typical of Hollywood and should surprise no one. As for us, we're sticking to the belief that what the movies need is good pictures. The aim of picturemakers should be to establish the sort of emotional experience that one enjoys when reading a great book or watching a great play—which is a sense of participation by reason of detachment, and is not the experience of getting sent. We're beginning to think that great pictures, although not beyond the skill of Hollywood, are beyond its aspiration. And unless one's aspirations are in good order, one's business chances are dim indeed.—E. B. WHITE, *The Second Tree from the Corner*

Chapter 3

THE PRACTICE
OF WRITING

In later chapters, we shall discuss principles of structure and style that can help students write more effective sentences and paragraphs. We shall also, in later chapters, discuss particular types of writing that students may be asked to do. The purpose of this chapter is to give a general view of the practice of composition and to guide students as they prepare to meet their early writing assignments.

We are using *practice* in a double sense, first as it is used in the adage "Practice makes perfect." Short papers, or informal themes, generally between five and six hundred words, are often assigned early in college English courses to develop ease in expression and the ability to handle larger writing projects. They are practice—the development of proficiency—for communication to come, both during and after college years. There is no doubt that this practice in writing is valuable: at the end of a term of composition, students nearly always express themselves more competently and more easily than they did at the beginning, largely as a result of writing and receiving criticism on their short compositions.

Practice also means *process, operation, procedure.* We shall discuss here the method, the step-by-step process, of writing substantial, well-organized, clear, and interesting themes.

Before we discuss the process of composition, however, it is wise to consider briefly some of the common problems of theme writing in relation to the whole practice of writing. For, although writing themes is valuable, and although it is satisfying to a number of students, other students find it arduous and even painful. Obstacles, some imagined, some real, block them in their approach to a writing assignment.

One problem is produced by the student's feeling that writing themes is forced communication. Instead of waiting until he is ready and eager to express his ideas, he is obliged to communicate at a certain time, at a prescribed length, usually in a designated form (expository, narrative, descriptive), and sometimes on one of a list of topics assigned. This regulated, unspontaneous writing seems to many students unnatural and difficult; a common protest is, "I have to be in the mood before I can write; I couldn't write anything good this week because I wasn't in the mood."

This attitude is understandable, but the student who takes it gives himself a mental handicap. If he will examine communication in general, he will find that forced communication is by no means peculiar to college English. In the business of living, the report is due tomorrow; the speech is set for Tuesday; the thesis must be finished before the established date for the awarding of degrees; the editor expects the article in time for the January issue; the class will assemble to hear the lecture at nine; the letter must be answered today. Communication is often forced, often prescribed in length and subject and form. The practice of writing in English courses is, in part, practice for meeting other deadlines, other responsibilities that leave little time for concern about one's mood. One may not be in the mood to study psychology, or to prepare for an examination, or to write the examination; but he gets into the mood, or rather, he forgets about his mood, by getting to work. The business of writing a theme should be handled in the same way. Worry about a lack of freedom, spontaneity, and "inspiration" is simply a form of procrastinating. So, indeed, is any sort of worry about a writing assignment. The remedy is systematic work.

A second, more genuine problem in theme writing is the problem of the reader, the audience for whom the paper is written. We have said earlier that the audience is an important factor in successful communication: material, language, attitude, and tone must, to some extent at least, be adjusted to it. But themes are often written in an unusual sort of vacuum; there seems to be no definite reader at whom to aim. The student sometimes just writes, in a baffled desperation, hoping the composition will turn out well, but having no clear idea of how appropriate his subject is, how fully he needs to explain an activity or process, how much knowledge he can take for granted on the part of the unknown reader, what standards, other than the standard of technical correctness, he is expected to meet.

The most obvious audience for the theme is, of course, the instructor. He reads the papers; on his response depends the student's grade. Some college freshmen, bearing these facts in mind, adopt what seems to them the shrewd course and write, not what they think or feel, but what they assume the instructor wants them to think and feel. Such students frequently misjudge their teachers. At least the good instructors manage to keep a sense of humor, have some memories of their own college days which would surprise their students, and are likely to lean over backward in judging themes that contain opinions opposite to their own. Students who wish to please these instructors can do so by honest, direct writing. They will do such writing (and so get the best grades) when they are actually trying to communicate an experience or an idea that seems to them worth communicating. Unless a student has convincing evidence to the contrary, he will be wise to assume that his teacher will be a fair and understanding reader and that the best way to impress is to do sincere, thoughtful writing.

As a further solution to the problem of the reader and a further aid to good writing, it is well to have in mind not just the teacher, but the kind of audience that most serious writers really write for and hope to be judged by—an audience of well-informed, intelligent people who are interested in the world they live in, who recognize and appreciate good informal writing, who will not read dull, wordy material but will respond readily to lively concrete expression, who welcome humor that is in keeping with the subject, who will read sympathetically or open-mindedly anything that reveals the writer's experience or knowledge or considered opinions.

It is valuable, too, for a student occasionally to write for particular audiences, for much of the communicating that he will do later—writing letters or reports and talking to small or large groups—will be aimed at special audiences. Writing a theme for the class and then reading it to the class is a good procedure. Another good practice is stating in an introductory note that a theme is aimed at a particular audience and then aiming the theme at that audience: for example, writing an editorial aimed at college students, a fund-raising letter to people who might contribute to a charity, a report for someone who has presumably requested such a report, a letter of application to a prospective employer, a criticism of a book for someone who has not read the book, information about fraternity rushing for an incoming freshman. In aiming at such audiences, it is necessary to consider the needs, knowledge, and interests of the audience; and in writing for a general audience of intelligent, well-informed people it is wise to remember that even they do not necessarily have specialized knowledge.

In summary, if the student will direct most of his writing at the intelligent, well-informed, sympathetic audience, assuming that his instructor is a member of that audience, and if he will occasionally direct a theme at a clearly defined particular audience, he will escape the frustrating experience of writing for no audience at all. He will also be practicing the kind of writing that, in the future as well as the present, he should be able to do.

A third problem, finding something to write about, will be considered in the next section, where we begin to discuss the writing process. Though choosing a subject is an initial problem for many students, it is also the first of five stages in planning and writing a theme. These stages or steps in composition are:

1. Choosing the subject
2. Planning the paper
3. Writing the first draft (or drafts)
4. Revising
5. Making the final copy

The most important single point for the student writer to keep in mind is that writing a theme should be thought of, and executed, *as a series of steps.* The early steps may overlap; for example, by the time the writer has fixed on a subject, he often has in mind a rough outline of his projected paper. But no step should be omitted, and no step should be hurried. Good themes are built gradually; and they are built by systematic procedure, thought, and care.

I. SOMETHING TO SAY

A good theme has substance. It shows a mind at work, observing, thinking, and communicating its observation and thought to a reader. Such thoughtful and substantial communication is certainly not beyond the power of any college student. Anyone who has lived for seventeen years or more has much to say that is worth saying. And yet the thin, trivial theme, not worth the time consumed in writing or the time wasted in reading it, is all too common; and the lament, "I can't think of anything to write," is all too familiar to teachers of English.

Often the student who says that he can't "think" of anything to write about has done no actual thinking. He has for five days waited passively for an idea to strike, and on the sixth day has begun to worry. Neither waiting nor worry is likely to produce good results. If he has thought actively about a subject for his paper, he has frequently made the mistake of thinking abstractly and beyond his own experience. He has thought of such topics as world peace, race relations, life in America, the educational system; and he is naturally confused. These topics are too vague and large. But in specific events he has witnessed, people he has actually known, opinions he has formed, concrete information he has acquired, he has hundreds of subjects for papers. About these things that he knows, he has something to say.

Suppose the assignment is to write an informal narrative theme that presents a vivid personal experience. "I can't think of anything to write," a student may say. "Nothing interesting has ever happened to me." This is absurd. He may mean that he has never been a jet pilot, has never been in a riot, and has never been the victim of a holdup. Perhaps not; but if he had been, he would still be at a loss for a theme subject, because a habit of mind makes him glance over his own experience and dismiss it as worthless. He should examine it closely. Every human life is full of experiences and events, not necessarily dramatic or sensational, but important at the time, and representing true segments of the experience of living. The student to whom nothing interesting has happened has run home from school every day for months in fear of the gang waiting around the corner; he has wondered about death and God at his grandfather's funeral; on a camping trip he has been lost in the woods; he has watched a large building burn; he has visited a part of his city or a part of his country unknown to him before; he has learned that his girl is going to a party with his friend; he has felt lost and strange on his first day at college. These are only a few of the dozens of possible subjects he has for his narrative paper.

Suppose the assignment is to write a theme that gives information about something the writer knows from firsthand experience; the theme is to be impersonal, focused on giving information about some business, or process, or specialized activity. The student, a girl this time, has never worked in a factory or a grocery store; she knows nothing about cars; she cannot set a lobster trap; she does not collect stamps; she has never been a waitress. She is in despair. But she has been a swimming instructor at a summer camp; she has collected money for school projects in various sections of her town; she has been assistant editor of her high-school paper; she has built stage sets and managed lighting for school plays; she has been on a committee studying air pollution in her community. About these things and many others, she has special, firsthand knowledge.

With the right kind of thinking about what he actually knows, the student has the problem not of finding something to write about, but of choosing the best subject from the many that are available. The best subject will usually be the one most real and interesting to him, about which he has the most exact knowledge, the most vivid impressions. Anything can be made real and interesting to a reader—literally anything, from shoe polish to a music festival, from an autopsy to a walk along a country road—if the writer knows about it, if he is himself interested in it, and if he communicates it concretely. A paper cannot be porous and thin and trivial if it is packed with definite statements, exact particulars, specific examples, concrete details, images, and sensations.

Close observation of one's own experience, reflection on that experience, and accurate, detailed recording are the essentials of something to say.[1]

II. PLANNING THE PAPER: ORGANIZATION AND FOCUS

Some planning of the paper has already been done by the time the writer has chosen the subject. That is, the writer has necessarily thought through the topic sufficiently to see that it can be developed; he probably has in mind three or four points he can make, and perhaps an illustration or two. But he is seldom mentally prepared to sit down at once and write the theme. More systematic planning is needed.

A. The Informal Outline

Most students find it useful, as a step toward writing, to jot down a rough outline of their early ideas about the subject, and, as their thinking and planning proceed, to work with that outline, adding new ideas as they come, deleting others, rearranging the material. A formal outline is unnecessary for a short informal paper; it may, indeed, be an actual hazard in writing because, looking logical and finished, it may bind the writer to a plan that is not the best for his material. The rough outline, however, is a convenient way of keeping track of ideas and seeing the relationship between them; and it has the virtue of being highly flexible.

Below is a copy of a rather full rough outline for a theme on the writer's changing ideas of happiness; the outline had been enlarged and amended during several days of intermittent thinking about the theme:

MY CHANGING IDEAS OF HAPPINESS

1. As a child, having everything I wanted
    candy
    Xmas presents (Uncle John)
    ~~dog I couldn't have (unhappiness)~~
    best bike in the neighborhood
    self-centered, thought everyone *circus*
        existed to give me things, *movies*
        Material things.
    ~~2. Doing what I wanted   circus, movies~~

[1] Because concrete development is such an important part of substance and interest, the student may find it useful to read the full discussion of concrete expression, beginning on page 127, before he writes his early informal themes.

2 8. Older, happiness in being independent
⌐ different, but like (1) because
   still selfish
   hated parents' authority
   earning own money
   going off in woods *having car*
   going into city alone
⌐ wanted to show off, be thought
   important

3 4. Now, doing some good is happiness
more   church (influence)
considerate ← appendix—doctors and nurses
of others   decided to be doctor
                  still like things and independence,
                  but less important now

The kind of planning represented by an outline like this pays dividends; and, for most writers, the planning should be on paper, not simply in the mind. Since the written plan can be viewed more wholly and clearly, the writer can apply to it, more easily than to a mental plan, certain fundamental questions about the content and organization of the theme. The questions to ask about any projected paper are:

1. Is the subject too large for a short theme?

Often the writer has tried, initially, to handle too much in five or six hundred words. The development of so much material will necessarily be sketchy. He needs to select only one phase of his subject—one division in his outline—and develop it fully for his theme. If, for example, the writer of the outline just quoted had originally planned a paper on all his changing ideas, including changing ideas of happiness, changing tastes in reading, and changing attitudes toward girls, his very large topic would have necessitated his leaving out most of the detail that gives the paper on happiness its individuality and substance.

Sometimes a student knows, from criticism of his papers in the past, that he needs to narrow the subjects on which he writes; but still, when he thinks about a new topic, he has difficulty in seeing why it should be limited. Such a writer will probably be helped by reading with particular care the material (beginning on page 174) on developing paragraphs. Absorbing a sense of solid paragraphs and the worth of such paragraphs may enable him to view more critically the plan of his projected paper. He may see more easily that full and meaningful development of major points in his outline would result in a paper of several thousand words, and that one part of his topic is adequate and suitable for one short theme. Possibly the discarded parts can be saved for rainy days to come.

2. Does the paper seem to be well focused?

Focus is often lost, or perfected, in the actual writing of the paper, but the writer can, by examining his outline, see if any of his material is irrelevant or not strictly relevant to the main idea. In the outline above, the point about the unhappiness of not having a dog appears irrelevant to the discussion of what constituted happiness at that time. Wisely, the writer struck it out.

Study of an outline may also suggest that overlapping main points could well be combined, that discussing them separately might weaken the focus of the paper by giving disproportionate weight to one section. The writer of the quoted outline saw that point 2 was logically a subordinate part of point 1, not worth separate development.

3. Is the arrangement of material good?

The writer of the outline above rearranged certain subtopics, but the chronological arrangement of his main points was made inevitable by his material. Often, however, the main points need to be shuffled, for better continuity or better building to a climax. Working out good connections between ideas usually comes later in the process of composition, but in this early stage the writer needs to see that he has a clear basic pattern and that the reader can be led logically and smoothly from one idea to the next. Steady focus and clear arrangement of material work together to produce the unity and coherence characteristic of a good theme.

These questions can also, of course, be applied to a first draft of a paper; and some writers prefer to start with a rough draft instead of an outline, with the intention of drastically revising and reorganizing the rough draft, and probably writing three or four drafts before the paper is in final form. In other words, they partially merge steps 2 and 3 (planning the paper, writing the first draft) in the practice of writing. It is, however, harder to eliminate parts of a paper than it is to strike out jottings in an outline, and harder to change the order of material that is written out with some fullness and continuity. For this reason the outline as a step preliminary to writing is likely to produce a better focused and better organized theme. A first draft based on a well-planned outline may need considerable revision, but the arrangement of material will probably be good; the writer can, therefore, give his attention to other problems of form and development.

B. The Statement of Purpose

Before beginning his first draft, the writer should consider his exact intention in writing the paper (aside from completing an assignment), and the audience for whom the paper is written. Let us say that the assignment is an informative theme aimed at the intelligent general audience discussed earlier in this chapter. With this assignment, the writer has a number of choices in regard to style and tone. If his purpose is purely to inform, he may wish to write the paper in an impersonal style, excluding references to himself and to his experience with and attitude toward the subject. If, on the other hand, some evaluation, persuasion, entertainment, or sharing of experience is appropriate to his material and is a secondary part of his intention, he may wish to write more personally, and to establish a personal, informal writer-reader relationship. If he is giving information about a process or activity (refinishing furniture, or training a dog, for example) in which he expects his reader to be engaged, he may even address his paper directly to the reader.

Having thought through the relationships of his material, his intention, his attitude toward the audience, and his style, the writer is ready to formulate a concise statement of his purpose in the theme he is about to write. These are examples of clear and useful statements of purpose:

> My purpose is to give objective information about what the photographer looks for in taking pictures, to a reader who has only an average knowledge of photography.

> My purpose is to give directions which will enable the reader with little knowledge of gardening to have a successful rose garden.

> My purpose is to give an informal and (I hope) entertaining report on baby-sitting to a reader inexperienced in this work.

> My purpose is to give the beginning fisherman information about trout fishing, and, by using some of my personal experience, to persuade him to try this exciting sport.

> My purpose is to describe the March Against Death in Washington (November 1969) so that a reader who was not there will feel the solemnity of the occasion.

Such a statement of purpose, somewhat modified, may be used at the beginning of the paper itself. Whether or not it is used in the paper, the clearly formulated statement of purpose will crystallize the writer's thinking and will help to give focus and consistency to his writing.

III. WRITING THE FIRST DRAFT

Many considerations may crowd the student's mind as he begins the first draft of his theme. As we have suggested before, one idea that should be held steadily in mind is that he is not simply writing a paper; he is writing a paper for someone else to read. His writing is not only expression, but also communication.

A. Writing for a Reader[2]

If the paper is informative, the writer should remember, as he writes his first draft, to supply background information that his audience might need, and to define terms that are technical or are used in some other special way. Definitions are sometimes given in footnotes; it is generally better, though, to work them into the text of an informal theme. Sometimes definition can be accomplished inconspicuously by the use of an appositive. For example, in a paper on sailing, one might define *boom* by writing, "During this operation it is important to watch the boom, the pole extending along the bottom of the sail." Sometimes a fuller definition is needed. The sentence "A let ball is served again," from a paper on how to play tennis, would be obscure to many readers; the writer needs to pause and explain the term in some such manner as this: "A ball is called *let* when it goes over the net and into the correct court, but touches the net on the way over. The server is permitted to serve another ball in place of the *let* ball."

If the writer is giving instructions or directions, he should be sure to include every step in a process—for example, to tell the inexperienced carpenter to sandpaper the surface before he puts on the second coat of varnish, or the inexperienced gardener to water the lawn after he applies chemical fertilizer in midsummer.

Although consideration of the reader obliges the writer to supply necessary definition and detail, it also obliges him not to state or labor the obvious. Statements like "At one time, hunting animals was necessary for man to survive, but in this country today hunting is largely a sport" are not worth making; they insult the reader's intelligence.

If the theme being drafted is not an informative paper, but is an informal recollection or a reflective personal essay like the one outlined on page 81, awareness of the audience is important in a somewhat different way. The writer needs to remember that he is describing people, places, and events that the reader probably does not know. The reader can read the paper, but not the author's mind, and only on the basis of detail actually set down can he understand and share the experiences presented. Persuasive writing also requires the writer to put himself in the place of the reader—to imagine how he would react to dogmatically-stated or unsupported opinions, or to a failure to consider reasonable arguments on the other side of the case.

B. Proportion and Transition

The informal outline represents a logical arrangement of steps or ideas, and, if it is a full outline, it includes a number of examples, reasons, or details

[2] This subject is discussed further in Chapter 9, "Informative Writing."

to support and develop the main points. The outline does not necessarily, though, indicate the relative importance of sections of the paper, or the amount of development they will need for clarity or for the emphasis the writer wants to give them. The proportions of the paper may be further shaped in revision, but in the first draft the writer should briefly cover the less important parts of his material, and point up, by full development, the most important parts. Ideas or aspects of the subject that seem equally significant should probably have something like equal development.

In the first draft, too, the writer should try to link his ideas so that the reader can easily follow the logic of his organization. Concluding a paragraph with a sentence that leads into the next paragraph, or beginning a paragraph with a sentence that refers clearly to a statement at the end of the preceding paragraph will enable the reader to move with no sense of disconnection from one block of the material to the next. Transitional words and phrases like *however, in addition, the third reason, the following day, after this step* make plain the sequence of ideas or actions and the relationship between them.

C. Uninterrupted Writing

It is generally wise, particularly if one is working from a good outline, to write the first draft in one sitting and at a fairly steady pace, without pausing long or worrying much over mechanical difficulties and small details. This does not mean that the student should write carelessly, even in a first draft. On the contrary, it is most desirable for him to learn to write reasonably clean and competent first drafts—he is often judged, on examinations, for example, by his ability to do this. But stopping in the process of writing the draft of a theme to look up the spelling of a word or the use of a comma, or to work over an awkward sentence, may break the writer's train of thought and interfere with the forward movement of the composition. Since it is possible for him to revise his work—since, indeed, he is expected to do so—he can defer nicety of expression for the sake of getting down on paper his unbroken sequence of ideas. Thoughtful planning, then uninterrupted first writing, and finally careful revision usually produce the best results.

IV. REVISION

Revision is the stage of writing that students most often neglect, sometimes because they write their papers too late to have much time for revision, sometimes because they have understandable difficulty in seeing weaknesses in their own work, sometimes because they are lazy. And yet, revision is very important; and working over a paper can be the most rewarding part of the whole writing process. Polishing a sentence, eliminating a useless phrase, finding the word that says exactly what one means, changing a routine beginning to an arresting one, joining two poorly related paragraphs with a neat transition, adding one or two details to bring a hazy picture into sharp focus—such changes make the difference between mediocrity and excellence; and they give the writer the sense of craftsmanship, of deep satisfaction and sometimes excitement, which comes from knowing that a thing is as perfect as one can make it. Teachers of English know that when a student with an average or below average record has once written a good paper, he is likely to write more good papers. The reason for this phenomenon is complex; but one element in it is that the student, having once had the experience of craftsmanship, having once stretched himself to do his best work, is no longer content with half-hearted imperfection.

Very occasionally, when a student is immersed in a subject or an experience (and when he is well trained and fluent), he can write a first draft that requires no revision: the development of the idea is complete and clear; the details, long present in his mind, are set down vividly for the reader; no word needs to be changed. But, nearly always, such finished writing comes from thoughtful and painstaking revision.

Revision, to be effective, should be done, not as soon as the first draft is completed, but at least twenty-four hours, preferably three or four days, later. (This means, obviously, that writing a theme should not be postponed until the night before the paper is due.) The completion of the first draft sometimes leaves the writer in a state of exhausted discouragement, sometimes in a glow of pride in achievement. Both states are frequently unjustified; and both blind him to the actual merits and defects of what he has written. Even if he has no distinct feeling of discouragement or sense of accomplishment, he is not an able critic just after his paper is written because he knows so well what he *intended* to say. Two or three days later, looking at the draft which has grown somewhat strange, he will be able to see what he failed to say. He may even— it has happened—be uncertain about what he meant. He will, certainly, look at the paper with a view closer to that of the alien reader who will ultimately see and judge it; and he is therefore, at this later time, able to make effective revision.

A part of the process of revision should be *reading the paper aloud.* Awkward phrasing, thoughtless repetition of words, repeated sentence patterns, and wordiness are more striking to the ear than to the fast-moving eye. Also, since reading aloud is slower than glancing over the page, small details of spelling and punctuation will receive more notice. The author should do this reading aloud, let us repeat, not when the theme is fresh and meaningful in his mind, but after an interval. He can hear then, if he listens, what the paper is, without the overtones of what he intended it to be.

The critical scrutiny and revision of the paper, like the whole writing practice, should be systematic. The writer should closely examine his paragraphs: do they have topic sentences or topic ideas? are they well developed? are the transitions between paragraphs smooth and clear? His sentences: are they grammatically correct? are they sufficiently varied? His words: is he sure of their meanings? are all of them necessary? could one exact word be substituted for the five he has used? are their connotations right for his purpose? are they correctly spelled? And his punctuation: does it indicate accurately the pauses, and the strength of the pauses, which the reader needs for immediate understanding? The student should scrutinize his paper particularly, of course, for errors or weaknesses that have been called to his attention before. The student who makes numerous blunders in writing will profit from reading his paper several times, looking for one type of fault in each reading, instead of trying to correct everything at one time. Systematically reading once for paragraph development, a second time for punctuation, and a third time for exact use of words will produce better results than trying to concentrate simultaneously on three very different problems.

Much more elusive than punctuation or paragraph development, and harder for the student to check in his own writing, is the clarity of thought and expression in the theme. There is sometimes, in the work of inexperienced writers, a kind of *fogginess*, whether basically in thinking or in expression it is often difficult to say. Reading a composition that has this quality, one has the feeling that somehow the wheels have slipped; there is a gap in thought, or between thought and expression; the sense is blurred. It is impossible to define this fogginess precisely, because there are so many varieties of it. The following short passages, taken from freshman themes, will illustrate:

The most important use of hypnotism is as an anesthetic. This use can be second only to the cure of neuroses. [Awkwardly phrased; but the basic fault is in the writer's failure to think through the idea. If the use as an anesthetic can be second to another use, then logically it is not "the most important use."]

It is impossible to determine how old leprosy is, for we cannot tell whether the leprosy recorded in 1500 B.C. was the same as that which now scourges man as it has for more than 3000 years. [Another example of foggy thinking. Having said that the leprosy recorded in 1500 B.C. is not necessarily the same leprosy that we know now, the writer assumes at the end of the sentence that it is the same.]

The trance stage of hypnotism is such a deep state that many people have been mistaken for dead while in it. The fact that bodies have often been found in caskets shows that people have been pronounced dead while being in trance. [This absurd statement is an example of a gap in expression, possibly in thinking too, although it is hard to believe that the point that the bodies had moved after they were enclosed in the caskets was absent from the writer's mind. Something was absent from his mind, however, when he failed to put that essential point on paper.]

My love of literature will occupy an outstanding niche on my ladder of success. [An example of a fuzzy, imperfectly visualized figure of speech. Niches are, by their nature, recessed, not outstanding; and it would be a most extraordinary ladder which had a niche.]

The loss of working hours must be increased if the company is to meet its production goal. [An example of foggy expression. The working hours, of course, not the loss of them, must be increased; or the loss must be decreased.]

My earliest recollection of first going to school occurred when I was five years old. [Another example of blurred expression. Going to school, not the recollection of it, occurred when the writer was five years old.]

Writing sentences like these in a first draft is understandable; failing to improve them before the paper is turned in is hardly excusable.

In revising his papers, the student should examine the clarity of his thinking and his expression, asking himself these three questions: Have I thought the ideas through, logically and carefully? Have I said exactly what I mean? Have I put on paper every link in my chain of thought, every detail that the reader needs to know? Clarity in thought and expression is particularly hard to judge immediately after the first writing of the paper. After an interval, gaps in communication and inexactness in wording are often so conspicuous that the writer wonders how he could have thought that he had made his meaning clear.

Finally, before he makes the last copy of his theme, the writer should examine, as thoroughly and critically as he can, the texture of the whole composition. A good theme is like a good piece of cloth, tightly woven, substantial, consistent in its quality. Mechanical errors—in spelling, punctuation, grammar—are tears in the cloth. Choppy sentences and disconnected paragraphs make breaks in the weave. Wordiness and undue triteness are shoddy places. Inexact or roundabout phrasing and, above all, lack of detail produce a thin, sleazy fabric. Removing actual errors is only part of the process of revision. It is basic, of course; but a more important part is working for the tight structure, the precise and finished phrasing, and the packed, concrete expression that make the good theme.

V. FINAL FORM

Preparing the final copy of the paper is the easy step in the process of writing. One needs only to keep in mind a few simple requirements, designed to facilitate the handling, grading, and filing of large numbers of themes.

A typewritten paper should be double-spaced, on standard $8\frac{1}{2}$ by 11-inch paper. A theme in longhand should be written on lined paper of the same size ($8\frac{1}{2}$ by 11) with widely spaced lines (about $\frac{1}{2}$ inch apart) so that the lines of writing will not be illegibly intermingled. Longhand papers are written neatly and clearly, in dark ink. In both typewritten and handwritten manuscripts, only one side of the paper is used. The title is centered near the top of the first page, with double space between it and the text below. Substantial margins are left on both sides of the page. The pages are arranged in order and are numbered. The paper is folded and endorsed according to the form established by the institution or the department. Most English instructors want themes folded lengthwise, with the student's name, course and section number, instructor's name, subject of the theme, and the date the theme is due written or typed on the outside, at the top of the folded manuscript.

Although the final copy of a paper should be finished and clean, most teachers do not object to a few minor revisions in the completed manuscript, provided it remains neat and legible. Words to be changed, if they cannot be erased, should have a line drawn through them, with the correct word written above the word struck out. (Unwanted words put in parentheses are confusing to a reader; the parentheses are used incorrectly and misleadingly when they enclose words not meant to be read.) If words are to be inserted, they too should be written between the lines, with a caret ($\wedge$) inserted to show where they should be read. The paragraph symbol (¶) should be used in the margin to show that a paragraph break, overlooked in typing, is intended here.

The completed manuscript should be read carefully to pick up any mechanical slips. An instructor reading great numbers of papers cannot make distinctions between errors of carelessness and errors of ignorance. An error is, necessarily, an error. "The girl who typed this for me made some mistakes" is not a valid excuse for mechanical deficiencies in a theme. The writer is obligated to check his typist as well as himself. His final copy should in all respects represent the best work he is able to do.

CHAPTER REVIEW

Below is a summary of the main ideas in the chapter. If your reading has been adequate, you should be able to supply the particulars necessary to develop these summary statements.

1. The communication in theme writing is no more forced than the communication necessary many times in everyday living.

2. The student can simplify the problem of what audience to write for by aiming most of his informal themes at an intelligent, well-informed general audience, and occasionally, with the approval of his instructor, writing for a particular audience.

3. The practice of composition should be thought of and executed as a series of systematic steps.

4. In choosing subjects, the student should avoid large abstract topics, and should draw on his own experience, observation, information, and thought.

5. It is advisable to make an informal outline, and to work out the organization of the paper by revising that outline, before starting to write the first draft.

6. A concise statement of purpose will help to give focus and consistency to the paper.

7. The student should allow himself ample time for revision, a very important part of the writing process.

8. Revision is most effective if it is done at least twenty-four hours after the first writing of the paper. Reading the paper aloud should be part of the revision.

9. The good theme, besides being mechanically correct, has substance, good organization, effective transitions between sentences and paragraphs, concrete development, clear thought, and apt, precise expression.

EXERCISES

The six student themes below, not arranged in order of merit, range from excellent to very poor. Read carefully, criticize, and grade the themes. The assignment was to write a paper of at least 500 words that would interest the reader and give him clear information about something the writer knew from firsthand experience. The theme was to be impersonal, focused on the process or activity rather than on the writer's own experience with it.

In criticizing each theme, consider its technical correctness (spelling, punctuation, sentence structure, etc.), its focus and organization, paragraph development, style and choice of words, and the clarity and interest of the whole paper.

1. MAY HE REST IN PEACE

To most people, the word cemetary brings a cold shiver to their spines, usually accompanied, when the subject is brought up by the sudden impulse to quickly change the subject. Nevertheless, since I found myself closely connected to one of these institutions two summers ago and so was able to learn just how its many processes are accomplished, I shall try to explain these processes and show that they are not as easily achieved as they sometimes appear to be.

My connection with the cemetary in which I worked was that of a grave digger. This job, as some people will think, is not by any means the only task of a cemetary. There are several preliminary processes that must be accomplished before the grave is actually dug.

At the notification of a client's death, the cemetary officials must look up the brief history of the deceased which they have on file. This material; date of birth, place of birth, date of death, place of death, residence and cemetary lot number, is copied on two cards. One of these cards is kept in the office for further reference while the other is sent to the maintenance department. This process is similar to the filing card system which all of you experienced just a month ago.

One member of the maintenance department, after receiving this card, finds the lot number and with two impliments, loosens the sod surrounding the lot in order that the grave may be dug just that much quicker. These lots are, according to their location, sometimes either in a muddy area or even in an area of hard clay. This is an important factor in determining the length of time that should be taken to dig a grave. As sometimes happens, two or even three funerals are scheduled for one day, so naturally it is a great advantage to know just what type of soil must be removed.

At this point, the laborors move into action. Knowing that the decision and timing of the funeral itself depend primarily on their speed, these laborors immediately begin removing what they call the "top" of the grave. This "top" consists of 2½ feet of soil. This soil is set aside, later to be used later for the "fill in" after the funeral. More soil is removed until the depth of six feet has been reached. At this point the grave is complete. The walls are checked to see that all are straight and now the laborious part of the process has come to an end.

The only remaining job before the funeral is that of preparing the so called "decorations". These "decorations" consist of a casket lowering device, several large sections of artificial grass to be spread about the grave and in some cases, a tent and four or five chairs to be used by relatives and close friends of the deceased.

Soon the funeral procession is sighted entering the cemetary. All employees, of course, make themselves scarce during the funeral procedure. Soon afterwards, however, they are seen again. This time they are completing their job by removing the "decorations", "filling in" the grave with the soil previously set aside and last but not least, placing the flowers in an orderly fashion, over the fresh grave.

You may be sure that at the end of the day these laborers leave the cemetary with a satisfied feeling within. They know that they have just completed a job well done and hope that someone has also left the cemetary that day with perhaps a lighter heart then they entered with, knowing now that their loved one has been put to rest in the dignified manner that he well deserved.

2. STAR GAZING

Ever since the dawn of time, man has been fascinated by the night sky. Ancient man saw many patterns in the sky to which he gave names and told stories about their origins. Today, as then, many people are intrigued by the stars and the moon. However, to a large majority of people the heavens are a great mystery. To become a star gazer and to be able to recognize the major stars and constellations takes determination, a strong neck, and a good star map. With these three things anyone can soon become an "expert" on the night sky.

One of the most difficult parts of learning to recognize the constellations is trying to see the so-called pictures they are supposed to depict. One of the easiest ways to overcome this obstacle is to forget that "Orion" is supposed to be a hunter and "Cygnus" a swan and think instead of their geometric shapes. After one has achieved this, the stars will soon begin to fall into recognizable patterns.

Another hazard of star gazing is the probability of gaining an extremely stiff neck. A chaise lounge may alleviate this problem to some extent; however, even when one is viewing the sky from a reclining position, the neck is still apt to become rather sore. This and the cold night air are quite frequently the prime factors in the decision of a person to give up star gazing as a lost cause.

However, once these obstacles have been disposed of, one can find a great deal of satisfaction in spending an evening studying the stars or in simply observing them. There is the personal satisfaction of being able to point out the major stars and constellations to friends and of being able to distinguish between the stars and the planets. There is also the satisfaction gained from contributing something to science. Professional astronomers are often greatly aided by the observations of an amateur. This can be done on a person's own or through such organizations as the American Association of Variables Star Observers. In this field astronomers depend almost entirely upon the data compiled by the members of the "AAVSO".

With the aid of a small telescope, the serious star gazer can study the stars more thoroughly. He can observe such objects as the moon, the moons of Jupiter, or the rings of Saturn. If there are a number of persons interested in astronomy living fairly close to one another, they will often form an astronomy club. They will either exchange information or do some joint star gazing.

For a number of young people star gazing is more than a hobby; it becomes what they hope will be their future profession.

In conclusion, a knowledge of the heavens is something anyone who truly wants it can have. Star gazing may be a future vocation, a serious avocation, or a relaxing pastime. Once one becomes a star gazer, the heavens become increasingly more fascinating. New secrets will be revealed as time goes by. All one needs to be admitted to this out-of-the-ordinary world is a little determination, a strong neck, and a good star map.

3. THE VOICES OF PAQUIMÉ[3]

We, the people of Paquimé, speak across the ages. But he who wants to hear must listen closely, and must seek through sweat and science, for our voices are dim with time. And we no longer have words—in their stead must serve the speech of tool and pot, of architecture and art, of jewelry, and of the bones we left behind. These, the marks of our toils and triumphs, our hopes and our tragedies, have inscribed the story of a great city ineradicably upon the earth.

High up in the foothills of the Sierra Madres, 5000 feet above the sea, lay a fertile mountain-rimmed river valley. Although it was a desert area, there was enough rain to clothe the land; the plains bloomed with sage and mesquite then as they do now. The far hills abounded in timber and game. Here we chose to settle, and we chose well. Surrounded by mountains, we were secure to build and grow. Our fields of corn and beans and squash flourished; our settlement became a great city, the thriving center of trade and culture for all the peoples of what is now called Mexico and the South-Western United States. We named the city "Paquimé," a word which

---

[3] The writer of this paper had spent some time with an archaeological expedition, and so was writing from first-hand experience.

has been passed down through the generations, and is all that remains of a once great language.

Architecture was perhaps the most impressive aspect of our culture. We did not write—yet we built pre-planned apartment houses four and five stories high. The foot-thick walls of oven-baked adobe brick, plastered over smoothly and tinted in delicate pastel colors, kept us warm in winter and cool in summer. Our ceremonial structures included a large cross-shaped platform oriented almost exactly true North, several truncated pyramids of effigy design, and porticoes of stone capitals atop wooden pillars, a design never before found in the New World. But by far the greatest of our architectural achievements was the intricate system of canals and reservoirs that irrigated our fields and brought water for miles across the desert directly into our homes.

We were not only engineers, but artisans too. Only listen to the voice of jewelry wrought from shell and turquoise and jade, gold and copper and bone—bracelets, rings, pendants, hair ornaments; a copper bell in the form of a turtle, its shell exquisitely incised by a complicated wax process that died with the artist. Listen to the whispers of common kitchen utensils in which we stored, cooked, and ate our food: the graceful symmetry of a jar painted red and black in geometric designs; the delicate simplicity of a lacquered and incised black bowl; the good-humored charm of a fat little pot in the shape of a bird, or a horned toad, or a man sitting with his knees drawn up. Only listen, and the voices will tell that we were a people who enjoyed life, who loved beauty, a people who could laugh.

Paquimé reached its height of achievement about 800 years ago, when it housed some 10,000 people, and covered an area of almost 250 acres. And it was a beautiful city, where now the weather-beaten walls slowly crumble back into the earth from whence they came. But suddenly, cataclysmically, our whole culture was destroyed. Our disappearance is as mysterious to those who seek to know our history as is our origin. The uncovered bones of a few solitary survivors show that they were attacked and killed in a last futile stand against some powerful adversary. But what happened to the many thousands who once dwelt in the great city? For most of us had gone before this final catastrophe befell our comrades. We fled in terror from some great disaster, leaving our homes and possessions behind—leaving a voice to speak down through the years. The wind blows; and the clinging dust covers and cradles all. But beneath the earth, the voices of pottery and adobe brick whisper on. The answers are there, for him who has the patience and knowledge to hear. Listen and we shall tell the triumphant story of our development . . . listen again, and our voices will relate the tragic tale of our fall.

4. THE DANCE OF DEATH

Working for a tree expert may seem like a silly and easy job, but actually it is a very difficult one, and calls for a great deal of skill.

How many times have you seen men working in trees and said to yourself, look at those grown men playing, they probably haven't the mentality to do anything else. If you have said this, you have the wrong impression.

The first day that you work for a tree expert, you will be given a one hundred and twenty foot rope, called the Life Line by most tree climbers. You will throw one end of the rope over a cross-bar or beam in the warehouse and spend the whole morning learning to tie knots. Two knots inparticular: one is called the saddle knot, and the other is the slip knot. The saddle knot determines your comfort while in the tree. The slip knot, which by the way does not slip, determines where you can go in the tree.

In the afternoon your teacher will take you out and put you in a small maple tree. Doing this you are learning the pruning techniques, and also getting the feel of your rope. This tree is usually only twenty or thirty feet high. You go to the very top of the tree, and loop your rope over the highest crotch. You have to choose this crotch depending upon the strength of the wood. For instance, in an Elm tree you can choose a small crotch and in a Maple tree, you must choose a large one. Then you slip into your saddle, which was tied before climbing the tree, take the other rope and tie the slip knot around this rope with the tail rope left from the saddle knot. When this is done, you are completely secure and it is practically impossible to fall out. You may stay in these small trees for a week or two, until you can move around in the tree with some ease, and have some faith in the fact that your rope will hold you.

At this point, you will consider yourself an expert, and suggest that you get into some larger trees. When your teacher elects a good size Elm tree, you can consider yourself in the tree business. To most people climbing an Elm tree would be a simple task, but when a climbing line is the difference between life and death, climbing becomes a frightening job. Particularly when you climb forty or fifty feet above ground with nothing holding you or to grab on to if you should happen to slip.

Once you are in your rope and test it to see if all the knots are tied correctly, you are completely secure and it is practically impossible to fall out of the tree.

After gaining confidence in yourself and your rope, you can dance around the tree with little fear and a great deal of agility. As stated before, it is almost impossible to fall out of a tree, but slackness, or sheer carelessness can turn your movement among the branches into a *Dance of Death*.

5. GLAMOUR FOR SALE

It isn't very big when you look at it from the street, squeezed in between a Bell Shop on one side and a restaurant, refuge for teen-agers, on the other. The big red neon sign, however, proudly proclaims to the shoppers the whereabouts of Carroll's Cosmetic Shoppe with two "p's" and an "e." The show windows on either side of the entrance give tempting promises of the treasures to be found within. Very rarely does a woman stop to glance over the display and then pass on to another store. Some magnetic force seems to draw her in, for no woman is immune to beauty.

Inside there are innumerable things to interest the prospective buyer. On the right are men's shaving sets, designed for Christmas gifts, shampoos, razor blades, and other necessary articles. Further down, still on the right, is a display of perfumed soaps in all shapes, sizes, and colors. At the extreme end comes an entire section devoted to bath powder, talc, and cologne. The names alone are enough to make any one want to try them—Black Magic, Shangri-la, Taboo, Mountain Heather, Tweed, Arpège, Kiss and Tell. Each promises an allure far beyond the wildest hopes. At the other side of the store is the perfume and the make-up bar. At the perfume bar tiny dram bottles are filled from larger, more elaborate ones, each reflected several times in mirrors effectively placed. Most of the customers would gasp if they knew that this small section of the store itself is worth several thousand dollars. At the make-up bar anything and everything is sold to "make Madame beautiful." Lipsticks come in any brand and color with nail polish to match. Beauty creams, powder, rouge, astringents, wrinkle-removers, false eyelashes, hair tints and endless preparations gaze placidly down from their shelves.

From nine to five-thirty every day the store is in a constant turmoil but always with perfect propriety—never rowdy or out-of-hand. The girls, each a walking advertisement of her business, never allow themselves to become ruffled or impatient. If, as rarely happens, the store is not able to comply with the customer's desires for a particular shade of lipstick or certain blends of perfumes, immediately something similar is suggested in an effort to satisfy. Confronted with a good salesperson the poor customer never has a chance. She never before suspected that she was without so many necessities. In fact she begins to wonder how she was able to exist.

After five-thirty the scene changes abruptly. Everyone relaxes and becomes human again. Laughter peals out as the girls get ready to go home. The manager beams down on everyone and urges her to try a dash of that new perfume for her date tonight. At last the store is dark and quiet except for the mice racing overhead in the stockroom. How do I know all these things? I spent the Christmas season there as "a walking advertisement" myself.

6. THE EDUCATION OF A MOUSE

Just as the metal ear-punch made its clear, round hole of identification in the mouse's ear, the small rodent successfully sank its sharp front teeth into the bare thumb of the experimenter. The ensuing squeaky yelp of the mouse was barely audible beside the loud exclamation of the experimenter. Although this simple incident had the immediate effect of sending the unfortunate human to look for an antiseptic and a bandage, it gave him some comfort by indicating that the energetic mouse would probably be a keen student. Thus ended the first step in the education of Beaver, as the experimenter thereafter called the sharp-toothed creature, a seemingly insignificant laboratory mouse.

Beaver's classroom was a simple maze constructed in the shape of a capital letter T. His course of study was learning to make a right turn when he came to the crosspiece in the maze.

Since communication between mice and men is rather difficult, the experimenter needed an uncomplicated teaching aid. After consulting some of the authorities of mouse education, he selected the method of using water as a reward for every correct turn. Well-housed laboratory mice are ordinarily given plenty of water; therefore, in order for water to serve as a satisfactory reward, Beaver had to be kept on a routine of water deprivation. Water was available to him only two hours per day. The maze was equipped with a full water bottle at the end of the right arm (right half of the crosspiece) and an empty water bottle at the end of the left arm. Hence, not only was Beaver rewarded for a correct turn, but he also was given a negative reward for an incorrect turn.

The trial-and-error method had previously been found to be most successful in training mice and consequently was selected by the experimenter for Beaver's training. Immediately after he had completed twenty hours without water on the fifth day of deprivation, Beaver was placed in the maze and allowed to wander.

However, Beaver did not wander—he sat without a hint of motion. After the passage of a predetermined minute, the experimenter prodded the recalcitrant rodent with a pencil. Beaver cautiously took a few mincing steps and then abruptly relapsed into his former sedentary position. The first unpromising lesson concluded when Beaver exhausted his allotted two minutes in the maze, still sitting motionless.

According to the design of the experiment, Beaver's second lesson began twenty-four hours after the first. In the second lesson, Beaver moved of his own accord within a few seconds. He began to cautiously explore the maze, stopping occasionally to sniff at imperfections in the wooden walls. After a few moments of indecision upon reaching the crosspiece, he chose the left arm. As soon as he entered the arm, a gate was quietly closed behind him to prevent the possibility of getting a positive reward after making the incorrect turn. The two minutes ended without his finding the empty water bottle.

The succeeding lessons were similar except that Beaver found the empty water bottle on the fourth lesson and tried in vain to extract water from it. Finally, in the twentieth lesson, he chose the right turn, found the water bottle, and received the reward. In the twenty-fourth lesson, he completed five successive correct turns and thereby attained the criterion of learning specified beforehand in the experiment's design.

This illustrative story of the "education" of a simple little mouse may seem insignificant. However, such rudimentary education is basic to the research of experimental psychologists. Hence, the training of a mere mouse like Beaver, no matter how silly such training seems, may yield the key to the eventual understanding of human behavior.

Chapter 4

THE STRUCTURE
OF SENTENCES

Students who have had the good luck to hear English well spoken during their formative years, and who have read widely and well, may have little technical knowledge about the structure of sentences, and yet be good readers and good writers. Such students are skillful in the use of English because their experience has helped them to develop an "ear for language." Even these students, however, can benefit in their writing and in their reading if they become more consciously aware of the rich variety of structures and patterns possible in English sentences; for increased awareness can lead to rewarding experimentation in their own writing and to a fuller and more discriminating appreciation of craftsmanship in the writing of others.

Students who do not have a highly developed ear for the patterning of sentences—and many college freshmen belong to this group—can find that study of structure will serve them well. Because they lack the analytical knowledge necessary for following complicated sentence patterns, many college students (not only freshmen) have difficulty in understanding what they read; they are likely to lose the continuity of involved sentences and to miss important meanings. And in writing—practical as well as artistic writing—the briefest, clearest, and most effective expression can be achieved only by one who knows how to use the structures discussed in this chapter.

The seven most common patterns of declarative English sentences are:

    s   v
1. Students read. (subject—verb: s-v)

    s   v   o
2. Students buy books. (subject—verb—object: s-v-o)

    s   LV   c
3. Students are people. (subject—linking verb—noun complement:[1] s-LV-c)

    s   LV   c
4. Students are young. (subject—linking verb—adjective complement: s-LV-c)

    s   v   o   o
5. He gave me money. (subject—verb—indirect object—object: s-v-o-o)

    s   v   o   c
6. They elected him chairman. (subject—verb—object—objective complement: s-v-o-c)

    s   v   o   c
7. We thought him honest. (subject—verb—object—objective complement: s-v-o-c)

Notice that patterns 6 and 7, though similar, are not identical because the objective complement in one is a noun and in the other an adjective. Other sentence patterns derived from those above are expletive patterns (*There is a salesman at the door*); passive patterns (*The report was read by the committee*); and question patterns (*Where am I?*).

Elements in the basic patterns may, of course, be phrases, and some of them may be clauses, rather than single words:

    s   v   o
All the people in town are saying that he has gone [A Pattern 2 sentence: s-v-o; s and v are phrases; o is a clause.]

    s   LV   c
What he hopes to accomplish is what I don't understand. [A Pattern 3 sentence: s-LV-c; s and c are clauses; LV is a single word.]

When words in sentences are arranged in one of these basic patterns, the word order is said to be *normal*. Except in questions and expletive patterns, the subject normally precedes the verb, and the object or complement follows the verb. Normal order, though sometimes changed or inverted for stylistic reasons, is so well established that we derive meaning from the arrangement of words: *The dog attacked the postman* means one thing and

---

[1] Verbs and complements are discussed in the Handbook, page 380.

The postman attacked the dog another, because we take for granted the subject-verb-object order in sentences of this pattern.

The basic patterns are expanded and combined in a number of ways to produce varied sentences. To aid him in constructing mature and logical sentences from the simple patterns, the writer needs to understand the principles of parallelism, modification, subordination, and consistency.

I. COMPOUND STRUCTURES AND PARALLELISM

Starting with a simple subject-verb-object sentence, *John enjoys skin-diving,* we can compound the entire pattern:

     s   v   o   s   v   o

John enjoys skin-diving, and Susan enjoys fishing.

Or, we can compound any or all of the basic sentence elements:

     s   s   v   v   o   o   o

John and Mary practice and enjoy sailing, swimming, and skin-diving.

Equal parts of a compound construction *(John, Mary; practice, enjoy; sailing, swimming, skin-diving)* are called coordinate, and parallelism is the principle of usage which requires that coordinate elements in a compound construction be given the same grammatical form. The parallel form serves to bind together the coordinate elements and to show that they have the same function in the sentence.

Words, phrases, clauses, and even sentences may be expressed in parallel form. When the parallel locutions are similar in length and rhythm as well as in grammatical construction, they are said to be *balanced;* balanced structures are often used to express comparison or contrast. The following passages illustrate the skillful use of parallelism and balance:

The world is *a comedy to those who think, a tragedy to those who feel.*—HORACE WALPOLE, *Letter to Sir Horace Mann*

But, in a larger sense, *we cannot dedicate, we cannot consecrate, we cannot hallow,* this ground. The brave men, *living* and *dead,* who struggled here, have consecrated it, far above our poor power to *add* or *detract.* The world *will little note nor long remember what we say here;* but it *can never forget what they did here.*—ABRAHAM LINCOLN, *Gettysburg Address*

Those whose lives are fruitful *to themselves, to their friends* or *to the world* are *inspired by hope* and *sustained by joy:* they see in imagination *the things that might be* and *the way in which they are to be brought into existence.*—BERTRAND RUSSELL, *Proposed Roads to Freedom*

Now the trumpet summons us again—*not as a call to bear arms, though arms we* *need—not as a call to battle, though embattled we are—*but a call to bear the burden of a long twilight struggle *year in* and *year out, "rejoicing in hope, patient in tribulation"*—a struggle against the common enemies of man: *tyranny, poverty, disease* and *war itself.*—JOHN F. KENNEDY, *Inaugural Address*

Faulty parallelism occurs in two situations: (1) when the same grammatical form is not used for logically coordinate elements, and (2) when locutions which are not logically coordinate are expressed in parallel form. The following sentences illustrate deviations from the principle of parallelism:

FAULTY: His work was writing letters and to answer the phone. [The two phrases, both complements of *was,* should have the same form.]
REVISED: His work was *writing* letters and *answering* the phone.

FAULTY: I had never learned before to take notes on cards and that I should summarize the material in my own words. [The two objects of *learned* should be in the same form.]
REVISED: I had never learned before *to take* notes on cards and *to summarize* the material in my own words. [*Or*] I had never learned before *that* I should take notes on cards and *that* I should summarize the material in my own words.

FAULTY: Vivian is small, pretty, and president of student government. [Since the noun construction is not logically coordinate with the two adjectives, it should not be treated as if it were.]
REVISED: Vivian, who is small and pretty, is president of student government.

FAULTY: She said he was young, naive, and didn't want to see him. [The elements are not logically parallel.]
REVISED: She said *that* he was young and naive and *that* she didn't want to see him.

In the faulty sentences above, the meaning is clear; the revisions improve the form and preciseness of the sentences without affecting the sense. In complex passages, though, faulty parallelism may seriously confuse the reader about the relationship of ideas, and therefore about the meaning of sentences. The following passages show how parallelism, well used, is a means of packing a number of closely related ideas and details into a single sentence, and keeping their relationship clear by the use of parallel forms. The first, from a modern novel, is a picture of the color, sound, and sensation of an autumn day; the second, from a nineteenth-century essay, is a statement about the effects of education and mental enlargement. As you read the passages, consider how difficult it would be to follow the writers' ideas through their long sentences without the help of the parallel structures; note, too, the rhythm and power, as well as the complex clarity, produced by skillful parallelism.

Around them, above them, below them—from the living and shining air of autumn, from the embrowned autumnal earth, from the great shapes of the hills behind them with their molten mass of color—dull browns, rich bitter reds, dark

bronze, and mellow yellow—from the raw crude clay of the piedmont earth and
the great brown stubble of the cotton fields—from a thousand impalpable and
unutterable things, there came this glorious breath of triumph and delight. It was
late October, there was a smell of smoke upon the air, an odor of burning leaves,
the barking of a dog, a misty red, a pollenated gold in the rich, fading, sorrowful,
and exultant light of the day,—and far off, a sound of great wheels pounding on
a rail, the wailing whistle, and the tolling bell of a departing train.—THOMAS
WOLFE, *Of Time and the River*

But the intellect which has been disciplined to the perfection of its powers, which
knows, and thinks while it knows, which has learned to leaven the dense mass of
facts and events with the elastic force of reason, such an intellect cannot be partial,
cannot be exclusive, cannot be impetuous, cannot be at a loss, cannot but be patient,
collected, and majestically calm, because it discerns the end in every beginning, the
origin in every end, the law in every interruption, the limit in each delay; because
it ever knows where it stands, and how its path lies from one point to another.—
JOHN HENRY NEWMAN, *The Idea of a University*

Students frequently improve their writing when they think, not simply
of avoiding faulty parallelism, but of consciously using parallel structures to
build tighter, more mature sentences. Parallelism, like the techniques that we
shall discuss in the next two sections, is a means of inserting, or embedding,
one or more sentences in a single concentrated sentence. Since we shall return
to this point in the following chapter, a brief illustration will suffice here:

> FIVE SENTENCES: The students had a number of demands. They wanted the abolition
> of ROTC, beginning now. They insisted that scholarship aid be increased. They
> protested that parietal rules were outdated. Furthermore, they demanded more
> student power in educational policies.

> ONE SENTENCE WITH PARALLEL STRUCTURES: The students demanded the phasing out
> of ROTC, increased scholarship aid, liberal parietal rules, and more student
> power in educational policies.

II. MODIFIERS AND APPOSITIVE STRUCTURES

As the illustrations near the end of the preceding section show, the compounding of sentence elements and the addition of modifiers work together
to expand simple sentence patterns. Without compounding, however, we can
enlarge a sentence by modifying any or all of its basic elements:

> The tree sheds its leaves.
> The large beech tree in my neighbor's yard always sheds its dark red leaves late
> in the fall when other trees are bare.

In elaborate sentences, the modifiers of the basic elements may themselves be
modified, as *red* is modified by *dark* in the sentence above. (This example

of modifying also illustrates the principle of embedding sentences. Implicit in the enlarged sentence above are three basic sentences: "There is a beech tree in my neighbor's yard. It sheds its leaves late in the fall. By then, other trees are bare.")

The nature of English grammar, the fact that we have a relatively unin-flected language, requires that modifiers, for clarity, be close to the locution they modify. Usually, adjective phrases immediately precede or follow the locution they modify:

> The woman, *straightening her hat grimly,* picked up the struggling child.
> *Straightening her hat grimly,* the woman picked up the struggling child.

Adjective clauses follow the locution they modify:

> The girl *who is stroking the cat* is my roommate.[2]

Adverbs modifying adjectives or other adverbs precede the locution they modify:

> During the *unseasonably* hot weather, he walked *very* slowly.

Adverbial phrases and clauses, and single adverbs modifying verbs are often movable:

> She *carefully* opened the door.
> She opened the door *carefully.*
> *Carefully* she opened the door.
>
> The students celebrate *when the team wins a game.*
> *When the team wins a game,* the students celebrate.

In sentences like those just above, considerations of style and emphasis, rather than grammatical usage, determine the position of modifiers. In a sentence like the one below, however, the adverb is awkwardly separated from the verb it modifies:

> AWKWARD: He understood the material he had read clearly.
> REVISED: He clearly understood the material he had read.

A modifier is called *misplaced* when its position is such that it appears to modify the wrong word, and *dangling* when the word it should modify has been omitted.[3]

---

[2] It is worth noting that when both an adjective phrase and an adjective clause follow a noun, the phrase precedes the clause: *The girl in the blue sweater who is stroking the cat is my roommate.* Changing the order of modifiers would produce an awkward and possibly ambiguous sentence: "The girl who is stroking the cat in the blue sweater . . . ."

[3] For further analysis and illustration of dangling and misplaced modifiers, see "Modifiers" in the Handbook, page 410.

MISPLACED: There is a meeting this afternoon about morality *in the Vice President's office.* [The last phrase seems to modify *morality;* the Vice President would not feel flattered.]

DANGLING: *Running down the street,* the house came into view. [Grammatically, the sentence says that the house was running; the actual runner has been left out of the sentence.]

MISPLACED: She wore a chain around her neck *of hammered gold.*

DANGLING: I heard his sad story *before dying.*

Sentences containing misplaced modifiers can usually be made satisfactory simply by changing the word order so that the modifier stands as close as possible to the word it modifies:

She wore a chain *of hammered gold* around her neck.

Sentences with dangling modifiers need to be recast so that the dangling modifier is changed to a subordinate clause containing the subject of the action:

As we ran down the street, the house came into view.

Or, the modifier may be kept and the rest of the sentence changed to include the word properly modified, in a position as close as possible to the modifier:

Running down the street, we saw the house.

Dangling and misplaced modifiers are usually merely absurd, as the above sentences demonstrate; they seldom distort the factual meaning intended, but they do cast doubt on the good sense as well as the grammatical competence of the writer. Very occasionally they are misleading:

Being an only child, my mother gave me everything I wanted. [The sentence says the mother was an only child; probably another meaning is intended.]

Patrolling three hundred miles to the north, the enemy has a secret air base. [If the writer meant that he, not the enemy, was patrolling, he gave misinformation.]

Hopeless about her condition, the doctor cheered her by describing the new drug. [Is the doctor hopeless, as the sentence says?]

The students listened while the Dean talked rebelliously. [If, as seems probable, the students listened rebelliously, the adverb *rebelliously* is misplaced, and the sentence is misleading.]

Appositive structures are particular kinds of modifiers. An *appositive* is a noun, pronoun, noun phrase, noun clause, or noun plus modifiers (sometimes called a noun cluster) standing beside another noun and denoting the same person or thing.

The tree, *a large beech in my neighbor's yard,* sheds its leaves late. [A noun cluster is in apposition with the subject of the sentence.]

The professor unresponsively heard Edna's excuse, *that she had slept through her ten o'clock conference.* [A noun clause is in apposition with the object, *excuse.*]

An appositive is usually not separated from its noun by intervening modifiers, but it may be separated by a modifier that identifies the noun.

SATISFACTORY SEPARATION: The flowers in the garden, *petunias and geraniums,* have bloomed all summer.

AWKWARD SEPARATION: The flowers in the garden, which we planted in June and which have bloomed all summer, *petunias and geraniums,* are still beautiful.

An *apposed adjective* is an adjective, or an expression used as an adjective, that occupies the same position as an appositive.

The dog, *playful and affectionate,* jumped into his master's lap.

Margaret, *unprepared for his words and unwilling to believe them,* could only stare at him.

Apposed adjectives have a special usefulness when the writer wants to give, in one sentence, a number of descriptive or identifying details about a noun. Suppose, for example, one wants to modify the subject of the sentence *The man went home* by saying that the man was tall, thin, and old, and that he was discouraged and lonely. Since three of these qualities are physical and two psychological, they are not logically coordinate.

AWKWARD: The tall, thin, old, discouraged, lonely man went home.

IMPROVED BY THE USE OF APPOSED ADJECTIVES: The tall, thin old man, now discouraged and lonely, went home.

As one learns to use appositive structures, he sees that these structures, which conventionally follow the term they modify, can often be moved so that they stand on the left side of their term. Reversing the appositive pattern is a way of varying sentence structure, and the reversal sometimes produces a more effective sentence.

CONVENTIONAL ORDER: This young man, an experienced politician, is managing the governor's campaign.

REVERSED: An experienced politician, this young man is managing the governor's campaign.

CONVENTIONAL ORDER: Christine, unhappy and anxious, waited for the phone to ring.

REVERSED: Unhappy and anxious, Christine waited for the phone to ring.

The use of appositive structures and other modifiers is, like the use of parallelism, a matter of style, not simply of grammatical structure; we shall return to it in the next chapter.

III. SUBORDINATION

When a writer uses two or more basic sentence patterns in sequence, or when he combines two or more patterns in a single sentence, he needs to consider the relationship of the statements. They may be appropriately compounded, but they often require subordination. Subordination means expressing in dependent clauses, or phrases, or single words, ideas which are not significant enough to be expressed in a main clause or an independent sentence. Compound structures and parallelism establish the relationship between equal elements; subordination and subordinating connectives establish the relationship between unequal elements.

Children, as everyone knows, express themselves in basic patterns: "I have a cat. The cat is yellow. Jimmy has a dog. His dog is big. It is brown. I like cats better." Or they may link the ideas: "We rode on the bus, and we went to the fair, and there were a lot of people, and I wanted a balloon, and Daddy bought it." These structures give equal weight to unequal ideas and fail to establish an exact relationship between the ideas. Adults, the educated reader assumes, will see more clearly the connections between their ideas; avoiding choppy "primer" sentences and sprawling "and-and" sentences, they will combine ideas in coherent, logical structures.

By means of subordination, mature writers achieve emphasis, economy, and clarity in writing: emphasis, because the important idea is usually expressed in a main clause, and less important ideas are subordinated to it; economy, because whole sentences can often be reduced to single words; and clarity, because subordination and subordinating conjunctions work together to show exact relationships between unequal parts of the sentence. Subordination is, then, like parallelism and modification, an element of style, and we shall discuss it further in the next chapter. At present we are concerned chiefly with the principles of subordination, and with the failures in communication produced by failures to subordinate intelligently.

The following passages illustrate lack of subordination, a common fault in student writing:

> LACK OF SUBORDINATION: The house was white. It stood on a hill. The hill was north of town. [Choppy "primer" sentences; three ideas are given equal weight in separate short sentences.]
> SUBORDINATION: The white house stood on the hill north of town. [The two less important sentences are reduced to a word and a phrase.]

> LACK OF SUBORDINATION: He went away. I have been unhappy.
> SUBORDINATION FOR CLOSER AND CLEARER RELATIONSHIP: I have been unhappy since he went away.

> LACK OF SUBORDINATION: I was afraid to see him and I didn't go to the party.
> SUBORDINATION: Because I was afraid to see him, I didn't go to the party.

> LACK OF SUBORDINATION: I received the notice and I went to the Dean's office.
> SUBORDINATION: As soon as I received the notice I went to the Dean's office.

> LACK OF SUBORDINATION: My parents wanted me to study but I wasn't interested in studying. I enjoyed going around with the crowd too much. My high-school

marks were not very good. Now I have come to college and I intend to work harder. I want to get better grades. [Here the writer appears incapable of thinking through the relationship between ideas which are obviously related and are not of the equal importance he gives them in his immature sentences.]

SUBORDINATION AND CONDENSATION: Although my parents wanted me to study, I was more interested in going around with the crowd; as a result, my marks in high school were not very good. In college I intend to work harder and to get better grades.

A second common fault is the use of inexact subordinating connectives:[4]

INEXACT: *As* I was trying to finish my paper that night, I drank a pot of black coffee. [*As* in this sentence can mean *while,* or *since* or *because.*]

REVISED: *While* I was trying to finish my paper that night, I drank a pot of black coffee. [*Or*] *Because* I was trying to finish my paper that night, I drank a pot of black coffee.

INEXACT: I read in the paper *where* the negotiations were successful.

REVISED: I read in the paper *that* the negotiations were successful.

A third fault may be expressing the major idea of a sentence in a subordinate clause instead of putting it in a more emphatic main clause. The following sentences illustrate this "upside-down subordination":

POOR: I read in today's New York *Times* about a position with your company for which I am applying.

MORE EFFECTIVE: I am applying for the position with your company which I read about in today's New York *Times.*

POOR: When he suddenly picked up a rock and threw it at me, I was talking to him.

MORE EFFECTIVE: While I was talking to him, he suddenly picked up a rock and threw it at me.

Context and the writer's purpose will usually determine which of several ideas should be emphasized by being expressed in a main clause. In the example below, the method of subordination chosen would depend on what idea the writer considered most important.

LACK OF SUBORDINATION: He came at eight o'clock, and Helen was sitting by the fireplace, and she was gazing moodily at the burning coals.

METHODS OF SUBORDINATION: When he came at eight o'clock, *Helen was sitting by the fireplace,* gazing moodily at the burning coals. At eight o'clock *he found Helen* gazing moodily at the burning coals as she sat by the fireplace. Sitting by the fireplace, *Helen was moodily gazing* at the burning coals when he came at eight o'clock. At eight o'clock, when Helen was sitting by the fireplace, moodily gazing at the burning coals, *he came.*

---

[4] For further information about connectives, see page 398.

The degree of subordination a writer uses is also determined by context, or by the total effect he wants his writing to have. Oversubordination, a fourth fault, occurs when the writer piles too many ideas into dependent clauses or phrases and so produces an awkward or unwieldy sentence, or a sentence inappropriate in its context.

> AWKWARD: The farmhouse, where John and his family spend vacations, a sprawling white building which overlooks a meadow where cows graze in the summer and a pond where children skate in winter, was built by John's great-grandfather.
>
> REVISED: The sprawling white farmhouse, where John and his family spend vacations, was built by John's great-grandfather. It overlooks a meadow where cows graze in the summer and a pond where children skate in winter.

Oversubordination sometimes occurs in student writing, but more common is undersubordination—giving too much emphasis to minor ideas that do not deserve that emphasis.

Weakness in subordination is a mark of immature writing and immature thinking. Since it indicates that the writer has not been able to see the relationship between the parts of a complex idea, and to grasp the relative value of those parts, lack of subordination or faulty subordination provokes irritation and skepticism in a thoughtful reader. Skillful subordination, on the other hand, clarifies and emphasizes important ideas, and gives the reader the impression of an able mind at work.

IV. CONSISTENCY

Consistency is harmony or congruity within a sentence, or between closely related sentences. As the writer builds sentences by compounding and parallelism, by modification, and by subordination, he should maintain consistency among the parts of the sentences. Faulty parallelism is one kind of inconsistency, since the writer shifts the structure of coordinate elements, or fails to make grammatical form consistent with the function of the sentence elements. Other inconsistencies are sudden, unnecessary shifts in subject; in person or style; and in the voice, mood, or tense of verbs.[5] Such shifts force the reader to adjust, often in mid-sentence, to a change from past to present tense, from indicative to imperative mood, from active to passive voice. The shifts are rarely confusing, as far as sense is concerned, but they are distracting and awkward, and, like dangling modifiers and faulty subordination, they may cause the reader to question the writer's competence.

The following sentences show inconsistencies of the sort that may easily occur in hasty writing. The inconsistencies should be removed in revision.

---

[5] See "Faulty Relationships of Sentence Elements," page 413 in the Handbook for other examples of inconsistencies.

INCONSISTENT: You fill the tube with air; then the tube is put in the casing. [Active to passive, and a shift in subject]
REVISED: You fill the tube with air; then you put the tube in the casing.

INCONSISTENT: Horatio left for the office as soon as his breakfast had been eaten. [Active to a conspicuously weak passive—unless someone else ate Horatio's breakfast]
REVISED: Horatio left for the office as soon as he had eaten his breakfast.

INCONSISTENT: When the mother died, the men in Roaring Camp have a meeting and decided to care for the baby. [Shift in tense]
REVISED: When the mother died, the men in Roaring Camp had a meeting and decided to care for the baby.

INCONSISTENT: The captain's mate must be at the dock at six o'clock; you must check the equipment and be ready to help early-comers on board. [Shift from third to second person, from impersonal to personal style]
REVISED: The captain's mate must be at the dock at six o'clock to check the equipment and help early-comers on board.

INCONSISTENT: Learn as soon as possible the arrangement of books in your library; if one can find the books he wants without help from the librarians, much time is saved. [Imperative to indicative; personal to impersonal; active to passive]
REVISED: The student will save time by learning the arrangement of books in his library, so that he can find the books he wants without help from the librarians.

Since many inconsistencies are unnecessary shifts from active to passive voice, it is appropriate here to say a word about the weakness, in general, of passive verbs. They are useful when the doer of the action is unknown or is relatively unimportant; for example, one naturally says *The eclipse can be seen at four o'clock* rather than *People can see the eclipse at four o'clock,* because the eclipse is more important in the sentence than the viewers of it. Frequently, though, passive verbs are less emphatic than active verbs, and they often produce involved, wordily indirect, or vague sentences:

INEFFECTIVE: A good play was seen last night by Jack and me. [Involved and indirect]
IMPROVED: Jack and I saw a good play last night.

INEFFECTIVE: The grating of wheels on the driveway was heard. [Vague; uninformative. Heard by whom?]
IMPROVED: I heard the grating of wheels on the driveway. [*Or*] The wheels grated on the driveway.

One other inconsistency deserves mention here, even though it is more a matter of style than of structure: an undesirable shift in usage.

INCONSISTENT: After an impressive service in the small but beautiful chapel, the campers hit the hay.
REVISED: An impressive service in the small but beautiful chapel ended the campers' day.

The following paragraph, in which the sentences range from simple to complex patterns, shows compound and parallel structures, modifiers and appositive structures, and subordination working together to produce consistent and varied sentences.

The sun had come round to a clearer portion of the sky and its glare was overpowering. Leventhal took off his jacket. The heat of the pavement penetrated his soles and he felt it in the very bones of his feet. In a long, black peninsular yard a row of scratchy bushes grew, dead green. The walls were flaming coarsely, and each thing—the moping bushes, the face of a woman appearing at a screen, a heap of melons before a grocery—came to him as though raised to a new power and given another quality by the air; and the colors, granular and bloody, black, green, blue, quivered like gases over the steady baselines of shadow. The open door of the grocery was like the entrance to a cave or mine; the cans shone like embedded rocks. He had a momentary impression of being in a foreign city when he saw the church the superintendent had mentioned—the ponderousness, the gorgeousness, the decay of it, the fenced parish house, the garden, and the small fountain thick with white lead and flimsily curtained with water.—SAUL BELLOW, *The Victim*

CHAPTER REVIEW

If your reading of this chapter has been adequate, you should be able to explain and give examples of the following, and to answer the questions below.

the most common patterns	appositives
of declarative sentences	apposed adjectives
compound structures	subordination
parallelism	upside-down subordination
balance	oversubordination
dangling modifiers	consistency
misplaced modifiers	

1. What is meant by normal order?
2. What are the two kinds of faulty parallelism?
3. How may an appositive structure be placed in relation to the term it modifies?
4. What are four faults in subordination?
5. What particular inconsistencies does the skillful writer avoid?
6. Under what circumstances are passive verbs preferable to active verbs? Under what circumstances are active verbs preferable?

EXERCISES

I. In each of the following sentences, identify the subject, the verb, and the object, indirect object, or complement if the sentence has one. What is the basic pattern of each sentence?

1. Leonard admitted that he was sometimes wrong.
2. To laugh at Sylvia is to make an enemy.
3. Avoiding faulty parallelism is advisable.
4. Where Ted has gone is what his parents wonder.
5. The dog was jumping over the fence.
6. All your friends will do whatever you wish.
7. No one can believe that Jack is guilty.
8. Doing one's best is a satisfaction.
9. Believing the worst is depressing.
10. Many of the students think that the faculty enjoys examinations.
11. Most of the audience considered the speech stupid.
12. The teacher reluctantly gave Hubert's term paper a D minus.
13. This unhappy young man is now wondering what to do.
14. The board of trustees made the youngest member president.

II. By using compound structures, or modifiers, or both, expand each of the sentences in Exercise I.

III. In the passage written by Saul Bellow (page 110), point out examples of (a) compound structures, (b) appositive structures, (c) effective use of modifiers, (d) subordination of one idea to another.

IV. Revise any of the sentences below which need to be revised to improve parallelism and eliminate inconsistencies.

1. Tom took his seat in the classroom, looked at the examination, and, with a reproachful glance at the professor, begins to write.

2. This book is interesting, lively, and also an informative piece of writing.

3. He was admitted to knighthood by a formal ceremony, dressed in the hauberk and donned the helmet.

4. He prayed for patience and understanding and that there would be no war.

5. The more you know about language, the more convinced one becomes of the importance of context.

6. Friendships I will make here and how to be tolerant of others will be valuable all my life.

7. Because he was a scholar, deeply learned in ancient civilizations, I thought that when he talked about the Greeks he would know his stuff.

8. When a man comes home after a day full of problems, you don't want to be faced with more problems.

9. Stevenson wrote essays, novels, was a poet, and traveled extensively.

10. My employer is a kind man; he often lets you go home early.

11. After traveling all day and wishing he had never undertaken the journey, Herbert arrived home tired, hungry, irritated, and his feet sore.

12. Being too early, even if it wastes valuable time, is better than to get there late.

13. We never tired of exploring the old house; happy hours were spent there.

14. She said he was old and a poor dancer and to leave her alone.

15. Mary is an excellent student, a good athlete, and attractive.

16. The book presents his experiences in Europe, how he met prominent people, and his hopes for peace.

17. Gretchen is active in the church, the D.A.R., the League of Women Voters, and doing her own housework too.

18. He hoped to gain from his education a knowledge of physics, valuable connections, and how to get along with people.

19. The writer should make an outline first; now begin the actual writing of the paper.

20. Kenneth works steadily, conscientiously, and having confidence that he will not only graduate from college but able to go to graduate school too.

21. As I walked upstairs, my sister's angry voice was heard.

22. Before Jack goes to see Nina, he made sure that his hair was combed and his shoes polished.

23. Marcia is always complaining that the television in the lounge is too loud and about her roommate's record player.

24. Harry likes to swim, dance, and to take long walks.

25. Uncle Charlie took me to Florida in December and when it was Christmas vacation.

V. Point out any dangling, misplaced, awkward, or ambiguous modifiers in the sentences below, and revise any sentences that need revision.

1. The girl who looks bored with red hair is my date.

2. He left word for her to call when she came home from work immediately.

3. At the time of the explosion the girl said she was in the outer office.

4. I visited my grandfather's grave whose name I bear.

5. Jason fell out of the apple tree and broke his arm which he had climbed to cut off a limb.

6. He promised on his way home to send the money order.

7. The sun greeted me as I came out of the house with a golden glow.

8. The housemother found the girls who had disobeyed rules in the vestibule with their dates.

9. Laura felt that she needed more time to write her paper badly.

10. Driving on Main Street, a black cat crossed my path.

11. Driving furiously down the street, Jerry missed two children who ran out from the curb barely.

12. Since puppyhood I had not seen my brother's dog, but she greeted me enthusiastically.

13. Waking early in the morning and remembering the events of yesterday, Cheever groaned and tried to go to sleep again.

14. Reviewing the material, sleep overcame me.

15. When a young boy, I ran away from home.

16. When a young boy, my father told me he ran away from home.

17. They discussed getting married frequently, but they made no decision.

18. At the age of ten, my grandfather gave me a gold watch.

19. Ann was almost asleep when she heard the horn blowing with irritation.

20. Standing on the dock, the boat was visible for a long time before it rounded the bend.

21. In the dining room of the inn, old and dilapidated, the women played cards after lunch.

22. Ruth told the secret to Bill in confidence, thus making at least four people who knew it.

23. Waiting for the train, there was nothing left to say.

24. With money from his summer job, Arthur is able to join a fraternity better.

25. Hubert was afraid that he only would receive a C in the course.

VI. Examine the lack of subordination or faulty subordination in the following passages, and revise the passages that need revision. Would any of the passages be satisfactory in a particular context?

1. Richard received three D's last semester and he has been elected president of his class.

2. The bus was crowded. There were no seats. We had to stand.

3. I like his sister while I do not care for him.

4. When I nearly fell over the body in the hall, I was just coming into the house.

5. We left early in the morning so we could get a good start, and we arrived in Chicago late that night, but then we had difficulty in finding a room at a motel.

6. Eliot had wandered for two hours until he decided to ask directions.

7. This is the chapter that Professor Lee wants us to read so that we will be prepared tomorrow when he gives us the quiz that he has promised.

8. Although Kay won first prize for her watercolor, she had been painting for only two years.

9. It was ten of nine. The class began at nine. I had to hurry.

10. Just as the game ended, our team had reached the five yard line.

11. Irene was tired and she was hungry but she had to go home and get dinner and it didn't seem fair.

12. Joe asked me for a date and so did Roger, and I decided to study instead of going out tonight.

13. Jim was depressed by the newspaper account where a man killed his wife and two children as he felt he was unable to provide for them.

14. When we got home, there was my aunt who lives in Buffalo, who had driven over to see us when we were gone.

15. My first date was with a medical student. He was in his second year at medical school. He was tall. He was handsome. He was the one all the girls in the dormitory wanted to meet. He was supposed to come at nine o'clock and he was late. He came at nine-thirty. I met him at the door. I was afraid he hadn't wanted to come at all and that was the reason he was a half hour late. I was very nervous. I wanted to make a good impression.

VII. For each of the exercises below, compose three sentences, each of which incorporates the three statements now made in separate sentences. By means of subordination, emphasize a different statement in each of your three sentences, and be sure that you are using modifiers, appositive structures, and parallel structures accurately.

1. Professor Blackstone teaches history. He is a tall, gaunt man. He is an excellent teacher.

2. Dorothy is wearing a red jacket. She is a pretty girl with brown hair. She is leading her grey poodle.

3. This book has nine hundred pages. It is a history of philosophy. In my opinion, it is scholarly but dull.

4. The flowers were pink roses. Arnold brought them to Lois on her birthday. She accepted them ungraciously.

5. The pigeons sit on the roof of the house. They flutter and coo all day. They are a nuisance to us.

Chapter 5

THE SENSE
OF STYLE

We have seen, in Chapter 4, that parallelism, use of modifiers, subordination, and consistency are matters both of conventional grammatical structure and of style. When the writer thinks beyond grammatical expression and is concerned with really effective expression, he is thinking about style. Style is a hard-to-define quality of excellence or distinction. Sometimes a writer has a worthwhile idea or experience to communicate, and expresses it in language that is conventionally acceptable or correct; still his writing may be so colorless, boring, and ineffectual that his readers will stop reading after the first few paragraphs, or, if they continue, will be unimpressed or unconvinced by what he says. Such a writer fails in communication, not because he lacks material, and not because he makes blunders, but because his writing has no characteristic flavor, no distinctive quality to interest the reader. His style is poor; or, as we sometimes say, he has no style.

There is, of course, no single "good style" or "right style," for style is highly individual. It is compounded of many elements including the writer's personality, his thought, his conscious or unconscious slanting, his tone, his choice of words, his arrangement of words, the length and rhythm of his sentences. A particular style cannot, then, be imposed on a writer; in a way, style cannot be taught, because it is the result of the writer's accurate and effective expression of himself—an individual unlike any other. But by analyzing and practicing techniques that are used in really good writing, the student can learn much about how to develop a style of his own.

Nearly all interesting and effective writing has these characteristics: it is economical in language; it is exact and original in phrasing; it is sufficiently concrete to communicate clear images and impressions; its sentences are varied to avoid monotony and to produce a positive, planned effect; it gives precise emphasis to important words and ideas. The purpose of this chapter is to analyze and discuss the techniques by which these elements of style are achieved.

I. ECONOMY AND CONCISENESS

The briefest expression is not always the best. Writing stripped to bare statements of facts, without supporting and elaborating detail, will lack both clarity and interest; great literature loses its quality of greatness if it is reduced to a factual paraphrase. At the same time, in effective prose every word counts. No words occupy space without contributing either factual or attitudinal meaning. Economical and concise expression comes, then, not simply from using fewer words, but from choosing words that work, and so warrant the space they take in the sentence.[1]

We shall give examples in this section of various types of wordiness, and show how one or two working words can effectively replace five or six slack words. The reader should bear in mind, however, as he reads the examples given here, what has been said earlier about the importance of context. In brief examples, phrases and sentences are necessarily presented without context. It is possible to imagine certain contexts in which the wordy expressions criticized here would be acceptable, or even desirable: a wordy phrasing of an idea may, for instance, establish an informality or an attitude of modesty that the communicator wants to establish; in conversation, if one does not immediately think of the exact word, a roundabout phrasing is usually preferable to a long, awkward pause in which one gropes for the right word. Context can never be disregarded, and brief examples, taken out of context, may be changed by particular contexts.

With these qualifications, we can consider various ways of achieving economy and conciseness in writing.

A. Avoiding Padding and Jargon

The first step in economical expression is recognizing and eliminating useless words. *Padding* is a term for words and phrases which add nothing except

---

[1] The exclusion of irrelevant detail, an aspect of both economy and focus, is discussed later in this chapter (page 134) and in Chapter 3, "The Practice of Writing." Our emphasis here is on stylistic economy in words, sentences, and short passages.

unnecessary length to a sentence, which clutter it and obscure its meaning. Usually padding can simply be struck out, leaving the sentence cleaner and clearer without the dead weight of this meaningless verbiage; sometimes, when the padding is removed, some rephrasing or substitution is required. Common types of padding are illustrated in the phrases and sentences below:

1. Awkward and meaningless repetition of the idea:

six *in number*	came punctually *on time*
large *in size*	*resultant* effect
recur *again*	*so* consequently *as a result*
each *and every*	*complete* absence
true fact	*habitual* custom
necessary requisite	sunset *in the west*
important essential	*of a* useful *character*
at the age of ten *years old*	biography *of his life*

2. Wordy delaying of the subject:

There are many students *who* should not be in college. [Many students should not be in college.]

There is one circumstance *which* is in his favor. [One circumstance is in his favor.]

There are two reasons *that* I have for not going: *the first is that* I have an exam to study for; *the second is that* I have no money. [I have two reasons for not going: I have an exam to study for, and I have no money.]

3. Wordy phrasing:

He spoke to me *concerning the matter of* my future. [about my future]

I am interested in work *along the line of* radio. [work in radio]

A large percentage of people are gullible. [Many people]

I consulted a lawyer *with regard to* the bill. [about]

I wish to ask your advice *in respect to the matter of* raising funds for the organization. [about raising funds]

My *field of* work is *that of* teaching. [My work is teaching.]

Some two hundred and fifty years ago, Alexander Pope wrote of such wordiness:

> Words are like leaves; and where they most abound
> Much fruit of sense beneath is rarely found.

Padding is not always as deliberate as its name may indicate; sometimes, like fat around the waist, it just appears; very frequently, though, it springs from the lazy hope (conscious or only half-conscious) of meeting a writing assign-

ment by filling space with words. Padding is not an acceptable substitute for
the "fruit of sense."

A kind of wordiness closely akin to padding is *jargon.* Jargon is verbose,
puffed-up, pretentious language, full of unnecessarily long and formal expressions, and inappropriate borrowings of semitechnical terms from such
fields as sociology, psychology, education, and economics. The writer of
jargon hopes to achieve dignity and impressiveness by his learned poly-
syllabic words. He achieves, instead, pomposity and obscurity. As the following examples show, jargon often consists of the "heavy words" discussed in
Chapter 2:

> She rendered a vocal selection. [She sang.]
> He could not discharge his financial liabilities. [pay his debts]
> The individual rejoined in the negative. [He said no.]
> He was the recipient of the munificent presentation. [He received the costly
> gift.]
> The book contains many picturized representations. [pictures]
> She is receiving instruction in driver education skills. [is taking driving lessons]
> The weather bureau predicts precipitational activity. [rain]
> In the initial instance. . . . [In the first place]
> Terminate the illumination. [Turn off the lights.]

Sir Arthur Quiller-Couch has ridiculed jargon (he includes in the term
what we have called "padding") by jargonizing the famous "to be or not to
be" soliloquy in *Hamlet.* These are Shakespeare's lines:

> To be, or not to be—that is the question:
> Whether 'tis nobler in the mind to suffer
> The slings and arrows of outrageous fortune
> Or to take arms against a sea of troubles,
> And by opposing end them. To die—to sleep—
> No more; and by a sleep to say we end
> The heartache, and the thousand natural shocks
> That flesh is heir to. 'Tis a consummation
> Devoutly to be wish'd.

The translation into jargon:

To be, or the contrary? Whether the former or the latter be preferable would
seem to admit of some difference of opinion; the answer in the present case being
of an affirmative or of a negative character according as to whether one elects on
the one hand to mentally suffer the disfavor of fortune, albeit in an extreme degree,
or on the other to boldly envisage adverse conditions in the prospect of eventually
bringing them to a conclusion. The condition of sleep is similar to, if not indistinguishable from that of death; and with the addition of finality the former might
be considered identical with the latter: so that in this connection it might be
argued with regard to sleep that, could the addition be effected, a termination

would be put to the endurance of a multiplicity of inconveniences, not to mention a number of downright evils incidental to our fallen humanity, and thus a consummation achieved of a most gratifying nature.—SIR ARTHUR QUILLER-COUCH, *On the Art of Writing*

The piece below, "What If an Educator Had Written 'The Lord's Prayer'?" satirizes a type of jargon to which some educational theorists, and others, seem to be addicted. First, for comparison, here is the simple language of "The Lord's Prayer" from the King James version of the New Testament:

> Our Father which art in heaven, Hallowed be thy name.
> Thy kingdom come. Thy will be done in earth, as it is in heaven.
> Give us this day our daily bread.
> And forgive us our debts, as we forgive our debtors.
> And lead us not into temptation, but deliver us from evil:
> For thine is the kingdom, and the power, and the glory, for ever.   Amen.

WHAT IF AN EDUCATOR HAD WRITTEN "THE LORD'S PRAYER"?

> Our Father figure who resides in the upper-echelon domain,
> May Thy title always be structured to elicit a favorable response.
> Reward us today, bread-wise,
> And minimize our unfavorable self-concept, resulting from credit over-extension,
> As we will strive to practice reciprocal procedures.
> And channel us, not into temptation-inducing areas,
> But provide us with security from situations not conducive to moral enrichment.
> For Thine is the position of maximum achievement in the power structure,
> Not to mention the prestige-attainment factor that never terminates.
>
> Amen
> —TOM DODGE, in English Journal, January 1971

Padding and jargon are the worst enemies of concise expression, but they are also easy to recognize and eliminate. The way to avoid them is to keep one's writing as simple and direct as possible.

B. Cutting Clauses

Cutting clauses is a method of subordination. It means reducing clauses, either independent or dependent, to concise phrases or even single words that do the work of the whole clause. The following sentences will illustrate this reduction. The reader should note that the revised sentences are better not only because they say the same thing in fewer words, but also because they are free of weak clauses and are therefore more emphatic.

UNCUT: The wind which blew through the cracks made a whistling sound. [two clauses, one independent, one dependent]

REVISED: The wind whistled through the cracks. [one clause; an exact verb cuts out five words]

UNCUT: He walked down the street as if he had a purpose. [two clauses, one independent, one dependent]
REVISED: He walked purposefully down the street. [one clause; an adverb takes the place of six words]

UNCUT: As he walked through the crowd he bumped with his shoulders people who were in the way. [three clauses, one independent, two dependent]
REVISED: He shouldered his way through the crowd. [one clause]

Appositive structures can be useful in replacing clauses. These structures —appositives and apposed adjectives—are effective means of securing not only economy and conciseness but also clarity, concreteness, variety, and emphasis. A student who wants to write well should examine the use of such structures in his reading and should experiment with them in his writing. The following sentences show how different kinds of appositive structures cut clauses:

UNCUT: Kenneth Roberts was a well-known author who wrote historical novels; his best work was his fifth novel which was *Northwest Passage*. [four clauses]
REVISED: The best work of Kenneth Roberts, a well-known writer of historical novels, was his fifth novel, *Northwest Passage*. [one clause; two appositives (*Northwest Passage,* and *a well-known writer* plus the phrase *of historical novels*) replace the wordy clauses]

UNCUT: Mr. Helm is a friend to cherish and he is a foe to dread; he is the best man on our school board.
REVISED: Mr. Helm—a friend to cherish and a foe to dread—is the best man on our school board. [use of a compound appositive (*friend* and *foe* with their modifiers) reduces the three clauses to one]

UNCUT: The children were happy and gay; they played in the street which was wet with rain.
REVISED: The children, happy and gay, played in the rain-wet street. [apposed adjectives (*happy* and *gay*) and a compounded adjective (*rain-wet*) cut two clauses]

UNCUT: John was now out of patience and he was also out of breath; he was so angry that he stammered.
REVISED: John, now out of patience and out of breath, was so angry that he stammered. [the phrases *out of patience* and *out of breath* serve as apposed adjectives, and replace two clauses]

Skillful parallel expression may also, as we have pointed out earlier, help to cut clauses and produce clearer and more concise expression:

UNCUT: It seemed to me, as I told her, that she should take the noon train. I advised her to make her reservations early. I also thought she should wire Aunt Mary that she was coming.

CUT AND IMPROVED BY PARALLELISM: I advised her to take the noon train, to make her reservations early, and to wire Aunt Mary that she was coming.

In the following example, parallelism provides more polished as well as more economical expression:

UNCUT: He asked just a few simple things of life. He wanted one or two small luxuries, like wine with his dinner. It was important to him to be absorbed in whatever work he did. And he yearned for romantic love.

IMPROVED BY PARALLELISM: He asked of life, quite simply, wine with his dinner, absorption in his work, and romance in his love.

James Thurber, in the paragraph below, was writing about "which-clauses," but his half-serious advice may also be applied to other weak clauses:

It is well to remember that one "which" leads to two and that two "whiches" multiply like rabbits. You should never start out with the idea that you can get by with one "which." Suddenly they are all around you. Take a sentence like this: "It imposes a problem which we either solve, or perish." On a hot night, or after a hard day's work, a man often lets himself get by with a monstrosity like that, but suppose he dictates that sentence bright and early in the morning. It comes to him typed out by his stenographer and he instantly senses that something is the matter with it. He tries to reconstruct the sentence, still clinging to the "which," and gets something like this: "It imposes a problem which we either solve, or which, failing to solve, we must perish on account of." He goes to the water cooler, gets a drink, sharpens his pencil, and grimly tries again. "It imposes a problem which we either solve or which we don't solve and . . ." He begins once more: "It imposes a problem which we either solve, or which we do not solve, and from which . . ." The more times he does it the more "whiches" he gets. The way out is simple: "We must either solve this problem, or perish." Never monkey with "which." Nothing except getting tangled up in a typewriter ribbon is worse.—JAMES THURBER, *Ladies' and Gentlemen's Guide to Modern English Usage*

C. Choosing Words That Work

Economy and conciseness come, above all, from using exact words that convey immediately and accurately a complex idea. Colorless and general verbs like *walk, go, said, look,* can often be replaced by concrete verbs that convey the action more vividly and exactly. We have seen examples of the value of strong verbs in cutting clauses (He *shouldered* his way through the crowd. The wind *whistled* through the cracks). In the following examples, an accurate verb can do in one stroke the work of a weak verb and a qualifying phrase:

He *walked* down the street *in an unsteady way.* [tottered or lurched or staggered—whatever he actually did]

He *sat* in the chair *looking idle and lazy.* [lolled]
She *looked* at him *in an angry way.* [glowered, glared]
He *looked* at her *with his mouth open.* [gaped]
He *took* the bank funds *and ran away with them.* [absconded with]
He *had funny expressions on his face* as he talked. [grimaced]

Loose, wordy expression is frequently the result of the writer's not know-ing, or not being careful enough to use, the precise name for a thing or a process. The following sentences illustrate the economy of accurate naming; the name may eliminate one or more weak clauses:

The teacher leaned on the *little stand that held his notes.* [lectern]
The conductor lifted *the stick that he uses to direct the orchestra.* [his baton]
We read a *fourteen-line poem* by Shakespeare. [sonnet]
He *hit a drive that curved to the right and went* into the woods. [sliced his drive]
She *led the queen from her hand, hoping that if the person on her left had the king he would play it and she could take the trick with the ace on the board.* [finessed her queen to the ace on the board]

As we pointed out earlier, in discussing varieties of English, formal words may be more precise than their informal equivalents. Sometimes, therefore, semiformal or formal words are necessary for economical and concise expres-sion. The following sentences are taken from freshman themes written in class, with little time for revision. The sentences would have been improved if the wordy informal locutions, most of them clauses, had been replaced by accurate, more formal words:

It seemed it just had to happen the way it did. [It seemed inevitable.]
Once the words were said, they couldn't be taken back. [The words were irrevocable.]
He had no weak point where he could be attacked. [He was invulnerable.]
She faced two courses of action and didn't know which one to choose. [She was in a dilemma.]

The use of accurate words offers endless possibilities for improvement, and will be considered further in the next section.

It is very important for the reader, as he thinks about this discussion of economy and conciseness, to understand that elaboration of a general state-ment for clarity and vividness, and repetition for desired emphasis are *not* wordiness. On the contrary, added detail often makes a meaningless state-ment rich and meaningful by enabling the reader to feel and see the particular things the writer felt and saw. Repetition of words or phrases may drive home an idea, or may create an atmosphere or arouse an emotion which is an important part of the writer's communication. The longer phrasing of an idea is sometimes preferable to the short one, for sometimes the very length and rhythm of a longer sentence establish a tone or a feeling that is part of the full meaning intended. The long locutions below are examples; their length as well as their phrasing carries the desired tone of solemnity and dignity:

> Fourscore and seven years ago, our fathers brought forth on this continent . . . .
> SHORTER, BUT LESS EFFECTIVE: Eighty-seven years ago our fathers made here . . . .

> The President of the United States gave an address.
> SHORTER, BUT LESS EFFECTIVE if one wishes to emphasize the dignity of the occasion: Nixon spoke.

Economical and concise expression is one of the most striking traits of really good English. But when an inexperienced writer understands this and begins to prune his writing, there is some danger that he will cut out the vital as well as the useless parts. Economy, properly understood, is not achieved simply by brevity, and never by sacrificing words or details that contribute positively either to the development of sense or to the communication of atmosphere or emotion. True economy and conciseness come from removing the lazy clutter of padding, jargon, weak clauses, and purposeless circumlocution, and replacing it with clear, strong, working words.

II. EXACT WORDS

We have discussed exact words in relation to economy. The purpose of this section is further to consider ways of extending one's command of words, and of developing an awareness of words both as tools of thought and as elements of style.

A. Original Expression

One of the obstacles to exact and individual writing is the trite expression, or *cliché*. Clichés are phrases that have become stale through overuse; once new and vivid, they have lost their force and have become mere words, incapable of carrying fresh meaning. The principal categories of trite expressions are:

1. Too-familiar combinations of words, like *tired but happy, icy chill, with bated breath, doting parents, fast and furious, depths of despair.*

2. Worn-out quotations, like "home sweet home," "lean and hungry look," "improve each shining hour," "cradle of the deep," "in the spring a young man's fancy," "all the world's a stage."

3. Worn-out figures of speech, like *sly as a fox, pretty as a picture, tired as a dog, sober as a judge, caught like a rat in a trap, trees like sentinels.*

No one can entirely avoid overused phrases, in speech or in writing; and indeed it is sometimes difficult to distinguish between clichés and expressions which, though used for years, have never become outworn but are an accepted and ageless part of our language; for example, is "damn with faint praise" a frayed quotation or simply familiar idiom? Furthermore, a cliché in an unusual context, or a cliché spoken ironically, or a cliché twisted to have a different meaning in context, may be witty and effective. An example is the use by James Thurber, in the passage quoted in the preceding section, of the cliché *multiply like rabbits;* unexpectedly applied to which-clauses, the trite expression has freshness and humor. It is unreasonable to say, therefore, that worn-out phrases, quotations, and figures of speech should never be used. One can, however, say that they should not be used unconsciously, or as lazy substitutes for more individual and more exact expression. Habitual triteness is evidence that the writer is not really thinking about his subject or making a serious effort to communicate it. He is, instead, taking refuge in ready-made phrases that hazily approximate his meaning. Consider, for example, the following passage:

> Her fond parents thought her a budding genius; but although she worked like a dog and was always burning the midnight oil, she had no sense of the finer things of life. All work and no play made Jill a dull girl.

What is the person described actually like? What, if he were forced to emerge from his thicket of clichés, would the writer have to communicate?

Akin to clichés in their effect on style and communication are vague words incapable of conveying precise meaning. We shall discuss concrete expression later in this chapter; here we shall comment only on certain stock adjectives and expressions of value-judgment. *Horrible,* for example, in judgments like "a horrible person," "horrible furniture," "a rather horrible lecture," conveys a drift of attitudinal meaning; but *uncouth, garish, disorganized* might convey more exactly what the writer had in mind. *Nice, fine, real, good, bad, immature, attractive* are other words too often used as vague terms of approval or disapproval when more precise words could be used.

Eliminating triteness and vagueness does not in itself produce distinctively original expression, but it clears the way for the originality that is well within the power of every college student—the accurate and interesting expression of his own observation and thought.

B. Extending Vocabulary

College students learn a number of new words—basic terms and technical names used in their courses—almost automatically. Such words, part of a body of information, absorbed over a period of time and used by the student when he talks or writes about the subject, are learned in the best possible way. Unfortunately, this natural acquisition of words is usually too slow, and the words are often too specialized, to provide the vocabulary which the student should have, both for ease in reading complex material and for the greatest flexibility and choice in his writing. He needs to supplement the natural increase in vocabulary by actively acquiring new words. There is no easy way to do this. The best way is to read widely and to learn the meanings of new words one encounters, following a procedure that fits the word into one's information and experience. The procedure should consist of three steps: (1) finding the definition of the word in the dictionary if it is not adequately defined by the context in which it occurs; (2) seeing how the word is used in its context; (3) trying to use the word, in a similar sense and construction, to make it a permanent part of vocabulary.

As he reads, the student interested in enlarging his store of words should be particularly attentive, not only to new words, but also to words which are near the border of his vocabulary. We "know" words, of course, in different degrees—well enough to recognize them and gather their meaning from context, well enough to know their general meaning or meanings without any context, well enough to use them accurately. A few moments' study of a word only faintly familiar, the meaning of which can be grasped from the context, will make it more nearly a word that one can use with assurance.

As important to the student writer as learning new words and sharpening his knowledge of familiar words is learning to use the vocabulary he already has, to find the exact word among the words he knows. Books of synonyms can be valuable aids in finding, or reminding oneself of, the exact word. If the writer looks up in Roget's *Thesaurus*[2] a word that is not quite right but is akin to the word he wants, he will probably find in the list of synonyms the precise word, which he knows—perhaps well—but which failed to come to mind. He may also be led to think about these related words, and to make a further investigation of words that he knows imperfectly. It is inadvisable to use synonyms with which one is not familiar, because synonymous words differ, sometimes widely, in shade and degree of meaning. For example, three of the synonyms for *hate* listed in Roget's *Thesaurus*—*disfavor, malice,* and *loathing*—obviously cannot be used interchangeably. *Webster's Dictionary of Synonyms* is a particularly good reference book because it indicates differences between synonyms.

Frequently the student who is apologetic about his small vocabulary, or who excuses unclear expression on the basis of limited vocabulary, does not realize how large his vocabulary actually is. He has never taken the trouble to use it. He needs to extend his active vocabulary, thoughtfully drawing on the great store of words that are familiar to him, in order to communicate his exact meaning.

C. Words That Make Distinctions

As students of language and meaning repeatedly remind us, the word is not the thing. Words are merely symbols that stand for complex objects or

---

2 Roget's *Thesaurus* is available in a paperback edition.

ideas. But these verbal symbols, used by one who understands and uses them well, can with accuracy convey complex meaning, make subtle distinctions, differentiate finely between similar referents. And a knowledge of words produces a mental discrimination between objects and ideas which might otherwise be blurred.

"Her mother is in a dangerous condition." The accurate user of words will not only speak or write, but will *think* more exactly, because he has the verbal means of dissecting the general idea: "Is her mother's condition *serious* or *critical?*" *Serious* and *critical* are still words with some range of meaning. But, in this context, they are words which make distinctions; they are the tools of a mind which makes distinctions, and which can make them more readily because it thinks in accurate words.

Making distinctions is the essence, too, of clear communication. The writing of a person whose vocabulary is imprecise is like the playing of an unskillful pianist who, even in a simple composition, strikes wrong notes or hits two keys instead of one. Such a communicator calls an *agnostic* an *atheist;* confuses *censure* and *censor;* says an *obsequious* person is *obedient;* speaks of *defying* the rules when he intends to *circumvent* them. The drift of his communication may be clear, but no part of it is sharply clear, because his words do not differentiate between subtly different things.

The following question-examples (which cannot be answered without more context) will illustrate the kind of differentiation that produces preciseness:

Mr. Jones has lost five thousand dollars. Is this a *misfortune* or a *catastrophe?*

Sylvia does almost everything her roommate tells her to do. Is she *responsive, suggestible,* or *weak-willed?*

The professor threw away his cigar before he went into class. Did he *discard* it or *relinquish* it?

Don McDonald made ten thousand dollars this year in his lumber business. Is he a *shrewd* businessman or a *sagacious* one?

He tries to get attention. Does he *invite* it, *solicit* it, or *demand* it?

Dorothy, sitting in class, is thinking about her first experience in school. Does she *remember* it or *recall* it? Does she *hear* the lecture or *listen to* it?

Professor Hamilton described to his class the exact form for their reports. Was he giving *suggestions, instructions,* or *orders?* Was his manner *positive* or *peremptory?*

Herb appeared not to see the sarcasm in the remark. Did he *ignore* it or was he *oblivious of* it?

Mr. and Mrs. Brown have frequent disagreements. Do they *argue, quarrel, wrangle,* or *bicker?* Their neighbors try to help and advise them. Are the neighbors *intervening, interceding, mediating,* or *interfering?* Is the advice *generous* or *gratuitous?*

John ran into a tree and smashed the front end of his father's car. He said that he fell asleep at the wheel because he had studied history until four o'clock the night before. Did he offer this fact in *excuse* or in *extenuation?* Did his father *chide* him, *reprove* him, *remonstrate with* him, or *berate* him about the accident? Was John *ashamed* or *contrite?*

The reader will note that not many of the words used in these examples are formal words, beyond the range of the average student's vocabulary; most of them are informal, familiar words that carry a particular shade of factual or attitudinal meaning.

As the college student increases his awareness of words, adds to his vocabulary, and learns to use accurately and fluently the words he already knows, he feels a new mastery of language. As he makes verbal distinctions, he makes finer mental distinctions. And he gives his readers a sense of what Walter Pater has called "mind in style" when he formulates his thought in the exact, the inevitable word.

III. CONCRETE EXPRESSION

Students who have had training in writing themes have generally been told repeatedly to use concrete words and to develop their material with concrete detail. Frequently, though, the reason for this advice is obscure; the instructions are regarded as the whim of certain teachers; the idea of concreteness has, in short, remained abstract, remote from the students' immediate, genuine understanding.

The purpose of this section is two-fold: First, we shall summarize a number of related principles about concrete and abstract statement, some of which have been discussed in earlier sections of this book. Second, by a series of examples, we shall try to demonstrate the values of concrete expression and the methods of achieving it. The illustrative material here and in the succeeding sections on variety and emphasis should be read with care. Theory and advice about techniques can be helpful in improving one's style, but more valuable is developing an ear for language—a sense of and feeling for the quality, texture, and rhythm of different kinds of prose.

A. The Principles That Underlie Concrete Expression

1. Abstract words (*truth, right, justice, religion, extremism,* for example) frequently do not have the same meaning for different people. They are necessary in language for expressing general ideas and arriving at judgments and conclusions; and they are powerful words, carrying as they so often do a heavy emotional charge. But because of their multiple meanings and emotional associations, they may confuse rather than clarify; at best, unless they are defined by concrete illustration, they leave only a vague idea of what

the writer had in mind when he used them. Concrete words, on the other hand, point to things which have existence in the physical world, on the nature and meaning of which people can agree. Concrete words like *horse, tree, typewriter* call up an image of the object named. It is true, of course, that there are different kinds of horses, trees, and typewriters; still, in a context, the label carries a reasonably definite meaning. Concrete words, therefore, communicate more exactly the image or idea that the writer had in mind.

2. Concrete words and details supply answers to questions like how large? how fast? how far? how heavy? how many? what kind? what color? what examples are there? what reasons? what supporting facts or statistics? Such particulars are often essential to clear communication. The second sentence below is clearer and more informative than the first:

> If you are driving at a moderate rate, you can stop your car in a short time, but you will have traveled a considerable distance.
>
> When you put on your brakes at forty miles an hour, you can stop in three and three-fourths seconds, but you will have traveled 132 feet.

3. In striving for exact expression, the writer often needs to choose, not simply between abstract and concrete words, but between fairly concrete and more concrete words. Words are more concrete (or less abstract) as they give more particulars about the thing they refer to. The following list illustrates an ascending scale from concrete to abstract, from definite to indefinite meaning: *collie, dog, animal, living creature, thing.* The most concrete word, *collie,* calls to mind a number of specific details (pointed nose, long hair, bushy tail, etc.). *Dog* is relatively concrete; at least we can assume that it refers to a four-footed domesticated mammal larger than a rat and smaller than a pony. *Animal* does not tell us much about the referent, but it is more informative than *living creature* (which includes fish, insects, etc.) and a good deal more informative than *thing,* which could refer to literally any thing.

4. Concrete words and details, besides giving more explicit information, evoke more definite feelings than abstract statements. We have seen that charged abstract words often produce a strong emotional response; but that response may be a cloud of feeling, aroused by the word, unfocused on any particular situation, and possibly far removed from the idea in the communicator's mind. With concrete words the feeling is different. If someone tells us he shot a collie, he produces a more definite feeling in us than if he says he shot a thing. Compare these two sentences:

> He treated his daughter cruelly.
>
> He beat his little seven-year-old daughter Eleanor with a heavy belt until red welts stood out on her thin shoulders and arms.

The first sentence gives only a vague general impression and so does not arouse interest, sympathy, or indignation. The second, a concrete presentation, supplies the age and name of the child and a picture of the flailing belt and the welts on thin shoulders and arms; we better understand and more sharply feel the cruelty. Concrete communication gives the reader the sense of being present in the situation or experience; of seeing what the writer saw, touching and smelling and hearing as the writer did. The reader comes closer, therefore, to sharing the writer's inside knowledge.

B. Methods and Examples

One method of achieving concreteness is the *substitution* of concrete terms for general or abstract terms. In the sets of examples below, the meaning becomes clearer as the phrasing moves from abstract to concrete:

She went out to get
- some food.
- some vegetables.
- some carrots.

From his window he can see
- a masterpiece of nature.
- a tree.
- a red maple.

She
- is in an awkward situation.
- is in trouble with the bank.
- has overdrawn her account.

The garden was getting some water.
The spray was turned on the flower garden.
Roses and delphiniums bent under the iridescent spray.

Carol is sad.
Carol has suffered a loss.
Carol's father died last week.

The most concrete expressions, *carrots, red maple,* etc., communicate most exactly the writer's meaning. Also, we can see in some of these examples that as the factual meaning is clarified, the reader's feeling is correspondingly clarified: we know better how to respond to the fact that Carol's father has died than to the statement that Carol is sad; "The garden was getting some water" creates only a hazy impression, but we may respond, with some feeling sprung from memory or association, to the clearer picture of roses and delphiniums bent under the iridescent spray.

A second, closely allied, method of attaining concreteness is the *expansion* of a general statement by the *addition* of specific examples and details. The following sentences illustrate such expansion:

A dangling modifier often produces a ridiculous sentence.
A dangling modifier often produces a ridiculous sentence—for example, "Walking up the hill, the moon shone brightly."

Having a wonderful time.

Having a wonderful time swimming and surf-boarding and dating the beautiful redhead you introduced me to last summer.

Jean's house was disorderly.
Jean's house was disorderly: there were papers on the floor, glasses and beer bottles on the mantel, and egg-smeared plates on the table.

In these sentences, too, the added concrete detail, besides giving more factual information, deepens or defines attitudinal meaning: for example, since "disorderly" means different things to different people, we can have a more definite feeling about Jean's house as we mentally see the nature of the disorder there.

In most passages of effective concrete writing, *substitution* and *expansion* work together to enable the reader to visualize or better understand the factual and attitudinal meaning of the writer. The two methods, possibly separate steps or considerations in the process of thinking and writing, are closely interwoven in the finished composition. For example:

Our dog attacked someone today.
Our Irish setter came around the corner of the house this morning with part of the grocery boy's black-and-white jacket in his mouth.

We can say that in the second sentence the more concrete *Irish setter* is substituted for *dog, grocery boy* for *someone, this morning* for *today;* and other details in the sentence expand, define, and make graphic the idea of *attacked.* Actually, though, substituted words and added details combine almost inseparably to present a picture rather than to make a summary statement as the first sentence does.

Some longer passages may illustrate more clearly the force of concrete words and amplifying concrete details as they work in combination. The passage below is part of a split-second reconstruction of an automobile accident. The entire report is an expansion of the general statement that a driver was instantly killed when his car crashed into a tree; the concrete facts and details within the slow-motion expansion give precise information and also communicate a sense of horror which the general statement cannot convey.

The car's front 24 inches have been completely demolished, but the rear end is still traveling at an estimated speed of 35 miles an hour. The driver's body is still traveling at 55. The half-ton motor block crunches into the tree. The rear of the car, like a bucking horse, rises high enough to scrape bark off low branches.
The driver's fear-frozen hands bend the steering column into an almost vertical position. The force of gravity impales him on the steering-wheel shaft. Jagged steel punctures lung and intercostal arteries. Blood spurts into his lungs.—E. A. WALZ and C. WALL, "Slow-Motion Picture of High-Speed Death"

The paragraph below expands with concrete examples the idea that human lots are unaccountably varied. Here the details, with their range and contrast, supply the reader with material for speculation about this profound mystery:

It is a curious speculation, yet not irrelevant to our enquiry, how human lots are cast, so strangely varied they are. You are born and no reasons given, a man or a woman, an Arab or an Andaman islander, an African pygmy or an Egyptian Pharaoh, a Chinese coolie or an English gentleman, a St. Thomas or an Ivan the Terrible. You are ushered into the world in the Stone Age, the fifth or fifteenth century, a vegetarian or a cannibal, of base or noble stock, the child of half-witted parents or of Viking breed, an imbecile or a fanatic. You inherit, according to the accident of your birth, a family blood-feud, a belief in Voodoo and a string of fantastic fetishes, or a Christian creed of love and charity. You are a warrior or a serf as Heaven decrees, are exposed as an infant born in ancient Sparta, die in middle life bitten by a poisonous snake in India, or live as a respectable German merchant to a ripe old age. One of a million million possible lots is yours. Is it accidental, an act of God, or, as some have conjectured, a selection made by yourself in a previous state? How profound a mystery lies behind these so manifestly unequal conditions of human existence! And what justice is it, if one man languishes most of his life on a bed of sickness, and another enjoys health and happiness or sits upon an imperial throne? Nature strews these inequalities of place, time, heredity, circumstances with a monstrous partiality. On what principles you are allotted good looks, a musical ear, a sunny temper, an affectionate disposition, a talent for figures, or denied these qualities does not appear. We are, the maxim runs, as God made us, and there the matter perforce must end.—W. MACNEILE DIXON, *The Human Situation*

A third way of achieving concreteness is the use of *figures of speech,* particularly similes and metaphors, which make or imply comparisons. In similes the comparison is stated, and is usually introduced by *like* or *as:* He had a laugh *like* thunder; she was as changeable *as* New England weather. In metaphors the comparison is implied: her *kittenish* ways; the *merry-go-round* of modern living. Although figurative language is sometimes considered purely literary and rare in everyday usage, actually figures of speech are an important part of common language. Slang is largely figurative: *snowed, smashed, mad as a wet hen, hot air, loaded* (wealthy), *wet blanket.* And common idiom is full of such figures of speech as *cauliflower ears, bury the hatchet, tall tale, red tape, sandwiched, skeleton in the closet, break the ice, cold shoulder, fifth wheel, rainy day* (hard times), *family tree.* Figures of speech are, in fact, the very lifeblood of language; and one of their principal values is that they make a general and abstract idea specific by associating it with something concrete and familiar.

Figurative language should be used with discretion, for it presents two pitfalls: strained or inappropriate comparisons (*her eyes glowed like a lighthouse light*); and trite expressions (*busy as a bee, white as a sheet, snake in the grass*). But good, fresh comparisons are one of the most valuable tools of the writer interested in communicating his ideas clearly and vividly.

Figures of speech may be used primarily to clarify factual meaning, as in the following appraisal of twentieth-century England:

England is not the jewelled isle of Shakespeare's much-quoted passage, nor is it the inferno depicted by Dr. Goebbels. More than either it resembles a family, a rather stuffy Victorian family, with not many black sheep in it but with all its cupboards bursting with skeletons. It has rich relations who have to be kow-towed to and poor relations who are horribly sat upon, and there is a deep conspiracy of silence about the source of the family income. It is a family in which the young are generally thwarted and most of the power is in the hands of irresponsible uncles and bedridden aunts. Still, it is a family. It has its private language and its common memories, and at the approach of an enemy it closes ranks. A family with the wrong members in control—that, perhaps, is as near as one can come to describing England in a phrase.—"England Your England," *A Collection of Essays by George Orwell*

More often, though, the value of figurative language lies in its power not only to clarify ideas, but to stir the senses and to particularize emotion by calling to mind sharp images. Much of the power of Biblical prose lies in its concrete imagery—the representation of such abstract ideas as *wisdom, God, love,* in terms of concrete, familiar experience:

I shall light a candle of understanding in thine heart, which shall not be put out.
He shall come down like rain upon the mown grass.
Set me as a seal upon thine heart, as a seal upon thine arm; for love is strong as death; jealousy is cruel as the grave; the coals thereof are coals of fire, which hath a most vehement flame.

The appeal of this famous passage from John Donne lies in the vivid figurative phrasing of the abstract idea of the brotherhood of men:

No man is an island, entire of itself; every man is a piece of the continent, a part of the main: if a clod be washed away by the sea, Europe is the less, as well as if a promontory were, as well as if a manor of thy friends or of thine own were; any man's death diminishes me, because I am involved in mankind. And therefore never send to know for whom the bell tolls; it tolls for thee.

Two brief examples from modern fiction illustrate further the picture-making quality and appeal to the senses of figurative language:

Night was fully come when they reached town. Across the land the lights on the courthouse clock were like yellow beads above the trees, and upon the green afterglow a column of smoke stood like a balanced plume.—WILLIAM FAULKNER, *Sartoris*

In the high heavens rode a veiled moon, magnified by the mist of an early spring day. A single poplar gathered up the white moonlight in her young, shimmering leaves and trickled it down like a waterfall. A single ray glowed like a fish around Alain's legs.—COLETTE, "The Cat"

The passage below, from an essay by Robert Louis Stevenson, could be summarized in the abstract sentence "The changes brought by death are terrible." Notice how this general idea is made poignantly meaningful and real by a combination of the methods we have been discussing: the general statement is followed by three figures of speech which picture, and convey a feeling about, the coming and the effect of death, and finally by three concrete details (chairs, walks, beds) which evoke images and by means of them communicate three aspects of loneliness:

The changes wrought by death are in themselves so sharp and final, and so terrible and melancholy in their consequences, that the thing stands alone in man's experience, and has no parallel upon earth. It outdoes all other accidents because it is the last of them. Sometimes it leaps suddenly upon its victims like a Thug; sometimes it lays a regular siege and creeps upon their citadel during a score of years. And when the business is done, there is sore havoc made in other people's lives, and a pin knocked out by which many subsidiary friendships hung together. There are empty chairs, solitary walks, and single beds at night.—ROBERT LOUIS STEVENSON, "Aes Triplex"

The following paragraphs by Thomas Wolfe are part of a long passage in which, by calling up particular sights, smells, and sounds, he communicates the meaning of the word and the idea "October"; in the last sentences, figurative language is used to further sharpen the sense impressions and the emotional significance of autumn fires.

The corn is shocked: it sticks out in hard yellow rows upon dried ears, fit now for great red barns in Pennsylvania, and the big stained teeth of crunching horses. The indolent hooves kick swiftly at the boards, the barn is sweet with hay and leather, wood and apples—this, and the clean dry crunching of the teeth is all: the sweat, the labor, and the plow is over. The late pears mellow on a sunny shelf; smoked hams hang to the warped barn rafters; the pantry shelves are loaded with 300 jars of fruit. Meanwhile the leaves are turning, turning, up in Maine, the chestnut burrs plop thickly to the earth in gusts of wind, and in Virginia the chinkapins are falling.

There is a smell of burning in small towns in afternoon, and men with buckles on their arms are raking leaves in yards as boys come by with straps slung back across their shoulders. The oak leaves, big and brown, are bedded deep in yard and gutter: they make deep wadings to the knee for children in the streets. The fire will snap and crackle like a whip, sharp acrid smoke will sting the eyes, in mown fields the little vipers of the flame eat past the black coarse edges of burned stubble like a line of locusts. Fire drives a thorn of memory in the heart.—THOMAS WOLFE, *Of Time and the River*

The inexperienced writer, unlike the writers we have been quoting, frequently assumes that his readers know intuitively, and therefore do not need to be told, the contents of his mind. He believes that when he has written "She wore a strange hat," he has described the hat, because the image of green feathers and yellow veil is completely clear in his own mind. Or, thinking of a gray farmhouse, beaten by rain, set in an expanse of treeless, plowed acres, he feels that he has conveyed that picture when he writes "The countryside was dreary." The skillful writer understands that it is his obligation (and his satisfaction) as a writer to give the reader a sense of the whole experience—the elements in it, the shades of feeling, as much of the outside and inside knowledge of the writer as it is possible to communicate. When the reader is supplied with the facts, observations, and sensations that are the bases of the whole experience, he can more nearly grasp the total meaning, factual and emotional.

C. Concreteness, Economy, and Substance

As the student-writer begins to work seriously on the concrete expansion of his ideas, he may face the problem of the proper balance between concrete expression and economical expression: How many facts and details should he include? Should some be sacrificed for the sake of economy? In the passage from Thomas Wolfe quoted above, for example, could not the writer have omitted some of the many details, and have more concisely communicated the feeling of "October"? Such questions are not easily answered; they involve individual taste and judgment. However, three points about the relationship of concrete development and economy are worth keeping in mind: First, if the detail is not strictly relevant to the central topic, or if it does not contribute positively to the idea or atmosphere of the passage, focus as well as economy demands that it be excluded. Second, underdevelopment is, however, a greater danger than overdevelopment in student writing; one very seldom has too much *relevant, contributing* detail. Third, nothing is less economical than a series of bare abstract statements that carry only vague meaning; they waste the lines that could be occupied by meaning-weighted words.

Both concrete and abstract words are essential for the effective use of language; abstract words for conveying general ideas and judgments, and concrete words for conveying particulars. It is easier, though, to say nothing or little-or-nothing in abstract terms than in concrete terms; to be concrete one must first *think* in specific terms, but one can make well-worn abstract statements without thinking at all. The student who wrote that he "came to college to be moldered morally, mentally, and physically" was writing abstractly and without thought; the only possible interest in his statement is produced by his unintentional (he wasn't thinking here either) but perhaps apt use of "moldered" for *molded.* The writer who is never concrete may well molder mentally, while the reader dozes; the concrete writer must be alive in body (receptive to sense impressions) and in mind—and there is hope for him morally too. Perhaps because thinking concretely is hard and generalizing is easy, the most common weakness in student papers is "thin" writing—vague, unoriginal, unthoughtful, lacking in substance.

The following very poor freshman theme will illustrate; the assignment was to write a well-organized paragraph on the student's reason for coming to college.

One good reason why I came to college is to acquire a higher education. I believe that a college education is the only way in which a young man may equip himself to cope with the many difficult tasks and obstacles which he will encounter in life. During college life, the student has to carry on a great many responsibilities which will indeed prove themselves to be a tremendous factor in future life. Another of the beneficial factors of college life are the activities which will be a true asset in the near future. A college education is a necessity for my chosen profession. Whether I am successful in my ambition or not, I will still have a priceless education which I may be dependent upon, a priceless education which will prove beneficial in both society and livelihood. In this day of scientific triumphs, no man can be successful in a profession without attending a school of higher learning. The acquisition of knowledge is not only essential for the enjoyment of higher standards of living and the finer things of life, but also is a source of self-satisfaction and pleasure. Knowledge provides an individual with a broad perspective, thereby giving an opportunity to enjoy a fuller and better life.

Poor writing like this shows, perhaps more clearly than good writing, the close interrelationships that always exist between the elements of style and between style and thought. The paper above is full of abstract, almost meaningless statements; the reader is left with numerous unanswered questions like what responsibilities? what activities? what profession? what do you mean? Because it takes so long to say so little, the paper is extremely wordy; everything it says can be expressed in a single sentence: "I came to college because I think college responsibilities, activities, and education will prepare me for my chosen profession and for a richer social and personal life." Also as a result of lack of real substance, the expression is repeatedly trite. And all of these weaknesses—in concreteness and clarity, in economy, and in originality—come from the writer's failure to think, about his subject, or about communicating it to a reader.

The following passage makes some relatively concrete statements, but it is still thin writing, the material inadequately developed:

When I hear the word "Maine" I think of the winters I spent there when I was a boy. Winter in Maine was so different from summer. It was hard in many ways, for we had frequent blizzards, and we lived in an isolated farmhouse. But I remember many things that were pleasant, like playing in the snow and the coziness of the house inside when there was a storm outside.

Now read this passage from another student theme. The writer here, by recording specific details, recollections, and sensations, gives his paper substance; he brings to life for the reader the experience and the pleasure of the boy during the Maine winter:

For all its force and fury, winter was mainly memorable to the boy for little things; sights and sounds that hit his sharpened senses like a silver hammer: the soft glow of early lamplight; the ticktack of sleet on frosted windowpanes; the song of the wind in the chimney; the gray blur of the sheep snuggled in their pen at night-fall; the look of the cows chewing their cuds; the morning crackle of birch bark in the kitchen stove; the stirring jangle of sleigh bells; the stillness of winter woods. Winter's ways were so different from those of the slow, sweet scroll of summer, on which buds swelled into blossoms, sunshine melted into rain, day drifted into night. But winter had many enchantments. The boy felt their quick tug as he trudged home from school, bent low to the gale, and suddenly saw through the swirling snow the smoke of his own chimney; as he jumped shivering into bed and felt the warm, flannel-wrapped soapstone which his mother had tucked between the blankets; as he raced downhill on his sled with the ends of red scarf streaming out behind him.

He felt the enchantment most of all at night when a blizzard was beating in baffled fury against the stout walls of the farmhouse. How good was the snugness of that sanctuary. Never did the kitchen seem so warm and cheerful, the lamplight quite so bright. By the time his mother had brought her sewing close to the lamp and his father's stockinged feet were propped up on the open oven, the boy would have the corn popper waiting. First he tried the top of the stove with a spit-wet finger. The sizzle mustn't be too sharp or too soft—only a trained ear could catch the proper pitch.

Another example of porous, thin, abstract writing:

I remember the little boy I was many years ago. There was nothing distinctive about him. Like other children of that age, he amused himself with his own toys and his own games. He was, I'm afraid, often into mischief. Then he grew older, and one day he was ready to go to school.

And now, this excellent paragraph from another freshman theme:

The little boy's exact age was that of children still able to create their own toys—the challenge of a ball to be caught; the enchanting beckon of an unwatched ladder to make one tall; the swift decisiveness of a scissors, teaching that lines cut away leave empty spaces. And music, too. His music was in the midnight-creak of stairs leading down from his room, or the patter of rain, or the clatter of horses' hoofs on a tar road. His days were for testing, touching, stretching, and trying. He learned that wood was hard, and solid for its weight; that swinging was not all fun, that someone had to push; that Pussy scratched sometimes. He heard a church bell, he saw a rainbow, he felt velvet, he tasted dirt, he smelled wet grass, he poked at a worm. It was the age of the boundless world, when marbles are soldiers. But, as he grew older, each one turned into a marble again, and one day they were forgotten somewhere, where children's toys are always forgotten.

In summary, abstract words, with their power to generalize, to relate, and to arouse feeling, are indispensable. But the writer who is interested in making clear exactly what he means, or in sharing his experience with others, will write as concretely as possible, and will define his abstractions with concrete examples, figures of speech, and concrete details. Concreteness is not hard to achieve; it comes, though, from a habit of mind that many inexperienced writers have not developed—the habit of remembering and setting down the actual observations, facts, and thoughts which are the basis of a general statement, and which make that general statement understandable and real to the reader.

IV. VARIETY IN SENTENCES

Although the inexperienced writer is not always aware of it, sound and rhythm are very important parts of effective style. Repetition can be consciously and artistically used; but an undesirable repetition of the same sound, the same sentence length, and the same sentence structure will be irritating to a trained reader, or will lull him into disinterest. Sometimes an unwisely repeated sentence structure produces an effect like that of the recitation of poetry by third-grade pupils: the real meaning is lost in the monotonously repeated rhythm.

Variety in sentences is very closely related to effective emphasis, which we shall discuss in the next section. Indeed, it is difficult to separate the two qualities, even for purposes of discussion. We shall, however, point out in this section certain types of monotony that the skillful writer avoids, and outline some of the techniques by which he varies his sentence patterns. In applying these techniques, he must also apply the principles of emphasis.

A. Kinds of Monotony

Careless repetition of words, illustrated in the sentences below, is a kind of monotony easily recognized and easily avoided:

Time has proved that Ibsen was a writer ahead of his *time*. Most of his plays are *timely* today.

We admired the *location* where his new house was to be *located*.

All of the members of the *community gathered* at these *community gatherings*.

I am *attracted* by the *current attraction* at the *current* festival.

Less easily recognized is the monotonous or awkward repetition of sound; for example, in unintentional rhyme, distracting alliteration, or the piling up of syllables harsh to the ear or difficult to pronounce. Reading one's writing aloud is the cure for unconscious repetitions like these:

My hopes faded *away* on a *day* last *May*.

He gave no expla*nation* for his interpre*tation* of the situ*ation*.

After this *success*, I am *seriously searching* for *similarly simple subjects*.

You must cope immediate*ly* with his problem, if not entire*ly* efficient*ly*, at least seeming*ly* confid*ently*.

Monotony in sentence length and repetition of sentence pattern are perhaps less conspicuous than repeated sound; but, unless patterned sentences are used judiciously, for deliberate emphasis, they are even more ineffective and awkward than thoughtlessly repeated sounds and words. The following passages illustrate some of the common types of monotonous sentence patterns:

> He walked down the street. He scanned the numbers on the houses. He found the one he wanted. He went up the steps. He hesitated a moment. Then he rang the bell. [Repeated choppy sentences, with the same subject-verb order: *he walked, he scanned, he found,* etc.]

> He walked down the street and scanned the numbers on the houses. He found the one he wanted and went up the steps. He hesitated a moment and then rang the bell. [Simple sentences with compound predicates]

> Walking down the street, he scanned the numbers on the houses. Finding the one he wanted, he went up the steps. Hesitating only a moment, he rang the bell. [Repeated introductory phrases]

> As he walked down the street, he scanned the numbers on the houses. When he found the one he wanted, he went up the steps. After he had hesitated for a moment, he rang the bell. [Repeated dependent clauses before the main clause]

> He scanned the numbers on the houses as he walked down the street. He went up the steps when he found the one he wanted. He rang the bell after he had hesitated for a moment. [Dependent clauses trailing the main clause]

B. Varying Sentence Patterns

The first step in achieving variety in sentence movement is, of course, recognizing monotonous sentence patterns. Reading the passage aloud and actually hearing it is probably the surest way of detecting the repeated rhythm. The monotony should then be remedied by the following techniques:

1. Varying the length of sentences; using occasional short sentences among longer ones, or occasional long sentences if the prevailing style is terse. This passage from a short story illustrates such variation:

> He heard no dogs at all. He never did hear them. He only heard the drumming of the woodpecker stop short off and knew that the bear was looking at him. He never saw it. He did not know whether it was in front of him or behind him. He did not move, holding the useless gun, which he had not even had warning to cock and which even now he did not cock, tasting in his saliva that taint as of brass which he knew now because he had smelled it when he peered under the kitchen at the huddled dogs.—WILLIAM FAULKNER, "The Bear"

2. Using parallel and balanced constructions, not continuously, but as a change from simpler constructions. Robert Louis Stevenson, writing on style, simultaneously described and demonstrated the value of varied parallelism:

> Nor should the balance be too striking and exact, for the one rule is to be infinitely various: to interest, to disappoint, to surprise, and yet still to gratify; to be ever

changing, as it were, the stitch, and yet still to give the effect of an ingenious neatness.

Related to parallelism and balance is *antithesis,* an arrangement of opposed words or sentence elements to emphasize contrast:

Read not to contradict and confute . . . but to weigh and consider.—FRANCIS BACON

. . . give me liberty, or give me death!—PATRICK HENRY

3. Intermingling loose and periodic sentences. In loose sentences, the sentence continues after the main thought has been expressed:

We know that the young prince died, although we know little more.

In periodic sentences, the meaning is suspended until the end of the sentence:

About the subsequent events, the terrified repledging of loyalty, the whispered conspiracies, the promises exchanged behind locked doors, *we know but little.*

Frequent and elaborate periodic sentences are more characteristic of formal than of informal style. Occasional periodic sentences, however, are excellent for varied movement as well as for the heightened suspense and emphasis of the sentences themselves.

4. Changing the usual subject-verb-object order of some sentences:

He could never forgive this. [subject-verb-object]
This he could never forgive. [object-subject-verb]

At the last minute Sally rushed in. [subject-verb]
At the last minute in rushed Sally. [verb-subject]

5. Changing the position of modifiers and parenthetic elements for variety in movement and for better emphasis:

He met a most attractive girl at the party.
At the party he met a most attractive girl.
He met, at the party, a most attractive girl.

Consequently, he is no longer interested in Marie.
He is, consequently, no longer interested in Marie.
He is no longer interested, consequently, in Marie.

As we have said earlier, appositive structures conventionally follow the term they modify, in the appositive position, but they may be moved so that they precede the term; some structures—apposed adjectives in particular—may be separated from their term. Their movability, therefore, can be used for sentence variety:

The small boys, breathless and expectant, waited for the clown to appear.
Breathless and expectant, the small boys waited for the clown to appear.
The small boys waited, breathless and expectant, for the clown to appear.

[It may be worth noting that there are limits to the movability of such adjective structures; if the sentence read *The small boys waited for the clown to appear, breathless and expectant,* the adjectives would seem to modify *clown.*]

By means of some of these devices, the walking-down-the-street passages on page 138 could be revised and varied as follows:

He walked down the street, scanning the numbers on the houses. When he found the one he wanted, he walked up the steps, hesitated a moment, and then rang the bell.

[*Or*]

He scanned the numbers on the houses as he walked down the street. Finding the one he wanted, he went up the steps and hesitated a moment. Then he rang the bell.

C. Variety and Emphasis

Sentence variety is closely related to emphasis because as the writer begins to vary his sentence length and structure and to change the position of modifying elements, he must consider what ideas he wants to emphasize by structure and position. Variety in sentences is not merely a matter of form and style. It is organic expression, in which sound and structure and rhythm all contribute to the full meaning the writer wishes to communicate. The short passage below illustrates some of the techniques we have been considering and the relationship between variety and emphasis. The first of the three sentences begins, not with the subject, but with an adverb and part of the verb, and ends with parallel phrases. The second is an example of balance and antithesis. In the third, a longer sentence, the main verb and the object twice precede the subject and are emphasized both by the inverted order and by repetition.

Never have the nations of the world had so much to lose or so much to gain. Together we shall save our planet or together we shall perish in its flames. Save it we can, and save it we must, and then shall we earn the eternal thanks of mankind and, as peacemakers, the eternal blessing of God.—JOHN F. KENNEDY, Address to the United Nations, September 25, 1961

The following two paragraphs are from *The Autobiography of Lincoln Steffens;* below the passage is a partial analysis of the methods Steffens uses to achieve both variety and emphasis.

[1] It was conversation I was hearing, the free, passionate, witty exchanges of studied minds as polished as fine tools. [2] They were always courteous; no two ever spoke together; there were no asides; they all talked to the question before the house, and while they were on the job of exposition anyone, regardless of his side, would contribute his quota of facts, or his remembrance of some philosopher's

opinion or some poet's perfect phrase for the elucidation or the beautification of the theme. [3] When the differences rose the urbanity persisted. [4] They drank their California wine with a relish, they smoked the room thick, and they pressed their views with vigor and sincerity and eloquence; but their good temper never failed them. [5] It was conversation. [6] I had heard conversation before; I have heard conversation sometimes since, but rarely, and never like my remembrance of those wonderful Saturday nights in San Francisco—which were my preparation for college.

[7] For those conversations, so brilliant, so scholarly, and so consciously unknowing, seemed to me, silent in the background, to reveal the truth that even college graduates did not know anything, really. [8] Evidences they had, all the testimony of all the wise men in the historical world on everything, but no decisions. [9] None. [10] I must go to college to find out more, and I wanted to. [11] It seemed as if I had to go soon. [12] My head, busy with questions before, was filled with holes that were aching voids as hungry, as painful, as an empty stomach. [13] And my questions were explicit; it was as if I were not only hungry; I was hungry for certain foods. [14] My curiosity was no longer vague.

[1] Loose sentence, medium length, with the complex appositive following the main clause.

[2] Long sentence; a series of short statements followed by a long, complex one, with parallel phrasing.

[3] Short sentence; a subordinate clause preceding the main clause which contains the main idea.

[4] Long sentence; parallel clauses.

[5] Short emphatic restatement of the topic idea of the paragraph.

[6] Long sentence with parallel phrasing, mounting rhythmically to a climax. "Conversation" repeated for emphasis.

[7] Long periodic sentence, with parallel phrasing and skillful placing of modifiers. "Conversation" repeated at the beginning for emphasis and transition.

[8] Object-subject-verb order to emphasize "evidences" and contrast "decisions" at the end of the sentence; long appositive.

[9] One word sentence for emphasis, after three rather long sentences.

[10] Compound sentence.

[11] Short complex sentence.

[12] Longer complex sentence with interrupting modifiers.

[13] Three clauses, the closely related ideas separated for emphasis.

[14] Short emphatic statement of the topic idea.

An even more striking example of organic expression, that is, of fitting the expression to the whole purpose, is the following passage from Virginia Woolf, an artist in modern prose. In the first paragraph, long complicated sentences are used to describe the complexity of darkness and sound and light; short sentences are used for dramatic action and realization: "Orlando leapt to his feet"; "The Queen had come." The short-sentence pattern of the second paragraph might seem, in a hasty eye-reading, to violate all prin-

ciples of sentence variety. More careful reading will show that those short
sentences are functional; they are used deliberately to communicate Orlando's distraught state of mind and at the same time his frantic, separate
actions. The reader should note, too, how skillfully the short-sentence
pattern is broken, just before it would become monotonous.

After an hour or so—the sun was rapidly sinking, the white clouds had turned
red, the hills were violet, the woods purple, the valleys black—a trumpet sounded.
Orlando leapt to his feet. The shrill sound came from the valley. It came from
a dark spot down there; a spot compact and mapped out; a maze; a town, yet girt
about with walls; it came from the heart of his own great house in the valley,
which, dark before, even as he looked and the single trumpet duplicated and
reduplicated itself with other shriller sounds, lost its darkness and became pierced
with lights. Some were small hurrying lights, as if servants dashed along corridors
to answer summonses; others were high and lustrous lights, as if they burnt in
empty banqueting halls made ready to receive guests who had not come; and others
dipped and waved and sank and rose, as if held in the hands of troops of serving
men, bending, kneeling, rising, receiving, guarding, and escorting with all dignity
indoors a great Princess alighting from her chariot. Coaches turned and wheeled
in the courtyard. Horses tossed their plumes. The Queen had come.

Orlando looked no more. He dashed down the hill. He let himself in at a wicket
gate. He tore up the winding staircase. He reached his room. He tossed his stockings to one side of the room, his jerkin to the other. He dipped his head. He
scoured his hands. He pared his fingernails. With no more than six inches of looking glass and a pair of old candles to help him, he had thrust on crimson breeches,
lace collar, waistcoat of taffeta, and shoes with rosettes on them as big as double
dahlias in less than ten minutes by the stable clock. He was ready. He was flushed.
He was excited. But he was terribly late.—VIRGINIA WOOLF, *Orlando*

Because monotony is a common weakness in college writing, most students will profit by reading their themes aloud and listening carefully for
monotonously repeated patterns. At first the process of breaking the pattern
by changing the wording, structure, or length of some sentences may be
purely mechanical. But as the writer deliberately—even laboriously—practices putting a verb before its subject now and then, interrupting a conventional sentence with modifiers and appositives, using some periodic sentences,
tying related ideas together in parallel constructions, changing his pace with
long and short sentences, he begins to develop a sense of the organic relationship between the pattern of sentences and the pattern of thought. From
telling himself, "I ought to have a short sentence among all these long ones,"
he progresses to "This idea should hit hard; I'll put it by itself in a short
sentence." Instead of thinking, "I have four subject-verb-object constructions
in a row; better change one or two," he thinks, "The object here is the most
important word in the sentence; I'll pull it out of its normal position to give
it emphasis." At this point he is no longer merely avoiding monotony; he is
beginning to achieve that functional and organic variety which is an important part of effective expression.

V. EMPHASIS

Emphasis in writing is more of a problem than emphasis in speaking. In speech, we depend a great deal on gestures, facial expressions, long pauses, and particularly on tone of voice to stress important words and ideas. The amateur in writing often attempts to reproduce the accents of speech by underlining and capitalizing, by frequent use of exclamation points, and by intensives like *very, so, most, frightfully, perfectly:*

> I was so very tired at the end of the day, but I felt that I had <u>never</u> had such a perfectly wonderful time. It was simply marvelous!! I wouldn't have missed it for <u>anything</u>! And I met the most wonderful Man!

Such devices for emphasis may be appropriate in informal correspondence, where they suggest to the reader the vocal stress the writer would have given the words; but they are not effective in more impersonal writing, where the writer's vocal tone is much less relevant. Skillful writers seldom rely on mechanical devices or many intensives for emphasis; they get emphasis by their choice of words, sentence form, and arrangement of sentences in the paragraph and of paragraphs in the whole piece of writing.

Here and there in the preceding sections of this book we have discussed a number of weaknesses which make writing unemphatic. It will be well to review them briefly before we discuss further ways of achieving effective emphasis:

1. *A thoughtlessly repeated sentence pattern is unemphatic.* It gives the same weight and the same rhythm to ideas that are actually varied and therefore should be distinguished by varied expression.

2. *Improper subordination destroys emphasis.* In the example below, lack of subordination gives equal stress to unequal ideas; the most important idea, therefore, is not emphasized:

> I was walking around Walden Pond. It was a cool day last September. I saw a child fall in the water.

Upside-down subordination, that is, putting the main idea in a subordinate clause or phrase, may rob that idea of its proper emphasis:

> He made his third proposal, which she accepted.
> He eluded his opponent, crossing the goal line.

3. *Overuse of the passive voice is unemphatic* because the passive is often weak, wordy, and indirect. Weak passives like the ones in the following sentences should be avoided in favor of more emphatic active statements:

> This paper is late because difficulties were run into by the writer.
> As we opened the gate, a snarling dog was seen on the steps.
> Many hours are spent by students in talking about their work instead of doing it.

4. *Clichés are unemphatic* because they are forceless and dull, and because they suggest laziness or indifference on the part of the writer.

5. *Abstract words are unemphatic* when they are thoughtlessly used in place of a clearer, more precise concrete word; "wildlife," for example, instead of "sea gull."

6. *Padding, jargon, weak clauses, and circumlocutions are destroyers of emphasis.* Their wordiness waters the meaning of the sentence and sometimes actually submerges it.

7. *Euphemism, a kind of circumlocution we have not discussed before, is another enemy of emphasis.* Our word *euphemism* is derived from the Greek *eu* meaning "well" and *phanai,* "to speak"; the Greek word *euphēmizein* mean "to use fair words, or words of good omen." Now, however, *euphemism* is a term applied to a mild, soothing, usually vague expression substituted for a precise, or blunt, or less agreeable term. It is a linguistic device by which people avoid talking about, and often thinking about, unpleasant realities. Examples of euphemisms are:

passed away or *departed from this world,* for "died"
perspire, for "sweat"
expectorate, for "spit"
social disease, for "syphilis"
lung affliction, for "tuberculosis"
indisposed, for "sick"
mortician, for "undertaker"
paying guest, for "boarder"
sanitation engineer, for "garbage collector"
deferred payment, for "installment buying"
defensive maneuver, for "retreat"
plant food, for "manure"

There are, of course, certain social and conversational situations in which euphemisms may be desirable. For example, good judgment would suggest saying "plant food" if the person to whom one is talking considers "manure" a shocking word; and tact and kindness might recommend "he passed away" or some other euphemism for death in conversation with one recently bereaved. But increasingly in modern writing euphemisms are rejected, because they are roundabout, inexact, hesitant, and weak. Like other vague terms and circumlocutions, they carry the reader away from, instead of bringing him close to the real meaning. In general, they should be used only when a situation involving personal feelings demands a delicate avoidance of fact. Normally the factual term should be used because it is more precise and more emphatic.

The writer who has learned to choose exact words, to subordinate skillfully, and to avoid wordiness, triteness, monotony, weak passive constructions, and euphemisms, has gone far toward emphatic expression. His writing will become more effective as he also learns to use *pause, position,* and *repetition* for emphasis.

A. Emphasis by Pause

In speech, the pause is a common and effective device for emphasis. A pause before a word or statement arouses interest in what is to come; a pause after a word or statement stresses its importance by giving the audience time to absorb it. In writing, commas, dashes, semicolons, periods, paragraph breaks, and chapter divisions all create pauses that emphasize the material immediately preceding and following the pause. The degree of emphasis depends on the length of the stop indicated by the punctuation. Beginnings and ends of sentences and beginnings and ends of paragraphs derive much of their emphasis from the fact that the beginnings follow, and the ends are followed by, full stops. We have discussed earlier the emphatic quality of the occasional very short sentence. It is emphatic not only because it differs from the sentences around it, but because its few words stand between, and are emphasized by, two stops. Advertising commonly uses short sentences and even one-sentence paragraphs, so that each idea will make its impact separately and emphatically on the mind of the reader.

A writer who is addressing an intelligent audience will, of course, take care that the ideas emphasized by his pauses are worthy of stress. He will use pauses to throw emphasis exactly where he wants it in the sentence or the paragraph, and in the exact degree. The following examples show how different kinds of pause work to create different emphases:

> He was flushed, he was excited, but he was terribly late.
> STRONGER EMPHASIS BY MEANS OF HEAVIER PAUSES: He was flushed. He was excited. But he was terribly late.

> First Mrs. Brown arrived, then Mrs. Jones, and last of all Mrs. Fitzpatrick.
> STRONGER EMPHASIS, BY MEANS OF ADDITIONAL PAUSES, on Mrs. Fitzpatrick and the fact that she arrived late: First Mrs. Brown arrived, then Mrs. Jones, and, last of all—Mrs. Fitzpatrick.

> I swear that this is not at all unusual.
> STRONGER EMPHASIS ON "NOT" AND "AT ALL" because they precede and follow the pause of a sentence interrupter: This is not, I swear, at all unusual.

> SHIFT IN EMPHASIS (AND IN MEANING) BY A SHIFT IN PAUSE (context would determine the best emphasis):
> However, Malcolm refused to give serious thought to this important question.
> Malcolm refused to give serious thought, however, to this important question.
> Malcolm refused, however, to give serious thought to this important question.
> Malcolm, however, refused to give serious thought to this important question.

> GREATER EMPHASIS ON THE LAST TWO SENTENCES BY MEANS OF A PARAGRAPH PAUSE:

He crept along, on his hands and knees again. The seconds passed like individual units, almost as if he heard a clock ticking. He could have sobbed every time he heard a man mutter in his sleep. They were all around him! He seemed to exist in several parts now; there was the sore remote protest of his palms and kneecaps, the choking swollen torment of his throat, and the unbearable awareness of his brain. He was very close to the final swooning relaxation a man feels when he is being beaten unconscious and no longer cares whether he can get up. Very far away he could hear the murmuring of the jungle in the night.

At a curve in the trail he halted, peered around, and almost screamed. A man was sitting at a machine gun about three feet away.—NORMAN MAILER, *The Naked and the Dead*

B. Emphasis by Position

Position is closely related to pause because, as we have just seen, pauses create positions of emphasis. Since the beginning and, particularly, the end of a sentence naturally receive the greatest emphasis, those positions should be occupied by words that the writer wishes to stress.

The delayed beginning, which we have mentioned as a type of padding, often wastes the emphatic first place in the sentence on non-contributing words:

There are many men who enjoy beating their wives.
MORE EMPHATIC: Many men enjoy beating their wives.

It was on Christmas Eve that I finally made up my mind.
MORE EMPHATIC: On Christmas Eve I finally made up my mind.

There is some hope on his part of getting home Friday.
MORE EMPHATIC: He has some hope of getting home Friday.

Avoiding such wasted emphasis is not, however, enough. One should use sentence beginnings to emphasize important elements that, in a conventional arrangement, would be buried in the middle of the sentence. The following examples show the emphasis given words and phrases when they are taken out of their normal position and put in place of the subject at the beginning of the sentence:

Sorrowfully she turned and walked down the road. [The adverb *sorrowfully* is emphasized by being taken out of its normal position after *turned*.]
Evidences they had . . . but no decisions. [The object is emphasized by being put before the subject and verb.]
Desperately he struggled to untie the last knot.
John I admire; *his brother* I detest.

Such inversion, or changing of the normal sentence order, should, of course, be practiced with great discretion. The force of the unusual order is lost, and the writing becomes stilted and strained, if an unconventional pattern is used repeatedly.

The end of the sentence is a position even more emphatic than the beginning, partly because it is followed by the period stop, and partly because there is a well-established general expectation that important things come last. In informal speech, sentences frequently trail off in weak modifiers and afterthoughts. In writing, such sentences should be revised to end strongly with words and ideas that merit a prominent position and receive an added emphasis from it.

> UNEMPHATIC: Julia made a vehement protest, however.
> MORE EMPHATIC: Julia, however, made a vehement protest.
>
> UNEMPHATIC: We loudly denounced him as soon as he came.
> MORE EMPHATIC: As soon as he came we loudly denounced him.
>
> UNEMPHATIC: We were surprised at his daring, not at his knowledge.
> MORE EMPHATIC: We were surprised, not at his knowledge, but at his daring.
>
> UNEMPHATIC: He was patient with their conversation in the next room, but he slammed the door when they turned on the radio.
> MORE EMPHATIC: He was patient with their conversation in the next room, but when they turned on the radio he slammed the door.[3]

Here are two sentences about Leonardo da Vinci's *Last Supper:*

Leonardo painted the Last Supper on the damp wall of the refectory, oozing with mineral salts. The effort to see the Eucharist as one taking leave of his friends, not as the pale Host of the altar, was strange after all the mystic developments of the middle age.

Walter Pater, in *The Renaissance,* wrote them this way:

On the damp wall of the refectory, oozing with mineral salts, Leonardo painted the Last Supper. . . . Strange, after all the mystic developments of the middle age, was the effort to see the Eucharist, not as the pale Host of the altar, but as one taking leave of his friends.

In Pater's first sentence, the main clause is emphasized by its position at the end; in the second, the two important ideas, "strange" and "as one taking leave of his friends," are given emphasis by a sentence arrangement that puts them at beginning and end.

The strongest sentences build to a climax. The elaborate periodic sen-

---

[3] The reader should be reminded that particular contexts might well justify some of the sentences we have marked "unemphatic." If, for example, the last sentence (about the radio and the slamming of the door) occurred in a discussion of this man's aversion to radio, the clause "when they turned on the radio," even though it is subordinate, might be important enough to deserve the end position.

tence, with its thought suspended until the end of the sentence, is a striking example of climactic arrangement:

To those among us, however, who have lived long enough to form some just estimate of the rate of the changes which are, hour by hour in accelerating catastrophe, manifesting themselves in the laws, the arts, and the creeds of men, it seems to me, that now at least, if never at any former time, the thoughts of the true nature of our life, and of its powers and responsibilities, should present themselves with absolute sadness and sternness.—JOHN RUSKIN, *Sesame and Lilies*

But in less elaborate sentences, too, parallel elements should be arranged in an order of increasing importance.

And now abideth faith, hope, charity, these three; but the greatest of these is charity. [The final clause states what the position of *charity,* last in the series, has already suggested.]

> The lark's on the wing;
> The snail's on the thorn:
> God's in his heaven—
> All's right with the world!

A jug of wine, a loaf of bread—and thou
Beside me singing in the wilderness.

Not for just an hour, not for just a day,
Not for just a year, but always.

And so, when their day is over, when their good and their evil have become eternal by the immortality of the past, be it ours to feel that, where they suffered, where they failed, no deed of ours was the cause; but wherever a spark of the divine fire kindled in their hearts, we were ready with encouragement, with sympathy, with brave words in which high courage glowed.[4]—BERTRAND RUSSELL, "A Free Man's Worship"

Violation of the natural order of climax robs a sentence of its force, unless the anticlimax is used deliberately for humor. The two sentences below illustrate intentional anticlimax; the writer wishes to emphasize the items which by most standards are the least important:

At the end of nine holes, the minister had lost his temper, his religion, and his golf ball.

Colonel McGunthrie has survived World War II, the Korean War, and forty years of marriage to Mrs. McGunthrie.

The following sentences are examples of thoughtless anticlimax:

[4] Reprinted from *Mysticism and Logic* by Bertrand Russell, by permission of W. W. Norton and Company, Inc. Copyright, 1929, by the publishers.

It was a stupendous performance, and very good.
She had no illusions. She distrusted her husband, herself, and her friends.
We find these psychological reactions in frogs, in guinea pigs, in men, and in rats.

In paragraphs, as in sentences, the position of elements is important. The principles of emphasis are much the same: the first and last sentences of the paragraph hold the positions of greatest emphasis; good paragraphs, like good sentences, begin strongly and build to a strong ending.

C. Emphasis by Repetition

We have said a good deal about wordy and ineffective repetition: the needless repetition of ideas ("punctually on time"), the careless repetition of words and sounds ("gathered at the gathering," "interpretation of the situation"), and the thoughtless repetition of the same sentence pattern. Repetition can be, however, one of the most effective means of emphasis. Skillfully used, it impresses key words and phrases on the reader's mind, creates emotional effects, and binds together sentences in a paragraph.

Specific examples will show, more clearly than any amount of general statement, the force of effective repetition. By repetition, Coleridge in *The Ancient Mariner* produces an effect not carried by the simple statement, "I was alone on a wide sea with no one to pity me." Read the stanza several times, letting the repetitions sink in—*alone, all, wide,* and the *s* sounds in *sea, saint, soul:*

> Alone, alone, all, all alone,
> Alone on a wide, wide sea!
> And never a saint took pity on
> My soul in agony.

Count and *counting* are repeated by William James to emphasize the idea that separate actions do count in the formation of habits and of character:

Every smallest stroke of virtue or of vice leaves its never so little scar. The drunken Rip Van Winkle, in Jefferson's play, excuses himself for every fresh dereliction by saying, "I won't count this time!" Well! he may not count it, and a kind Heaven may not count it; but it is being counted none the less. Down among his nerve-cells and fibres the molecules are counting it, registering and storing it up to be used against him when the next temptation comes. Nothing we ever do is, in strict scientific literalness, wiped out.—WILLIAM JAMES, *Psychology*

Thomas Wolfe often uses repetition to create atmosphere and feeling. In the following passage, the phrase *in the night, in the dark* is repeated for lyric emphasis and power; it integrates the separate details in the paragraph:

Father, in the night time, in the dark, I have heard the thunder of the fast express. In the night, in the dark, I have heard the howling of the winds among great trees, and the sharp and windy raining of the acorns. In the night, in the dark, I have heard the feet of rain upon the roofs, the glut and gurgle of the gutter spouts, and the soaking gulping throat of all the mighty earth, drinking its thirst out in the month of May—and heard the sorrowful silence of the river in October. The hill-streams foam and welter in a steady plunge, the mined clay drops and melts and eddies in the night, the snake coils cool and glistening under dripping ferns, the water roars down past the mill in one sheer sheet-like plunge, making a steady noise like wind, and in the night, in the dark, the river flows by us to the sea.—THOMAS WOLFE, *Of Time and the River*

In the opening sentences of a novel by Robert Penn Warren, the repetition of the phrase *coming at you* works with sentence rhythm to give the reader an experience of motion, speed, and monotony:

To get there you follow Highway 58, going northeast out of the city, and it is a good highway and new. Or was new, that day we went up it. You look up the highway and it is straight for miles, coming at you, with the black line down the center coming at and at you, black and slick and tarry-shining against the white of the slab, and the heat dazzles up from the white slab so that only the black line is clear, coming at you with the whine of the tires. . . .—ROBERT PENN WARREN, *All the King's Men*

The following beginning of a short story illustrates more subtle and complex repetition. Repeated, but carefully varied, compound-sentence structures and repeated words—*fall, cold, wind, blew*—combine to emphasize details of sensation, setting, and mood:

In the fall the war was always there, but we did not go to it any more. It was cold in the fall in Milan and the dark came very early. Then the electric lights came on, and it was pleasant along the streets looking in the windows. There was much game hanging outside the shops, and the snow powdered in the fur of the foxes and the wind blew their tails. The deer hung stiff and heavy and empty, and small birds blew in the wind and the wind turned their feathers. It was a cold fall and the wind came down from the mountains.—ERNEST HEMINGWAY, "In Another Country"

Effective emphasis, involving as it does so many of the principles and techniques of good expression, might well be the subject of a whole book on writing. Effective emphasis occurs when the writer knows surely what he wants to say, when he says it in strong concise words, and when he uses sentence form and rhythm, order and position, pause, and controlled repetition to produce the exact stress he desires.

CHAPTER REVIEW

If your reading of the chapter has been adequate, you should be able to explain and to illustrate each topic in the following outline of the chapter:

I. Economy and conciseness
   A. Avoiding padding and jargon
      1. Padding
         a. Awkward and meaningless repetition of the idea
         b. Wordy delaying of the subject
         c. Wordy phrasing
      2. Jargon
   B. Cutting clauses
      1. Techniques of cutting clauses
      2. Use of appositives and parallelism
   C. Choosing words that work
      1. Accurate verbs
      2. Accurate names
      3. Accurate formal words
II. Exact words
   A. Original expression
   B. Extending vocabulary
   C. Words that make distinctions
III. Concrete expression
   A. The principles that underlie concrete expression
   B. Methods and examples
      1. Substitution
      2. Expansion
      3. Figures of speech
   C. Concreteness, economy, and substance
IV. Variety in sentences
   A. Kinds of monotony
      1. Careless repetition of words and sounds
      2. Monotony in sentence pattern
   B. Varying sentence patterns
      1. Varying length
      2. Using some parallel and balanced constructions
      3. Intermingling loose and periodic sentences
      4. Varying the subject-verb-object order
      5. Changing the position of modifiers, parenthetic elements, and appositive structures
   C. Variety and emphasis
V. Emphasis
   A. Destroyers of emphasis
      1. Repeated sentence patterns
      2. Improper subordination
      3. Overuse of the passive voice
      4. Clichés
      5. Thoughtlessly used abstract words
      6. Padding, jargon, weak clauses, and circumlocution
      7. Euphemism
   B. Emphasis by pause
   C. Emphasis by position

  1. Sentence beginnings
  2. Sentence endings
  D. Emphasis by repetition

EXERCISES

I. The following varied passages represent different kinds of effective expression. Analyze the style of each passage to see what makes the expression of the ideas distinctive and memorable. Consider the elements of style discussed in this chapter: economy and conciseness; exact and original phrasing; concrete expression; variety in sentences; emphasis by pause, position, and repetition. Consider, too, language, tone, use of figurative language, parallelism and balance, antithesis, use of modifiers and appositive structures, alliteration, sentence rhythm, charged words, and, whenever you know the context, the communicator's intention and attitude, and the appropriateness of the language used.

Veni, vidi, vici. (I came, I saw, I conquered.)

Liberté, égalité, fraternité.

Life, liberty, and the pursuit of happiness.

United we stand, divided we fall.

Sighted sub sank same.

Blood, sweat, and tears.

The land of the free and the home of the brave.

Is life so dear or peace so sweet as to be purchased at the price of chains and slavery? Forbid it, Almighty God! I know not what course others may take, but as for me, give me liberty, or give me death!—PATRICK HENRY, Speech in the Virginia Convention, 1775

With malice toward none; with charity for all; with firmness in the right, as God gives us to see the right, let us strive on to finish the work we are in; to bind up the nation's wounds; to care for him who shall have borne the battle, and for his widow, and his orphan—to do all which may achieve and cherish a just and lasting peace among ourselves, and with all nations.—ABRAHAM LINCOLN, Second Inaugural Address, 1865

I wish to preach not the doctrine of ignoble ease but the doctrine of the strenuous life.—THEODORE ROOSEVELT, 1899

We are accepting this challenge of hostile purpose because we know that in such a Government, following such methods, we can never have a friend; and that in the presence of its organized power, always lying in wait to accomplish we know not what purpose, there can be no assured security for the democratic Governments of the World. We are now about to accept gauge of battle with this natural foe of liberty and shall, if necessary, spend the whole force of the nation to check and nullify its pretensions and its power. We are glad, now that we see the facts with no veil of false pretense about them, to fight thus for the ultimate peace of the world and for the liberation of its peoples, the German peoples included: for the rights of nations great and small and the privilege of men everywhere to choose their way of life and of obedience. The world must be made safe for democracy.— WOODROW WILSON, Address for Declaration of War Against Germany, 1917

If it had not been for these thing, I might have live out my life talking at street corners to scorning men. I might have die, unmarked, unknown, a failure. Now we are not a failure. This is our career and our triumph. Never in our full life could we hope to do such work for tolerance, for joostice, for man's onderstanding of man, as now we do by accident. Our words—our lives—our pains—nothing! The taking of our lives—lives of a good shoemaker and a poor fishpeddler—all! That last moment belongs to us—that agony is our triumph.—BARTOLOMEO VANZETTI, Statement after Receiving Sentence, 1927

I am certain that my fellow Americans expect that on my induction into the Presidency I will address them with a candor and a decision which the present situation of our Nation impels. This is preeminently the time to speak the truth, the whole truth, frankly and boldly. Nor need we shrink from honestly facing conditions in our country today. This great Nation will endure as it has endured, will revive and will prosper. So, first of all, let me assert my firm belief that the only thing we have to fear is fear itself—nameless, unreasoning, unjustified terror which paralyzes needed efforts to convert retreat into advance.—FRANKLIN D. ROOSEVELT, First Inaugural Address, 1933

We shall go on to the end, we shall fight in France, we shall fight on the seas and oceans, we shall fight with growing confidence and growing strength in the air, we shall defend our Island, whatever the cost may be, we shall fight on the beaches, we shall fight on the landing grounds, we shall fight in the fields and in the streets, we shall fight in the hills; we shall never surrender, and even if, which I do not for a moment believe, this Island or a large part of it were subjugated and starving, then our Empire beyond the seas, armed and guarded by the British Fleet, would carry on the struggle, until, in God's good time, the New World, with all its power and might, steps forth to the rescue and the liberation of the old.—WINSTON CHURCHILL, Speech after Dunkirk, 1940

The ordeal of the twentieth century—the bloodiest, most turbulent era of the Christian age—is far from over. Sacrifice, patience, understanding and implacable purpose may be our lot for years to come. Let's face it. Let's talk sense to the American people. Let's tell them the truth, that there are no gains without pains, that we are now on the eve of great decisions, not easy decisions, like resistance when you're attacked, but a long, patient, costly struggle which alone can assure triumph over the great enemies of man—war, poverty and tyranny—and the assaults upon human dignity which are the most grievous consequences of each. . . .

That, I think, is our ancient mission. Where we have deserted it we have failed. With your help there will be no desertion now. Better we lose the election than mislead the people; and better we lose than misgovern the people. Help me to do the job in this autumn of conflict and of campaign; help me to do the job in these years of darkness, of doubt, and of crisis which stretch beyond the horizon of tonight's happy vision, and we will justify our glorious past and the loyalty of silent millions who look to us for compassion, for understanding and for honest purpose. Thus we will serve our great tradition greatly.—ADLAI E. STEVENSON, Speech of Acceptance of the Presidential Nomination, 1952

In the long history of the world, only a few generations have been granted the role of defending freedom in its hour of maximum danger. I do not shrink from this responsibility—I welcome it. I do not believe that any of us would exchange places with any other people or any other generation. The energy, the faith, the devotion which we bring to this endeavor will light our country and all who serve it, and the glow from that fire can truly light the world.

And so, my fellow Americans, ask not what your country can do for you, ask what you can do for your country.

My fellow citizens of the world, ask not what America will do for you, but what together we can do for the freedom of man.

Finally, whether you are citizens of America or citizens of the world, ask of us here the same high standards of strength and sacrifice which we ask of you. With a good conscience our only sure reward, with history the final judge of our deeds, let us go forth to lead the land we love, asking His blessing and His help, but knowing that here on earth God's work must truly be our own.—JOHN F. KENNEDY, Inaugural Address, 1961

Darkness had no place in the life of Eleanor Roosevelt, and it has even less place in her remembrance. For hers was a radiance that warmed the cold, beckoned to the lost, and kindled hopes where none had ever flamed.—ADLAI E. STEVENSON, on the first anniversary of Mrs. Roosevelt's death, 1963

Finally, brethren, whatsoever things are true, whatsover things are honest, whatsoever things are just, whatsoever things are pure, whatsoever things are of good report; if there be any virtue, and if there be any praise, think on these things.—The Epistle of Paul to the Philippians

Read not to contradict and confute; nor to believe and take for granted; nor to find talk and discourse; but to weigh and consider. Some books are to be tasted, others to be swallowed, and some few to be chewed and digested; that is, some books are to be read only in parts; others to be read, but not curiously; and some few to be read wholly, and with diligence and attention.—FRANCIS BACON, "Of Studies"

Sir, a woman's preaching is like a dog's walking on his hinder legs. It is not done well; but you are surprised to find it done at all.—SAMUEL JOHNSON

A foolish consistency is the hobgoblin of little minds, adored by little statesmen
and philosophers and divines. With consistency a great soul has simply nothing to
do. He may as well concern himself with his shadow on the wall. Speak what you
think now in hard words and tomorrow speak what tomorrow thinks in hard words
again, though it contradict everything you said today.—"Ah, so you shall be sure
to be misunderstood?"—Is it so bad, then, to be misunderstood? Pythagoras was
misunderstood, and Socrates, and Jesus, and Luther, and Copernicus, and Galileo,
and Newton, and every pure and wise spirit that ever took flesh. To be great is to
be misunderstood.—RALPH WALDO EMERSON, "Self-Reliance"

Connie went to the wood directly after lunch. It was really a lovely day, the first
dandelions making suns, the first daisies so white. The hazel thicket was a lacework
of half-open leaves, and the last dusty perpendicular of the catkins. Yellow celan-
dines now were in crowds, flat open, pressed back in urgency, and the yellow glitter
of themselves. It was the yellow, the powerful yellow of early summer. And primroses were broad, and full of pale abandon, thick-clustered primroses no longer shy.
The lush, dark green of hyacinths was a sea, with buds rising like pale corn, while in
the riding the forget-me-nots were fluffing up, and columbines were unfolding their
ink-purple riches, and there were bits of blue bird-eggshell under a bush. Everywhere the bud-knots and the leap of life!—D. H. LAWRENCE, *Lady Chatterley's Lover*

That night I was at the bottom, without money or friends, cold, hungry, and
tired, without hope, not knowing where to turn. I think I was a little lightheaded,
from not having had enough to eat. I crossed the Drive, and started down the long,
deserted corridor of the Mall.

In front of me, the spaced, even rows of lights shone yellow in the shadowy air;
I heard the crisp sound of my own footsteps on the pavement; and behind me the
hiss and whisper of traffic turned homeward at the end of day. The city sounds were
muted and far away, they seemed to come from another time, from somewhere in
the past, like the sound of summer, like bees in a meadow long ago. I walked on, as
though through the quiet arches of a dream. My body seemed light, without weight,
made up of evening air.

The little girl playing by herself in the middle of the Mall made no sound
either. She was playing hopscotch; she went up in the air with her legs apart, and
came down again as silent as dandelion seed.—ROBERT NATHAN, *Portrait of Jennie*

How many winters had he lived in the Voralberg and the Arlberg? It was four
and then he remembered the man who had the fox to sell when they had walked
into Bludenz, that time to buy presents, and the cherry-pit taste of good kirsch,
the fast-slipping rush of running powder-snow on crust, singing "Hi! Ho! said
Rolly!" as you ran down the last stretch to the steep drop, taking it straight, then
running the orchard in three turns and out across the ditch and onto the icy road
behind the inn. Knocking your bindings loose, kicking the skis free and leaning
them up against the wooden wall of the inn, the lamplight coming from the window,
where inside, in the smoky, new-wine smelling warmth, they were playing the accor-
dion.—ERNEST HEMINGWAY, "The Snows of Kilimanjaro"

In the late summer of that year we lived in a house in a village that looked across the river and the plain to the mountains. In the bed of the river there were pebbles and boulders, dry and white in the sun, and the water was clear and swiftly moving and blue in the channels. Troops went by the house and down the road and the dust they raised powdered the leaves of the trees. The trunks of the trees too were dusty and the leaves fell early that year and we saw the troops marching along the road and the dust rising and leaves, stirred by the breeze, falling and the soldiers marching and afterward the road bare and white except for the leaves.—ERNEST HEMINGWAY, *A Farewell to Arms*

So the next morning he and Aleck Sander went home with Edmonds. It was cold that morning, the first winter cold-snap; the hedgerows were rimed and stiff with frost and the standing water in the roadside drainage ditches was skimmed with ice and even the edges of the running water in the Nine Mile branch glinted fragile and scintillant like fairy glass and from the first farmyard they passed and then again and again and again came the windless tang of woodsmoke and they could see in the back yards the black iron pots already steaming while women in the sunbonnets still of summer or men's old felt hats and long men's overcoats stoked wood under them and the men with crokersack aprons tied with wire over their overalls whetted knives or already moved about the pens where hogs grunted and squealed, not quite startled, not alarmed but just alerted as though sensing already even though only dimly their rich and immanent destiny; by nightfall the whole land would be hung with their spectral intact tallowcolored empty carcasses immobilized by the heels in attitudes of frantic running as though full tilt at the center of the earth.—WILLIAM FAULKNER, *Intruder in the Dust*

The road rose again, to a scene like a painted backdrop. Notched into a cut of red clay crowned with oaks the road appeared to stop short off, like a cut ribbon. Beside it a weathered church lifted its crazy steeple like a painted church, and the whole scene was as flat and without perspective as a painted cardboard set upon the ultimate edge of the flat earth, against the windy sunlight of space and April and a midmorning filled with bells. Toward the church they thronged with slow sabbath deliberation. The women and children went on in, the men stopped outside and talked in quiet groups until the bell ceased ringing. Then they too entered.—WILLIAM FAULKNER, *The Sound and the Fury*

Certainly the travelers were not looking their best. They had crept off the train which brought them from the interior, stiff from trying to sleep fully clothed in their chairs, sore in their minds from the recent tearing up of their lives by the roots, a little gloomy with some mysterious sense of failure, of forced farewell, of homelessness no matter how temporary. Imperfectly washed, untidy and dusty, vaguely not-present in eyes dark-circled by fatigue and anxiety, each one carried signed, stamped papers as proof that he had been born in a certain time and place, had a name of his own, a foothold of some kind in this world, a journey in view for good and sufficient reasons, and possessions worth looking into at international frontiers.—KATHERINE ANNE PORTER, *Ship of Fools*

How could I help but think of the past towards which we were returning across the dense thickets of time, across the familiar pathways of the Greek sea? The night slid past me, an unrolling ribbon of darkness. The warm sea-wind brushed my cheek —soft as the brush of a fox. Between sleep and waking I lay, feeling the tug of memory's heavy plumb-line: tug of the leaf-veined city which my memory had peopled with masks, malign and beautiful at once. I should see Alexandria again, I knew, in the elusive temporal fashion of a ghost—for once you become aware of the operation of a time which is not calendar-time you become in some sort a ghost. In this other domain I could hear the echoes of words uttered long since in the past by other voices. . . . Kisses made more passionate by remorse. Gestures made in the amber light of shuttered rooms. The flocks of white doves flying upwards among the minarets. These pictures seemed to me to represent the city as I would see it again. But I was wrong—for each new approach is different.—LAWRENCE DURRELL, *Clea*

There was a long rivulet in the strand: and, as he waded slowly up its course, he wondered at the endless drift of seaweed. Emerald and black and russet and olive, it moved beneath the current, swaying and turning. The water of the rivulet was dark with endless drift and mirrored the high-drifting clouds. The clouds were drifting above him silently and silently the seatangle was drifting below him; and the grey warm air was still: and a new wild life was singing in his veins.

Where was his boyhood now? Where was the soul that had hung back from her destiny, to brood alone upon the shame of her wounds and in her house of squalor and subterfuge to queen it in faded cerements and in wreaths that withered at the touch? Or, where was he?

He was alone. He was unheeded, happy, and near to the wild heart of life. He was alone and young and wilful and wildhearted, alone amid a waste of wild air and brackish waters and the seaharvest of shells and tangle and veiled grey sunlight and gayclad lightclad figures of children and girls and voices childish and girlish in the air.—JAMES JOYCE, *A Portrait of the Artist as a Young Man*

A few light taps upon the pane made him turn to the window. It had begun to snow again. He watched sleepily the flakes, silver and dark, falling obliquely against the lamplight. The time had come for him to set out on his journey westward. Yes, the newspapers were right: snow was general all over Ireland. It was falling on every part of the dark central plain, on the treeless hills, falling softly upon the Bog of Allen and, farther westward, softly falling into the dark mutinous Shannon waves. It was falling, too, upon every part of the lonely churchyard on the hill where Michael Furey lay buried. It lay thickly drifted on the crooked crosses and head-stones, on the spears of the little gate, on the barren thorns. His soul swooned slowly as he heard the snow falling faintly through the universe and faintly falling, like the descent of their last end, upon all the living and the dead.—JAMES JOYCE, "The Dead"

II. Keeping in mind the passages of excellent prose in Exercise I, read the following passages and feel the difference. The sentences below contain many of the enemies of effective expression: padding, jargon, weak clauses, thought-less repetition, clichés, inexact phrasing. Revise the sentences, expressing the ideas in concise and emphatic English.

1. One bad trait which he has is that he is of a selfish nature.

2. He announced himself to be in favor of terminating the employment of three sales representatives.

3. Because of the fact that I think that exercise is a necessary requisite to health, it is my habitual custom to take a walk every day.

4. It was over Labor Day that we made a trip in the car, driving to Lake Madison for the Labor Day weekend.

5. There are two ways in which our opinions differ in respect to this institution of higher learning; they are, namely, that John feels that the pursuit of knowledge is made secondary to social activities and I do not; furthermore, he also thinks that teachers of outstanding quality are few and far between whereas I, on the other hand, think that by and large my professors are literally excellent.

6. She went to bed in the wee small hours, tired but happy after her day of honest toil.

7. Dr. Black is one of the most outstanding lecturers I have ever heard lecture, I believe.

8. It was during the time that I was in the Army that I became a sadder and wiser man in regard to the less desirable attributes of human nature.

9. As a matter of fact, she anticipates participating in the next dramatic production which will be given by the Dramatic Club.

10. America was started with the first formation of the Declaration of Independence which was in 1776.

III. Improve the following sentences by substituting an exact word or phrase for each of the italicized locutions.

1. The cabinet was pine with *a thin layer of walnut on top of the pine*.

2. The car *slid* over the ice *and then it went* into the fence.

3. His hair was *uncombed and standing up in various directions*.

4. He was teasing the dog by *stretching the rubber band and releasing it in the dog's face*.

5. He has to *make a list of the contents of his book in alphabetical order*.

6. She was not skillful in her drawing *in showing the relationship of things in regard to distance*.

7. He *penned a communication in which he gave his support to* the committee's action.

8. He had been a member of the club *ever since it was founded*.

9. He was a *man who was running* for *the office of* mayor.

10. His conversation was *full of witty thoughts tersely expressed*.

11. He *looked* at her *with a self-satisfied and affected smile*.

12. He made a touchdown by *starting in one direction, then turning and going in the other*.

IV. Consider the different shades of meaning in the sets of words below. In what context, or for what purpose, would each word be exact in its factual and attitudinal meaning?

1. spend, waste, squander
2. regard, respect, veneration
3. firm, stubborn, resolute
4. frightened, scared, terrified
5. patient, enduring, long-suffering
6. tame, docile, spiritless
7. underprivileged, poor, impoverished
8. sad, miserable, wretched
9. happy, joyous, ecstatic
10. satisfied, contented, complacent
11. young, immature, childish
12. assured, self-confident, overbearing
13. frail, delicate, fragile
14. miscalculation, error, fault
15. order, command, decree
16. indolent, lazy, shiftless
17. lethargic, passive, stoical
18. show, display, flaunt
19. unusual, erratic, eccentric
20. resentful, spiteful, malicious
21. inefficient, incompetent, incapacitated
22. untidiness, mess, chaos
23. leave, desert, abandon
24. duty, debt, obligation
25. guess, assume, believe
26. noisy, boisterous, rowdy
27. willful, obstinate, perverse
28. gloomy, morose, morbid
29. informed, knowing, wise
30. acute, sensitive, perceptive

V. As an exercise in economy and emphasis, write short news items, consisting of no more than three sentences, in which you include the facts listed below. Decide how many sentences are needed to convey clearly the information in each list, and which details should be subordinated to more important details.

1. There was a heavyweight fight.
   It took place Friday night.
   It was televised locally but not nationally.
   Jake Morris is the state champion.
   He won the fight.

He weighs 187 pounds.
He comes from Chicago.
The fight was ten rounds.
Jake's opponent was Rocky Smith.
Rocky weighs 178 pounds.
He comes from St. Louis.
Jake was ahead all through the fight.
The decision was unanimous.

2. The state commissioner of agriculture talked about rainmaking.
He made a speech on the radio.
Rainmaking has been recommended to relieve the drought in the southern part of the state.
The drought has lasted three months.
The commissioner said the value of rainmaking was uncertain.
He said the wind patterns were too variable for control of the rainmaking.
He said this last Thursday.

3. Marjorie White rode her bicycle into Boston.
She rode ten miles.
She did this yesterday.
She went to the Massachusetts General Hospital.
She went to see her father.
Her father was hurt in an accident last week.
Her father is Jeremiah White.
His name is on the danger list at the hospital.
The Whites live at 703 Willow Road, Somerville.
Marjorie is eight years old.

VI. Summarize the factual meaning of each of the following passages from Shakespeare. In each passage, point out the figures of speech. What meaning does the figurative language add to the literal, factual meaning of the lines?

> 'Tis better to be lowly born
> And range with humble livers in content
> Than to be perked up in a glistening grief
> And wear a golden sorrow.

> Though yet of Hamlet our dear brother's death
> The memory be green; and that it us befitted
> To bear our hearts in grief, and our whole kingdom
> To be contracted in one brow of woe. . . .

> Leave her to heaven
> And to those thorns that in her bosom lodge
> To prick and sting her.

> Have stooped my neck under your injuries,

> And sigh'd my English breath in foreign clouds,
> Eating the bitter bread of banishment.
>
> Pluck from the memory a rooted sorrow,
> Raze out the written troubles of the brain.

VII. Improve the style of the following passages by varying the sentence structures.

1. I called the doctor and he came at once. He examined my father, and he said there was nothing to worry about. He prescribed some medicine, and I went to the drugstore to get it.

2. At first, I disliked this teacher. Later, I appreciated his methods. Consequently, I do not trust my first impressions of teachers. At present, I am keeping an open mind.

3. She heard the doorbell ring. She went to answer it. A seller of brooms and mops was there. She told him she had enough brooms and mops. He went away when he heard this.

4. A tall, white-haired woman of fifty, Miss Brown taught English. Serious in her work, she demanded accuracy. Realizing that most of us were going to college, she prepared us for the College Boards.

5. When Edward first applied for a job, he was very nervous. While he was waiting in the outer office, he almost decided to leave. When he saw the boss, he felt more confident. After he got the job, he was thankful.

VIII. Rewrite the following sentences, making them more interesting and more exact by using concrete words and details. The rewritten version may consist of more than one sentence.

1. He bought several articles of clothing for which he had to pay a large sum.
2. I read a book until late last night.
3. She put the utensils into a large container.
4. We had a conversation about a controversial question.
5. He had been indulging in a certain amount of entertainment during his stay in the city.
6. As he stepped onto the porch, the bundle he was carrying broke open and the contents spilled.
7. She wore a brightly colored costume.
8. He belongs to some radical organizations.
9. His business is selling machinery.
10. She was worried about losing an important paper.
11. This sentence is poorly constructed.
12. He spoke on matters of local interest, denouncing communist infiltration into education.
13. The committee decided to raise funds for local improvements.
14. I am busy today with a number of social engagements.
15. He performed a good deed.
16. When the teacher wasn't looking, we were likely to misbehave.

17. The vehicle moved along the road at a rapid rate.
18. I hid in the far corner of the yard, among the trees and flowers.
19. She was the picture of health.
20. My little brother is always asking me absurd questions.
21. Because of his misdemeanors, he came within the grip of the law.
22. A member of the faculty influenced me in choosing my vocation.
23. I voted for Brown for Congress because he has a good record.
24. He does well in games that require physical endurance.
25. She constantly irritates me in little ways.

IX. Write a paragraph of at least 200 words in which, by means of accurate concrete statement and detail, you expand one of the general statements below.

1. It was a dismal rainy night.
2. I was impressed with his efficiency.
3. The world looks different in the very early morning.
4. The house belonged to another age.
5. People on the subway are interesting.
6. So late at night, the dormitory seemed strange.
7. This neighborhood is restful (*or* depressing).
8. I like the view from my window.
9. At this time of year the campus is attractive.
10. Already one sees signs of approaching winter.
11. College has changed a few of my ideas.
12. I am learning some interesting things in college.
13. My college teachers are not what I expected.
14. The audience was rude.
15. He gave a dull (*or* effective) speech.
16. The room expressed the personality of its owner.
17. He (she) tried to appear sophisticated.
18. His dress and actions led me to believe he was not a student.
19. Exploring the moon is less important, I think, than improving the earth.
20. I want to do work that seems to me socially useful.

X. Cut clauses in the following passages by using an appositive or an apposed adjective structure in place of one or more of the clauses.

1. My partner's name is Mr. Hickenlooper; he is in New York today.
2. This grey old man is a veteran of three wars. He speaks clearly and forcibly.
3. My father, my brother, and I know the secret, but no one else does.
4. His hobbies are collecting stamps, playing golf, and driving fast cars. These hobbies provide him with different kinds of recreation.
5. Let me introduce you to Mr. Politico. He has been mayor of his city; also he has been a state senator, and he will be our next senator in Washington.
6. I think his first two objections are valid. The first is that the cost is too great, and the second is that the bridge cannot be completed soon enough.
7. The quarterback, who was battered and tired, limped toward the showers.

8. Carol felt unwilling to go and yet she felt reluctant to remain, and so she stood on the doorstep and waited.

9. Henry and Mary joined in the game. At first they were puzzled and later they were enthusiastic.

10. Jerry acted at times like a child and at other times like a man. He was a puzzle to his parents.

11. Little Tom appeared at the top of the stairs; he was wearing his new cowboy suit, and he was no longer tear-stained and sullen.

12. Jack Holden, who was the red-haired center, was discouraged now but still determined. He talked earnestly with his teammates.

XI. Examine the sentences in Exercise X after you have reduced clauses to appositives. In how many of the revised sentences could the appositive structures be moved so that they precede the noun or stand in another position in the sentence? How many of the sentences would be improved by some manipulation of the appositive structures? Example:

UNREDUCED: Terence, who was carrying a bat in one hand and a glove in the other, swaggered down the street.

REDUCED: Terence, carrying a bat in one hand and a glove in the other, swaggered down the street.

POSSIBLE VARIATIONS: Terence swaggered down the street, carrying a bat in one hand and a glove in the other. Carrying a bat in one hand and a glove in the other, Terence swaggered down the street.

Chapter 6

THE STRUCTURE
OF PARAGRAPHS

Perhaps the best way to understand the function of the paragraph is to consider the history of organizing written matter into units. Indenting for a paragraph serves as a mark of punctuation, and paragraphing, like other devices for indicating pause, emphasis, or separation, became a convention of writing because it serves a purpose. Early manuscripts consisted of one unbroken page after another without punctuation, capitalization, or separation of words, and with no marking off of paragraphs. Such manuscripts put too much tax on the reader, for he was obliged to blunder along, trying to find where words ended, where the pauses were, which words were proper names, and where one block of thought or detail ended and another began. During the early Middle Ages a series of devices was introduced to enable a writer to convey his meaning more efficiently, and to make reading less arduous. Division into paragraphs was one of these devices. At first such divisions were indicated not by indenting, as at present, but by the use of a mark much like our present symbol, ¶. Our word *paragraph* (*para,* beside, and *grapho,* to write) grew out of this practice. Indentation for paragraphs in writing is paralleled in public speaking by a pause longer than the usual pause after a sentence, or by a gesture or movement indicating that the speaker has completed one small phase of his subject and is going on to another.

Anyone who understands how language works knows that communication is usually most effective when the audience is given a general idea of the subject and then is supplied with organized blocks of expression, each dealing with a phase of the subject and each clearly related to the preceding and succeeding blocks. In writing, paragraphs constitute such blocks. For good writing, therefore, good paragraphing is essential. If the paragraphs are poorly made or unsuccessfully cemented together, the whole structure of the communication is unsound.

For convenience in discussion, paragraphs are often divided into three types: expository paragraphs that give information or explain an idea, belief, problem, or process; descriptive paragraphs that describe people, places, actions, or experiences; and narrative paragraphs that tell a story or part of a story. The three kinds of paragraphs are often used in the same piece of writing, and a single paragraph may contain expository and descriptive and narrative elements: for example, a writer may make his facts or opinions concrete and clear by describing a scene or by telling a story. Still, the division of paragraphs into types is convenient because paragraphs with different purposes are developed differently.

About narrative paragraphs it is very difficult to generalize. Since they present one phase in the action of the story, their length and composition depend entirely on the emphasis the writer wishes to give that part of his narrative. We shall be chiefly concerned in this chapter, therefore, with writing good expository (informative or evaluative or persuasive) paragraphs and descriptive paragraphs, and with examples to clarify the generalizations of the text.

I. UNITY IN PARAGRAPHS

Most unified expository paragraphs have a *topic sentence,* that is, a sentence which expresses the central idea of this block of the composition. The topic sentence usually stands at or near the beginning of the paragraph, as a clear introductory statement of the new phase of the subject about to be discussed; but sometimes it comes in the middle of the paragraph, and sometimes at the end. In descriptive (and narrative) paragraphs, the topic sentence is frequently implied rather than stated; for example, a writer may set down a number of details about wind, cold, bare trees, etc., which give a single impression of bleakness, without the explicit statement "It was a bleak day." Such paragraphs have a *topic idea* rather than a topic sentence. A paragraph of any type has unity when it develops one topic sentence or topic idea, and when every statement in the paragraph contributes to the development of that topic sentence or idea.

The following paragraph illustrates failure in unity:

Many older students have difficulty for a while in their courses in college. Having been out of school for several years, they have lost the habit of study and the power to concentrate. Formulas in chemistry and mathematics, which are recited readily by students fresh from high school, are only dim memories to them. Their age and the greater sense of responsibility most older students have is an advantage to them. Many of them have held responsible jobs or positions in the armed services, and now many of them have families dependent on them. Consequently, they are serious about getting an education.

[This paragraph has two topic ideas: (1) older students have difficulty in their courses; (2) they have the advantage of age and a sense of responsibility. There are two possible remedies for this paragraph disunity: one is to introduce the paragraph with a topic sentence which covers both ideas—"Many older students have both disadvantages and advantages in college"; a second, and better, remedy is to split the paragraph into two paragraphs, developing more fully each of the two ideas. The second is better because the ideas are underdeveloped as they stand.]

Another failure in unity is illustrated in the first paragraph of a theme on baby sitting:

Baby sitting is an excellent job for a girl who likes children and is willing to follow instructions. The work is easy, and she will have pleasant associations with her charges and their parents. [She should find out from the beginning what her privileges are and how much pay she will receive.] She will also gain experience that will be most helpful when she has a home and children of her own.

[The first sentence is the topic sentence of the paragraph, further developed by sentences two and four. The bracketed third sentence is irrelevant. It should, perhaps, be the topic sentence of a later paragraph about practical matters to be agreed on by baby sitter and employer.]

The following paragraph, the conclusion of a paper describing the life of a surveyor's assistant, has a somewhat different kind of disunity: the details in the first sentence contribute to a central impression of difficulty and tedium which is contradicted by the last sentence; the writer appears to have changed his mind about what his topic idea is:

Working hard from sunrise to sunset, tramping tedious miles in search of lost boundaries, repeating the same monotonous tasks each day, being outdoors in all kinds of weather—such is the life of the surveyor's assistant. It is a healthful and exciting life for the college student looking for summer employment.

Achieving unity in paragraphs is not difficult, but it does require effort and attention. Students should consciously build their paragraphs around topic sentences or topic ideas and learn to examine the structure of paragraphs as they revise their papers. Unity can be tested very simply by these two questions: What is the topic sentence or topic idea? Is every statement in the paragraph clearly relevant to this topic sentence or topic idea?

II. COHERENCE, TRANSITION, AND STRUCTURE

The sentences in a paragraph, besides being relevant to a single topic sentence or idea, must be clearly related to each other. One sentence should lead into the next, one idea coherently follow another, so that the reader is carried forward without confusion.

The clear connection between statements comes, first, from a logical arrangement of a sequence of ideas. A number of patterns of arrangement or organization will be fully discussed and illustrated in a later section of this chapter. Some of them are: setting down events in chronological order; making a general statement and clarifying it with particulars; proceeding from the whole problem to its separate parts, from cause to effect, or from question to answer. In practice, these patterns are often combined, and the pattern or patterns chosen will, of course, depend on the material. But a paragraph, to be coherent, must have some logical arrangement of details. The structure of the paragraph represents the structure of the writer's thought.

The paragraph below, on training a puppy, is weak in coherence and clarity because the writer has failed to follow the step-by-step, chronological pattern which his material requires:

While the puppy is still very young, he can learn simple commands. To teach him "Come," the owner sits on the floor a little distance away, pats the floor and says "Come" as he pulls on the puppy's leash. Before this, the puppy should get used to wearing his collar. After wearing it several times, he should have a leash attached to it. If he resists, his trainer pulls him gently across the floor. The dog should be petted and praised when he comes without being dragged. He can learn "Sit" and "Lie down" in much the same way: the owner repeats the command and at the same time pushes the puppy into the desired position.

[The coherent, logical order is: While the puppy is still very young, he should learn to wear a collar, and then get used to having a leash attached to the collar. Now he is ready to learn simple commands. To teach him "Come," the owner sits on the floor, etc.]

In the paragraph above, *Before this* at the beginning of the third sentence should have warned the writer that he was violating his natural time-order; because of this violation, the clause *if he resists,* at the beginning of the fifth sentence, is not logically related to the immediately preceding sentences. The writer of the paragraph below also uses a chronological pattern, but he makes his time-structure clear by the expressions *in the weeks and months, at first, gradually, finally:*

In the weeks and months that followed I tried to understand and accept Dad's death. At first I had a thousand daydreams of his return. Always, he was tired from a long, long trip, but alive and well. Gradually, though, my fantasies and hopes died away. I stopped listening for his voice; I stopped searching for his face in crowds. Finally I knew in my heart that he never would return. The god of my childhood was gone, and there was nothing.

The examples above show that a second way of achieving coherence is the use of effective transitions. Besides arranging his ideas in logical order, the writer must take care that the connections between his statements are made clear to the reader. Transitions within paragraphs are words, phrases, or structures which supply the reader with a smooth and orderly passage from one idea to the next. Common ways of establishing transitions between sentences in a paragraph are:

1. Using sentence connectives such as *therefore, however, on the other hand, at the same time, meanwhile, afterward, then, yet, for example*. Such connectives may show that sentences are related by time, by cause-effect, by contrast, or by expansion of a general statement.

2. Repeating a key word that has occurred in the preceding sentence; or using a term clearly equivalent to a term in the preceding sentence or a term clearly in contrast to one in the preceding material.

3. Using an unmistakable pronoun reference to a word or idea in the preceding sentence.

4. Putting parallel thoughts in parallel constructions to show the relationship between them.

5. Using subordination and subordinating conjunctions to clarify the relationship between important and less important ideas, and to help the reader grasp the main ideas of the paragraph.

The writer of the following confusing paragraph probably had arranged his ideas in logical sequence, but, in writing, he omitted so many connectives and subordinated so poorly that it is difficult to follow his thought:

POOR IN COHERENCE: I have decided one thing. The principal reason for enrolling in an educational institution is to obtain an education from books. Extracurricular activities teach much. I am eager to participate while in college. The problem of my poor high-school preparation is too large to be solved in a short time. My grades are low. I will not participate in extracurricular activities until I have found an answer.

IMPROVED IN COHERENCE: I have decided one thing: the principal reason for enrolling in an educational institution is to obtain an education from books. Although extracurricular activities teach much and I am eager to participate in them before I finish college, I have an immediate problem of low grades because of my poor high-school preparation. Until I have solved this problem I will not participate in extracurricular activities.

The passage below is analyzed in some detail to show how transitions, skillfully used, reveal structure and clarify meaning.

[1] These insecticides are not selective poisons; they do not single out the one

species of which we desire to be rid. [2] Each of them is used for the simple reason that it is a deadly poison. [3] It therefore poisons all life with which it comes in contact: the cat beloved of some family, the farmer's cattle, the rabbit in the field, and the horned lark out of the sky. [4] These creatures are innocent of any harm to man. [5] Indeed, by their very existence they and their fellows make his life more pleasant. [6] Yet he rewards them with a death that is not only sudden but horrible. [7] Scientific observers at Sheldon described the symptoms of a meadow lark found near death: "Although it lacked muscular coordination and could not fly or stand, it continued to beat its wings and clutch with its toes while lying on its side. Its beak was held open and breathing was labored." [8] Even more pitiful was the mute testimony of the dead ground squirrels, which "exhibited a characteristic attitude in death. The back was bowed, and the forelegs with the toes of the feet tightly clenched were drawn close to the thorax. . . . The head and neck were outstretched and the mouth often contained dirt, suggesting that the dying animal had been biting at the ground."

[9] By acquiescing in an act that can cause such suffering to a living creature, who among us is not diminished as a human being?—RACHEL CARSON, *Silent Spring*

The opening sentence of the first paragraph, linked to preceding material by the subjects *These insecticides* and *they,* might be considered the topic sentence. Since, though, this sentence is negative, one might more exactly say that the first six sentences state and restate with different emphases the topic idea that these unselective poisons bring horrible death to innocent creatures as well as to undesirable species. Concrete details in the second half of the paragraph develop the more general ideas at the beginning.

Sentence 2 in the first paragraph is linked to sentence 1 by *Each of them* and by the repetition of *poison* (poisons). The first three sentences of the paragraph are bound together by partial parallel structures: they begin with equivalent subjects *(These insecticides, Each of them, It)* closely followed by the verb.

Sentence 3 begins with a clear pronoun reference *(It)* to each of the poisons; *therefore* links sentences 2 and 3 in a cause-effect relationship; and *poisons* repeats and emphasizes a key word. *All life* contrasts with *the one species* in sentence 1 and, in a different way, with *deadly* in sentence 2.

In sentence 4, *These creatures* refers to the creatures named in sentence 3.

Indeed at the beginning of sentence 5 indicates that this will be an emphatic restatement of the idea of the preceding sentence. *They* and *their* are pronoun references to the innocent creatures, and *his* refers to man.

Yet in sentence 6 leads the reader to expect contrast with the preceding sentence; contrast occurs not only in the whole statement but also in *death* as opposed to *life* in sentence 5 and in *horrible* in contrast to *pleasant.* Again pronoun references—*he* and *them*—connect the sentences.

The sentences numbered 7 are related to preceding material by the repetition of *death.* Also, detail in the quoted matter repeats the idea of *horrible.*

Even more pitiful, at the beginning of the sentences numbered 8, links

8 to 7; it promises further expansion and more graphic expansion of the general idea of horrible death. Again, the key word *death* is repeated and is echoed in *dying animal.*

In the last sentence, *such suffering* refers to the detail in the preceding material, and *living creature* contrasts with *dying animal* near the end of the sentence before. Skillful use of the life-death motif does much to give the passage unity.

Sentence 9 might have been joined to the preceding paragraph. Miss Carson probably chose the one-sentence paragraph as a way of emphasizing both the image of the dead ground squirrel and the final question. In context, the question receives even greater emphasis because it closes a chapter of *Silent Spring.*

In descriptive and narrative paragraphs, and sometimes in expository paragraphs, poor coherence may be produced by a careless shift in the point of view from which people, places, or events are observed.[1] The following paragraph is part of a narrative in which all the events are recorded through the observation and consciousness of a fifteen-year-old girl:

> Jennie slipped into her sister's room and shut the door. Now the music was far away, and she could no longer hear the bright laughing voices or see the dancing. She didn't have to watch Greta smiling up at John as they danced perfectly to the sad sweet music. No one would find her here and make her go back to the party; no one would think of looking here, if anyone cared enough to look at all. She sat down at the dressing table and stared at her face in the mirror. Stiff, strained, ugly. But there were steps in the hall, voices. The closet was the only place to hide. Panicky, she rushed to it, huddled behind the rustling dresses, drew the door closed as the door of the room opened. Her sister's voice—and Greta's. "I won't have anyone telling me what to do," Greta was saying. Her mouth was not smiling now, but was hard and cruel.

> [Since Jennie is in the closet and cannot see Greta's mouth, the last sentence shifts from the point of view which has been established. For better consistency, the last sentence might read: Her voice told Jennie that her mouth was no longer smiling but was hard and cruel, as Jennie had seen it before.]

III. EMPHASIS IN PARAGRAPHS

We have said earlier, in discussing the principle of emphasis, that good paragraphs, like good sentences, should begin and end strongly. If a paragraph has unity, if it is a necessary block in the paper, and if its structure is sound, emphasis usually takes care of itself. A paragraph that builds logically to a climax, with its topic sentence at the end, is naturally emphatic. A paragraph

---

[1] Point of view, or angle of observation, in descriptive and narrative writing is discussed fully in Chapter 12, "Descriptive Writing."

that begins with its topic sentence may, however, be in some danger of tapering off at the end unless the writer has in mind the importance of the end position. A paragraph beginning with its topic sentence may end emphatically with a striking example or detail, as does the paragraph by Rachel Carson; or it may end with a restatement or enlargement of the topic idea; or it may invite the reader to go on to the next paragraph.

The following paragraph, from the student theme previously quoted (page 167), enlarges, in its last sentence, the topic idea stated in its first sentence:

> There was nothing that Dad couldn't do. He could put a squirming brown worm on a hook, dive from the highest tower into the deep water below, or take our automobile apart and fix it. Once, when our old Buick was back together again, there was a small square part left over; but the car ran just the same. I knew it would, because Father was an engineer. He built bridges, big buildings, a tunnel for my electric train, and a pen for the quivering gray rabbit that he brought home in his coat pocket. Dad could even play the piano and sing "Columbia the Gem of the Ocean." Sometimes I felt sorry for all the other boys in the world whose fathers were such ordinary men.

The paragraph below, from another student theme, develops one phase of the experience related in the paper, and leads the reader, in its last sentence, into the next phase:

> Today, as I gaze over a gauze mask, my body wrapped in white and my hands in rubber, the operating room seems strangely unreal. Yesterday it was a room full of excitement and things to learn. Now its white walls seem to hold something far different. I can hardly convince myself that I am here not as an observer but as an instrument nurse. Suddenly I feel that I have no right to hold this position. Many doctors have told me of my responsibility. Mine is almost as great as theirs, they maintain, for if I mix the wrong drugs, have the wrong instruments ready, or have improperly sterilized equipment, the operation will be as much a failure as if the surgeon's scalpel slipped. The patient's life is in my hands, and I can't be too careful. I have checked everything twice, suction apparatus, sterile gauze, sterile sheets, sutures, needles. . . . Now the doctor is coming; the operation will begin.

IV. TRANSITIONS BETWEEN PARAGRAPHS

Much of what has been said about making clear connections between sentences within the paragraph applies to connections between paragraphs in a well-organized paper. Paragraphs, like the sentences that compose them, must have an arrangement that is basically logical and effective; they must also be linked in such a way that the reader is led easily from one of these units of composition into the next. Each paragraph, developing its single topic idea, at the same time is, and must clearly be, a part of an unbroken chain. In long papers, short transitional paragraphs which summarize briefly the preceding ideas and relate them to the idea following are often used to join long paragraphs or sections of the paper. In short papers, the common transitional devices are these:

1. Concluding a paragraph with a sentence that introduces the next phase of the action. The last paragraph quoted in the previous section is an example, with its concluding sentence, "Now the doctor is coming; the operation will begin."

2. Using in the first sentence of a paragraph a connective or a transitional word or phrase: *furthermore, therefore, as a result, in addition, on the contrary.*

3. Beginning a paragraph with a sentence that refers clearly to a statement at the end of the preceding paragraph or to its topic idea.

The following paragraph beginnings illustrate some of the common ways of linking paragraphs:

> The *second* difficulty is overcrowded classrooms. [The first difficulty has been discussed in the paragraph before.]
>
> *Such objections* can be answered easily. [*Such objections* refers clearly to the material in the preceding paragraph.]
>
> *Many high schools, then, are not giving the preparation the student needs.* Should this fact be ignored by the colleges, or accepted as a real problem? [The first sentence summarizes the ideas of the preceding paragraph. The question introduces the topic idea of this paragraph.]
>
> *A week later,* the merchants of the town decided to take action.
>
> The increased cost of living, *however,* has invalidated *these gains.*
>
> *Besides using these questionable methods,* salesmen are expected to make actual misrepresentations about the superior quality of expensive goods.
>
> Pedestrians, *as well as drivers,* would benefit by *this change* in traffic regulations.

Obvious connections like *Now let us look at the other side of the question* should be avoided as much as possible; they are preferable to no connections at all, but they are mechanical and labored. It is worth mentioning, too, that connectives like *therefore, however, consequently,* etc. receive emphasis when they stand at the beginning of a clause, sentence, or paragraph. Such emphasis may be desirable, but often a sentence is more effective if the connector is buried and the emphatic beginning position is used for more important words.

> CLEAR, BUT WITH UNDUE EMPHASIS ON THE CONNECTIVE: These contradictions have been the result of divided responsibility. Therefore, the students should now accept sole responsibility.
>
> IMPROVED: These contradictions have been the result of divided responsibility. The students, therefore, should now accept sole responsibility.

Good transitions between paragraphs are an inconspicuous but essential part of a good composition. They keep the organization of the paper clear;

they prevent the reader's falling into a gulf between paragraphs, or having to leap from one thought to another; they give him a sense of continuity and progress, from the beginning of the paper to the end.

V. LENGTH OF PARAGRAPHS

It is impossible to lay down hard-and-fast rules about the length of paragraphs, because paragraph development and length differ widely with the importance of the idea being discussed, the nature of the composition, and the purpose of the writer. Convention usually prescribes the use of a new paragraph for each new speech in written dialogue, however brief or fragmentary that speech is. In advertising, as we have noted earlier, short paragraphs are used to facilitate reading and to give separate emphasis to each idea. For the same reasons, paragraphs in newspapers and in business letters are usually short. Even in formal writing, one occasionally finds a one-sentence paragraph used for sharp emphasis, or for transition between long paragraphs. In narrative writing, where a new paragraph is used for each new phase of the action of the story, some paragraphs may be long because certain phases of the action need full presentation; others may be very short because the action is minor or brief. The proper length of paragraphs cannot, then, be established dogmatically, but must be determined by the nature and complexity of the material and by the intent of the author. We can only suggest here an approach to the question of how long paragraphs should be in the informative, evaluative, and persuasive writing that most college students are required to do.

In the next section on the organization and development of paragraphs, we are quoting as examples 22 expository and descriptive paragraphs, most of them from modern writing. The shortest of these paragraphs is 113 words, the longest 293 words; the average length of the 22 paragraphs is about 170 words. The average paragraph in this fairly typical selection, then, would occupy between a half and two-thirds of a double-spaced typed page. We offer this calculation, obviously not as a rule, but as a rough guide to the student in judging the length of his own paragraphs; except in narrative writing or newswriting, his paragraphs should rarely exceed 300 words and rarely fall below 100. More than three paragraphs on a single page should, therefore, be a signal to him to re-examine his paragraphing; the length may be suitable to his subject, but the short paragraphs suggest that his material is not adequately developed. Also, the writer should look again at paragraphs longer than a manuscript page; they may be justified, but their unusual length suggests that two phases of the idea or action have been thoughtlessly run together.

VI. DEVELOPMENT AND ORGANIZATION
OF PARAGRAPHS

Although short paragraphs are not necessarily faulty, inadequately developed paragraphs are. A common weakness in student writing is the sketchy
paragraph which, though it deals with an important phase of the subject,
consists only of a topic sentence with a qualifying statement or two. Such
skeleton paragraphs, lacking flesh, thought, vitality and color, convey little
or no meaning to the reader. They give the impression of mental malnutrition
—usually a correct impression. They are likely, too, to lead to another failure:
the writer, seeing, as he looks at his manuscript, that his paragraphing is
choppy, often tries to improve the appearance of his paper by combining
paragraphs, with the result that he throws into one disunified paragraph
two or more underdeveloped topic ideas. His realization that undeveloped
paragraphs are a weakness in writing is, of course, commendable. The treatment for these starved paragraphs, however, is not to swell them by the addition of inappropriate bones, but to develop the flesh and substance that they
should have.

If a topic sentence or topic idea is worth including in a paper, it is worth
sufficient development to make it meaningful and interesting to the reader.
And, as we have pointed out earlier, a logical plan of development, suited to
the material, is essential to coherence and clarity. In the following pages we
shall discuss and illustrate nine methods of developing paragraphs. These
methods, which are also ways of developing longer pieces of writing, are
closely related, and they are, as we have said, frequently used in combination.
For convenience we shall discuss them separately under the headings *chronological arrangement, general-to-particular or particular-to-general arrangement, analysis, contrast and comparison, definition, cause and effect, reasons,
question to answer or problem to solution, patterns in description.*

This paragraph is short—for emphasis. We have tried to choose illustrative paragraphs that not only effectively demonstrate a method but also have
something to say. Read them carefully, for thought, content, and quality of
writing, before analyzing them for technique. Technique is important, but
good writing has substance as well as technique.

A. Chronological Arrangement

Chronological arrangement, or setting down events in their natural time-
order, is used in paragraphs of simple narrative, paragraphs explaining a simple process, and paragraphs recording a continuous chain of action or occurrence. Ordinarily such paragraphs do not have a topic sentence; the topic
idea is the coverage of one step or one phase of a longer or more complex ac-

tion. In addition to arranging events in time-sequence, the writer usually needs some connectives to keep the sequence clear.

In the following paragraph about the early history of the earth, the words *new, gradually, eventually,* establish the time-pattern, and the verbs *began* and *became* carry the idea of change through time:

> The new earth, freshly torn from its parent sun, was a ball of whirling gases, intensely hot, rushing through the black spaces of the universe on a path and at a speed controlled by immense forces. Gradually the ball of flaming gases cooled. The gases began to liquefy, and Earth became a molten mass. The materials of this mass eventually became sorted out in a definite pattern: the heaviest in the center, the less heavy surrounding them, and the least heavy forming the outer rim. This is the pattern which persists today—a central sphere of molten iron, very nearly as hot as it was 2 billion years ago, an intermediate sphere of semiplastic basalt, and a hard outer shell, relatively quite thin and composed of solid basalt and granite.— RACHEL L. CARSON, *The Sea Around Us*

B. General-to-particular or Particular-to-general Arrangement

In a paragraph developed by *general-to-particular* arrangement, the topic sentence, a summary statement of the idea, stands at or near the beginning of the paragraph, and is followed by facts, statistics, instances, details, or examples that support and clarify it. General-to-particular arrangement is essentially concrete expansion of an idea, and it is probably the most useful of all the methods of paragraph development for the student to understand and to practice in his own writing.

The paragraphs below illustrate the use of different kinds of particulars to substantiate and elaborate a general statement. In the first, a descriptive paragraph, the topic sentence, "Kit liked it all," is followed by six incomplete sentences which *expand* and *particularize* "all"; they give a series of concrete pictures of what Kit liked. The last sentence of the paragraph pulls the details together and restates the topic idea:

> Kit liked it all. The whitewashed, crumbling, flat-roofed, one-story *adobe* houses, with their mica windows guarded by iron bars or painted wooden shutters. The narrow, unpaved, winding lanes and alleys leading to the plaza and its naked cottonwoods. The long, shadowy, echoing *portales,* the rigid *vigas* thrusting their ends out through the walls, the heavy sagging gates of the hidden *patios.* The irrigated gardens, the fields, and the twin red-brown communal houses of the Indian pueblo up the stream. The soft gloom of the quiet interiors with their queer modeled fireplaces, their strings of red peppers, their gay Indian rugs, stacked along the walls for seats by day and beds by night, their Pueblo pottery and baskets, their silver-mounted saddles hung on pegs, their *santos* and grotesque holy pictures. Outside, their chimneys made of broken pots, their beehive ovens, and the white, white bread that was baked in them. Mountain, and meadow, and '*dobe* wall, Kit liked them all.
> —STANLEY VESTAL, *Kit Carson*

The topic idea of the next paragraph is stated in the first three sentences, and is supported by numerous *brief concrete examples* and *statistics:*

If nature gave us logic, she appears to be singularly lacking in what she bestows. For she herself drives no straight furrow, and exhibits an inconsistency which in a man would be accounted madness. Her habit is to turn upon herself, wound and afflict herself, undoing with her left hand what she has done with her right. What more inharmonious than that she should send hailstones to the destruction of her own blossoms and fruits, tempests upon the crops she has herself ripened to the harvest? The meteorite that, in 1908, fell in Siberia, about 100 tons in weight, destroyed the forest in which it fell for a radius of about forty miles. The lightning splits the tree, and sets the forest aflame. The sand of the desert or the encroaching sea turns fertile fields into barren wastes, and reduces whole populations to distress or starvation. It is her own features which nature thus rends and mangles. Wild beasts destroy 3000 persons every year in India, and 20,000 die of snake-bite. There are 700 million sufferers from malaria in the world. Forty per cent of the children born in Central China perish from cold or famine before they are a year old. —W. MACNEILE DIXON, *The Human Situation*

The author of the following paragraph states, qualifies, and restates his topic idea in the opening sentences, and then supports his thesis with four examples probably familiar to many readers:

It is not difficult to recognize the widespread longing for the state of complete laziness and passivity. Our advertising appeals to it even more than to sex. There are, of course, many useful and labor saving gadgets. But this usefulness often serves only as a rationalization for the appeal to complete passivity and receptivity. A package of breakfast cereal is being advertised as *"new—easier to eat."* An electric toaster is advertised with these words: ". . . the most distinctly different toaster in the world! Everything is done for you with this new toaster. You need not even bother to lower the bread. Power-action, through a unique electric motor, *gently takes the bread right out of your fingers!"* How many courses in languages, or other subjects, are announced with the slogan "effortless learning, no more of the old drudgery." Everybody knows the picture of the elderly couple in the advertisement of a life-insurance company, who have retired at the age of sixty, and spend their life in the complete bliss of having nothing to do except just travel.—ERICH FROMM, *The Sane Society*

In the paragraph below, one *long illustration* makes concrete and clear the abstract idea stated in the topic sentence—that people react, not to objective events, but to their often distorted mental images of those events:

The only feeling that anyone can have about an event he does not experience is the feeling aroused by his mental image of that event. That is why until we know what others think they know, we cannot truly understand their acts. I have seen a young girl, brought up in a Pennsylvania mining town, plunged suddenly from entire cheerfulness into a paroxysm of grief when a gust of wind cracked the kitchen window-pane. For hours she was inconsolable, and to me incomprehensible. But when she was able to talk, it transpired that if a window-pane broke it meant that a close relative had died. She was, therefore, mourning for her father, who had frightened her into running away from home. The father was, of course, quite thoroughly alive as a telegraphic inquiry soon proved. But until the telegram came, the cracked glass was an authentic message to that girl. Why it was authentic only a prolonged investigation by a skilled psychiatrist could show. But even the most casual observer could see that the girl, enormously upset by her family troubles, had hallucinated a complete fiction out of one external fact, a remembered superstition, and a turmoil of remorse, and fear and love for her father.—WALTER LIPPMANN, *Public Opinion*

Particular-to-general arrangement is a less common method of paragraph development than general-to-particular. Sometimes, though, a writer starts with particular details or examples and builds to a more general idea at the end of the paragraph. In the paragraph below, a famous scientist answers a question—how many original species produced the multiple forms of life on earth—by first giving particular pieces of evidence and then stating his conclusion. (This paragraph illustrates both particular-to-general arrangement and question-to-answer.)

It may be asked how far I extend the doctrine of the modification of species. The question is difficult to answer, because the more distinct the forms are which we may consider, by so much the arguments fall away in force. But some arguments of the greatest weight extend very far. All the members of whole classes can be connected together by chains of affinities, and all can be classified on the same principle, in groups subordinate to groups. Fossil remains sometimes tend to fill up very wide intervals between existing orders. Organs in a rudimentary condition plainly show that an early progenitor had the organ in a fully developed state; and this in some instances necessarily implies an enormous amount of modification in the descendants. Throughout whole classes various structures are formed on the same pattern, and at an embryonic age the species closely resemble each other. Therefore I cannot doubt that the theory of descent with modification embraces all the members of the same class. I believe that animals have descended from at most only four or five progenitors, and plants from an equal or lesser number.—CHARLES DARWIN, *The Origin of Species*

C. Analysis

Analysis means breaking a complex problem, term, or concept into its various parts. Analysis as a method of development is more often used in long pieces of writing than in single paragraphs; in such longer pieces, one or more paragraphs may be devoted to each part of the divided subject. Paragraphs too, however, are developed by analysis when the writer, instead of discussing his topic as a whole, breaks it, for clarity, into its components.

Bertrand Russell, to make clear what he means by the abstract term *patriotism,* breaks the complex idea into its component parts: love of home, liking for compatriots, pride, etc. This paragraph illustrates climactic arrangement of ideas and also the use of analysis as a method of definition.

Patriotism is a very complex feeling, built up out of primitive instincts and highly intellectual convictions. There is love of home and family and friends, making us peculiarly anxious to preserve our own country from invasion. There is the mild instinctive liking for compatriots as against foreigners. There is pride, which is bound up with the success of the community to which we feel that we belong. There is a belief, suggested by pride but reinforced by history, that one's own nation represents a great tradition and stands for ideals that are important to the human race. But besides all these, there is another element, at once nobler and more open to attack, an element of worship, of willing sacrifice, of joyful merging of the individual life in the life of the nation. This religious element in patriotism is essential to the strength of the State, since it enlists the best that is in most men on the side of national sacrifice.[2]

D. Contrast and Comparison

In a paragraph developed by contrast or comparison or both, the writer sets side by side two or more people, things, or situations, and demonstrates the differences, or similarities, or differences and similarities between them. Like general-to-particular arrangement, contrast and comparison develop a general idea by making it detailed and concrete.

Theodore C. Sorensen, writing about President John F. Kennedy and his father, Ambassador Joseph P. Kennedy, announces his pattern of contrast in the opening topic sentence of the paragraph below. Sentences within the paragraph are structured to emphasize difference rather than similarity and also (appropriately in a book about President Kennedy) to emphasize the traits of the father less than the traits of the son:

Father and son could scarcely have been more different. The "very few" members of the National Association of Manufacturers who supported his election, the President smilingly remarked to their 1961 convention, must have been "under the impression that I was my father's son." Both had a natural charm—but the father, though very emotional underneath, was often dour and gruff while his son kept outwardly calm. Both had a winning Irish smile—but the father was capable of more angry outbursts than his infinitely patient son. Both had a tough inner core, capable of making hard decisions and sticking to them—but the father had a more aggressive exterior compared to his son's consistently gentle composure. The father's normal conversation was often filled with hyperbole—his son's speech, in private as in public, was more often characterized by quiet understatement.—THEODORE C. SORENSEN, *Kennedy*

[2] From *Why Men Fight* by Bertrand Russell, Appleton-Century-Crofts, Inc. Copyright, 1917. Used by permission of the publishers.

Stuart Chase, describing the Grand Coulee Dam, sees in it an achievement comparable to, and greater than, the construction of the Great Pyramid six thousand years ago. In the following paragraph he uses both comparison and contrast to convey his ideas about the dam, and to build to his topic sentence at the end of the paragraph:

One of these masses is built of cut stone, the other of poured concrete. One took 50,000 men twenty years to build, the other will take 5,000 men six years, in a task not only three times greater but vastly more complex and dangerous. Both structures relied on the labor of those who would otherwise have been unemployed. Egyptian peasants in the off season built Cheops; American workingmen and engineers shelved by a great depression are building Grand Coulee. Pyramids were houses for the dead. Dams are centers of energy for the living. It is better, I think, to live in the age of the Great Dams than in the age of the Great Pyramids.— STUART CHASE, *Idle Money Idle Men*

A useful type of comparison is *analogy*. An analogy clarifies an unfamiliar idea or situation by stating it in terms of (i.e., comparing it with) a more familiar situation. Edward Bellamy, in *Looking Backward,* writes from the point of view of one who has awakened in the year 2000 and is looking back at the undesirable social structure of his own day; in the following paragraph he explains the complex social and economic structure of the 1880's by comparing it to a simple thing, familiar to his readers—a stagecoach:

By way of attempting to give the reader some general impression of the way people lived together in those days, and especially of the relations of the rich and poor to one another, perhaps I cannot do better than to compare society as it then was to a prodigious coach which the masses of humanity were harnessed to and dragged toilsomely along a very hilly and sandy road. The driver was hunger, and permitted no lagging, though the pace was necessarily very slow. Despite the difficulty of drawing the coach at all along so hard a road, the top was covered with passengers who never got down, even at the steepest ascents. These seats on top were very breezy and comfortable. Well up out of the dust, their occupants could enjoy the scenery at their leisure, or critically discuss the merits of the straining team. Naturally such places were in great demand and the competition for them was keen, every one seeking as the first end in life to secure a seat on the coach for himself and to leave it to his child after him. By the rule of the coach a man could leave his seat to whom he wished, but on the other hand there were many accidents by which it might at any time be wholly lost. For all that they were so easy, the seats were very insecure, and at every sudden jolt of the coach persons were slipping out of them and falling to the ground, where they were instantly compelled to take hold of the rope and help drag the coach on which they had before ridden so pleasantly. It was naturally regarded as a terrible misfortune to lose one's seat, and the apprehension that this might happen to them or their friends was a constant cloud upon the happiness of those who rode.

In the paragraph below, the author, a former president of the University

of California, uses brief analogy to describe the modern multiversity and to
contrast it with older kinds of universities:

> The "Idea of a University" was a village with its priests. The "Idea of a Modern
> University" was a town—a one-industry town—with its intellectual oligarchy. "The
> Idea of a Multiversity" is a city of infinite variety. Some get lost in the city; some rise
> to the top within it; most fashion their lives within one of its many subcultures.
> There is less sense of community than in the village but also less sense of confinement.
> There is less sense of purpose than within the town but there are more ways to excel.
> There are also more refuges of anonymity—both for the creative person and the
> drifter. As against the village and the town, the "city" is more like the totality of
> civilization as it has evolved and more an integral part of it; the movement to and
> from the surrounding society has been greatly accelerated. As in a city, there are many
> separate endeavors under a single rule of law.—CLARK KERR, *The Uses of the
> University*

E. Definition

Definition as a method of paragraph development means, not quoting a
dictionary definition, but discussing fully and specifically the meaning of a
word or a term so that the reader understands exactly what it stands for in
the context of this piece of writing. Definition of this sort is particularly
necessary when the author is using abstract terms which have different meanings for different people, when he is limiting his subject more than it usually
is limited, or when he is writing on a topic likely to be unfamiliar to his
readers. Full and exact definition paragraphs are often the most important
part of a paper; without them the composition may be obscure or misleading.

Clear definition may be accomplished by one or more of these methods:
by *analysis* (division of the subject into its parts); by *negation* or *exclusion*
(showing what the term does *not* mean); by *restatement* (repetition in different words of the core of the definition); by *particular instances* or *examples;*
and by *contrast* and *comparison.*

Definition by analysis has been illustrated by the paragraph on patriotism,
page 178. In the paragraph below, a transitional paragraph, the author starts
to define "creative thought" by *negation*—telling his readers that it is not
like the three types of thinking he has discussed before:

> This brings us to another kind of thought which can fairly easily be distinguished
> from the three kinds described above. It has not the usual qualities of the reverie,
> for it does not hover about our personal complacencies and humiliations. It is not
> made up of the homely decisions forced on us by everyday needs, when we review
> our little stock of existing information, consult our conventional preferences and
> obligations, and make a choice of action. It is not the defense of our own cherished
> beliefs and prejudices just because they are our own—mere plausible excuses for
> remaining of the same mind. On the contrary, it is that peculiar species of thought

which leads us to *change* our mind.—JAMES HARVEY ROBINSON, *The Mind in the Making*

Definition by *restatement* is shown in the following paragraph. The author defines the field of anthropology by repeating, in different terms, that anthropology is concerned with all cultures and not solely with our own:

The distinguishing mark of anthropology among the social sciences is that it includes for serious study other societies than our own. For its purposes any social regulation of mating and reproduction is as significant as our own, though it may be that of the Sea Dyaks, and have no possible historical relation to that of our civilization. To the anthropologist, our customs and those of a New Guinea tribe are two possible social schemes for dealing with a common problem, and in so far as he remains an anthropologist he is bound to avoid any weighing of one in favor of the other. He is interested in human behavior, not as it is shaped by one tradition, our own, but as it has been shaped by any tradition whatsoever. He is interested in the great gamut of custom that is found in various cultures, and his object is to understand the way in which these cultures change and differentiate, the different forms through which they express themselves, and the manner in which the customs of any peoples function in the lives of the individuals who compose them.—RUTH BENEDICT, *Patterns of Culture*

The term "loaded words" (the words we have called "charged") is defined by a series of *examples* in this paragraph from S. I. Hayakawa's *Language in Action:*

In short, the process of reporting is the process of keeping one's personal feelings out. In order to do this, one must be constantly on guard against "loaded" words that reveal or arouse feelings. Instead of "sneaked in," one should say "entered quietly"; instead of "politicians," "congressmen" or "aldermen"; instead of "office-holder," "public official"; instead of "tramp," "homeless unemployed"; instead of "Chinaman," "Chinese"; instead of "dictatorial set-up," "centralized authority"; instead of "crack pots," "holders of uncommon views." A newspaper reporter, for example, is not permitted to write, "A bunch of fools who are suckers enough to fall for Senator Smith's ideas met last evening in the rickety firetrap that disfigures the south edge of town." Instead he says, "Between seventy-five and a hundred people were present last evening to hear an address by Senator Smith at the Evergreen Gardens near the South Side city limits."

A combination of *analogy* and *contrast* is used by Max Eastman in the first paragraph of *Enjoyment of Poetry* to define the term "poetic people":

A simple experiment will distinguish two types of human nature. Gather a throng of people and pour them into a ferry-boat. By the time the boat has swung into the river you will find that a certain proportion have taken the trouble to climb upstairs, in order to be out on deck and see what is to be seen as they cross over. The rest have settled indoors, to think what they will do upon reaching the other side, or perhaps lose themselves in apathy or tobacco smoke. But leaving out those apathetic, or addicted to a single enjoyment, we may divide all the alert passengers on the boat into two classes—those who are interested in crossing the river, and those who are merely interested in getting across. And we may divide all the people on the earth, or all the moods of people, in the same way. Some of them are chiefly occupied with attaining ends, and some with receiving experiences. The distinction of the two will be more marked when we name the first kind practical, and the second poetic, for common knowledge recognizes that a person poetic or in a poetic mood is impractical, and a practical person is intolerant of poetry.

F. Cause and Effect

Cause-and-effect arrangement of material, like analysis, is used less frequently in paragraphs than in longer articles which trace developments over a period of time and show how one occurrence or situation produces or is produced by another. Paragraphs organized on this plan may, like longer pieces of writing, start with the cause of the problem or condition under discussion and move forward to its effect; or, the writer may start with an existing situation (effect) and move back to its cause.

In the paragraph below, an historian discusses the fact that human beings, from very ancient times, have imagined ideal worlds or Utopias; he begins with the cause (the psychological conditions that produced a longing for something beyond the actual world) and proceeds to the effect:

In the long history of man on earth there comes a time when he remembers something of what has been, anticipates something that will be, knows the country he has traversed, wonders what lies beyond—the moment when he becomes aware of himself as a lonely, differentiated item in the world. Sooner or later there emerges for him the most devastating of all facts, namely, that in an indifferent universe which alone endures, he alone aspires, endeavors to attain, and attains only to be defeated in the end. From that moment his immediate experience ceases to be adequate, and he endeavors to project himself beyond it by creating ideal worlds of semblance, Utopias of other time or place in which all has been, may be, or will be well.—CARL BECKER, *Modern Democracy*

The following paragraph has a different cause-effect pattern. James Baldwin discusses the results or effects of the long interracial drama in this country (cause), and then considers the potential further effect of the experience Americans have gained:

The time has come to realize that the interracial drama acted out on the American continent has not only created a new black man, it has created a new white man, too. No road whatever will lead Americans back to the simplicity of this European village where white men still have the luxury of looking on me as a stranger. I am not, really, a stranger any longer for any American alive. One of the things that distinguishes Americans from other people is that no other people has ever been so deeply involved in the lives of black men, and vice versa. This fact faced, with all its implications, it can be seen that the history of the American Negro problem is not merely shameful, it is also something of an achievement. For even when the worst has been said, it must also be added that the perpetual challenge posed by this problem was always, somehow, perpetually met. It is precisely this black-white experience which may prove of indispensable value to us in the world we face today. This world is white no longer, and it will never be white again.—JAMES BALDWIN, "Stranger in the Village," *Notes of a Native Son*

G. Reasons

Closely related to the pattern of effect-to-cause development is the method of giving reasons for an attitude, a belief, or a course of action. In a lecture on the role of the United States in world affairs, Adlai Stevenson first says that Americans need to develop a new attitude toward world problems, and then gives reasons for the attitudes they now hold. This paragraph also illustrates general-to-particular development of an idea.

One of our hardest tasks—if we hope to conduct a successful foreign policy—is to learn a new habit of thought, a new attitude toward the problems of life itself. Fortitude, sobriety and patience as a prescription for combating intolerable evil are cold porridge to Americans who yesterday tamed a continent and tipped the scales decisively in two world wars. Americans have always assumed, subconsciously, that all problems can be solved; that every story has a happy ending; that the application of enough energy and good will can make everything come out right. In view of our history, this assumption is natural enough. As a people, we have never encountered any obstacle that we could not overcome. The Pilgrims had a rough first winter, but after that the colony flourished. Valley Forge was followed naturally by Yorktown. Daniel Boone always found his way through the forest. We crossed the Alleghenies and the Mississippi and the Rockies with an impetus that nothing could stop. The wagon trains got through; the Pony Express delivered the mail; in spite of Bull Run and the Copperheads, the Union was somehow preserved. We never came across a river we couldn't bridge, a depression we couldn't overcome, a war we couldn't win. So far, we have never known the tragedy, frustration and sometimes defeat which are ingrained in the memories of all other peoples.—ADLAI E. STEVENSON, *Call to Greatness*

H. Question to Answer, or Problem to Solution

Asking a question and supplying an answer, or stating a problem and suggesting a solution often require more extended development than is possible in a single paragraph. Paragraphs are developed this way, however, when the question or the problem is one aspect of a larger problem under discussion. The question, or the statement of the problem, stands at or near the beginning of such a paragraph, and the answer or solution at the end; together they constitute the topic idea of the paragraph. The following question-to-answer paragraph about teaching is also developed by analogy:

To pass from the overheated Utopia of Education to the realm of teaching is to leave behind false heroics and take a seat in the front row of the human comedy. What is teaching and why is it comic? The answer includes many things depending on whether you think of the teacher, the pupil, the means used, or the thing taught. But the type situation is simple and familiar. Think of a human pair teaching their child how to walk. There is, on the child's side, strong desire and latent powers: he has legs and means to use them. He walks and smiles; he totters and looks alarmed; he falls and cries. The parents smile throughout, showering advice, warning, encouragement, and praise. The whole story, not only of teaching, but of man and civilization, is wrapped up in this first academic performance. It is funny because clumsiness makes us laugh, and touching because undaunted effort strikes a chord of gallantry, and finally comic because it has all been done before and is forever to do again.—JACQUES BARZUN, *Teacher in America*

The following example is the first paragraph of an essay on what the author calls "the crisis of American masculinity." Both the opening question and the partial answer at the end of the paragraph state the problem that is the subject of the essay; both are clarified by chronologically arranged details within the paragraph:

What has happened to the American male? For a long time, he seemed utterly confident in his manhood, sure of his masculine role in society, easy and definite in his sense of sexual identity. The frontiersmen of James Fenimore Cooper, for example, never had any concern about masculinity; they were men, and it did not occur to them to think twice about it. Even well into the twentieth century, the heroes of Dreiser, of Fitzgerald, of Hemingway remain men. But one begins to detect a new theme emerging in some of these authors, especially in Hemingway: the theme of the male hero increasingly preoccupied with proving his virility to himself. And by mid-century, the male role had plainly lost its rugged clarity of outline. Today men are more and more conscious of maleness not as a fact but as a problem. The ways by which American men affirm their masculinity are uncertain and obscure. There are multiplying signs, indeed, that something has gone badly wrong with the American male's conception of himself.—ARTHUR M. SCHLESINGER, JR., *The Politics of Hope*

I. Patterns in Description[3]

Descriptive paragraphs often do not have the clearly logical structure of most of the paragraph patterns discussed in the preceding pages. They have, however, an organization and logic of their own, dependent on the material and the effect the writer wishes to produce.

Frequently, as we have said before, paragraphs of description have a topic idea rather than a topic sentence; and they are usually developed by a series of concrete details that convey a sharp sense of a person, place, or experience.

[3] For a fuller discussion of descriptive writing, see Chapter 12, "Descriptive Writing."

(The paragraph from *Kit Carson,* page 175, is an example.) The topic idea will determine the writer's selection of detail; his particulars, in a descriptive passage, should contribute to a central or dominant impression—for instance, an impression of disorder, or cheerfulness, or calm, or bustling activity.

Having selected the descriptive details to create this dominant impression, the writer will generally arrange them in the paragraph according to one of two principles: First, his arrangement may be an orderly one, based on the space-relationship of the items included; the observer may, for example, record his observations as he looks from left to right, or from far to near, or from near to far, or up one side of a street and down the other. Second, the arrangement may be impressionistic: details may be set down in no particular space-pattern, but as they strike the consciousness of the observer. Such impressionistic description is often used in narrative writing to give the reader simultaneously a sense of a scene or situation and an understanding of the character who observes it; the character and his state of mind are revealed by what catches his interest, what is important to him, and by how logically or unsystematically his attention moves from one detail to another; we know him better from seeing how his "principle of selection" works.

The paragraph below is an example of orderly, near-to-far description:

Below him, bounding from rock to rock, ran the brook, laughing in the sunlight and tossing the spray high in the air in a mad frolic. Across this swirling line of silver lay a sparse meadow strewn with rock, plotted with squares of last year's crops— potatoes, string beans, and cabbages, and now combed into straight green lines of early buckwheat and turnips. Beyond this a ragged pasture, fenced with blackened stumps, from which came the tinkle of cow bells, and farther on the grim, silent forest—miles and miles of forest seamed by a single road leading to Moose Hillock and the Great Stone Face.—F. H. SMITH, *The Fortunes of Oliver Horn*

In the following impressionistic paragraph, the attention of the observer moves from a general impression of the cold scene, down to the street, up to the dominant posters, down to the street again, and then to the distance:

Outside, even through the shut window pane, the world looked cold. Down in the street little eddies of wind were whirling dust and torn paper into spirals, and though the sun was shining and the sky a harsh blue, there seemed to be no color in anything except the posters that were plastered everywhere. The black-mustachio'd face gazed down from every commanding corner. There was one on the house front immediately opposite. BIG BROTHER IS WATCHING YOU, the caption said, while the dark eyes looked deep into Winston's own. Down at street level another poster, torn at one corner, flapped fitfully in the wind, alternately covering and uncovering the single word INGSOC. In the far distance a helicopter skimmed down between the roofs, hovered for an instant like a bluebottle, and darted away again with a curving flight. It was the Police Patrol, snooping into people's windows. The patrols did not matter, however. Only the Thought Police mattered.—GEORGE ORWELL, *Nineteen Eighty-four*

Many paragraphs, as we have seen, are developed by some combination of the methods of chronological arrangement, general-to-particular or partic-ular-to-general arrangement, analysis, contrast and comparison, definition, cause and effect, reasons, question to answer or problem to solution, and description. The method or methods used will depend on the nature of the material. How fully the writer develops particular paragraphs will depend, too, on his material and on the importance of these paragraphs in the paper. A paragraph of any type is well developed when the topic idea is sufficiently expanded to be meaningful to the reader, when the organization is clear, and when the length of development accords with the weight that this phase of the subject, or of the action, should have in the balanced development of the whole piece of writing.

VII. FIRST AND LAST PARAGRAPHS

Because beginning and concluding paragraphs occupy the positions of great-est emphasis, they deserve special attention.

The primary purpose of a beginning paragraph is to launch the subject and to interest the reader in it. Too often college writers have the idea that a first paragraph should "lead up to the subject." As a result, they often waste the important beginning of a paper in dull, laborious introductory remarks like "I intend to discuss three reasons . . . ." or "In this paper I hope to prove . . . ." Instead of wasting words, they should start at once to discuss or to prove, with a directness and vigor that immediately attract the reader. These tedious leading-up-to-the-subject paragraphs can often simply be struck out in the process of revision; the second paragraph, which actually gets into the subject, is likely to be a more effective beginning. Even worse than a merely dull and wasted beginning paragraph is the apologetic introduction: "Interior decorating is a very complicated business which I don't know much about, but I did work for a month last summer . . . ." The reader, unless he is unhap-pily obliged to grade the paper, is at once discouraged from reading further. Good beginning paragraphs are direct and sure and interesting. An episode or a snatch of conversation focused on the subject, a vivid situation or scene, an emphatic statement of an opinion, a clear definition of the topic to be dis-cussed—these make effective beginnings because they awaken curiosity or interest.

The last paragraph of a paper should emphasize the idea the writer wishes to leave with the reader, and should give the reader a sense of finality and completion. The concluding paragraph is particularly important because, since it is last, it is likely to fix the reader's impression of the whole paper. That impression will be poor if the writer ends apologetically: "Of course I haven't been able to do justice to this subject." And the impression will be clouded if the writer concludes his paper with a collection of afterthoughts and incidental details which he feels should be mentioned, but for which he has not found room in the body of the composition. Such details should be either omitted or incorporated earlier, for placed at the end they scatter the reader's thoughts, and divert his attention from the main ideas. A final paragraph must be sharply focused.

A common type of conclusion is the summary, which briefly reviews the principal points covered in the paper. In a long paper, which has dealt with complex material, the summary ending is often desirable, even necessary. In a short informal paper, however, it is usually not desirable, because it seems mechanical and unnecessary; a reader of any intelligence does not need, and does not care, to be told what he has read within the last two minutes.

A thoughtful arrangement of the material in a paper in climactic order often automatically solves the problem of achieving an emphatic ending. If the writer is presenting four reasons for a belief he holds, or three or four arguments in favor of a course of action, and if he puts his most important point last, the development of that paramount reason or that particularly telling argument will serve as an emphatic conclusion.

Good closing paragraphs sometimes suggest a solution for a problem described in the paper. They may call on the reader to take some definite action. They may stimulate action or thought by posing a question: "Citizens have the power to demand better television programs. When will they exercise that power?" They may give an example of how the advocated plan or idea has operated. They may restate, emphatically and in different terms, the topic idea of the paper. These last paragraphs should be carefully constructed, and carefully phrased, to give the exact emphasis and impression that the writer hopes the reader will carry away.

CHAPTER REVIEW

If your reading of the chapter has been adequate, you should be able to answer the following questions:

1. What is the function of the paragraph?
2. How can paragraph unity be tested?
3. What is meant by coherence? By what methods is it attained?
4. What are the common ways of making transitions or connections between sentences within a paragraph? Between paragraphs?
5. Why is it impossible to lay down hard-and-fast rules about the length of paragraphs?
6. What advice is given to the student as a guide in determining the proper length of his paragraphs?

7. Explain clearly how paragraphs are developed by

chronological arrangement
general-to-particular and particular-to-general arrangement
analysis
contrast and comparison
definition
cause and effect
reasons
question to answer or problem to solution

8. According to what principles are descriptive paragraphs usually organized?

9. What are the important things to keep in mind about first paragraphs? About last paragraphs?

EXERCISES

I. The following passages, most of them from modern writing, illustrate various kinds of paragraph development. Students may find it useful to apply these questions to each paragraph:

1. What is the topic sentence or topic idea?
2. By what method or methods is the paragraph developed?
3. Does the paragraph end strongly? If so, how has the writer accomplished the emphatic ending?
4. If two successive paragraphs from the same source are printed, why has the writer broken the passage into two paragraphs?
5. By what means does the writer tie together the sentences of his paragraphs?

(1)

We travel together, passengers on a little space ship, dependent on its vulnerable reserves of air and soil; all committed for our safety to its security and peace; preserved from annihilation only by the care, the work and I will say the love we give our fragile craft. We cannot maintain it half fortunate, half miserable, half confident, half despairing, half slave—to the ancient enemies of man—half free in a liberation of resources undreamed of until this day. No craft, no crew can travel safely with such vast contradictions. On their resolution depends the survival of us all.—ADLAI E. STEVENSON, Speech to the Economic and Social Council in Geneva, Switzerland, July 9, 1965

(2)

He [Sam Houston] was fiercely ambitious, yet at the end he sacrificed for principle all he had ever won or wanted. He was a Southerner, and yet he steadfastly maintained his loyalty to the Union. He was a slaveholder who defended the right of Northern ministers to petition Congress against slavery; he was a notorious drinker who took the vow of temperance; he was an adopted son of the Cherokee Indians who won his first military honors fighting the Creeks; he was a Governor of Tennessee but a Senator from Texas. He was in turn magnanimous yet vindictive, affectionate yet cruel, eccentric yet self-conscious, faithful yet opportunistic. But Sam Houston's contradictions actually confirm his one basic, consistent quality: indomitable individualism, sometimes spectacular, sometimes crude, sometimes mysterious, but always courageous. He could be all things to all men—and yet, when faced with his greatest challenge, he was faithful to himself and to Texas. The turmoil within Sam Houston was nothing more than the turmoil which racked the United States in those stormy years before the Civil War, the colorful uniqueness of Sam Houston was nothing more than the primitive expression of the frontier he had always known. —JOHN F. KENNEDY, *Profiles in Courage*

(3)

"Absurd" originally means "out of harmony," in a musical context. Hence its dictionary definition: "out of harmony with reason or propriety; incongruous, unreasonable, illogical." In common usage in the English-speaking world, "absurd" may simply mean "ridiculous." But this is not the sense in which Camus uses the word, and in which it is used when we speak of the Theatre of the Absurd. In an essay on Kafka, Ionesco defined his understanding of the term as follows: "Absurd is that which is devoid of purpose. . . . Cut off from his religious, metaphysical, and transcendental roots, man is lost; all his actions become senseless, absurd, useless."— MARTIN ESSLIN, *The Theatre of the Absurd*

(4)

The ugliest example [of strong prejudice in contemporary civilization] is racial prejudice. Even though few reputable historians continue to find the key to civilization in the innate superiority of the white, the Nordic, or the Anglo-Saxon race, this vulgar theory still colors the thought and feeling of a great many men who do not openly commit themselves to it. In the Anglo-Saxon world, indeed, feeling about color is so strong and deep that men assume it is instinctive, and even the tolerant are likely to be repelled by the thought of racial intermarriage; whereas such feeling has actually been rare in history. All peoples have been pleased to regard themselves as superior, but few have identified their superiority with the color of their skin. And since the great majority of the world's population are what Americans call colored, and consider naturally inferior, it becomes necessary to repeat that this attitude is strictly a prejudice, inconsistent with the principles of democracy and Christianity, and with no scientific basis whatever. Biologically, races are not pure or sharply defined, racial differences are only a small fraction of man's common inheritance, and the clearest differences—as between white skin and yellow, long heads and broad, straight hair and kinky—have no clear importance for survival. Historically, mixed races have usually produced the golden ages, all races have proved capable of civilization, and no race has led the way throughout history. The 100 per cent American today is a parvenu who owes 99 per cent of his civilization to a mongrel antiquity.—HERBERT J. MULLER, *The Uses of the Past*

(5)

The best illustration of the difference between normal and neurotic fear was given by Sigmund Freud himself. A person in an African jungle, he said, may quite properly be afraid of snakes. That is normal and self-protective. But if a friend of ours suddenly begins to fear that snakes are under the carpet of his city apartment, then we know that his fear is neurotic, abnormal. In attempting to estimate our own fears we may profitably apply Freud's serviceable yardstick. It would be quite normal for a Polish mother to fear that her children might die of starvation, but when a wealthy American mother comes into my study and tells me that her children are dying of slow malnutrition, I suspect that her fear is a morbid and neurotic shadow, based on her own feelings of guilt, fear, and hatred.[4]

(6)

Leeuwenhoek's day of days had come. Alexander had gone to India and discovered huge elephants that no Greek had ever seen before—but those elephants were as commonplace to Hindus as horses were to Alexander. Caesar had gone to England and come upon savages that opened his eyes with wonder—but these Britons were as ordinary to each other as Roman centurions were to Caesar. Balboa? What were his proud feelings as he looked for the first time at the Pacific? Just the same, that Ocean was as ordinary to a Central American Indian as the Mediterranean was to Balboa. But Leeuwenhoek? This janitor of Delft had stolen upon and peeped into a fantastic sub-visible world of little things, creatures that had lived, had bred, had battled, had died, completely hidden from and unknown to all men from the beginning of time. Beasts these were of a kind that ravaged and annihilated whole races of men ten million times larger than they were themselves. Beings these were, more terrible than fire-spitting dragons or hydra-headed monsters. They were silent assassins that murdered babes in warm cradles and kings in sheltered palaces. It was this invisible, insignificant, but implacable—and sometimes friendly—world that Leeuwenhoek had looked into for the first time of all men of all countries.

This was Leeuwenhoek's day of days. . . .—PAUL DE KRUIF, *Microbe Hunters*

(7)

The warm kitchen air was like a stupor. This was the steady heart of the house. Ghostly moonlight might wash up to the sill, fragile fancies pervade other rooms: here strong central life went calmly on. In the range red coals slept deep, covered and nourished for the long night. The tall boiler, its silvery paint flaked and dulled, gave off drowsy heat. Under the table the cat Virginia, who was not to be shocked, lay solidly upright with her paws tucked in, sated with scraps and vibrating a strong stupid purr. The high grimed ceiling was speckled with motionless flies, roosting there after a hard day. Packages of groceries, series of yellow bowls and platters, were ranged on the shelves in comfortable order. This was not a modern kitchen, shiny, white and sterile, like a hospital. It was old, ugly, inconvenient, strong with the memory of meals arduously prepared; meals of long ago, for people now vanished.[5]

4 Reprinted from *Peace of Mind* by permission of Simon and Schuster, Inc. Copyright, 1946, by Joshua Loth Liebman.
5 From *Thunder on the Left.* Copyright, 1925, by Christopher Morley. Published by J. B. Lippincott Company.

(8)

There are two philosophies of medicine: the primitive or superstitious, and the modern or rational. They are in complete opposition to one another. The former involves the belief that disease is caused by supernatural forces. Such a doctrine associates disease with sin; it is an aspect of religion which conceives diseases as due to certain forms of evil and attempts to control them by ceremonial and superstitious measures or to drive them away by wishful thinking. On the other hand, rational medicine is based on the conception that disease arises from natural causes; it associates sickness with ignorance. Civilized man tries to control the forces causing disease by material, not spiritualistic, means; he does not view disease as supernatural or the outcome of sin against moral laws, but rather as resulting from the violation of sanitary laws. He recognizes that knowledge is the sole means of preventing it. The measures he relies upon both to prevent and cure disease are those which have resulted from scientific investigation and which have been proved to be effective by experience.—HOWARD HAGGARD, *Devils, Drugs and Doctors*

(9)

I (to quit hiding behind the generalization of "the male") hate women because they almost never get anything exactly right. They say, "I have been faithful to thee, Cynara, after my fashion" instead of "in my fashion." They will bet you that Alfred Smith's middle name is Aloysius, instead of Emanuel. They will tell you to take the 2:57 train, on a day that the 2:57 does not run, or, if it does run, does not stop at the station where you are supposed to get off. Many men, separated from a woman by this particular form of imprecision, have never showed up in her life again. Nothing so embitters a man as to end up in Bridgeport, when he was supposed to get off at Westport.—JAMES THURBER, *Let Your Mind Alone*

(10)

Now, many civilized peoples have been content to accept their religion as a symbolic representation, tacitly if not openly. The Greeks and Romans took for granted that every people should have its own gods, and felt free to adopt foreign ones; the practical Chinese entertained hosts of deities, in a spirit of skepticism as well as hospitality; the deeply religious Hindus always assumed that Brahma had many different manifestations. All could respect the sacredness of other religions. The Western world, however, has had a radically different tradition. The Israelites introduced a very literal belief in a jealous God, who would tolerate no rivals. When Christianity took over the God of Israel, it intensified his concern with right belief; he punished not only the worship of other gods but erroneous opinion about his own unknowable nature. Mohammedanism, regarding itself as a purer form of these religions, was even more literal in its dogma.—HERBERT J. MULLER, *The Uses of the Past*

(11)

I went to the woods because I wished to live deliberately, to front only the essential facts of life, and see if I could not learn what it had to teach, and not, when I came to die, discover that I had not lived. I did not wish to live what was not life, living is so dear; nor did I wish to practise resignation, unless it was quite necessary.

I wanted to live deep and suck out all the marrow of life, to live so sturdily and Spartan-like as to put to rout all that was not life, to cut a broad swath and shave close, to drive life into a corner, and reduce it to its lowest terms, and, if it proved to be mean, why then to get the whole and genuine meanness of it, and publish its meanness to the world; or if it were sublime, to know it by experience, and be able to give a true account of it in my next excursion. For most men, it appears to me, are in a strange uncertainty about it, whether it is of the devil or of God, and have *somewhat hastily* concluded that it is the chief end of man here to "glorify God and enjoy Him forever."—HENRY THOREAU, *Walden*

(12)

Of late years a determined attempt has been made to rewrite history in economic terms. But this does not go deep enough. Man's thought and social life are built on his economic life; but this, in its turn, rests on biological foundations. Climate and geology between them decide where the raw materials of human industry are to be found, where manufactures can be established; and climate decides where the main springs of human energy shall be released. Changes of climate cause migrations, and migrations bring about not only wars, but the fertilizing intermingling of ideas necessary for rapid advance in civilization.—JULIAN HUXLEY, *Man in the Modern World*

(13)

It is obvious that the relation of teacher to pupil is an emotional one and most complex and unstable besides. To begin with, the motives, the forces that make teaching "go," are different on both sides of the desk. The pupil has some curiosity and he wants to know what grownups know. The master has curiosity also, but it is chiefly about the way the pupil's mind—or hand—works. Remembering his own efforts and the pleasure of discovery, the master finds a satisfaction which I have called artistic in seeing how a new human being will meet and make his own some part of our culture—our ways, our thoughts, even our errors and superstitions. This interest, however, does not last forever. As the master grows away from his own learning period, he also finds that mankind repeats itself. Fewer and fewer students appear new and original. They make the same mistakes at the same places and never seem to go very far into a subject which, for him, is still an expanding universe. Hence young teachers are best; they are the most energetic, most intuitive, and the least resented.—JACQUES BARZUN, *Teacher in America*

(14)

There are five ways to get wealth—to make it, to buy it, to find it, to have it given to you, and to steal it. Finding and giving are matters of chance or personal whim, and do not occur in any regular way. Stealing is frequently similar, and even when carefully organized on a large scale it is not recognized by society as a proper activity. Consequently, the science which deals with wealth limits itself to making and buying. This science is called economics.

The word "wealth" is used in the preceding paragraph, and all through this book, in a definite, scientific sense. In its broadest sense it may be considered to mean all material things that are, or by any possibility may be, useful to human beings, except their own bodies. It is customary, however, among students of economics to limit the definition of wealth to things that are owned by human beings, and this is logical because only things that are owned create economic problems. Let us, therefore, for the purposes of this book associate our definition of wealth invariably with the idea of ownership.—HENRY PRATT FAIRCHILD, *Economics for the Millions*

(15)

The tractors came over the roads and into the fields, great crawlers moving like insects, having the incredible strength of insects. They crawled over the ground, laying the track and rolling on it and picking it up. Diesel tractors, puttering while they stood idle; they thundered when they moved, and then settled down to a droning roar. Snub-nosed monsters, raising the dust and sticking their snouts into it, straight down the country, across the country, through fences, through dooryards, in and out of gullies in straight lines. They did not run on the ground, but on their own roadbeds. They ignored hills and gulches, water courses, fences, houses.

The man sitting in the iron seat did not look like a man; gloved, goggled, rubber dust mask over nose and mouth, he was a part of the monster, a robot in the seat. The thunder of the cylinders sounded through the country, became one with the air and the earth, so that earth and air muttered in sympathetic vibration. The driver could not control it—straight across country it went, cutting through a dozen farms and straight back. A twitch at the controls could swerve the cat', but the driver's hands could not twitch because the monster that built the tractor, the monster that sent the tractor out, had somehow got into the driver's hands, into his brain and muscle, had goggled him and muzzled him—goggled his mind, muzzled his speech, goggled his perception, muzzled his protest. He could not see the land as it was, he could not smell the land as it smelled; his feet did not stamp the clods or feel the warmth and power of the earth. He sat in an iron seat and stepped on iron pedals. He could not cheer or beat or curse or encourage the extension of his power, and because of this he could not cheer or whip or curse or encourage himself. He did not know or own or trust or beseech the land. If a seed dropped did not germinate, it was nothing. If the young thrusting plant withered in drought or drowned in a flood of rain, it was no more to the driver than to the tractor.—JOHN STEINBECK, *The Grapes of Wrath*

(16)

The civilized man has built a coach, but has lost the use of his feet. He is supported on crutches, but lacks so much support of muscle. He has a fine Geneva watch, but he fails of the skill to tell the hour by the sun. A Greenwich nautical almanac he has, and so being sure of the information when he wants it, the man in the street does not know a star in the sky. The solstice he does not observe, the equinox he knows as little; and the whole bright calendar of the year is without a dial in his mind. His note-books impair his memory; his libraries overload his wit; the insurance office increases the number of accidents; and it may be a question whether machinery does not encumber; whether we have not lost by refinement some energy, by a Christianity intrenched in establishments and forms, some vigor of wild virtue. For every Stoic was a Stoic; but in Christendom where is the Christian?—RALPH WALDO EMERSON, "Self-Reliance"

(17)

Religions, being products of different cultures, naturally differ in all kinds of ways: in their inherited symbols and ceremonials; in the ways in which they express their truths; in vestment, vessel, and architecture. These things are secondary. In relation to them we can show the same courtesy we would exhibit when we enter a home in a foreign land. The furniture of that home is different; the etiquette and language are different; but in their basic humanness, those who live in the foreign home and build their hopes, habits, and affections around it are people like ourselves. We can respect them as people.

It is so with the religions. Differences of outer form make no real difference if at the heart of each religion there is the belief that man is a creature of dignity whose proper destiny it is to grow into maturity of selfhood. We can live happily with any religion that grandly and staunchly holds to this belief. We cannot live happily with any other.—H. A. OVERSTREET, *The Mature Mind*

(18)

Consider how perfectly Harding met the requirements [of the Republican bosses in 1920]. Wilson was a visionary who liked to identify himself with "forward-looking men"; Harding, as Mr. Lowry put it, was as old-fashioned as those wooden Indians which used to stand in front of cigar stores, "a flower of the period before safety razors." Harding believed that statesmanship had come to its apogee in the days of McKinley and Foraker. Wilson was cold; Harding was an affable small-town man, at ease with "folks"; an ideal companion, as one of his friends expressed it, "to play poker with all Saturday night." Wilson had always been difficult of access; Harding was accessible to the last degree. Wilson favored labor, distrusted business men as a class, and talked of "industrial democracy"; Harding looked back with longing eyes to the good old days when the government didn't bother business men with unnecessary regulations, but provided them with fat tariffs and instructed the Department of Justice not to have them on its mind. Wilson was at loggerheads with Congress, and particularly with the Senate; Harding was not only a Senator, but a highly amenable Senator. Wilson had been adept at making enemies; Harding hadn't an enemy in the world. He was genuinely genial. "He had no knobs, he was the same size and smoothness all the way round," wrote Charles Willis Thompson. Wilson thought in terms of the whole world; Harding was for America first. And finally, whereas Wilson wanted America to exert itself nobly, Harding wanted to give it a rest. At Boston, a few weeks before the convention, he had correctly expressed the growing desire of the people of the country and at the same time had unwittingly added a new word to the language, when he said, "America's present need is not for heroics but healing; not nostrums but normalcy; not revolution but restoration; . . . not surgery but serenity." Here was a man whom a country wearied of moral obligations and the hope of the world could take to its heart.—FREDERICK LEWIS ALLEN, *Only Yesterday*

(19)

As a first approximation, we may say that science emerges from the other progressive activities of man to the extent that new concepts arise from experiments and observations, and the new concepts in turn lead to further experiments and observations. The case histories drawn from the last three hundred years show examples of fruitful and fruitless concepts. The texture of modern science is the result of the interweaving of the fruitful concepts. The test of a new idea is therefore not only its success in correlating the then-known facts but much more its success or failure in stimulating further experimentation or observation which in turn is fruitful. This dynamic quality of science viewed not as a practical undertaking but as development of conceptual schemes seems to me to be close to the heart of the best definition. It is this quality which can be demonstrated only by the historical approach, or else learned by direct professional experience.—JAMES B. CONANT, *On Understanding Science*

(20)

So, too, the lifelessness, the hopelessness, the despair of the winter sea are an illusion. Everywhere are the assurances that the cycle has come to the full, containing the means of its own renewal. There is the promise of a new spring in the very iciness of the winter sea, in the chilling of the water, which must, before many weeks, become so heavy that it will plunge downward, precipitating the overturn that is the first act in the drama of spring. There is the promise of new life in the small plant-like things that cling to the rocks of the underlying bottom, the almost formless polyps from which, in spring, a new generation of jellyfish will bud off and rise into the surface waters. There is unconscious purpose in the sluggish forms of the copepods hibernating on the bottom, safe from the surface storms, life sustained in their tiny bodies by the extra store of fat with which they went into this winter sleep. —RACHEL L. CARSON, *The Sea Around Us*

(21)

Looking at President Nixon's political accomplishments after his first year in the White House is like walking through a supermarket. The shelves, of course, are still being stocked and many remain empty, which doesn't make it easy to reach an overall judgment. But some of the wares are now on display. I can see new and promising policies of solid nutritious value that should be assets to the national diet. I can see some that have only been relabeled, some whose labels sound misleading, others whose packaging seems more important than the content. In some cases the cyclamate ingredient probably exceeds the standards established by the Food and Drug Administration; in others, the claims made for quality and weight might well arouse the suspicions of Mrs. Virginia Knauer, the redoubtable lady who looks after consumer interests. Altogether, looking over the shelves, I find it difficult to determine the store's buying policies.—HENRY BRANDON, "Nixon After the Honeymoon," *Saturday Review*

II. Read again the paragraphs used for illustration in the text of this chapter, and pick out the topic sentence or state the topic idea of each paragraph. Within the paragraph, what transitional devices does the author use?

Chapter 7

LANGUAGE
IN ACTION

We have considered a number of principles that underlie the working of language and the understanding and skillful use of English, and have discussed in some detail matters of sentence structure, paragraph development, and style. Now we are ready to examine the complex play and interplay of all these principles and techniques: to see how choice of words, choice of detail, concrete or abstract expression, figurative language, sentence structure, sentence length, organization, paragraph structure and length, slanting, factual meaning, and attitude work together in a composition of some scope to achieve the writer's intention. This chapter presents an example of language in action.

Properly to serve our purposes, the example to be analyzed should have certain characteristics: it should be written in informal or high informal English and addressed to an intelligent general audience; it should be developed with skill and subtlety, and should illustrate as many as possible of the principles of effective writing; it should deal with a topic of interest to college students, and should have something of significance to say. In short, it should be worthy of close examination both for its subject matter and its style.

We have chosen "The Business of a Biographer" by Catherine Drinker Bowen because it seems to us to meet these requirements. The essay, published in *The Atlantic Monthly* in 1951, recounts the author's experiences in preparing a book about John Adams and the American Revolution, and deals specifically with the biographer's business—his problems, procedures, techniques, and obligations. But Mrs. Bowen is also discussing matters that any writer must consider if he wants to write well. One of the problems she is concerned with is the perennial one of how to interest a reader. She not only states that a writer must be interesting—this, as we and other authors of rhetorics know, is easy to do; she puts her precepts into practice and demonstrates that it is possible to write interestingly about how to be interesting. Students who wish to improve their own writing can find the essay valuable for the light it throws on the craft of the writer.

"The Business of a Biographer" is printed on the left-hand pages of this chapter. The student should read the essay straight through, seeing the plan of development, responding to the whole effect, and *ignoring* the comments printed on the opposite pages. *After* his first reading, when he is ready to analyze the essay, he should examine it again, this time considering the comments and questions on the right-hand pages.

Mrs. Bowen (1897——) is a well-known biographer whose works include *Beloved Friend,* a life of Tchaikovsky; *Yankee from Olympus,* a biography of Justice Oliver Wendell Holmes; *The Lion and the Throne,* the life and times of Sir Edward Coke; *John Adams and the American Revolution;* and *Francis Bacon.* Among the honors she has received is the National Book Award for nonfiction.

THE BUSINESS OF A BIOGRAPHER*

CATHERINE DRINKER BOWEN

1

[1] Gertrude Stein once gave a talk before—oddly enough—the boys of Choate School. "It is the business of an artist," she told them, "to be exciting."
[2] It is the business also of an historian. History is, in its essence, exciting; to present it as dull is, to my mind, stark and unforgivable misrepresentation. And if history be, as Webster has it, the story of nations, biography the story of men—then by that same token, biography should prove, intrinsically, more exciting even than history. Biography is more immediately comprehensible; it is something our experience lets us know, in the Keatsian phrase, upon our pulses.
[3] Choice of subject is, for the biographer, a vital part of the total creative

---

* Copyright 1951, by the Atlantic Monthly Company, 8 Arlington Street, Boston 02116, Massachusetts.

COMMENTARY

on

"THE BUSINESS OF A BIOGRAPHER"

[1] The first two paragraphs of the essay could be combined in one paragraph, having as its topic idea the thesis that art, history, and biography are intrinsically exciting and should be made exciting. With her very short opening paragraph, however, Mrs. Bowen emphasizes the idea *exciting*, which is to be a recurrent theme in the essay. Gertrude Stein was a highly individualistic, experimental writer. Readers of the *Atlantic* could be expected to place this allusion and to find mildly humorous the thought of Gertrude Stein with a schoolboy audience. Thus the allusion and the comment *oddly enough* establish early a pleasant, informal reader-writer relationship.

[2] *It is the business also* links this paragraph to the first paragraph by repetition of key words and the connective *also*. Paragraph 2 supplies brief definitions and establishes the author's attitudes toward history and biography: *exciting* and *more exciting* are, of course, favorably charged expressions, and *stark and unforgivable misrepresentation* is an unfavorably charged locution applied to dull presentations of history. Thus far, most of Mrs. Bowen's sentences have been short and have begun with the subject and verb. Sentence 3 in this paragraph (*And if history be . . . .*) is somewhat longer, and it varies the sentence pattern; it begins with a subordinate clause containing the definitions, and emphasizes the idea that biography should prove even more exciting than history, by expressing this idea in the main clause at the end of the sentence. The tone of *to my mind* and *our experience lets us know* continues to establish a personal, informal reader-writer relationship. How would you paraphrase *something our experience lets us know . . . upon our pulses?*

[3] In this paragraph the author suggests the general chronological organization of the essay: she will start with her choice of subject—itself determined by her interest

effort. Sometimes it is not even an individual that lights the biographical spark, but only a period in history. Such was, for example, my own experience with my last book, *John Adams and the American Revolution*. I had published three biographies set in the nineteenth century, and each of them had spilled over, at its outset, into an earlier period. With each I had been given a glimpse, tantalizing, provocative, into the Century of Enlightenment, that Century of Reason—extraordinary and vivid time when our American world was young and yeasty, when men of faith, men of intellect and staunchest character, threw down a king and fashioned a government to their very liking. "When, before the present epocha," wrote John Adams to his friend Wythe in 1775, "had three millions of people full power and fair opportunity to form and establish the wisest and happiest government that human wisdom can contrive?"

[4]   Reading those words, I had felt a stirring at the roots of my hair. Exciting? . . . I remembered a young historian, the ink yet damp upon his doctoral thesis, who had said to me with all the vigor and confidence of his twenty-odd years, "Now I have my training, I'm going to write and make some money. I'm not going to teach. I plan to take—well, some period of history, and *hop it up* the way you biographers do."

[5]   Hopping up, I learned, is done with morphine, marihuana. But we biographers do not hop up history!—I told my young friend quickly. Does one hop up the Rocky Mountains, or a hibiscus flower? On the contrary, we ourselves are moved by this astonishment of height, this redness of red; we desire to reproduce this astonishment, this good news granted by earth or sky. So it is with history, if one be history-minded, and so it was with me when first I read John Adams's letters, his essay *On the Canon and Feudal Law,* his legal brief in defense of the British soldiers on trial for their lives after the Boston Massacre. The life of any active man reflects his times, and with Adams this is peculiarly, startlingly true. Nothing that he said, nothing he did could have been said or done in any other era.

[6]   Adams's philosophy, moreover, was extraordinarily pertinent to the times in which I found myself living at the moment. This was February, 1945, and America was fighting a war. To our deeply troubled minds there had already been introduced, that spring, ideological problems which were to come after the war: problems of government, of federation. What, we had begun to ask ourselves, is the meaning of sovereignty? I wanted to study history through the eyes of a man interested in these problems, a man conscious of the word federation—a word that may well bring states or nations from the constant fear of war to the joyful practice of peace.

[7]   John Adams from his twentieth year was a student of law, a student of governments past and present. He was a constitution maker. Even before Independence was declared, he taught the various colonies how to compose their several state governments. Adams put, in short, a canvas bottom under

in the Eighteenth Century—and later proceed chronologically through her five years of work on the biography. Words like *tantalizing, provocative, extraordinary,* and *vivid* continue to express her feeling about history and biography. What is the difference in meaning between *tantalizing* and *provocative?* Sentence 5 (*With each I had been given a glimpse . . . .*) conveys feeling not only by choice of words but also by sentence length and rhythm; notice the use of appositives (*that Century of Reason—extraordinary and vivid time . . . .*) and of parallelism (*when our American world . . . when men of faith . . . .*). In its context, *yeasty,* in sentence 5, is a metaphor. Explain its appropriateness here. Do you like the alliteration of *young and yeasty?* What is the meaning of *very* in the phrase *very liking?*

[4] *Reading those words* links paragraph 4 to paragraph 3, and the one-word incomplete sentence *Exciting?* reiterates and emphasizes a major theme. In four paragraphs Mrs. Bowen has directly or indirectly quoted five people (Gertrude Stein, Webster, Keats, John Adams, the young historian); this habit of quotation is a characteristic of her style that will be even more apparent in later sections of the essay. The quotations, skillfully woven into the account of the biographer's work, give the impression of a mind that absorbs and relates materials from reading and from experience. Consider the implication and the tone of the expression (sentence 3) *the ink yet damp upon his doctoral thesis.*

[5] The expressions *hopping up* and *hop up,* explained both by context and by the first sentence of the paragraph, are shifts from the high informal English used in most of the essay. What are the purpose and effect of the shift in levels? The concrete comparison of history to the Rocky Mountains and a hibiscus flower expresses in another way the attitude toward history already expressed. Sentence 4 (*On the contrary . . . .*) contains some interesting attitudinal and figurative language: *this astonishment of height, this redness of red . . . this good news granted by earth and sky;* the last phrase is another appositive structure. The last sentences of the paragraph deal with the author's early reading, before her final choice of a subject; they also introduce an idea that has been suggested earlier and will be developed later— that John Adams was in a special way a man of his time.

[6] Paragraph 6 is a paragraph of reasons for Mrs. Bowen's interest in John Adams. Notice the position of connectives and modifiers in the paragraph; *moreover* (sentence 1), *To our deeply troubled minds* (sentence 3), *that spring* (sentence 3), and *we had begun to ask ourselves* (sentence 4) might all occupy different positions in the sentences in which they appear. What are the alternative positions, and why do you think the author arranged the sentence elements as she did? How would you explain the meaning of *sovereignty* as the word is used in sentence 4? Of *ideological* in sentence 3? The last sentence in the paragraph contains two appositive structures, one following the other. The expression *from the constant fear of war to the joyful practice of peace* is an example of balance and antithesis (the expression of contrasting ideas in parallel and balanced structures). Why is *joyful practice of peace* a better phrase than "joyful time of peace"?

[7] This short paragraph has a particular-to-general organization. Three of its four sentences begin *John Adams, He, Adams;* notice that sentence 3 breaks the pattern with a subordinate clause preceding the same subject, *he.* Visualize the figure of speech in the last sentence—the guy ropes to Britain, the canvas bottom that kept the colonies from falling through to chaos. Is the main idea clear? Does the figure

the American Revolution, so that when the guy ropes to Britain were cast off, the colonies did not fall through to chaos, bloodshed, and a new paternalism. [8]   Casting about, before my choice was fully made, I read the published biographies of Adams. There are not many, only five or six. I looked up Adams in the biographical dictionaries; I paged through the nine large volumes called *Life and Works of John Adams,* edited in the 1850s by John's grandson, Charles Francis Adams, our Minister to England during the Civil War. I read such published letters as I could find, notably those to Benjamin Rush of Philadelphia, to John Winthrop of Massachusetts who was Adams's teacher of mathematics at Harvard in the 1750s. I read the superb correspondence with Thomas Jefferson when the two were old men, living in retirement. I lingered long over the little volume called *Familiar Letters of John Adams and his Wife, during the Revolution.* I read also the letters of John's daughter Abigail and the later letters of John's wife, written during John's presidency. I went through most of the books written by John's descendants —and the Adamses of Massachusetts were a writing tribe. *The Education of Henry Adams* tells much about Braintree, where John's boyhood was spent; so do the biographies and autobiographies of the various Charles Francises and the eight-volume *Memoirs* written by John's eldest son, John Quincy Adams, sixth President of the United States.

[9]   All doubts fled. I had chosen my hero—or more exactly, he had chosen me. I knew by now the basic facts of Adams's life; it would be for me as biographer to make the facts live. Should this high aim be achieved, I was aware it would be due not alone to the manner of presentation but to the manner of research. Reading hundreds of books and manuscripts, how does the biographer know which passages to copy down? He doesn't know, he guesses, and the instinct behind his guess can make or mar the finished product. It is laborious work, this copying in research libraries, hour after hour and day after day, using a soft pencil for the sake of one's wrist and begging the librarian for a table by the daylight.

[10]   In this process of research, I employ no helpers, no apprentices, no Ph.D. students to do my reading for me, nor even the subsequent filing and cross-filing of notes. It would be dangerous; something vital might be overlooked. Painting a portrait, does the artist hire an apprentice to choose his colors, decide the pose in which the subject will sit or the texture of the frame in which the portrait will hang? This copying in libraries, this eventual choice of incident is half the biographical battle, perhaps more than half. While the biographer reads, he is actually in process of composition; he recites passages to his friends on the telephone, he talks continually of his great discoveries.

[11]   Selection of material depends, of course, on the type of biography one intends to write. The choice here is plain. Either one desires to dig out and reveal hitherto unpublished material, thereby gaining kudos in the academic

seem to you effective? Might paragraph 7 be combined with paragraph 6, or is there good reason for making it a separate paragraph?

[8]   Paragraph 8, a paragraph of concrete particulars, serves a double purpose: it describes the author's continued preliminary reading—part of the process of choosing her subject; and it supplies the reader with information, some of which will be referred to later, about sources and about the Adams family. Some students are unreasonably reluctant to use the pronoun *I*, but Mrs. Bowen has used it nine times in this paragraph. What purpose is served by this repetition? In paragraph 8 the author needs to use *read* (or a word of similar meaning) very frequently, and there is danger of tiresome repetition or of over-obvious efforts to find synonyms. Skim the paragraph to see how she handled her problem.

[9]   In the chronological development of the essay, paragraph 9 completes one phase of the writing process, choosing the subject, and introduces the next, the actual research. Paragraphs 10, 11, and 12 deal with other aspects of research. The five short independent clauses that open paragraph 9 are followed by a semiperiodic complex sentence (*Should this high aim be achieved . . . .*). The paragraph, though not long, combines several methods of paragraph development: cause-effect, question-to-answer, and general-to-particular arrangement. Note the frequent repetition in the paragraph: *chosen . . . chosen* (sentence 2), *facts . . . facts* (sentence 3), *manner . . . manner* (sentence 4), *know . . . know* (sentences 5 and 6), *guesses . . . guess* (sentence 6). Do you consider this repetition desirable or undesirable?

[10]   *In this process of research* is a clear transition from paragraph 9 into paragraph 10. The comparison (also an analogy) of the biographer and the portrait-painter makes concrete the topic idea that the biographer must do all his own work because research is part of composition. Mrs. Bowen mentions the artist's colors, the pose of the subject, and the texture of the frame in which the portrait will hang. What are, or what might be, the equivalents of these three things in a biographical portrait? The author will make further use of the biography-portrait analogy later. She has a way of introducing an idea briefly and then building on it in a later passage.

[11]   In this paragraph of contrast, the author defines and describes the type of biography she proposed to write. What is the meaning and suggestion of *kudos* in sentence 3? How else does Mrs. Bowen slant in favor of one type of biography and against the other type? What part of the context helps to make clear the distinction between what is historically "new" and what is biographical *news*?

world (with a likely raise from assistant professor of history to a full professor-
ship)—or one desires to write a book that will be bought and read. My ambition, quite frankly, was to introduce John Adams to as many people as I could.
Repeatedly, during research, I reminded myself of this aim. Otherwise, I
might be tempted into following false clues, spend precious hours copying
some incident which, while it may have been historically "new," was patently
not biographical *news*—a matter altogether different. Whatever did not stand
as illustration of Adams's character or Adams's part in forming the American
States, must be thrown out. There were times indeed, when I almost wept with
vexation, putting broken manuscripts, faded newspaper columns from me on
the library table, or turning them face down against temptation.

[12]   So strongly did I hold to this purpose that in my first year of reading
I wrote it out, filing it in the folder marked *Preface to Book:* "The facts on
which my narrative is based are available to everyone. I do not scorn what
the academic historian calls secondary material, or tertiary or septuagenary
—so long as it is proven authentic. I aim not to startle with new material but
to persuade with old, and I shall use a narrative form because for me it is the
most persuasive. Fictionalized biography is the current label; I myself do not
admit a phrase which, besides being doubtful English, does not express what
I am trying to do. Call this book, rather, a 'portrait' of John Adams. I shall
draw a portrait, and like Saint-Mémin with his profiles, I shall use the *physionotrace:* I shall find instruments with which to measure, and then go ahead
and paint. In brief, I shall study the available evidence and on the basis of it,
build pictures which to me are consistent with the evidence. All my reading,
all my research will be directed toward two goals: the understanding of John
Adams's character; and the understanding of how it felt to be a citizen of the
Eighteenth Century."

2

[13]   The contract with my publishers allowed me five years; I sat down and
portioned carefully the time that remained. I would give myself two full
reading years, then twelve months to write out what I call the *chronology*
of my narrative—that is, a straight, unvarnished succession of facts, names,
dates which trace my hero's movement from place to place. Knowing where
one's hero is at each given week—if not each day—is the first necessity in
biography, and by no means easy to achieve. There would be, I knew, gaps of
weeks and even months when I should lose John Adams between Braintree
and Boston as dismally as though he had journeyed to Samarcand.

[14]   So much for three years. The remaining two, I could devote to brooding about John Adams. I could think of him as walking, talking, studying,
riding circuit, arguing cases in court, or resting at Braintree with his family.
I could determine upon those scenes which best would illustrate character
and times; I could cease collecting facts and begin visualizing my subject in

[12]   The opening sentence links paragraphs 11 and 12 with the reference *this purpose,* and makes clear that Mrs. Bowen will further discuss the aim described in paragraph 11. The closely-related material is probably put into two paragraphs rather than one because paragraph 12 contains a later and more precisely-formulated statement. If you have read Chapter 3 of this book, you will recognize the quoted passage in paragraph 12 as an elaborate version of the "statement of purpose" recommended for student themes. Mrs. Bowen will later say more about the "narrative form" of biography; here she is briefly defining, by negation, contrast, and restatement, the kind of portrait she hopes to draw. In the third sentence (*I do not scorn . . . .*) what does *septuagenary* mean? Why did the author use it instead of a simpler expression? Notice that she here develops further the biography-portrait analogy introduced earlier. (Saint-Mémin was a French-American artist who engraved profile portraits of many distinguished Americans in the early Nineteenth Century.) Since the term *fictionalized biography* is frequently applied to biography that takes liberties with facts in the manner of the historical novel, it is not surprising that Mrs. Bowen rejects the label as inapplicable to what she is trying to do.

In the first section of the essay, the author has established her theme that the business of a biographer is to be exciting; and she has discussed the first "biographical spark," her preliminary reading, her final choice of a subject, her general method of research, and the controlling purpose, formulated in the first year, which would determine her selection of material and her method of presentation. Paragraph 12 and section 1 of the essay end strongly with the statement, in parallel structure, of the double goal foreshadowed earlier, in paragraphs 3–7: *the understanding of John Adams's character; and the understanding of how it felt to be a citizen of the Eighteenth Century.*

[13]   If part of the "business" of a biographer is being exciting, another part is the painstaking preparation for the actual writing of the book. In section 2 Mrs. Bowen begins a closer analysis of the very practical "business" of planning, and of finding, recording, and absorbing material. Paragraph 13, like many of the author's paragraphs, begins with the topic sentence; it analyzes the work of the first three years, with emphasis on the necessity, and the difficulty, of knowing where one's hero is at a given time. The last sentence of the paragraph would be clear if it read: "There would be, I knew, gaps of weeks and even months when I should lose John Adams." What does the last half of the sentence as Mrs. Bowen has written it contribute to the meaning?

[14]   *So much for three years,* a transitional expression written as a sentence, leads into the work of the last two years. The second sentence of the paragraph is an example of inverted order, with the object (*the remaining two*) placed before the subject and verb so that *three years* and *the remaining two* are in close sequence. Mrs. Bowen uses concrete particulars to develop her "brooding" about John Adams, and at the same time restates and develops the statement of purpose at the end of section 1: *character and times* echoes the double goal of understanding John Adams and understanding how it felt to be a citizen of the Eighteenth Century; the plan to interweave Adams and history further expands the goal; and *determine upon those*

terms of action. My story would have a protagonist as well as a hero: the United States of America was my protagonist. Its birth, its growth moved parallel with Adams's own coming of age. I must weave and interweave, move from Adams to history, from history to Adams. . . . To accomplish this, twenty-four months seemed all too short—twenty-four months to write my book.

[15] My schedule determined, I ploughed into the second year of research, traveling about the country to interview Adamses when they would permit it, and to interview historians for the exchange of ideas concerning govern-ment practical and theoretical. In the end, I found myself the possessor of hundreds of slips of yellow paper, cut to half the size of ordinary typewriter paper and covered with writing, the source carefully copied on the upper left-hand corner. My first files were chronological, with the exception of cer-tain large subjects such as *Boston, streets and buildings* . . . or, *Washington, George* . . . or, *Philadelphia, appearance of* . . . or, *Statistics of Population, 1700–1776.* Or, simply and quite terrifyingly, the file marked IDEAS.

[16] I began to cross-file again, narrowing my chronology from decades to years, then to months, weeks, days, meanwhile committing to memory as many facts as I could, in the hope they would pop up at the needed moment. (In 1774, the Province of New York ordered *Liberty and Prudence* as the watermark for its official letter paper. In 1745, New England men sent 9000 cannon balls into Louisburg before the fortress surrendered.) The work fell of itself into three divisions: (1) Research about *things.* That is, how did the streets of Braintree look in 1745, in '65, in '74? How did John Adams's mother dress, what did Harvard students of the mid-Eighteenth Century eat and drink, what outdoor games did they play? (2) Research about *people,* their characters, affiliations, actions, beliefs. And (3) research about *ideas,* those philosophies and principles by which the Eighteenth Century lived, wrote its books, and created its governments.

[17] For the physical scene I found it necessary to visit Braintree in all four seasons. In the small tidy farmhouse where John was born, I went up narrow stairs, looked out a boy's dormer window onto February snow. I walked by Black's Creek when November held the salt grass stiff. John's great-great-granddaughter walked with me to show how she too had gone smelting in childhood between those marshy banks. I climbed Penn's Hill in June as Abigail Adams had climbed it to see the Battle of Bunker Hill across the Bay. In Boston, the old State House still stands, and in Philadelphia, Independence Hall. All the bustle of the twentieth century cannot efface the spirits that walk within these walls.

3

[18] But I spent far less time on the physical scene than on that other, harder quest. The Eighteenth Century is not to be trifled with. What made

scenes and *visualizing my subject in terms of action* further explain the narrative form. The terms *protagonist* and *hero* commonly designate the same thing—the main character in a drama, novel, or story. What seems to be the difference in meaning between the words as Mrs. Bowen uses them? Notice that the choice of these words, suggestive of dramatic action, supports the initial theme that biography should be exciting. What technique is used to give the paragraph an emphatic ending?

[15] Like many of the paragraphs in the essay, this one develops a general idea (*second year of research*) with concrete particulars and examples. The opening sentences are good illustrations of cutting clauses. Ideas incorporated in the first sentence are: My schedule was determined. I ploughed into the second year. I traveled about the country. I interviewed Adamses. . . . I interviewed historians. We exchanged ideas concerning government. . . . Notice how many possible clauses are similarly cut to phrases in sentence 2. In these two sentences, do you agree with the author's choice of the most important idea for expression in the main clause? If you have written research papers, following the procedure of taking notes on slips or cards, Mrs. Bowen's system of recording the source of her information and organizing her notes under headings will be familiar. The incomplete sentence that ends the paragraph is part of the *or . . . or* series in the preceding sentence, and might have been attached to that sentence. Is there good reason for writing it as a separate sentence? For writing *ideas* in capital letters?

[16] Dealing with the next phase of research, paragraph 16 is developed by concrete examples and analysis of the three divisions into which the research fell. Some of the examples of the facts to be ascertained or memorized seem inconsequential. What is the effect of including this kind of example?

[17] This paragraph, an expansion of division (1) in the preceding paragraph (research about things), may seem, in a first reading, to lack unity: the opening sentence, about visits to Braintree, seems to be the topic sentence, to be developed with details about the visits; but the last two sentences shift to Boston and Philadelphia. What is the topic idea of the paragraph? This is a particularly good example of packed writing. The concrete details enable the reader to visualize the farmhouse, the stiff salt grass, the marshy banks of the creek, etc. More importantly, perhaps, they communicate the author's sense of involvement in her living materials as she looks out John Adams's dormer window, walks with John's great-great-granddaughter where he walked and went smelting, climbs Penn's Hill as Abigail Adams climbed it during the battle of Bunker Hill, and feels the living spirits in the old State House and Independence Hall.

We have made little comment thus far on the variety, usually a subtle variety, in the author's sentences. In paragraph 17, sentence 1, a simple sentence, has a short phrase before its main clause. Sentence 2 opens with a phrase and a subordinate clause, followed by the main clause with a compound predicate. Sentences 3, 4, and 5 all begin with the subject and verb and have a subordinate clause following the main clause; but these similarly constructed sentences are varied in length (12, 19, and 22 words) and in the use of modifiers. The short (13 words) next-to-last sentence begins with a phrase and is a compound sentence, though the second clause is elliptical—the predicate, *still stands*, is understood but not expressed. The last sentence is complex, with the main clause at the beginning; it ends strongly with the alliterative phrase *walk within these walls.*

The paragraph makes an emphatic section ending, both because it is good in de-

that century different from our own was not man's clothing but his out-
look, his view of body and soul—a view so altered by time that only deepest
immersion, a deliberate, disciplined shutting of the eyes would bring it back.
Later, I was to say so, in an essay on *Sources and Methods* that was included
in my bibliography. I mailed it to my publishers with the completed manuscript. Back, in due time, came my galley proofs from Boston, with an editorial query on the margin, "Author: Don't you mean *opening* of the eyes?"
[19]   I did not mean opening, and said so by return mail. I meant a closing
of the eyes, a shutting out of our boasted scientific "progress." . . . In John
Adams's day, Galen's four fluid humours still governed the body—the
sanguine, the phlegmatic, the choleric, the melancholic. Harvard in 1751
debated the truth of Copernicus's theory. The narrowing of one's mind to
this strange constriction is a struggle painful, almost impossible. The Age
of Enlightenment has tales to tell that wash our world away. Gone are
Pasteur, Lister, and the germ theory of disease. Gone is Darwin. Special
creation, spontaneous generation rule the universe. Newton, Descartes, Bacon,
Harvey have not yet obliterated the long medieval darkness. Over our shoulders peer Ramus, Abélard and the schoolmen, with Fra Castoreus and Meister
Eckhart.
[20]   It is another world, and the biographer must somehow enter it. To
help on that awful journey, I sought every avenue that offered, spending
hours in the map rooms of libraries, to familiarize myself with old Braintree,
old Boston, old Worcester, with the Great Plymouth highway running down
from the north and with the Connecticut River that divided Massachusetts
of 1750 almost as the Mississippi divides our country today. Searching for the
faces, the authentic features of my subjects, I combed museums, art reference
libraries, print rooms, comparing an Adams nose by Copley with an Adams
nose by Stuart and deciding, in the end, that Saint-Mémin's physionotrace
was more trustworthy than the draughtsmanship of the masters. As for
Eighteenth Century newspapers, that gossipy sheet called *The Boston Gazette*
became more recognizable to me than the New York *Times* for 1950. I
could even distinguish between the anonymous gentlemen who wrote for
the newspapers (most of whom turned out to be Sam Adams).
[21]   In the Boston Public Library, I found some three thousand volumes
from John Adams's own collection. I took them from the shelves, read
John's inked marginal notes, and what I read made me laugh aloud. An
impudent scholar surely, this Adams, of the sort that Carlyle calls "original
men, the first peculiarity of which is that they in some measure *converse with
the universe at first hand.*"
[22]   Taking stock, I saw that I was done with the period of intensive
reading; it was time to give shape to what I had found. Nevertheless I was
troubled; it is a crisis which every writer longs for and every scholar fears.
I wanted to read more, learn more, even copy more; the file marked *Things*

tail and in style, and because the closing sentences evoke the spirits of John Adams
and the United States—hero and protagonist.

[18] The first two sentences of this paragraph carry the reader smoothly from the
physical scene discussed in the preceding paragraph to other aspects of the
Eighteenth Century. The transition causes one to wonder, though, about the reason
for starting a new section here. Section 2 has outlined the research to be done and
shown the author in quest of one kind of knowledge; section 3 recounts the continued quest up to the end of the time allotted to research and reading. Sections 2
and 3 seem, therefore, to be logically a single section of the essay; and, incidentally,
their combined length is approximately that of each of the other sections. It looks as
though Mrs. Bowen liked paragraph 17 (as we do) and wanted to give it additional
emphasis by ending a section with it. The section break also throws emphasis on
the "harder quest," for understanding of the Eighteenth Century.

In paragraph 18, two short sentences are followed by a long sentence that states
the topic idea of this paragraph and paragraph 19; notice the use of appositives in
this sentence, and the figures of speech in *deepest immersion, a deliberate, disciplined shutting of the eyes.* In what sense are *immersion* and *shutting of the eyes* in
logical as well as grammatical apposition? The three shorter sentences at the end of
the paragraph are varied in structure and in sentence beginnings: the first of the
three has an adverb preceding the subject-predicate; the second begins subject-verb-
object; the third begins with two adverbial modifiers followed by verb and then
subject.

[19] This paragraph could be attached to paragraph 18, since it continues the
discussion of closing of the eyes, and since it expands with concrete particulars the
topic sentence or idea of paragraph 18. The paragraph break may be justified
because it emphasizes the metaphor of the shutting rather than the opening of the
eyes.

Paragraph 19 is stylistically interesting in two ways: the sentences are uniformly
short and emphatic—the longest, which lists the four humours, is 20 words and the
others range from 3 to 15 words; and the author uses a number of inversions. The
verb precedes the subject in *Gone are Pasteur . . . , Gone is Darwin,* and *Over our
shoulders peer Ramus . . . .* Natural order in the fifth sentence would be "The
narrowing . . . to this strange constriction is a painful, almost impossible struggle,"
but Mrs. Bowen writes *struggle painful, almost impossible.* What do the sentence
length and the inversions contribute to the meaning of the paragraph? The sentence
The Age of Enlightenment has tales to tell that wash our world away is interesting
for its use of alliteration (*tales to tell, wash our world away*); for the figure *wash;*
and for the use of *Age of Enlightenment* instead of Eighteenth Century—is this
meant to be ironical? What is the meaning today of *sanguine, phlegmatic, choleric,*
and *melancholic,* and how did the words come to have these meanings? See your
dictionary. Can you explain *special creation* and *spontaneous generation?*

[20] Having said that her research fell into three divisions—research about things,
about people, and about ideas—the author has given details about her study of the
physical scene (paragraph 17), and details about the ideas of the Eighteenth Century
(paragraph 19), but has said nothing directly about people. In paragraphs 20 and 21
we have a discussion of her research which includes things, people, and ideas. Notice,
at the beginning of paragraph 20, the travel figure (a sustained metaphor) in

to do was not exhausted by half. The temptation was great and insidious;
I had witnessed historians who went on digging up facts until they grew
too old to write their books at all. In a New England library I had met two
learned professors, deep in manuscript and notebooks—beautiful, lined
notebooks, with *Category A* and *Category B* traced in red ink and black.
Each professor took me out to lunch, kindly showed me his notes, and
confided with a sigh, "How I dread the day when I finish reading in libraries
and have to put all this material together and write my book!"

[23] It is, indeed, a common occupational disease of historians. When I
feel it stealing over me, I remind myself of what Justice Holmes told one
of his secretaries: "There comes a time, young feller, when a book has to be
written!"

[24] For me the time had come.

4

[25] For the actual writing of my tale, modern biography offered two
literary forms: the critical and the narrative. In the first, the author remains
eternally present, telling the reader what to think and bolstering all pronouncements with quotations from the original source, or leaving a shrewd
margin for error by employing such phrases as, "We consider . . . the
records tell us . . . it is probable that . . ."

[26] The bulk of my biography would have no such handy props. Choice
of the narrative form had set upon me an extra burden, an extra technical
procedure; I must make my characters three-dimensional instead of two. It
was the artist's task as distinct from the scholar's—and *it is the business of
an artist to be exciting.* The words went over in my mind, and there were
hours when the cold hand of fear lay on me.

[27] I could not, for instance, employ the frank critical statement that my
hero in youth was shy, nor quote a reminiscent Adams acquaintance in proof
of shyness. The reminiscence was penned thirty years later, when Adams
had become the reverse of shy. To quote it would destroy utterly the illusion
of reality, the hard-won empathy, immediacy, the sense of being *there.* How
then, could I convey to my reader the fact that John was shy? Only in one
way: I must show him being shy. From John's *Autobiography,* written half
a century after the event, I had learned briefly of that fateful day when
the boy, at sixteen, journeyed ten miles from Braintree to take his examinations for Harvard College. Quite obviously, those were, for John, fearful
and significant hours. I must transcribe them; I must translate them from
reminiscence to reality. I must let my reader travel to Cambridge with John,
walk invisible beside his pony, trudge with him across Harvard Yard and
up the steps to face his four examiners and that large, handsome, distin-

another world, enter it, journey, every avenue. What is the meaning of *awful* in sentence 2? Is the word appropriate in its context? The paragraph is developed by particularization of *every avenue that offered.* We have commented on the short sentences in paragraph 19: 11, 15, 20, 9, 15, 13, 10, 3, 7, 12, and 15 words. In contrast, the sentences in paragraph 20 are 11, 58, 47, 24, and 22 words long. How is the length of sentences 2 and 3 suited to the content? The reference to Saint-Mémin's physionotrace echoes Mrs. Bowen's statement of purpose at the end of section 1. Samuel Adams, a cousin of John, was a leader in the American Revolution and a signer of the Declaration of Independence. What is the purpose of the parenthetical reference to him?

[21] Mrs. Bowen is still talking about research in libraries. Is there any reason for splitting this short paragraph from the related material in paragraph 20? What facts about John Adams does the paragraph communicate? What attitudes toward him? How would you paraphrase the italicized phrase from Carlyle?

[22] [23] [24] These three paragraphs have a single topic idea: that the time for actual writing had come and that it was a difficult time. What purpose is served by breaking what could be a single paragraph into three? In particular, does the single-sentence last paragraph seem justified in context? The last part of sentence 2 (paragraph 22) is a good example of balance: *every writer longs for and every scholar fears.* The difficulty of beginning the actual writing is developed with three illustrations: historians who grow too old to write their books, the two professors with their notebooks, the statement of Justice Holmes. How do the three illustrations differ? Is the difference relevant to the paragraphing the author uses? In sentence 4 of paragraph 22, what does *insidious* mean? In the last sentence of paragraph 23, what is the effect of Justice Holmes's use of *feller* instead of *fellow?*

[25] [26] *For the actual writing* links paragraph 25 and section 4 to the preceding material and introduces the next phase of the whole process of composition. It is soon apparent, however, that section 4 itself does not follow a strict chronological pattern; it is an analysis of the obligations and problems imposed by the narrative form. Paragraphs 25 and 26 could be one paragraph contrasting the critical and narrative forms; the only reason for breaking them into two seems to be to sharpen the contrast. The writing is quite heavily charged here; by what unfavorably and favorably charged words does the author make narrative biography seem preferable to critical? *It is the business of an artist to be exciting* is, of course, a repetition of the theme introduced early in the essay. *Cold hand of fear,* in the last sentence of paragraph 26, is a personification and might be considered a cliché. Does it seem unduly trite as it is used here? In the same sentence what is meant by *the words went over in my mind?*

[27] Paragraph 27 clarifies by concrete illustration the difference between the critical and narrative forms stated in more general terms in the two preceding paragraphs. It is both informative and persuasive in its effect, since the reader can feel for himself the difference between simply being told that young Adams was shy, and being taken with him through his experiences at Harvard. Here, as elsewhere, the packed concrete detail makes the paragraph interesting; so does the quality of the writing, particularly the techniques of emphasis and variety. Sentence 3 ("To quote it would destroy utterly the illusion of reality, the hard-won empathy, immediacy,

guished, and terrifying individual, President Holyoke of Harvard College. It was not for me to write, "We can therefore imagine John's feelings as he confronted the President of Harvard." I must do more than that, I must stand with my reader before that polished desk; with John I must answer the questions put in Latin, with John freeze to paralysis when he cannot recall the Latin word for *morality.*

[28]   And in my method will be no deception. The reader knows I am not God, knows I cannot actually be inside John's mind—and knows by now, I sincerely trust, that behind my narrative is historical source and historical evidence without which I would not presume to take young Adams to Harvard Hall or anywhere else. Should the evidence anywhere conflict, I shall sacrifice my narrative. Experience tells me I must forever be prepared for such sacrifice, not in large things—the facts of our Revolutionary history are by now well ascertained—but in those small descriptive details that bring a scene alive. When first I wrote of young Adams's journey to Cambridge, for instance, I had him walk the ten miles on foot, alone and frightened. The very act of walking seemed characteristic of his mood. When I discovered he had a pony, it altered somehow the very climate of the journey.

[29]   In this connection, when five of my Adams chapters appeared serially in the *Atlantic,* I received a letter from a distinguished college professor, himself a biographer. He approved my chapters, he said cordially. "I wish," he went on, "to take advantage of your research. But I am puzzled. You have written Adams's conversation in such a manner that I cannot tell which words he actually spoke. In the published volume, will your documentation support these conversations?"

[30]   I told the professor that it would be for him rather than for me to say if my published bibliography proved adequate. My own conscience was clear. Each public utterance of John's, whether a speech in Congress, an essay in the *Boston Gazette,* or a legal brief used in court, was historical, actual, directly from source even if paraphrased. My ambition had been to persuade people to read historic documents such as Adams's essay *On the Canon and Feudal Law,* his *Instructions to the Braintree Representatives in 1765.* It was, indeed, more than an ambition with me; it was an obsession. Americans must know these glorious pages, these inspired paragraphs.

[31]   Unfortunately for the biographer, readers will not suffer lengthy quotations. At sight of set-in paragraphs, readers flee; they are gone, lost, the book is closed. The thought was awful to me. I must devise ways, I must lend a hand to my readers. . . . Could not James Otis, sitting in the *Gazette* office, read aloud the best lines from some long-drawn page? Or John himself, riding down from circuit court in Falmouth, rehearse his forthcoming essay *On the Canon and Feudal Law?* Or Sam Adams, journey-

the sense of being *there"*) is an example of emphasis by the repetition of closely related ideas, and also of climactic arrangement; try moving *the sense of being there*
to another place in the series and see the loss of emphasis. In this sentence, what
does *empathy* mean? The seven repetitions of *I must* convey a sense of obligation to
make the material immediate to the reader. Sentences in the paragraph are varied in
length—27, 15, 19, 14, 10, 35, 10, 12, 43, 20, 40 words—and also in structure. One
kind of structural variety is the question-answer pattern (*How then, could I convey
to my reader the fact that John was shy? I must show him being shy.*). Another is
the use of parallelism as in the sentence beginning *I must let my reader travel to
Cambridge . . . .* In the last sentence of the paragraph, the first two *I must* clauses
are run together with only a comma between them. Do you see a reason for this
punctuation? In the last part of the sentence, the structure is varied by putting *with
John* before the subject and verb *I must answer,* and another *with John,* for emphasis, before the second verb, *freeze.* In the last clause of this last sentence, why is
cannot recall a better form of the verb than *could not recall?*
[28]   Paragraphs do not usually begin with *and.* The connective serves to emphasize the coordination of ideas in the author's mind: she will create scenes partly
imaginative *and,* at the same time, true to historical evidence. The detail about
John's pony, mentioned in the preceding paragraph, is a good example of the way
narrative effect will be sacrificed to historical fact if the two conflict. Notice the
alternation of long and short sentences in the paragraph, and also the varied
sentence beginnings. Sentence 1 begins with a connective and a phrase followed by
verb, then subject. The much longer second sentence, with parallel predicates and
the emphatic repetition of *knows,* begins subject-verb. Short sentence 3 begins with
a subordinate clause. Sentence 4, a complex sentence containing a complete sentence
(an absolute construction) begins subject-verb. Sentence 5 starts with a subordinate
clause, sentence 6 with subject-verb, sentence 7 with a subordinate clause. Notice,
too, the way the sentences are constructed to end strongly.
[29]   The transition *In this connection* is not immediately clear in its reference: the
reference at first seems to be to John's pony or his journey, instead of to the topic
idea of the preceding paragraph—that in the narrative method there is no deceiving
of the reader, no departure from historical evidence. The principal function of
paragraph 29 is to serve as a transition into the next five paragraphs, which deal
with the problems, in narrative biography, of conversation and historical accuracy.
[30] [31]   The two paragraphs rather than one for the discussion of John Adams's
public utterances can be defended because paragraph 30 is focused on the author's
purpose in drawing directly from the historical sources, and paragraph 31 on the
best method of bringing these sources to the reader. Mrs. Bowen's concern for the
reader has been constant: her ambition has been to introduce John Adams to as
many people as possible, to make the facts live, to let the reader share Adams's
experiences; now she must "lend a hand" to readers who would find long quotations
from historical documents unpalatable. *These glorious pages, these inspired paragraphs,* at the end of paragraph 30, and *The thought was awful to me,* in paragraph
31, are, of course, expressions of strong personal feeling. Would a more objective
statement that Americans ought to know these historical sources accomplish the same
purpose? Does Mrs. Bowen's tone also indicate some personal feeling toward the

ing with John in the coach to Philadelphia, could quote Hawley's shrewd letter of advice to the Congressional delegates from Massachusetts.

[32] So much for Adams's historical utterances. His private conversations were another matter. The sense of them, the emotional or critical content, I took from Adams's Diary or letters, then paraphrased into dialogue, taking care to have the sentences as brief as possible. Over even these insignificant phrases I labored long, testing words with the *Oxford English Dictionary* to make sure I fell into no anachronism. (Readers have demurred at my putting the word *propaganda* into Adams's mouth, yet the *Oxford English Dictionary* gives 1718 as the first date of use. Readers of *Yankee from Olympus* objected to my using *sabotage* in our Civil War era; it came direct from a Boston newspaper of 1861.)

[33] To reproduce the speech of a past era is impossible. Attempting to catch even the echo of a rhythm that is gone, I took to bed with me each night for years, some seventeenth or eighteenth century book and read myself to sleep . . . Burton, John Selden, Isaak Walton, Sir Thomas Browne, John Bunyan; I chose chatty, facile writers who were at home in the vernacular and who wrote, I felt sure, as they talked. *The Letters of George Third* were a treasury of conversational idiom, John Aubrey's *Brief Lives* (1680) a very mine of phrases: "They *culled out* their *greatest shillings* to lay in the scale against the tobacco." . . . Or, "He *addicted himself* but little to the study of the law, being a *great waster.*"

[34] The device even of private conversation I used as sparingly as possible and never for any purpose but one—to reveal character, emotion, the state of being of my subjects. In real life, people do talk, and had not Plutarch, Herodotus, Thucydides, Tacitus used dialogue to illuminate history?

[35] Academic historians, accustomed to write only in the critical form, are slow to recognize the difficulties of the straight narrative method. They are apt to call it "popularization," and their implication is not flattering. Yet among classic historians are those who acknowledge not only the difficulties but the value of historical narrative. In his brilliant essay, "The Muse of History," George Macaulay Trevelyan says:—

[36] "It is in narrative that modern historical writing is weakest, and to my thinking it is a very serious weakness—spinal in fact. Some writers would seem never to have studied the art of telling a story. There is no 'flow' to their events, which stand like ponds instead of running like streams. Yet history is, in its unchangeable essence, 'a tale.' Round the story, as flesh and blood round the bone, should be gathered many different things—character drawing, study of social and intellectual movements, speculations as to probable causes and effects, and whatever else the historian can bring to illustrate the past. But the art of history remains always the art of narrative. That is the bed rock."

professor? If so, what is it? Two run-together sentences occur near the beginning of paragraph 31: *they are gone, lost, the book is closed,* and *I must devise ways, I must lend a hand to my readers.* Can you see a reason for using commas instead of semicolons between the independent clauses? Why does Mrs. Bowen in sentence 2 of paragraph 31 say in four different ways that the readers are gone? The last three sentences in paragraph 31, following the ellipsis (. . .), give the impression of the author's thinking aloud about concrete devices for making the documentary material interesting. The three sentences are similar in movement in that a participial phrase follows the subject in each, but the structure is varied by making two of the sentences questions and the last a declarative sentence.

[32] [33] [34] The incomplete sentence opening paragraph 32 is a transition closing the discussion of Adams's public utterances; sentence 2 introduces the subject-matter (private conversations) of a block of three paragraphs. Paragraph 32 describes the derivation of the dialogue used in the biography and part of the method of giving it historical accuracy; paragraph 33 is about a second method used to give the dialogue some of the flavor of Eighteenth Century speech, and, like paragraph 32, it ends with two examples. Paragraph 34 closes the discussion of conversation and cites authority for using dialogue to illuminate history. Might the three paragraphs, or two of the three, be written as one? What do the following expressions mean in context: in paragraph 32, *anachronism* (Would the context make the meaning clear if one did not know the word?); in paragraph 33, *facile, vernacular,* and *addicted;* in paragraph 34, *illuminate history?*

[35] [36] The first two sentences of paragraph 35 might have been placed near the beginning of the section, when the author is commenting on the two forms; they are more effective here because we understand more clearly now what the difficulties of the narrative method are, and how inappropriate "popularization" is to Mrs. Bowen's work. Section 4 as a whole has been an explanation, defense, and justification of the narrative method, a subject about which Mrs. Bowen has strong feelings, as her language has shown. Paragraph 36 also quotes an authority, a distinguished British historian, in support of historical narrative. The quotation is in a separate paragraph because it is conventional to separate long quotations from the text, either in this way, or by putting them in smaller type, or by setting the paragraph in from the margin. (Mrs. Bowen has said that at the sight of set-in paragraphs, readers flee.) We have commented on the occasional figurative language the author uses; notice how much more figurative is the language of the quoted paragraph: *spinal, flow, stand like ponds instead of running like streams, as flesh and blood round the bone, bed rock.* The emphatic last two sentences of the quotation make an emphatic ending for this section on narrative biography.

5

[37]   Acceptance of the narrative form was my first biographical step. But
it was after all only an artistic decision, not a piece of writing. I had worked
for three years; I had done my research, I had set down my chronology. Yet
no character or place had actually been introduced to the reader. How then
should the tale be opened, how closed? Was I to open with birth and close
with death? It was at about this time that a novelist, a writer of detective
stories, remarked to me, "What an easy time you biographers have, compared with us fiction writers! The shape of your book is laid out ready to
hand, before you even begin to write."
[38]   I said, "What shape, exactly?" The novelist told me it was self-evident:
—"Birth, education, marriage, death."
[39]   He could not have been more mistaken. Life has no shape, artistically
speaking, any more than grief has a shape, or jealousy, or love, or any of
those large angry things. It is for the writer to find a shape, find boundaries,
a circumference within which he may freely move according to his abilities.
If he tries to encompass the universe within his book, he will surely get
lost, and getting lost is a sin the experienced writer can never permit himself.
Nothing will repel the reader more quickly than an author who wanders
from his tale. . . . John Adams lived for ninety years. Was I to tell the
full story of those years? Should I write of Adams as lawyer, as political
philosopher, as diplomat to France and Holland, as President? What particular bias would guide me? Why, in short, was I writing this book?
[40]   Once more I asked myself the vital question—a question elementary,
yet it would seem, neglected by writers of history. For my beginning, John
Adams himself gave the philosophic clue; his story must open, not at his
birth but when Adams was ten—the year, he told Dr. Rush much later,
when he "first became a politician." This was 1745, the famous year of the
Louisburg victory, a moment of great significance both for hero and protagonist, for Adams and history.
[41]   I went on, yet as I proceeded, it became plain my story was sickening
from surfeit of material; I was not creating a living character as I had hoped
to do. I was setting down a mere list of events, an Adams calendar, with no
space to explain why things happened or how the men felt who brought
these things to pass.
[42]   In much perturbation of spirit, I made the decision to end in the year
1776, with the Declaration of Independence, when Adams was only forty. To
sacrifice the Old John Adams was no easy decision. This was a glorious old
man, as appealing at eighty as he was at thirty. I had looked forward to describing those years of retirement at Quincy, when an ex-President of the
United States signed his letters so cheerfully, "The Farmer of Stony Fields."
To end in 1776 would be to sacrifice the wonderful correspondence with Jef-

[37] [38] The repetition of the word *narrative* supplies an immediate transition; then the opening sentences supply a general transition from section 4, a brief summary of the three years of work, and a lead into the topic sentence (*How then, should the tale be opened, how closed?*). This question introduces a question-to-answer or problem-to-solution pattern: the question is developed and restated in different words in paragraphs 37, 38, and 39, and is answered in succeeding paragraphs. Breaking paragraph 38 off from paragraph 37 half-observes the convention of using a new paragraph for each new speech in dialogue; however, since paragraph 38 contains two speeches, it seems that the break is used, rather, to emphasize the question *What shape, exactly?* and the novelist's mistaken answer.

[39] Paragraph 39 has considerable variety in sentences. The short, emphatic opening sentence is followed by three longer ones, complex and compound-complex in structure, suited to their content—the complex materials that the writer must shape. At the end of the paragraph the use of both short statements and short questions, and the use of a longer question in a series of short ones, give variety. Repetition of what is basically the same question, repetition of *shape* and *lost,* and use of the related figurative words *boundaries, circumference, freely move, encompass the universe, wander*—all emphasize the central idea. *Bias* (next to last sentence) may be defined as a "tendency or inclination, especially one which prevents unprejudiced consideration of a question." Is this precisely what Mrs. Bowen means by the word? Earlier she has answered in one way the question *Why was I writing this book?*—she wanted to introduce John Adams to as many people as possible. In the context of this paragraph, what more specific meaning does the question have? Sentence 2 is well turned and rather philosophical. Is it surprising that Mrs. Bowen includes love in her list of "large angry things"?

[40] In sentence 1 the author again uses an appositive structure, *the vital question —a question elementary,* to clarify and emphasize an idea. She has effectively used a large number of such structures in the course of the essay. The "vital question" seems to be the one about the opening and closing of the tale, introduced in paragraph 37 and since then asked in other ways. *For my beginning,* in sentence 2, starts to answer the question. In that sentence, why does the author say *philosophical clue* instead of "historical clue"? The last sentence of the paragraph re-emphasizes, in another appositive structure, the relationship of *hero and protagonist, Adams and history,* which will guide the author's shaping of her materials.

[41] In the first sentence, the words *my story was sickening from a surfeit of material* combine alliteration, personification, and metaphor. Though her style is not highly figurative, Mrs. Bowen is attentive to figures of sound and figures of speech.

[41] [42] [43] These three paragraphs constitute a block in the larger problem-to-solution pattern: paragraph 41 indicates that the problem remained even though the author was not starting with Adams's birth; paragraph 42 records the decision to end in 1776, and is developed with reasons for the author's unhappiness about sacrificing Adams's later years; paragraph 43 communicates acceptance of the 1776 ending as an effective solution to the problem.

Paragraph 42 contains a good deal of charged language to convey the author's "perturbation of spirit" about omitting the years after 1776: *glorious old man,* ferson—above all, to sacrifice the most dramatic death scene in American history. What climax could possibly substitute for dying on the Fourth of July? Moreover, I am suspicious of a biography that skimps the death scene of its hero. "It imports us to know how great men die as to know how they live."

[43]   History came to my rescue. The Declaration of Independence was itself a kind of death; it marked the end of an empire. There were Americans who recognized this fact in all its significance, and who greatly mourned, even as they rejoiced. The Fourth of July, 1776, would be an ending and—for America, my protagonist—a beginning. The Fourth of July was a death and a resurrection, the very Easter of our national spirit.

[44]   Within my circle, within my stated circumference, I had room now to move, room to paint a scene or two, describe an incident to the full. I could let John Adams sit by his farmhouse window and *think*. Sitting and thinking was characteristic of Adams; again and again his Diary records, "At home, without company, thinking." I had space, now, to describe the room where John sat, describe the old Plymouth Road beyond his window, the hard-packed snow, the squeak of sled runners as neighbors hauled their wood by oxcart to the town. And when my "big" scenes fell due, such as for instance, the Boston Massacre, I could allow three entire chapters to Adams's defense of the British soldiers involved on that fateful night of March Fifth. I could print Adams's legal brief in its entirety, using every device in the calendar of biographical technique—describe the courtroom, the rain against long windows on those cold autumn days of 1770. I could have the sound of military bugles drift up from where British frigates lay armed and watchful in Boston Harbor down the hill.

[45]   My circle was closed, my boundaries defined; I knew what my first scene would be and my last. My book had now an end and a beginning—but then so, for example, has Wednesday. On Wednesday the sun rises and sets. Yet if the world is to be interested in what one does on Wednesday, one has to meet with trouble on Wednesday—meet an obstacle and conquer it. Or we can let the obstacle conquer, choosing tragedy for our Wednesday story.

[46]   Conflict, the book trade calls it. Suspense. As biographer, I could not scorn this technique of the craft. My story needed it. John Adams was, all in all, a happy man. *"Les hommes heureux,"* say the French, *"n'ont pas d'histoires."* I myself do not hold with such cynicism. Surely, Wordsworth's Happy Warrior is the truly happy man? And to be a warrior, a man must have fought for something, fought with something—perhaps with the devil, perhaps with his own soul. Life that possesses no conflict possesses no victory.

[47]   What then, was the conflict in John Adams's first forty years? What made those years exciting *for him?* What, in short, was my over-all plot? Once more, history herself gave answer and plot: *How John Adams brought America to Independence.*

[48]   Herein lay personal conflict in plenty, though John Adams never carried a gun. When he took sides with the revolutionists, Adams sacrificed,

appealing, wonderful correspondence, most dramatic death scene in American history. The last sentences of the paragraph, about death, lead into the realization in the next paragraph that the Declaration of Independence was a kind of death. Paragraph 43 also contains charged language, though not charged words of personal attitude; the proper names (*Declaration of Independence, Fourth of July, America, Easter*) carry clusters of emotional meaning for many people, as do *end of an empire, mourned, rejoiced, ending, beginning, death,* and *resurrection.* The last sentence, which ends the paragraph strongly, derives some of its emphasis from the fact that it repeats part of the preceding sentence, makes skillful use of allusion and metaphor, and builds to a climactic ending. The phrase *the very Easter of our national spirit* aptly climaxes the ending-beginning, death-and-resurrection metaphor that has been slowly and carefully developed in this paragraph and in the preceding one.

[44]   This is one of the author's good paragraphs of particularization; it also has something of a cause-effect organization: the limited scope of the book, referred to in *Within my circle,* has the effect of allowing fully-developed scenes. Notice the author's awareness of the importance of sense detail: in her scenes she will create visual images—the old Plymouth Road and the courtroom, for example; she will communicate sensations such as cold—the hard-packed snow, the cold autumn and the rain; she will include sound—the squeak of sled runners, the sound of bugles.

[45]   The beginning of the first sentence, *My circle was closed,* effects a deft transition by pointing back to the beginning of paragraph 44, *Within my circle,* and also completing the circle figure.

[45] [46] [47]   In writing about the business of a biographer, Mrs. Bowen has discussed various principles and techniques that are applicable to other kinds of composition. The author chooses her subject after preliminary thought and reading; she selects material in accordance with a central purpose, rejecting what is interesting but not relevant to that purpose; she labels and classifies her notes; she decides on her literary form; she makes a skeleton chronology (a kind of outline) of the book; she further limits the subject so that she can deal with it fully; she presents dramatically, instead of summarizing, important scenes; she remembers and includes details to give the reader a sense of reality; she is mindful of the reader's needs and interests. Paragraphs 45, 46, and 47 deal with a final problem in narrative writing: the story must have not only a beginning and an end, but also a central conflict.

The paragraphing in this part of the essay seems unduly choppy. The first sentences of paragraph 45 summarize the preceding material and lead into the topic sentence (*Yet if the world is to be interested . . . one has to meet with trouble. . . .*), which is further developed in paragraph 46. These two paragraphs could be written as one. Paragraph 47, a brief question-to-answer paragraph, is perhaps justifiably made a separate paragraph, since it applies the general statements about conflict to John Adams's first forty years, and since the author wants to emphasize this material. The analogy of a story and a Wednesday in paragraph 45 is a skillful and economical device for making the point that a beginning and an end are not enough for interest. Notice that the author's sentences, particularly in paragraphs 46 and 47, are, though varied in movement, nearly all short. (An exception is the next-to-last sentence in paragraph 46, with its parallel structures.) Might the short sentences and the short paragraphs be used for the same reason—emphasis and drama as the author works out the problem of suspense and conflict? Can you think of any other defense for the author's paragraphing? In paragraph 46, does Mrs.

or so he thought, every material thing that made life worth while. By 1770, he was the leading lawyer of Massachusetts; he was offered many more cases than he could handle. The law courts were royal courts, their judges crown-appointed. When they closed, John's means of livelihood was gone. John was greatly ambitious for his three sons, especially for the eldest, John Quincy, who, John wrote his wife, "has genius." It was Adams's ambition to send John Quincy to Harvard, then to London to study law at the Inner Temple. He desired John Quincy to know the world, not grow to manhood in the narrow atmosphere of farm and township. When Adams chose the patriot side, he took as it were his vow of poverty, relinquished consciously and with sadness all ambition for his son. There was no way he could know this same son would one day be President of the United States. "I am melancholy for the public," he wrote his wife Abigail in the summer of '74, "and anxious for my family. I go mourning in my heart all the day long, though I say nothing."

[49]   I had now my conflict, my "plot." It was my hope that this general plot would suggest a separate, specialized plot for every one of my thirty-two chapters. I desired each chapter to be an entity, a tale that might be read aloud and the book laid down until next evening. I hoped to devise chapter endings that would lead the reader on. I had a writing motto: *Will the reader turn the page?* Traced on yellow cardboard the words hung over my desk, a terrible warning.

[50]   Somebody asked Charles Dickens about his rules of composition, the artistic principles by which he proceeded. "I have only one artistic principle," he said. "That is, to rouse the emotions of my readers."

[51]   Between novelist and biographer the difference is profound. The one invents situations that will rouse a reader's emotions; the other brings out the significance of situations that already exist. Both are concerned with *la recherche du temps perdu,* both wish to uncover the nature or motivations of man. "It is the business of an artist to be exciting." A large order, an ambition high and difficult. *Will the reader turn the page?* Ours is a vocation which carries great hazard; Justice Holmes used to say that no author could become truly conceited because every two years or so he exposes himself anew to the ridicule of the public.

[52]   There is no art that does not demand virtuosity. "If you own a hundred thousand francs' worth of craftsmanship," Degas told a pupil, "spend five sous to buy more." It is the business of a biographer to know his subject. And then, summoning such techniques as he has mastered through practice of his calling, he will settle upon literary form, upon circumference and plot—making it his business then to project his story with all the vigor his endowments will permit.

Bowen assume that her readers can translate the French saying, "Happy men do not have histories," or does context supply the translation? Notice the way the word *conflict* appears in the first sentence of paragraphs 46, 47, 48, and 49, and neatly stitches the four paragraphs together.

[48] In this general-to-particular paragraph, the topic sentence, *Herein lay personal conflict in plenty . . . ,* is developed with specific facts about John's livelihood, his ambition for his son, and the results, as he saw them, of siding with the revolutionists. His own statement about his frame of mind makes an especially effective ending for the paragraph. The paragraph is well written. The sentences in general are longer than in the preceding paragraphs, with some variety in length (13, 21, 19, 10, 9, 21, 20, 20, 25, 19, 22, 14 words), and considerable variety in structure. For example, of the 12 sentences in the paragraph, 3 begin with subordinate clauses, only 5 begin with subject-verb. We have commented earlier on Mrs. Bowen's skillful use of quotation; notice the amount of quotation and allusion that she uses and will continue to use in this section.

[49] Paragraph 49, opening with a transitional sentence, advances the chronology of the essay well into the writing process. It again emphasizes the author's awareness of the reader, and suggests another principle of composition—the importance of chapter endings. The paragraph has several of the appositive structures that Mrs. Bowen uses very frequently: *my conflict, my plot; an entity, a tale.* After three similar sentence beginnings (*I desired, I hoped, I had*), the last sentence begins with a modifier preceding the subject-verb; it ends strongly with *a terrible warning,* a phrase that might have been placed after *words. Terrible* means "exciting terror" or "severe"; it is also used colloquially to mean "extremely unpleasant or bad." In what sense is the author using the word?

[50] [51] These paragraphs could be made one, since the quotation from Dickens serves to introduce the contrast and comparison of the two kinds of artists. Does the shift from contrast to comparison seem to you too abrupt? *A la Recherche du temps perdu (Remembrance of Things Past)* is the title of a long novel by Marcel Proust, and Mrs. Bowen reasonably assumes that her readers know the meaning of the phrase. Paragraph 51 is interesting in that it brings together in an orderly way the early theme (*It is the business of an artist . . . .*) and the writing motto, and at the same time gives the impression of recollections and anxieties crowding into the writer's mind. This effect is heightened by the incomplete sentence (*A large order . . . .*) between the quoted sentence and the motto, by the shortness of those three sentences, and by the emotional language: *large order, high and difficult, great hazard.*

[52] *Virtuosity* is one of the more formal words used in the essay. Does it mean the same thing as *craftsmanship* in the quotation from Degas? As *business* in sentences 3 and 4? The last two sentences are a neat, nonmechanical summary of the essay, in which Mrs. Bowen uses her title for the first time. The business of knowing the subject has been discussed in sections 1, 2, and 3 of the essay; literary form in section 4; circumference and plot in section 5; and the projection of the story with vigor all through the essay, from the opening theme *It is the business of an artist to be exciting* to the repetition in paragraph 51 of *Will the reader turn the page?* Being exciting may seem easy, natural, spontaneous; the author has shown us that in the biographer's art, as in other arts, it is the product of laborious and systematic effort, immersion in the material, problem-solving, and care.

Chapter 8

EVERYDAY USES
OF ENGLISH

Certain special skills in English may have far-reaching importance. A student's method of reading, and the quality of his notes and examinations may not only determine his grade in a course, but may also influence his attitude toward a whole field of learning. Getting a position one wants sometimes depends on a letter. The ability to speak to large and small groups may establish a student's leadership in campus affairs, and may also affect his business or professional activities and his role in his community. In this chapter we are assembling suggestions about reading for study, taking notes, writing examinations, writing business letters, and public speaking—some of the everyday uses of English about which the college student needs to be informed.

I. READING FOR STUDY

Students who have done poorly on quizzes and examinations often say, "But I read the material over three times"—or "four times." They usually *have* read the material three or four times, but that fact is not a credit to them; it is evidence that they are in a groove of ineffectual reading. The last two or three readings have been of little or no value because they have been simply repetitions—diluted repetitions—of the first unskillful reading. In the following pages we shall outline a method of study to replace the unsystematic and unproductive procedure of reading an assignment again and again.[1]

These are the common weaknesses in the reading of college students:

1. Missing main ideas; confusing minor points with major points.

2. Failing to see the connection between points; missing the broad development of the theme or idea.

3. Not understanding, or misunderstanding, the author's terminology, and so not understanding the meaning of whole paragraphs or chapters.

4. Taking notes that misrepresent the organization and emphasis of the material, and that are, consequently, useless either for daily preparation or for review.

No simple remedy can be prescribed for all of these weaknesses; inadequate background in the field, inadequate reading experience, and inadequate vocabulary are often at least partially responsible for them, and there is no quick, easy cure for such deficiencies. But most students find a marked improvement in their grasp of a subject as soon as they learn a technique or method of study. The method may differ slightly with different material, but reading for study should, in general, consist of these four steps:

1. *A preliminary survey* (if the material is expository), which gives the reader a skeleton outline of what the author is going to say, and enables him to fit particular facts and details into a pattern when he begins to read. This preliminary survey is made by looking at the table of contents, which usually lists the main points discussed in each chapter of a book; and, chiefly, by leafing through the pages assigned and making a mental note of the headings and subheadings by which the author has indicated the organization of his material. Most college texts have such headings, in capital letters, in boldface type or italics, or in marginal notations. (With books that do not have headings or marginal notations, the best way to get an idea of the organization and general development is to skim along looking at topic sentences. The first or second sentence of a paragraph will usually be a topic sentence.) Often, too, the first paragraphs of a chapter state what is to be covered in the chapter, and the concluding paragraphs summarize what has been said; reading these paragraphs may be a valuable part of the preliminary survey. With a little practice, students can make an efficient survey of thirty or forty pages in five or ten minutes. These minutes are well spent. Having in mind the outline of the material, and the names, at least, of the main points, the

---

[1] Suggestions about reading particular kinds of writing—informative, evaluative, and persuasive—are made in Part 2, *Understanding Kinds of Prose.*

student can read with a sense of direction, and knowledge of the whole plan. This initial survey does much to prevent the first two of the weaknesses in study listed above—missing the main ideas, and failing to see connections between ideas.

2. *Reading the material through* to see the development of the ideas observed in the preliminary survey, *without stopping* to re-read difficult passages, to look up words, or to take notes. The reading should be as rapid as is consistent with the student's understanding of the material, and the reading should be continuous. It is wise to mark with a check in the margin passages that seem important, and with a check or question mark passages that are unclear; but breaking the reading by puzzling long over a passage, or by stopping to take notes, will interfere with one's grasp of the sequence and development of ideas. Also, one is likely to waste time with such stops: a momentarily unclear passage may be clarified by the later context; and notes taken before the reader knows surely what is most important in the material are likely to be useless or misleading.

3. *Checking through the material, and re-reading with care any sections that are difficult or obscure.* This is a very different procedure from simply reading the assignment over again. The reader should look once more at section headings, and at paragraph beginnings; if he can mentally fill in their content, he can go on to the next section without re-reading the material here. He should concentrate on passages about which he is vague, or which, in his first reading, he has checked for later consideration. This is the stage of reading for study in which one may profitably spend fifteen minutes over a few lines of poetry, a formula, or a paragraph of philosophical reasoning.

An important part of this process of checking and selective re-reading should be fixing in mind not only the topic ideas of the assignment, but the meaning of key words *as the author uses them.* We have listed as a common study fault the misunderstanding of the author's terminology. Sometimes the student needs to consult his dictionary in order to understand the author's language; more often he needs to consider carefully the context and the author's explanation of a troublesome word or term. In economics, for example, a number of familiar words, like *wealth, goods, cost, scarcity,* are used in special senses; students have difficulty in understanding a text in economics if they assume that they know the meaning of such words, and fail to read carefully the economist's definition of them. Historians may use the word *revolution* to describe social or economic change; students who take for granted that "revolution" always involves violent upheaval will be misled by overlooking the writer's definition of the word.

Part of checking and selective re-reading, too, should be active thinking about the material presented, and perhaps some criticism or evaluation of the author's opinions and techniques. Critical judgment is not always pos-

sible for the student reading material in a field new to him. But thinking
about the material, being alert and curious about new ideas and the implications of those ideas, and relating those ideas to his own interests and
experience are certainly important parts of good reading in any field, and of
education in general.

4. *Taking notes.* Since good notes represent, in concise form, the organization and the most important ideas of a body of material, the student is in
no position to take useful notes until he knows the organization and the
central ideas of what he is reading. Steps 3 and 4 in this process of reading
for study may be combined; that is, the reader may take notes as he checks
the material and re-reads the difficult passages. But he should not take notes
until he has completed his first reading of the assignment, and until the
outline of the material and the major ideas are clear to him.

Many students make their notes on reading too full, too cluttered with
nonessentials. Good notes should contain the main ideas of the selection
read, the important subordinate points, and only enough supporting example
or detail to clarify the larger ideas. Notes are generally most usable if they
are in informal outline form, with major ideas, definitions, principles, etc.
numbered or underlined, with less important material grouped under them,
and with spaces left between divisions of the material, so that the notes do
clearly reflect the emphasis and organization of the piece of writing.[2]

When one studies from his own books, it is a good practice to underline
important ideas, perhaps with a system of marginal notation or numbering
that shows the relationship between the ideas. Such underlining may be
the basis for notes, or it may take the place of notes. Like taking notes, the
underlining should be done *after* the first reading, and it should be selective.
Too much underlining defeats the purpose of emphasizing the most significant material; pages on which nearly everything is underlined are less helpful when one reviews them than pages on which there are no marks at all.

II. TAKING NOTES

The most efficient system for taking notes from different sources, in preparation for writing a paper, is using note cards; each card is labeled with the
source of the material and with a heading that tells exactly what part of
the subject it deals with; the cards can then be grouped and arranged in the
right sequence as one organizes the material he has collected. This method
of taking notes is described fully in the chapter on the research paper.
Taking notes on other kinds of reading has been discussed in the preceding

2 The informal outline for notes is illustrated on page 228, in the discussion of taking
notes on lectures.

section of this chapter. We shall be concerned here with taking notes on lectures—a use of English important to college students, but one with which many entering students are not familiar.

Good note-taking is largely the product of experience. Notes improve as the student learns what to expect from different lecturers; learns better how to write as he listens; and sees, as he tries to use his notes for review, just what their deficiencies are. The following suggestions may, however, help to shorten the period of trial and error through which a number of students go before they learn to take usable lecture notes.

A. Materials for Efficient Note-taking

Good equipment is essential for good notes. The student who, with a blunt pencil stub, takes notes in a small, pocket-sized notebook or on the backs of envelopes, is defeating his purpose. The purpose of his notes is to recall the lecture clearly, in its whole development and continuity; but his method produces a hard-to-read, unclear, fragmented record. He should, therefore, equip himself with a pencil or pen that writes easily and legibly, and with a large notebook, preferably $8\frac{1}{2}$ by 11 inches, and preferably loose-leaf.

Such a notebook has a number of advantages. It will hold all of the material—reading notes, lecture notes, assignments, etc.—for all of the student's courses; labeled index tabs or markers can divide the notebook into sections and simplify locating the material for a particular course. The loose leaves facilitate the rearrangement of material; for example, a student may wish to keep in separate sections his reading notes and his class notes for a course, but may wish to combine and correlate them when he reviews for an examination. Also, as the notebook becomes crowded during the college year, older material and notes can be removed from the loose leaf notebook, and filed somewhere else in manila folders. The $8\frac{1}{2}$ by 11-inch size is the right size for mimeographed material distributed in some classes, and for compositions written on standard $8\frac{1}{2}$ by 11-inch paper. The greatest advantage of the large notebook for lecture notes (and notes on reading) is that the student can scan the large page and quickly see the relationship of ideas, the pattern and development that his notes represent.

B. Judging What Is Important

Judging what is important in a lecture is the chief problem in note-taking. The best notes are not a transcription of the lecture; often they are brief. The student must listen, and select, so that he gets down in his notes: (a) the central thesis or the several main ideas of the lecture; (b) the principal subordinate ideas; and (c) just enough supporting fact, example, or detail to clarify the larger ideas when he reviews them after a lapse of time. (He may also, of course, jot down things that interest him, that he wants to look up, that puzzle him, or that he wants to remember.)

Teachers differ in the amount of guidance they give their note-taking audiences: some indicate very clearly the plan of the lecture and may even put a preliminary outline on the board; others speak more informally and casually, hope that their students will listen and think rather than mechanically record, and believe that the pattern of the lecture will emerge as students think over the material. Nearly any lecturer, though, does provide signposts and aids to distinguishing between main ideas, significant subordinate points, and material that merely illustrates or provides additional detail or is designed to keep the students awake. Students should be alert to these signposts. The principal ones are:

1. *The lecturer's introductory remarks,* which usually state the topic to be discussed and often sketch its main parts: "We shall consider this morning the causes of the French Revolution"; "Our subject today will be three forms of municipal government."

2. *Transitional expressions* that mark the divisions of the lecture and show that a new main idea or another subordinate point worth noting is about to be introduced: "The next major cause was . . . ."; "The second point to keep in mind is . . . ."; "Another reason for this situation was . . . ."; "Next we see . . . ."; "Also in this connection . . . .".

3. *Rules, definitions, facts, or principles stated slowly,* or stated with emphasis, or repeated, or written on the board.

4. *Summaries* of material covered, indicating what the major ideas have been.

Judging what is important in lectures becomes easier as a course goes on, partly because the student gets used to his teacher's method of lecturing, and partly because he knows more about the purpose and content of the course. As one's knowledge in any field expands, so does his sense of the way new information fits into it. He has a frame of reference by which he can place and evaluate fresh material. For this reason, whenever possible, the student should do assigned reading in the course, or collateral reading, *before* he comes to a lecture on the same or related material. His background of information will help him follow the lecture and grasp the relative significance of ideas. Reviewing notes on previous lectures may also supply some of this helpful background.

C. Taking Organized Notes

Clearly-organized notes depend, of course, on understanding the organization of the lecture. Also, though, the student should realize that his notes on the page should be a skeleton of the lecture: main ideas should stand out sharply and should be numbered, or underlined, or spaced for emphasis. Supporting ideas or details should be grouped under them, to make one block on the page or pages of notes. For example, here are efficient notes on a lecture on part of the material in Chapter 2 of this book:

Varieties of English—
  Produced by different educ. and social situations.
  Varieties overlap and change, but certain differences.
  I. Nonstandard Eng.
  Usually not written except in fiction (dialect).
  Misuse of words, grammar.
              Ex. They was tired after they clum the hill.
  Limited vocab.
  Slang and shoptalk—overlap standard Eng.
      (Shoptalk—used by people in same occupation.)
      (Objections to slang—not original, not clear, poor impression.)
  II. Standard Eng.
      A. Formal
        More often written than spoken. Educ. people to educ. people.
        In scholarly articles, formal lectures, tech. writings, some poetry and other
            literature.
        Characteristics: long sentences, parallelism, balance, interrupting modifiers,
            triads (sets of 3), allusions.
        Usually impersonal.
        Contractions not used.
        Exact vocab.
                Ex. psychosomatic, contentious
      B. Informal
        Most commonly used language of educated people.
        Ranges from high informal (editorials, literature) to more informal articles
            and serious conversation.
        Sentence length and construction more like speech; allusions to generally
            understood events.
        College students should aim at high informal Eng. in most writing. (Written
            informal Eng. more careful and precise than spoken.)
      C. Colloquial
        Conversational Eng. more often spoken than written.
        Has constructions and vocab. of relaxed speech of educated people.
Eng. should be appropriate to: user
                                audience
                                occasion
  Inappropriate formal Eng. is pompous; "heavy."
                Ex. Wend my way to my place of residence. (go home)
  Many students need to raise level of usage, to use more exact words, and prepare
      to be effective with well-educ. groups.

Notes in informal outline form, like those above, are generally more useful than running summaries of the lecture: the main points and divisions stand out more clearly; spacing indicates the blocks of the lecture, and indentation can show the relative importance of parts of the material. If a lecturer has suggested his outline ("There are four principal reasons for the present tension in world affairs"), the student can easily number or underline each of the four reasons. If an outline is not announced, or if the lecture is loosely organized, the note-taker should do the same with what appear to be the main points. Later, as he looks over his notes, he may see that what he numbered major point III is logically subordinate to II; but even so, his outline form has helped him to see the proper relationship between ideas.

D. Short Cuts

Working out sensible short cuts will enable the student to listen more, write less, and still take good notes. Some standard abbreviations that he can learn to use in note-taking are:

ex.	—example	∴	—therefore
e.g.	—for example	vs.	—contrary to or opposed to
i.e.	—that is	esp.	—especially
bk.	—book	b.	—born
c.	—about	d.	—died

Also, he should develop a system of individual abbreviations like those used in the notes quoted above. These should, of course, be completely intelligible to him, but some shortening of words (for example, indiv. for individual, char. for characteristic) does not seriously interfere with the readability of notes and does save writing time.

Another efficient practice in taking notes on a packed or rapidly delivered lecture is to get down just enough of the idea to identify and recall it, then to leave several blank lines, and go on to the next point. The blank lines can be filled in after class while the memory of the lecture is still fresh.

E. Revision

Editing, reorganizing, and revising lecture notes may not be necessary after one develops proficiency, but it is usually advisable for the inexperienced note-taker. Such revision should be done as soon as possible after the lecture, since part of it may be expanding the notes with remembered facts and details. A number of students type their notes as, or after, they revise; the greater clarity of the typed pages makes them more useful for review. Revision has the very real value, not only of providing better notes, but also of fixing the material in mind.

A final suggestion. One student's notes are often not meaningful to another person, because of individual systems of abbreviation and differences in method; and students should take their own notes and not rely on the work of others. Nevertheless, the student who feels that his note-taking is ineffective may find it helpful to look at notes taken on the same lectures by an able student who is willing to lend them. The good notes may offer hints about what to listen for and how to follow the organization of a particular lecturer.

III. WRITING EXAMINATIONS

College students do not need to be told that writing good examinations is an important practical matter. Often, of course, students fail examinations because they lack sufficient knowledge. That lack may be due fundamentally to a difficulty with language—to an inability to read well and to grasp the content and organization of the material in the course. But we are concerned here, not with insufficient knowledge, but with the actual taking of the examination; with the kind of failure, or poor result, of which the student says, "I really knew the material, but I guess I didn't do a good job on the exam." This kind of failure often comes from incompetence in the use of English.

We shall discuss in this section five aspects of writing good examinations. It will be clear that we are talking primarily not about the purely objective examination that requires only a true-false judgment or the selection of a term, but about the examination that is at least partially essay and discussion. Students will have examinations of this type particularly in English, history, government, sociology, economics, and philosophy.

A. Reading the Questions

The poor reading of questions written in clear and simple English is a major cause of unsatisfactory examination papers. It is commonly responsible, first, for a careless omission of parts of questions. If an examination question asks students to "define and give an example of each of the following," nearly always one or two students in a class of twenty-five or thirty will define the terms without giving examples. It is unlikely that they could think of no examples; more probably, as soon as they read the word *define*, they stopped reading and plunged into writing on the question as they understood it. The instructor reading these papers may surmise what has happened; but he expects his students to be able to read, and he cannot give credit for the part of the answer that is not there. Frequently, too, students leave out a whole question on an examination. Because they cannot answer the question? Perhaps; perhaps not. The instructor cannot guess; he can only deduct the 15 or 20 per cent allotted to this part of the test.

The student can avoid these costly errors of omission by taking a few minutes at the beginning of the hour to read all of the questions *carefully* before he begins to write. This preliminary reading has another value: it enables the student to make some estimate of the time he will need on each part of the examination, and to budget his time as he writes. Sometimes the instructor has suggested on the question sheet the number of minutes to be spent on each part; when he has, the suggestions should be noted and followed as closely as possible, for college examinations are meant to be completed. The wise student will also try to allow a few minutes at the end of the hour for reading his paper, and for checking it with the question sheet to be sure that nothing is omitted.

Another failure in reading, often serious, is the failure to note directions about the *form* of the answer. Nearly always the form is prescribed in directions like "discuss briefly," "discuss as fully as time allows," "outline," "list five reasons," "write a short essay," "in a few sentences summarize . . . ." These directions are important. They are designed to test the extent of the student's knowledge, or his ability to select the main ideas, or his ability to organize complex material or to assemble many facts in a short time. There is always a reason for the directions; and the student who outlines when he is asked to write an essay, lists ten causes when he is asked to discuss three, writes a sprawling account when he is asked to state clearly in one sentence, fails to give evidence of the *kind* of knowledge for which he is being tested.

B. Definition

We have mentioned the examination question that asks students to define terms they have studied. Because this is a common type of short-answer question, and because longer essay questions may also require definitions of terms, skill in defining is important in writing examinations. A good definition nearly always does two things: (1) it puts the subject into the genus, or class, to which it belongs; (2) it differentiates the subject from other members of that class:

> A conjunction is a word [classification] used to connect words, phrases, clauses, or sentences. [Differentiation from other words.]

The following attempts at defining, from examination papers on the material in this book, illustrate typical failures in definition. They may clarify, by contrast, the techniques of good definition.

> Context determines the meaning of a passage. [Not a definition, because it tells what context *does* without telling what it *is:* that is, the first step in definition, classifying *context* as surrounding material, has been omitted. One unfamiliar with context could conclude from this attempt at definition that context means a skillful reader.]

> An independent clause is a group of related words containing a subject and verb. [All right as far as it goes; the term is classified and differentiated from phrases

and single words. But an independent clause is not distinguished from a subordinate clause; *and is capable of standing alone as a sentence* should be added for
complete differentiation.]

A euphemism does not cause shock or unpleasantness. [A correct, though negative, statement about euphemism, but not a definition because the word is not
classified. A good day, a peaceful sleep, an enjoyable party—hundreds of things—
do not cause shock or unpleasantness.]

Context is where the surrounding material sheds light. [Meaningless definition
because of faulty expression. In a good definition, the genus is given as a noun,
and not as a *where, when,* or *if* clause: *Context* is the *surrounding material; golf*
is a *game; a robin* is a *bird.*]

A euphemism is when you say he passed away for he died. [One restricted example; no definition. Both basic steps, classification and differentiation, are omitted.
This statement defines *funeral* as well as it does *euphemism.* Here too the definition form is incorrect; a euphemism is a mild soothing term; it is not "when you
say."]

C. Substantial, Packed Answers

A good answer to an essay or discussion question is a little composition; it
presents the problems of any theme. The steps in the writing process must be
taken quickly in writing examinations, but they are essentially the same: the
student must assemble and select his material, being sure that all of it is
clearly focused on what the question asks for; he must organize it; he must
write it correctly and clearly and with as much *relevant concrete detail* as
time and the directions on the examination permit.

This relevant concrete detail often makes the difference between a good,
substantial examination paper and a mediocre or poor one; and the failure
to include detail often comes, not from scanty information, but from vague,
general, thoughtless expression. Consider the following answer, written on
an examination question that asked students to state clearly the function
of a number of characters in the short story in which each appeared. This
answer was written about the second stranger in Hardy's story "The Three
Strangers":

The second stranger was introduced by the author to give the story excitement
and suspense. His appearance at the cottage was important because it furthered
the action of the story.

"Excitement and suspense"? In what way? "Furthered the action of the
story"? Certainly; so does any character in any well-planned story. The
answer is almost meaningless; and yet oral questioning showed that the
student who wrote it was familiar with the details of the story. He was
capable of writing a good, well-packed answer like this one:

The second stranger, the brother of the condemned man, by fleeing when he saw his brother and the hangman in Shepherd Fennel's cottage, caused the company to pursue him, and so enabled his brother to escape. His explanation when he was caught made the situation clear to the reader.

We have said before that the successful writer does not assume that his reader knows intuitively, without needing to be told, the contents of his mind. This is never more true than in writing examinations. The job of the student is to assure his reader, beyond any doubt, of the fullness and accuracy of his knowledge. Packing his answers with specific detail is one of the best ways of showing his thorough grasp of the material.

Since inclusion of detail takes writing time, able students learn to save time by practicing the techniques of economy. Without sacrificing detail, they avoid noncontributing words and lengthy phrasing. They learn to reduce clauses to appositives or participial phrases or single words; to write, for example, "the bloodless, three-day revolution" instead of "the revolution was bloodless and was accomplished in three days." The following answer to a question about the Reform Bill of 1832 contains all the detail essential to a good answer, but the writer has used more than twice the number of words he needs:

> The Reform Bill was carried out in England in 1832. It was put through by the Whigs. It did two things: first it did away with the old rotten and pocket boroughs as they were called, and second it made a new distribution of the number of seats; as a result of this, the new towns would be better represented in parliament.

This is a precise, economical phrasing of the same material:

> The Whig Reform Bill of 1832 in England eliminated the rotten and pocket boroughs, and redistributed parliamentary seats for better representation of the new towns.

Another example of wordy expression is the following answer to a question asking for identification and explanation of a phrase in a short story:

> The "three hunting hawks" are in the story "In Another Country" written by Hemingway. It is about soldiers who were wounded in World War I in Italy. The three hunting hawks are three Italian soldiers. The story is narrated by an American who has been given some medals for bravery just as the Italian boys have. But he feels he has not earned his medals in the same way they have earned theirs. He feels in his heart that he is not really brave and he thinks they are, so he thinks of them in his mind as three hunting hawks who are not afraid of anything.

The writer could have written:

> The "three hunting hawks" in Hemingway's "In Another Country" are three Italian soldiers who, like the American narrator of the story, have been wounded in World War I in Italy. All four boys have the same medals for bravery, but the American, feeling that he has not earned his and that he is not really brave, thinks of the others as three fearless hunting hawks.

One objection to wordiness on examinations is that the student who wastes time on unnecessarily long answers may not be able to complete the examination. Another objection is that wordiness suggests imprecision and a general lack of proficiency.

D. Focus

Accurate detail produces the substantial, packed answer, but it must be relevant detail. Few things are more exasperating to a busy instructor than wading through material that is not pertinent to the question. The inclusion of irrelevancies on examinations sometimes comes from the student's failure to focus mentally on the question, from a general fogginess about what is asked for. Sometimes it is deliberate evasion: knowing very little about the question asked, the writer hopes to receive credit by writing on a slightly different subject. Sometimes, more innocently but no more wisely, the student includes irrelevant material out of an impulse to display all he knows, whether it is asked for or not. The effect, in any case, is to convince the instructor that the student is confused and unsure of the material since he has not written a coherent, well-organized, well-focused answer.

E. Expression

Good examination papers, besides covering the questions completely according to directions, and being clearly organized, specific, and well-focused, are legible and literate. Students have been known to protest, when instructors in other departments have criticized their handwriting, grammar, spelling, and sentences, that "this is not an English course." Students who have read this book will, we hope, not be inclined to take this attitude; any course is an English course in so far as it requires meaningful communication in English. Most students cannot write as effectively under pressure as they can with time for thought and revision, but they can express themselves clearly and with reasonable correctness. Frequent misspellings of common words, unreadable words and phrases, jumbled or ungrammatical sentences in which the meaning is obscure, interpose a barrier to communication; they are irritating to the reader, and they give an impression of the writer's incompetence which no amount of factual information about the subject can wholly remove.

Inappropriate English also creates an unfavorable impression. Examination papers are seldom written in very formal English, but they should maintain a good level of informal usage and avoid, by all means, lapses into language that is out of key with the occasion and the subject under discussion ("Hamlet was disturbed and unbalanced when he found his father had been bumped off"). Part of competence in any field is the ability to discuss the subject in appropriate language.

The student who has trouble with examinations often finds it very profitable to read the papers written by good students. Actually seeing excellent answers to questions on which he has written poorly, noting what material has been selected and what omitted as inconsequent or irrelevant, and how the material has been organized and presented, may be of practical help to him in writing other examinations in that course.

In general, students will find that their examination papers improve if they follow these rules:

1. Read all the questions carefully before starting to write.

2. Budget time to ensure completing the examination.

3. Work for direct, economical expression without sacrificing relevant detail.

4. Realize that organization and expression are important; they are worth the time they may take.

5. *Answer the question, the whole question, and nothing but the question.*

IV. WRITING BUSINESS LETTERS

The basic requirements of a good business letter are that it state its business clearly, concisely, and courteously, and that it follow certain conventional patterns of usage. A business letter has six parts: the heading, the inside address, the salutation or greeting, the body of the letter, the complimentary close, and the signature.

Heading

120 Lowell Street
Petersburg, Illinois 62675
February 1, 1972

Inside
Address

Brown, Day and Company
55 Fifth Avenue
New York, New York 10003

Salutation

Gentlemen:

Body

Complimentary
Close

Very truly yours,

Signature

William A. Platt

William A. Platt

1. *The heading,* in the upper right-hand corner, gives in three lines the street address of the writer, the city and state, the ZIP number, and the date. (If one is using paper with a letterhead, only the date is required in the heading; the date is either centered under the letterhead or written flush with the right-hand margin.) The heading of a typewritten letter is single-spaced and is usually in block form, as in the example above. The indented form may, however, be used; it is more common in letters written in long-hand than in typed letters:

120 Lowell Street
Petersburg, Illinois 62675
February 1, 1972

The form chosen should be used consistently throughout the letter, that is, in the heading, the inside address, and the address on the envelope. Punctuation at the ends of the lines is unnecessary.

2. *The inside address* gives the name of the person or company to whom the letter is written, and the complete address. It follows the form (block or indented) of the heading, is also single-spaced in a typed letter, and is set flush with the left-hand margin, usually three to six spaces below the last line of the heading.

When a person's position is included in the inside address, it is generally placed on the same line as his name; if this makes the line awkwardly long, the title may be put on a second line, or it may be divided in this way:

```
Professor John F. Carter, Chairman
Department of Economics
Tufts University
Medford, Massachusetts 02155
```

Names of states may be abbreviated in the inside address and the heading if the abbreviation produces a better balance in the length of the lines.

3. *The salutation,* or greeting, of the letter is written flush with the left-hand margin, two spaces below the last line of the inside address. It is followed by a colon.

The salutation used depends on the degree of formality the writer considers appropriate for this letter. Conventional salutations in order of decreasing formality, are: *My dear Sir* or *My dear Madam* (very formal); *Dear Sir* or *Dear Madam; My dear Mr. Brown; Dear Mr. Brown.* The last salutation is now most commonly used if the writer knows the name of the person who will receive the letter. If the addressee is a company or group, the salutation will be *Gentlemen, Dear Sirs* (now less frequently used), *Mesdames* (very formal plural of *Madam*), or *Ladies.*

4. *The body* of a typewritten letter is usually single-spaced, with double spaces between paragraphs. The paragraphs may be indented, but in most business correspondence now there is no indentation; the double spaces mark the paragraph divisions. Since business letters should be easy to read, paragraphs are frequently short.

A generation or two ago, business correspondence was frequently carried on in a jargon which was a peculiar combination of curt efficiency and elaborate formality: *Yours of the 5th instant received and contents duly noted; In reply to your esteemed favor of the 8th inst. would say . . . .* This jargon has, fortunately, dropped out of current usage. Simple, direct expression is now characteristic of business correspondence. The body of the business letter, unlike its other parts, is no longer conventionalized; within certain limits it may, and should, express the personality of the writer.

In general, business letters are still formal and impersonal; but the degree of formality and impersonality depends upon the situation and the writer's purpose. His purpose must guide him, too, in his choice of material, his arrangement of it in the letter, and his use of language. Some business letters are purely factual and informative, but many of them are also persuasive; the tone of the letter may be as important as the factual meaning in accomplishing the aim for which the letter was written.

5. *The complimentary close* is written slightly to the right of the middle of the page and two or three spaces below the last line of the body of the letter. A comma is usually placed after the close. Only the first word of a closing phrase is capitalized.

The complimentary close should be consistent with the salutation, and both should be chosen for their harmony with the tone of the letter. A very formal letter beginning *My dear Sir* might close *Yours respectfully, Respectfully yours,* or *Very respectfully yours.* A letter beginning *Dear Sir* would consistently close with *Yours truly, Yours very truly,* or *Very truly yours.* A less formal letter, addressed to a business acquaintance, and beginning *Dear Mr. Brown,* might close with *Sincerely yours, Sincerely, Very sincerely yours, Cordially yours,* or *Cordially.*

The participial close (*Hoping for the favor of an early reply; Trusting that this answers your question*) is no longer considered good form.

6. *The signature* is always handwritten. Unless a letterhead carries the writer's name, the name is typed below the signature, to ensure legibility.

A professional title (*Dr.* Thomas Sand) is never used before the signature. If the letter requires mention of the writer's professional status, this form is used:

Thomas Sand

Thomas Sand, M.D.

A married woman signs her own name, not her husband's, and indicates her status parenthetically:

Marjorie J. Carson

(Mrs. Frank Carson)

[*Or*]

(Mrs.) Marjorie J. Carson

Letters of application, sometimes the most important compositions that students write, deserve special attention. A letter of application, to be considered favorably, must follow the conventional business-letter form outlined above. It must be neatly typed and neatly spaced on the page or pages, and it must be free from mechanical errors. In all details it should convey an impression of the writer's competence and his care in composing this letter.

Generally speaking, a letter of application should discuss, or at least mention, the six points listed below. These requirements for the letter may be modified by particular circumstances; for example, the applicant may, as part of his application, be asked to fill out blanks which cover some of these six points; he may be writing his letter to a person who is acquainted with his work, so that discussing it fully would be unnecessary. The average letter of application, however, should cover this material:

1. *The application itself*—a clear statement of the position applied for and the fact that the writer is applying. If an acquaintance of the person to whom he is writing has told him of a possible opening, or has suggested that he write the letter, he will probably begin his letter with that information and proceed in the same paragraph to the statement that he wishes to apply for the position.

2. *Qualifications*—the education and experience of the applicant. This is usually the longest and most detailed section of the letter. If the writer's experience has been considerable, he will emphasize it, and will probably limit the discussion of his education to a statement of the degree or degrees he holds, the dates of the degrees, and the institutions from which he received them. On the other hand, if the applicant has little experience, he will need to deal fully with his education and cite the particular courses he has taken that prepare him for the position he is seeking.

3. *Personal information*—age, health, interests, community activities, marital status. This section of the letter, though less important than the writer's qualifications, is still important because it gives a picture not simply

of the worker but of the human being in whom the prospective employer is interested.

4. *References*—the names, positions, and addresses of people willing to vouch for the ability and character of the applicant. Three or four references are usually given, and the applicant should ask the people in advance for permission to use their names.

5. *Salary*—often not mentioned in a letter of application; but it may be advisable for the writer to make a statement about the salary that he would expect or that he understands is attached to the position, to prevent later misunderstanding.

6. *Request for an interview*—with information about the writer's availability, free time, telephone number—anything that will make it easy for the receiver of the letter to get in touch with him. The interview is so important that getting it is frequently the real purpose of the letter of application. The letter fails in its intention if the reader is not convinced that the writer is worth seeing; it may fail, too, if arranging the interview is not made easy and convenient.

Letters of application often have an accompanying fact sheet or résumé on which facts about the applicant are listed under the headings *Education, Experience, Personal Data, References.* Such a sheet is particularly useful if the writer needs or wishes to present a great deal of detail—for example, a long record of previous employment, or, if his experience is limited, a long list of relevant courses he has taken. If a fact sheet is attached, the information in the letter itself may be simplified, but it should include all the material the writer wants most to emphasize.

A letter of application presents a very interesting problem in communication. The facts in the letter, the applicant's actual record, will, of course, determine to a considerable extent the response of the reader; but the way the facts are presented, the emphasis they are given, the tone of the letter, the total impression the reader receives of the total person writing may determine his response even more. A skillful letter of application attracts attention without dramatics and without violating conventions. Within the bounds of a rather formal style it communicates a personality. It is both honest and effectively slanted. It persuades without pressing; it conveys self-confidence without conceit.

V. PUBLIC SPEAKING

In order to become an effective public speaker, one needs a knowledge of the principles of public speaking, some expert criticism, and numerous opportunities to speak and to hear other speakers. Since a good course in public speaking supplies these essentials, the best thing to do is to take such a course.

This brief section on public speaking is intended to supply some guidance and to make the student feel less at a loss when he has occasion to speak.

A good speech and a good written composition have much in common, and most of what we have said about writing is applicable to public speaking. There are certain important differences, though, between planning a speech and planning a paper, and there are additional things to say about practicing, delivering, and criticizing speeches.

In planning a speech one needs to keep in mind that the speaker and the writer have different relationships to their audiences. A writer may if he wishes make his communication so impersonal that one gets little impression of the man behind it. A speaker cannot; his audience watches his movements, gestures, and facial expressions and hears his voice; it judges not only the speech but the speaker. A good speaker gives his audience a sense of participation; he keeps in mind the information, the experience, the loyalties, the attitudes, the ideas, the common background that his hearers have or are likely to have; he stresses those things that he has in common with his hearers; he points his whole discourse at the particular selected group that he is addressing. Adlai E. Stevenson, for example, in the opening paragraphs of a speech to the National School Boards Association, spoke modestly of his knowledge compared with that of his audience, and then emphasized the common concern with education of his audience and himself:

I was flattered by your invitation to make the keynote speech at this convention— in part because I thought I was through with keynotes and conventions. But for me who knows so little about education to talk to you who know so much makes me very uneasy. And at the moment I feel as unsupported and insecure as Hillaire Belloc's water beetle:

Who traveled on the water's face
With ease, celerity and grace;
But if he stopped to try and think
Of how he did it, he would sink!

You have asked me to speak to the subject of "Improving Education—A Free People's Responsibility." Certainly the improvement is imperative, and certainly it is the responsibility of all of us; because all of us, in one way or another, are teachers and teach ourselves and others. Parents are teachers. Churchmen are teachers. Editors are teachers. Friends are teachers. Even politicians should be teachers.

But our chief concern today is with the part of teaching that goes on in the public schools where the shape of the future is cast.

In a different situation, addressing the Institute of Life Insurance, Mr. Stevenson humorously recognized a gap between himself and his audience (and in recognizing, closed it), paid tribute to the business of the audience, then moved to his theme of "our" deficiencies:

I understand that this audience, the Institute of Life Insurance, represents the largest aggregation of investment capital in the world. Well—this is a most unusual environment for a Democrat! And I must say that there have been occasions in the past when I would have welcomed even more the attention and good will—and contributions—of businessmen of such influence and affluence.

I know it is customary at meetings of this kind to tell you how important, useful and wise you are. That wouldn't be hard to do with the life insurance business, which has pioneered in the development of greater economic security for our citizens and advanced and improved our housing, education and health.

But I want to talk not about our virtues and triumphs but about our faults and failures. For in a matter of days we enter a new decade. Just as a hundred years ago, on the eve of the Civil War, we entered the decade of the '60s that proved decisive to our republic, so in this century we are entering the same decade—on the eve of trials equally decisive. Therefore it seems to me not a time for uncritical self-congratulation but for critical self-examination. Shaw wrote: "The more things a man is ashamed of, the more respectable he is." Well, I don't think we are as respectable as we like to think.

Since these two speeches were largely persuasive, the relationship between the speaker and the audience was, of course, especially important. Members of an audience are not likely to be persuaded to accept an attitude or to perform an action unless they like the speaker and feel that they have something in common with him. In informative speeches, the situation is somewhat different, for the speaker is not asking the audience to do anything or to accept any controversial belief. Since he is primarily concerned with presenting his subject clearly, he is likely to be less personal and more objective. The fact remains, though, that the audience must respect the speaker if it is to respect his knowledge, and the speech will not be effective if the speaker misses his particular audience by assuming that his hearers have more knowledge than they have and so talking over their heads, or by underestimating them and so talking down to them. The informative speech will gain in interest and clarity when the speaker makes allusions aimed at the special knowledge and interests of his particular audience and when he adapts his remarks to the particular occasion. All of this adjustment to and consideration of the audience is part of tone.

Speeches that aim at sociability or entertainment—after-dinner speeches, for example—also call for the establishment of a certain rapport, a kind of genial sharing, between speaker and audience. To be amused we need to like the person who is attempting to amuse us. Here too, tone is very important. A speaker is most likely to entertain when he shows a friendly regard for his audience and its opinions and when he does not appear to take himself too seriously. Mark Twain, Will Rogers, and Bob Hope—in fact all good entertaining speakers—have succeeded in amusing and entertaining audience not only by wit, humor, and shrewd observation but also by adapting the tone of their remarks to the audience and the circumstances.

Another difference between written and spoken communication is that most people find it more difficult to follow development of thought when they listen than when they read. In reading it is always possible to turn back a page or two and pick up the thread or to reread a paragraph or a sentence that is not immediately clear. For the listener there is no turning back and no opportunity to pause and reflect on an idea. Good speakers take into account these differences between reading and listening. They try to use shorter and less complex sentences than in writing, to repeat or to summarize more frequently, to give examples more often, to develop fewer main points, to make the main points and the organization unmistakably clear, so that their audience will not lose the continuity, or will be able, if it does, to pick up the thread again.

Although the speaker needs to be aware of the differences between speech and writing, the actual steps in preparing a speech are similar to those followed in preparing a composition. They may be listed as follows: (1) choosing an appropriate subject, (2) making an outline and perhaps writing a draft of the speech, (3) practicing the speech, (4) delivering the speech.

A. Choosing an Appropriate Subject

A good subject fits the speaker and the audience and the occasion. It fits the speaker when it leads him into subject matter which he knows or can find, and in which he has a real interest. A speaker who chooses a subject about which he knows little, and in which he is only faintly interested, invites suffering; a dull, plodding speech is painful to listen to and painful to give.

Even when the subject suits the speaker, it may not suit the occasion and the audience. At a formal faculty dinner a doctor gave a graphic account of recent advances in surgical techniques. The subject matter was good, the doctor was interested in it, and the audience was made up of educated people, but the *occasion* called for sociable after-dinner remarks and not for talk about scalpels and blood. An example of a subject unsuitable to the *audience* was supplied by an evangelical young English instructor. Asked to address a high-school study hall, he chose to discuss Matthew Arnold's idea of culture and he talked for forty minutes with deep conviction but with no concessions to the interests of his hearers. He was later considerably embarrassed when he learned that the high-school teachers had barely succeeded in keeping his restless audience in order. The choice of subject is important; when the speaker knows beforehand the audience and the occasion, there is little excuse for an inappropriate choice.

B. Outlining the Speech

After a speaker has chosen his subject, he is ready to select the substance of his speech and to organize it. For the informal theme an outline is desirable; for a speech of any length it is essential. The writer's outline may do no more than block out the rough organization; the speaker's outline, because it will serve as a kind of prompter when he practices his speech, needs to be much more detailed and more carefully planned. Except under very special circumstances, good speakers do not memorize their speeches word for word. They may, after they have made a thorough outline, write out a draft of the speech so that they can look at what they are going to say and check the transitions between ideas, but when they actually practice the speech they refer to a revised outline and not to the draft, and they memorize an abbreviated form of the outline but not the draft. If they wish to have notes available when they speak, the abbreviated outline serves that purpose too.

In making his detailed outline the speaker should not only consider the body of the speech, the argument or information; he should give special attention to the introductory remarks and the conclusion. The purpose of the introductory remarks is usually three-fold: (1) to gain the attention of one's hearers and to establish a favorable relationship with them, (2) to state specifically the subject of the talk, and (3) to bring home to the members of the audience the significance of the subject to them. In short, the introduction usually indicates what the speech is about and puts the audience in a friendly and receptive frame of mind. The body and conclusion of the speech are similar to the body and conclusion of a piece of writing except for the differences of style, development, transitions, and the like that we have already considered. The conclusion of the speech, like the introduction, needs to be pointed at the particular audience and needs to be planned, and later phrased, with special care.

C. Practicing the Speech

Once the speaker has drawn up a suitable outline, he is ready to practice his speech aloud, looking at the outline as he does so, and timing himself to see that his speech is of proper length. In order to deliver a speech effectively it is desirable to practice it at least four times. While practicing, one should memorize his outline, or at least the key words of the outline. Some speakers feel more comfortable if they have an abbreviated key-word outline available when they actually deliver the speech. Such notes, however, should be used only to bolster one's sense of security; the speaker should practice until he can give his speech easily without referring to them.

In addressing an audience the speaker is likely to find it hard to keep in mind all the points that are required for good delivery. A good speaker must speak loudly enough to be heard, must enunciate clearly, must use pauses and voice emphasis effectively, must not talk too fast, must speak easily without *ah's* and *uh's,* must be independent of his notes and able to watch his audience and adjust to it. In practicing a speech, therefore, the speaker should go through the whole routine as if he were actually on the platform and the audience were before him. He should decide how he is to stand, what he is to do with his hands, how fast and how loudly he is to talk, what words he will emphasize and where he will pause, so that when he does address his audience he will be doing again what he has been doing in practice. Good habits established during practice will go far to ensure good delivery.

D. Delivering the Speech

If a speaker has chosen a subject that is important to him, has adapted it to the audience and the occasion, and has practiced his speech until he is able to deliver it well, he has reason to feel confidence in his speech and in himself. It would be unrealistic, though, to say that such a speaker has nothing to worry about. There is still the problem of stage fright.

The best way to avoid or to lessen stage fright is to know something about it. Everyone, even speakers and actors of long experience, suffers from a feeling of tenseness before the performance, and such tenseness is natural and in fact desirable. A speaker, like an athlete, needs to be keyed up beforehand to do well. Another consoling fact is that a speaker's nervousness is much more apparent to him than it is to his audience; the student speakers who are praised by classmates for being at ease on the platform are usually the first to admit that they felt extremely nervous. Since stage fright is a form of self-consciousness, one can reduce his nervousness, not by ignoring the audience as most fearful speakers tend to do, but by looking at it, thinking about it, talking to it. When a speaker shifts his attention from himself and forces himself to focus on his subject and his audience, stage fright disappears, public speaking loses its terrors, and the speaker begins to enjoy himself.

One way to achieve effective delivery is to be aware of some common faults and to know how to avoid them. The faults mentioned below will serve as a kind of check list for the inexperienced speaker.

1. *Starting too abruptly.* Inexperienced speakers are frequently so eager to get through the ordeal of speaking that they walk rapidly to the platform and rush breathlessly into their subject. Experienced speakers pause for a moment before they say anything. They know that they will feel more at ease if they become physically adjusted before they start speaking. Often they arrange notes or wipe their glasses or shift the light. They usually look at the audience and take a deep breath. Insufficient air in the lungs will cause a speaker to gasp and to speak jerkily. After the initial pause, good speakers address the audience directly, first mentioning the names of distinguished people present and then going on to "Ladies and gentlemen" or some appropriate term of address. If they have been introduced, they often make brief extemporaneous remarks alluding to the introduction before they begin their prepared speech. Such remarks put the speaker and the audience more at ease.

2. *Not looking at the audience.* This is a cardinal sin in public speaking. One should look at his audience as he begins to speak and should continue to look at it throughout his talk. What is called "eye contact" is very important; it gives the audience a sense of being in direct communication with the speaker, and it gives the speaker a chance to see when the audience is restless or perplexed or unable to hear.

3. *Poor enunciation.* The time to improve enunciation is during the practice period before the speech is given. Saying the speech and having a friend point out faults will help. The permanent cure for poor enunciation is forcing oneself to enunciate with reasonable clarity all the time.

4. *Inappropriate volume.* Speaking too softly to be heard in all parts of the room is a fault easy to correct if, as we have suggested above, one is watching his audience; he can see if people are straining to hear, and can increase his volume. Too much volume for a small room is a less common fault, to which there is not necessarily a clear audience-reaction—audiences are generally polite and try not to wince even though they are being shouted at. The best way to avoid speaking too loudly is to think in advance about the size of the room and of the audience, and to practice what seems the right volume. In a classroom that seats about twenty-five students, for example, one probably needs to speak only a little more loudly than he does in normal conversation.

5. *Forgetting the speech.* This fault is usually a result of inadequate preparation or of trying to memorize a set speech word for word. If one knows and speaks from his outline, he may speak in sentences that are not so well turned, but he will not be at a loss because he cannot remember a particular phrase, and his speech will sound like a speech and not like a recitation.

6. *Distracting facial expressions, posture, mannerisms.* Practicing a speech before a mirror is one good way to see and to correct one's own faults. Another is to get criticisms from one's friends. In speech classes, one gains from the criticisms of the instructor and of classmates.

7. *Lack of emphasis, monotony.* The speaker who knows exactly what he wants to say and who feels that his subject is important seldom fails to give effective emphasis. He then talks with much the same stress that he would use in conversation. It is wise, also, to give considerable thought to emphasis as one practices a speech.

8. *"Uh" or "ah" habit.* People usually say "uh" or "ah" because they are momentarily at a loss for a word and feel that they should fill the silence while they think. There are several ways to avoid this distracting habit: *(a)* speaking more slowly; *(b)* deliberately pausing where pauses are justified —at the end of a sentence, for example—and thinking ahead during the pause; and *(c)* realizing that a moment of silence is less conspicuous than an "uh," and resolutely saying nothing until the right word comes.

9. *Too hasty ending.* There are at least two very ineffective ways of ending

a speech: just stopping, without preparing the audience by words or by voice for the ending; and mumbling the last few words and then fleeing from the platform. Both the wording of the conclusion and the voice of the speaker ought to announce that the speech is at an end, and the movements of the speaker afterward ought not to suggest flight. It is generally assumed that only the wicked flee when none pursueth.

E. Learning by Critical Listening

One of the defects of a brief discussion of public speaking is that a full use of examples is impossible. The reader can, however, find examples in the speeches that he hears, and can learn something from a critical examination of almost any speech. Some of the points to consider in examining a speech are:

1. The actions of the speaker at the very beginning of the speech.
2. The introduction—the speaker's way of gaining the favorable attention of his audience, indicating the general content of his speech, and arousing interest in his subject.
3. The organization.
4. Transitional devices.
5. The means used to develop the material concretely.
6. The ways in which the speech is adapted to the particular audience and occasion.
7. The language the speaker uses—level of usage, choice of words, sentence structure, clarity and economy and subtlety of expression.
8. The use of the voice—volume, rate, pauses, voice emphasis.
9. Movement, posture, gesture.
10. Eye contact with the audience.
11. The use of language and of voice to achieve finality at the conclusion.

Although critical analysis of speeches can be helpful in showing one what to practice and what to avoid, only practice itself will make a good speaker.

EXERCISES

I. The following answer to an examination question on the crisis in Russia in 1917 is correct in fact but wordy in expression. Rephrase the answer to give the same information in direct, economical sentences.

There were two revolutions that took place in Russia in 1917. The first one happened in the spring of that year and was carried through by the Moderate Socialists and Democrats who succeeded in overthrowing the government of the Czar. The second revolution occurred in the fall of the same year. It was at this time that Lenin returned to Russia. This second revolution overthrew the Russian Republic and established the Bolsheviks in power. Perhaps the main difficulty of the Republican government was the necessity of keeping up the war effort in spite of the fact that economic conditions in Russia were poor. It was this situation that gave the Bolsheviks their opportunity.

II. If you are receiving less than A in a course, get an examination written by an A student and compare your examination paper with his. (This is to be done, of course, when the papers are returned, not during the examination.) In what specific ways could your paper have been improved?

III. Write a business letter to the bursar of your college, explaining that you have been charged a laboratory fee for a course that you are not taking.

IV. Write your insurance company an account of an automobile accident in which you have been involved.

V. The letter of application below has many weaknesses in content, form, and tone. Point out as specifically as you can the faults that would make the letter a failure, and suggest ways of improving it.

April 2, 1972
1632 Washington Ave.
Cambridge, Mass.

Hazen and Milton, Inc.
Federal St.
Boston, Mass.

Sirs:
It has been brought to my attention that you may have an opening in your firm for an up-and-coming chemist. I am writing to offer my services since I am desirous of living near Boston. I could start work in July, after I have a short vacation.

I have majored in chemistry at Carlyle College and will graduate in June with a well-rounded education. I have also held responsible jobs in the summers and am not afraid of hard work.

I am twenty-one years of age and as yet unmarried. I have blue eyes and brown hair, and am in excellent physical condition. I have been a member of the golf team and the swimming team and enjoy other sports as well.

My references are Prof. James Ware of the chem department at Carlyle, and Rev. Fred Ransom of the Unitarian Church in Cambridge. They can tell you of my work and character.

I am home for spring vacation and will be in Cambridge all week. Kindly contact me at the above address, or call 864–0192.

Respectfully submitted,
Kenneth Rock

VI. Following the suggestions about writing letters of application, write a skillful letter applying for the kind of position you hope you will be applying

for ten years from now. You will, of course, need to give a fictitious account of
your experience during this ten-year period.

VII. Make a list of the faults in public speakers which you find most trying. Consider teachers, lecturers, and other speakers whom you have heard.

VIII. Suppose you have been asked to give an informal talk to a group of
secondary school students who are interested in attending your college or
university in the future. Which of the following subjects would seem to you
most appropriate, which least appropriate, and why?

1. The importance of studying philosophy
2. The place of fraternities (or sororities) in my college
3. Varieties of trees on the campus
4. How I got along with my roommate
5. How to study for college examinations
6. Customs and traditions of the college
7. The poetry of Robert Browning
8. Campus slang
9. The advantages of a small college (or a small university, or a large university, or
a country college, or a city college, or a coeducational college, or a noncoeducational
college)
10. A history of the college library
11. Restaurants within walking distance of the college
12. What every freshman should know about writing themes
13. Student-faculty relations
14. The role of students in educational policy
15. The campus theater

Choose from the list above a topic in which you have some interest, and
make an informal outline that would serve as the basis for a speech on that
subject.

PART 2

Understanding Kinds of Prose

Chapter 9

INFORMATIVE
WRITING

The function of purely informative writing is to convey verifiable facts and ideas as objectively as possible. Informative communication presents, explains, and interprets factual meaning. It answers one or more of the following questions: *What is it? Who is it? How is it done? How does it operate? How did it develop? What are the facts? What do the facts mean?*

Although expressions of attitude and personal judgment are excluded from writing intended to convey *only* factual meaning, a writer's intention is frequently complex, and a communication primarily informative may have secondary and supporting purposes. Thus a writer may entertain or use other persuasive devices to make his information more palatable or of more immediate concern to an audience; or interpreting facts may lead him to value judgments.

A great deal of our daily communication is, of course, noninformative or only partly informative. But for much of what we know, we are dependent upon factual writing; and we need, every day of our lives, the ability to communicate informatively. We must be able to give directions, to support our opinions with factual evidence, to clarify old thoughts and new ideas, and to communicate facts that we have gleaned from lectures, from conversation, from observation or research, and from reading.

The basic requirements of good informative prose are these:

1. The writer must know his subject thoroughly.

2. He must present it clearly to an audience which does not have his knowledge.

3. Without distorting the facts, he must adjust his method of presentation and his style to the particular audience he is addressing, and must make his material interesting to that audience.

I. KNOWING THE SUBJECT

This first requirement of good informative writing needs little elaboration. But it may be worth pointing out that a writer does not know his subject, in the sense of being prepared to write about it, until he knows it in a focused and organized way. He may have worked for years in an apple orchard, and yet he is not ready to write a paper on the work behind the harvest until he has thought through the successive stages of the familiar routine, sifted the major from the minor tasks, and decided which of a hundred remembered details will be most informative to a reader and which should be excluded as irrelevant or noncentral. A student may have spent several weeks reading about prisons in preparation for the writing of a research paper; but he does not know that subject, even though his mind and his note cards are full of it, until he has limited the broad topic to something he can handle, has correlated his data, has weighed conflicting evidence, and has thought about a plan of presentation.

Knowing the subject also involves a reasonable knowledge of as many facts as possible. The responsible informative writer knows and states the facts on both sides, the exceptions to the rule, and the degree of probability in his conclusions; he is careful not to slant by suppressing relevant fact.

II. PRESENTING MATERIAL CLEARLY

An organized knowledge of the subject is one guarantee of clear presentation. However, the very thoroughness of a writer's knowledge may produce weaknesses in his communication unless he remembers constantly that his readers —some of them, at least—know less than he does. An able scholar is not always a good teacher of college freshmen; sometimes he takes too much for granted, and mistakenly assumes that his students understand terms and ideas that are familiar and elementary to him. So it may be with the writer. He needs to remember *(a)* to define any terms which might be unfamiliar to the reader; *(b)* to supply background and detail which an uninformed reader cannot supply for himself; *(c)* to plan an organization suitable to the material and helpful to the reader in understanding it.

A. Definition of Terms

Definition is so important in many kinds of writing (including college examinations)[1] that it seems wise not only to emphasize the need for defining terms in informative writing, but also to discuss briefly the techniques of clear definition. A good definition nearly always does two things: (1) it puts the subject into the genus, or class, to which it belongs; (2) it differentiates the subject from other members of that class. A sentence definition will illustrate the principle:

> Hockey is a game [classification] in which opposing teams, using sticks curved at one end, try to drive a disk or ball into the opposing team's goal. [Differentiation, from other games, other team games, and other games which use sticks.]

Longer definitions may proceed from these two basic steps to further means of clarification. The following definition of *epic* classifies the subject, differentiates epic poetry from other poetry, breaks it into two main divisions, and cites examples in each division:

> EPIC: A poem of dramatic character dealing by means of narration with the history, real or fictitious, of some notable action or series of actions carried out under heroic or supernatural guidance. Epic poetry may be divided into two main classes: *(a)* the popular or national epic, including such works as the Greek *Iliad* and *Odyssey,* the Sanscrit *Mahabharata,* and the Teutonic *Nibelungenlied;* and *(b)* the literary or artificial epic, of which the *Aeneid,* Ariosto's *Orlando Furioso,* Tasso's *Jerusalem Delivered,* and Milton's *Paradise Lost* are examples.[2]

In some kinds of informative writing, the author may need to give extended definitions of terms. In short informative papers, brief definitions are more common. As we have suggested in an earlier chapter, the brief definitions can often be worked inconspicuously into the account of a process or activity, sometimes by means of appositive structures: "Under these circumstances, the designer chooses India paper, a very thin printing paper."

B. Thorough Coverage

Informative writing may lack clarity because the writer takes for granted other kinds of knowledge, besides the meaning of terms, and so leaves gaps in his material which the reader may not be able to fill in. Thorough coverage means avoiding such gaps by providing needed context or background, by covering every step in a process, by including important warnings about what *not* to do, and presenting information in concrete, specific terms.

---

1 Definition is discussed further in the section "Writing Examinations," page 231.

2 From *The Reader's Encyclopedia,* ed. William Rose Benét. Copyright, 1948. Thomas Y. Crowell Company.

A comment, for example, on the last speech of William Pitt the Younger —"I return you many thanks for the honour you have done me, but Europe is not to be saved by any single man. England has saved herself by her exertions, and will, as I trust, save Europe by her example."—might be unclear without historical context. If the reader aimed at is a general reader, not an historian, he should be told that Pitt was Prime Minister of England, that the English naval victory at Trafalgar had recently occurred, and that the speech was a reply to a toast proposed to Pitt as the "Saviour of Europe."

In giving instructions, directions, and explanations, the writer should be sure to include every step in a process. This excerpt from a recipe in a cookbook omits parts of the process as well as definition of terms:

> Add the eggs, flour, and baking powder. Pour the mixture into a shallow pan and bake in a moderate oven till done.

An inexperienced cook might not know that the eggs should be beaten, the flour sifted, and the pan oiled; "moderate oven" is vague, and "till done" unhelpful. The following directions are clearer:

> Add the eggs, well-beaten. Sift the flour and baking powder together, and add them to the mixture. Transfer the mixture to a shallow oiled pan, and bake it at 350 degrees for twenty minutes.

Almost as useful to an uninformed reader as positive instructions, may be warnings about possible missteps, or instructions about what not to do: "Do not use weed-killer on the parts of your lawn where there is clover, or you will lose your clover."

Finally, whenever detailed information will increase clarity, the writer supplies accurate figures for time, space, amounts, sizes, and specific names for processes, parts, and materials. In everyday experience, nearly everyone has received directions like "After you leave the village, turn right on Elwood Road," and has learned that it would have been more helpful to be told: "Drive three and a half miles from the second stop light in Elwood Village and then look for Elwood Road. Turn right on Elwood Road."

C. Patterns of Organization

The question of what terms to define and what material to include for thorough coverage can be answered by giving thoughtful consideration to the reader's needs. The major problem in presenting material clearly is working out the best possible organization. Because organization depends so much on the nature of the material, general comment on it is of little value. We shall discuss briefly in the following pages eight organizational systems or patterns most commonly used in informative writing. These patterns are sometimes used alone, sometimes in combination. They extend to longer pieces of writing the methods of paragraph development discussed and illustrated in Chapter 6.

1. Chronological arrangement

Chronological arrangement means setting down events in the time-order in which they occur. It is the arrangement naturally used in the writing of history, in biography, and in articles that trace the development of a movement or situation. It is also used in giving instructions or following a simple process from beginning to end. The writer needs to keep the time-relationship of events clear to the reader by means of transitional expressions like *immediately after, while these events were taking place, the next day, for twenty years there were no further advances; then . . . , as soon as this step is completed.*

2. Definition

We have said that brief definition of terms which a reader may not know is vital to clear communication. The extended definition, in which the writer devotes several pages or an entire article or book to clarifying a term, is also common in informative writing. Long articles and even books have been written to define such terms as *corporation, democracy, university, aggression, neurosis, race, existentialism.*

Like brief definitions, extended definitions put the subject into a genus or class, and differentiate it from other members of its class with which it might be confused. Extended definitions also clarify the subject in one or more of these ways: (1) by giving examples; (2) by comparing the subject with something familiar to the reader; (3) by comparing and contrasting it with related subjects; (4) by tracing its history or development; (5) by negating or excluding—showing what it does not mean or does not include as the author is using it; (6) by restating in different words the essentials of the definition; (7) by analyzing—breaking the subject into its components, and examining each part.

3. Analysis

Analysis, though related to definition, is not merely a method of definition. It is a major technique in informative writing, and requires separate treatment.

Analysis is a method of dividing a complex subject into its main parts, examining each of those parts, and showing their relationship to one another and to the whole. In a complete or formal analysis, each of those parts is in turn divided, then each of the subdivisions is further divided, and so on down to the last possible unit. In nontechnical informative writing, partial or informal analysis is one of the two most important methods of making material clear; definition, with which it is often used, is the other. When a writer says near the beginning of his paper, "There are three main elements in the Philippine situation," or "Six different kinds of bird calls can be distinguished," or "The problem created by fraternities is fourfold," he is introducing an analysis of a subject too complex to be treated as a whole.

It may be useful to examine some specific plans of analysis. The principle in each case is the same—breaking the whole into its parts—but the detailed pattern of analysis varies with the material.

The analysis of a mechanism (an electric razor, a gasoline engine, a carburetor, a kerosene stove, an electric door chime, etc.) usually falls into three large divisions: (1) the description of the whole mechanism; (2) the analysis of its main functional parts; (3) the operation of the mechanism. This is a typical outline:

ANALYSIS OF A MECHANISM

I. Description of the mechanism
   A. Definition
   B. Function
   C. Principle or principles on which it works (gravity, friction, etc.)
   D. Main functional parts
II. Construction of the mechanism
   A. First main part
     1. Definition or description
     2. Function
     3. List of its subordinate parts (if the writer wants to carry the analysis further)
   B. Second main part $\Big\}$ (developed like A)
   C. Third main part
   D., E., etc. (if there are more main parts)
III. Operation of the mechanism

The analysis of a process (changing a tire, playing badminton, baking sponge cake, cleaning upholstered furniture, setting up a darkroom, training a bird dog, laying asphalt tile, etc.) is likely to have four large divisions, because a process not only has main parts or steps, but also, nearly always, requires equipment or supplies. Unless the equipment is very simple, it is better described in a separate section of the paper than brought in suddenly when it is needed in the process.

ANALYSIS OF A PROCESS

I. Definition of the process
   A. Description of it as a whole

B. Purpose (or value)
II. Requirements for carrying out the process
    A. Materials necessary
        1. Tools
        2. Other supplies
    B. Conditions necessary
III. Main steps in the process
    A. First main step
        1. Description
        2. Materials
    B. Second main step ⎱
                    ⎰ (developed like A)
    C. Third main step ⎰
    D., E., etc. (if there are more steps)
IV. Results of the process

4. Cause-and-effect arrangement

Cause-and-effect arrangement is the pattern in which a writer discusses the causes of an event or set of circumstances, and then the effects—for example, the causes for the failure of the League of Nations and the effects of that failure on international affairs and world history. Many current articles, both popular and scholarly, are based on this plan of organization. Examples are: the causes of campus revolt, and the effects of that revolt; the causes of the war in Vietnam, and the present effects and probable future effects of that war. Within the cause-effect pattern, the writer often uses analysis; that is, he divides "cause" into three or four main causes, and "effect" into three or four main effects.

Sometimes a writer reverses the order, starting with the effects of a development or event, and then discussing its causes. This is particularly true when the effects (or possible effects) are dramatic, and when the writer wants to attract the interest of a large audience.

5. Reasons

The pattern of giving reasons for an action or a situation is used largely in interpreting historical data and reaching a conclusion about why a person or a group behaved as it did. This organization is closely related to effect-to-cause arrangement, since "reasons" and "causes" may be similar. It is also a kind of analysis, in which a total or complex reason is broken into its components. The writer first describes a situation or action, and then gives the reasons for it, usually in order of climax—building to the most important reason at the end. Examples of topics that can be developed in this way are: Henry VIII's reasons for his quarrel with the Church; reasons for dropping the atomic bomb on Hiroshima in World War II; reasons for the downgrading of Stalin in Russia in 1956; reasons the State Department may not accept the latest Russian disarmament plan.

6. Question-to-answer or problem-to-solution arrangement

Giving reasons for an action is a form of question-to-answer organization, since the writer asks "Why?" and in the course of his discussion answers the question. Question-to-answer organization may be used in interpreting facts of the past—Why did the United States enter the war in Korea?; in predicting future developments on the basis of known facts—What action is Congress likely to take on foreign aid?; or in analyzing a current problem—Is mass culture resulting in mediocrity? Is the four-day week possible? Are demonstrations an effective form of protest? What is the answer to the current drug problem? Question-to-answer articles are frequently evaluative; on the basis of the facts he assembles, the writer arrives at a judgment.

Problem-to-solution arrangement is similar in that it starts with a statement of a problem, analyzes the problem, and suggests a solution or several solutions. For example, a writer discussing the problem of overcrowded colleges might conclude that a combination of larger lecture classes and more independent work by students would do much to solve the problem. Problem-to-solution articles are also frequently evaluative or persuasive as well as informative.

7. General-to-particular or particular-to-general arrangement

General-to-particular arrangement means starting with a general, comprehensive statement, and then giving particular or specific facts and examples to support it. Particular-to-general arrangement means starting with a series of facts or examples, and, on the basis of them, arriving at a conclusion.

In writing which aims to give the reader the gist of the information as quickly and economically as possible, the general-to-particular pattern is more common than the particular-to-general. News stories, summaries of news, and most long reports usually state first a generalization or a series of generalizations, and supply particulars later. Feature articles and informative essays, especially those which aim to persuade as well as to inform, are likely to start with particulars and lead the reader gradually to share the writer's conclusions. A news story, for example, would headline and summarize in its first paragraph statistics about the number of people killed, injured, or left destitute by a flood. A feature article or an editorial designed both to inform and to arouse sympathy for the stricken community, might start with particular examples of an orphaned child and a homeless old couple, and proceed from these persuasive, interest-evoking examples to a more general picture of the havoc.

8. Contrast and comparison

We have mentioned earlier the use of contrast and comparison as a method of definition. Contrast, or comparison, or a combination of the two may also be the basic pattern of a long article. A writer may, for example, compare and contrast the earlier and later novels of Sinclair Lewis; or the programs of the New Deal and the New Frontier; or the political records of two candidates for office. If the subjects being compared are complex, they are broken by analysis into their main parts and compared part by part.

These eight organizational patterns—chronological arrangement, definition, analysis, cause-and-effect arrangement, reasons, question-to-answer or problem-to-solution arrangement, general-to-particular or particular-to-general arrangement, and contrast and comparison—are, as we have seen, often closely related and are sometimes used singly, sometimes in combination.

In good informative writing, the organization, besides being fundamentally clear and logical, must be pointed out so that the reader can follow it easily. Indicating at the beginning of the paper its pattern of organization is one way to aid the reader. Another is emphasizing the steps in the development or the relationship of points by means of expressions like *the third problem is . . . the next step is . . . in addition to this equipment the player needs . . . an hour later . . . in the second place . . . this instrument serves two purposes.*

The whole problem of making material clear involves an important question that we have not adequately considered: *Clear to whom?* This brings us to the third requirement of good informative writing: the writer must adjust his material and his style to the needs and interests of his audience.

III. ADJUSTING MATERIAL AND STYLE TO AN AUDIENCE

The writer, planning the presentation of his material, must first of all ask himself: How much do my readers know? The answer to this question is not easy for the student writer, who often has the feeling of aiming at no audience at all. And yet he must make some assumptions about his readers before he can decide how to handle his material. He may (with the instructor's approval) state the kind of reader he would like to write for, and consistently aim his paper at that reader. The best general assumption to make, though, is that he is writing for an intelligent audience that does not have specialized knowledge in any field.[3] Particularly in analyzing processes and mechanisms, it is wise to assume that the intended readers must have any uncommon term

[3] This question of the audience for student themes is discussed more fully in Chapter 3.

and any step in the process clearly explained. There is a practical reason for this: much of the informative writing done by the student is essentially training for later informative writing; at present he may necessarily write about simple subjects of which nearly every reader has some knowledge—how to change a tire, how to paddle a canoe, how an orange juicer operates; but the techniques of organizing this material and presenting it as if the reader knew little about it are the techniques he may sometime use in writing articles and reports and interoffice memos about more complex subjects which his readers will not already understand.

Besides deciding how much his readers (or hypothetical readers) know, the informative writer needs to consider carefully his attitude toward his subject: Is his intention partly evaluative or persuasive? If so, how much shall he let his feelings about the subject enter into his information? He needs to consider with equal care the tone of his writing. Tone establishes the writer-reader relationship, an important, though often subtle, element in any communication. What kind of relationship does the writer want to establish with his readers: formal and impersonal? informal and personal? very informal, chatty, and intimate?

Examples will clarify some of these differences in attitude and tone. The passage below is an article on *skunk* from *The Columbia Encyclopedia:*

> **skunk,** carnivorous, nocturnal mammal of the weasel family. The common or striped skunk of the United States, Mexico, and Canada has thick black fur with two white stripes on the back. It is usually a little over 2 ft. long including the long, bushy tail. Because it destroys many insect pests it is protected in many states. Its ability to spray from the vents under the tail an oily liquid with an offensive, persistent odor protects it against most enemies. In the North the animals sleep through the winter. The small, slender spotted skunk *(Spilogale)* has several white stripes or lines of spots. It inhabits part of the SE and central United States, Mexico, and Central America. In the fur trade it is of less value than the striped skunk. The hognosed skunk *(Conepatus)* ranges from the SW United States through most of South America.[4]

The following passage (the first four paragraphs of an article called "Mephitis, the Skunk," originally published in *The American Mercury*) is another treatment of the same subject:

> Cree Indians call him *Sikak;* mammalogists label him *Mephitis mephitis,* and his pelt, which this year is enjoying a great vogue among the ladies, is apt to be camouflaged beguilingly as *Alaska Sable* or *Black Marten.* Plainest and commonest name of all, certainly the most richly fraught with disparaging implication, is plain *skunk.*
>
> Seldom, however, do we make any effort to know Mephitis better, or to under-

[4] Reprinted from *The Columbia Encyclopedia,* Second Edition. Copyright 1950 by Columbia University Press.

stand him and his skunkly way of life. We are content to believe (as a writer un-
charitably alleged three hundred years ago) that this glossy, plume-tailed cousin of
the weasels is only an "evil-smelling child of the devil," and a rapacious poultry-
thief. It is too bad that we subject little Sikak to such unrelenting ostracism, for we
miss becoming acquainted with one of the most amiable of all our wood-folk.

It is usually late in April or in May that the baby skunk is ushered into life. He is
one of a litter that may contain almost a dozen, and the place of his birth is most
often a vault-chambered burrow in the frozen earth. This root-smelling underground
cavity has been patiently lined with dry leaves and matted grasses against the chill of
spring nights. The baby skunk's universe is a warm and pungent darkness, its silence
broken only by tiny whimperings and the soft pad-pad of his mother's sharp-clawed
paws as she goes and comes on periodic foragings for May-beetles and crickets.

It is necessary that the baby's life should be sequestered in this careful fashion,
for newborn Mephitis is a helpless mite no larger than a meadow mouse. His little
eyes, which will be black and bright as berries, are sealed tight shut as a kitten's.
For two weeks and more he remains unseeing and defenseless. His father retires to a
distant earth-tunnel of his own. It is the mother skunk who must lick and pat and
smooth his soft new fur, must procure unaided a sufficiency of food to insure that
she shall have an adequate milk supply for her prodigious brood.[5]

The expression of attitude toward the subject is very different in these
two pieces. In the first, the attitude is impersonal; the author is merely reporting facts, both favorable (the skunk destroys insect pests) and unfavorable
(the offensive, persistent odor of its spray); he is not concerned with arousing
feeling about the animal. In the longer article, the author sets out, by means of
two stylistic devices, to make his subject appealing and attractive: first, he
humanizes the skunk by naming it and referring to it in the kind of terms
usually associated with a human baby (*Mephitis, cousin, little Sikak, baby's
life, newborn Mephitis*); second, he uses a number of other favorably charged
locutions (*most amiable, helpless mite, little eyes, defenseless, soft new fur*).
The writer is working hard, perhaps too hard, to personalize the skunk and
so to make his writing interesting.

The writer-reader relationship is also different in the two pieces. In the
first it is impersonal; the writer keeps himself out of the communication. In
the second it is personal; the biographer of Mephitis does not use "I" or address his readers directly as "you," but he identifies himself with his readers
(*we are content, we miss,* etc.) even though he does not actually belong to the
group which fails to understand skunks, and he writes conversationally (*it is
too bad, all our wood-folk*). This personal writer-reader relationship is consistent, of course, with his personalizing of the skunk, and is another interest-
arousing technique.

Many readers would say that the second passage, with its personal touch

[5] From *Down to Earth* by Alan Devoe. Copyright, 1940, by Alan Devoe. Reprinted by
permission of Coward-McCann, Inc.

and human appeal, is more interesting than the first. Not everyone, however, would agree. It is certainly true that the passage uses devices for interest, as the encyclopedia article does not; but some readers might object that it is sentimental in its handling of the subject and that it labors the devices of *little Sikak, helpless mite, little eyes,* etc. until they are not really interesting. Readers sensitive to style might point out, also, a certain overelegance and straining for effect in the numerous adjective-noun and verb-adverb combinations, and in other heavy and wordy expressions: *camouflaged beguilingly, richly fraught, disparaging implication, rapacious poultry-thief, unrelenting ostracism, vault-chambered burrow, root-smelling underground cavity, ushered into life, it is necessary that the baby's life be sequestered in this careful fashion, procure unaided a sufficiency of food to insure that she shall have an adequate milk supply for her prodigious brood.* Furthermore, a reader who wanted to learn quickly the main facts about skunks would prefer the brief factual account. Informative writing, like other writing, should be interesting; but *Interesting to whom?* is a question as difficult as *Clear to whom?*

The professional writer can, by studying the publication at which he is aiming, estimate reasonably well both the knowledge his readers have and the kind of style and tone they are likely to expect. The student writer, lacking this advantage, can only consider thoughtfully three things—his assignment, his material, his hypothetical audience—and exercise his best judgment about the most appropriate style, approach to the material, and attitude toward the reader.

Whether or not to use the first person ("I" or "we") in informative writing, and whether or not to use direct address to the reader ("You should first understand the principle") are questions related both to the material and to the writer-reader relationship. These matters of mechanics produce a surprising number of problems; anyone who has struggled with the problems in his own writing is both amused and sympathetic when, in his reading, he finds evidences of the similar struggles of other writers. "I" is often too personal in semiformal or formal writing; also it may focus attention on the writer rather than on the subject matter. The editorial "we" is less personal, but it may create confusion because "we" may at one point in the writing mean the author or authors and, at another point, mean all-of-us—author and audience. Writers sometimes resort to "the writer of this article has found it advisable" as a desperate way out of the difficulty. Direct address to the reader is the clearest form for directions or advice which the reader is expected to follow: "you will need" is simpler and better than "the amateur carpenter needs," or "the would-be fisherman needs." But "you" can cause trouble too. Writers of English texts, for example, sometimes involve themselves in sentences like "It is imperative that the college student learn to punctuate correctly," because the simple "You must learn to punctuate correctly" would be poor in tone for a reader who felt that he had already learned to punctuate correctly. The indefinite "you," unless it is used with discretion, can also produce such startling statements as "You should be buried in an oak coffin," or "The fact that you are an illegitimate child need not wreck your life."

In view of these hazards, it is generally best to avoid direct address except in one of two situations. The first is in giving advice or directions to an audience expected to profit personally from such instructions; here, as we have said, the "you" technique works simply and well. The second situation occurs when the writer, giving information about something remote from the reader's knowledge, feels that he can make his information more vivid and meaningful if he carries the reader directly into an experience. For example, an article about life in London in the eighteenth century might begin, "If you had lived in London in 1750, you would have seen . . . ."; or an article on deep-sea diving might begin, "When you, wearing your two-hundred-pound diving dress, are standing on the bottom of the ocean . . . ." The reader has certainly not lived in 1750, and he may think it just as unlikely that he will ever be standing on the bottom of the ocean. These articles, in other words, are not directive; but association with the experience sometimes makes information more immediate and interesting to the reader. Factual writing, in some instances like these, can be a kind of communication of experience.

IV. READING INFORMATIVE WRITING

Because most college students are required to write informative themes, reports, and research papers, our focus in this discussion of informative writing has been chiefly on the problems of the writer. However, an understanding of these problems and of the techniques of informative prose will be helpful in reading as well as in writing. Reading and writing are interactive: reading supplies models for writing, and examples of applied principles; writing makes one more attentive to the methods of other writers, and therefore a more perceptive reader.

In reading informative prose, one should be particularly alert to (a) the writer's definitions of terms, and (b) his indications of pattern or organization. A writer defines a term for one of two reasons: because he expects it to be unfamiliar to his readers, or because he is using it in some special sense. In either case, he thinks the term is important. The reader needs to understand it, as it is used, in order to understand the whole communication.

Having in mind the organizational patterns discussed in this chapter is helpful in reading, for an informative writer usually indicates in his opening paragraphs what his basic organization is going to be. If he says, "We now have a new concept of political morality," the reader can expect extended definition of this new concept with, perhaps, some contrast to the old; if he says, "Four major problems confront the Security Council," the reader can expect a four-part analysis; if he says, "The duck farmer's day begins at five o'clock," the reader can expect to be taken chronologically through the day. Being attentive to such indications of pattern helps the reader to see the development as he goes along, and to emerge from his reading with an organized knowledge of the material. Noticing the writer's transitions (*on the other hand, the third problem is, the next step,* etc.) also helps one to follow the development. In some kinds of informative writing—textbooks and reports, for example— headings in capital letters, italics, or boldface type further point out the organization and emphasize main ideas.

Finally, the reader should judge, in so far as he can, the value and completeness of the information presented, the soundness of the reasoning and of the conclusions drawn from the facts, and the appropriateness of any attitudinal elements or devices for interest that the writer uses. The reader's first obligation is to understand fully what the writer has said. His final obligation, as a critical reader, is to make some appraisal of the worth of the piece of writing.

TOPICS FOR WRITING

I. Some of the sixteen topics below are specific; others need to be rephrased in terms of the writer's concrete experience. The topics are intended primarily to suggest a number of possible subjects for informative papers. Read the list slowly, rewording the topics to fit your experience and checking any about which you have material for writing. If you were, in fact, writing papers on the subjects you have checked, what method or methods of organization would you be likely to use? Would you need to limit any of the topics?

1. Publishing a literary magazine
2. Training an animal
3. Playing a sport
4. Learning to paint in watercolor
5. Repairing a mechanism
6. Seeing a part of the country (or a country) strange to you before
7. A significant event on campus
8. Gaining a new perspective on a current problem
9. Bird-watching as a hobby
10. Student-faculty relationships in high school and in college
11. The meaning to you of an abstract word such as *education, loyalty, success, happiness, patriotism*
12. Working in a library, office, or store
13. The special language, including slang, of a group to which you belong
14. Race relations in an integrated school

15. Working with retarded children
16. An experiment in education

II. Write a coherent 500- or 600-word summary of one of the essays read in your English course. Your summary should follow the development of ideas in the essay, should be clear and economical, and should include all important ideas.

III. Write a theme on your past experience with English which will give your teacher useful information about you as a student of English. Make your paper a thoughtful, analytical, honest discussion of your abilities, or your tastes, or your weaknesses, or your problems in reading, writing, or speaking English.

Organize your theme around a central idea or around several closely related ideas. Develop these ideas fully, and make the paper interesting by using specific details and examples.

Suggested Topics

My Changing Taste in Reading
The Kind of Writing I Like To Do
The Kind of Writing I Should Like To Be Able To Do
Why I Dislike Writing Themes
The Training in English That I Need
My Principal Problem or Problems in English
The Influence of My Early Training on My Use of English
The Effect of My Reading on My Writing

IV. Study a cartoon that seems to you particularly effective; write a paper in which you describe the cartoon in detail and explain its implications to a reader who has not seen it. The cartoon should have some subtlety, and should be suitable for full description and comment. Your purpose in this paper should be clear description, and intelligent and unbiased interpretation for an audience which may agree or may disagree with the implications of the cartoon. If your writing is successfully objective, the reader will be unable to determine your own point of view, but he will grasp in full the meaning and suggestion of the cartoon. (To enable your instructor to judge the success of your writing, you will need to turn in the cartoon with the theme.)

Chapter 10

EVALUATIVE
WRITING

Evaluative writing is found in reviews of books, movies, plays, and concerts; in newspaper editorials; in commentaries on current affairs; and in critical books and articles of many kinds. The writer makes a judgment of a work or a situation, and imparts that judgment to his readers.

The evaluative or critical use of language is similar to the informative in that it requires knowledge of as many facts as possible, and sound reasoning about the facts; but the critic's conclusions go beyond verifiable fact into the realm of values. In some respects, too, evaluation is similar to persuasion, since persuasion also deals with values and judgments, and since the critic's judgments may influence those of his readers. But evaluation at its best is objective and nonpartisan; the critic's primary purpose is not to influence his readers, but to arrive at and to express the truest judgment to which his knowledge and his standards can lead him.

I. WRITING EVALUATIONS

The writer of an evaluation may use any of the patterns of organization discussed in the preceding chapter. The most common patterns in critical writing are (1) general-to-particular arrangement, in which the writer first expresses his judgment—of a book, for example—and then gives supporting facts, examples, and details; (2) contrast and comparison, in which a work under consideration is compared to other works by the same artist or writer, or to other works in the field; or in which one critical opinion is contrasted with another; (3) analysis—the breaking of a complex topic like a governmental policy into its separate parts, and the criticism of each part and finally of the whole; (4) the pattern of question-to-answer or problem-to-solution, in which the writer's judgment of a situation leads him to recommend a course of action. The soundest evaluations, whatever their pattern, give reasons for the value judgments they express.

In contemporary society, the writer of evaluation has unworthy models —particularly those editorial writers and news commentators who, under the guise of evaluation, consciously slant their facts, make emotional misstatements and unfounded judgments, work for special interests, and appeal to the prejudices of their audience. The writer of evaluation has, however, good models too: those critics who, with a background of knowledge, give their best judgment of a book, a play, an art exhibit, a music festival; those columnists who study all sides of a situation, report the facts, weigh the evidence, and state an opinion; those statesmen who, in a scrupulously nonpartisan way, analyze a policy and make recommendations about it. Critics like these provide a general standard for good criticism: it is informative and logical and unbiased; it appeals to the reason, not merely the feeling, of the audience; and it gives as fully as possible the basis of the critical judgment.

Since criticism of books, essays or plays is often assigned in college, we shall consider briefly the kind of evaluative writing in which the student acts as critic. He should read the work he is to evaluate, with these two questions in mind: *What is the author's purpose? How well does he succeed in achieving his purpose?* Answering the first question will involve deciding whether the author's purpose is to inform, to evaluate, to persuade, or to communicate experience, or whether it is multiple; it will also involve determining the nature of the work, its scope, and the ways in which the author may have limited his subject. Sometimes an author will supply, in a preface or in explanatory notes, information about his purpose. For example, the journalist Tom Wolfe, author of *The Electric Kool-Aid Acid Test,* appends an author's note to that book. Besides detailing the sources he used in writing his account of a group of hippies, Wolfe says in the note that he tried not only to tell what the group did but also "to re-create the mental atmosphere or subjective reality" of their experience; he adds that he has tried to show that, for the members of the band of "Pranksters," the events described in the book were both a group adventure and a personal exploration. Sometimes, too, especially in the preface to a nonfiction book, the author will indicate how and why he has limited the coverage of his topic.

Answering the second question, *How well does he succeed in achieving his purpose?* will involve noting particular matters of organization, method, substance, and style, and also arriving at one kind of judgment of the author's work—an objective judgment of his success in what he was trying to do. Having arrived at this appraisal of the work, the student-critic may proceed to ask a third question: *What is the value of the work?* In answering this question, he makes another judgment, this time not in terms of the author's purpose, but in terms of his own tastes and standards. The two judgments may, of course, coincide: the student may feel that the author has accomplished (or not accomplished) his purpose and has also produced a satisfying (or unsatisfying) work. But the two judgments may differ: granting that the author has succeeded in doing what he set out to do, the reader may find the work shallow and trivial, or offensively morbid, or unreal in the view of life it gives.

In writing his evaluation, the student should cover these three points:

1. What the work is about; its nature, scope, structure, and content, and the author's purpose in writing it.
2. What the student's evaluation is
   a. in terms of the author's purpose
   b. in terms of the student's own standards for an informative, or convincing, or satisfying, or artistic work of this kind.
3. What the student's evidence is for the judgment he arrives at.

If the audience the student is writing for is familiar with the work—if, for example, he is writing for a class in which everyone has read this book—the section of his paper describing its content will be very brief. If, on the other hand, he is writing for the college magazine or for any general audience unacquainted with the book, he will need to describe and summarize it in some detail in order to make his subsequent analysis and criticism clear. In any case, though, an evaluation should not be primarily summary or synopsis of the work. And the writer should, by quotations and examples and specific references, support his critical opinion and let his readers see for themselves why he arrived at it.

In evaluating poems and short stories, the writer will include the material outlined above. He may, however, give slight emphasis to the author's purpose because the general purpose—to communicate experience—may be evident. And much of the student's evaluation will probably be technical analysis of the work. The author's style—choice of words, choice of details, imagery, metaphor, patterns of sound—and the author's technical and artistic skills are likely to be very important in appraising his achievement.

II. JUDGING EVALUATIONS

A critic may, in an evaluation of some length, give detailed reasons for his opinions; he may support them with a mass of factual evidence, and may refer to or criticize the opinions of others. The reader is given the whole basis of the evaluation, and he can judge it by asking himself if the facts seem to be fairly selected, and if the reasoning from the facts is sound. He may not agree with the evaluation, because his standards and values may differ from those of the writer, but if he judges it to be fair, intelligent, and honest, then it deserves his attention and respect as one man's considered judgment on this subject.

In short articles, the writer usually cites only a few facts and instances to support or explain his evaluation. A book reviewer, for example, may quote a passage or two and refer to several specific instances of questionable fact or of careful scholarship in the book. Very short book reviews, because of limited space, may give no factual evidence to support the writer's evaluation. And certain newspaper columnists, sometimes for reasons other than limitations of space, fail to supply facts on which their judgment is presumably founded.

The reader has real problems in judging criticism that gives little or no factual evidence to support the writer's conclusions. The best guide is probably the author's record and reputation: Is he a recognized authority? Have his training and experience equipped him to make sound judgments in this field? Does he have prejudices that influence his evaluations? Have his past evaluations been reasonable and trustworthy? The repute of the newspaper or magazine in which an article appears may further help one judge the worth of the evaluation. Nearly every publication has a consistent slant on some matters, and is not completely impartial in selecting the material it prints. On the other hand, a number of publications maintain a high standard, and anything they publish has been adjudged valid by a careful editorial staff.

Familiarity with other opinions on the same subject is also useful to the reader of evaluation. College students should be familiar with *The Book Review Digest,* which gives excerpts from various reviews of the same book. The reviews are often contradictory in their judgments; the reader sees that a single judgment is not necessarily the truth about the book; the weight of critical opinion, however, may support or may cause doubt about the opinion expressed in a particular review that he is trying to appraise. Reading several of the reviews quoted in the *Digest* (and preferably reading the book itself), and deliberately reading newspapers, magazines, and columnists with different slants will help one judge other people's evaluations. More important, it will help one form considered judgments of his own.

Finally, the reader of the short evaluation can ask himself whether or not the writer seems to be fair-minded, and whether or not he is giving as much factual support of his judgment as space allows. If he is filling space with name-calling and with appeals to emotion instead of with evidence and reasons, the reader is justified in questioning his integrity and therefore his evaluation. If the evaluation seems to be fair-minded and founded on solid knowledge, the reader will not necessarily accept it, but, as we have said before, he will respect it as an honest, informed opinion.

TOPICS FOR WRITING

I. Below are ten limited topics, which may suggest others, for evaluative papers.

1. Your twelfth-grade English course
2. House rules (or absence of rules) in the house or dormitory where you live
3. Rules governing use of the college library
4. Fraternities on the campus
5. The role of students in determining educational policy
6. An evening with television
7. The "relevance" of one or two required courses
8. The idea of ungraded college courses
9. Reducing undergraduate colleges and universities to three instead of four years
10. The selective service system: fair or unfair?

II. Following the suggestions in this chapter, write an evaluation of a book, play, film, art exhibit, television show, or concert. Include as much specific detail as possible to support your judgment.

III. Clip from a magazine or newspaper a short review of a book or film, and write an analysis and appraisal of the review. In planning your paper, consider the following questions: (a) What is the reviewer's judgment of the work he is reviewing? (b) What kinds of evidence does he give in support of his judgment? (c) What is the general plan of the review? For example, does the reviewer state his judgment early and then give reasons or evidence; or does the review build from particulars to a judgment at the end? (d) What is your opinion of the review, and what are the reasons for your opinion?

IV. Read two or three reviews of the same book and write a comparison of the factual content, attitude, and intention of the articles. Include in your paper a judgment of the reviews: which seems to you the best, which the worst, and why?

V. Write a paper in which you compare, contrast, and evaluate any two selections on the same general subject read in your English course and approved by your instructor for this assignment.

VI. Compare a movie or television play with the book on which it is based, giving reasons for your judgment that one is better than the other.

Chapter 11

PERSUASIVE
WRITING

The term *persuasive writing* covers a range of material. It includes the formal argument used in debates, in courts of law, and in much reflective and philosophical writing; such argument appeals chiefly to reason. It also includes various kinds of formal and informal inducement which may appeal largely to feeling.

The writer of persuasion often presents and explains facts; he is often persuading his audience to accept a judgment he has made; and, knowing that people respond to the problems and emotions of other human beings as they cannot respond to impersonal facts and figures, he may communicate human experience—real or fictitious—to achieve his purpose. What distinguishes persuasive writing from other types of communication is neither its content nor its form, but its primary intention: persuasion is consciously aimed at directing human actions and at molding human attitudes. The persuasive writer is committed to a purpose, sometimes of changing his readers' beliefs and behavior, sometimes of confirming or bolstering with new data the beliefs they already hold.

The principal methods of persuasion are (1) persuasion by logical argument, (2) persuasion by appeal to emotion, (3) persuasion by irony and ridicule. Though these methods overlap and are frequently used in combination, they are best clarified by separate discussion.

Tone and attitude are important parts of successful persuasion. We shall comment on them further in the following pages; here we only suggest a general principle: usually, and especially if the audience aimed at is an intelligent audience, temperance and restraint are more persuasive than immoderation in argument or in the expression of feeling. A fable tells of the sun and wind in rivalry to cause a man to remove his cloak. The wind lashes and buffets him, and the man protectively wraps his cloak more tightly about him. The sun shines warmly and benignly, and the man responds by taking off his cloak. Gentle persuasion is usually more effective than force in causing people to change the cloak of their opinions.

I. PERSUASION BY LOGICAL ARGUMENT

The closely organized logical argument usually follows a basic plan of this kind: (1) The writer or speaker states the question clearly and fairly, defining any terms that might be ambiguous, and limiting the argument to the specific issues that he regards as important; he may in this preliminary step of his argument consider the history of the question and its present significance. (2) He states his position and supports that position by citing facts and authorities, and by reasoning from the evidence he presents. (3) He recognizes and refutes any outstanding arguments against his ideas. (4) He summarizes his argument and emphasizes the merits of his position or his proposal. Less formal arguments are likely to include these four steps too, but to follow a more personal, less orderly plan.

The writer of convincing argument must have studied his subject thoroughly. He must know exactly what the major issues are, so that he will not waste words in arguing trivial side issues or points on which there is general agreement. He must have not merely facts and authorities to support his position, but trustworthy, representative, up-to-date facts and reputable authorities. He must know his subject well enough to know more than one side of it. Argument, unlike some other kinds of persuasion, assumes opposition; understanding that opposition, being able to concede its strength on some points, but also to demonstrate its weakness on vital points, may be a large part of successful argumentation. In order to see weaknesses in opposing views, and in order to evaluate his own evidence and to arrive at sound conclusions, the writer needs, in addition to knowledge, skill in logical reasoning.

The reader of argument also needs this skill. If he is a critical reader, he will ask two questions about a piece of argumentative prose: Is the evidence good? Is the reasoning sound? In answering the first question he will be helped immeasurably, of course, if he has read and thought about the subject, if he himself has some command of the facts and some acquaintance with the recognized authorities in the field. But without this knowledge he still can make valid judgments about the evidence on which the writer's conclusions are based. He can see how well the writer's statements are substantiated. Some of them may be unsubstantiated, or practically so: "leading scientists agree," or "as psychologists tell us," or "the facts are well known," or "experiments have proved" is not equivalent to quoting scientists, psychologists, facts, or results of specific experiments. Some statements may have unreliable substantiation because the sources are unauthoritative or prejudiced: "the Podunk *Post-Examiner* of February 10, 1970, says . . . ."; "the last issue of *Popular Reading* contains an article which settles this issue for all time"; "John Smith's authoritative study [written in 1945] says the last word on college football"; "the *Democratic Digest* gives an impartial account of the political situation." The reader can also recognize the citing of irrelevant or dubious authority— Thomas Jefferson, for example, quoted to support an argument against national health insurance; or a famous chemist quoted on foreign policy, or a prominent businessman on modern art. Persons competent in one field are not necessarily authorities in another. Finally, a reader can make some judgment of the evidence by asking himself how much of it there is, and whether the writer seems to have minimized or ignored evidence on the other side.

In answering the second question—Is the reasoning sound?—the reader is aided by a knowledge of logic. Frequently, while reading or listening to argument, one has an elusive sense of illogic in the thinking, a feeling of something's-wrong-but-I-can't-put-my-finger-on-it. A knowledge of the two kinds of logical thinking called *induction* and *deduction,* and of the common errors in logic, called *fallacies,* makes it easier to detect weaknesses in reasoning and also to recognize and to practice sound reasoning.

A. Induction

Induction is the kind of reasoning by which we examine a number of particulars or specific instances and on the basis of them arrive at a generalized conclusion. The scientist reasons inductively when he observes a series of phenomena and arrives at a conclusion or hypothesis which explains the phenomena and enables him to predict that under certain circumstances a particular phenomenon will take place; if in the course of time further observation supports his hypothesis and if no exceptions are observed, his conclusion is generally accepted as truth and is sometimes called a law. In everyday living, too, we arrive at conclusions by induction. Every cat we encounter has claws; we conclude that all cats have claws. Every rose we smell is fragrant; we conclude that all roses are fragrant. An acquaintance has, on various occasions, paid back money he has borrowed; we conclude that he is frequently out of funds but that he pays his debts. Every Saturday morning for six weeks the new paper boy is late in delivering the paper; we conclude that he sleeps on Saturday mornings and we no longer look for the paper before nine o'clock.

In each case we have reasoned inductively from a number of instances; we have moved from an observation of some things to a generalization about all things in the same category.

Occasionally, in restricted situations, it is possible to examine every instance. For example, a teacher may note that student A is present in class today, student B is present, C is present, and so on through the whole class list; by simple counting, the teacher can conclude that all members of the class are present today. Ordinarily, though, it is impossible to examine every instance—the claws of every cat, for example, or the nervous system of every cockroach, or every case of diphtheria, or every ruptured appendix, or the opinion of every voter. One must make an inductive jump from the instances he can know to a conclusion embracing things of the same sort that he cannot know. Inductive reasoning arrives, therefore, not at "truth" or "law," but at probability. The probability grows stronger and the induction becomes sounder when a substantial number of instances are examined, when the instances examined are typical, and when the exceptions, if any, are infrequent and explainable.

A conclusion based on too few instances or on untypical instances is called a **hasty generalization.** It is the most common fallacy in inductive reasoning, and is responsible for much misinformation and prejudice: "Negroes are lazy." "Why do you say that?" "Well, we had a Negro cook who was the laziest mortal I ever saw, and look at Bob Jones—he doesn't even try to get a job." The speaker is, of course, generalizing on the basis of only two examples, assuming that these examples are typical, and ignoring the countless exceptions. The hasty generalization may also occur in scientific research; further research may reveal exceptions which modify or invalidate the earlier conclusion.

Cause-effect induction is reasoning about why things happen and about the relationship between them. We observe effects and arrive at a conclusion about their cause; or we observe a set of circumstances (causes) and draw a conclusion about their effects; or we observe some effects and reason from them that there will be other effects. A doctor examines a patient, learns his symptoms, and from the data makes a diagnosis; he has started with the effects of the illness and reasoned to the cause of them. In cause-to-effect thinking the process is reversed because we can see the causes and, usually with the help of past inductions, can predict the effects. A student visits football practice two days before the opening game; he observes that two players are fighting on the field, that the captain and the coach are on bad terms, that the team's best passer is on the bench with a broken arm, and that the backfield is slow; seeing these causes, he predicts that this will not be a successful team. Effect-to-effect thinking is chain reasoning which also usually relies on past inductions: "That little accident [cause] smashed the right front fender [observed effect]; Father will be angry and will make me pay for a new fender [further effect reasoned on the basis of past instances]; I won't be able to take Jane to the prom [ultimate effect]."

A great deal of scientific research deals with causal relationships; that is, with observing and describing those orderly connections between elements and events in the universe, on the basis of which causes can be assigned and effects predicted with accuracy. In our daily thinking, too, we make numerous cause-effect inductions, many of which, however, lack scientific exactitude; they need to be verified before they can be held as logical conclusions. The following effect-to-cause inductions are fairly typical of the kind of reasoning we hear and perhaps do every day. During a storm, the back door slams with such force that the glass breaks; we assume that the wind blew the door. A friend is obviously depressed on the day grades come out; we say that he is badly disappointed in his grades. An engagement is broken a month after the engaged girl's family loses its money; we conclude that the engagement was broken for that reason. All these inductions need further verification, for the cause in each case may well be different from the one assigned: the door may have been slammed by a member of the family who is happy to have the storm blamed for it; the friend may be depressed and the engagement may have been broken for any number of reasons.

These examples illustrate two common fallacies in cause-effect induction. The first fallacy is oversimplifying, and attributing to a single cause effects which actually have complex causes. "I failed the course because the teacher was unreasonably hard" is sometimes an example of this oversimplification. Other examples are: "The atomic bomb won World War II"; "The problem of our cities is unsolved because we have spent billions on the space program"; "The reason for the high cost of living is the program of farm subsidies."

Often closely related to oversimplifying the cause is the logical fallacy of seeing a cause-effect relationship between events that have only an accidental time relationship. This fallacy is called **post hoc ergo propter hoc,** Latin for "after this therefore because of this." A common instance of this reasoning is a statement like "I won't vote for the Democrats again. Six months after they got into office the city tax rate went up ten dollars." It is possible, of course, that the Democrats were responsible for the tax increase; but it is also possible that any administration would have found higher taxes necessary. Asserting without proof a cause-effect relationship simply because one event follows another is as illogical as asserting that breakfast causes lunch. Many superstitions are maintained by this *post hoc ergo propter hoc* thinking. A superstitious person walks under a ladder, and an hour later, for reasons entirely unrelated to that incident, has a quarrel with a good friend; he forgets or ignores the real causes of the quarrel, falls into the logical confusion of after-I-walked-under-the-ladder-therefore-because-I-walked-under-the-ladder, and is confirmed in his original faulty induction that walking under ladders brings bad luck.

Induction by analogy occurs when one observes that two things are similar in some ways, and then reasons, from the observed likeness, that they are also similar in other ways. For example, Sir Isaac Newton observed that certain combustible substances—oils, turpentine, camphor, etc.—had refractive powers two or three times greater than might be expected from their densities. He reasoned by analogy that the diamond, with its very high refractive powers, was also combustible. This inference was correct.

Reasoning from analogy is dangerous, however, and argument by analogy alone is seldom convincing, because analogous situations or objects have differences as well as similarities and the differences may outweigh the similarities. Sir David Brewster, a nineteenth-century physicist and biographer of Sir Isaac Newton, pointed out that if Newton had reasoned from analogy the combustibility of greenockite and octahedrite, which also have high refractive powers, he would have been wrong. His reasoning about the diamond simply happened to be right. Long observation of Mars has given astronomers a body of data from which they have arrived inductively at a number of conclusions about that planet. Some people have reasoned by analogy that since Mars has atmosphere, temperatures, and seasonal changes comparable to earth's, it must also have life like ours. This conclusion is questionable; it disregards the observed differences between the two planets.

Analogy is not logical proof. In informative writing it is a useful method of clarifying a difficult subject. Skillful analogy also has great persuasive power. But it should be used in conjunction with, not as a substitute for, more strictly logical reasoning; and it is effective only when the similarities are striking and the differences slight between the things being compared. The following induction by analogy is weak because the comparison is farfetched and the differences are glaring:

> Even the most durable machines break down if they are worked constantly for long periods of time. Their parts wear out; they become inefficient. Are students supposed to be stronger than machines? Do they deserve less attention and care? We should have shorter assignments and longer vacations.

The following famous passage illustrates effective analogy. The comparison is used not to prove, but to describe and to persuade:

> In the field of world policy I would dedicate this Nation to the policy of the good neighbor—the neighbor who resolutely respects himself and because he does so, respects the rights of others—the neighbor who respects his obligations and respects the sanctity of his agreements in and with a world of neighbors.—FRANKLIN D. ROOSEVELT, *First Inaugural Address*

B. Deduction

Inductive reasoning, as we have seen, moves from individual circumstances or instances to a conclusion; this conclusion, unless every possible instance has been examined, expresses probability; the probability is as strong as the weight of evidence that supports it. Deduction is reasoning from stated propositions or premises to a conclusion. If the conclusion follows logically from the premises and if the premises are true, deduction arrives at proof or certainty.

All men are mortal.
John is a man.
Therefore John is mortal.

The statement above is a **syllogism,** the pattern in which, in formal logic, a deductive argument is expressed. The syllogism consists of three statements—a major premise, a minor premise, and a conclusion drawn from the premises.

A syllogism like the preceding one—called a *categorical* syllogism—contains three and only three main terms, each of which appears twice, but not twice in the same statement. The terms are given these names: the **major term** is the predicate of the conclusion; the **minor term** is the subject of the conclusion; and the **middle term** appears in both premises. The major term in the syllogism above is "mortal," and the premise in which it appears is called the **major premise.** The minor term is "John," and the premise in which it appears is called the **minor premise.** The middle term, "man/men," appears in both premises.

Diagraming the syllogism sometimes makes the relationship of statements clearer:

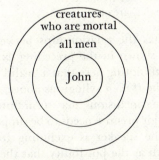

If all men are included in the larger group of mortal things (major premise), and if John is included in the group of all men (minor premise), then John is inevitably included in the group of those who are mortal (conclusion).

Categorical syllogisms like the one we have been considering may make affirmative or negative statements; they can be represented by the formulas *All X is Y; Z is X; therefore Z is Y,* or *No X is Y; Z is X; therefore Z is not Y:*

MAJOR PREMISE: All dogs are carnivorous.
MINOR PREMISE: My cocker is a dog.
CONCLUSION: Therefore my cocker is carnivorous.

MAJOR PREMISE: No dogs live forever.
MINOR PREMISE: My cocker is a dog.
CONCLUSION: Therefore my cocker will not live forever.

Different phrasings of the major premise produce other patterns of the syllogism. One of these is the *if-then* pattern, in which the major premise expresses a cause-effect induction. The form of this syllogism is *If X, then Y; X; therefore Y*, or *If X, then Y; not Y; therefore not X:*

MAJOR PREMISE: If college administrators are responsive to student criticism, then violent protest ceases.
MINOR PREMISE: Administrators in my college are responsive to student criticism.
CONCLUSION: Therefore violent protest will cease.

MAJOR PREMISE: If college administrators are responsive to student criticism, then violent protest ceases.
MINOR PREMISE: Violent protest in my college has not ceased.
CONCLUSION: Therefore administrators are not responsive to student criticism.

Another form of the syllogism is established by the *either-or* major premise. The pattern is *Either X or Y; not X; therefore Y*, or *Either X or Y; not Y; therefore X:*

MAJOR PREMISE: Either the keys are on the table, or they are in the car.
MINOR PREMISE: They are not on the table.
CONCLUSION: Therefore they are in the car.

MAJOR PREMISE: Either the keys are on the table, or they are in the car.
MINOR PREMISE: They are not in the car.
CONCLUSION: Therefore they are on the table.

When a syllogism has the relationships between terms and between premises and conclusion shown in the preceding examples, its argument is said to be *valid*. It is worth noting here that a "valid" argument is not necessarily *factually true*. In the *if-then* syllogisms above, for example, the major premise, and therefore the conclusions, may seem untrue; certainly the cause-effect statement in the major premise needs to be supported. And the *either-or* argument is untrue if the speaker is excluding from his major premise possible alternatives—such as the possibility that the keys are in his pocket. Perhaps the point about validity and truth will be clearer if we look at more obvious examples:

MAJOR PREMISE: Irishmen have hot tempers.
MINOR PREMISE: He is Irish.
CONCLUSION: Therefore he is hot tempered.

MAJOR PREMISE: Poisonous snakes should be killed.
MINOR PREMISE: Garter snakes are poisonous.
CONCLUSION: Therefore garter snakes should be killed.

These two arguments are "valid" because they have the logical form of the categorical syllogism. However, the conclusions are unreliable because the major premise of the first syllogism is a hasty generalization, and the minor premise of the second syllogism is a misstatement of fact. In judging the truth or reliability of a deductive argument, one must ask two questions: Are the premises true? Is the argument valid? If the answer to both questions is "yes," the deduction can be accepted as true.[1]

C. Fallacies

We have mentioned earlier the common fallacies in inductive reasoning: hasty generalization, oversimplification of complex causes, *post hoc ergo propter hoc* argument, and faulty analogy. The most common fallacies in deductive argument come from (*a*) questionable or incorrect premises, and (*b*) the faulty relationship of parts of the syllogism. Fallacies in relationship sometimes produce a slippery illogic in the reasoning, difficult to detect. For example, in the categorical syllogisms illustrated in the last section, the subject of the major premise is the predicate of the minor premise; the form of the syllogism is, as we have noted, *All X is Y; Z is X; therefore Z is Y.* In the following syllogism of somewhat the same pattern, the terms are shifted:

> All tigers are felines. (*X is Y*)
> My cat is a feline. (*Z is Y*)
> Therefore my cat is a tiger. (∴ *Z is X*)

The illogic here is made apparent by the absurdity of the conclusion; but it may not be so apparent in a similarly constructed syllogism:

> All communists say Russia doesn't want war.
> He says Russia doesn't want war.
> Therefore he is a communist.

Diagraming such arguments is a good way of seeing why they are invalid:

 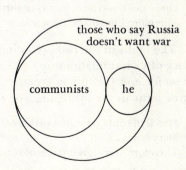

---

[1] True premises and a valid argument can produce only a true conclusion. Untrue premises, as we have seen, can produce questionable or untrue conclusions. But it may be worth noting that a conclusion may happen to be true even though it is drawn from false premises: All cats are birds; all pigeons are cats; therefore all pigeons are birds. The conclusion here is true for reasons other than those stated in the premises.

My cat and *he* are in the large circles of *felines* and *those who say Russia doesn't want war,* but not necessarily in the smaller circles of *tigers* and *communists.* There is no established relationship between the terms (tigers and my cat; communists and he) except the fact that they are both members of a larger group.

Another fallacy is in conclusions drawn from negative premises. If one premise in a categorical syllogism is negative, the conclusion must be negative in a valid argument; if both premises are negative, no conclusion can be drawn.

> VALID: Only freshmen are attending the meeting.
> John is not a freshman.
> Therefore John is not attending the meeting.

> INVALID: No freshmen are attending the meeting.
> John is not a freshman.
> Therefore John is attending the meeting.

No conclusion can be drawn from the last two negative premises; John may or may not be attending the meeting.

In a valid argument, the conclusion follows inevitably from the premises. *Non sequitur* (Latin for "it does not follow") is the fallacy of leaping to a conclusion not warranted by the premises. Drawing a conclusion from negative premises is one form of *non sequitur.* Other examples are:

> Anyone who works hard deserves a vacation now and then.
> I work hard.
> Therefore my parents should give me a trip to Bermuda.

> Men who have made sacrifices for their country should be honored.
> I have made sacrifices for my country.
> Therefore I should be President.

The faults in the two preceding syllogisms are closely related to another fallacy of logical relationship—*the shifting of the meaning of terms between the major and the minor premise.* The shifted meaning is equivalent to a fourth term in the syllogism. For example:

> Man is the only creature capable of reason.
> Mary is not a man.
> Therefore Mary is incapable of reason.

The meaning of *man* has been shifted from *mankind* in the major premise to *male* in the minor premise. Other examples of shifted meanings are:

> Men who have devoted themselves to the service of the community should hold public office.

I have devoted myself to the service of the community by running a bakery for fifteen years.

Therefore I should hold public office.

Government employees who are sympathetic with Russian policy should be discharged.

This government employee belonged in 1943 to an organization which was friendly toward Russia.

Therefore he should be discharged.

We seldom encounter the complete syllogism except in discussions of logic and in very formal argument. More usual is a reduced form of the syllogism in which one or two of the three parts, though implied, are not stated. The reduced syllogism is called an **enthymeme.** Sometimes in the enthymeme the conclusion of the syllogism is omitted because it is obvious: *Students who are found cheating on examinations fail the course; Clarence has been found cheating on an examination;* [the obvious omitted conclusion: therefore Clarence will fail the course]. Sometimes the minor premise is omitted for the same reason: *I like candidates who speak their minds; I'm going to vote for you;* [omitted premise: you speak your mind]. Sometimes both the minor premise and the conclusion are omitted because the major premise adequately communicates them: *I date only men who have cars;* [omitted: you don't have a car; therefore I won't have a date with you]. Most frequently the major premise is omitted because the communicator assumes (often wrongly) that it is universally accepted and so does not require proof or even statement. One of the most useful skills of the hearer or reader of argument, therefore, is the ability to supply the omitted major premise. By recognizing that premise and examining it critically, he can better judge the reliability of the argument. The enthymemes below are familiar informal arguments; the major premise on which each one is based is put in brackets.

Jim must have been in a fight; he has a black eye. [Major premise: All black eyes are the result of fights.]

So he forgot he made the appointment. What can you expect? He's a college professor. [Major premise: College professors usually forget appointments. *Or,* College professors are absent-minded.]

He must be a grind! He got all A's last semester. [Students who get A records are grinds.]

He can't be a good doctor. He's in favor of socialized medicine. [No good doctor is in favor of socialized medicine.]

You're crazy, saying the meat tastes spoiled. I got it at the store just an hour ago. [Meat is always fresh when it is bought at stores.]

What a coward. He's a conscientious objector, you know. [All conscientious objectors are cowards.]

Naturally he's a delinquent. He reads ten comic books a week. [Reading comics always produces delinquency. *Or,* If one reads many comic books, then he will be a delinquent.]

Of course it's true; I read it in the paper. [Everything printed in the newspapers is true.]

They won't be happy together; he's two years younger than she. [Marriages are always unhappy if the man is younger than the woman.]

I think they'll be very nice neighbors. They have a new Cadillac. [People are nice neighbors if they have a new Cadillac. *Or,* If people have a new Cadillac, then they'll be nice neighbors.]

We're not talking about the same girl. The one I knew last summer had blond hair. [Once a blonde always a blonde.]

His mother has trained him to be neat around the house; he'll make a wonderful husband. [Any man who is neat around the house is a wonderful husband; also, a man trained by his mother to be neat around the house will continue to be neat when he is married.]

Two logical fallacies not peculiar to induction or to deduction, but involving the quality of the whole argument, are *begging the question* and *ignoring the question.*

Begging the question is assuming, without proof, the truth of a proposition which actually needs proof. If an arguer says, "This senseless language requirement should be abolished," he is, with the word *senseless,* begging the question; the question is whether or not the language requirement is senseless; if it is, it should of course be abolished; simply calling it senseless is not a logical argument in its disfavor. "This corrupt political machine should be replaced by good government" is another example of begging the question. No proof is offered that the government under attack is a "corrupt political machine," or that the government supported by the speaker will be "good." Both propositions are simply assumed. *Arguing in a circle* is one form of begging the question:

People who are poor lack ambition because if they didn't lack ambition they wouldn't be poor.

The study of literature is worthwhile because literature is a worthwhile subject.

Such argument in a circle is sometimes baffling, particularly when the argument is long and the circular motion is therefore difficult to detect. What the arguer in a circle does, technically, is offer as proof of his first proposition a second proposition which can be proved only by proving the first.

Ignoring the question is diverting attention from the real issues, or shifting the argument to some other ground. It has many forms. Name-calling, introducing irrelevant facts, and using other devices of charged language may be means of ignoring the real question. Sometimes a new argument is introduced in an effort to obscure the original issue: "I told you, Dorothy, I can't afford to buy you a coat this winter." "I don't see why not. Susan Jones has a new coat. I should think you'd want me to be well dressed. It's a good thing someone in this family takes some pride in appearance. You haven't even shaved today." Arguing that an accused murderess should be acquitted because she is the mother of three children, and that a candidate should be mayor because he is the veteran of two wars are examples of ignoring the question by shifting from the central issues; the questions here are "Did she commit the murder?" and "Will he make a good mayor?" What is called argument *ad hominem* (to the man) is a way of ignoring the question by a shift from reasonable consideration of a measure or proposal to an attack on the character of the opponent; his ancestry, his religion, the fact that his first wife divorced him, that his son was arrested for speeding, etc. may be introduced to appeal to prejudice while the real question—the merits and defects of the proposal itself—is ignored. When the English quartet called the Beatles first appeared in this country, their singing and playing received some adverse criticism. Among the replies[2] to one critic's unfavorable judgment were these arguments: "You're jealous of them—jealous because you'll never make as much money in your whole life as they have in one year"; "Maybe if you had as much talent as a writer as they have in singing, your articles might be better"; "You may as well crawl back into your cave." These are examples of ignoring the question, and argument *ad hominem*.

D. The Texture of Logical Thought

Although we have separated induction and deduction for purposes of discussion, the two processes work together in most acts of reasoning. A simple illustration of the interplay between them is this: A friend asks you one afternoon to go with him to a movie at the neighborhood theater. You say, "No; it's Saturday." Behind your refusal lies an induction, based on instances in your own experience, that on Saturday afternoons many school children attend this theater and are very noisy. You make a quick deduction: Every Saturday afternoon this theater is full of noisy school children; this is Saturday; therefore the theater will be full of noisy school children. Another inductive-deductive process also takes place. You have arrived at the generalization that you do not enjoy a movie if you cannot hear all of it. You reason: I do not want to go to a movie if I cannot hear all of it; I will not be able to hear all of it today (because of the noise of the children);

2 Printed in the Boston *Globe*, February 12, 1964.

therefore I do not want to go to this movie on this day. Still another reasoning process about your relationship with the friend who has asked you to go to the movie may occur. From your past experience with him you may have induced: Jack is not offended if for some good reason I refuse his invitations. Now you may deduce: I am refusing this invitation for a good reason; therefore Jack will not be offended. In this kind of thinking, the inductions and deductions are almost automatic. In more complex reasoning they are formulated only after conscious and disciplined thought.

We have said earlier that induction is important in scientific thinking: it enables human beings to arrive at generalizations and hypotheses about the world they live in, to see cause-effect relationships, and, on the basis of established probabilities, to make predictions and produce effects by controlling causes. As a science advances and its inductive hypotheses are further substantiated, the substantiated hypotheses supply premises from which deductive conclusions are drawn. One kind of reasoning leads to and supports the other. In the same way, in a logical argument, observed instances have perhaps led the speaker or writer inductively to the position he takes in the argument. From his inductions he may reason deductively about what should be done in a particular situation.

Closely interwoven though the two kinds of reasoning are, it is useful to have some knowledge of their differences, of the different kinds of reliability they can arrive at, and of the common fallacies in each kind of thinking. Being able to reduce a confusing argument to syllogistic form will enable one to see more clearly its premises and its validity. Being alert to hasty generalization, to faulty cause-effect reasoning, to conclusions that do not follow the premises, to question-begging, and to ignoring of the question will help one judge the soundness of an argument. One who has some familiarity with logic is less likely than others to slip into the logical weaknesses that often occur in the writing of college students. The scrupulous, reasonable writer checks the data from which he draws conclusions; gives a fair consideration to all the facts, not only those which accord with his point of view; both avoids hasty generalization and takes pains to support his generalizations with facts and instances. He takes pains, too, to qualify when qualifying is needed, not to overstate or to make assertions beyond his knowledge: he guards against imprecise statements like "Students learn tolerance in college" (All students?); "Parents fail to understand our values" (All parents? All values?); "Our generation has never known poverty" (What about those in slums, in depressed areas?). The careful writer also avoids *if-then* and *either-or* propositions which illogically exclude other possibilities; examples are "If the administration censors student publications, the intellectual life of the university will die"; "Either we win the war in Southeast Asia or we surrender to the Communists." The writing of many students becomes tighter, more exact, when they consciously subject it to the tests of reason. A knowledge of the processes of logical thought, in short, provides instruments of analysis with which one can better examine the texture of his own argument and the arguments of others.

E. Tone

In persuasion by logical argument, the writer may be formal or informal in his attitude toward his audience; but he is usually less concerned with ingratiating himself than with winning their respect. For this respect, he depends largely on the quality of the argument itself. If he presents the issues fairly; if he is reasonable in considering opposing points of view; if his evidence is good and his thinking clear and sound; if he respects the intelligence of his audience and assumes that they will not be convinced by slippery illogic and devices like arguments *ad hominem,* he will almost certainly gain a respectful hearing for what he has to say.

As a rule, the most skillful argument is reasonable in tone as well as in thought; it gives the impression of trying to arrive at truth, not merely to win a case; it is good tempered, and free from dogmatism and conceit. Fighting-mad arguments and dogmatic statements do sometimes affect already-sympathetic or prejudiced audiences; but they are likely to alienate and offend an impartial audience. Benjamin Franklin, wise in argument and diplomacy, wrote in his autobiography:

I made it a rule to forbear all direct contradiction to the sentiments of others, and all positive assertion of my own. I even forbade myself . . . the use of every word or expression in the language that imported a fix'd opinion, such as *certainly, undoubtedly,* etc., and I adopted, instead of them, *I conceive, I apprehend,* or *I imagine* a thing to be so or so; or it *so appears to me at present.* When another asserted something that I thought an error, I deny'd myself the pleasure of contradicting him abruptly, and of showing immediately some absurdity in his proposition; and in answering I began by observing that in certain cases or circumstances his opinion would be right, but in the present case there *appear'd* or *seem'd* to me some difference, etc. I soon found the advantage of this change in my manner; the conversations I engag'd in went on more pleasantly. The modest way in which I propos'd my opinions procur'd them a readier reception and less contradiction; I had less mortification when I was found to be in the wrong, and I more easily prevail'd with others to give up their mistakes and join with me when I happened to be in the right.

And this mode, which I at first put on with some violence to natural inclination, became at length so easy, and so habitual to me, that perhaps for these fifty years past no one has ever heard a dogmatical expression escape me. And to this habit (after my character of integrity) I think it principally owing that I had early so much weight with my fellow-citizens when I proposed new institutions, or alterations in the old, and so much influence in public councils when I became a member; for I was but a bad speaker, never eloquent, subject to much hesitation in my choice of words, hardly correct in language, and yet I generally carried my points.

II. PERSUASION BY APPEAL TO EMOTION

Persuasion by appeal to emotion is accomplished chiefly by the use of charged language. Since the devices of charged language have been discussed fully in the early sections of this book, it will be necessary here only to recall the most commonly used techniques: slanting by emphasis and selection of detail; the use of charged abstract words, charged words of personal attitude, charged proper names, and other charged expressions; irony and ridicule; the "right-on-our-side" technique. Heavily and irresponsibly charged language may employ irrelevant or untrue "facts," name-calling, and the false appearance of logical reasoning to arouse emotion.

All these persuasive devices may be used consciously, craftily, and dishonestly. It is important to remember, though, that some of the most moving human utterances are not calculated appeals to emotion, but sincere expressions of feeling, from the heart to the heart. Such honest expressions of emotion, accompanied by logical argument or evaluation, or springing from a deeply-felt human experience, are worthy of the highest respect:

We shall go on to the end, we shall fight in France, we shall fight on the seas and oceans, we shall fight with growing confidence and growing strength in the air, we shall defend our Island, whatever the cost may be, we shall fight on the beaches, we shall fight on the landing grounds, we shall fight in the fields and in the streets, we shall fight in the hills; we shall never surrender, and even if, which I do not for a moment believe, this Island or a large part of it were subjugated and starving, then our Empire beyond the seas, armed and guarded by the British Fleet, would carry on the struggle, until, in God's good time, the New World, with all its power and might, steps forth to the rescue and the liberation of the old.—WINSTON CHURCHILL, Speech after Dunkirk, 1940.

Intreat me not to leave thee, or to return from following after thee: for whither thou goest, I will go; and where thou lodgest, I will lodge: thy people shall be my people, and thy God my God: where thou diest, will I die, and there will I be buried: the Lord do so to me, and more also, if ought but death part thee and me.—The Book of Ruth

Tone and attitude are especially significant in writing that persuades wholly or partly by appeal to emotion. The writer nearly always makes an effort to establish friendly relations with his readers, and to emphasize attitudes and loyalties that he shares with them. Because this friendly, personal tone is so common, and so valuable in setting the stage for persuasion, it is sometimes difficult to judge whether a writer is sincere, or whether he is shrewdly playing on the feelings of his audience. (The apparent concern of some radio and television announcers about the problems of the listener, and their enthusiasm for sharing the products they advertise seems to be, for example, convincing to part of their audience.) In judging the genuineness of a writer's tone and attitude, it is useful to appraise his whole record—is his feeling of enthusiasm or admiration or distaste one which he has consistently expressed for his present subject, or does he achieve, synthetically, the same feeling for different subjects? It may be useful, too, to reduce the communication as nearly as possible to its factual meaning, to see exactly what factual substance it has. And, the reader can often judge tone and attitude in the light of the context of circumstances—do the circumstances warrant the expressions of attitude with which the writer tries to influence his readers?

Two elements of style, rhythm and repetition, are also of special importance in persuasion that appeals to emotion. The sound and rhythm of sentences and the movement of a whole piece of prose may in themselves convey and inspire feeling. Controlled repetition of key words and phrases often has cumulative emotional force. The reader, and particularly the writer of language that evokes feeling, should study rhythm and repetition. The two elements of style are effective in the passages quoted above from the Bible and from Churchill's speech to Parliament at a time of crisis; they work effectively, too, in less formal and literary prose. We have cited earlier in this chapter Franklin D. Roosevelt's enunciation of the "good neighbor policy." Let us look at it again, not this time for its use of persuasive analogy, but for the added force the analogy gains from sentence rhythm and the repetition of significant words. The following passage strips the statement to its factual meaning without regard for style:

> In the field of world policy I would dedicate this Nation to the policy of the good neighbor. He resolutely respects himself and, therefore, the rights of others, his obligations in the world, and the sanctity of his agreements with other people.

Compare the original statement:

> In the field of world policy I would dedicate this Nation to the policy of the good neighbor—the neighbor who resolutely respects himself and because he does so, respects the rights of others—the neighbor who respects his obligations and respects the sanctity of his agreements in and with a world of neighbors.

III. PERSUASION BY IRONY AND RIDICULE

Irony and ridicule are methods of persuading by making attitudes opposed to those of the writer seem undesirable or absurd. They may be used, as we have pointed out earlier, to appeal to emotion. They may also be used to appeal, through wit, to intelligence. Irony and ridicule are not the same; it is possible to be ironical without ridiculing, and to ridicule without irony; but the two devices are often blended in persuasive writing.

Ridicule may be simply defined as mockery, intended to produce unsympathetic laughter. It is an effective device of persuasion, not when it is directed at the audience, but when the writer and his audience are allied in mockery of the subject or action or attitude under discussion. *Irony* is a more complex term and idea. The word is derived from the Greek *eironeia,* meaning dissimulation or understatement. *Verbal irony* now is a figure of speech in which the real meaning is different from, sometimes the opposite of, the apparent or literal meaning. Examples of verbal irony are "A delightful examination, wasn't it?" and "We had a lovely time; it didn't matter a bit that he sent me pink roses for my orange dress and walked me six blocks to the dance in the rain." By an extension of meaning, *fictional irony* (sometimes called *dramatic irony* or *tragic irony*) occurs when a character in fiction or drama says, sees, or does something, the real significance of which is understood by the audience but not by the character himself. Another kind of fictional irony (the *irony of fate*) is produced by an unexpected turn of events or an outcome different from the one anticipated; for example, a woman labors for ten years to pay for a diamond necklace which she bought to replace one she borrowed and lost, only to find at the end of the story that the necklace she borrowed was paste.[3]

These different types of irony have in common the element of contrast— between what is said and what is meant, between what is not understood and what is realized, between what is expected and what occurs; contrast, in short, between what things seem to be and what they actually are. A reader must be able to perceive the contrast in order to appreciate or even understand irony. Irony therefore demands intellectual activity on the part of the reader.

Recognizing verbal irony in speech is usually easy, because the speaker's facial expression and tone of voice belie the literal meaning of his words. Verbal irony in writing is harder to recognize; the reader may take literally a passage written ironically unless he is alert to possible contrast between the writer's words and his intentions. The reader of irony is likely to move, rapidly, through three mental steps: (1) it's strange that a serious and respectable writer should mean this; (2) this is too much; he can't possibly mean it; (3) of course he doesn't mean it; he's being ironical. For example, Jonathan Swift's *A Modest Proposal,* written in the eighteenth century to satirize the callous attitude of the English toward poverty-stricken Ireland, suggests with apparent seriousness that Irish children be sold for food to wealthy English families. The introduction of the proposal is misleading to an unsuspecting reader; Swift hopes to serve the nation, he says, by offering a "fair, cheap, and easy method" of making the numerous, ragged, burdensome Irish children "sound, useful members of the Commonwealth." As he goes on, the reader is quickly jolted from *this is strange* to *he can't possibly mean it* by the contrast between normal, humane attitudes and a statement like this:

---

[3] "The Necklace," by Guy de Maupassant.

I have been assured by a very knowing American of my acquaintance in London that a young healthy child, well nursed, is, at a year old, a most delicious, nourishing, and wholesome food, whether stewed, roasted, baked, or boiled; and I make no doubt that it will equally serve in a fricassee or a ragout.

The next paragraph, with its outrageous detail, can hardly leave in doubt the ironical intention of the treatise:

I do therefore humbly offer it to public consideration, that of the hundred and twenty thousand children already computed, twenty thousand may be reserved for breed; . . . that the remaining hundred thousand may, at a year old, be offered in sale to the persons of quality and fortune through the kingdom, always advising the mother to let them suck plentifully in the last month, so as to render them plump and fat for a good table. A child will make two dishes at an entertainment for friends, and when the family dines alone, the fore or hind quarter will make a reasonable dish, and seasoned with a little pepper or salt will be very good boiled on the fourth day, especially in winter.

Irony is sometimes, as in Swift's *A Modest Proposal,* harsh and biting; this heavy irony is very close to sarcasm, and frequently ridicules the situation or subject it is criticizing. Often, though, irony is light and good humored; such light irony, which may or may not be accompanied by ridicule, is a common form of wit. Ironical writing is, therefore, often humorous; and humor, skillfully and appropriately used, is itself a means of persuasion. The reader laughs with the communicator at something else. The columnist Art Buchwald, writing in the late New York *Herald Tribune* about paperback book publishers who make nonpornographic books pornographic by the pictures and strange descriptions they put on the covers, says that if the trend continues, some familiar books will be described in these terms:

Snow White and the Seven Dwarfs—The story of a ravishing blond virgin who was held captive by seven deformed men, all with different lusts.

Cinderella—A beautiful passionate woman bares her naked foot to the man she loves while her stepmother and stepsisters plot to cheat her out of the one memorable night in her life.

Alice in Wonderland—A young girl's search for happiness in a weird depraved world of animal desires. Can she ever return to a normal happy life after falling so far?

Tom Sawyer—A gang of sub-teen-age hoodlums paint the town white, and commit mayhem and murder to satisfy their desires.

This type of irony and ridicule is a kind of *reductio ad absurdum*—reduction to absurdity of a trend or proposal; *reductio ad absurdum* is also used in serious logical argument to disprove a proposition by showing that if it were carried to its logical conclusion, its consequences would be absurd.

In general, the difference between irony and sarcasm is that sarcasm is personal and bitter. Irony, even heavy irony, is apparently less bitter because it is impersonal. The writer seems to be detached, self-possessed, judicious, not emotionally involved in the subject he is discussing. Because irony requires a perception of basic contrasts, and because it usually gives an impression of calm restraint, it is particularly effective with an intelligent audience. Such an audience is receptive to persuasion by a writer whose wit, intelligence, and apparent objectivity they enjoy and admire.

Successful persuasion by irony and ridicule is not easy to write. Nor is it easy to give instructions about writing a kind of prose that has so many forms and that requires a particular cast of mind: some people readily perceive the incongruous, the ridiculous, the contrasting elements in a situation, while others do not. It is possible, though, to point out three common weaknesses in the attempts at persuasive irony and ridicule of inexperienced writers. The first is the weakness of inappropriate or misdirected humor. Flippant comments thrown into a serious discussion, ridicule used to avoid the trouble of critical evaluation, and supposedly humorous gibes at an object worthy of understanding or sympathy are not persuasive; they raise questions about the writer's taste and judgment. A second weakness is produced by a lack of detachment and objectivity. When a writer shows a strong personal bias or an intrusive personal hatred toward a subject which he is trying to criticize by irony and ridicule, the reader is likely to shift in attention from the subject to the author, and to wonder what makes him so fanatical or bitter or vituperative; what, in short, is the matter with him. Such a shift is, of course, not persuasive in its effect. A third common weakness comes from the writer's fear that his readers will miss the point. He labors and verbally underlines his attempts at irony ("I love this course, the way I love spinach and cod-liver oil, if you know what I mean") to a point of distraction and irritation for an intelligent audience. The writer of persuasive irony and ridicule should have confidence in his readers; he should give them the pleasure of personal discovery and appreciation of the intended meaning.

TOPICS FOR WRITING

I. Write a 500- or 600-word paper in which, by means of reasonable argument, you persuade the reader to accept an opinion that you hold or a course of action that you recommend. Choose a limited subject on which you are well informed and on which you have seriously reflected. If the paper is intended for a particular audience, state this in an introductory note.

II. Clip from a newspaper or magazine an editorial or commentary that seems to you a successful piece of persuasion. Write a paper analyzing the article and covering these points: the kinds of reasoning you find; devices of persuasion other than logical argument; the author's tone. Plan to hand in the article with your paper.

III. The following subjects for persuasive papers are stated as propositions that the writer would support by facts, examples, authority, reasoning, and any other appropriate persuasive devices. Examine the statements and rephrase any that you would rephrase if you were writing a paper on the general topic. Would you further qualify any of the statements? Would you limit the subject if you were planning a paper of 500 or 600 words? How?

1. Contrary to widespread opinion, most college students do want an academic education.

2. Girls are no longer slaves to the dictates of fashion designers.

3. Public demonstrations are a legitimate and effective form of protest.

4. Great tragedy can be written about common, "unheroic" men and women.

5. The seriousness of the current "drug scene" has been exaggerated.

6. A thirty-hour work week would be a mistake because even now people do not know what to do with the leisure they have.

7. Marshall McLuhan has a significant message for my generation.

8. There should be no compulsory busing of children to schools outside their neighborhoods.

9. Militant groups like the Black Panthers have done irreparable harm to the cause of civil rights.

10. What is called nonconformity is, in fact, frequently rigid conformity.

11. All students, including those who will go to college, should have some vocational training in secondary school.

12. Changes are needed in the admissions policies of this college.

IV. Ten topics for evaluative papers are listed on page 270. A subject for evaluation ("Fraternities on the Campus," for example) can usually be restated as the thesis of an argument ("Fraternities Serve No Useful Purpose on This Campus"). Examine the topics on page 270 and consider how you might change them to theses for persuasive papers.

Chapter 12

DESCRIPTIVE WRITING

In modern writing, description is usually a subordinate part of an essay or a narrative, rarely an independent unit. It is, however, an important part of communication, particularly the communication of experience. It may be used to convey outside, factual knowledge—to draw pictures of people and places and to give information about activities. More often it is used to call up pictures and at the same time to convey inside knowledge—the mood, feeling, and state of mind of the observer.

The basis of good description is close observation and vivid concrete details which enable the reader to visualize the person or scene described. A mere accumulation of details may, however, produce a blurred, conglomerate impression instead of a sharply drawn image. The descriptive writer therefore selects details that produce a unified effect, and arranges those details according to some principle or pattern that makes visualizing and sensory perception easy for the reader. *Dominant impression* is the technical term for the unified effect or central theme to which descriptive details contribute.

Since describing people and describing places involve somewhat different techniques, it is best to consider them separately.

292

I. DESCRIBING PEOPLE

When, in actual experience, we meet a person we have not seen before, we usually get a quick first impression either of his general appearance or of some outstanding feature. Further observation shows us the particulars which produce that general impression and other features which make up this individual. Thus we may note immediately that a man looks shabby and worn, and then observe such details as his too-tight overcoat with only one button, his shapeless hat, and his bent shoulders. Or, we may be struck by a woman's extraordinary height before we consciously notice the color of her hair, the expression of her face, or her clothes.

A writer, in describing people, is likely to use this pattern of natural observation: some outstanding quality followed by more closely observed details. He seldom describes the person systematically from head to toe, but instead chooses a few striking traits of appearance, manner, or dress. Also— and this is very important—he selects at least some details which *individualize the character;* which differentiate him from similar people; which make him not simply a type, but distinctly, uniquely himself.

The following passages are brief illustrations of individualizing detail:

He was a small, skinny boy, his chin pointed, and his eyes so bright they had deceived Ralph into thinking him delightfully gay and wicked. The coarse mop of black hair was long and swung down, almost concealing a low, broad forehead. He wore the remains of shorts and his feet were bare like Jack's. Always darkish in colour, Simon was burned by the sun to a deep tan that glistened with sweat. —WILLIAM GOLDING, *Lord of the Flies*

Doctor Parcival was a large man with a drooping mouth covered by a yellow mustache. He always wore a dirty white waistcoat out of the pockets of which protruded a number of the kind of black cigars known as stogies. His teeth were black and irregular and there was something strange about his eyes. The lid of the left eye twitched; it fell down and snapped up; it was exactly as though the lid of the eye were a window shade and someone stood inside the doctor's head playing with the cord.—SHERWOOD ANDERSON, *Winesburg, Ohio*

Point of view is a technical term for the angle of observation in descriptive and narrative writing. The identity of the observer and his attitude toward what he sees determine the point of view. Point of view, in turn, determines the way a person is described. In description of people, the observer may be the author frankly slanting his material and shaping the reader's judgment of the person; or he may appear to be a completely objective reporter, even though he is, in fact, slanting by his selection of detail. The observer may, in narrative description, be another character who likes or dislikes or does not understand the person he is describing.

In the following passage, the author is openly influencing the reader's judgment by including his own opinions clothed in charged expressions like *semi-rattlesnake, decidedly bad, uncouth and unpicturesque:*

He was a prim-faced, red-nosed man, with a long thin countenance and a semi-rattlesnake sort of eye—rather sharp, but decidedly bad. He wore very short trousers, and black cotton stockings: which, like the rest of his apparel, were particularly rusty. His looks were starched, but his white neckerchief was not; and its long limp ends straggled over his closely buttoned waistcoat in a very uncouth and unpicturesque fashion.—CHARLES DICKENS, *Pickwick Papers*

The paragraph below is an example of the objective point of view. The description consists of factual statements which appear to be verifiable. Note, too, how the various details contribute to the dominant idea of the respect this character inspires:

Peter Randall was one of the most highly respected farmers of Monterey County. Once, before he was to make a little speech at a Masonic convention, the brother who introduced him referred to him as an example for young Masons of California to emulate. He was nearing fifty; his manner was grave and restrained, and he wore a carefully tended beard. From every gathering he reaped the authority that belongs to the bearded man. Peter's eyes were grave, too; blue and grave almost to the point of sorrowfulness. People knew there was force in him, but force held caged. Sometimes, for no apparent reason, his eyes grew sullen and mean, like the eyes of a bad dog; but that look soon passed, and the restraint and probity came back into his face. He was tall and broad. He held his shoulders back as though they were braced, and he sucked in his stomach like a soldier. Inasmuch as farmers are usually slouchy men, Peter gained an added respect because of his posture.—JOHN STEINBECK, "The Harness," *The Long Valley*

In the following paragraph from a short story, the author describes a little Negro girl as she seems to her white playmate. The reader experiences Pinky through Susie's mind, with Susie's attitude and selection of detail:

There was a scurrying, as of a frantic little animal, along the path from Aunt Hester's cabin, and Pinky dropped on the ground beside her. She wasn't very black —her satiny yellow skin merely looked as if she had a good tan—and Aunt Hester had trained her stiff black hair to lie flat to her head. Susie loved the feel of Pinky's skin, and the smell of the magnolia balm Aunt Hester greased her hair with, and the fresh starchy smell of Pinky's calico dresses. She loved everything about Pinky with all her heart.—SARA HAARDT, "Little White Girl"

Real people are almost never entirely static or motionless. If they are, their immobility is so unusual that it is an individualizing characteristic. Movement, gestures, physical attitudes, and speech are inseparable parts of personality. Good description, therefore, *vitalizes a character;* that is, it shows him in some typical pose or activity. In brief description, the pose or activity may serve better than an enumeration of physical traits to give a sense of the whole person:

> The woman with the pink velvet poppies wreathed round the assisted gold of her hair traversed the crowded room at an interesting gait combining a skip with a sidle, and clutched the lean arm of her host.—DOROTHY PARKER, "Arrangement in Black and White"

Extended description—in novels, for example—sometimes starts with a passive sketch of the character, and then shows him in revealing action:

> Mr. Chadband is a large yellow man, with a fat smile, and a general appearance of having a good deal of train oil in his system. Mrs. Chadband is a stern, severe-looking, silent woman. Mr. Chadband moves softly and cumbrously, not unlike a bear who has been taught to walk upright. He is very much embarrassed about the arms, as if they were inconvenient to him, and he wanted to grovel; is very much in a perspiration about the head; and never speaks without first putting up his great hand, as delivering a token to his friends that he is going to edify them.
> "My friends," says Mr. Chadband. "Peace be on this house! On the master thereof, on the mistress thereof, on the young maidens, and on the young men! My friends, why do I wish for peace? What is peace? Is it war? No. Is it strife? No. Is it lovely, and gentle, and beautiful, and pleasant, and serene, and joyful? O yes! Therefore my friends, I wish for peace, upon you and upon yours."—CHARLES DICKENS, *Bleak House*

Mr. Chadband's bear-like motion, his raised hand, and his habits of speech not only vitalize him, but also differentiate him from other large fat men. In the following paragraph, a dominant impression of decayed beauty and elegance is heightened by individualizing detail and by the contrast between the character's general immobility and her constantly-moving hands:

> She was perhaps fifty years old and she had been a fine beauty not so long ago. Her face was smooth and wax-colored, her small round mouth was painted bright red, the small, clever-looking black eyes were sketched in and lengthened with dark blue smudges, her lightly tinted reddish hair was cut short and curled around her forehead and ears. She was slender except for a lazy little belly, and her clothes were very expensive-looking; shabby as they were, they were still much too elegant for her present occasions. She wore enormous pearls in her ears, around her throat, on two fingers of her left hand. On her right she wore what appeared to be a light-colored much-flawed emerald, big as a robin's egg and surrounded by small diamonds. These hands, very narrow, fine, heavily veined, and old-looking, were in constant movement. Thumbs turned in lightly to the palm, the hands moved aimlessly from the edge of the table to her lap, they clasped and unclasped themselves, spread themselves flat in the air, closed, shook slightly, went to her hair, to the bosom of her gown, as if by a life of their own separate from the will of the woman herself, who sat quite still otherwise, features a little rigid, bending to read the dinner card beside her plate.—KATHERINE ANNE PORTER, *Ship of Fools*

II. DESCRIBING PLACES

In describing places, as in describing people, the writer follows the principle of selecting details which contribute sharply to a dominant impression, and which individualize the place so that it is not merely typical but has a quality of its own. The following description gives a dominant impression of bareness and poverty; the room described is individualized by the possessions of its occupant. This passage also illustrates one of the close relationships between description of people and description of places. The boy who lives in this room is not presented, but he is indirectly described by his surroundings. The passage is an example of *suggestive description:* the reader understands more than he is explicitly told.

> The room was furnished with what the college issued: a desk, placed dead center under the overhead light, a table, three wooden chairs, a bed, a bureau, and an empty fireplace, the brick floor of which was free of ashes and cigarette butts. One shelf of the bookcase was almost filled with textbooks, a one-volume edition of Shakespeare, and a Bible. On the table were two notebooks and a dictionary, a cup and saucer, a plate, and a small electric stove with a saucepan on it. A calendar and two pine cones had been arranged on the mantelpiece in an effort at decoration. There was a framed photograph of a middle-aged woman on the bureau, and two neckties hung from a corner of the mirror. The room looked as if its occupant had moved in that afternoon and would leave tomorrow.—OLIVER LA FARGE, "Prelude to Reunion"

Point of view in describing places is more complicated than point of view in describing people. It involves, in addition to the attitude or psychological position of the observer, his physical position relative to the scene he is presenting. Is he moving or stationary? If he is moving, by what means of locomotion, and how fast? If he is stationary, is he below, or above, or on the same level as what he observes? Is he standing, or sitting, or lying on his back? His physical position will make a great deal of difference in what he sees, and the reader must understand that position in order to visualize the scene.

Point of view in the sense of the psychological attitude of the observer also influences selection and arrangement of detail. If the feeling of the observer about what he sees is more important than the scene itself, the description is likely to follow an *impressionistic pattern,* in which details are set down in no order except the order in which they impress, or strike the attention of the observer. Such impressionistic description, with its focus on inside responses, is sometimes called *subjective,* in contrast to *objective* writing which focuses on outside objects. Impressionistic description reveals the principle of selection operating in the observer; it is a useful method of showing his state of mind and indirectly characterizing him; it is, therefore, another technique of suggesting more than is actually stated. The dominant impression in this kind of writing is usually a consistent emotional tone, because all the recorded details are colored by the feelings of the person who sees them.

The following passage is an example of impressionistic description. No effort is made to describe the scene systematically; instead, details are set down as they impinge on the consciousness of a spoiled and wealthy woman who emerges from an exclusive shop on a winter afternoon and for a moment feels herself unsheltered in the world. The "little box" referred to in the passage is an extravagant trifle that she has considered buying.

The discreet door shut with a click. She was outside on the step, gazing at the winter afternoon. Rain was falling, and with the rain it seemed the dark came too, spinning down like ashes. There was a cold bitter taste in the air, and the new-lighted lamps looked sad. Sad were the lights in the houses opposite. Dimly they burned as if regretting something. And people hurried by, hidden under their hateful umbrellas. Rosemary felt a strange pang. She pressed her muff to her breast; she wished she had the little box, too, to cling to. Of course, the car was there. She'd only to cross the pavement. But still she waited. There are moments, horrible moments in life, when one emerges from shelter and looks out, and it's awful. One oughtn't to give way to them. One ought to go home and have an extra-special tea.[1]

When a writer is primarily interested in presenting the scene itself rather than the reactions of the observer, he follows an *orderly pattern* designed to give the reader an orderly objective picture of what the observer (either author or character) sees. The basis of this orderly pattern may be a logical relationship of details. For example, the passage about the college student's room on page 296 describes first what the college has provided, and then what the student has added to the room. Other orderly patterns of this kind are based on contrast: between the age of a house, for example, and the modernity of one room; or between a first impression and a modified second impression; or between the familiar, in a place revisited, and the unfamiliar.

The most common orderly patterns in describing places are, however, based on space-relationships between elements in the scene. If the observer is moving, the reader follows him in his progress with the help of space-connectives like *at the top of the hill, around the corner, half way up the stairs.* If the observer is stationary, the reader can visualize the scene when details are set down in some consistent pattern such as left-to-right or right-to-left (in the description of a room or a landscape); near-to-far or far-to-near (in the description of a large or complex scene); up-to-down or down-to-up (in the description of a building, a hill, or a street). The following short example of orderly description uses a near-to-far arrangement of detail:

They stood together, looking out across the country, down over the orchard,

[1] From Katherine Mansfield, "A Cup of Tea," *Short Stories of Katherine Mansfield,* © by Alfred A. Knopf, Inc.

beyond the road, across the lower fields and the woods of the point to the lake. The wind was blowing straight down the lake. They could see the surf along Ten Mile Point.—ERNEST HEMINGWAY, "The Three-Day Blow"

In practice, the impressionistic-subjective point of view and the orderly-objective point of view are frequently combined. A writer often wishes to present simultaneously a picture of the scene and the mood of the person who observes it. The passage below contains an example of orderly near-to-far description and at the same time communicates the feeling of the observer:

He was standing in the sunny window. Geraldine went up to him. She put her hand on his arm and gave it a gentle squeeze. How pleasant it was to feel that rough man's tweed again. Ah, how pleasant! She rubbed her hand against it, touched it with her cheek, sniffed the smell.

The window looked out on to flower beds, a tangle of michaelmas daisies, late dahlias, hanging heavy, and shaggy little asters. Then there came a lawn strewn with yellow leaves with a broad path beyond and a row of gold-fluttering trees. An old gardener, in woollen mitts, was sweeping the path, brushing the leaves into a neat little heap. Now, the broom tucked in his arm, he fumbled in his coat pocket, brought out some matches, and scooping a hole in the leaves, he set fire to them.

Such lovely blue smoke came breathing into the air through those dry leaves; there was something so calm and orderly in the way the pile burned that it was a pleasure to watch. The old gardener stumped away and came back with a handful of withered twigs. He flung them on and stood by, and little light flames began to flicker.[2]

The preceding passage illustrates a final principle: effective description of places *vitalizes the scene and appeals to the reader's senses.* The most common fault of weak description is that it presents a dead black and white drawing, without movement, without color, without sound, with nothing but a bleak visual representation of the scene. It is like a map or a poor photograph in which objects are too remote and too still to seem real. The following description of a night scene (which also contains a brief description of a person) carries the reader into an experience by letting him know the character's multiple sensations of feeling, sight, and hearing:

It was high here, and the air moved with grave coolness. On either hand lay a valley filled with silver mist and with whippoorwills; beyond these valleys the silver earth rolled on into the sky. Across it, mournful and far, a dog howled. Bayard's head was as cool and clear as a clapperless bell. Within it that face emerged clearly at last: those two eyes round with grave astonishment, winged serenely by two dark wings of hair. It was that Benbow girl, he said to himself, and he sat for a while, gazing into the sky. The lights on the town clock were steadfast and yellow and unwinking in the dissolving distance, but in all other directions the world rolled away in slumbrous ridges, milkily opaline.—WILLIAM FAULKNER, *Sartoris*

[2] From Katherine Mansfield, "Widowed," *Short Stories of Katherine Mansfield,* © by Alfred A. Knopf, Inc.

Just as we know people in their complexity of appearance, expression, speech, and motion, so we know places in a complexity of sight and sound and smell, and sometimes the taste and often the feel of things. The skillful writer brings a place to life, and communicates to the reader all the physical impressions and sensations that are part of experiencing that scene.

III. CHARACTER IN SETTING

We have seen in the preceding pages that descriptions of people and of places are often interwoven, to show a character's reaction to his environment, or to characterize him by means of the setting in which he lives. In the following passage a dominant impression of energy and eagerness is created both by the character's appearance and by her typical activity; the appearance of her house further contributes to this dominant impression.

She was cutting down the old year's chrysanthemum stalks with a pair of short and powerful scissors. She looked down toward the men by the tractor shed now and then. Her face was eager and mature and handsome; even her work with the scissors was over-eager, over-powerful. The chrysanthemum stems seemed too small and easy for her energy.

She brushed a cloud of hair out of her eyes with the back of her glove, and left a smudge of earth on the cheek in doing it. Behind her stood the neat white farm house with red geraniums close-banked around it as high as the windows. It was a hard-swept looking little house, with hard-polished windows, and a clean mud-mat on the front steps.

Elisa cast another glance toward the tractor shed. The strangers were getting into their Ford coupe. She took off a glove and put her strong fingers down into the forest of new green chrysanthemum sprouts that were growing around the old roots. She spread the leaves and looked down among the close-growing stems. No aphids were there, no sowbugs or snails or cutworms. Her terrier fingers destroyed such pests before they could get started.—JOHN STEINBECK, "The Chrysanthemums"

The two paragraphs below characterize and contrast two women through an impressionistic description of their rooms. The point of view, that of a young girl who sometimes cleans the rooms, controls the selection of detail: the narrator is chiefly concerned with the surfaces that must be cleaned or set in order.

As I watched her [Miss Pride], taking in with admiration each detail of her immaculate attire and her proud carriage, I heard, from the adjoining room, embedded in a yawn, the waking squeal of Mrs. McKenzie, a garrulous and motherly old woman whom I had always disliked. Her room was no pleasure to clean: her bed was strewn with corsets and short-sleeved night-dresses, and on her bedside table, I often found drying apple cores which I removed gingerly, having in my mind an image of her with her sparse hair unpinned sitting up in bed cropping with her large false teeth. Upon the bureau, amongst sticky bottles of vile black syrups and tonics and jars of fetid salve, there lay her bunion plasters and her ropes of brown hair which she sometimes arranged in a lofty cone on top of her head. Usually she was in the room when I entered and she saluted me with disgusting moonshine as "mother's little helper" or asked me if my "beauteous mamma" was sick.

Now in Miss Pride's room, there was never anything amiss. Perhaps once or twice a summer, I found a bottle of imported wine or whiskey on her writing desk; this was the only medicine she took and she took it regularly in small quantities. On the bureau, the china hair receiver did not receive a wisp of hair, and there were neither spots nor foreign objects upon the white linen runner. A hat-pin holder, sprouting long, knobbed needles, two cut-glass cologne bottles, and a black glove box, shaped like a small casket, were reflected in the clear swinging mirror. Though I should have loved to dearly, I had not the courage to investigate the drawers which were always neatly shut, but I was sure that they were in scrupulous order. The other old ladies, almost without exception, allowed the feet of stockings and the straps of camisoles to stream from each gaping tier like so many dispirited banners.—JEAN STAFFORD, *Boston Adventure*

Presenting character in setting, or setting as a part of characterization, is likely to give the reader a sense of depth and reality; he is brought into the total experience he might have if he were in the position of the observer.

TOPICS FOR WRITING

I. Write a description of a person whom you know. Select details that will individualize the person; show him engaged in some action that will further reveal him to the reader.

II. Write a description of a place you know. Give particular attention to point of view and pattern, and to vitalizing the scene.

III. Write a paper in which you simultaneously describe a person and a place by presenting a character in his own environment. Your purpose should be to communicate to the reader a vivid sense of the person and the scene.

IV. As an experiment with point of view, write two descriptions of the same person, as he appears to two observers. Consider carefully the state of mind or perhaps the character and experience of the observers. For example, one observer may know the person well and the other know him only slightly; one observer may admire him and the other be indifferent to him. It should not be necessary to state explicitly the attitudes of the two observers; that will be made clear by what they see.

V. Following the general plan of the preceding assignment, write two descriptions of the same place, using two points of view. The points of view might differ because one observer is seeing the place for the first time, and the other is revisiting the place that has emotional associations—pleasant or unpleasant—for him.

Chapter 13

AUTOBIOGRAPHY, SIMPLE NARRATIVE, ESSAY

I. AUTOBIOGRAPHY AND SIMPLE NARRATIVE

Simple narratives are not necessarily autobiographical, but we are, for two reasons, discussing in combination these types of writing often assigned in English courses. The student's narrative writing is likely to be best—most vivid and most original—when he uses autobiographical material. Also, the problems and the techniques of writing autobiography and writing simple narrative are much the same.

The simple narrative is the short, uncomplicated story in which events are set down in natural time-order. It is related on the one hand to the narrative essay—an essay that tells a story in order to clarify an idea—and on the other hand to the short story. It differs from the essay in that the latter emphasizes an idea; the simple narrative invites the reader to share the happenings—usually human experiences—that it presents. For example, a composition entitled "Moving Day" might be an essay if all the recorded events of the day were focused on a central idea that possessions are more trouble than they are worth; it would be a simple narrative if the writer presented in vivid detail the experience of moving from a familiar to a strange place, for the sake of the experience itself. Both autobiography and simple narrative aim at the communication of experience.

The simple narrative differs from the short story chiefly in its simplicity of structure. The complex short story often departs from natural time-order and begins in the middle or near the end for purposes of unity and concentration; it maintains suspense about how the plot will develop; it often builds to a climax; and it frequently leaves the reader with a mind full of suggestions about what is going to happen after the story itself has ended. The simple narrative, besides following a simple chronological order, has little or no suspense, does not necessarily mount to a climax, and ends simply and completely with the final occurrence in a chain of events—with the end of a day, for example, or the close of school, or the parting with a friend.

One might conclude, from this comparison, that the simple narrative is a colorless and unexciting literary form. This is not true. It is often the best method of presenting genuine experience; of writing about real people and real events, just as they were, just as they happened, without the distortion which too often occurs when an inexperienced writer is called upon to produce a formal essay or a short story. Simple narrative is the natural form for writing about subjects like these: First Date; I Get (or Lose) My First Job; The New Neighbors; The New Teacher; English and I; Childhood by the Sea; Grandmother Comes to Visit; The Day I Joined the Circus; Family Reunion; My Brother and I. Such topics are, of course, autobiographical. They draw on the rich reservoir of knowledge that any writer has in his own past experience.

A. Selection and Focus

The simple narrative is usually a running account of something that happens over a period of time—the events of a day, or several days, or several years. Since its structure is simple, the writer must select from all that happened in that time, and must focus sharply on a single line of development. If, for example, he is writing about his experience in trying, through a whole summer, to catch a particular large bass, he will rigidly subordinate, or perhaps omit entirely, the other activities of the summer.

Similar selection and focus produce the best autobiographical writing. With so much material available, the writer of a short autobiography is in danger of trying to cover too much, and so making his paper a bare and uninteresting listing of events. Selection will enable him to develop fully a limited amount of material and to make the recorded experience real to a reader. Autobiographical writing will be most successful if it is focused on one of these topics:

1. A particular experience or event that was important to the writer.
2. A place that has been meaningful to him.

3. A single chain of events—for example, falling in and out of love in the course of a few months; becoming committed to a social or political cause.

4. A unit or phase of experience, like the end of childhood.

5. A relationship—with a member of the writer's immediate family, or a relative, or a friend who influenced him in some significant way.

6. A growing interest—in music, or literature, or people.

7. A changing idea or attitude—for example, about education, or religion, or one's family, or one's self.

B. Technique

Autobiography is normally written in the first person; usually simple narrative is, too. The first-person point of view is not a requirement, and there are impersonal narratives; but the writer is frequently recording his own experience, or, as an interested observer, is recording a sequence of events or actions about which he has close knowledge. The first-person form, which is direct and which gives a sense of immediate contact between writer and material and between writer and reader, generally fits this kind of communication. However, there are writers who dislike the first person—who feel blocked or constrained when they must write "I" and "me." Such writers may be helped by the simple device of thinking of and writing about their experience as if it had happened to someone else. In the following paragraph from an autobiographical essay, the writer looks back, as at another person, to record a phase of his boyhood:

Night came and went, and came again and went again, and I remember a little boy with a bicycle, a little boy who never tired of running, who stopped only when he ate, and who grew older before I really got to know him. He lived in a hurry, never having time for such trivialities as the dentist or an errand; the gang was always waiting, and he had promised the fellows, and after all. . . . His best argument was that Johnny's mother let Johnny, and Johnny's best argument was that all the fellows were going. He was a boy who loved old clothes that were changed only when Mother villainously stole them out of his room at night, a boy to whom anything could be interesting for a day or so: piano lessons, a chemistry set, or a book on hypnotism. He always met "swell" new friends, and the world was full of "swell" things, and he could be anything he wanted—an engineer, an explorer, or a pilot.

An interesting technical study for both the writer and the critical reader of any kind of narrative is the balance between summary and presentation of material. *Summary* is general statement which gives the net result of action. *Presentation* is the full and dramatic development of scenes of action. This is summary:

My family couldn't understand why I didn't show more sadness at my brother's death.

This is presentation:

> In the quiet house smelling of flowers, I felt out of place because my eyes were dry. Sadness was part of me, but I did not feel I was as sad or mournful as I should be. I saw Mother looking at me strangely.
> "You're a bad boy, Jackie," Aunt Edna said. "You shouldn't go over to Sonny's house for comic books while poor Jim lies in there in a casket."
> "He doesn't even cry, Aunt Edna," said Bobby.
> "I bet he won't even cry at the funeral," said Hennie.
> But I wanted to cry.

This is another summary:

> I was very proud of the new white dress I was going to wear to the party.

The following paragraph presents, this time not by including actual dialogue, but by adding concrete detail:

> I stood in front of Mamma's long mirror in the big bedroom looking at my new white dress. It was one of the prettiest I had ever had. Mamma had sewed two blue stars from the five-and-ten on the wide square collar and navy blue buttons all the way down the front. Maybe someone would think I had a big brother in the Navy. That would be swell. I had a blue bow in my hair that matched, too. One curl was hanging lower than the others, so I poked at it and walked around the room with my neck stiff to see if it was going to fall down. Mamma called up to ask me if I had found my clean white socks in the drawer. She asked if I wanted a ride to the party, but I told her no, because none of the kids ever got rides from their mothers and fathers. They said it was sissy. Anyway, I didn't want to wrinkle my dress before anyone saw it.

In general, presentation is more effective than summary because it takes the reader into the full scene; but full presentation of trivial or repetitious scenes can become boring to a reader. The writer of narrative or auto- biography must decide what is important enough to be presented, and what can well be summarized or partly summarized. The balance he works out will determine the movement or *pace* of his narrative. In a narrative or auto- biography of some length, the pace may be very leisurely; that is, the writer may take time to recall and set down a wealth of remembered detail about a scene or an experience. An example is the following passage from Mark Twain's autobiography, part of a much longer passage in which he lets early memories of a farm come flooding back:

> As I have said, I spent some part of every year at the farm until I was twelve or thirteen years old. The life which I led there with my cousins was full of charm, and so is the memory of it yet. I can call back the solemn twilight and mystery of the deep woods, the earthy smells, the faint odors of the wild flowers, the sheen of rain-washed foliage, the rattling clatter of drops when the wind shook the trees, the far-off hammering of woodpeckers and the muffled drumming of wood pheasants in the remoteness of the forest, the snapshot glimpses of disturbed wild creatures scurrying

through the grass—I can call it all back and make it as real as it ever was, and as blessed. I can call back the prairie, and its loneliness and peace, and a vast hawk hanging motionless in the sky, with his wings spread wide and the blue of the vault showing through the fringe of their end feathers. I can see the woods in their autumn dress, the oaks purple, the hickories washed with gold, the maples and the sumachs luminous with crimson fires, and I can hear the rustle made by the fallen leaves as we plowed through them. I can see the blue clusters of wild grapes hanging among the foliage of the saplings, and I remember the taste of them and the smell. I know how the wild blackberries looked, and how they tasted, and the same with the pawpaws, the hazelnuts, and the persimmons; and I can feel the thumping rain, upon my head, of hickory nuts and walnuts when we were out in the frosty dawn to scramble for them with the pigs, and the gusts of wind loosed them and sent them down. I know the stain of blackberries, and how pretty it is, and I know the stain of walnut hulls, and how little it minds soap and water, also what grudged experience it had of either of them. I know the taste of maple sap, and when to gather it, and how to arrange the troughs and the delivery tubes, and how to boil down the juice, and how to hook the sugar after it is made, also how much better hooked sugar tastes than any that is honestly come by, let bigots say what they will. I know how a prize watermelon looks when it is sunning its fat rotundity among pumpkin vines and "simblins"; I know how to tell when it is ripe without "plugging" it; I know how inviting it looks when it lies on the table in the sheltered great floor space between house and kitchen, and the children gathered for the sacrifice and their mouths watering; I know the crackling sound it makes when the carving knife enters its end, and I can see the split fly along in front of the blade as the knife cleaves its way to the other end; I can see its halves fall apart and display the rich red meat and the black seeds, and the heart standing up, a luxury fit for the elect; I know how a boy looks behind a yard-long slice of that melon, and I know how he feels; for I have been there.

In shorter compositions, the writer may not wish to present so fully, and he will necessarily quicken his pace by summarizing a good deal if he is covering a long period of time. He should plan his paper, not as a chain of equal parts, but as a chain that links key scenes. When he comes to an action or experience that is important, or particularly entertaining or revealing, he should expand his summary into a partially or fully developed scene. The best preparation for the writing of autobiography or narrative is, first, selecting the material, and, second, jotting down in rough outline form a list of the most significant scenes. These will be presented, with detail proportionate to their importance, and they will be linked by transitional and summary passages which carry the reader smoothly through time, from one scene to the next.

II. THE REFLECTIVE PERSONAL ESSAY

The general term *essay* is used for pieces of writing dissimilar in content and style. A piece of writing primarily informative may be called a factual essay, an

historical essay, or a biographical essay. Evaluative and persuasive compositions may be classified as critical or editorial or philosophical essays. Descriptive pieces may—depending on their content—be called character essays,
nature essays, or simply descriptive essays. And when narrative or autobiography is used to clarify an idea, the result may be the narrative essay or
autobiographical essay.

Essays are also divided into two large groups: (1) formal essays, characterized by serious treatment of serious ideas, by formal organization and style,
and often (though not always) by dignified and impersonal tone; (2) personal
or informal essays, characterized, as the name indicates, by less formal style
and organization, and frequently by a relaxed, genial, conversational tone.
College students have probably read formal essays by writers like Francis
Bacon and John Stuart Mill, and informal essays by writers like Charles Lamb,
James Thurber, and E. B. White.

Students frequently do their best writing when they attempt what we call
the reflective personal essay. This is a composition that communicates meaningful personal experience on which the writer has seriously reflected. Thus it
has the natural, easy style and tone of the informal essay and, at the same time,
much of the substance and essential seriousness of the more formal essay. The
writer, usually with the help of description and narration, recreates his experiences for the reader, evaluates them, and leads the reader to share both the
experiences and a set of values which they imply or to which they are related.

There are no rules for writing reflective personal essays, no pattern to
follow—though the best of such essays are skillfully constructed around some
basic pattern and unified by some basic theme. The essayist's material and his
attitudes toward it will determine his structure, his choice of details, and his
tone. E. B. White's reflective personal essay "Walden" was prompted by a visit
to Walden Pond where Henry David Thoreau had lived nearly a hundred
years before. Written in the form of a personal letter to Thoreau, the essay
records in a chronological pattern the incidents of two days, and explains to
"Dear Henry" the changes modern civilization has brought to travel and to
Walden Pond and its surroundings. The tone is that of a letter to a friend—
informal and affectionate; it is also humorous, witty, and a little nostalgic for
the natural beauty Thoreau saw at Walden and for the simplicity Thoreau
advocated. A quiet indictment of the complexities and the materialism of
modern living emerges from White's observations. James Baldwin's essay
"Notes of a Native Son" has a very different structure and tone. This essay,
beginning with the death of the author's father and the birth on the same day
of his sister, moves back to past experiences, forward, back to the past again,
and finally forward to focus on the father's death, the drive to the graveyard
through riot-scarred Harlem, and the meaning to Baldwin of the total experience he has recounted. The deceptively casual movement in time and place
enables the author to start dramatically with one of his central themes—the

opposition of death and birth—and then to develop, in their context, inter-woven oppositions of blackness and whiteness, love and hate, parent and child, innocence and experience, reality and unreality. By the end of the essay, some of the themes have coalesced; the oppositions have been modified and have shifted into new oppositions; and the "notes" have moved into a tightly struc-tured pattern. The tone of the essay is grave and intense, suited to the subject-matter.

The preceding examples are meant to show how diverse in content, form, and tone reflective personal essays are. The student-writer has the idea for a reflective essay in any experience or observation significant to him. In plan-ning and writing his paper, he needs to keep in mind the principles of con-creteness: it is not enough for him to say that his experiences were significant, thought-provoking, or productive of new attitudes or values. With his use of substantial and vivid detail, he will show his readers why these things are so.

TOPICS FOR WRITING

I. On pages 302–303 we have listed a number of topics—some specific and others more general—for simple narratives and autobiographical writing. Look again at these topics, think about them in terms of your own experience, and jot down any ideas they suggest to you.

II. Delve into your past and reproduce, in 500 words or more, a single episode that was important or upsetting or in some way vivid and memorable to you. Think about things like this: your first experience with death; a quarrel; a moment of triumph, or shame, or humiliation, or fear, or joy, or anger, or grief, or deep peace. Force your memory to grasp every detail of the episode: every impression of sight, sound, muscular activity, temperature, taste, touch, tone of voice, expression, and play of thought. Understate rather than overstate the emotion that accompanied the experience. Present the recollection so concretely that the reader will understand, without being told explicitly, how you felt.

III. Successful reflective personal essays, usually 1000 to 2000 words long, have been written on the following subjects:

My Education Not from Books
What I Believe
My Changing Ideas of Happiness
The Road I Have Traveled
Experience (or age, or college, or books, or people) Has (or have) Changed My Way of Thinking
My Town
The Importance of Books (music, people, work, religion) in My Life

My Quest for Peace of Mind
What I Have Learned in College
The Process of Growing Up
A Problem I Have to Solve
Taking Stock of Myself
My Ideas of Good and Evil
The Generation Gap as I See It
The Meaning to Me of Freedom

Chapter 14

THE RESEARCH
PAPER

The research, or library, paper is the long paper which, unlike the informal theme, is based on the student's reading and study, and on data systematically assembled for this paper. It is usually at least 2000 words long. The purpose of assigning it in freshman English courses is to give students training in using the library, in gathering material, in taking efficient notes, in using footnotes, and especially in organizing and writing a composition of some length. Writing a long paper is different from writing several short ones that total the same number of words. Since the material is more complex, the long paper presents greater problems of organization, logical arrangement of material, transition between sections, and clarity. A source paper rather than an informal essay is usually assigned to give practice in handling long papers, because the substance is supplied by the sources—students need not create it—and because the training in using the sources and giving credit to them in footnotes may be as valuable as the training in writing. All in all, work on the research paper teaches skills which students will need when they write term papers in college, and which many of them will use later when they prepare reports, graduate papers and theses, articles, and even speeches.

To students unfamiliar with the technique of research, some of the methods outlined in this chapter, particularly methods of taking and labeling notes, may seem unnecessarily laborious and involved. Students who have had experience with investigative papers realize, however, that these methods are used because they are efficient; they simplify the organization and writing of the paper, and ensure its accuracy. To those who may not see, as they begin work on the research project, the value of following the instructions given in this chapter, we can only say that the methods recommended here are tested methods, and that the reasons for using them will become apparent as work on the paper proceeds.

Requirements for the completed research paper differ slightly in different institutions, but most instructors expect it to have these parts:

A title page, that is, a page blank except for the title of the paper and the usual endorsement.

A preface which states precisely the scope of the paper, makes any necessary acknowledgments of help or advice received, comments on the type of reader for whom the paper is written, and states exactly how the writer has limited his subject and what his intention is. In general, the research paper should be written for the intelligent layman who has no special knowledge about the subject of the paper; if the writer needs to assume some special knowledge, he should make this clear. The preface may be only a paragraph, or it may be several pages long. The research paper itself will be impersonal, but the preface may be personal; it may, if the writer wishes, tell his reasons for investigating this subject. If he has been forced to limit his topic in some unusual way, or to omit some phase of it which a reader might expect to find included, the limitation or omission should be explained in the preface. Since the preface is, for the instructor, one standard by which to judge the paper, the student should take particular care to state precisely the purpose and scope of his work.

A formal outline that represents fully and accurately the contents of the paper.

The text of the paper, typed, with numbered pages, with footnotes in correct form, and with any drawings, charts, or other illustrations that will contribute to interest or clarity. The paper is written in appropriate English, which for nearly all research subjects is high informal or possibly formal English.

A bibliography, in which all books and articles used in writing the paper are listed alphabetically, according to the author's last name.

An appendix, if the paper needs one. The appendix is the place for long quotations, tables of statistics, maps, and drawings, which are useful for reference but too bulky to include in the text of the paper.

It will be apparent that the research paper is a large project—total work time may amount to sixty hours or more; and the actual writing is only one of the final stages. The work preliminary to writing—choosing the subject, assembling a bibliography, taking notes, and organizing the notes—will occupy something like three-fourths of the time allotted to the whole paper.

I. CHOOSING THE SUBJECT

In choosing a subject, the student should be guided first by his own interest and curiosity. The research paper is, as we have said, a large project; it involves a great deal of work; it is important, therefore, that the student investigate a subject that will be genuinely interesting to him.

Choosing a topic about which one already has considerable information is usually unwise. Since the research paper must be carefully documented—that is, since the sources of information must be given in footnotes—the student who writes on a subject he already knows must go through the boring procedure of reading and taking notes on material already familiar to him, to be sure of accurate detail and of adequate documentation. More important, he will miss the satisfaction of exploring a new field of knowledge. The wise student, therefore, chooses a field beyond the bounds or on the fringes of his present knowledge: some subject he has run across in his reading, or has heard mentioned in one of his courses; of which he has thought "I'd like to know more about that sometime," but which he might not find time to investigate without the stimulus of this assignment.

With his subject tentatively selected, or with two or three interesting topics in mind, the writer should at once take the second step in choosing his subject: he should look in the card catalogue in the library, in reference books, and in the various magazine indexes to be sure there is enough printed material available for a substantial research paper. He should not be easily discouraged; material can be found on almost any topic if one looks hard enough and long enough. But the material is not always available in the library or libraries to which the student has access. He should be *sure* that he will be able to find the sources of information he needs *before* he begins intensive work on the paper.

A third step in choosing the subject is limiting it to a topic that can be adequately handled in 2000 or 3000 words. Topics like The Negro Revolution, The Napoleonic Wars, The History of Medicine, The Modern Theater, are obviously not appropriate for a student paper; a volume or volumes would be needed to treat any one of them adequately. Good papers can, however, be written on certain phases of these immense subjects. The Philosophy of Dr. Martin Luther King, Jr., The Battle of Waterloo, Recent Developments in Heart Surgery, The Advantages and Disadvantages of the Arena Stage—these are more limited subjects that might be chosen from the broader fields. In order to limit his topic and to decide which phase of it will be most interesting to him, the student should read (without taking notes) several general accounts; for example, articles in encyclopedias, chapters in history texts, or magazine articles. Frequently a limited subject will be limited still further: the student will find, as he gets more deeply into his research, that the

topic is still too broad. He should, however, make some limitation at the outset, and other limitations as soon as possible before he wastes valuable time in
taking notes on material that will be outside the scope of his final topic.

Some subjects on which successful research papers have been written are
listed below. They represent a variety of interests, and may suggest topics
of interest to the reader. Most of them illustrate, too, a reasonable limitation
of a wide field; in some cases the writer of the paper limited the subject still
further as he learned more about it.

Myths of the Navajo Indians
Symbolism in Oriental Rugs
The Early History of Stained Glass
Byron and the Cause of Greek Freedom
Keats and Fanny Brawne
Ruskin's Controversy with Whistler
Browning's Courtship of Elizabeth Barrett
Attitudes toward War in Selected Novels of World War I and World War II
Early Plays of Eugene O'Neill
Coffee Houses in England in the Eighteenth Century
Customs of the Troubadours
Viking Explorations on American Shores
Benjamin Franklin as a Scientist
Lincoln and Anne Rutledge
The Assassination of Lincoln
Barnum and Tom Thumb
The Last Days of Hitler
Early History of the Quakers
The Doctrine of Papal Infallibility
The Assassination of Thomas à Becket and T. S. Eliot's *Murder in the Cathedral*
The Evolution of Christmas Customs
A Comparison of Christmas and Hanukkah
Doctors in the Middle Ages
The Sounds Fish Make
Migration of Birds
New Hope for Mentally Retarded Children
Advances in Group Therapy
The Black Muslim Movement
Causes of High School Dropouts
The Cuban Crisis of 1962
The John Birch Society
The Television Debates in the Presidential Campaign of 1960
Evolution of the Peace Corps
Origins of the War in Vietnam
The Theory and Practice of "Vietnamization"
The Meaning of "The New Left"

A Report on Television and Violence
The Controversy Over Drugs
What We Can Learn from the Moon

II. MAKING THE BIBLIOGRAPHY

The work of making the bibliography, that is, the formal list of books and articles on which the paper is based, begins before the subject of the paper is finally selected, and continues, as the writer discovers new sources, until he is ready to write the first draft. A substantial working bibliography should, however, be assembled *before* the student begins to take notes. Some of the items in this preliminary bibliography may prove disappointing when he examines them; some of them he may not be able to find; but his bibliography will give him an initial survey of the field and of the work before him. The bibliography should be kept in standard form on 3 by 5-inch bibliography cards; a *separate* card should be used for *each* book or article.

This system of bibliography cards has been adopted because it is convenient. In the finished bibliography at the end of the research paper, all sources used in writing the paper are listed alphabetically according to the last name of the author (or, if no author is mentioned, according to the first important word in the title); author, work, and facts of publication are given in consistent form. The student should carefully follow this standard form in making out his bibliography cards. When the time comes to prepare the final bibliography for his paper, he will be well paid for his exactness. He can easily alphabetize his cards according to the first word on each one; all the necessary data will be there, and in the correct form and order; his bibliography can simply be typed from his cards.

A bibliographical entry for a book is in this form:

```
Mead, Margaret. Culture and Commitment. New York: Doubleday and
     Company, Inc., 1970.
```

Notice that:

1. The order of information is *(a)* author, *(b)* title, *(c)* place, publisher,[1] and date of publication.

2. The author's last name is first, to facilitate alphabetizing the bibliography.

3. The three main parts of the entry are separated by periods.

4. The title of the book is underlined to represent italics in print.

---

[1] Usage is somewhat divided on the inclusion of the publisher; but the *MLA Style Sheet,* Second Edition (New York: MLA, 1970) , advises that the publisher's name be included in bibliographic entries.

If the book has two authors, the form is as follows:

Bloomfield, Morton W., and Leonard Newmark. <u>A Linguistic
    Introduction to the History of English.</u> New York: Alfred A.
    Knopf, 1963.

If a book has three authors, the three names are usually given, as in the
first entry below. If there are more than three authors, the name of the first
author listed on the title page is used, followed by *et al.* (a Latin abbreviation
meaning "and others"), or by the English "and others."

Barnet, Sylvan, Morton Berman, and William Burto. <u>Aspects of the
    Drama</u>. Boston: Little, Brown and Company, 1962.

Foerster, Norman, and others. <u>Literary Scholarship: Its Aims and
    Methods</u>. Chapel Hill: The University of North Carolina
    Press, 1941.

If the book is a collection of essays or articles edited by one or more people, this form is used:

Stearn, Gerald Emanuel, ed. <u>McLuhan: Hot and Cool</u>. New York:
    New American Library, Inc., 1967.

Belcher, William F., and James W. Lee, eds. <u>J. D. Salinger and
    the Critics</u>. Belmont, California: Wadsworth Publishing
    Company, Inc., 1962.

An entry for a translated book is written:

Camus, Albert. <u>Resistance, Rebellion, and Death</u>, trans. Justin
    O'Brien. New York: Alfred A. Knopf, 1961.

A bibliographical entry for an article may have one of these slightly different forms:

Albee, Edward. "The Decade of Engagement," <u>Saturday Review</u>, 53
    (January 24, 1970), 19-20.
Albee, Edward. "The Decade of Engagement," <u>Saturday Review</u>, LIII
    (January 24, 1970), 19-20.
Albee, Edward. "The Decade of Engagement," <u>Saturday Review</u>,
    January 24, 1970, pp. 19-20. [<u>Or</u>: 24 Jan. 1970, pp. 19-20.][2]

Notice that:

1. Although the entries above have minor differences in form, the order
in each is (a) author, (b) title of the article, (c) name of the periodical, (d) issue
of the periodical and page numbers of the article. In choosing the form for
bibliographical entries, students should be guided by the preference of the
instructor and should use the form consistently in the bibliography.

---

[2] The *MLA Style Sheet* now recommends Arabic rather than Roman numerals, as in the
first entry. It further notes that volume numbers may be omitted if the complete date of the
publication is given, as in the last entry.

2. A period follows the author's inverted name; the other items are separated by commas.

3. The title of the article is put in quotation marks; the name of the periodical is underlined to represent italics in print.

4. When both volume and page numbers are given, the abbreviations vol. (for volume) and pp. (for pages) are not used.

An entry for an article in a magazine that is part of a newspaper is written:

DeMott, Benjamin. "The Sixties: A Cultural Revolution,"
    The New York Times Magazine, December 14, 1969, pp. 28-31,
    122-127.

An entry for an encyclopedia article reads:

Albright, Spencer D. "Congressional Committees," The
    Encyclopedia Americana, 1960, VII, 516-17.

An unsigned article in an encyclopedia, magazine, or newspaper is listed with the title of the article first, and is alphabetized by the first important word in the title—*Changing* in this entry:

"The Changing Library," Newsweek, 75 (February 16, 1970), 33.

An article, story, or essay that is part of a collection is entered in this form:

MacLeish, Archibald. "The Conquest of America," Ten
    Contemporary Thinkers, ed. Victor E. Amend and Leo T.
    Hendrick. New York: The Macmillan Company, 1964.

Source books for controlled research papers often contain excerpts from longer works, as well as complete articles. The bibliographical form for such an excerpt is:

Bradley, Andrew Cecil. Shakespearean Tragedy. London, 1904.
    Excerpt in Interpreting Hamlet, ed. Russell E. Leavenworth.
    San Francisco: Howard Chandler, 1960.

Notes to be used in the actual writing of the research paper are *not* taken on bibliography cards. It is often useful, however, as work on the paper proceeds, to make on these cards brief notations on the availability of the book or on its value.

A bibliography is gathered from three principal sources: (a) the card catalogue in the library, (b) periodical indexes, (c) encyclopedias and reference books. The following pages will provide a brief introduction to these sources. For more detailed information, a good book to consult is Jean Key Gates' *Guide to the Use of Books and Libraries*,[3] available in a paperback edition.

[3] New York: McGraw-Hill Book Company, 1962.

A. The Card Catalogue

The card catalogue is an alphabetical file which lists all books in the library by author, by title, and by subject. It also gives information about the publication and the size and content of the book; and it supplies the library call number to enable the user of the library to locate the book on the shelves.

An *author card,* alphabetized in the card catalogue according to the author's last name, has a heading like this:

```
          White, Theodore Harold, 1915–

E              The making of the President, 1960. New
840            York, Atheneum Publishers, 1961.
.W5            400 p.      25cm.
```

A *title card* for the same book has the title of the book typed at the top; the card is alphabetized according to the first important word in the title (not by *a, an, the*):

```
    The making of the President, 1960


          White, Theodore Harold, 1915–

E              The making of the President, 1960. New
840            York, Atheneum Publishers, 1961.
.W5            400 p.      25cm.
```

Usually the student starting work on a research paper will not know the authors and titles of books that might be useful to him. He will, therefore, look up in the card catalogue the subject of his paper, and related subjects. A *subject card* for the book by Theodore H. White classifies it under the heading "Presidents" and the three subheadings shown below:

```
┌─────────────────────────────────────────────────────┐
│                                                       │
│        PRESIDENTS - U.S. - ELECTION - 1960.           │
│                                                       │
│        White, Theodore Harold, 1915–                  │
│                                                       │
│   E              The making of the President, 1960. New│
│   840            York, Atheneum Publishers, 1961.     │
│   .W5            400 p.     25cm.                      │
│                                                       │
│                                                       │
└─────────────────────────────────────────────────────┘
```

The student making his own card for this book will omit some of the data on the library card, and record only what he needs for his own final bibliography and for his convenience in locating the book. His bibliography card will be in this form:

```
┌─────────────────────────────────────────────────────┐
│  White, Theodore Harold. The                          │
│  Making of the President, 1960.                        │
│  New York: Atheneum Publishers, 1961.                 │
│                                                       │
│                                                       │
│   E                                                   │
│   840                                                 │
│   .W5                                                 │
│                                                       │
└─────────────────────────────────────────────────────┘
```

The author, title, and facts of publication appear exactly as they will appear in the finished bibliography at the end of the paper. The library call number is recorded so that the student can later find the book without again consulting the card catalogue. If he is using more than one library, he should write the name of the library beside the call number, also to save trouble when, sometime later, he wants to locate the book.

In using the card catalogue, the student will find it helpful to remember that cards are filed word by word, rather than letter by letter. A letter-by-letter sequence is New England, Newfoundland, Newgate, New Hampshire, New York; a word-by-word sequence is New England, New Hampshire, New York, Newfoundland, Newgate. Also, abbreviations like *St., Dr., U.S.* are filed as if they were spelled out: *Saint, Doctor, United States.* Names beginning with *Mac, Mc,* and *M'* are filed as though they all began *Mac.*

B. Indexes to Periodicals

The periodical indexes list, usually by author and subject, in one alphabet, the contents of journals and magazines. They are an excellent source for bibliography, particularly for up-to-date material. The most generally useful index is the *Readers' Guide to Periodical Literature,* which indexes, by author, title, and subject, most of the important American periodicals and some foreign publications. It is published twice a month (except in July and August), and is cumulated in large volumes. Abbreviations used in the entries are explained at the beginning of each issue; and a check-list of the periodicals subscribed to by his library enables the student to see easily what articles he will be able to find.

Entries in the *Readers' Guide* (and in other indexes) are in this form:

> **Civil rights**
> UNITED STATES
> Battle begins on civil rights. il US News 56:31-
> 2 F 10 '64
> Crushed by the coalition. Time 83:14 F 14 '64
> Russell sounds call for civil-rights fight. US
> News 56:8 F 3 '64
> X factor is race. S.Alsop. il Sat Eve Post 237:10
> F 8 '64
> **Civil rights demonstrations**
> Race trouble in a model city; Atlanta. il US
> News 56:78 F 10 '64
> Spring offensive; Negroes plan the future. P.
> Watters. il Nation 198:117-20 F 3 '64

In noting the references on his bibliography cards, the student should translate these abbreviated entries into the form correct for his final bibliography. A card for the first entry would read:

"Battle Begins on Civil Rights," *U.S. News and World Report,* 56 (February 10, 1964), 31-32.

In addition to the *Readers' Guide to Periodical Literature* (1900 to date), students should be familiar with the following useful indexes:

Agricultural Index, 1916 to date.
Annual Magazine Subject-Index, 1908 to date.
Art Index, 1929 to date.
Biography Index, 1946 to date.
Book Review Digest, 1905 to date.
Catholic Periodical Index, 1930 to date.
Cumulative Book Index, 1928 to date. (Indexes all books published in the English language.)
Dramatic Index, 1909–1950.
Education Index, 1929 to date.
Engineering Index, 1884 to date.
Essay and General Literature Index, 1934 to date. (Analyzes and indexes parts of books, which would not be listed in the card catalogue.)
Index to Legal Periodicals, 1908 to date.
Industrial Arts Index, 1913–1957. (Indexes material on business, finance, engineering, applied science.)
International Index to Periodicals, 1907 to date.
Monthly Catalogue of United States Government Publications, 1895 to date.
New York Times Index. (Indexes current events from 1913 to date.)
Nineteenth Century Readers' Guide, 1890–1899.
Poole's Index to Periodical Literature, 1802–1907.
Psychological Abstracts, 1927 to date.
Public Affairs Information Service, 1915 to date.
Quarterly Cumulative Index Medicus, 1927 to date. (Indexes medical books, journals, and articles.)
Writings on American History, 1906 to date.

C. Encyclopedias and Other Reference Books

Encyclopedias and other reference books are useful both as sources of information and as bibliographical aids. We have said that reading an account in an encyclopedia, for a general view of the research subject, is often a good beginning of work on the paper. Also, standard encyclopedias usually list, at the end of an article, a well-selected bibliography for further reading in the field. In addition to the *Encyclopaedia Britannica*, the *Encyclopedia Americana*, and the one-volume *Columbia Encyclopedia*, students should be familiar with special encyclopedias and reference works which give more detailed information, and specialized bibliographies, in particular fields. Some of the most useful of these works are:

Encyclopaedia of the Social Sciences, 1937.
Langer's Encyclopaedia of World History, 1952.
McLaughlin and Hart's *Cyclopedia of American Government*, 1914.
Dictionary of American History, 1942.

Palgrave's *Dictionary of Political Economy*, 1923–26.
Bailey's *Cyclopedia of American Agriculture*, 1907–09.
Grove's *Dictionary of Music and Musicians*, 1954.
Munn's *Encyclopedia of Banking and Finance*, 1949 (supplement, 1956).
Bryan's *Dictionary of Painters and Engravers*, 1903–05.
Baldwin's *Dictionary of Philosophy and Psychology*, 1925.
Hastings' *Encyclopaedia of Religion and Ethics*, 1908–27 (revised).
Catholic Encyclopedia, 1907–22 (revised).
Jewish Encyclopedia, 1925.
Cambridge Ancient History, 1923–39.
Cambridge Medieval History, 1911–36.
Cambridge Modern History, 1902–26.
Cambridge Bibliography of English Literature, 1941–57.
Runes' *Dictionary of Philosophy*, 1942.
Van Nostrand's *Scientific Encyclopedia*, 1958.
The Reader's Encyclopedia of World Drama, 1969.
John Canaday, *Lives of the Painters*, 1969.
Encyclopedia of World Art, 1959.
Encyclopedia of Painting, 1955.
Winchell's *Guide to Reference Books*, 1951 (with supplements).
Gates' *Guide to the Use of Books and Libraries*, 1962.
Galin and Spielberg, *Reference Books: How to Select and Use Them*, 1969.

In connection with reference books, the student should be familiar with the annual supplements to encyclopedias, and other yearbooks which are excellent sources for recent facts and statistics:

Americana Annual
Britannica Book of the Year
Collier's Year Book
New International Yearbook
Statesman's Yearbook
World Almanac and Book of Facts
Yearbook of the United Nations
Yearbook of World Affairs

For biographical material, the best sources of information are:

American Men of Science
Biography Index
Century Dictionary of Names
Chambers's Biographical Dictionary, 1961, 1969
Contemporary American Authors
Current Biography
Dictionary of American Biography
Dictionary of National Biography (British)
International Who's Who
Twentieth Century Authors
Webster's Biographical Dictionary

Who's Who (mainly British)
Who's Who in America
Who's Who in History

An hour or two of browsing in the reference room of the library, locating and examining the various indexes and reference works, is time well spent. Work on the research paper would be valuable if it taught students only this: how to use a library, how to find material on any subject they may need to investigate.

III. BUILDING THE OUTLINE

We have already suggested that the student read a few general treatments of his subject very early in the research project. This preliminary reading— in encyclopedias or textbooks—may help him limit his subject and may supply him with a starting bibliography. Another advantage is that it gives him, from the beginning, some idea of the main divisions of his paper, or the points he will probably cover, or the questions he will need to answer. He can at once make a tentative outline that will grow and change as he reads and gathers material for his paper.

For example, a student planning to write a paper on the battle of Trafalgar can tell from reading one or two accounts of the battle that a possible outline of his paper might be:

1. Background—Napoleon's idea of invading England
2. Nelson's battle plan
3. The battle
4. Results

The purpose of such a tentative outline is two-fold. First, the rough outline, even though the student changes it as he learns more about the subject, keeps him mindful of the focus and organization of his paper. Second, it enables him to label his notes with headings from the outline which show where a particular piece of information fits into the plan of the paper. The student with the informal four-point outline above can label his notes "Background," or "Battle plan," or "Battle," or "Results" as soon as he begins to take them. As his information grows, his changing outline will include more details; he can then label his notes more specifically with headings and subheadings of an expanded, formal outline like this:[4]

   I. Situation in 1805
     A. Napoleon's invasion plans

---

[4] A number of instructors prefer sentence outlines to topical outlines for research papers. A sentence outline of this material and discussion of the sentence outline can be found on pages 475–479.

      B. French and Spanish fleet at Cadiz

  II. Nelson's command of the English fleet at Cadiz

      A. His plan for victory

         1. Memorandum

         2. Reaction to plan

      B. Condition of his fleet

         1. Smallness of fleet compared to that of enemy

         2. Loss of ships sent to Gibraltar

         3. Request for additional force

 III. Preliminaries to attack

      A. October 19

      B. October 20

      C. Dawn of October 21

 IV. The advance to attack

      A. Nelson during advance

         1. Presentiment of death

         2. Prayer for victory

         3. His immortal signal

      B. Arrangement of ships in advance

         1. In leeward division

         2. In windward division

  V. The battle

      A. Attack of leeward line

         1. Firing on *Royal Sovereign*

         2. Action against *Santa Anna* and *Fougueux*

      B. Attack of windward line

         1. Firing on *Victory*

         2. Attack on *Bucentaure*

         3. Engagement with *Redoubtable*

            a. Damage to French

            b. Injury to Nelson

         4. Other ships in the fighting

      C. English successes in center and rear

         1. *Redoubtable*

         2. *Fougueux*

         3. *Bucentaure*

         4. *Santissima Trinidad*

         5. *Santa Anna*

         6. *Belleisle*'s action against the enemy

      D. Entrance of enemy van

         1. Defeat of two

         2. Flight of three others

         3. Flight of Dumanoir with remainder

 VI. Results of battle

      A. Immediate

         1. Death of Nelson

         2. Ships captured by English

     B. Long-run
       1. English superiority on the sea
       2. Cancellation of Napoleon's invasion plans

Many instructors, knowing the value of the expanding outline, require a tentative short outline early in the research project, and a more detailed outline after the work is well underway. Whether or not it is required, the student should build his outline as he builds his paper. The use of the outline in taking notes and writing the paper will be discussed further in the following sections.

IV. TAKING NOTES

In taking notes on the material he reads for his research paper, the student should bear in mind two things: first, that his paper will be written from these notes, after he has read a great deal of material, and after particular references have become blurred with others and are no longer fresh and clear in his mind; second, that he will be required to footnote his material, giving the source, including the exact page, from which he has taken his information. His notes, therefore, must be full enough to recall the material; they must accurately record its source. They should also be taken, and labeled, in such a way that they can easily be arranged in convenient order for the writing of the paper.

Scholars have worked out an efficient system for noting, filing, and organizing material:

All notes are taken on cards, 3 by 5, 4 by 6, or 5 by 8 inches. Students usually find 4 by 6-inch cards the most convenient size.

Each note card carries the exact source, including the page number, from which the material on the card is taken.

Each card carries a heading which describes its content and shows where this material fits in the outline of the paper.

The material on each card concerns only one subdivision of the paper.

Each note card also shows clearly whether the material is quoted from the source, or is summarized.

Below are two sample note cards. The first, a note for a research paper on the migration of birds, is an example of summary; the second, for a paper on the philosophy of Thomas Hardy, shows by its form that it is an exact quotation. In general, very few notes should be quotations. Sometimes, of course, it is important to quote exactly in the research paper the opinion of one authority on a controversial subject, or the wording of an historical document; sometimes an idea is so strikingly expressed that one wishes to use the perfectly turned sentence or phrase. In such cases, the material should be copied accurately on the note card and clearly enclosed in quotation marks.

But most material is not worth full quotation; and an acceptable research paper is never a series of quotations or near-quotations.

Whitlock, *Migration of Birds*   Cold

110 cold by itself not sufficient direct influence on majority of species to leave home to which they are devotedly attached

111 with increasing cold, daily migration in search of food have to be prolonged to distance where return during daylight is impossible

Summary Notes

Cecil, *Hardy*   Religion

223 "He found it impossible to believe the Christian hope..... But he can only be respected for the honesty which compelled him to accept a philosophy of the universe so repugnant to the deepest instincts of his heart. And still more must he be honored for that elevation of soul which enabled him to maintain the Christian temper without the help of the Christian consolation."

Quotation

Unconscious plagiarism,[5] consisting of staying too close to the wording and organization of one's sources, is a recurrent danger in writing research papers. Although the material is taken from other authors, the language and the arrangement of ideas should be the writer's own. If he presents, as his own writing, sentences or paragraphs in which the sequence of ideas is that of his source and the wording is only slightly changed, he is making illegitimate, though perhaps not consciously dishonest, use of sources. This

[5] For a fuller explanation of plagiarism, see pages 503–505.

unintentional plagiarism occurs when the student takes verbatim notes without enclosing the material in quotation marks, plans to put it in his own language later, but forgets by the time he starts writing that the notes are not already in his own words. The way to avoid this danger is to digest the material as one reads and condense it in one's own words on the note cards. For example, a student is taking notes on the following passage from a book on the "theatre of the absurd":

Inevitably, plays written in this new convention will, when judged by the standards and criteria of another, be regarded as impertinent and outrageous impostures. If a good play must have a cleverly constructed story, these have no story or plot to speak of; if a good play is judged by subtlety of characterization and motivation, these are often without recognizable characters and present the audience with almost mechanical puppets; if a good play has to have a fully explained theme, which is neatly exposed and finally solved, these often have neither a beginning nor an end; if a good play is to hold the mirror up to nature and portray the manners and mannerisms of the age in finely observed sketches, these seem often to be reflections of dreams and nightmares; if a good play relies on witty repartee and pointed dialogue, these often consist of incoherent babblings.

But the plays we are concerned with here pursue ends quite different from those of the conventional play and therefore use quite different methods. They can be judged only by the standards of the Theatre of the Absurd, which it is the purpose of this book to define and clarify.—MARTIN ESSLIN, *The Theatre of the Absurd*

The note card below is poor because, although parts of the passage are omitted, the notes follow very closely the wording of the source and the sentence structure of Mr. Esslin. If the material appeared in this form in the research paper, it would be, though unintentionally, plagiarized:

```
         Esslin, Theatre of the Absurd   Characteristics

   xvii  Plays in this new convention, when
         judged by standards of another, will
         seem impertinent and outrageous.  If a
         good play has a cleverly constructed
         story, these have none.  If a good play
         is judged by subtlety of character and
         motivation, these present mechanical
         puppets.  If a good play has a fully
         explained theme, these have neither be-
   xviii ginning nor end.  If a good play holds
         mirror up to nature, these seem like
         dreams and nightmares.  If a good play
         has witty repartee, these often consist
         of incoherent babblings.  But these
         plays pursue ends quite different from
         those of the conventional play and
         therefore use different methods.
```

The following note card is good. The student has summarized the material in his own words and has recorded it economically. (The author's name without the title of the book is adequate identification of the source when only one work by this author is used; if more than one work is used, the title, or a short form of it, should be recorded on the note card.)

```
Esslin                              Characteristics

xvii  Conventional standards do not apply to
      these plays.  Instead of having conven-
      tional plot, characterization, motiva-
      tion, clearly unfolding theme, realistic
      representation of life and manners, and
xviii sensible dialogue, they are often form-
      less, dreamlike, irrational.  They use
      a new convention for different aims.
```

It is impossible to overemphasize the importance of labeling each note card, both with its exact source, and with a heading ("Cold," "Religion," and "Characteristics" on the cards above) which describes the material on the card. These descriptive labels, as we have said in the preceding section, should match a heading in the student's growing outline of his paper. At first, they may be rather general. As the outline with its various subdivisions takes shape, they can be increasingly specific. The value of this labeling becomes most apparent when the student has finished gathering material and is preparing to write his paper. He can, without reading all the material on his cards, pull out and put into separate piles all those cards having the same heading; he then arranges the piles in the best order for discussion in the paper; he is ready to begin writing from notes in logical sequence, with no necessity of leafing through a notebook, or scanning large sheets of paper for particular bits of material that he remembers having somewhere. This flexibility of the note cards—the fact that they can be shuffled and arranged—is the principal reason for using them; but much of their value is lost unless each card is complete with source and heading.

Worth re-emphasizing, too, is the importance of putting on any one card *only* material which concerns *one subdivision* of the paper. If one reads, for example, an article on the Lincoln-Douglas debates, and wishes to make from it two brief notes—one on the first debate, another on the effects of the debates —it is a temptation to put the two short notes on one card. A little reflection will show, however, that those two pieces of material belong in different parts of the paper; a single card can be in only one place in a pile of note cards; the two notes should, therefore, be put on different cards, each with its informative label. It is more trouble, of course, to make out two cards; it is more trouble in general to take careful notes than it is to take slipshod ones. But the writer is well repaid for his effort by the ease with which a paper can be written from accurate, intelligible, systematic notes.

As he reads and takes notes, the student should make some evaluation of his sources. Obviously sources are not of equal worth. They may even contradict one another. How is the student, not himself a specialist in the field, to judge the authority of what he reads? The reputation of the author is often a guide; his qualifications as an expert can sometimes be checked in the biographical dictionaries; his work may be referred to with respect or criticized adversely by other writers in the field, so that an estimate of him gradually emerges from other sources. The publication in which an article appears should be considered in evaluating it: an article in a reputable magazine is more to be trusted than a feature story in the Sunday newspaper; an article from a paper or magazine with a definite political slant should be read with that slant in mind. The style and tone of a book or article are not infallible measures of its soundness; but, generally speaking, a work that is documented either with footnotes or with sources introduced into the text is more reliable than a popular, undocumented account; a novelized biography, for example, may be lively and interesting and generally accurate, but for reliable facts about the subject one would consult a more scholarly work. Finally, the date of the book or article is relevant in evaluating it. The most recent work is not invariably the best, but it has the benefit of previous scholarship; and in some fields, science and technology particularly, sources are quickly outdated. The student should be sure that he has seen the most recent material on this subject, and that any older material that he uses checks with the latest data.

V. WRITING AND FOOTNOTING THE PAPER

When the student feels that he has gathered enough material for his paper, he is ready for two last preliminaries to the actual writing of the first draft. First, he should thoughtfully revise the outline which has been growing and changing as he has taken notes and thought about his paper. This outline may be changed still further during the writing of the paper; that is, the writer may find, when he gets into the material, that certain parts of it need to be rearranged for better development, coherence, or emphasis. But a full outline, which shows the material in logical sequence and organization, is necessary for the second step toward writing.

This second step consists of arranging the note cards in sequence, following the order of the outline. If the student has labeled his cards carefully, it will not be necessary, as we have said before, to read all of the notes, but only to look at the headings, which will correspond, roughly at least, to the headings and subheadings in the outline. With his note cards arranged in this logical sequence, and with his outline before him, the student is ready to study the cards dealing with the opening section of his paper, and to begin to write.

Paragraph by paragraph, writing the research paper is much like writing any theme. But the material is so much more complex than it is in a short paper that, as we have said, it presents special problems. The writer, in addition to having the organization of his paper clearly in mind, must take special care to keep that organization clear to the reader by means of skillful transitions between paragraphs and sections of the paper, and by means of occasional summary statements or paragraphs that pull together the preceding material and lead into the next phase of the development. He must be sure that he is explaining, fully enough for a general audience, the terms, processes, or events which have by now become thoroughly familiar to him. And he has a special problem, of course, in handling the footnotes in a research paper.

There are two kinds of footnotes: those that give additional information about a point that cannot be developed easily or coherently in the text of the paper, and those that give exact references to sources. Most of the footnotes in a student research paper will be of the second type. These footnotes are used in a paper of this kind for three reasons. First, they observe a code of scholarship: they give credit where credit is due; they honestly acknowledge the debt of the writer to other writers whose information and ideas he has used. Second, the footnotes give support to what would otherwise be the writer's unsupported, and perhaps questionable, word: they say in effect to the reader, "This is not a mere fancy of mine; So-and-so, an authority in the field, has this idea." Third, the footnotes give the exact source of the information so that the interested reader can readily find the reference if he wishes to check it or to read further on a particular point. Reference footnotes, in short, are evidence of the honesty, the soundness, and the exactness of the paper.

Knowing what to footnote is a problem for inexperienced writers, and no simple, rigid rules can be provided. It will be helpful to study the footnoting —to see what kind of material is footnoted—in the research paper printed at the end of this chapter. Also, these general principles will supply guidance:

1. Footnote any direct quotation.
2. Footnote any borrowed map, chart, or diagram.
3. Footnote any borrowed ideas, opinions, conclusions, and patterns of organization, even though they are not in the language of the source.
4. Footnote any factual information which has been taken from sources and which is not common knowledge.

Just what constitutes common knowledge, what facts are so generally accepted that they need no footnotes, is often hard to decide. Footnoting too little is, however, a more serious fault than footnoting too much. "When in doubt, footnote" is a good safe rule.

A footnote number is used *at the end* of a borrowed passage, and is raised slightly above the typed line. The footnote itself, preceded by this number, and paragraphed, is commonly set at the bottom of the page. Footnotes are numbered from 1 on each page, or, preferably, they are numbered continuously from the beginning to the end of the paper. Typical student research papers have at least three or four footnotes to a typed page. In good research papers the footnote references on each page are varied; they show that the student has brought together, in his own synthesis, material from different sources.

The *first* footnote reference to a book or article is usually a full reference, including the author's full name (in natural order) and the place and date of publication. Below are examples of first footnote references to a book, to a signed article, and to an unsigned article:

> ¹Alfred Werner, <u>Post-Impressionist Painting</u> (New York, 1964), p. 41.

> ²Arthur Schlesinger, Jr., "The Lowering Hemisphere," <u>The Atlantic</u>, 225 (January, 1970), 79.

> ³"Revolution Without Plan," <u>Newsweek</u>, 75 (February 9, 1970), 34.

Notice that the information in these first footnote references[6] is much like that given in the bibliography; but in the footnotes the authors' names are in natural order, since they are not being alphabetized; commas are used to separate the parts of the footnote; and a specific page reference tells exactly where this piece of information appeared in the book or article. When both volume and page are given, as in the second and third footnotes above, the numbers are not preceded by *vol.* and *p.* If the volume of a magazine is not included, or if a one-volume work is referred to, *p.* for *page* or *pp.* for *pages* accompanies the page reference.

Later footnote references to the same source are simplified: they may be reduced to the author's last name and the page number; references to an unsigned article may be reduced to the name of the magazine or newspaper and the page number:

> Werner, p. 49.

> Schlesinger, p. 82.

> <u>Newsweek</u>, p. 37.

[6] First footnote references include the publisher when a bibliography is not appended to the paper. The form is: Alfred Werner, *Post-Impressionist Painting* (New York: McGraw-Hill, 1964), p. 41. Some instructors prefer the longer form even though a bibliography supplies the name of the publisher. Usage is divided, and students should follow the wishes of the instructor about the fullness of first footnote references.

When more than one work by the same author is referred to in the paper, the title or a short form of the title must be used in later footnotes; the name of the author and the page number alone would not, of course, tell which of his works was referred to. Similarly, when more than one issue of a magazine is referred to, the title of an unsigned article, or a short form of the title, or the issue of the magazine must be used to identify the reference.

Ibid.[7] (an abbreviation of the Latin *ibidem,* "in the same place") is used to refer to a source named in the immediately preceding footnote. *Ibid.* is followed by a comma and a page reference if the page is different from that in the preceding footnote; it stands alone when the material annotated comes from the same page of the same source named in the footnote just before:

> [1]Daniel Lang, <u>Casualties of War</u> (New York, 1969), p. 50.
>
> [2]<u>Ibid</u>. [reference to p. 50 of Lang's book]
>
> [3]<u>Ibid</u>., p. 63 [reference to a different page of Lang's book]
>
> [4]"My Lai: An American Tragedy," <u>Time</u>, 94 (December 5, 1969), 30.
>
> [5]<u>Ibid</u>. [reference to p. 30 of the <u>Time</u> article]

Besides *ibid.,* a number of conventional abbreviations and symbols are used in footnotes. The most common, some of which we have already mentioned, are listed below. The student may not use all of them in his research paper, but he should know their meanings in order to understand their use by other writers.

> *op. cit.*—an abbreviation of the Latin *opere citato* meaning "in the work cited." It is used in place of the title in footnote references subsequent to the first full reference: Werner, *op. cit.,* p. 49. In accordance with the *MLA Style Sheet,* we recommend the simpler form (Werner, p. 49), but students should understand the use of *op. cit.,* for they will encounter it in a number of scholarly publications, particularly in older scholarly writing.
>
> ch., chs. *or* chap., chaps.—chapter, chapters
>
> cf. (Latin *confer*)—compare. The English *see* is often more accurate.
>
> ed.—edition *or* edited by *or* editor
>
> e.g. (Latin *exempli gratia*)—for example
>
> *et al.* (Latin *et alii*)—and others
>
> f., ff.—following. Pp. 2 f. means page 2 and the page following; pp. 2 ff. means page 2 and the pages following. An exact reference, such as pp. 2-5, is preferable to pp. 2 ff.

---

[7] The notes below and in the research paper at the end of the chapter follow the practice of underlining (i.e., italicizing) *ibid.* Some journals and publishers are now dropping this convention of italicizing Latin abbreviations. The student should follow the preference of his instructor.

l., ll.—line, lines

n.—note

n.d.—no date; used in bibliography and footnotes when a book or pamphlet carries no date of publication.

p., pp.—page, pages

passim—here and there. This symbol is useful when material is condensed from a number of pages. The reference pp. 79–90 *passim* means that here and there, scattered through the pages, the material was found. *Passim* should not be used when a more exact citation is possible.

sic—thus, so. It is inserted in brackets to indicate that an error in expression or spelling appeared thus in the original source.

vol., vols.—volume, volumes. As we have said, when a reference requires both volume number and page number, the symbols for volume and page are omitted: *Encyclopaedia Britannica,* 10, 480.

Some special problems in footnoting are:

1. **Reference to an encyclopedia article.** If the article is signed with the initials rather than the name of the author, the student should find the author's name in the alphabetized list of contributors at the beginning of volume I of the encyclopedia, and should write the footnote in this form:

> Henry William Carless Davis, "Charles the Great," Encyclo-paedia Britannica, 1957, 5, 256-257.

A later footnote reference to this article, if no references to other works by Davis intervene, could read:

> Davis, p. 258.

If an encyclopedia article is unsigned, the first footnote reference will have this form:

> "Sartre, Jean-Paul," The Reader's Encyclopedia, 1965, 2, 898.

A later reference could be shortened to:

> The Reader's Encyclopedia, 2, 899.

2. **Reference to a book which has several authors.** A full reference includes the full names of the authors if there are no more than three:

> Edward A. Bloom, Charles H. Philbrick, and Elmer M. Blistein, The Order of Poetry: An Introduction (New York, 1961), pp. 33-34.

A later footnote reference to this book, if no references to other writings by the same group of authors intervene, could read:

> Bloom et al., p. 67.   Or: Bloom and others, p. 67.

3. Reference to an edited book:

John Milton, <u>Paradise Lost</u>, ed. Merritt Y. Hughes (New York, 1962), p. 82.

A later footnote, if no references to other works by Milton intervene, could read:

Milton, p. 89.

4. Reference to a translation:

Thomas Mann, <u>Joseph and His Brothers</u>, trans. H. T. Lowe-Porter (New York, 1948), p. 251.

A later reference, if no references to other works by Mann intervene, could read:

Mann, p. 400.

5. Reference to a selection that is part of a book:

Alfred Harbage, "Shakespeare's Audience: Modern Appraisals," <u>Shakespeare: Modern Essays in Criticism</u>, ed. Leonard F. Dean (New York, 1961), p. 9.

A later footnote, if no references to other works by Harbage intervene, could read:

Harbage, pp. 13-14.

6. Reference to an excerpt that is part of a book—a book of source materials for a controlled research project, for example:

John Thomas Codman, <u>Brook Farm, Historic and Personal Memoirs</u>, Boston, 1894, excerpt in <u>Autobiography of Brook Farm</u>, ed. Henry W. Sams (Englewood Cliffs, New Jersey, 1958), p. 232.

A later footnote could read:

Codman, p. 236.

7. Reference to a work which the student has not read, cited or quoted in a book or article he has read:

Samuel Beckett, <u>The Unnamable</u>, quoted in Wylie Sypher, <u>Loss of the Self in Modern Literature and Art</u> (New York, 1962), pp. 149-150.

In writing the first draft of his paper, the student will probably waste time and divert his attention from the presentation of his material if he stops to write footnotes in correct form for his finished paper. *It is important, however, to make a record of footnotes as one writes the first draft;* the sources are noted on the cards; it is obviously a waste of time and effort to write the paper without footnotes and then to go through the cards a second time to find and write down the sources. An easy and efficient way of keeping track of footnotes in the first draft is to put a very brief notation—usually author and page will do—in parentheses where the footnote number will be in the final copy. Many students find it useful to underline this embryonic footnote in red or blue pencil, or to put it in red or blue parentheses, so that it stands out from the text of the paper. Later, this brief notation can be expanded into correct footnote form, dropped to the bottom of the page, and given its proper number. Keeping track of sources in the first draft, like making careful bibliography and note cards, will save trouble in the long run, and ensure accurate documenting of the paper.

VI. REVISING AND COMPLETING THE PAPER

Most instructors, before they read and judge a research paper, examine its outline, bibliography, and footnotes. This initial survey is partially a check on correct form, but it is more than that. The outline represents the scope and organization of the paper; the bibliography gives some indication of the amount of reading done and the value of the sources the student has found and used; the footnotes show to some extent how well he has drawn together materials from different sources and integrated them into a paper which, though composed of borrowed data, is genuinely his own. In a good research paper, the outline, bibliography, and footnotes are in proper form; also, and more important, they give initial evidence of these qualities in the paper: logical organization, adequate coverage of the subject, sufficient documentation, and skillful integrating of scattered materials.

Although the machinery of the research paper is important, students should not become so absorbed in it that they neglect what is, after all, essential to excellence in any composition—good writing. Even though a research paper represents many hours of hard work, even though it is elaborately and correctly footnoted, it is not a good paper if it is incompetently written. Careful revision is, therefore, very important.

The length of the research paper and the complexity of its content make the inexperienced writer susceptible to faults which in a short paper he probably would avoid. Six of the most common of these faults are listed below. Some of them have been discussed earlier, but they deserve special comment in connection with revising and completing the research paper. Easy to fall into, they are also easy to correct in revision. The six faults:

1. *Lack of transition between sections of the paper.* This fault usually is a result of writing different sections of the paper at different times, and thinking of them as separate units. Units they are, but they are also parts of a whole; their close relationship must be established by transitional phrases

and sentences that lead the reader from one part of the paper into the next. In the following sentence, the writer of a student research paper on the early history of jazz makes a smooth transition from New Orleans jazz to Dixieland jazz:

> While New Orleans was enjoying its last days as jazz capital, groups of white musicians, seeing the success of the Negroes, attempted to imitate them, and in doing so created what is called the Dixieland style.

By means of the following transitional paragraph from a paper on Cro-Magnon man, the reader is saved what would have been a confusing leap from the Cro-Magnons back to the Eolithic age:

> Before studying the Cro-Magnon race, it is necessary to have some knowledge of the epochs that preceded it. Our pre-history has been divided into three chronological classifications . . . .

2. *Choppy sentences.* Choppy sentences are often simply careless, but sometimes they come from the mistaken idea that items of information from different sources should be put in separate sentences. Material from different sources is frequently, and quite properly, welded into a single sentence; two or more footnotes may be used in one sentence to give the sources of the combined material. The following excerpt from a paper on the assassination of Lincoln will illustrate:

> Booth savagely reeled about, put the knife into his right hand, and slashed the Major's arm;[22] then he leapt from the box down to the stage twelve feet below.[23]

Short, choppy sentences are even more objectionable in a research paper, presumably a mature piece of work, than in an informal theme.

3. *Choppy paragraphs.* Short, underdeveloped paragraphs sometimes are caused by a misconception similar to the one which produces choppy sentences: the student mistakenly thinks that the material from each source should be presented in a separate paragraph. More often, choppy paragraphs come from using a paragraph break at each minor division in the outline of the paper. Organizing paragraphs around a topic sentence is the cure for this serious weakness. A third-level subdivision in the outline (I, A, 1) is often the topic idea of a solid paragraph; the points under it (*a, b, c*) are not likely to require separate paragraphs, because these points are essentially the facts and details that support the topic idea. Paragraphs should bind together, not separate, such closely related subordinate points.

4. *Unconscious repetition of material.* Some repetition, for emphasis, or for purposes of summary, may be desirable in dealing with complex material. But the use of the same material more than once without reference to its earlier use gives the impression that the writer, blindly stumbling through his note cards, has lost track of what he has already said. If it is desirable to

call the reader's attention to facts previously discussed in the paper, a phrase like "we have seen that," or "as has been said before" will indicate that the repetition is purposeful and that the writer has a sure grasp of all the material in the paper.

5. *Unconscious contradiction.* This fault, seriously confusing to the reader, is closely related to unconscious repetition of material. It occurs when the writer, having on his note cards the differing opinions of two authors, sets them down as if both opinions were facts. The writer who does this is, of course, using his note cards thoughtlessly. If the opinions of both authors appear to have some merit, if neither can fairly be rejected, they should be introduced in some such manner as this:

> There is some difference of opinion about the exact date when the first music that could be called jazz was played. Robert Goffin, in *Jazz from the Congo to the Metropolitan,* says that the first bands were formed in the 1880's.[4] Other authorities, however . . . .[5]

(Introducing sources into the text in this way, even when no contradiction is involved, often makes a clearer and more readable paper. Only the page reference is needed in the footnote when author and title are given in the text.)

6. *Unawareness of dates.* We have said earlier that the student should be sure that he is not using outdated sources. He should, moreover, be conscious of the dates of relatively recent sources. If in his paper he makes a statement like "Very recently a new development has occurred," and if the source of his statement is an article published in 1945, he has given misinformation. Checking of the manuscript with the dates in the bibliography will prevent such blunders in the final copy.

It seems hardly necessary to say that the writing in the research paper should be technically correct. Errors in agreement, parallelism, and reference are inexcusable in so important a paper. Run-together sentences and impressionistic incomplete sentences are out of place in writing of this kind; they are incongruous with the formality of footnotes and the serious and scholarly tone of the whole paper.

Because the paper is formal, contractions like *can't, won't, couldn't* are usually avoided; and abbreviations should be used with caution—*Pres., Prof., Sen., Mass., U.S.,* for example, should be written out. Personal comment should be restricted to the preface; the text of the paper should be written in impersonal style.

This requirement of impersonal style in the formal paper does not mean that the writer's personality and judgment are excluded from the paper. On the contrary, in his selection of material, his arrangement of it, his expression of ideas, the words he chooses, the sentences he writes, the conclusions he may draw from the data he has assembled, the writer dominates the paper. He makes clear and interesting to a reader a subject that is clear and interesting to him. His phrasing is impersonal because his purpose in writing is to present, not himself or his experience, but the subject on which he has chosen to work and to write.

Checking the form of the outline, bibliography, and footnotes; examining transitions; inspecting for choppiness; eliminating unconscious repetition, contradiction, and confusion of dates; correcting mechanical errors; making the style consistent in level and tone as well as finished and exact—all of this takes time in a long paper. The foresighted student, therefore, plans to finish the draft of his paper at least a week before the paper is due, so that he will not be hurried in his revision. He may also need to allow several days for preparing the final copy. A usual requirement is that the research paper be typed. The typing itself takes some time, of course; and even skillful typists may make mistakes, particularly in copying footnote references from a draft which has been a good deal revised. The student should allow time, not only for thorough revision, but for careful proofreading after the paper is typed. It is most unfortunate when the painstaking work of weeks is marred or obscured by hasty work on the last stages of the paper.

Strange though it may seem to the student who has read this chapter and has yet to begin work on his own paper, many college students find the research paper the most enjoyable and rewarding work that they do all term. As they proceed systematically to assemble a bibliography, to take notes, to shape the outline of the material, what seemed at first a complicated and formidable task turns out to be simply a series of steps; no step is difficult in itself; and each one produces satisfying, tangible progress. Students who believe that they have no imagination are particularly likely to enjoy the research paper; it does not call for imagination, but for skill in finding, organizing, evaluating, and presenting material. Writing a long paper gives one confidence about handling other writing assignments, and nearly always a fluency that makes subsequent writing easier. In work on the research paper there is, too, the pleasure of learning, of becoming something of an authority on a subject in which one is interested. Because it is a large project, the research paper is more likely than the short paper to give the conscientious writer the satisfaction that comes from orderly procedure, sustained effort, and solid achievement.

SUMMARY

The student is not expected, even after he has carefully read this chapter, to remember all the details about sources, note-taking, bibliography and footnote form. He should use this chapter for reference as he works on the research paper, rereading the section on bibliography before he gathers his bibliography, the section on taking notes when he is ready to take notes, the section on footnotes when he is ready to use them.

Below are a number of instructions or admonitions that summarize the most important things to keep in mind during work on the research paper:

1. Choose a subject in which you are interested.

2. Limit the subject so that it can be covered adequately in a paper of this length.

3. Be sure that there is enough available material before you decide finally on a subject.

4. Gather your bibliography from the card catalogue in the library, from periodical indexes, and from encyclopedias and reference books. (As your work proceeds, you will probably add to your bibliography other sources that you discover in the bibliographies and footnotes of books and articles you read.)

5. Put the entries on your bibliography cards in correct form.

6. Take notes on cards, using separate cards for separate pieces of information.

7. Record on each note card the exact source, including the page number, of the material.

8. Give each note card a heading or label which tells exactly what the material on the card is about.

9. As early as possible make a tentative outline of the paper, so that headings on your note cards can correspond to headings in the outline.

10. Take summary notes rather than full quotations unless you have reason to quote directly from the source. Summarize the material in your own words.

11. Bear in mind that all sources are not of equal value.

12. Remember that your paper should integrate material from different sources. Your footnotes will reflect this integration.

13. Be sure that you understand clearly when and how to use footnotes. Study the footnotes in the research paper that follows, to see:

(*a*) where the footnote numbers are placed;

(*b*) how the information in the footnotes is arranged and punctuated;

(*c*) how footnote references are simplified after the first reference to the book or article; and

(*d*) how *ibid.* is used.

14. Put footnotes (though not necessarily in full and correct form) into the first draft of the paper.

15. Refer to the material in this chapter and to the section on outlining, page 473 ff., to be sure that bibliography and outline as well as footnotes are in correct form.

16. Allow ample time to revise the writing in the paper. Guard particularly against the faults discussed in the last section of this chapter.

17. Examine the research paper printed in the following pages, seeing its organization and development, and using it to clarify any matters of form or conventional usage that are unclear to you.

RACING FOR THE MOON: AMERICA'S PROJECT APOLLO

Susan Lawsine Ries

English 1 A

May 25, 1964

- ii -

PREFACE

I believe that this nation should commit itself to
achieving the goal, before this decade is out, of landing a
man on the moon and returning him safely to earth. No
single space project in this period will be more exciting,
or more impressive, or more important for the long-
range exploration of space . . . .

John F. Kennedy[1]

———

Why the great hurry to get to the moon...? We have
already demonstrated that, in everything except the power
of our rocket boosters, we are leading the world in scientific space exploration. From here on, I think we
should proceed in an orderly way, building one accomplishment on another, rather than engaging in a mad effort to win a stunt race.

Dwight D. Eisenhower[2]

———

[1]Quoted in Jay Holmes, America on the Moon (Philadelphia and New
York, 1962), p. 203.
[2]Quoted in Richard Witkin, "Pros and Cons," America's Race for
the Moon, ed. Walter Sullivan (New York, 1962), p. 147.

- iii -

These two statements refer to Project Apollo, America's manned
1970 lunar-landing program, which, during its brief existence, will
cost at least 20 billion dollars.³ It will tax the abilities of the
National Aeronautics and Space Administration ten major centers and
most of its 30,000 employees.⁴ Five thousand industrial firms will
be contracted to work on it, and 15,000 other companies will be indirectly involved in its development.⁵ An unprecedented venture,
charged to succeed within a decade, the Apollo project has assumed
some of the aspects of a war-time "crash program"⁶: major scientific
and engineering talents are fervently devoted to it; duplications of
effort and expenditure occur; there is public confusion over some
of its objectives; and—as the above quotations illustrate—the
question of its relative importance is subject to much debate.

The purpose of this paper is to describe the aims and procedures
of Project Apollo, and then to discuss this controversial program
with reference to its ten-year time limit. For some critics of
Apollo, the controversy centers on the necessity of manned, versus
unmanned, lunar exploration. Because of limited space, I have
chosen to ignore this issue and to concentrate on the critical
question which interests me more: is a lunar landing by 1970 an indispensable objective for America? The paper is addressed to all
persons who are interested in Project Apollo and who would like to
evaluate it for themselves.

Because the program is a continuing operation, it is difficult
to keep abreast of the advances that are being made in theory and in
technology. Even though I have attempted to use the most recent
source materials, it is possible that the descriptive portion of
this paper may be outdated in the near future. The evaluative section of the paper, however, will continue to be relevant as long as
there are thinking Americans.

-----

³Hugh L. Dryden, "Footprints on the Moon," National Geographic,
125 (March, 1964), 357.

⁴Ibid.

⁵Ibid.

⁶Edwin Diamond, The Rise and Fall of the Space Age (New York,
1964), p. 7.

– iv –

OUTLINE

I. Development of American manned lunar-landing program
   A. Origin
      1. Russian "firsts" in space
      2. President Kennedy's Message to Congress, May 25, 1961
   B. Supervision
   C. Three planned stages
      1. Project Mercury
      2. Project Gemini
      3. Project Apollo
   D. Lunar Orbital Rendezvous Technique

II. Reasons for accelerated development of program
   A. Political
      1. Importance of space race in Cold War
      2. Psychological effect on Americans and allies
   B. Military
      1. Possibility of enemy aggression from space
      2. Military potential of lunar base
   C. Economic
      1. Technological "spin-off"
      2. New concepts in industry
      3. Future remedy for unemployment
   D. Scientific
      1. Advancement of life sciences
      2. Impetus to all scientific fields

III. Arguments for deceleration of program
   A. Political
      1. Transient importance of space race for neutral nations
      2. Criticism of space race
   B. Military
      1. Developing Russian-American cooperation in space
      2. Lack of military value in lunar base
   C. Economic
      1. "Problem of priorities"
      2. Future economic consequences of program
   D. Scientific
      1. Conclusions of Space Science Board on scientific value
         of program
      2. Effect on Russian science of massive space effort

IV. Conclusion

- 1 -

RACING FOR THE MOON: AMERICA'S PROJECT APOLLO

Sputniks and Luniks were already impressive history when Russia
astounded the world with another "first" in space. On April 12,
1961, Major Yuri Gagarin was orbiting the earth![7] In America, the
National Aeronautics and Space Administration's three-year-old Project Mercury was still in its final stage of development. Its objective was a manned flight of three or more orbits, and a safe re-
entry to earth.[8] Americans would wait ten long months before
Astronaut John H. Glenn's triumphant ride in Friendship 7 accomplished this goal on February 20, 1962.[9]

At the time of Major Gagarin's orbiting, the United States had
no official plans beyond Project Mercury for manned space exploration. But the new Kennedy Administration had reviewed our space
program and concluded that a lunar landing within the decade was
vital—as the late President emphasized in his May 25, 1961 Message
to Congress.[10] Amazed and alarmed by Russia's demonstrated superiority in space technology, the Congress agreed that appropriations
for a lunar program were necessary. On August 7, 1961, H. R. 6879
was voted into law: NASA was to receive $1,671,750,000 for the
Fiscal Year 1962,[11] and Project Apollo was born.

Scores of NASA officials have supervised the development of our
manned lunar-landing program, but those with primary responsibilities are: James E. Webb, Administrator of NASA; Dr. Hugh L. Dryden,
Deputy Administrator; Dr. Robert C. Seamans, Jr., Associate Administrator; and Dr. George E. Mueller, Associate Administrator for
Manned Space Flight.[12] As they have conceived it, the program is to

----

[7]Martin Caidin, Red Star in Space (New York, 1962), p. 221.
[8]NASA, One...Two...Three...and the Moon (Washington, D.C.,
1962), p. 2.
[9]NASA, America in Space (Washington, D.C., 1963), p. 17.
[10]Holmes, p. 203.
[11]Ibid., p. 205.
[12]Until September, 1963, the Office of Manned Space Flight was
headed by D. Brainard Holmes.

- 2 -

progress in three stages toward its 1970 goal. Project Mercury, the
first stage, was successfully completed on May 16, 1963, with Astronaut L. Gordon Cooper's twenty-two orbit mission.[13] During the
project almost fifty-four hours of space flight time[14] were accumulated by our first six astronauts: Shepard, Grissom, Glenn, Carpenter, Shirra, and Cooper. The 384 million dollar program provided
experience in science-industry-government coordination, in systems
engineering, and in operational and flight control procedures.[15]
Project Mercury was also valued for its in-flight scientific experiments, which have contributed to our understanding of space
phenomena.[16]

The second stage of the program, Project Gemini, will commence
this year (1964) with three flights, the third of which will be
manned. Delayed two years by technological and developmental problems, its mission schedule now extends into 1967.[17] To the progress
of our lunar program Gemini will contribute two-men flights of
longer duration—from four to fourteen days—and practice in rendezvous and docking[18] techniques.[19] The Gemini spacecraft, powered by
the Titan II engine with 430,000 pounds of thrust,[20] can alter its
orbit in flight and control its re-entry to descend to any selected
recovery site.[21] As a result of these advances in the spacecraft,
much more responsibility can be assumed by the astronauts in flight
than was the case in Project Mercury. The Gemini astronauts will

[13]NASA, America in Space, p. 19.
[14]Dryden, p. 362.
[15]1965 NASA Authorization Hearings before Subcommittee on Manned
Space Flight of the Committee on Science and Astronautics, U.S.
House of Representatives (Washington, D.C., 1964), p. 371.
[16]Ibid.
[17]Ibid., p. 373.
[18]In space science terminology, "rendezvous" and "docking" refer
to the procedure by which two objects meet, at a preconceived time
and place, and join together, while orbiting in space.
[19]Harold Schmeck, Jr., "Project Gemini," America's Race for the
Moon, p. 37.
[20]Dryden, p. 371.
[21]1965 NASA Authorization Hearings, p. 381.

– 3 –

have logged 860 hours of space flight and have become proficient in
all of the rendezvous techniques necessary for a manned lunar landing, when Project Gemini is completed.[22]

The climactic third stage of the lunar program, Project Apollo,
will begin its flight schedule in 1966. Before its major objective
is attempted, preliminary activity will include qualification
flights for the newly developed Saturn IV and Saturn V[23] launch vehicles, flight tests for the Apollo spacecraft itself, lunar exploration by unmanned spacecraft, and a simulated lunar mission.[24] The
spacecraft to be used for the project will accommodate three men,
and contain three modules, or units: the Command Module, head-
quarters for the lunar astronauts; the Service Module for the pro-
pulsion and life-supporting systems; and the Lunar Excursion Module
(LEM) for the actual lunar descent.[25]

The procedure outlined for the manned lunar journey is known as
the Lunar Orbital Rendezvous Technique. This is a multi-stage
process, as explained by Dr. Hugh L. Dryden in his National Geographic article, "Footprints on the Moon."[26] The Apollo spacecraft,
launched from Cape Kennedy, will orbit the earth while its trajec-
tory is computed for reaching the moon seventy hours later. When
this computation has been made, the restartable engine of the Saturn
V's third stage will be activated to attain "escape velocity."[27]
Once the spacecraft is in a circular orbit ninety miles above the
moon, two of the three astronauts will enter LEM, detach it from the
Command Module, and go into a separate elliptical lunar orbit. They
will then descend in LEM for a lunar landing, maintaining communication at all times with the Command Module. After landing and explor-

---

[22]Ibid., p. 374.

[23]For comparison with the Titan II engine mentioned above, the
Saturn V, in its first stage alone, will be capable of 7.5 million
pounds of thrust power, according to Dr. George Mueller's testimony
included in the 1965 NASA Authorization Hearings, p. 414.

[24]Ibid., p. 405.

[25]Gladwin Hill, "Journey by Phonebooth," America's Race for the
Moon, pp. 60-61.

[26]Ibid., pp. 85-87.

[27]This is the speed (24,200 MPH) necessary to break free of the
earth's gravitational pull and thus extract the spaceship from earth
orbit.

,– 4 –

ing the lunar surface, the two astronauts must blast off in LEM—
somehow executing a launching procedure which requires the supervision of one hundred men on earth—to rendezvous with the "mother
ship." Another difficult task awaits the astronauts on the return
trip: re-entry into a narrow path of the earth's atmosphere, 300
miles wide and 40 miles deep. If this is overshot, the vehicle will
catapult off into space; if it is undershot, the astronauts will be
crushed by forces of up to 350 g's.[28] Besides the risks involved in
the LEM rendezvous with the Command Module and the spacecraft's re-
entry to earth, the three men will face exposure to the Van Allen
Radiation Belt, possible solar flares, and the high and low extremes
of lunar temperature.[29]

With such a complex and dangerous mission ahead, the Apollo astronauts are undergoing strenuous training. The trio selected as the
first lunar crew will be outstanding representatives of this nation's courage and capability. Relying upon their performance,
America will aim for the moon.

Thus Project Apollo[30] develops, transforming 1950 science fiction into 1970 scientific fact. Almost all Americans excitedly anticipate a lunar landng, but there is controversy over how it
should be achieved. Must we race for the moon—or might we more
leisurely reach for it, with more carefully planned objectives and
less concentrated effort and expense? Many people laud Project
Apollo as an urgently required national goal; others criticize it
as a needlessly accelerated undertaking. To understand these conflicting viewpoints, let us examine them in more detail.

Those who defend our accelerated lunar project advance political, military, economic, and scientific arguments in support of it.
Their political argument is based on the importance of the space
race between the United States and the Soviet Union. Premier Khru-
shchev, they say, has encouraged use of this contest as a "yard-

---

[28]One g is equal to the amount of the earth's gravitational pull
which we all encounter in normal activity; the gravitational load
that the astronauts would encounter in decelerating too abruptly
would "crush them like ants under a boot," says Dr. Dryden.

[29]The temperature during lunar daylight reaches as high as 240°
F.; the lunar night temperature falls as low as minus 271° F.

[30]In this section of the paper the term "Project Apollo" will
refer—as it often does in common usage—to all three phases of the
lunar program.

- 5 -

stick" of each society's status and worth.[31] As a result, space competition has become the most publicized and dramatic phase of the
Cold War, and the performances of Project Apollo and its rival Russian lunar program will be closely observed by uncommitted nations
of the world. Impressed by the winning country's superior technology, they will be strongly attracted to the political system that
fostered that country's progress. L. V. Berkner summarizes this
argument in his article, "The Compelling Horizon," in the May, 1963,
issue of the Bulletin of the Atomic Scientists:

> These new vistas of space science and technology have
> inspired men everywhere to a new level of aspiration....
> In a world involved in a political struggle between contest-
> ing ideologies, man instinctively recognizes that the
> rewards and acclaim will...go to the side that can best
> satisfy these aspirations.[32]

A second political reason for the project, related to the first,
is the psychological effect that the success of Project Apollo will
have on our national morale. By landing first on the moon, say
Apollo supporters, we will restore our own and our allies' confidence
in American supremacy in space.[33]
Military arguments in favor of Apollo stress the potential of
space for enemy aggression against the Free World. Our "spy" satellites and other counterweapons contribute importantly to American
space defense.[34] But still other defense projects must operate, if
we are to insure against any military menace from space.[35] The
Apollo program helps develop such projects, says General Bernard
Shriever, Commander of the Air Force Systems Command, because:

> All the mechanics of operation involved in a lunar landing
> and return—propulsion, guidance, rendezvous, controlled
> landing—are vital to the U.S. military posture.[36]

[31]Holmes, p. 138.
[32]19, 8.
[33]Holmes, p. 20.
[34]Editors of Fortune,The Space Industry (Englewood Cliffs, New
Jersey, 1962), pp. 20-23.
[35]Ibid.
[36]Holmes, p. 145.

— 6 —

Brigadier General H. A. Boushey proceeds beyond this point in his
military reasoning, contending that the moon itself has great
military potential. In his opinion, all future American space
efforts will depend heavily on the establishment of a lunar base.[37]

Advancing economic arguments for Project Apollo, proponents
talk of "spin-off," of new concepts in industrial organization,
of the favorable effect of space research expenditures on the
economy, and of the project as a remedy for unemployment. "Spin-
off" is defined as those technological products and processes which
can be adapted for use in our daily lives.[38] "Spin-off" products
include: ceramic cookware tolerant of sudden temperature changes,[39]
dehydrated concentrated foods requiring no cooking or refriger-
ation,[40] medical sensors for remote observation of hospital
patients,[41] and compact, self-sustaining power units.[42] "Spin-off"
processes have led to: the development of stronger materials with
more diversified characteristics; an increase in reliable
miniaturized equipment; and advances in automation techniques, for
a myriad of industrial uses.[43] Smaller electronic computers—another
"spin-off" product—have acted as a major stimulus for industrial
automation.[44]

Industrial organization has also been influenced by Project
Apollo's emphasis on research and development. In spacecraft
production attention must be focused on industrial scientists and
engineers whose opinions are reflected in major company decisions.
This new collaboration between scientist and executive may help
lessen the bureaucratic tendency of big business.[45]

---

[37]Diamond, p. 112.

[38]Dryden, p. 391.

[39]Ibid.

[40]Ibid.

[41]Holmes, p. 183.

[42]Fortune, p. 97.

[43]Ibid., pp. 95-96.

[44]Dryden, p. 391.

[45]Fortune, p. 91.

- 7 -

Even more important, the large research expenditures for our
space program insure a faster rate of national economic growth.
According to economist Leonard Silk, the technological advances
resulting from space research lead to greater efficiency in
industrial production. This makes it possible either to reduce the
cost of a retail product or to increase wages without an infla-
tionary rise in prices. Thus, the productivity of both labor and
capital is expanded, and there is a corresponding increase in
economic progress.[46]

The "spin-off" from Apollo and the project's emphasis on research are having an immediate and beneficial effect on the American
economy, according to supporters of the project. They say that the
lunar program might also serve another economic purpose, if
disarmament should become a reality and leave thousands of workers
unemployed: NASA could supply Apollo contracts to industrial plants
no longer needed for defense.[47] And, being a civilian-administered
agency, it would do so without incrementing the defense-industry
power complex.[48]

Finally, the scientific importance of the project is considered
by its defenders. "Some people say we will find nothing on the moon.
Yes—but what kind of nothing?" asks Dr. Edward Teller.[49] If
hypothetical moon-people were to train their telescopes on earth,
would they not conclude that the vast oceans, deserts, and green
fuzz of our planet held little of interest?[50] Apollo advocates point
to the moon's scientific significance for geologists and biologists
especially. By investigating the lunar surface[51] and interior,[52]

---

[46]Diamond, p. 66.

[47]Holmes, pp. 178-182 passim.

[48]Ibid.

[49]Otto Binder, Victory in Space (New York, 1962), pp. 172-173.

[50]Ibid.

[51]The earth's atmosphere and oceans gradually erode its surface
features over millions of years, but the moon—with its lighter
atmosphere and lack of oceans—retains its original surface.

[52]Depending on whether or not the moon's interior has an iron
core, one of the opposing theories of planetary origins—collision
or condensation—can be validated.

- 8 -

geologists hope to find clues to the origin of the solar system.[53]
Biologists await the discovery of any primitive life forms which
may exist on the moon. Study of these could lead to an explanation
of the beginnings of life on earth and knowledge of where life
might exist in other parts of the universe.[54] A Washington Post
reporter, Howard Simons, states:

> Whatever is learned about the moon will become part of
> a cosmic Rosetta Stone that will help explain the earth
> and its geologic history and that of the entire solar
> system.[55]

In addition to advancing the life-sciences specifically, the lunar
program, as part of our entire space effort, will serve as "a great
impetus" to basic research in all scientific fields.[56] For these
reasons, supporters of the project argue, Apollo is justified
scientifically.

They conclude that the implications of the space race, the
threat of military menace from space, the economic benefits provided
by Apollo, and the scientific advances it encourages, all combine
to make Project Apollo essential to American security and progress.

Most critics of the project agree with its supporters on the
importance of an American lunar-landing program, but argue that
there is no necessity for this program's accelerated development.
They make the following points.

First, they ask, does the space race influence international
relations to the extent which has been suggested? Contrary to this
political argument for Apollo, collected data indicate no relationship—after the world-wide revaluation of Soviet technology—between
a nation's prowess in space and other nations' favorable opinions
of it.[57] Furthermore, Russia and America are so well-matched in

---

[53]Homer E. Newell, The Mission of Man in Space (Washington,
D.C., 1963), pp. 8-10.

[54]Holmes, p. 21.

[55]Howard Simons, "We Know So Shamefully Little about the Moon,"
reprinted by NASA from the Washington Post (Washington, D.C., 1963),
p. 8.

[56]Leonard S. Silk, "The Impact on the American Economy," Outer
Space, ed. Lincoln P. Bloomfield (New Jersey, 1962), p. 78.

[57]Diamond, p. 25.

— 9 —

technological ability that the advancement of one over the other in
space performance is hardly possible for any length of time.[58]

> And there is no reason to suppose that this fact is
> lost to decision-makers and leaders everywhere. Thus,
> in the peaceful areas of space, it is unlikely that
> accomplishment per se at a given time will produce
> major and permanent shifts in attitudes toward either
> of the contenders.[59]

For some Apollo critics, speed in the space race is not the
central issue; their major objection is to the existence of the
space race itself. They denounce the "necessity-of-a-space-race-
theme" as a reductio ad absurdum of an inspiring challenge to
humanity.[60] Instead of imitating and competing with the Russians,
says James R. Killian, Jr. (President Eisenhower's first scientific
adviser),the United States should be concentrating on its own
scientific objectives in space, continuing to establish its preeminence in this important area.[61] With our involvement in the space
race, these critics continue, we have lost sight of the fact that
rocket power and space "firsts" are not a valid standard of a
nation's comprehensive progress and achievement.[62]

In debating the military necessity for Apollo, again there are
two rebuttals. Some critics ask: although the military possibilities
of space cannot be discounted, should the developing Russian-
American cooperation in space be ignored? On August 16, 1963, the
First Memorandum of Understanding was signed by these two countries,
establishing their joint participation in launch coordination of and
data exchange from weather satellites, data exchange from
magnetometer-equipped satellites for the World Magnetic Survey,

---

[58]Donald N. Michaels, "Prospects for Human Welfare," Outer
Space, p. 61.
   [59]Ibid., p. 62.
   [60]Edwin Diamond, "The Rites of Spring," Bulletin of the Atomic
Scientists, 19 (May, 1963), 27.
   [61]Holmes, p. 193.
   [62]Diamond, "The Rites of Spring," p. 27.

– 10 –

and space communications experiments.[63] This is only a beginning to
international collaboration in space, these critics admit, but
Russia—beset this year with economic and political problems—might
be amenable to future co-sponsored ventures.[64] Such an optimistic
view is, at present, an unproved hypothesis, but so, the critics
remind us, is the pessimistic view of nuclear bombs in orbit. That
the first view is as valid as the second has been demonstrated by
Russian-American communal endeavor in the International Geophysical
Year of 1957, and in the exploration of Antarctica.[65]

Other critics of Apollo agree with its supporters that the
military space threat is real. But this group of critics argues
that there would be little military value in a lunar base; the
technological and logistic problems involved in shooting a weapon
from the moon to a particular point on earth are too complex. Dr.
Lee A. DuBridge, President of California Institute of Technology,
questions in the following manner the possibility of accomplishing
this feat: could a duck hunter, shooting from a car traveling at
2200 miles per hour, hit the left wing of a spinning bird with a
bullet that followed a curved path and took two days to reach its
target?[66]

Third, the economic necessity of Project Apollo is discussed by
its critics. They concede that Apollo "spin-off" is technologically
and theoretically valuable to the American economy. But, they
reason, we have an unsolved "problem of priorities":[67] this
glamorous lunar venture is diverting economic resources from more
essential government projects here on earth. These projects are
designed to increase human resources (e.g., through better education and employment programs) and fulfill human needs,[68] and thus
are of as great importance as Apollo "spin-off" to the economy.

---

[63]Adlai E. Stevenson, "Statement Made in the Political and Security Committee of the United Nations, December 2, 1963," Department of State Bulletin, 49 (December 30, 1963), 1012.

[64]Diamond, The Rise and Fall of the Space Age, p. 10.

[65]Hugh Odishaw, ed. The Challenge of Space (Chicago, 1962), p.
237.

[66]Diamond, The Rise and Fall of the Space Age, pp. 112-113.

[67]James R. Killian, Jr., "Shaping a Public Policy for the Space
Age," Outer Space, p. 185.

[68]Ibid.

– 11 –

Also, the critics point out, this "spin-off" value may be offset
by the final economic consequences of Apollo. We are spending billions of dollars annually on a hastily conceived and poorly organized space program.[69] The failures and delays of such a program
could seriously undermine world confidence in American technology.[70]
There is the possibility, too, that American space and defense expenditures will exceed 90 billion dollars by 1970.[71] The grossly unbalanced national budget that would result could lead to recession
for the rest of the economy.[72] Thus, the critics conclude, both the
stability and the comprehensive progress of our economy could be
adversely affected by the project.

Questioning the scientific reasons for haste in developing Project Apollo, its opponents cite a 1962 report from the Space Science
Board of the National Academy of Sciences. This report admonished
NASA for exaggerating the scientific purpose of the project, and for
allowing its accelerated progress. Describing Apollo as "primarily a
technological and engineering effort," the report stated that the
scientific value of the project will come after the accomplishment
of its actual objective, i.e., to land American astronauts on the
moon. But, the report continued, if the manned lunar exploration
which will follow is to yield maximum scientific gains, its aims
and procedures must be scientifically planned beforehand. And, concluded the report, this scientific planning requires time which the
presently accelerated project does not afford.[73]

In addition to these scientific arguments for decelerating
Apollo, the critics refer to the effect of the massive Russian space
effort on other areas of science in that country. There is evidence,
they say, that the rest of Soviet science has been retarded, not advanced, by their space effort. The United States, they warn, must
not allow this to happen here: our space program must be motivated

---

[69]Ibid., p. 188.

[70]Ibid., p. 185.

[71]Fortune, p. 85.

[72]Ibid.

[73]"Conclusions of Space Science Board of the National Academy of
Sciences—Summer, 1962," Bulletin of the Atomic Scientists, 19
(May, 1963), 18-19.

– 12 –

by scientific aims and conducted in scientific order, not recklessly
accelerated by the desire for political prestige.[74]

To summarize, the critics of Project Apollo reason that the much
publicized space-race theme has been overstated, that the military
potential of the moon is practically nonexistent, and that economic
and scientific progress would be better furthered by a moderately
paced program.

In conclusion, the ultimate challenge, thus far, of our existence merits our best effort in response. If scientific order and
dignified progress are to characterize our lunar project, we must
reach, rather than race, for the moon.

---

[74]Killian, p. 184.

BIBLIOGRAPHY

(Sources referred to in footnotes)

Berkner, L. V. "The Compelling Horizon," Bulletin of the Atomic Sci-
     entists, 19 (May, 1963), 8-10.
Binder, Otto. Victory in Space. New York: Walker and Company, 1962.
Bloomfield, Lincoln P., ed. Outer Space. Englewood Cliffs, New Jer-
     sey: Prentice-Hall, Inc., 1962.
Caidin, Martin. Red Star in Space. New York: The Crowell-Collier
     Press, 1963.
"Conclusions of Space Science Board of the National Academy of Sci-
     ences." Bulletin of the Atomic Scientists. 19 (May, 1963),
     18-19.
Diamond, Edwin. The Rise and Fall of the Space Age. New York:
     Doubleday and Company, Inc., 1964.
Diamond, Edwin. "The Rites of Spring," Bulletin of the Atomic Scien-
     tists, 19 (May, 1963), 26-29.
Dryden, Hugh L. "Footprints on the Moon," National Geographic, 125
     (March, 1964), 356-402.
Editors of Fortune. The Space Industry. Englewood Cliffs, New Jer-
     sey: Prentice-Hall, Inc., 1962.

– 13 –

Holmes, Jay. America on the Moon. Philadelphia and New York: J. P.
    Lippincott and Company, 1962.
NASA. America in Space. Washington, D.C.: Government Printing
    Office, 1963.
NASA. One...Two...Three...and the Moon. Washington, D.C.: Government
    Printing Office, 1963.
1965 NASA Authorization Hearings before the Sub-Committee on Manned
    Space Flight of the Committee on Science and Astronautics, U.S.
    House of Representatives. Washington, D.C.: Government Printing
    Office, 1964.
Newell, Homer E. The Mission of Man in Space. Washington, D.C.: Gov-
    ernment Printing Office, 1963.
Odishaw, Hugh, ed. The Challenge of Space. Chicago: The University
    of Chicago Press, 1962.
Simons, Howard. "We Know So Shamefully Little about the Moon,"
    reprinted from the Washington Post by NASA. Washington, D.C.:
    Government Printing Office, 1963.
Stevenson, Adlai E. "Statement Made in the Political and Security
    Committee of the United Nations, December 2, 1963," Department
    of State Bulletin, 49 (December 30, 1963), 1005-1012.
Sullivan, Walter, ed. America's Race for the Moon. New York: Random
    House, 1962.

SUPPLEMENTARY BIBLIOGRAPHY[8]

(Sources read, but not referred to in footnotes)

Buchheim, Robert W. and the Staff of the Rand Corporation. Space
    Handbook. New York: Random House, 1959.
Caidin, Martin. Rendezvous in Space. New York: E. P. Dutton and
    Company, 1962.

[8] Dividing the bibliography of a paper into two parts—sources referred to in the footnotes of the paper and sources read but not referred to—is not conventional practice. We
have found, however, that it makes students more aware of the number of sources they
actually use, and that it is helpful to teachers in making an initial survey of the paper.
Students should follow the preference of their instructor about dividing or not dividing
their bibliography in this way.

– 14 –

Clarke, Arthur C. The Exploration of Space. New York: Harper and
    Brothers, 1959.
Dean, James, George Gardner, Victor Seigel and Elbert Umstead.
    Space, The New Frontier. Washington, D.C.: Government Printing
    Office, 1963.
Ducrocq, Albert. Victory Over Space. Boston and Toronto: Little,
    Brown, and Company, 1961.
Gantz, Kenneth F., ed. Man in Space. New York: Duell, Sloan, and
    Pearce, 1959.
Lapp, Ralph E. Man and Space, The Next Decade. New York: Harper and
    Brothers, 1961.
"Space Technology Section," Aviation Week and Space Technology, 80
    (March 16, 1964), 107-140.

EXERCISES

I. Put the references below into proper footnote form, keeping them in their present order.

1. Page 53 of a book called A Story of Our Republic written by Melville Freeman and published in 1938 in Philadelphia by F. A. Davis Company.

2. Page 43 of an article called April Elegy, by Archibald MacLeish, which appeared in the Atlantic Monthly, volume 174, June, 1945.

3. Part of a news story on the death of Lincoln which appeared in the Boston Advertiser of April 14, 1865. The excerpt is quoted in an article in New England Magazine for December, 1903, volume 9; the article, entitled Living History, was written by H. King, and the quotation is on page 426. The title of the news story was President Assassinated.

4. Page 48 of a book by David Miller Dewitt, published in New York in 1909. The name of the book is The Assassination of Abraham Lincoln and Its Expiation.

5. Page 49 of the book cited in footnote 4.

6. Page 43 of the Atlantic Monthly article cited in footnote 2.

7. Page 400 in the article on Lincoln in Harper's Encyclopedia of United States History, published by Harper and Brothers in 1907 in New York. The article is in volume 5 of the encyclopedia.

8. Here and there in pages 17 to 38 of a book by Otto Eisenschiml entitled Why Was Lincoln Murdered? The book was published in 1937 by Little, Brown and Co. in Boston.

9. Page 37 of the book by Melville Freeman cited in footnote 1.

10. Page 50 of the book Why Was Lincoln Murdered? cited in footnote 8.

11. An article in Century Magazine, vol. 51, April, 1896, page 945. The article is called At the Death-bed of Lincoln, and was written by E. C. Haynie.

12. The same page of the same article cited in footnote 11.

13. Page 113 of a book by Adlai E. Stevenson called Putting First Things First, published in 1960 by Random House in New York. The reference is in an article called Lincoln's Faith in the book by Stevenson.

14. Page 50 of a book by Gordon Langley Hall published in New York by Holt, Rinehart and Winston in 1964. The name of the book is Vinnie Ream, the Story of the Girl Who Sculptured Lincoln.

15. Page 62 of the book cited in footnote 14.

16. Page 115 of the article cited in footnote 13.

17. Page 92 of a book called The Day Lincoln Was Shot published in New York in 1955 and written by J. Bishop.

18. Pages 336 and 337 of an article by E. Ryan published in the February, 1953 issue of the Catholic World, volume 176. The name of the article is Memories of Abraham Lincoln.

II. In so far as is possible with the data given, arrange the items in Exercise I in correct form and order for a bibliography. What additional information is needed?

III. The first ten footnotes of a poorly annotated paper on hypnotism are listed below. Point out the errors in the footnotes as they stand. Whenever it is possible without more bibliographical information, put the notes into proper form.

1. Raper, Howard W., *Man Against Pain*, 30.
2. Bromberg, W., *The Mind of Man*, page 161.
3. op. cit. 163.
4. Hypnotism Now Commonplace, "Literary Digest," March 7, 1936.
5. Raper, *Man Against Pain*, page 32.
6. "Journal of Amer. Med. Assoc.", Feb. 19, 1944, page 531
7. Ibid.
8. Bromberg, W., the Mind of Man, page 162.
9. *Power of Hypnotism*, "Science Digest," 41, 23, March 1957.
10. M. Silverman, How Medical Hypnosis Works, Sat Eve Post, April 27, 1957, vol. 229, 51.

IV. Below is the bibliography for a short investigative article on the alleged massacre at the Vietnamese village of My Lai 4 (Song My), first widely reported and commented on in late November and December, 1969. As preparation for the writing of a long research paper, students were asked to read several accounts of, or editorial comments on, the same event, and to write a short paper in which they compared the accounts and the attitudes expressed, and in which they used standard bibliography and footnote form. Items in this bibliography are numbered for easy reference to them in the exercise that follows the listing.

1. Crawford, Kenneth. "Song My's Shock Wave," *Newsweek*, 74 (December 15, 1969), 38.
2. "The Fallout from Song My," *Newsweek*, 74 (December 15, 1969), 40–41.
3. Hoffman, David. "Cong Helped Bury Dead at Song My," *The Boston Globe*, December 1, 1969, pp. 1, 20.
4. "The Killings at Song My," *Newsweek*, 74 (December 8, 1969), 33–34, 36, 41.
5. Lelyveld, Joseph. "The Story of a Soldier Who Refused to Fire at Songmy," *The New York Times Magazine*, December 14, 1969, pp. 32–33, 101, 103, 110, 112–114, 116, 118, 120–121.
6. "My Lai: An American Tragedy," *Time*, 94 (December 5, 1969), 23–24, 26, 28–30, 32.
7. "On Evil: The Inescapable Fact," *Time*, 94 (December 5, 1969), 26–27.
8. "The 'War Crime' Issue: Some Nagging Questions," *Newsweek*, 74 (December 8, 1969), 34–35.

Give the footnotes below the form that they should have in a finished paper:

Footnote 1: a reference to pages 33–34 in item 4 in the preceding bibliography.

Footnote 2: a reference to pages 23–24 in item 6 in the bibliography.

Footnote 3: a reference to pages 28–29 in item 6.

Footnote 4: a reference to page 34 in item 8.

Footnote 5: a reference to page 101 in item 5.

Footnote 6: a reference to item 1.

Footnote 7: a reference to page 20 in item 3.

Footnote 8: a reference to pages 112–113 in item 5.

Footnote 9: a reference to page 113 in item 5.

Footnote 10: a reference to page 40 in item 2.

Footnote 11: a reference to item 1.

Footnote 12: a reference to page 27 in item 7.

Footnote 13: a reference to page 26 in item 7.

Footnote 14: a reference to page 121 in item 5.

Footnote 15: a reference to page 30 in item 6.

Footnote 16: a reference to page 41 in item 2.

HANDBOOK

PART 3

Understanding Conventions:

A Handbook of Grammar, Rhetoric, Mechanics, and Usage

HANDBOOK

Section 1

CONVENTIONS
AND MEANING

Without conventions, the communication of meaning through words would be impossible. A word is a symbol that stands for and refers to an object, idea, or attitude; its basic meaning (what it refers to) is fixed by the customary use or convention of the language to which it belongs. If a writer, unclear about the meanings of words, says that he believes in "immorality" when he means *immortality,* or if he characterizes someone as "ingenious" when he means *ingenuous,* he fails to communicate; or, at best, he calls upon his reader to guess at the meaning intended but misstated. A convention is literally a "coming together." A speaker or writer and his audience are enabled to "come together" in understanding, to share experience and ideas, by their common acceptance of the conventional meanings of words.

Just as good English involves a knowledge of the established or agreed-upon meanings of words, it involves also—if the writer is at all concerned with the impression he will make on an informed audience—a knowledge of certain commonly accepted matters of usage. Most of this Handbook is concerned with these conventions of usage. Sometimes they are vital to the clear communication of meaning; when, as is often the case, they are not, an awareness of them is still important in much the same way that an awareness of other widely followed customs is important.

We live, of course, in times of rapid change—in attitudes, in dress, and in language; many once-established conventions are no longer observed; others may be thought to represent a stifling conformity. The wise nonconformist, however, understands the use of convention; when he chooses to depart from it, he does so purposefully and on principle, not unintentionally and blunderingly.

Some of the conventions of language, like many social conventions, are relatively unimportant matters of form, the observance of which depends on circumstances: a conventional rule for the use of the comma, for example, may be comparable to the conventional rule of speaking to strangers only after an introduction; neither the comma nor the introduction may be necessary. Other conventions, both of manners and of language, have a greater practical usefulness because they establish procedures which it is convenient to have established. For example, traditional good manners require a man to allow a woman to precede him through the door he has opened; having this practice established by convention is useful: it saves confusion and indecision at doors. Similarly, in language, certain uniform practices in capitalization, punctuation, and spelling are convenient for writers and readers: the writer is saved the trouble of working out his own system, and the reader is spared the greater trouble of adjusting to the personal eccentricities of each author. A writer may have good reason to take liberties with some of these conventional practices, just as a man may with good reason precede a woman through a door; but unless the reason is clear, he may appear to be discourteous and uninformed.

Still other conventions of manners and of language are so deeply rooted in custom or principle that one who violates them is likely to be considered ignorant or boorish by people trained in the conventions. The host who invites a guest to dinner and fails to provide a chair for him at the table violates a basic principle of hospitality; the writer who, through a comparable confusion of numbers, uses singular verbs with plural subjects violates a similarly basic principle of grammar. The person invited to eat the dinner or to read the book is justifiably annoyed; his impression of the host or of the writer is an unfavorable one.

This unfavorable impression brings us to the heart of the relationship between conventions and meaning. Ordinarily, the failure to observe conventions of language like those just mentioned does not interfere seriously with the factual part of meaning. The person who talks with his mouth full of food usually can be understood; but his listeners are not likely to be favorably impressed by what he is saying or to hope that he will continue his discourse. In a similar way, though a reader may be temporarily confused by misleading punctuation, by misplaced modifiers, or by vague pronoun reference, he can usually arrive at the factual meaning of the passage in spite of these obstacles. He will, however, feel an irritated disrespect for the writer who makes his communication needlessly difficult and will be offended by the writer's appar-

ent attitude of discourtesy and disregard for his reader. Under these circumstances, the writer's intention will almost certainly be defeated: a reader is not
easily persuaded or convinced by one with whom he is irritated, nor is he
likely to trust the information of a writer who seems imprecise or incompetent.
Understanding the conventions and scrutinizing one's writing to be sure that
no careless violations have crept in will not, in themselves, produce positively
successful writing. They will, though, free the writer from awkward and
misleading expression, and from the adverse criticism of his readers.

In discussing the conventions of grammar, usage, and mechanics, we have
tried to take into account the flexibility of language, and to indicate where
usage is divided, how usage may differ in formal and informal situations, and
what freedom the writer has in following or departing from certain conventions. As the student applies the conventions to his own writing, he should,
of course, be further guided by his instructor's standards of correctness and
appropriateness.

HANDBOOK

Section 2

SENTENCE ELEMENTS AND THEIR RELATIONSHIPS

1. NOUNS: PLURALS AND POSSESSIVES

A noun is traditionally defined as a word or group of words used to name a person, place, or thing. Nouns function in sentences as subjects, objects, and complements[1] of verbs or verbals, as appositives, as objects of prepositions, and as modifiers.

> *Subject: Tom* is here.
> *Direct object:* She bought the *books*.
> *Indirect object:* She gave her *mother* the money.
> *Complement:* George is her *husband*. He left, slamming the *door*.
> *Appositive:* Mr. Thompson, the acting *chairman*, called the meeting to order.
> *Object of a preposition:* He stood on the *corner*.
> *Modifier: Henry's* departure was well-timed.

Nouns show a change in form (i.e., are inflected) in the possessive case and, usually, when they change number.

1 For a discussion of complements, see page 380.

Plurals of Nouns

a. The plurals of nouns are generally formed by adding *s* or *es* to the singular. The letter *s* forms the plural when it can be added to the singular and pronounced without adding a syllable (*bath, baths; cat, cats*); the letters *es* form the plural when the singular ends in a sound (*s, ch, sh, z, x*) that cannot unite with *s* to form one syllable.

Among the exceptions to this rule are: (1) unchanging plurals (*deer, deer; Japanese, Japanese*); (2) *en* plurals (*child, children*); (3) *f* to *v* plurals (*thief, thieves*); (4) some foreign plurals (*alumnus, alumni*); (5) plurals in which vowels change (*man, men; foot, feet*); (6) plurals formed with *es* even though the noun does not end with *s, ch, sh, z,* or *x* (*Negro, Negroes*). If you are uncertain about how a particular word forms its plural, look it up in the dictionary.

b. Plurals of figures and letters are generally formed by adding an apostrophe plus *s*. *S* alone may be used if the apostrophe is not needed for clarity.

dotted both i's; pronounce s's clearly; three size 7's; IOUs

Possessive Case

a. Singular and plural nouns not ending in *s* or *z* add an apostrophe plus *s*.

the child's toy; children's toys; the woman's hat; the women's hats

b. Plural nouns ending in *s* or *z* add only an apostrophe.

the Smiths' house; ladies' clothes; babies' bottles

c. Singular nouns ending in *s* or *z* may add the apostrophe plus *s* or the apostrophe only.

Keats' poetry or Keats's poetry

d. To indicate joint or separate ownership, possessives are used as follows:

(1) When two or more people are mentioned as owning an object in common, only the last of the names is given possessive form:

Mary and John's records show their taste for symphonic music.

(2) When two or more people are mentioned as owning separate objects, each name is given possessive form:

Ted's and Marshall's books are still in our attic. [I.e., Ted's books and Marshall's books are still in our attic.]

e. When possession is attributed to inanimate objects, the *of* phrase may be preferable to the possessive case form.

the shoulder of the road [rather than the road's shoulder]

Usage is divided, however, and some of the numerous exceptions to this generalization are such common phrases as *a day's journey, a week's wages, a stone's throw, an hour's delay, the sun's rays, the earth's circumference, an arm's length.*

f. Possessive with the gerund.[2] **Nouns serving as modifiers of gerunds are usually given the possessive form, particularly in written English.**

We were all surprised by Eliot's refusing to go. [*Refusing*, a gerund, is modified by the possessive *Eliot's*.]

In colloquial usage, the noun modifying a gerund is often not given the possessive form.

EXERCISES

I. In the sentences below, point out the single nouns and the groups of words which function as nouns. What is the function in the sentence of each noun or noun construction?

1. That Tom was lazy was clear to his sisters.
2. Martha sold Jack a paper.
3. The boys know where they intend to go.
4. Alice is the president's wife.
5. To break the rule is to be suspended from college.
6. Harry raced down the street, fearing disaster.
7. My brother, a veteran of Vietnam, was the principal speaker.
8. Charles' parents, startled by his appearance, called their son a radical.

II. Give the plural for each of the following nouns (if necessary, consult your dictionary): *calf, potato, birch, alumna, cactus, shears, teaspoonful, Burmese, index, fish, brother-in-law, ox.*

III. Convert the possessives below, now expressed in *of* phrases, to possessives expressed by an apostrophe, or an apostrophe plus *s*. Should any of them not be changed?

1. The house of Mr. Jones and the barn of Mr. Benning were sold at the same time.
2. The leaves of many trees get summer blight.
3. The cars of my friends are new.
4. The novels of Dickens are in the reading room of the library.
5. The cost of clothes was higher at the end of the year.

2 For a discussion of gerunds, see page 382.

6. The toys of the babies were mixed with the toys of the puppy.

7. I enjoy the poetry of Blake more than the poetry of Burns.

8. The garden of the Robinsons is carefully tended; the garden of their neighbor is not.

2. PRONOUNS: CLASSES AND CASE

A pronoun is a word that takes the place of a noun. Pronouns therefore function in sentences as nouns do—as subjects, objects, appositives, objects of prepositions, complements, and modifiers.

Pronouns may be classed as personal, relative, interrogative, demonstrative, or indefinite.

The pronouns *I, you, he, she, we, they,* and *it* with all their forms (*me, mine, we, ours, us,* etc.) are called **personal pronouns.** They are inflected for gender, number, case, and person. When the word *self* or *selves* is added to a form of the personal pronoun, the resultant form (*myself, yourself, himself, ourselves, themselves*) is called a compound personal pronoun. Such pronouns may be reflexive (I hurt *myself*) or intensive (The President *himself* will be there).

Relative pronouns are two-function words. Like other pronouns, they stand in place of a noun, but they also connect a subordinate clause to some word in the main clause. Words often used as relative pronouns are *who, whom, whose, which, what, that,* and also the compound relative pronouns *whoever, whomever, whichever, whatever.* Of these, only *who* and *whom* and their compound forms are inflected for case. Relative pronouns are sometimes understood but not expressed:

The house [*that*] he lives in is on the corner.
The man [*whom* or *that*] we expected did not come.

Who, whose, which, and *what,* when they are used to introduce a direct or indirect question, are called **interrogative pronouns:**

Who wants another piece of pie? [Direct question]
They wondered *who* had taken the money. [Indirect]

This and *that* and their plurals *these* and *those* are called **demonstrative pronouns** when they are used to point out or call attention to a particular thing:

This is the last stop.
Those are not my shoes.

Certain pronouns which do not refer to definite persons or things are called **indefinite pronouns.** Examples are: *any, nothing, few, each, much, all, something, everyone.*

> *Each* should work for the good of *all.*
> *Everyone* is to bring *something.*

The case of a pronoun is determined by its function in its clause.

a. A personal pronoun is in the subjective case when it serves as a subject of a verb or as a complement of the verb *to be* (i.e., a predicate nominative), or when it is in apposition with a subject or with a complement of *to be.*

> *Subject of a verb:* I wonder where *he* has gone.
> *Complement of* to be: I believe that it was *she.*
> *In apposition with a subject:* Two applicants—Richard and *I*—were interviewed by the committee.
> *In apposition with a complement:* Only one person is the criminal, *he,* Marvin.

Although the complement of the verb *to be* is in the subjective case in formal usage, the colloquial *it's me* in place of the formal *it is I* is standard English.

b. A personal pronoun is in the objective case when it is the object of a verb, a verbal,[3] or a preposition; when it is in apposition with an object; or when it is the subject of an infinitive.

> *Object of a verb:* The students admire *him.*
> *Object of a verbal:* Finally remembering *me,* Harold smiled and shook hands.
> *Object of a preposition:* They laughed at *her.*
> *In apposition with an object:* The family met us—Hilda and *me*—at the airport.
> *Subject of an infinitive:* I didn't expect *him* to come.

c. A personal pronoun is in the possessive case when it expresses possession or when it is used to modify a gerund.

> Jane is wearing *her* skirt and *my* sweater.
> Everyone regretted *his* receiving the prize. [In this sentence the gerund *receiving* is the object of *regretted,* and *his* modifies *receiving.*]

d. The case of a relative or interrogative pronoun is determined by its function in its own clause.

> Give the ball to *whoever wants it.* [*Whoever* is the subject of the italicized subordinate clause in which it appears and so is properly in the subjective case. The subordinate clause is the object of the preposition *to.*]
> If we have a party, *whom shall we ask?* [*Whom* is in the objective case because it is the object of the verb *ask.* Many students of usage, though, would defend the use of *who.*]

---

3 If necessary, see "Verbs and Verbals" page 382.

The sentences below further illustrate some of the common problems involving case of pronouns.

He says that *we* freshmen must work together. [*We,* the subject of *work,* is in the subjective case.]

To *us* freshmen the sophomore rules seem unreasonable. [*Us* is the object of the preposition *to.*]

We were surprised to see James and *him* together after their quarrel. [Both *him* and *James* are objects of the infinitive *to see.* The use of the subjective *he* in such an expression should be avoided.]

He is a man *who,* I believe, will have his own way. [*I believe* is a parenthetical expression. *Who* is the subject of the subordinate clause *who will have his own way.*]

I saw *him* waving to his children. [*Him* is the object of *saw; waving* is a participle modifying *him.*]

We objected to *his* walking on our new lawn. [The gerund *walking* is the object of *objected to; his* modifies *walking.*]

They wondered *whom* he was taking to the dance. [*Whom* is the object of *taking* and is appropriate in formal English. In informal English and particularly in conversation, *who* can be defended.]

It wasn't Harold that asked the question; it was *I.* [*I* is here a complement of *was,* and strict formal usage therefore requires *I* rather than *me.* Some cultivated people would use *I,* some would use *me,* and many others would simply avoid the construction.]

He is taller than *I.* [Here *I* is in the subjective case because it is the subject of the elliptical clause *than I am tall.*]

EXERCISES

Underscore the preferable pronoun in each sentence. Explain your choice.

1. Will you join my parents and (I, me) for dinner?
2. The teacher would not start the lecture until (we, us) students quieted down.
3. The program was planned to help (we, us) students.
4. It is not necessary to ask (who, whom) will be the leading actor.
5. He wanted Martha and (I, me) to come.
6. Choose (whoever, whomever) you think can handle the job.
7. Such ruffians as (they, them) cause trouble for the rest of us.
8. If I were (they, them) I should refuse to buy an inferior stone.
9. Will you let Tom and (I, me) take the car?
10. (Him, his) arriving so late caused a good deal of comment.
11. He pointed out the man (who, whom) he said had helped him.
12. For some time there has been a coldness between Marion and (I, me).
13. We found (him, his) working on his term paper.
14. We found (him, his) watching television every night an annoyance.
15. I am grateful to (whoever, whomever) has worked on the program.

3. PRONOUNS: AGREEMENT   Agr

Some pronouns—indefinite pronouns, for example—do not customarily have and do not require antecedents; words like *anyone* and *everyone* are not dependent for meaning on a noun that has preceded them. Most pronouns, however, are used as substitutes for nouns and are dependent on those nouns, their antecedents, for their meaning. The antecedent is the word or words that would have to be repeated if the pronoun were not used.

A pronoun agrees with its antecedent in gender, number, and person.

Some problems of pronoun agreement stem from differences between formal and colloquial usage. Since words like *everyone, anyone, nobody* are grammatically singular, in formal usage they are followed by singular verbs and referred to by singular pronouns. Such words are, however, often plural in meaning, and in colloquial usage they are often followed by plural pronouns:

Formal: *Everyone* did *his* duty.
Colloquial: *Everyone* did *their* duty.

The principles of agreement stated below are based on the formal usage which most instructors will want their students to observe in written English.

a. In formal English, expressions that require a singular verb (*each, every, either, neither, many a, a person, anyone, everyone, no one, someone, anybody, everybody, nobody, somebody*) **require a singular pronoun when they serve as antecedents.**

Each of us has *his* private anxieties and *his* private joys.
Almost *everybody* in college knows that *he* will need to earn *his* living some day.
If *either* Martin or Ted hears of this, *he* will oppose it.
Everyone took off *his* hat and stood in silence while the body of the great man was lowered into the grave.

b. The masculine pronoun (*he, his, him*) is generally used to refer to a singular antecedent which is both masculine and feminine in meaning.

In this small coeducational college *a student* soon learns to speak to everyone *he* meets. [Although some of the students are girls, *he* (rather than *he or she*) is the preferable usage. *He or she* would be used only for a special emphasis.]

c. Collective nouns as antecedents may be followed by *it* or *they*. If the collective noun is thought of as a unit, *it* (or the possessive form, *its*) is the appropriate pronoun; if the collective noun is thought of as representing a group of individuals, *they* (*their, them*) is the appropriate pronoun.

The jury will give *its* verdict today. [The jury is thought of as a unit.]
The jury are returning to *their* homes today. [A group of individuals.]

d. When *one* is the antecedent, it usually is followed by *he* or *his*.

One should weigh *his* words when *he* speaks to the council.

In very formal style, a *one . . . one* sequence may be used:

One regrets that *one* is unable to do more.

e. The relative pronoun *who* is generally used to refer to people and not to things; *which* is generally used to refer to things and not to people; and *that* is used to refer to people or to things or to both.

a man *who* or *that* . . .
a house *which* or *that* . . .
the same man and the same house *that* we saw yesterday . . .
a group *which* or *that* meets every Saturday . . .
a group of home owners *who* object to their taxes . . .
the cat *that* ate the goldfish . . .

Since there is no possessive form for *which* or *that,* the possessive of *who* (*whose*) is often used to refer to things; "the dog *whose* master has abandoned him" is preferable to the awkward *which* construction: "the dog the master *of which* has abandoned him."

f. Inconsistencies in pronoun usage should be avoided. Inconsistencies are unnecessary and undesirable shifts from one person to another, from one number to another, or from one gender to another. Some inconsistencies can be corrected by substituting the right pronoun; others call for more substantial revision.

INCONSISTENT IN PERSON: When *I* was a freshman, the sophomores were strict in making *them* follow the rules. *You* were not safe if *you* walked on the grass or wore a high-school letter or failed to say "Sir" to upperclassmen. [A shift from the first person *I*, to the third person *them*, to the second person *you*. For consistency and for clarity this passage should be written in the first person.]

CONSISTENT: When *I* was a freshman, the sophomores were strict in making *us* follow the rules. *We* were not safe if *we* walked on the grass or wore a high-school letter or failed to say "Sir" to upperclassmen.

INCONSISTENT IN PERSON: When *a man* is hungry, *you* aren't satisfied with a frilly salad and a cup of tea. [A shift from the impersonal *a man* to the indefinite second person *you*.]

CONSISTENT: When *a man* is hungry, *he* is not satisfied with a frilly salad and a cup of tea.

INCONSISTENT IN NUMBER: *Everyone* in the class was looking at *his* watch. *They* thought the end of the hour would never come. [A shift from the singular *his* to the plural *they*. This passage could be improved by substituting *he* for *they*, but it still would not be entirely satisfactory.]

REVISED: *Everyone* in the class was looking at *his* watch and thinking that the end of the hour would never come. [*Or*] *Everyone* in the class was looking at *his* watch. It seemed that the end of the hour would never come.

INCONSISTENT IN GENDER: The dog barked and showed that *it* wanted to come in. I think that *he* remembered me. [A careless shift from *it* to *he*.]

CONSISTENT: The dog barked and showed that *he* wanted to come in. I think that *he* remembered me.

EXERCISES

Point out any errors or awkwardness in agreement between pronoun and antecedent in the following sentences, and correct the sentence by supplying the proper pronoun or, if necessary, by revising the sentence.

1. Each man and woman in the audience thought that the speaker had given them something to think seriously about.

2. Many a high-school boy will wish that they had studied more in high school and had prepared themselves better.

3. Everyone in the congregation gave as much as they could when the collection was taken.

4. The senior class was proud of its part in introducing the honor system.

5. The person chosen, whether a man or a woman, will find that the group will cooperate with them and will appreciate their service.

6. We saw the prisoners which had been leaders in organizing the penitentiary's baseball team.

7. No one was eager to give their time to the new organization.

8. One should practice the speech thoroughly so that they will be less nervous about facing the audience.

9. The committee made its report and said that their judgment was unanimous.

10. If any student considers the rule unfair, he or she should speak to a member of student council; they are always willing to listen.

4. PRONOUNS: REFERENCE   Ref

A pronoun should refer clearly to its antecedent. Writing becomes inexact and confusing when a pronoun may refer to more than one antecedent, when it is too far from its antecedent for clarity, or when it seems, because of its position, to refer to the wrong antecedent. Inexact thinking as well as inexact expression is often responsible for obscure or ambiguous reference. The most common types of faulty reference are:

a. Reference to an antecedent that is implied but not stated.

UNSATISFACTORY: Leslie has been interested in medicine since he was ten years old, and he plans to be *one* someday. [The pronoun *one* has no expressed antecedent.]

REVISED: Leslie has been interested in medicine since he was ten years old, and he plans to be a doctor someday.

b. Reference to a too-remote antecedent. If the pronoun and its antecedent are so distant from one another that the relationship is not immediately clear, the sentence or the passage should be revised by changing the construction or by substituting a noun for the vague or ambiguously used pronoun.

UNSATISFACTORY: She wore a ribbon on her hair *that* was green and crisp and new. [*That* appears to refer to *hair.*]
REVISED: On her hair she wore a ribbon *that* was green and crisp and new.

UNSATISFACTORY: The Supreme Court decided that the judge had shown prejudice in the case. Justice Holmes retired soon after. *That* made legal history, and lawyers argued over the case for years afterwards. [The reference of the pronoun *that* is obscure, but the sense of the sentence suggests that the pronoun is intended to refer to the court decision though the antecedent *decision* is not expressed. The passage should be revised.]

c. Ambiguous reference. The reference of a pronoun is ambiguous if the reader wavers even momentarily in choosing between two or more possible antecedents.

AMBIGUOUS: She refused to return the ring, *which* was what he wanted. [Does *which* refer to the ring or to her refusal to return it?]
REVISED: He wanted the ring, but she refused to return it. [*Or*] He was glad that she refused to return the ring.

AMBIGUOUS: The manager told the union official that it was not *his* duty to collect the union dues. [In this sentence it is not clear whether *his* refers to *manager* or to *union official.* Unless the context of such a sentence makes clear the reference of the pronoun, the sentence should be recast.]
REVISED: The manager told the union official that the union should collect its own dues. [*Or*] The manager said to the union official, "It is not my duty to collect dues for the union."

ACCEPTABLE: Mr. Thompson told his son that *he* could not join a fraternity unless *he* got better grades. [Here the reference of *he* and *he* causes no uncertainty; the general sense of the sentence makes the meaning immediately clear.]

d. Indefinite reference of *you*. In formal English the use of the pronoun *you* in the sense of *one* is out of place. In informal English the indefinite *you* can sometimes be used to give a sense of immediacy; misused, however, it may be incongruous and even ludicrous.

INAPPROPRIATE: Chaucer, born in the fourteenth century, wrote for his own age and for succeeding ages. He understood the psychological tensions of the Pardoner, though he lacked the organized psychological knowledge which is available to twentieth-century writers. *You* are astonished as *you* . . . [The indefinite and too-informal *you* is out of place in formal, impersonal writing of this kind.

More appropriate than *You are astonished as you* . . . would be *The reader* or *The modern reader* or *One* followed by *is astonished as he reads* . . .]

INAPPROPRIATE: Human nature is funny. Even if *you* have held up a bank and killed seven men, *you* may still be very gentle with your dog. [Here the *you* is undesirable because it involves the reader in a situation in which he has no part and in which, probably, he would prefer not to be involved. The writer does not really intend to address the reader; he has simply used *you* vaguely in order to get out of a difficulty.]

REVISED: Human nature is unpredictable. Even a man who has held up a bank and has killed seven men might still be very gentle with his dog.

EFFECTIVE: If *you* could have been present in the years of Barnum's greatest glory, *you* would have seen Annie Oakley . . . ; *you* would have watched Buffalo Bill . . . ; *you* would have heard the whoops of fleeing Indians and pursuing cowboys . . . ; *you* . . . etc. [Here the use of *you* serves to give the reader a more vivid sense of being present; use of the formal *one* would be out of place in this context.]

e. Reference to an inconspicuous or buried antecedent.

AWKWARD: The apartment house is the largest building on the street; it is the narrowest street in town. [*Street,* the antecedent of *it,* is buried in a prepositional phrase, and the reader expects *it* to refer to *apartment house,* the subject of the first clause.]

REVISED: The apartment house is the largest building on the narrowest street in town.

EXERCISES

Some of the following sentences are satisfactory. Others illustrate the faulty reference or the indefinite use of pronouns. Correct all unsatisfactory pronoun references. If necessary, recast the sentence.

1. In our school they don't let you smoke.
2. My mother said that my sister was an impudent child, and that she would see to it that she would never let her temper get out of control again.
3. While we were watching the man fishing on a pier, we saw him haul one in.
4. John is studying law because his father is one.
5. Whoever is going had better sign his name.
6. Mr. Banker bought John a coat but he thought it was too small for him.
7. Mary told her sister that she was not responsible for her actions.
8. The lightning struck the tree nearest the barn, but after burning for a few seconds it was extinguished by the rain.
9. The penalties for stealing are severe, but you don't usually think about penalties until after you are caught.
10. Jack gave him five dollars when he was a freshman in college.

11. The furniture van had not arrived, the telephone was still disconnected, and there was no food in the house. The dog was sick, too. This was very depressing.

12. Never beat a dog with your hand; use a newspaper; this will make him afraid of you.

13. She was angry when he tried to give her advice, which was not very helpful.

14. If you think Dick needs money, you should do it in a diplomatic way.

15. He carried the kitten in his car that was only three weeks old.

5. VERBS: PRINCIPAL PARTS   Prin

Verbs are words that assert, or express action, state of being, or occurrence; they are inflected to indicate tense, voice, mood, person, and number.

a. The principal parts of a verb supply the basic forms for all tenses of that verb.

The principal parts are three: (1) the present infinitive, *climb,* (2) the past tense, *climbed,* and (3) the past participle, *climbed.* On the basis of the way they form the past tense and past participle, verbs are classified as regular or irregular. A regular verb, like *climb,* forms the past tense and past participle by adding *d, ed,* or *t* to the present infinitive. An irregular verb is one that forms its past tense or past participle in some other way; for example, *go* (present infinitive), *went* (past tense), and *gone* (past participle). Regular verbs are more common than irregular verbs, but some of the most commonly used verbs are irregular.

b. To use the information given by the principal parts of verbs, it is necessary to know at least the following facts:

(1) The first principal part *(go)* supplies the form for the present tense (first and second person, singular, *go;* third person singular, *goes;* first, second, third person plural, *go)* and the present participle, *going,* and forms the future tense *(shall* or *will go)* with the help of the auxiliary *shall* or *will.*

(2) The second principal part *(went)* supplies the form for the past tense *(went).*

(3) The third principal part *(gone)* combines with auxiliaries to form the present perfect tense *(has* or *have gone),* the past perfect tense *(had gone),* and the future perfect tense *(shall* or *will have gone).*

Many errors in tense are caused by ignorance of principal parts or by failure to choose the proper principal part. One who writes *He drownded* for *He drowned* simply does not know the principal parts of *drown.* In *He come* for *He came,* the error is produced by the use of the first principal part instead of the second; in *He had went* for *He had gone,* the error is produced by the use of the second principal part instead of the third to form the past perfect tense.

c. In revising their papers, students should look up in the dictionary the principal parts of any verb about which they are uncertain.

Dictionaries may differ in their way of indicating principal parts, but any satisfactory dictionary supplies the information and explains in an introductory section headed "Explanatory Notes" or "Inflected Forms" what system is used.

d. Students should be sure that they know the principal parts of the verbs most commonly used:

PRESENT INFINITIVE	PAST TENSE	PAST PARTICIPLE
awake	awoke	awaked
	awaked	awoke
		awakened
begin	began	begun
bid (to offer)	bid	bid
bid (to command)	bade	bidden
	bid	bid
break	broke	broken
bring	brought	brought
burn	burnt	burnt
	burned	burned
burst	burst	burst
choose	chose	chosen
come	came	come
dive	dived	dived
	dove (*colloquial*)	
do	did	done
dream	dreamt	dreamt
	dreamed	dreamed
drink	drank	drunk
drive	drove	driven
drown	drowned	drowned
dwell	dwelt	dwelt
	dwelled	dwelled
eat	ate	eaten
fall	fell	fallen
fly	flew	flown
forget	forgot	forgotten
		forgot
freeze	froze	frozen
get	got	got
		gotten

PRESENT INFINITIVE	PAST TENSE	PAST PARTICIPLE
give	gave	given
go	went	gone
hang (a thing)	hung	hung
hang (a person)	hanged	hanged
	hung	hung
kneel	knelt	knelt
	kneeled	kneeled
lay (to place)	laid	laid
lead	led	led
lie (to recline)	lay	lain
lie (to make a false statement)	lied	lied
light	lighted	lighted
	lit	lit
lose	lost	lost
pay	paid	paid
raise (to lift)	raised	raised
rise (to get up, to come up)	rose	risen
see	saw	seen
set (to place)	set	set
shine	shone	shone
	shined	
show	showed	shown
		showed
shrink	shrank	shrunk
	shrunk	shrunken
sing	sang	sung
	sung (*rare*)	
sit	sat	sat
slay	slew	slain
slink	slunk	slunk
spit	spit	spit
	spat	spat
steal	stole	stolen
strive	strove	striven
	strived	strived
swim	swam	swum
tread	trod	trod
		trodden

PRESENT INFINITIVE	PAST TENSE	PAST PARTICIPLE
wake	woke	waked
	waked (*rare*)	woke
		woken (primarily British)
wear	wore	worn
weave	wove	woven
wring	wrung	wrung
write	wrote	written

EXERCISES

Underscore one of the words in parentheses and give the reason for your choice.

1. The boat (lay, laid) on its side in the harbor.

2. The boys had (swam, swum) about thirty yards before they reached the shore.

3. After you (sit, set) the book on the table, (lie, lay) down on the couch and take a nap.

4. When the seams (burst, bursted), she knew she had (wore, worn) the coat long enough.

5. The man (bid, bidded) five dollars for the chair.

6. As soon as the sun (rose, raised), we took the flag and (rose, raised) it on the flag pole.

7. After I had (laid, lain) in bed for two hours, I (waked, woken) and (lay, laid) out the clothes I wanted to wear for dinner.

8. When we have (given, give) our share, we still will not have (payed, paid) our full debt.

9. The sun (shone, shoned) and the birds (drank, drunk) from the fountain.

10. For many years he had (wore, worn) the coat which had been (weaved, wove, woven) in his native land, and he (wrung, wrang) his hands in grief when it was (stole, stolen) from him.

6. VERBS AND COMPLEMENTS

A predicate is a word or group of words which makes an assertion about a subject. In sentences like *Time flies* and *Who cares?* the verbs alone constitute a predicate. Other verbs require the help of noun or adjective structures to complete the thought and establish the meaning of the verb. The helping noun or adjective is called the complement of the verb.

A *transitive* verb takes an object (He *felled* the *tree*); transitive verbs therefore take complements, since a direct object may be called a complement. *Intransitive* verbs, except for a special kind called *linking* verbs, do not take complements. Words frequently used as linking verbs are *be, seem, become, appear,* and the verbs of the senses *(smell, feel, taste, look, sound).* They are called linking because they join or link their subject to a noun or adjective. The same verb, may, in different sentences, be a transitive verb, a simple (i.e., non-linking) intransitive verb, or a linking verb. Note the use of the verb *sound* in these sentences:

> **Used as a transitive verb:** *Sound* the trumpets. [Sound is followed by its direct object and complement, *trumpets.*]
> **Used as a simple intransitive verb:** The alarm *sounded.* [Here *sounded* needs no complement.]
> **Used as a linking verb:** Your suggestion *sounds* good. [Here *sounds,* an incomplete predicate, links *suggestion* to the adjective *good. Good* is a complement.]

a. Complements of transitive verbs. Since complements of transitive verbs ordinarily present no problems of grammar or usage, we shall simply list the most common complements. They are: (1) the direct object (Eleanor was sharpening a *pencil*), (2) the indirect object (He gave *me* a ticket), (3) the objective complement (The board made him *chairman.* Jack Sprat and his wife licked the platter *clean*), and (4) the subjective complement after a passive verb (He was made *chairman* by the board. He was made *uneasy* by the decision).

b. Complements of linking verbs: the subjective complement. The complement of a linking verb, called the subjective complement, may be a pronoun, a noun or noun-equivalent (word, phrase, or clause), or an adjective (word, phrase, or clause).

> It is *Tom.* [*Tom* is a predicate noun and the subjective complement of *is.*]
> His objection is *that travel costs are too high.* [A noun clause used as a predicate noun, the subjective complement of *is*]
> Lobbing is *returning a ball in a high curve.* [A gerund phrase used as a predicate noun, subjective complement of *is*]
> She is *tall* and *graceful.* [Subjective complements of *is,* these two predicate adjectives modify the subject, *she.*]
> The materials are *of the best quality.* [An adjectival phrase, used as the subjective complement of *are*]

Two difficulties may arise in connection with linking verbs. The first is that when the subjective complement is a pronoun, it is, in formal usage, in the subjective case to agree with the subject of the sentence: *This is he, that is she.* In colloquial usage, the pronoun-complement is often given the objective case, particularly in the expression *It's me.*

The second difficulty stems from the fact that a number of verbs may be used both as simple intransitives and as linking verbs; as simple intransitives they may be modified by adverbs, and as linking verbs they may have adjectives as complements. The following sentences will illustrate:

The dog smells good. [He has a pleasing odor. *Smells* is a linking verb, *good* an adjective-complement.]

The dog smells well. [He has a good sense of smell. *Smells* is an intransitive verb, *well* an adverb.]

She looked intent. [She appeared to be concentrating. *Intent* is an adjective following a linking verb.]

She looked intently. [She used her eyes to look fixedly at something. *Intently* is an adverb modifying *looked*.]

For further discussion of adjectives and adverbs, see page 395.

EXERCISES

Distinguish between adverbs and adjective-complements in the following sentences. Assuming that the sentence is grammatically correct, what does it mean, or what might it mean in a larger context?

1. The bell sounded loud.
2. The bell sounded loudly.
3. John came slowly.
4. John is slow.
5. Janet looked happy.
6. Janet looked happily.
7. Ralph appeared cautiously.
8. Ralph appeared cautious.
9. She looked careful.
10. She looked carefully.
11. The child is well.
12. The child is good.

7. VERBS AND VERBALS

Verbals may be generally defined as word forms that combine some of the characteristics of verbs with the characteristics of another part of speech. Verbals differ from verbs in that (1) verbs can undergo change in person and number, and verbals cannot; (2) verbs can make an independent predication or assertion, and verbals cannot.

a. Participles. Participles are usually defined as verbal adjectives. They have some of the characteristics of verbs: they can be transitive or intransitive, complete or linking, active or passive, and they can take complements and be modified by adverbs. In their work as adjectives, they modify nouns and pronouns and in general perform adjective functions. Forms of the participle are *knowing* and *having known* (active), and *being known, known,* and *having been known* (passive).

Three difficulties may arise in connection with participles:

(1) The confusion of participles used as verbals and participles that are part of a verb phrase. Used with auxiliaries in verb phrases, participles can be verbs and can make an independent predication; used as participles they cannot:

> Elsie has been *eating* between meals. [*Has been eating* is a verb phrase; it serves as the simple predicate of the sentence.]
>
> Joe hurried into town, *eating* a sandwich as he walked. [*Eating* is a participle modifying *Joe;* it does not serve as a predicate.]

Failure to distinguish between participles and verb phrases can produce fragmentary sentences.

(2) Dangling or misplaced participles. Participles should refer clearly to the noun or pronoun they modify.

DANGLING: Running across the campus, the bell rang.
REVISED: Running across the campus, I heard the bell.

MISPLACED: Leaping and growling, I saw the dog as I approached.
REVISED: I saw the dog leaping and growling as I approached.

(See "Modifiers," page 410.)

(3) Awkward participial structures used in place of a clause:

AWKWARD: Al being an old friend, I knew I could trust him.
REVISED: Since Al was an old friend, I knew I could trust him.

b. Gerunds. The gerund may be defined as a verbal noun. The forms of the gerund are identical with the forms of the participle, but it is usually easy to distinguish between the two if one remembers that the participle has the functions of an adjective and the gerund has the functions of a noun.

> *Gerund: Remembering* names is difficult for Gerald.
> *Participle:* Finally *remembering* the man's name, Gerald crossed the street and spoke to him.
>
> [In the first sentence *remembering* is the subject of *is,* and is modified by the adjective *difficult; names* is the direct object of the gerund. In the second sentence the participle *remembering* modifies the noun *Gerald* and is itself modified by the adverb *finally.*]

In their capacity as nouns, gerunds serve as subjects, objects, and complements of verbs, and in general perform the functions of a normal noun. Gerunds resemble verbs in that they can be transitive or intransitive, complete or linking, active or passive, and can have adverbial modifiers and complements in the same way that verbs can.

In formal usage, nouns and pronouns modifying gerunds are generally in the possessive case.

> *John's leaving* was a shock to her; *his coming back* is what she lives for.
> We resented *Don's consulting* the faculty committee.

In colloquial usage this convention is often ignored, and the objective rather than the possessive case is used. The objective case is appropriate in any kind of usage when stress is placed on the noun or pronoun:

> Can you imagine *Jim deciding* to go to graduate school? [The sense is "Jim of all people," or "Jim who has never seemed interested in study."]

Also, usage is divided when the modifier of the gerund is inanimate:

> The *barn's burning down* was a great loss to Mr. Johnson.
> [*Or*] The *barn burning down* was a great loss to Mr. Johnson.

c. Infinitives. The infinitive may be defined as a verbal that functions as a noun (*To live* is *to come* nearer to death), an adjective (There is a man *to admire*), or an adverb (He went *to ask* for information). It is commonly, though not always, preceded by *to*. As a verbal, the infinitive can be transitive or intransitive, complete or linking, active or passive; it can take complements and be modified by adverbs; it can also take a noun or pronoun as a subject and form what is loosely called an infinitive clause (We asked *him to bring the oars*). Like other verbals, it cannot form a complete predication. The forms of the infinitive are: *to forgive* and *to have forgiven* (active), and *to be forgiven* and *to have been forgiven* (passive).

When an infinitive is used as a modifier, it should, like a participle, refer clearly to the noun or pronoun it modifies.

> FAULTY: To flower in June, you should set out the plants by the middle of May.
> REVISED: To flower in June, the plants should be set out by the middle of May.

The *split infinitive* occurs when a modifier is placed between *to* and the other part of the infinitive: "to industriously work." Split infinitives should be avoided whenever they can be avoided without loss of effectiveness or accuracy; usually the modifier can with advantage be placed either before or after the infinitive.

> AWKWARD: It was strange to, without really trying, succeed.
> REVISED: It was strange to succeed without really trying.

> AWKWARD: He tried to cautiously determine how much she had heard.
> REVISED: He tried cautiously to determine how much she had heard.

The split infinitive is not, however, the sin against good usage which it has sometimes been labeled. Sometimes splitting an infinitive is necessary to preserve exact meaning. An authority on usage, George O. Curme, gives this example of an infinitive that must be split for the sake of exactness: "He failed to entirely comprehend it." Neither "He failed entirely to comprehend it" nor "He failed to comprehend it entirely" would have the same meaning.

EXERCISES

I. Identify the verbs, participles, gerunds, and infinitives in the following sentences.

1. Undisturbed by the clamor around him, Elmer continued to eat his supper.
2. Jean's arriving so early gave her hosts a problem to solve.
3. To waver is to risk losing what we have tried to win.
4. Having been thwarted in his efforts to see Linda, Bob, still determined, decided to write a letter to her.
5. Reading the assignment twice is a good procedure to follow.
6. Reading the assignment a second time, Bert had the feeling of mastering the material.
7. We asked her to bring the sandwiches, knowing that being asked would give her pleasure.
8. Having learned that Helen hated walking, I did not dare suggest walking to town.
9. Practicing makes the work easy to do.
10. We protested her leaving the party, and finally persuaded her to stay and go home with us later.

II. Revise the sentences below to eliminate the faulty or awkward use of participles, gerunds, and infinitives.

1. Walking along the road, the sun came up over my right shoulder.
2. To study efficiently, the room should be cooler.
3. Falling over the goal line, the touchdown was made.
4. He intended to quickly and quietly leave.
5. The days are long when doing unpleasant work.
6. To be productive, you should plant tomatoes before the first of June.
7. Him refusing to go aroused her anger.
8. Mary being my guest, I consulted her about the plans.
9. Jack said that laughing was good for the soul. Laughing as he said it.
10. He tried to superstitiously avoid walking under the ladder.

8. VERBS: AGREEMENT   Agr

A verb agrees with its subject in person and number.

Sentences in which the subject immediately precedes the verb and in which the subject is clearly singular or clearly plural offer no problems of agreement. Mistakes in agreement most often occur when intervening words blur the subject-verb relationship, when the verb precedes the subject, or when the writer is not sure whether a particular subject should be considered singular or plural.

Conventions that govern the agreement of the verb with its subject differ in formal and informal usage. In applying the rules listed below, the student should be aware that a number of them are flexible, and that a sentence in which a rule is mechanically followed may be stiff or awkward and may need to be recast.

a. A verb agrees with its subject in person and number—not with an expression mistakenly considered to be its subject.

(1) A verb agrees with its subject—not with a modifier of the subject.

The destruction of the ships and landing forces *has* [not *have*] *been accomplished.* [The subject is *destruction.*]

My understanding of many ideas *has* been clarified. [The subject is *understanding.*]

(2) A verb agrees with its subject—the number of the verb is not influenced by the subjective complement.

The problems of municipal government *are* [not *is*] his chief interest. [The plural subject, *problems,* requires a plural verb. If the subjective complement, *interest,* were made the subject, the sentence would read: "His chief *interest is* the problems of municipal government."]

(3) A verb agrees with its subject—the number of the verb is not influenced by phrases introduced by *with, in addition to, along with,* and the like.

The *man* with his six children *is* [not *are*] waiting at the door.
The *teacher* as well as the students *finds* the room too warm

In sentences like these, there seems to be an awkward disagreement between formal grammar and meaning. For this reason many people prefer to recast the sentences to make the subject plural:

The man and his six children *are* waiting at the door.
The teacher and the students *find* the room too warm.

(4) A verb agrees with its subject—not with the introductory adverbs *here* and *there.*

Here *come* the *professor and* his *wife.* [*Come* is plural because it agrees with the compound subject.]
Here *comes Dean Harlow.*
There *sits* our most distinguished *citizen.*
There *lie* our *enemies.*

(5) A verb agrees with its subject—not with the expletive *there*.

There *is* only one *reason* for their quarrels.
There *are* several *reasons* for his decision.

Two qualifications of this convention should be noted. In spoken English the convention is often waived, and one hears sentences like "There's Tom and Betsy." In written English, usage is divided when a sentence has an expletive and a verb followed by a series, the first item of which is singular: "In the room there *were* (or *was*) a scarred desk, a straight chair, and a couch with sagging springs."

b. Singular subjects joined by *or* or *nor* take a singular verb.

He did not know whether the *captain or* the *lieutenant was* responsible.
Neither *Arthur nor* his *father was* at home.

c. When a singular and a plural subject are joined by *or* or *nor*, the verb agrees with the nearer subject.

He did not know whether the *officer or* the *soldiers were* to blame.
He did not know whether the *soldiers or* the *officer was* to blame. [Sometimes following this convention will produce "correct" but awkward sentences. Such sentences should be recast to avoid the construction.]

d. When two subjects joined by *or* or *nor* differ in person, the verb agrees with the nearer subject.

Either James or *I am* willing to go.
Neither John nor *you are* capable of dishonesty.

Such sentences, too, are frequently awkward, and it may be wise to recast them:

Both *James and I are* willing to go.
John is not capable of dishonesty, nor *are you*.

e. Singular subjects joined by *and* take a plural verb unless the subjects are thought of as a unit.

Honesty and justice are required in a judge.
My *guide and counselor* [one person] *has served* me well.

f. The pronoun *each* and compound subjects modified by *each* and *every* take a singular verb.

Each of the carpenters *is bringing* his own tools.
Each magazine and newspaper has its special place on the stand.
Every tree and every bush was coated with ice; *every street was* dangerously slippery.

g. Collective nouns may take either singular or plural verbs, depending

upon whether they are thought of as referring to a single unit or to the individuals in the group.

> The *committee is meeting* this morning. [The committee is thought of as a unit.]
> The *committee are arriving* tonight and tomorrow, some by train and some by plane.
>
> The *number* of errors *accounts* for the grade.
> A *number* of students *are* leaving early.
>
> A *majority is* needed before a vote can be taken.
> The *majority were* on their feet before the vote was called for.

h. The pronouns *none* and *any* may take either singular or plural verbs, depending upon the sense of the sentence.

> None of the grass *was* burned.
> None of the leaves *are* raked.
>
> Any of these dates *is* convenient.
> Any of us *are* invited.

i. In mathematical calculations either a singular or a plural verb may be used.

> Two plus two *is* (or *are*) four.
> Three and three *is* (or *are*) six.

j. The antecedent of the relative pronouns *who*, *which*, and *that* determines the number and person of the verb of which the pronoun is the subject.

> It is *I who am* to blame, and it is *you who deserve* the praise.
> She is one of those determined *women who insist* on having the last word.[4]

k. In formal usage *one*, *no one*, *anyone*, *everyone*, and *someone*, and *nobody*, *anybody*, *everybody*, and *somebody* require singular verbs.

> *No one was* willing to bring up any new business because *everyone was* eager for the meeting to come to an end.
> *Everyone*—even the older people who did not dance—*was* having a good time at the party.

EXERCISES

In the following sentences, point out any subject-verb agreement that should be corrected in formal written English and revise any sentences that need revision.

---

[4] Margaret M. Bryant notes that although about five out of every six writers use the plural (one of those who *are*) in sentences of this kind, the singular (one of those who *is*) is also used by educated writers and occurs frequently in informal English. *Current American Usage*, p. 12.

1. Each voter in these three communities are planning to cast a ballot in this election.

2. My cousin along with several friends from New York are going to pay us a visit.

3. There is, the senator says frequently and forcibly, many reasons why all good citizens should vote.

4. Neither the president nor his representatives were able to attend the ceremony.

5. Neither of the professors were able to answer my question.

6. Every doctor and every dentist in town are free on Wednesday afternoons.

7. Each of the fighters were becoming tired by the end of the fifth round.

8. Everyone—male and female, young and old—like to attend barn dances.

9. He is one of those men who is called successful but who is merely rich.

10. War may be eliminated when the causes of war is understood.

11. Either Harry or I are ready to volunteer.

12. Neither he nor his partner are entirely blameless.

13. This collection of essays have been carefully chosen.

14. There's Janice and her brother.

15. Her principal interest are books.

9. VERBS: VOICE AND MOOD

Voice

Voice is the property of the verb which shows whether the subject of the verb acts or is acted upon. Active voice shows the subject acting; passive voice shows the subject acted upon.

> *Active voice:* Our team *won* the game.
> *Passive voice:* The game *was won* by our team.

The passive voice is useful, particularly when the doer of the action is unknown or is relatively insignificant. For example, the sentence "Someone has stolen the *Mona Lisa* again" is less effective than the passive statement "The *Mona Lisa* has been stolen again." Often, though, the passive is unemphatic, indirect, wordy, and vague. Since active statements are frequently more effective, one should use the passive only when there is good reason for doing so.

> *Weak passive:* Current events were discussed and long papers were written by us.
> *Active:* We discussed current events and wrote long papers.

> *Weak passive* (and unnecessary shift to passive in the middle of the sentence): As we entered the woods, a shot was heard.
> *Active:* As we entered the woods, we heard a shot.

Mood

Mood is the property of the verb which indicates whether the speaker is (1) making a request or giving a command (imperative), (2) expressing a supposition or wish (subjunctive), or (3) stating a fact or opinion or asking a question (indicative).

> *Imperative mood: Close* the window. Then please *sit* down.
> *Subjunctive mood:* If I *were* wealthy I could own a yacht.
> *Indicative mood:* His son *is* at home now. *Will* he *stay* long?

Some problems with mood arise in connection with the subjunctive, a mood little used in modern English. In some situations, however, it may be necessary to make a choice between the indicative and the subjunctive. Conventions for the use of the subjunctive are:

a. The subjunctive is used to express a condition that is contrary to fact.

> If I were you, I should accept the invitation.
> Even if he were wealthy, he would still wear old clothes.
> He would pay his share if he were able.

b. The subjunctive may be used to express strong doubt.

> *Subjunctive:* If it should be a rainy day, we shall not go. [Since the speaker is expressing doubt that the day will be rainy he uses the subjunctive.]
> *Indicative:* If it is a rainy day, we shall not go. [The indicative is used because the idea of doubt is not emphasized.]

> *Subjunctive:* If the teacher were to give a quiz, some of us would be sorry. [This sentence implies that the speaker does not expect the quiz to be given.]
> *Indicative:* If the teacher gives a quiz, some of us will be sorry. [This sentence does not indicate whether or not a quiz is likely.]

c. The subjunctive is used in *that* clauses expressing a recommendation, a demand, a request, a necessity.

> The committee recommended that the project be abandoned.
> He demanded that the bill be paid immediately.
> He asked that we be quiet.
> They demand that the rules be changed.
> I move that the petition be granted.
> It is essential that this law be passed.

Sentences like those just above can often be recast to avoid the formal subjunctive:

> The committee recommended abandoning the project.
> He demanded immediate payment of the bill.
> He asked us to be quiet.
> They demand a change in the rules.
> Passage of this law is essential.

The subjunctive also survives in modern English in certain exclamations and wishes like "so *be* it," "far *be* it from me to object," "peace *be* with you," "Heaven *help* us all."

Unnecessary shifts in mood—from indicative to imperative or imperative to indicative, for example—can produce awkward sentences. See "Consistency," page 108.

EXERCISES

I. Change the following passive statements to active statements. How many of them are improved by use of the active voice?

1. Your invitation was received by me today.
2. On the athletic field, students playing hockey can be seen.
3. By nine o'clock the book was read, the cat was put out, and he had gone to bed.
4. When the bell rang, students pouring out of the buildings were observed.
5. The President was elected by a large majority.

II. In each of the following sentences, choose the verb that seems preferable, and justify your choice.

1. The law requires that the defendant (have, has) benefit of counsel.
2. If the earth (was, were) square, some nations would want all four corners.
3. I wonder if the young man who just spoke to me (was, were) a college student.
4. Senator Borgam Patwell moved that the motion (be, was) postponed indefinitely.
5. Rosalind would like Russell better if he (were, was) a better correspondent.
6. If Thornton (was, were) ever kind, he was kind for a reason.
7. I should go for a swim today if the water (was, were) not so cold.
8. What could I say if the professor (was, were) to ask why I have been absent?
9. He requires that each student (give, gives) a five-minute speech.
10. The man asked if it (were, was) too late to get a ticket for the game.

10. VERBS: TENSE

The six main tenses of English verbs are:

Present tense: I walk.
Past tense: I walked.
Future tense: I shall (will) walk.
Present perfect tense: I have walked.
Past perfect tense: I had walked.
Future perfect tense: I shall (will) have walked.

The simple present tense often indicates habitual or timeless action: *I walk to school every day. Snow falls early in Maine.* The form *I am walking,* which indicates action occurring at present, is called the progressive present; and a third form of the present, *I do walk,* is called the emphatic present. The past tense has corresponding forms: *I was walking. I did walk.* Past action is also sometimes recorded in the present tense, or historical present. Future time is frequently expressed by constructions other than the future tense; for example: *I am going to walk, I expect to walk soon, I am about to walk.*

Knowledge of the following conventions will help to prevent the misuse of tenses.

a. Statements regarded as permanently true are expressed in the present tense.

> In the first grade the child learned that two and two *are* [not *were*] four.
> Socrates believed that the unexamined life *is* not worth living.
> People in the ninth century thought that the world *was* flat. [The past tense is correct here because the speaker does not regard the idea as true now.]
> Copernicus discovered that the earth *revolves* [not *revolved*] around the sun.

b. The historical present tense may be used effectively in the presentation of lively dramatic action, but is likely to be inappropriate when used for routine narrative.

> APPROPRIATE: A crowd has assembled now and is peering up at the man on the ledge of a tenth-story window. Other tenth-story windows are open, filled with gesticulating and shouting people. The man on the ledge is shaking his head. Now he has turned and is looking at the street below him. Suddenly . . .
> PROBABLY NOT APPROPRIATE: Before me on the library path I see Henry. I hardly recognize him under that battered old hat, and apparently he doesn't even see me. I pass him and go on to my history class.

c. Generally the past tense is used to refer to action completed in the past, and the past perfect is used to refer to action completed prior to some definite time in the past.

> When I *called* he *had* already *left.* [*Called,* past tense, represents action completed in the past. *Had left,* past perfect, represents action completed prior to the past action described by the verb *called.*]

d. The present perfect tense represents an action occurring at an indefinite time in the past and extending up to and perhaps through the present time.

> Richard *has been* on the honor roll three times. [*Has been* here means up to the present time.]
> Helen *has been waiting* for him to call. [This sentence implies that she is still waiting.]

e. The future perfect tense represents an action to be completed in the future prior to a definite time in the future.

> I *shall have left* before you arrive.
> By next week, all the students *will have gone* home.

f. The tense of subordinate clauses should be in logical sequence with the tense of the main verb.

I *had been* in college for two months before I *met* him. [Since being in college preceded the meeting, the past perfect tense and the past tense are properly used to show the time-relationship of events.]

I *think* that you *will* do well.

I *thought* that you *would* do well.

g. The time indicated by infinitives and participles should be adjusted to the tense of the main verb and the meaning of the sentence.

I was glad *to receive* the letters. [I.e., I was glad *when I received* the letters.]

I was glad *to have received* the letters. [I.e., at some time in the past I was glad that I *had already received* the letters.]

Having waited in the rain for three hours, Mark *was* thoroughly exasperated when Helen finally appeared. [Not "Waiting in the rain for three hours, Mark was thoroughly exasperated when Helen finally appeared." Since waiting preceded and caused the exasperation, the action referred to by the participle is previous to that of the verb, and the form *having waited* is therefore required.]

Casting fearful glances behind him, the boy *walked* by the graveyard. [Here the action of the participle and the action of the main verb occur simultaneously and the present participle is properly used.]

h. When direct discourse is changed to indirect discourse, the tense of verbs should be adjusted.

Direct discourse: Sara said, "I *love* to study history."
Indirect discourse: Sara said that she *loved* to study history.

Direct discourse: He asked, "*Have* you a date for Saturday night?"
Indirect discourse: He asked if I *had* a date for Saturday night.

Direct discourse: Dave said, "I *had planned* to go home this weekend until I *heard* from my parents."
Indirect discourse: Dave said that he *had planned* to go home this weekend until he *heard* from his parents. [Here the verbs are unchanged; there is no way of giving *had planned* a greater degree of past time, and *heard* must remain in the past tense to preserve the logical sequence of tenses.]

Shall and *Will, Should* and *Would.* Usage is divided on *shall* and *will* and on *should* and *would.* In formal usage, many careful writers still attempt to preserve some of the distinctions between them, and feel strongly that the distinctions should be made; other careful writers use *will* in place of the more formal *shall,* and *would* in place of the more formal *should.* In informal English, *will* and *would* are more commonly used; and it is often possible to use contractions (*I'll, I'd, he'll,* etc.) and so to avoid the problem. Statements **a** and **b** below describe traditional, formal usage.

a. To express simple futurity, *shall* (or *should*) is used in the first person and *will* (or *would*) in the second and third persons.

I shall (should) go.   We shall (should) go.
You will (would) go.   You will (would) go.
He, she, it will (would) go.   They will (would) go.

b. **To express determination, promise, or command, *will* is used in the first person, and *shall* is used in the second and third persons.**

I will.   We will.
You shall.   You shall.
He, she, it shall.   They shall.

c. *Would* **may be used in all persons to express determination.**

He warned me, but I *would* have my way.
I warned him, but he *would* have his way.
He warned you, but you *would* have your way.

d. *Should* **may be used in all persons to express possibility or supposition.**

Even if I (you, he) *should* be defeated, the cause will not be lost.

e. *Should* **in the sense of *ought to* is used in all three persons.**

If we are to consider our duty, you *should* go, I *should* go, and he *should* go.

f. *Would* **is used in all persons to express habitual action.**

I (you, he) *would* stop each day to see the progress the workmen had made on the new office building.

EXERCISES

I. Point out misuses of tense in the sentences below and revise any sentences that need revision.

1. These primitive people did not know that the world was round or that three and three made six.
2. Did you call him yet?
3. Marrying the editor's daughter, he was surprised when he learned that he was to start to work as office boy in the editorial department.
4. Pausing in the middle of his speech, he glanced at Ted and beckoned to him.
5. Although Carlyle wrote many volumes, he often said that silence was greater than speech.
6. At the dance that night there were many of the people that we saw in the afternoon.
7. The sky was gray and the wind shook the trees. The sun, which was shining this morning, is now obscured.
8. I called her each night ever since we went to the game together.
9. They have completed the project several days ago. Now they have started work on the new tunnel.

10. Although he was really terrified the night before, he now tried to pretend that he felt very calm.

11. Crossing the room, he opened the door.

12. Before the first of the month, he finishes his term paper.

13. Mary had been in college a year before she had learned how to study.

14. Walking past the housemother's room, Ida answered the telephone.

15. I have done so well in my courses last term that I decided to take an extra course this term.

II. Consider the use of *shall* and *will,* and *should* and *would* in the following sentences. Some of the uses are clearly correct; some are clearly incorrect; some are matters of taste; some could be correct if the sentence were interpreted in a certain way. Classify each sentence and comment on it. Correct any uses that are clearly wrong.

1. He shall attend the dinner if it is held at a convenient place and time.

2. Will you go to the party?

3. They are very likely to come, but what if they would be late?

4. I will be pleased to accept your invitation.

5. I will drown unless someone shall save me.

6. They should have come earlier; now the dinner is cold.

7. I warned him, but he would not listen.

8. When we were children, we would meet Father at the gate and he would give us sticks of candy.

9. He gave us the key in case he should not be there to let us in.

10. I should like to attend the concert but I don't think I will be able to go.

11. I would always help him when he would have let me.

12. We should have known that they should try to mislead us.

11. ADJECTIVES AND ADVERBS   Adj, Adv

Adjectives (words, phrases, and clauses) modify nouns and pronouns. *Descriptive* adjectives express a quality, condition, or characteristic of the noun or pronoun:

> The man, *old* and *stooped,* is still *vigorous.* [*Old* and *stooped,* apposed adjectives, and *vigorous,* a predicate adjective, characterize *man.*]

Limiting adjectives point out or identify particular members of a class:

> *This* man and *three* boys delivered *the* furniture to *my* house. [The four italicized words function as limiting adjectives.]

Adverbs (words, phrases, and clauses) usually modify a verb, an adjective, or another adverb. Sometimes they modify a whole sentence rather than a particular expression in the sentence:

> *Possibly* she has forgotten what day it is.

Simple adverbs supply answers to such questions as How? When? How much? Where? In what order or degree?

> She slept *late.*
> He talked *slowly.*
> Our work is *somewhat* harder *here* than it was *there.*
> He came *first* and stayed *longer* than anyone else.

Interrogative adverbs (*when, why, how, where*) introduce a question:

> *Where* did he go? *Why* has he gone?

A *conjunctive* adverb (sometimes called a transitional adverb or sentence connector) acts as a conjunction and at the same time acts as an adverb in that it modifies the action of its clause. Expressions commonly used as conjunctive adverbs are: *besides, indeed, in fact, also, moreover, furthermore, nevertheless, still, however, therefore, thus, hence, consequently, accordingly.*

> His nose was broken; *nevertheless* he fought on.
> They were very late; *in fact* they arrived when the dance was over.

Adjectives and adverbs are inflected to show degree of comparison:

Positive degree: *young* brother, *courageous* man, runs *fast,* moved *quickly.*
Comparative degree: *younger* brother, *more courageous* man, runs *faster,* moves *more quickly.*
Superlative degree: *youngest* brother, *most courageous* man, runs *fastest,* moves *most quickly.*

Some words are compared irregularly, by a change in form: *good, better, best; little, less* (or *lesser*), *least.*

Understanding of the following principles will help to avoid the misuse of adjectives and adverbs.

a. Adverbs modify verbs which express action. Adjectives serve as subjective complements of linking verbs (i.e., verbs that express little or no action and serve primarily to link the subject to what follows). Words often used as linking verbs are *be, seem, become, appear,* and the verbs of the senses (*smell, taste, feel, look, sound*).

> He *carefully* avoided the broken glass. [In this sentence it is clear that *carefully* is an adverb modifying *avoided.* This sentence presents no problem.]
> He looked *steadily* at the papers before him. [*Looked* is sometimes used as a linking verb, but here it is used to describe or convey action, and the adverb *steadily* tells how he *looked*—i.e., how he performed the action.]
> She looks *happy.* [Here *looks* serves only to join the subject *she* to the adjective *happy* and is a linking verb: it describes the subject and not the action. *Happy* is a subjective complement.]
> That small boy looks *mischievous.* [*Mischievous,* a subjective complement, describes the boy.]
> The small boy looked *mischievously* at his companion. [*Mischievously* describes the act of looking.]

He is doing *well* [not *good*] in his history course. [*Good* would be wrong here because an adverb is needed to modify the verb *is doing*.]

I can't tell whether he feels good or *bad*. [*Badly* in place of the adjective *bad* is often used colloquially.]

He felt his way *uncertainly* in the darkened room. [*Felt* describes an act; *uncertainly* describes how that act was done.]

b. With transitive verbs, adjectives may serve as objective complements— i.e., may serve to modify the object in a particular way.

She cooked the meat *tender*. [*Tender,* an adjective, applies to the state of the meat and is correct. To substitute *tenderly* for *tender* would be to change the sense of the sentence.]

She cooked the meat *quickly*. [*Quickly* is not an objective complement but is an adverb modifying *cooked*.]

We painted the barn *red*. [*Red,* an adjective, applies to the state of the barn and is an objective complement.]

c. Dictionaries supply important information about particular adverbs and adjectives.

One cause of errors in the use of adverbs and adjectives is uncertainty as to which part of speech a particular word may be. Can *slow,* for example, be used as an adverb? Looking up the word in a good dictionary will reveal that it is used as an adjective or as an adverb. If one looks up the word *considerable* he will learn that it is an adjective (or, colloquially, a noun) and not an adverb. Dictionaries also supply information about the way adverbs and adjectives form the positive, comparative, and superlative degrees.

d. Adjectives and adverbs should not be overused.

Adjectives and adverbs (and expressions used as adjectives or adverbs) are of course indispensable, but they should be used economically and exactly. When they are overused, they tend to clutter communication and to obscure the essential ideas. The skillful writer usually depends upon effective verbs and nouns to carry most of his meaning. He uses adjectives and adverbs to qualify and to make more precise the work done by verbs and nouns.

Overuse of modifiers is most likely to occur in pretentious or generally wordy expression. The best way to avoid this fault is to write honestly and unaffectedly, and to strike out or to express more briefly words, phrases, or passages that do not carry their share of meaning. (See "Economy and Conciseness" in Chapter 5.)

EXERCISES

I. In each of the following sentences choose one of the words in parentheses and explain the reason for your choice. (Sometimes the choice may depend on the sense intended.)

1. Mary plays golf as (well, good) as John does.
2. When you get to know her, she is a (real, really) sincere person.
3. Morris does not feel (good, well) about it; and Melvin, I understand, feels (bad, badly) and is very unhappy.
4. After weighing each of the three sisters, we discovered that Helen was the (heavier, heaviest).
5. Did the ride on the merry-go-round make you feel (bad, badly)?
6. He held the boat (steady, steadily).
7. That fish smelled (peculiar, peculiarly) to me.
8. You look (considerable, considerably) better today.
9. Although the dog looks gentle, he hears strangers however (quietly, quiet) they move, and he barks (ferocious, ferociously).
10. She looked (sick, sickly) to me.
11. He thought that he had been treated (bad, badly).
12. I have trouble with chemistry but I am doing very (good, well) in English.
13. She may smile (pleasant, pleasantly) now, but she looked (miserable, miserably) this morning.
14. He is the (older, oldest) of the three Harris boys.
15. He walked (slowly, slow) and (cautiously, cautious) down the dark road.

II. Write the comparative and superlative degrees of the following adjectives and adverbs.

far	tired	safe
beautiful	much	slow
gladly	handsome	slowly
old	bad	pleasant

12. CONNECTIVES
Con, Conj

Prepositions

A preposition is an expression used to connect a noun or pronoun to some other element in the sentence. The noun or pronoun, called the object of the preposition, may be a word, a phrase, or a dependent clause. A preposition may be a single word (*on, in, along,* etc.) or several words (*in accordance with, because of,* etc.).

> He argued *with* me. [*With,* a preposition, takes as its object the pronoun *me* to form the prepositional phrase *with me.*]

a. Prepositions should be used idiomatically.

Certain words are conventionally joined to certain prepositions to form idiomatic phrases. For example, *accuse* is followed by *of* (*accuse* him *of* the crime); *acquiesce* is followed by *in* (*acquiesce in* a decision); and *wait* is followed by *on* or *for* (*wait on* a customer, *wait for* a friend or a bus). Dictionaries give information about idiomatic usage, and the student should look up a word when he is uncertain about the preposition that conventionally follows it.

b. A preposition may be used at the end of a sentence. The effort to avoid prepositions at the ends of sentences sometimes produces awkward constructions. *We had many things to talk about* is a more natural sentence than *We had many things about which to talk.* If natural rhythm and idiom place a preposition at the end of a sentence, no convention of good usage requires that the sentence be changed.

Conjunctions

A conjunction is an expression that connects words, phrases, or clauses. Conjunctions differ from prepositional connectives in that prepositions always have an object expressed or understood and conjunctions do not.

> He was tired, *for* it was very late. [*For* is a conjunction joining two independent clauses. It does not have an object.]
> He did the work *for* five dollars. [*For* is a preposition, and its object is *dollars.*]

Conjunctions may be classified as *coordinating conjunctions, subordinating conjunctions,* and *conjunctive adverbs.*

Coordinating conjunctions connect elements of equal rank. The most common connectives of this kind, sometimes called pure conjunctions, are *and, but, for, or, nor.* So and *yet* may also be used as pure conjunctions.

> He is young *and* strong. [*And* connects *young* and *strong.*]
> The two nations fought on the land *and* on the sea. [*And* connects two phrases.]
> He may be old, *but* he is still a good swimmer. [*But* connects two independent clauses. In a sentence of this kind, a comma conventionally precedes the coordinating connective; if the comma is not needed for clarity or emphasis, it may be omitted.]
> Chester was late, very late. *And* Ann resented it, although she said nothing at the time. [*And* connects two sentences.]

Certain coordinating conjunctions are used in pairs and are called correlative conjunctions. Examples are *not only . . . but also, either . . . or, neither . . . nor, both . . . and.*

> *Both* Ted *and* I are going.
> *Neither* he *nor* she wants to marry.

Subordinating conjunctions connect clauses of unequal rank and show the relationship between them. Subordinating conjunctions are *after, although, as, because, before, if, since, so that, that, though, unless, until, when, where, whether, while.*

He did not speak *because* he was angry. [*Because* subordinates *he was angry* and connects it with the main clause of the sentence.]

When the situation is clearer, I can make a decision. [*When* connects the subordinate clause of which it is a part to the main clause *I can make a decision.*]

Conjunctive adverbs (also called transitional adverbs, transitional connectives, and sentence connectors) join two independent clauses or sentences, and at the same time modify the clause or sentence in which they occur. Expressions used as conjunctive adverbs are *accordingly, again, all the same, at the same time, also, besides, consequently, conversely, furthermore, for that reason, hence, however, indeed, in fact, likewise, moreover, nevertheless, notwithstanding, on the other hand, on the contrary, on that account, otherwise, rather, still, then, therefore, thus.*

The student council has refused to act; *for that reason* we are circulating a petition.

He is unmoved by emotional appeals; he is ready, *however*, to listen to reason.

The lectures stimulated discussion both on the campus and in town; the students are eager, *therefore*, to continue them next year.

The sentences above illustrate two points worth noting about conjunctive adverbs. (1) When a conjunctive adverb is the sole connective between two independent clauses in the same sentence, it is generally preceded by a semicolon. (2) Conjunctive adverbs, unlike coordinating and subordinating conjunctions, are movable; they do not necessarily stand at the head of the clause to which they belong, and a sentence is frequently improved when a conjunctive adverb is moved out of the emphatic head position.

a. Conjunctions should express clearly and exactly the relationship the writer intends.

The overuse or imprecise use of conjunctions like *as, so, while, and, but,* and *since* often produces ineffective writing. *As,* for example, is often used where *because,* or *for,* or *when,* or *since,* or *just as* would more clearly express the meaning. *So* is often used in sentences where *so that,* or *accordingly,* or *for this reason* would be more precise. *While* is sometimes used inexactly for *but* or *although. And* carries the general meaning of addition or continuity, but expressions like *consequently* and *again* may serve better in particular contexts. *But* is not always the best expression of contrast; sometimes *yet,* or *nevertheless,* or *however,* or *on the contrary* may be preferable. *Since* may be less exact than *because* or *for* in some sentences. The following sentences illustrate imprecise uses of conjunctions:

As I was on the beach, I could see the approach of the storm. [This sentence is ambiguous. It may mean *When* I was on the beach . . . or *Because* I was on the beach . . .]

While the road was very dark, we knew it well and could find our way. [*While*

is essentially a time-connective; *although* would be more exact in this sentence.]
   She received the letter *and* she called her parents. [*And* is a loose connective
here. *When* she received . . . or, *As soon as* she received . . . would more
clearly establish the relationship of the two clauses.]

b. Conjunctions should be appropriate to the style of a piece of writing.
   In the following sentences, heavy and incongruous connectives are used
inappropriately in simple, informal writing:

POOR: *Notwithstanding the fact that* he weighs only one hundred and fifteen
   pounds, Larry is a good athlete.
IMPROVED: Although he weighs only one hundred and fifteen pounds, Larry is a
   good athlete.

POOR: We didn't know *whence* the hired man came, or how long he would work
   for us.
IMPROVED: We didn't know where the hired man came from, or how long he would
   work for us.

POOR: I wasn't sick after eating the green apples, *whereas* Helen and Tom missed
   two days of school.
IMPROVED: Although I wasn't sick after eating the green apples, Helen and Tom
   missed two days of school.

POOR: My room, *albeit* small and dark, is the only place in the house where I can
   work in peace.
IMPROVED: My room, though small and dark, is the only place in the house where
   I can work in peace.

   On the other hand, certain connectives widely used in colloquial English
are not appropriate in written English unless the style is intended to sound
colloquial. Among those connectives is *like* used as a conjunction in place of
as or *as if* ("Write the paper *like* I told you to write it."). Comments on *like*
and other dubious connectives can be found in the Glossary of Usage, pages
486–502.

EXERCISES

   I. Choose the idiomatic prepositions in the following sentences. If necessary, consult your dictionary.

   1. We knew that he was capable (of, for) doing the work well.
   2. The child was accompanied (with, by) his mother.
   3. He is willing to abide (by, with) the rule.
   4. Jack dissented (with, from) the majority.
   5. My hat is identical (with, to) yours.

6. Bob is oblivious (of, to) the irony of the situation.
7. Sam is proficient (at, in) mathematics.
8. His misplaced humor is repugnant (for, to) me.
9. We all concur (in, with) the decision.
10. Dave is angry (with, at) all his friends.

II. Comment on the exactness and appropriateness of the connectives in the following sentences, and revise any sentences that need revision.

1. As I was driving to school, I decided to stop and see Mary.
2. Harold's brothers played golf and tennis while he enjoyed reading.
3. We're going hiking on Saturday; moreover we hope to do some mountain climbing Sunday.
4. I knew that he was guilty as I saw him fire the shot.
5. He looks like his father, but he talks like his mother does.
6. Dorothy has been depressed since Alec went to New York without saying goodbye.
7. We began to worry about her as it was near midnight.
8. I saw in the paper where another plane crashed.
9. I felt that she was deceitful as I heard her evade Ralph's questions.
10. He hurried so he would not be late.
11. She is an attractive girl, if she is not a good student.
12. My roommate makes the beds while I clean up the room.
13. Mrs. Boone is always sociable and pleasant; conversely, Mr. Boone is not.
14. He was on probation last term, and he is spending more time on his studies now.
15. Being as the weather was warm, we planned to have the party outdoors.

13. PHRASES AND CLAUSES

a. A phrase is a group of two or more grammatically related words which does not contain a subject and a predicate and which functions as a single part of speech.

Noun phrase: Talking to her friends is one of her chief pleasures. [The italicized phrase is the subject of the verb *is*.]
Verb phrase: By one o'clock he *will have finished* his examination. [The phrase consists of *finished,* the main verb, and its auxiliaries, *will* and *have*.]
Adjectival phrase: She lives in the house *with green shutters.* [The phrase modifies the noun *house*.] *Smiling sourly,* she watched him go. [The phrase modifies the pronoun *she*.]
Adverbial phrase: He executed the order *without delay*. [*Without delay* tells how he executed the order and so modifies the verb *executed*.]

b. A dependent (or subordinate) clause is a group of words which has a subject and a predicate, but which is a dependent part of a sentence.

Like phrases, dependent clauses do the work of a single part of speech, and they may be called noun or adjective or adverb clauses.

Noun clause: He denied *that life is short.* [The clause serves as the object of *denied.*] I know *he will come.* [*He will come* looks like an independent clause, but it is easy to see that the word *that*—I know *that* he will come—is understood here though it has been omitted. *That he will come* is the object of the verb *know,* and the clause is therefore a noun clause.]

Adjective clause: I returned to the town *where I was born.* [Modifies the noun *town.*]

Adverbial clause: The students celebrate *when examinations are over.* [Modifies the verb *celebrate.*]

c. An independent (or main) clause has a subject and predicate and makes, with the help of context, a complete assertion.

A simple sentence consists of one independent clause; a compound sentence of two or more independent clauses; a complex sentence of one independent clause and one or more dependent clauses; a compound-complex sentence of two or more independent clauses and one or more dependent clauses. An independent clause, therefore, may be a complete simple sentence, or part of a compound, complex, or compound-complex sentence. It may also be an absolute construction—a construction grammatically unrelated to the rest of the sentence.

Dogs chase cats. [This is a simple sentence as well as an independent clause.]

Jonathan's father loves his son, but *he loves his car too.* [Two independent clauses form a compound sentence.]

Tom said—*everyone listened intently*—that the film was banned in Boston. [The italicized clause is an absolute construction in a complex sentence.]

EXERCISES

Identify independent and dependent clauses in the following sentences.

1. Where you go I will go.
2. He said the weather was sure to improve.
3. Ruth cut the flowers, and Jane arranged them.
4. This is what he wants, and he is determined to have it.
5. I said, though it wasn't true, that I would miss him.
6. What you ask is almost impossible for us to do when we think what the consequences might be.
7. He robbed the bank while his confederates stood guard outside and the police were eating lunch.
8. The examination I took was very difficult.

9. Because the moonlight was beautiful and the night was warm, we stayed on the lake until everyone else had gone.

10. You may leave whenever you wish, but be sure you get home early.

14. FRAGMENTARY AND INCOMPLETE SENTENCES   PF, Frag

According to the broadest definition, a sentence is any locution spoken or punctuated as an independent unit of discourse. For practical purposes, we can say that a sentence is grammatically complete when it contains a subject and a predicate and, in context, makes an independent assertion.[5]

a. A fragmentary sentence is an unsatisfactory incomplete sentence. It is a subordinate part of a sentence written with a capital letter at the beginning and a period at the end.

The error of punctuating a fragmentary sentence as if it were a complete sentence is called the **Period Fault.** Basically, though, fragmentary sentences are produced, not by poor punctuation, but by the failure to recognize the elements of a sentence; most fragments result from the confusion of verbs and verbals, or the confusion of phrases or dependent clauses with independent clauses. Sometimes a fragment needs simply to be attached to the preceding or following sentence, of which it may be a dependent part; sometimes it needs to be rewritten so that it becomes an independent statement.

UNSATISFACTORY: He arrived late. *Having been detained at the office.* [A participial phrase written as a sentence]
REVISED: Having been detained at the office, he arrived late.

UNSATISFACTORY: I enjoy realistic writers. *Like Saul Bellow and John O'Hara.* [A prepositional phrase written as a sentence]
REVISED: I enjoy realistic writers like Saul Bellow and John O'Hara.

UNSATISFACTORY: I am taking three sciences. *Biology and chemistry and geology.* [Appositives written as a sentence]
REVISED: I am taking three sciences: [or a dash] biology, chemistry, and geology.

UNSATISFACTORY: At three o'clock he was ready to leave. *When suddenly he saw her hurrying through the crowd.* [A dependent clause written as a sentence]
REVISED: At three o'clock he was ready to leave. Suddenly he saw her hurrying through the crowd.

Fragmentary sentences like those above force the reader, who has learned to expect the completion of an idea within the conventional signs of the sentence, to stop and mentally correct the writing. Such fragments are considered

---

[5] Statements in the imperative mood (*Shut the door. Be ready at six.*) are classified as complete sentences even though the subject, *you,* is not expressed.

errors because they indicate incompetence; they suggest that the writer does not know the difference between a sentence and a part of a sentence.

b. Some grammatically incomplete sentences convey clearly and appropriately the meaning the communicator wishes to convey.

Such sentences are more common in informal than in formal writing. Exclamations, questions, answers to questions, certain transitional expressions, established formulas, and bits of dialogue are often quite properly written as sentences:

> *What an examination!*

> *Questions?* Of course I had questions. What I needed was answers, and I sought those answers in my reading.

> Is our policy the correct one? *Perhaps so.* We need, though, to be aware of certain obstacles.

> *To return now to the causes of this act of aggression.* [A transitional phrase leading into a new paragraph]

> *Nothing ventured, nothing gained.* [A familiar formula]

> *Going to the play tonight?*
> *No. Have to study. Exam tomorrow.*

Also, in narrative writing, particularly in modern fiction, one may find an impressionistic setting down, in incomplete sentences, of a character's thoughts, or of descriptive detail:

> It was a beautiful calm day. *Not a ripple on the water. Not a cloud in the sky.*

Deciding what can properly be punctuated as a sentence involves, like many other matters of English usage, the application of good judgment rather than rigid rules about what is and what is not an acceptable sentence. Since the careless or illiterate fragmentary sentence is jarring to an educated reader, many English instructors require students to mark with an asterisk any incomplete sentences they use, and to indicate in a note at the bottom of the page that the incomplete construction is intentional. Students whose sense of style is unsure will be wise to avoid incomplete sentences except in exclamations and in the writing of dialogue.

EXERCISES

I. In the passages below (1) revise or repunctuate any fragmentary sentences, and (2) point out any acceptable incomplete sentences and explain why you think they are acceptable.

1. Mr. Wilder is a self-made man. Having worked hard all his life and accomplished a great deal.

2. Let me help you. Since I happen to be here.

3. Knowing that she should apologize for her rudeness but lacking courage to face him after what she had said.

4. Chester is not planning to attend the dance. Because of financial difficulties.

5. Being deeply indebted to his godfather, Horace decided to give him a present. A wrist watch. Which would have permanent value. Hoping very much that his godfather would be pleased.

6. Rain on the windows. Rain sluicing down the street. The world was dismal with rain.

7. To my surprise, I received a C. Thus doing better than Albert.

8. Whether it was good or bad he didn't know. But at least it was over now. Settled, once and for all.

9. Would the Dean believe that the car had really broken down? Probably not.

10. Although eager to go, uncertain about what awaited me when I got there.

11. He came at nine. When I had given up hope.

12. Dorothea made a poor impression. In every way.

13. I missed the test. As a result of being ten minutes late to class.

14. Some columnists should be jailed for libel. Charles B. Muddle, for example.

15. I hope to be elected to Phi Beta Kappa. Chiefly to please my parents.

16. He was happily married, he enjoyed his work, he had high hopes for the future. Then the sudden disaster.

17. Though reading the material several times, still not comprehending it as well as I should.

18. Van studies till twelve-thirty every night. Being the studious type.

19. Jim spent all his money in Miami. Easy come, easy go.

20. The heat shimmered up from the pavement. Shimmered from the low buildings and the parked cars.

II. Read the passage below, with particular attention to the incomplete sentences. Why do you think the author chose to use them? What would be the effect on the passage of adding verbs to make the sentences grammatically complete?

Fog everywhere. Fog up the river, where it flows among green aits and meadows; fog down the river, where it rolls defiled among the tiers of shipping, and the waterside pollutions of a great (and dirty) city. Fog on the Essex marshes, fog on the Kentish heights. Fog creeping into the cabooses of collier-brigs, fog lying out on the yards, and hovering in the rigging of great ships; fog drooping on the gunwales of barges and small boats. Fog in the eyes and throats of ancient Greenwich pensioners, wheezing by the firesides of their wards; fog in the stem and bowl of the afternoon pipe of the wrathful skipper, down in his close cabin; fog cruelly pinching the toes and fingers of his shivering little 'prentice boy on deck. Chance people on the bridges peeping over the parapets into a nether sky of fog, with fog all round them, as if they were up in a balloon, and hanging in the misty clouds.

Gas looming through the fog in divers places in the streets, much as the sun may, from the spongy fields, be seen to loom by husbandman and ploughboy. Most of the shops lighted two hours before their time—as the gas seems to know, for it has a haggard and unwilling look.

The raw afternoon is rawest, and the dense fog is densest, and the muddy streets are muddiest, near that leaden-headed old obstruction, appropriate ornament for the threshold of a leaden-headed old corporation: Temple Bar. And hard by Temple Bar, in Lincoln's Inn Hall, at the very heart of the fog, sits the Lord High Chancellor in his High Court of Chancery.—CHARLES DICKENS, *Bleak House*

15. FUSED AND RUN-TOGETHER SENTENCES   CF, Run

a. A fused sentence is produced when two independent clauses NOT joined by a pure conjunction[6] are incorrectly written with no punctuation between them.

> The decision is difficult to refuse to help seems selfish. [The two independent clauses—*the . . . difficult* and *to refuse . . . selfish*—are said to be fused because there is no punctuation between them.]

b. A run-together sentence (or comma fault) is produced when two independent clauses NOT joined by a pure conjunction are unconventionally written with only a comma between them.

> The decision is difficult, to refuse to help seems selfish. [Here the same two independent clauses are said to be run together because the comma is used where a heavier mark is needed.]

Fused and run-together sentences, sometimes the result of careless punctuation, are more often the result of the writer's not recognizing independent clauses or not knowing how a sequence of two independent clauses is conventionally written and punctuated. When the clauses are felt to be closely related, the relationship may be expressed in the following ways:

(1) For emphasis, the clauses may be written as independent sentences.

They want to spend the summer in Michigan. I want to stay here.

(2) The clauses may be joined by a pure conjunction, or by a pure conjunction plus a comma.

They want to spend the summer in Michigan, but I want to stay here.

(3) The clauses may be written without a pure conjunction and separated by a semicolon.

They want to spend the summer in Michigan; I want to stay here.

---

6 *And, but, for, or,* and *nor* are the most common pure conjunctions. *So* and *yet* may also be used as pure conjunctions.

(4) The clauses may be linked by a conjunctive adverb (*however, therefore, nevertheless, consequently,* etc.) and separated by a semicolon, or written as two sentences. A comma in place of the semicolon or period would produce a run-together sentence.

> The plan merits serious consideration; therefore it would be unwise to vote on it at this meeting.
> The prospects for the early passage of the bill are not good. Senator Wylie, however, is still hopeful.

A general rule that will help students avoid both fused and run-together sentences is: Between two independent clauses in the same sentence not joined by *and, but, for, or,* or *nor,* use a semicolon.[7]

Fused sentences are likely to produce at least momentary confusion for the reader, and they are an annoyance: the reader is forced to make the separation of ideas that the writer should have made for him. Run-together sentences, too, can be annoying and confusing, particularly when modifiers intervene between the two clauses. The following run-together sentences will illustrate:

> Their parents have consented, according to rumor, they will soon be married. [One cannot tell which of the two statements is a matter of rumor. A semicolon should be used in place of one of the commas.]
> The party started late and lasted till dawn, therefore, the guests talked about it for weeks. [Does *therefore* belong logically with the first clause or with the second? One of the commas should be a semicolon.]
> They quarreled bitterly, late that night, he called to apologize. [A semicolon should be used after *bitterly* or after *night* to indicate whether the quarrel or the apology occurred late that night.]
> He was tired, after his winter of work, he decided to take a vacation. [A semicolon is needed after *tired* or after *work* to show with which clause the phrase belongs.]

Although fused and run-together sentences can sometimes be made satisfactory simply by putting a semicolon or a period between the independent clauses, often this change in punctuation is only a superficial technical improvement. For an effective sentence, an essentially weak structure needs to be revised.

> RUN-TOGETHER: I make many mistakes in writing, most of them are in spelling and punctuation.
> TECHNICALLY IMPROVED: I make many mistakes in writing; most of them are in spelling and punctuation.

---

[7] In a series of *more* than two parallel independent clauses in a sentence, commas are generally used: *Martha is bringing sandwiches, Sue is bringing salad, and Gina is bringing cake.*

REVISED: I make many mistakes in writing, most of them in spelling and punctuation.

FUSED: Jim has a good job he has had it since July.
TECHNICALLY IMPROVED: Jim has a good job; he has had it since July.
REVISED: Jim has had a good job since July.

c. Run-together sentences may be used in special situations.

In informal English, when the clauses are short and closely related and there is no danger of misreading, sentences are sometimes run together:

Jack likes him, I don't.

In modern narrative writing, too, one not infrequently finds closely related main clauses deliberately run together to give an effect of rapid movement, breathless action, or concurrent impressions or events. The following informal passages, each written by a careful modern craftsman, will illustrate:

A few frogs lost their heads and floundered among the feet and got through and these were saved. But the majority decided to leave this pool forever, to find a new home in a new country where this kind of thing didn't happen. A wave of frantic, frustrated frogs, big ones, little ones, brown ones, green ones, men frogs and women frogs, a wave of them broke over the bank, crawled, leaped, scrambled. *They clambered up the grass, they clutched at each other, little ones rode on big ones.* And then —horror on horror—the flashlights found them.—JOHN STEINBECK, *Cannery Row*

At first the Thompsons liked it [a tune repeatedly played on a harmonica] very much, and always stopped to listen. Later there came a time when they were fairly sick of it, and began to wish to each other that he would learn a new one. *At last they did not hear it any more, it was as natural as the sound of the wind rising in the evenings,* or the cows lowing, or their own voices.—KATHERINE ANNE PORTER, "Noon Wine"

In the passage below, from an essay, the author effectively runs together independent clauses to give the impression of quick anxieties crowding the mind of the biographer:

Unfortunately for the biographer, readers will not suffer lengthy quotations. At sight of set-in paragraphs, readers flee; *they are gone, lost, the book is closed.* The thought was awful to me. *I must devise ways, I must lend a hand to my readers.* . . .
—CATHERINE DRINKER BOWEN, "The Business of a Biographer"

The inexperienced writer should remember, however, that run-together sentences have no place in formal writing, that they are still widely objected to even in informal writing, and that they may be unclear. If the student wishes to use run-together sentences in informal narrative, he should probably, as with incomplete sentences, star the passage and indicate to his instructor in a footnote that his punctuation is deliberate. Students who are unsure should avoid this experimental punctuation.

EXERCISES

Correct the punctuation in the following fused and run-together sentences, and revise any sentences that would be improved by further revision.

1. Jane is a good friend when she makes a promise she always keeps it.
2. He is trustworthy, as far as I know, he has never been in trouble.
3. Today is the thirteenth of April this is my sister's birthday.
4. Mark came today to visit Steve was something he had wanted to do for a long time.
5. He is a Communist sympathizer, a man formerly associated with the Party testified to this before the committee.
6. He admired her courage above all the rest of her good qualities seemed secondary to this one.
7. I did not answer when he questioned me he eyed me suspiciously.
8. We knew what he had done, what he had intended, we did not know.
9. The boys walked slowly along the road the grass was burned.
10. This is the time of year when spring seems far away, when will winter end, we wonder.
11. He had traveled widely in this country, Latin America, and Canada, he had many friends in every part of the continent.
12. Tony has won his letter in football he is the only sophomore who has played in every game.
13. My father and grandfather were lawyers, therefore I have always been interested in law, I intend to make it my profession.
14. Ralph broke a date with Georgia last Saturday, consequently she is not speaking to him, although he has called her every night this week.
15. The international situation is not hopeless, on the contrary it seems much brighter than it did a month ago, and I have renewed faith in the United Nations.
16. He was born in 1887. He is eighty-five years old therefore he walks very slowly.
17. She told him she never wanted to see him again, moreover, she was exasperated that he even suggested a date.
18. My math teacher gave only two A's I think this is unfair.
19. John said he was resigning from the Student Council, he announced this yesterday.
20. The English book has a rule about using semicolons, in sentences like this, one can just as well use commas however, I can try it the other way.

16. MODIFIERS   DM, Mod

Modifiers should, for clarity, be close to the locution they modify, and should be so placed that they cannot appear to modify the wrong locution.

a. A modifier is called dangling when the word it logically modifies has been left out of the sentence.

(1) Dangling phrases.

DANGLING: Walking up the path, a stone lion stood in front of the museum. [According to the sentence, the lion walked up the path; the actual walker has been left out of the sentence.]

REVISED: Walking up the path, we saw a stone lion standing in front of the museum.

DANGLING: After opening the oven door, the chicken cooked more slowly. [The chicken did not open the oven door.]

REVISED: After I opened the oven door, the chicken cooked more slowly.

DANGLING: There was the village green, driving through the town.

REVISED: We saw the village green as we drove through the town.

Sentences containing dangling phrases are corrected by inserting the word that the phrase should modify (Walking up the path, *we* saw . . .), or by changing the phrase to a clause that has as its subject the real doer of the action (After *I* opened the oven door . . .).

(2) Dangling elliptical clauses. A dangling elliptical clause may be corrected by adding the words omitted in the incomplete clause.

DANGLING: When eight years old, my father was very severe about my smoking. [Since the person who was eight years old has been left out of the sentence, *When eight years old* appears to modify *my father*.]

REVISED: When I was eight years old, my father was very severe about my smoking.

DANGLING: While writing a letter to his brother, a pigeon flew into the room.

REVISED: While Jim was writing a letter to his brother, a pigeon flew into the room.

(3) Dangling infinitives.

DANGLING: To avoid eye strain, the lamp should have a hundred-watt bulb.

REVISED: To avoid eye strain, you should have a hundred-watt bulb in your lamp.

DANGLING: To enjoy television, the television room must be well planned.

REVISED: To enjoy television, one must have a well-planned television room.

b. A modifier is called misplaced when its position is such that it appears to modify the wrong word.

(1) Misplaced adverbs.

MISPLACED: He nearly wrote all of his term paper yesterday.

REVISED: He wrote nearly all of his term paper yesterday.

MISPLACED: He needed someone to help him review the material badly.

REVISED: He badly needed someone to help him review the material.

(2) Misplaced phrases.

MISPLACED: I saw a church as I walked up the hill with a white steeple.
REVISED: I saw a church with a white steeple as I walked up the hill.

MISPLACED: Snarling in anger, I saw the dog as I came into the yard.
REVISED: I saw the dog snarling in anger as I came into the yard.

(3) Misplaced clauses.

MISPLACED: I had an unhappy experience in my first year of high school which I shall never forget.
REVISED: In my first year of high school I had an unhappy experience which I shall never forget.

MISPLACED: He sat smoking his pipe on the front porch that he had just lighted.
REVISED: He sat on the front porch, smoking the pipe he had just lighted.

(4) Ambiguous modifiers.

AMBIGUOUS: When John applied for the position on the advice of his roommate he dressed very carefully. [The phrase *on the advice of his roommate* is a "squinting modifier"; its position is such that it may modify either the preceding or the following words.]
REVISED: On the advice of his roommate, John dressed very carefully when he applied for the position. [*Or*] When John, on the advice of his roommate, applied for the position, he dressed very carefully.

AMBIGUOUS: He said after the election he would take a vacation.
REVISED: After the election, he said he would take a vacation. [*Or*] He said that he would take a vacation after the election.

EXERCISES

Point out any dangling, misplaced, or ambiguous modifiers in the following sentences and revise any sentences that need revision.

1. Curled up on the sofa, the cat purred comfortably.
2. John almost shoveled all the snow from the walks and driveway.
3. When covered with syrup, you will enjoy a tasty dish.
4. She was a tall woman with black hair and a friendly smile about thirty years old.
5. After staying at home for three days, my cold was better.
6. The house was set in a pine grove with a beautiful view and blue shutters.
7. While quietly studying, the doorbell disturbed Jane.
8. After preparing for an evening alone, I heard him come in with annoyance.
9. The teacher called on Bryan to recite for the fourth time.
10. She looked at Oscar when he came in with a vacant stare, then started to play the piano again.
11. Horace found the material which the other members of the class had been unable to find in the public library.

12. After finishing high school, my father thought I should work for a year before coming to college.

13. Eleanor was criticized for taking a stand publicly against the decision of the student council by her sorority sisters.

14. I decided we should leave when the clock struck twelve.

17. FAULTY RELATIONSHIPS OF SENTENCE ELEMENTS   Cst

Most of this section is a review of faulty relationships, or constructions, discussed in other parts of the book. When a faulty relationship is treated fully elsewhere, we shall illustrate it briefly and give a reference to the fuller treatment.

a. Faulty agreement of subject and verb, or of pronoun and antecedent.

FAULTY: My *study* of history and French *have* heightened my desire to go to Paris.
REVISED: My *study* of history and *French has* heightened my desire to go to Paris.

FAULTY: The *students which* demonstrated last night are seeing the Dean today.
REVISED: The *students who* demonstrated last night are seeing the Dean today.

See "Verbs: Agreement," page 385, and "Pronouns: Agreement," page 372.

b. Faulty parallelism.

NON-PARALLEL: He objected *to the food* and *that the dining room was noisy.*
REVISED: He objected *to the food* and *to the noise* in the dining room.

See "Parallelism," page 425, and "Compound Structures and Parallelism," page 100.

c. Misrelated modifiers.

MISRELATED: *Writing my term paper* last night, *a bat* flew into the room.
REVISED: *When I was writing* my term paper last night, a bat flew into the room.

MISRELATED: The man who is riding the grey *horse with a cigar* is Major Banting.
REVISED: The *man with a cigar* who is riding the grey horse is Major Banting.

See "Modifiers," page 410, and "Modifiers and Appositive Structures," page 102.

d. Poorly related clauses.

LOOSELY RELATED: Ann was determined to appear in the play, *and* she had a sore throat.
REVISED: *Although* she had a sore throat, Ann was determined to appear in the play.

AMBIGUOUSLY RELATED: *As* I was only a few miles from St. Louis, I decided to call Henry.

REVISED: *When* I was only a few miles from St. Louis, I decided to call Henry. [*Or*] *Since* I was only a few miles from St. Louis, I decided to call Henry.

See "Subordination," page 105 and page 426, and "Connectives," page 398.

e. Faulty complements.

Faulty complements occur when an adverb instead of an adjective is used after a linking verb, when the noun-complement of a linking verb is not logically the equivalent of the subject, and when a pronoun-complement does not agree with the subject.

FAULTY: The garden smells *fragrantly* after the rain.
REVISED: The garden smells *fragrant* after the rain.

FAULTY: Integrity is *where one lives up to his principles.*
REVISED: Integrity is *living up to one's principles.*

FAULTY: My greatest difficulty in writing is *when I have to find a subject.*
REVISED: My greatest difficulty in writing is *finding a subject.*

FAULTY IN FORMAL USAGE: If I were *him,* I should act differently.
REVISED: If I were *he,* I should act differently.

See "Verbs and Complements," page 380.

f. Unnecessary and awkward shifts in subject, or in voice, mood, or tense of verbs.

SHIFT IN SUBJECT AND IN VOICE: When Jane went for the mail, a letter from home was found.
REVISED: When Jane went for the mail, she found a letter from home.

SHIFT IN VOICE AND IN MOOD: First sandpaper the surface carefully; then the varnish should be put on.
REVISED: First sandpaper the surface carefully; then put the varnish on.

See "Consistency," page 108, "Verbs: Voice and Mood," page 389, and "Verbs: Tense," page 391.

g. Inconsistency in style or usage.

SHIFT FROM PERSONAL TO IMPERSONAL STYLE: If you are diligent, you will do well; one must remember that college is primarily for study.
REVISED: If you are diligent, you will do well; you must remember that college is primarily for study.

SHIFT IN USAGE: Mrs. Grantham sought revenge by fouling up her rival's debut.
REVISED: Mrs. Grantham sought revenge by ruining her rival's debut.

See "Consistency," page 108.

h. Awkward separation of sentence elements.

Frequently, and appropriately, modifiers separate a subject and verb, a verb and its object or complement, or the parts of a verb phrase. For example, sentence elements are satisfactorily separated in the sentence: "The *secretary,* it appears, *is* deliberately *withholding* vital *information.*" Awkward separation of elements is needless separation that breaks the continuity and natural rhythm of the sentence.

AWKWARD: Jane had, after a long period of unrest, uncertainty, and anxiety, decided to go.

REVISED: After a long period of unrest, uncertainty, and anxiety, Jane had decided to go.

AWKWARD: John went to see, when the swelling and the pain in his ankle increased, the doctor.

REVISED: When the swelling and the pain in his ankle increased, John went to see the doctor.

i. Incomplete constructions.

Incomplete constructions occur when words that are grammatically necessary to complete the construction or the sense of the sentence are omitted.

INCOMPLETE: I write to my closest friends *with whom* I have much in common and *know me* as I am.

REVISED: I write to my closest friends *who know me* as I am and with whom I have much in common.

INCOMPLETE: He both *hopes* and fears *the time of* his graduation from college.

REVISED: He both *hopes for* and *fears the time of* his graduation from college. [*Or*] He looks forward with both hope and fear to his graduation from college.

INCOMPLETE: Girls are more interested in clothes *than horses.* [The sentence might be understood to mean "more interested in clothes *than horses are.*"]

REVISED: Girls are more interested in clothes *than in horses.*

INCOMPLETE: Herbert did better on the examination than *any member* of the class. [The sentence suggests that Herbert is not a member of the class. If he is, the sentence is incomplete.]

REVISED: Herbert did better on the examination than *any other member* of the class.

One kind of incomplete construction is used commonly, particularly in speech, and is considered standard English:

John was *as tall* if not taller *than his brother.*

Most teachers will want their students to complete the construction in writing:

John was *as tall as* if not taller than *his brother.* [*Or,* for a less awkward sentence] John is at least as tall as his brother.

j. Illogical constructions.

Illogical constructions occur when two things not of the same kind or construction are compared or placed in apposition.

ILLOGICAL: I like this *teacher* better than *any course* I have had.
LOGICAL: I like this teacher better than any I have had. [*Or*] I like this course better than any I have had.

ILLOGICAL: *Like most novels of Dickens, the heroine* is a generous, unsophisticated girl.
LOGICAL: This girl, like most of Dickens' heroines, is generous and unsophisticated.

ILLOGICAL: Robert's *ears are large, like his father*.
LOGICAL: Robert has large ears like his father's. [*Or*] Robert, like his father, has large ears.

ILLOGICAL: I read Carl Becker's *Modern Democracy, an historian* I greatly admire.
LOGICAL: I read *Modern Democracy* by Carl Becker, an historian I greatly admire.

k. Mixed constructions.

Mixed constructions occur when the writer carelessly fuses two different constructions.

MIXED: John's ambition is to be a lawyer and is working industriously to achieve his goal.
REVISED: John's ambition is to be a lawyer; he is working industriously to achieve his goal.

MIXED: When the chapel bell rang five times was the signal for a fire drill.
REVISED: When the chapel bell rang five times, we prepared for a fire drill. [*Or*] Five rings of the chapel bell signaled a fire drill.

EXERCISES

Revise any of the following sentences that need revision, to eliminate shifted, incomplete, and illogical constructions, and other faulty relationships of sentence elements.

1. The proposal of the students was more radical than the faculty.
2. I use my limited vocabulary as an excuse for my poor writing, though being inexcusable.
3. He was a short, bald-headed man who always looks as though he had slept in his clothes.
4. In making up an advertisement, one must be skillful, have a thorough knowledge of the product, well trained, and experienced.
5. You need more than a knowledge of the game to be a golf caddy; one must also be a student of human nature.
6. I like Audrey's perfume; she smells well.
7. If I were him, I would not change all the plans and they already made.
8. The buyer of a second-hand car should be able to recognize certain signs of

hard use; look, for example, at the floor pads and brake pedal and having in mind the condition of the springs.

9. Riding down the street, a dog ran in front of the car.

10. The grass was uncut and the blinds closed.

11. The man that is leading the dog in the leather jacket is my neighbor.

12. I am disgusted with the people he associates.

13. Joan finally, not to drag out the story too long and include every detail, decided to stay in school.

14. Robert has studied French for six years, where Martha has no knowledge of the language and not desiring to.

15. Professor Brown said in the office the papers were ready for us.

16. My reasons for writing on a topic other than the topic assigned is it did not interest me, thus making it difficult.

17. I like apples better than any fruit.

18. Tom is over at Jane's house who is his cousin.

19. After the excitement was all over was when we got there.

20. Jack thinks he will not be involved or even connected with the accident.

21. I never have and I still do not understand what a restrictive modifier is.

22. Hilary went to the headmaster for information was just what he needed to know.

23. Unlike most poetry, Robert Frost is not difficult to understand.

24. The teacher-student relationship in college is more impersonal than high school.

25. Like many other students, success in medicine is my ambition.

HANDBOOK

Section 3

STYLE AND RHETORIC: SUMMARY AND REVIEW

18. CHOICE OF WORDS   WW, Ch, Exp

The symbol **WW** (wrong word) in the margin of a theme generally means that the writer has used a nonexistent word or expression ("undoubtably"); has used a word ungrammatically ("The pipes bursted"); has fallen into inappropriate usage ("The situation was thoroughly fouled up"); has mistaken the meaning of a word ("He made no direct illusion to Russia in the speech"); or has used a word or expression loosely and inexactly ("He gave many causes for his choice"). The student should look up in the dictionary any word marked **WW**; should (if he finds it) determine its meaning and possibly its status; and should substitute in his theme a more exact or more appropriate word or expression.

Skill in the choice of words is a complex skill. The writer should:

a. Avoid padding, jargon, and vague, awkward, ill-phrased, or trite expressions.

b. Choose appropriate usage.

c. Use exact, concrete words, wherever possible, in place of abstract words (*red barn* instead of "building").

d. Use exact names (*lectern* instead of "little stand on the desk").

e. Use strong, working words (The siren *screamed* instead of "made a noise like a scream").

f. Choose words with exact connotations (She was *slender and lovely* instead of "skinny and lovely").

g. Be unsatisfied until the precise word or expression is found to convey the meaning intended.

For further discussion of choice of words or expressions, see Chapter 2, "Appropriate English"; "Exact Words" and "Concrete Expression" in Chapter 5; "Choosing Words That Work," page 121; and the discussion of "foggy" expression, pages 88–89.

19. COHERENCE   Coh

Coherence in writing is produced by logical order and clear connections between parts of the material.

The following passages illustrate a lack of coherence produced by faulty arrangement of material:

POOR IN COHERENCE: We did our best to explain what had happened, to John and Carol, having arrived two hours late at the dance because we had mistaken the time.

IMPROVED: When, having mistaken the time, we arrived two hours late at the dance, we did our best to explain to John and Carol.

POOR IN COHERENCE: When I met him again, he appeared to have changed his mind. This was four days later, and was in the morning.

IMPROVED: When I met him one morning four days later, he appeared to have changed his mind.

Failure to make clear connections between ideas produces incoherence in the following passages:

POOR IN COHERENCE: Her uncle was not comforted and she left. She would go the next day.

IMPROVED: Since she could do nothing to comfort her uncle, she left, promising to return the next day.

POOR IN COHERENCE: He was successful for three reasons. He sold a vitamin compound and he believed it was a good product. He was sincere in this. He was a good talker and could convince anyone on any matter and besides he liked people.

IMPROVED: He was successful for three reasons: he sincerely believed in the vitamin compound he was selling; he talked convincingly; and he liked people.

For further information related to coherence, see "Modifiers," page 410; "Faulty Relationships of Sentence Elements," page 413; "Parallelism," page 425; "Subordination," page 426; "Transitions," page 428; and "Unity and Focus," page 428. Coherence in paragraphs is discussed in Chapter 6.

20. CONCRETENESS   Abst

Concrete words are words referring to objects which have existence in the physical world, on the nature and meaning of which, therefore, people can to a considerable extent agree. Although abstract words (**Abst**) are necessary in discussing general concepts and conditions, concrete words are preferable, whenever they can appropriately be used, because they convey more exact factual and attitudinal meaning. For a full discussion of concreteness, see the section "Concrete Expression" in Chapter 5.

a. Concrete expression is achieved by substituting concrete words for abstract words.

ABSTRACT: The flowers were different colors.
CONCRETE: The chrysanthemums were bronze, yellow, and white.

b. Concrete expression is achieved by expanding general statements with concrete particulars and examples.

ABSTRACT: He is a good citizen.
CONCRETE: He is a good citizen. He has agreed to take charge of the Community Fund drive, and he has been chairman of the School Committee for three years.

c. Concrete expression is achieved by using concrete comparisons and figures of speech.

ABSTRACT: The length of time organic life has existed on earth is almost inconceivable.
CONCRETE COMPARISON: In order to understand the process of organic evolution, let us imagine a cord stretched from New York to Boston, each yard of which represents 10,000 years . . . .

ABSTRACT: People cannot live isolated from other human beings.
CONCRETE FIGURE OF SPEECH: No man is an island, entire of itself; every man is a piece of the continent, a part of the main . . . .

21. ECONOMY   Econ

For a full discussion of economy, see the section "Economy and Conciseness" in Chapter 5.

a. Economy is achieved by avoiding padding and jargon.

(1) *Padding* is a term for words and phrases that add nothing but length to a sentence.

PADDING: There are a large number of college students who find it difficult to do their work punctually on time, with the resulting effect that they receive poor marks which do not make them happy.

IMPROVED: Many college students find it difficult to do their work punctually; they receive poor marks as a result.

(2) *Jargon* is a term for verbose, "heavy" language.

JARGON: Ultimately I ascended the incline to view the conflagration.

IMPROVED: Finally I went up the hill to see the fire.

b. Economy is achieved by cutting weak clauses to phrases or to single words.

WORDY: Mr. Brown, who was my chemistry teacher, had a classroom manner which was very interesting.

IMPROVED BY CUTTING CLAUSES: Mr. Brown, my chemistry teacher, had a very interesting classroom manner.

c. Economy is achieved by the substitution of exact words for longer locutions.

WORDY AND INEXACT: She planted some bulbs of those little yellow and purple flowers that bloom early in the spring.

CONCISE: She planted some crocus bulbs.

WORDY: He looked at her with an expression of great displeasure and hostility on his face.

CONCISE: He scowled at her.

d. Concrete detail and repetition for emphasis should not be confused with wordiness.

BRIEF BUT UNINFORMATIVE: She seemed upset.

IMPROVED BY ADDITIONAL DETAIL: She talked rapidly, her eyes darting from his face to the handkerchief she was twisting in her hands. In the middle of a sentence she got up and left the room.

22. EMPHASIS   Emph

For a fuller discussion of emphasis, see the section "Emphasis" in Chapter 5, and the section "Emphasis in Paragraphs" in Chapter 6.

a. Emphasis is achieved by proportion.

In the whole composition, main ideas are emphasized by fuller development than is accorded less significant ideas.

b. Emphasis is achieved by pause.

Pauses created by chapter divisions, paragraph breaks, and marks of punctuation throw emphasis on the material immediately preceding and following the pause.

LESS EMPHATIC: At first I did not know what was required of me, but I know now.

MORE EMPHATIC: At first I did not know what was required of me. I know now.

c. Emphasis is achieved by position.

The beginning and end of a composition, a paragraph, and a sentence are the positions of greatest emphasis. They should be used to stress the important ideas.

UNEMPHATIC SENTENCE BEGINNING: There was a writer named Matthew Arnold who influenced my thinking.

MORE EMPHATIC: Matthew Arnold was a writer who influenced my thinking.

UNEMPHATIC SENTENCE ENDING: The situation is critical, I believe.

MORE EMPHATIC: The situation is, I believe, critical.

d. Emphasis is achieved by skillful repetition.

"This great Nation *will endure* as it has *endured, will* survive and *will* prosper. So, first of all, let me assert my firm belief that the only thing we have to *fear* is *fear* itself. . . ."

e. Emphasis is destroyed by:

(1) Thoughtlessly repeated sentence patterns.

(2) Improper subordination that gives stress to ideas not worth emphasizing.

(3) Overuse of the passive voice.

(4) Triteness.

(5) Padding, jargon, weak clauses, and circumlocutions.

(6) Euphemisms overused or inappropriately used.

(7) Abstract words thoughtlessly used.

f. Skillful writers do not rely for emphasis on mechanical devices like exclamation points, underlining, capitalization, and the use of intensives.

POOR DEVICES FOR EMPHASIS: It happened *so suddenly!* I was a victim of Fate. *What* was I to do in these ghastly circumstances?

23. FIGURATIVE LANGUAGE   Fig

In figurative language, words are used non-literally. The basis of most figurative language is comparison or association of two ordinarily separate things or ideas.

a. The most common figures of speech are:

(1) *Simile:* a non-literal comparison, usually introduced by *like* or *as,* of two things unlike in most respects but similar in others.

He shall come down *like rain upon the mown grass.*

(2) *Metaphor:* an implied non-literal comparison.

I am the *captain of my soul.*
The fog comes *on little cat feet.*
With *rue my heart is laden* for *golden* friends I've had.
A *dusty* answer.

(3) *Analogy:* a sustained comparison of two ideas or situations.

(4) *Metonymy:* a form of comparison in which an exact name for something is replaced by a term closely associated with it.

crown [for king], *sail* [for ship], *The kettle is boiling* [for The water in the kettle is boiling; or for The situation is coming to a head].

(5) *Personification:* a form of metaphor infrequently used in modern writing, which attributes human qualities to objects or ideas.

With how sad steps, O Moon, thou climb'st the skies!
How silently, and with how wan a face.

Duty commanded and he obeyed.

b. Appropriate figurative language serves to make expression concrete and vivid. (For illustrations, see "Concrete Expression" in Chapter 5.)

c. Trite figures of speech should be avoided.

Trite similes: *pretty as a picture, happy as a lark, fresh as a daisy.*
Trite metaphors: *budding genius, crack of dawn, lap of luxury.*
Trite personifications: *Father Time, Mother Nature.*

d. Mixed, or awkwardly combined, figures of speech should be avoided.

The *odor* of magnolias *shouted* a welcome.
In the argument he *brought his big guns* into play and *stifled* his opponent.
While he was courageously *battling* his way *through the sea of life, fate stepped in and tripped him up.*

e. Strained and inappropriate figures of speech should be avoided.

Trees were dressed in their best bibs and tuckers preparing for their farewell-to-summer ball.
Her smile was as warm as an electric heater.

24. GOOD PARAGRAPHS   ¶

For a full discussion of paragraphs, see Chapter 6.

a. A good paragraph in expository writing usually has a clear topic sentence or topic idea, which gives unity to the paragraph.

b. A good paragraph has coherent arrangement of material and clear transitions between sentences. (See "Transitions," page 428.)

c. Good paragraphs begin and end strongly.

d. Paragraphs in a paper should be linked to one another by transitions that make the organization evident to the reader. (See "Transitions," page 428.)

e. As a rough guide to paragraph length, the student should bear in mind that paragraphs in expository writing rarely exceed 300 words and rarely fall below 100.

f. Good paragraphs are usually concrete and fully developed.

g. Eight ways of organizing paragraphs, often used in combination, are:

    (1) chronological arrangement
    (2) general-to-particular or particular-to-general arrangement
    (3) analysis
    (4) contrast and comparison
    (5) definition
    (6) cause and effect
    (7) reasons
    (8) question to answer or problem to solution

h. The first and last paragraphs in a paper occupy positions of greatest emphasis, and should be written with particular care.

25. INTEREST   Int

Since human beings are interested in very different things, the techniques of being interesting differ with audience and circumstances. Student writing is likely to be most interesting when the student chooses a subject in which he himself is interested, and when he writes with the needs and interests of an audience in mind. He will then ask himself such questions as: What is my audience probably interested in? How much information about this topic do they probably have? At what points might they be puzzled and lose interest unless I explain more fully? How can I cause them to share my interest in this material?

One answer to the last question is: Be concrete. Use words, facts, examples, concrete comparisons, and details to stir the mind and senses of the audience and enable them to share the writer's knowledge and experience.

If passages in a composition are marked **int** (lacking in interest), the writer should examine them to see if the ideas are abstract and underdeveloped—if he has failed to set down on paper the concrete particulars needed to make the material interesting. It is also possible that the writing lacks interest because the writer is stating the obvious, because he is giving evidence of no real thought about the subject, or because his sentences are monotonously unvaried.

See "Writing for a Reader," page 85, "Concrete Expression" and "Variety in Sentences" in Chapter 5, and "Adjusting Material and Style to an Audience," page 259.

26. LEVELS OF USAGE   Lev

The term *levels of usage* refers to varieties of English: the differences in construction, pronunciation, and vocabulary produced by differences in education and in economic and social circumstances. For a full discussion of nonstandard English and of the three main varieties of standard English—formal English, informal English, and colloquial English—see Chapter 2, "Appropriate English."

a. Usage (formal, informal, or colloquial) should be appropriate to the subject, the audience, and the occasion.

b. Unless there is a positive gain in a shift, usage should be consistent in a passage or a composition.

c. Students should aim at high informal English in most of their writing.

d. In high informal writing, slang is usually out of place.

e. "Heavy" words, over-formal and pretentious for their context, should be avoided.

27. PARALLELISM   Par, ‖

Parallelism is the principle of usage which requires that coordinate elements in a compound construction be given the same grammatical form. Words, phrases, clauses, and even sentences may be put in parallel form. For a fuller discussion of parallelism, see "Compound Structures and Parallelism" in Chapter 4.

a. Faulty parallelism occurs when logically coordinate elements are not expressed in parallel form.

FAULTY: He is afraid to live and of death.
PARALLEL: He is afraid to live and to die. [*Or*] He is afraid of life and of death.

FAULTY: The mayor promised that he would build new sidewalks, provide new equipment for the schools, and reducing the taxes.
PARALLEL: The mayor promised that he would build new sidewalks, provide new equipment for the schools, and reduce the taxes. [Three verbs.] [*Or*] The mayor promised to build new sidewalks, to provide new equipment for the schools, and to reduce the taxes. [Three infinitives.] [*Or*] The mayor promised new sidewalks, new equipment for the schools, and reduced taxes. [Three nouns.]

b. Faulty parallelism occurs when elements not logically coordinate are expressed in parallel form.

FAULTY: He is tall, thin, and a Sigma Chi.
LOGICAL: He is a tall, thin Sigma Chi.

FAULTY: The teacher said Maynard was lazy, careless, and had better get to work.
LOGICAL: The teacher said that Maynard was lazy and careless, and that he had better get to work.

28. REPETITION   Rep

For a fuller discussion of awkward repetition see pages 137–138. For a fuller discussion of skillful repetition see pages 149–150.

a. Awkward and unnecessary repetition of words and sounds should be avoided.

AWKWARD: The *fact* is, I *do* my best *writing* when *doing factual writing*.
IMPROVED: I write best when I deal with facts.

AWKWARD: The *shipper* checks the *merchandise* which has been *shipped* in, then the *shipper* puts the *merchandise* into stock.
IMPROVED: The shipper checks the merchandise as it comes in and then puts it into stock.

b. Skillful repetition is an element of style, used for clarity and emphasis.

The only thing we have to *fear* is *fear* itself . . .
We shall fight on the beaches, *we shall fight* on the landing grounds, *we shall fight* in the fields and in the streets, *we shall fight* in the hills . . .

29. SUBORDINATION   Sub

Subordination means expressing in dependent clauses, or phrases, or single words, ideas not important enough to be expressed in main clauses or independent sentences.

For a fuller discussion of subordination, see "Subordination" in Chapter 4, and "Cutting Clauses," page 119.

a. Subordination is used to avoid:

(1) Choppy "primer" sentences:

CHOPPY: I have a teacher named Mr. Mulch. He teaches biology. He is very strict.
IMPROVED BY SUBORDINATION: Mr. Mulch, my biology teacher, is very strict.

(2) Sprawling "and-and" sentences:

SPRAWLING: The bell rings and he comes into class, and he takes attendance.
IMPROVED BY SUBORDINATION: As soon as the bell rings, he comes into class and takes attendance.

b. When subordination is used effectively, less important ideas are usually placed in subordinate constructions, and important ideas are expressed emphatically in independent clauses.

LACK OF SUBORDINATION (equal emphasis to ideas not equally significant): I was stepping off the curb and the truck hit me.
UPSIDE-DOWN SUBORDINATION: (emphasis on the less significant idea): When the truck hit me, I was stepping off the curb.
PROPER EMPHASIS ON THE MORE SIGNIFICANT IDEA: As I was stepping off the curb, the truck hit me.

c. An awkward series of subordinate clauses in a sentence should be avoided.

AWKWARD: He is the man who has bought the Nelsons' house for which he paid twenty thousand dollars which he borrowed from his brother-in-law.
IMPROVED: He borrowed twenty thousand dollars from his brother-in-law to buy the Nelsons' house.

d. Subordinating conjunctions should be grammatically correct and should express clearly the relationship between ideas.

POOR: He doesn't know *as* he can take the courses he wants.
REVISED: He doesn't know *that* (or *whether*) he can take the courses he wants.

POOR: *Whereas* Edward needs money, he is looking for a part-time job.
REVISED: *Because* Edward needs money, he is looking for a part-time job.

POOR: I read in the book *where* paragraphs should have topic sentences.
REVISED: I read in the book *that* paragraphs should have topic sentences.

For further discussion of the use of connectives, see "Connectives," page 398.

30. TONE

Tone is the manner of verbal expression that a speaker or writer adopts. It reveals his attitudes, chiefly attitudes toward his audience and himself. For a fuller discussion of tone, see the section "Appropriate Tone" in Chapter 2, and "Tone," page 285.

When passages in a student composition are marked for tone, the writer should examine them, perhaps read them aloud, to see if he has unintentionally been dogmatic, aggressive, pompous, or condescending; or if he has been inappropriately familiar, emotional, or sarcastic.

31. TRANSITIONS   Trans

Transitions are words, phrases, sentences, or even paragraphs, which show the reader the connections between the writer's ideas.

For further discussion of transitions within paragraphs, see page 167.

For further discussion of transitions between paragraphs, see page 171.

a. Transitions between sentences within a paragraph are established by:

(1) Using sentence connectives such as *therefore, however, on the other hand, consequently, at the same time.*

(2) Repeating a key word that has occurred in the preceding sentence, or using a term clearly equivalent to a term in the preceding sentence or a term clearly in contrast to one in the preceding material.

(3) Using a clear pronoun reference to a word or idea in the preceding sentence.

(4) Putting parallel thoughts in parallel constructions to show the relationships between them.

(5) Using subordination and subordinating conjunctions to clarify the relationships between important and less important ideas.

b. Transitions between paragraphs are established by:

(1) Concluding a paragraph with a sentence that leads into the next paragraph.

(2) Using in the first sentence of a paragraph a transitional word or phrase: *furthermore, as a result, in addition, on the contrary.*

(3) Repeating a key word used in the preceding paragraph.

(4) Beginning a paragraph with a sentence that refers clearly to a statement at the end of the preceding paragraph or to its topic idea.

(5) Using short transitional paragraphs to summarize the preceding ideas and relate them to the idea that follows.

32. UNITY AND FOCUS

A composition, a paragraph, or a sentence has unity and focus when it has a dominant idea to which all details within the unit are clearly relevant.

The fault of disunity in sentences is most commonly produced by (1) including material which is irrelevant or which appears to be irrelevant because of the absence of subordination or connectives, and (2) joining in one sentence apparently unrelated ideas, or too many ideas.

LACK OF UNITY: I have come to this college, which will be a hundred years old next year, to study business administration. [The age of the college is irrelevant to the main idea of the sentence.]

IMPROVED: I have come to this college to study business administration.

LACK OF UNITY: Charles Dickens wrote *Martin Chuzzlewit* in 1843, and I enjoyed it a great deal. [Two very different ideas are faultily joined in one sentence.]

IMPROVED: Charles Dickens wrote his enjoyable novel *Martin Chuzzlewit* in 1843.

LACK OF UNITY: Helen had always been afraid of the dark and now she was fifteen years old. [The two ideas seem wholly unrelated.]

IMPROVED: For as many of her fifteen years as she could remember, Helen had been afraid of the dark.

LACK OF UNITY: Children in grade school are likely to regard their teachers as gods, or sometimes as tyrants, and then later they realize that teachers are human and can be advisers and friends, and they change their attitudes, which is something I did rather late, but which I have done now. [This sprawling, overloaded sentence contains too many ideas for one sentence.]

IMPROVED: Children in grade school usually think of their teachers as gods or tyrants. Later, students realize that teachers are human beings who can be advisers and friends. I have arrived, rather tardily, at this more mature attitude toward my teachers.

Unity is closely related to coherence, emphasis, subordination, and the use of exact connectives. For further information about particular aspects of unity, see "Unity in Paragraphs" in Chapter 6, "Connectives," page 398, "Faulty Relationships of Sentence Elements," page 413, "Coherence," page 419, "Emphasis," page 421, "Subordination," page 426, and "Transitions," page 428.

Focus in a paper is achieved when the writer aims consistently, with a specific purpose, at a central subject. Focus requires the omission of extraneous matter, and the proportionate development of major and minor parts of the material. See "Planning the Paper: Organization and Focus" in Chapter 3, and "Selection and Focus" in Chapter 13.

33. VARIETY   Monot, Var

For a full discussion of variety (or, conversely, monotony), see the section "Variety in Sentences" in Chapter 5.

a. Monotonous repetition of words, sounds, and sentence structures should be avoided.

MONOTONOUS REPETITION: My general reaction to his action was that in general he acted wisely.

IMPROVED: I felt that in general he acted wisely.

MONOTONOUS CHOPPY SENTENCES: Joan came into the house. It was dark. The clock was striking seven.

IMPROVED: When Joan came into the dark house, the clock was striking seven.

MONOTONOUS SENTENCE PATTERNS: Having had a hard day at the office, Joe lost his temper quickly. Recovering from his anger, he regretted what he had said. Knowing that he was sorry, Martha accepted his apology.

IMPROVED: Joe, after a hard day at the office, lost his temper quickly. As soon as he recovered from his anger, he regretted what he had said, and Martha, knowing that he was sorry, accepted his apology.

b. Variety in sentence movement is achieved by:

(1) Varying the length of sentences.

(2) Using parallel and balanced constructions as a change from simpler constructions.

(3) Intermingling loose and periodic sentences.

(4) Changing the position of modifiers and parenthetic elements.

(5) Changing the subject-verb-object order of some sentences.

Sentence variety is closely related to subordination and to emphasis: in varying the movement of his sentences, the writer must consider what ideas he wants to emphasize by structure and position.

HANDBOOK

Section 4

PUNCTUATION

Punctuation rules are simply ways of stating the generally accepted, conventional meaning of punctuation marks. The able writer is aware of the important part such marks play in clarifying meaning and giving emphasis, and he departs from the conventions only when there is clear and positive advantage to be gained from doing so.

34. APOSTROPHE (')   Apos

a. The apostrophe is used to indicate the possessive case of nouns and of indefinite pronouns (*everyone's, everybody's, someone's, somebody's,* etc.). The apostrophe is NOT used to form the possessive case of personal pronouns (*his, hers, its, ours, yours, theirs*) or of the pronoun *who* (*whose*).

(1) To form the possessive of singular and plural nouns not ending in *s* or an *s* sound, use the apostrophe plus *s*.

Tom's shoes   day's work   man's fate   men's clothes
sons-in-law's hats   anybody's coat   anybody else's coat

(2) To form the possessive of plural nouns ending in *s,* use the apostrophe alone.

soldiers' uniforms   friends' houses   ladies' jewelry

431

(3) To form the possessive of singular nouns ending in *s* or in *s* sounds, use either the apostrophe alone, or the apostrophe plus *s*.

Burns's [*Or*] Burns' poetry

b. The apostrophe plus *s* is used to form the plurals of letters, figures, and signs when the apostrophe is needed for clarity; otherwise *s* alone may be used.

There are three *a*'s in Alaska.
The little girl wrote *1*'s for *7*'s.
He has learned his ABCs.

c. The apostrophe is used to indicate the omission of one or more letters or numbers.

They won't come, and we can't meet without them.
He said the 'gator [alligator] was dangerous.
"Abner was goin' down the road 'bout twenty miles an hour," Uncle Ike said.
Edna graduated in '66, and Marshall was in the class of '62.

EXERCISES

I. Insert the needed apostrophes in the following sentences:

1. There are two *r*s and two *i*s in Henrys last name.
2. She doesnt think its necessary to study.
3. That handwriting is either James or hers.
4. Its unlikely that hell arrive before eight oclock.
5. There were thirteen *and*s, eight *but*s and three *so*s in the first page of the theme.

II. Write the contractions for the following expressions; if no recognized contracted form exists, write *none*.

shall not	is not	she will
will not	can not	he will
would not	must not	it is
could not	should not	they are
are not	may not	we have
am not	might not	it has

III. Write the possessive singular and, if it exists, the possessive plural of each of the following:

she	man	army
it	woman	NLRB
he	child	country
one	president	fox
you	James	D.A.R.
I	Henry	lady

35. BRACKETS ([ ])

Brackets are most commonly used to enclose interpolations by the writer or the editor in quoted material.

"He [Calvin Coolidge] had the reputation of being a man of few words."
"That year [1860] he met Lincoln for the first time."
The little boy wrote, "I didn't mispell [*sic*] any words today."

Brackets may be used, as they are used in this book, to enclose comments on illustrative material. They also serve as parentheses within parentheses.

36. COLON (:)

The colon is a formal and specialized mark indicating introduction, anticipation, or amplification.

a. The colon is used to introduce a formal quotation or a formal listing of particulars.

In his speech of July 3, 1970, Senator Patwell said: "This un-American law . . ."
The college library has ordered the following books: . . .
The villagers showed their fear of the new machine: the women averted their eyes, the children became silent, and the men muttered uneasily to one another.

b. The colon is used to follow the salutation of a business letter.

Dear sir: Dear Mr. Nelson: Gentlemen:

c. The colon is used to separate: hours from minutes (12:15), a title from a subtitle (*The English Romantic Poets: A Review of Research*), and chapter from verse (John 3:3).

EXERCISES

Insert or substitute brackets and colons where they are needed in the following business letter; remove them where they are not needed, and supply the correct punctuation. If you are uncertain in choosing between brackets and parentheses see the discussion of parentheses on page 445.

801 Oregon Street
Urbana, Illinois 61801
January 2, 1972

Mr. Harold Mason, President
The Cornwall Company
56 Fifth Avenue
New York, N.Y. 10003

DEAR MR. MASON;

I am mailing to you today the following material: Chapters I, III, and V of Section One: Chapters II and IV of Section Two: and Chapters I and II of Section Three.

Your suggestions about: margins, numbering of pages, and use of headings are very helpful: they will solve some troublesome problems.

The two sentences that you were puzzled by [page 144, lines 8–12] do need revision. Below are the sentences as they originally were along with the changes that should be made;

Charles Fremont, grandson of Joclyn (should be Jocelyn) was born in Carecus (should be Caracas), Venezuela, on March 6 (should be March 8) at 8:29 A.M. His twin brother and loyal follower was born three hours later.

Please thank Mr. Edmonds for the research he has done and for his patience in reading the manuscript. My wife [who is doing the typing and who insists that my handwriting is illegible] also wants to thank Mr. Edmonds.

I hope to be able to send you the additions to Chapter VI of Section Two in a few days.

Cordially yours,
MARTIN S. BARRETT

37. COMMA (,)   C

The comma is the most frequently used mark of punctuation. Misuse of it produces not only mechanical errors, but also uncertainty and misunderstanding. A single comma is used to indicate a separation and a pause; commas in pairs are used to set off matter that constitutes some kind of additional unit but that does not need to be marked off by the longer and more emphatic pauses that would be indicated by a pair of dashes.

a. The comma is used to separate two independent clauses joined by *and, but, for, or,* or *nor.*

He promised to be here at six, but I don't expect him until seven.

Some handbooks on writing have stated this rule without qualification. Actually, the comma between independent clauses is often omitted, particularly if the clauses are not long. The comma after *six* is unnecessary in the sentence just cited; the sentence is perfectly clear without it. There is, however, a reason for this convention of using the comma between independent clauses joined by *and, but, for, or,* or *nor:*[1] frequently the subject of the second clause can momentarily be misread as the object of the first clause or the object of the preposition *for*. In the following sentences, commas are needed between clauses to prevent temporary misreading:

I did not have time to buy the gift for Father hurried me away. [One naturally reads *gift for Father*.]
I went to the railroad station to meet Mary and Frances went to the bus depot. [One reads *to meet Mary and Frances*.]
I must call for the doctor said to let him know. [One reads *call for the doctor*.]

Because such temporary confusion can easily occur, many teachers insist that their students follow the rule and always use a comma between independent clauses joined by *and, but, for, or,* or *nor*. Certainly that conventional usage is safe. The student who takes liberties with it should be sure that he is not causing his reader the annoyance of stumbling over an unclearly punctuated sentence.

b. A comma should NOT be used to separate two independent clauses which are NOT joined by *and, but, for, or,* or, *nor*. The use of a comma under these circumstances, when a semicolon or a period is needed, is called a Comma Fault, and a sentence so punctuated is called a Run-together Sentence. For a full discussion of the Comma Fault, see "Fused and Run-together Sentences," page 407.

c. The comma is generally used after an adverbial clause, a participial phrase, or any long phrase preceding the main part of the sentence.

Since I gave you my promise, I will be there.

Here, and in many other sentences of similar pattern, the comma after the introductory clause or phrase is not really necessary. But it is generally advisable to follow this rule of punctuation, or at least to be aware of it, for two reasons: first, there is a natural pause for emphasis before a main clause that begins in the middle of a sentence, and the comma marks that emphatic pause; second, the omission of the comma, like the omission of the comma between main clauses, frequently produces misreading. Commas are confusingly omitted in the following sentences, even though some of the introductory clauses and phrases are short:

---

[1] Note that the comma *precedes* the conjunction.

> While he was riding his horse lost a shoe.
> After all I had done my best to help him.
> By testing emotional reactions are determined.
> To one who is interested in farming land has beauty and character.

On the whole, it is easier to follow the convention of using the comma to set off the introductory clause or phrase than it is to examine each sentence to be sure that it is immediately clear. The use of the comma in this situation is never "wrong." The omission of it may be troublesome, because it may cause the reader to go back and to supply for himself the pause for clarity that should have been indicated by the writer.

Sometimes, as we have suggested, the comma after introductory expressions is used less for clarity than for the pause and emphasis that would occur in speech and in thought. The following sentences illustrate:

> Smiling shyly, she turned to go.
> Without waiting for his hostess to pick up her fork, Alan attacked the roast beef.
> Surprised at the good behavior of the large crowd, the police were helpful and friendly.

d. Commas are used to set off nonrestrictive modifiers; commas should not be used to set off restrictive modifiers.

> Charles Smith, who is ten years old, should know better than to throw stones. [Nonrestrictive modifier]
> People who live in glass houses shouldn't throw stones. [Restrictive modifier]

This conventional rule of punctuation is deeply rooted in common sense and logic. A restrictive modifier *identifies* or *restricts* the meaning of the word it modifies. It is not set off by commas because it is an essential part of the context and is necessary to fix or limit the meaning of the word:

> Students who are failing any course are requested to see the Dean. [*Who are failing any course* is a restrictive clause; it identifies the students requested to see the Dean.]

A nonrestrictive modifier gives *additional* information about an *already identified* subject. It is set off by commas because it is simply a parenthetical element or a conveyor of fact supplementary, not essential, to the main point of the sentence:

> My oldest sister, who married a British sailor, is visiting us. [*Oldest* clearly identifies the sister; hence, *who married a British sailor* is clearly a nonrestrictive modifier.]

Confusion or distortion of meaning may result from the illogical punctuation of restrictive and nonrestrictive modifiers. Consider the difference in meaning in the following sentences:

All our money, which we had left on the beach, was taken by the thief.

All our money which we had left on the beach was taken by the thief.

[In the first sentence the loss is apparently more serious: all our money was taken. In the second sentence, only the money which we had left on the beach was taken. The writer who has had three dollars stolen while he was swimming is probably giving misinformation if he records his loss in the form of the first sentence.]

The members of the football team, who ate at the hotel, have ptomaine poisoning.

The members of the football team who ate at the hotel have ptomaine poisoning.

[The coach would be more distressed by the situation represented in the first sentence.]

The examples of restrictive and nonrestrictive modifiers that we have been considering are clauses. In the sentences below, phrases give additional information about an identified subject; these nonrestrictive phrases are properly set off by commas:

Mary, now tired, returned to work.

Mother, concerned at the lateness of the hour, was awake when I came home.

Professor Greenleaf, having failed to hear the bell, talked on.

The logical punctuation of restrictive and nonrestrictive modifiers can usually be determined by reading the sentence aloud. If the modifier is naturally set off with pauses when one reads, it should be set off by commas in the written sentence.

e. Commas are used to set off words, phrases, or clauses that are thrown in as interrupters or parenthetical elements when the grammatical structure is complete without them.

He is, however, unwilling to accept the compromise.

War and unemployment, on the other hand, are ever-present dangers.

He, it is said, was more to blame than his son.

f. Commas are used to separate elements (words, phrases, or clauses) in a series.

Papers were strewn on the table, on the desk, and on the floor.

He enjoys hunting, fishing, and swimming.

He stated that conflict was imminent, that the opponents were well prepared, and that he felt uncertain of victory.

He was tired, he was hungry, and he was very late.

(When there is no danger of ambiguity or misreading, it is permissible to omit the comma before the final element in the series.)

g. Commas are used to set off a nonrestrictive appositive. (An appositive is a noun or a noun equivalent used to explain another noun construction which has the same referent.)

 Mr. Morgan, John's father, was pleased. [Nonrestrictive appositive; commas are needed.]

 The poet Milton was blind. [Restrictive appositive; commas should not be used.]

h. Commas are used to separate coordinate adjectives not joined by a conjunction.

 The tall, thin man shrugged his shoulders.
 We watched the dawn of a bleak, wintry day.
 The long, hot, difficult journey was nearly over.

The comma is *not* used when adjectives in series are not coordinate. In the sentences above, each adjective seems to modify the noun directly. In other series, each adjective modifies a complex of adjectives and noun. Examples are:

 They live in a red brick house. [Here *red* modifies the locution *brick house; red* and *brick* are not coordinate.]

 The tired old man staggered under the load. [*Tired* modifies *old man.*]

 The beautiful little blond dog was waiting at the door. [Here, each adjective modifies the whole expression that follows.]

i. Commas are used to set off nouns of address.

A noun of address, which names the person or persons spoken to, may be a sentence interrupter; but it may also be at the beginning or end of a sentence:

 Now, Jake, you know how it is.
 I appreciate your advice, Doctor, but I cannot follow it.
 Sir, may I change the time of my conference?
 Let us consider carefully, my friends.

j. Commas are used to set off a short direct quotation from the rest of the sentence.

 "All these people," she said, "are strangers to me."
 He said, "Are you going now?"
 "You must go now," he said.

k. A comma is used to separate the parts of dates, addresses, and geographical names.

 On August 17, 1967, his address was 14 Barton Street, Peoria, Illinois; later he moved to Cleveland, Ohio, to live near his sister. [But Zip Code numbers are not separated: Medford, Massachusetts 02155.]

l. A comma is generally used to set off a brief introductory expression.

Yes, I know what you mean.
Well, that's what he said.
No, Vivian is not practical.
Oh, I'm sorry to hear this.
In short, he was a remarkable man.

m. A comma is used to prevent misreading. (Sometimes the fact that commas are needed to prevent misreading is a hint that the sentence needs to be revised.)

Before, he had insisted on cash payment.
For him, to buy was better than to sell.

n. Commas are used (1) when they are needed to clarify meaning by marking a slight pause, and (2) when they are required by some of the established conventions stated in the rules above. Commas that are not justified by (1) or (2) should be omitted.

Commas should *not* be used to separate words that form an organic unit in the sentence; they should *not* separate a subject from its verb in a simple sentence, a verb from its object, an adjective from its noun, or a conjunction from the clause it introduces. The following examples illustrate a haphazard misuse of commas: the commas clutter the sentences, creating pauses where no pauses should occur.

Gay streamers and floating balloons, decorated the gymnasium.
The way to success, is often, a long and difficult, road.
Mother said, she disapproved of the plan.
I refuse to go unless, you go with me.
The angry, members of the committee, protested loudly, but, the chairman was firm.

The organic and therefore proper use of commas can often, as in these sentences, be determined by reading the sentence aloud. Unless a comma is demanded by some well-established convention, it should be used only when a slight pause is natural, or is needed for clarity or emphasis.

EXERCISES

I. Decide whether to use commas, semicolons, or no mark of punctuation in the places where there is a caret (∧) in the sentences below, and cite the rule that applies. (Before you do this exercise, see rules **a** and **b** under "Semicolon," page 452.)

1. The wind is blowing∧ but the sun is warm.
2. "I am willing∧" he said∧ "to give money to such a cause∧ and I do not want my name used in connection with it."

3. He was old∧ he was tired∧ and he was unwilling to learn new ways.

4. In the winter∧ there is snow to shovel∧ in the summer∧ there is grass to cut∧ in the fall∧ there are leaves to rake∧ only in the early spring is there leisure.

5. We waited at home until she returned∧ for Mother was worried about her∧ and Father was worried about the car.

6. He said∧ "My children are sick∧ my wife is ill∧ and I have no money."

7. The Arnolds brought ice, lemonade, and cookies∧ the Lanes brought frankfurts∧ rolls, and wood for the fire∧ and we brought potato salad, oranges, and a large thermos jug full of coffee.

8. Maynard gets sleepy as soon as he opens his chemistry book∧ he can read a detective story∧ though∧ until three in the morning.

9. Speech is silver∧ silence is golden.

10. If you ask him a question∧ he does not answer∧ if you tell him something∧ he forgets it immediately.

11. The driver slowed down∧ when he saw the police car∧ then he turned sharply into a country lane∧ and roared away.

12. He is very polite∧ in fact, he is too polite∧ and I distrust him.

II. In the sentences below, the expressions in italics are restrictive or nonrestrictive modifiers. Insert commas wherever they are needed for proper punctuation of these modifiers.

1. Marcella *who is very sensitive* often has her feelings hurt.

2. His hair *gray and sparse* made him look older than he actually was.

3. The men *who were the fathers of the American Revolution* would be surprised at the actions of some of their descendants.

4. He admits that history *which he calls his least interesting subject* is the course for which he studies least.

5. The subjects *which Edward likes best* are psychology and anthropology.

6. Tom *startled by the sudden question and only half awake* mumbled a reply and went to sleep again.

7. His latest book *on which he worked for seven years* is said to be inferior to his earlier books.

8. The sun *obscured by the cloud of smoke* cast a ray of light on the path ahead of us.

9. We saw our friend *still smiling and serene* open the door to the Dean's office.

10. Martin *who has never read a book in his life* says that he hopes to be a newspaper man and a critic.

III. Correct or revise all sentences in which commas are omitted or misused.

1. She asked for Fred and Mark and Walter felt slighted.

2. The birds disturbed Henrietta, sometimes, they woke her up just before dawn.

3. The address of the tall, thin, man is 12 Fifth Avenue, New York, New York, 10003.

4. "If I come to dinner," she said, "I'll have to bring my father who is visiting me, and a friend, who is visiting him."

5. He had to work hard for the firm of Hamilton, Cook, and Boggle makes heavy demands on the people, whom it employs.

6. I have swallowed too much salt and sand is in my hair.

7. I waited forty minutes for Betty and Joan are always late.

8. As I expected the invitation to the wedding came this morning.

9. Children, who are public nuisances, should be kept at home.

10. The play lasted for three hours, however the audience liked it.

11. No I cannot help you Hubert my friend.

12. Paul who is not concerned about his appearance, likes to wear comfortable, old clothes.

13. Professor I'd like to talk with you, if I could sometime about an exciting short story I read last night.

14. Irene's youngest brother Ned who has been in Vietnam for a year is back at home.

15. Everyone who was invited was there but Elsie a small slender girl, with red hair, had to leave early.

IV. In the passage below strike out any commas that are not *required* according to the conventions of punctuation.

Polly said, "It's too small, for a wedding announcement," and tore open the letter, as Jim went out to bring in the rest of the groceries, from the car. Below him, as he walked down, the steps of the cottage, the lake shimmered blue in the noonday sun. There were no more bundles in the car, and he slammed the door, listening to the sharp, crack in the clear, air. Everything was intensified like that here: sound and smell and color, and the sensations of sunlight and used muscles and refreshment after sleep. He sat down on the low, flat, boulder, at the meeting of the two paths, one zigzagging from the cottage down to the beach, the other winding up to the knoll with its single crooked, pine tree, overlooking the lake. The stone was warm from the sun. With the side of his shoe, he scraped together a pile of brown, pine needles, which covered the ground at his feet.

Polly came out on the porch. "Jim, Berda's in Boston and wants to come up this week-end. We haven't invited anyone else, have we?"

"I haven't." He grinned at his sister, over his shoulder. "How about your wide-eyed medical friends?"

"They can't come. And they are not wide-eyed," she added, good-naturedly.

38. DASH (−)

The dash, skillfully used, does much to clarify meaning; unskillfully used, it misleads the reader and suggests that the writer is using punctuation to suit his own convenience rather than to guide the reader. Dashes may be used singly or in pairs.

a. Dashes are used in pairs to set off interpolations to which the writer wishes to give greater emphasis than parentheses or commas would give them.

He said—you can imagine how this pleased me—that he would not accept my handwritten paper.

These three elements—fact, attitude, and intention—combine to produce the compound of meaning.

Charles, you must—don't scuff your feet and wear out your shoes—you must return Mr. Hazlitt's rake.

b. A single dash is used to mark an unexpected turn of thought, an abrupt suspension of sense, a sudden change in structure or a hesitation in speech.

He gave a—I'm sorry; I promised not to tell.

Beets, carrots, tomatoes, corn, chard, onions—all these I planted in the unfertile soil. At the end of the summer I had well-fed worms and a flourishing crop of— weeds!

Mary heard Tom say to her father, "Mr. Hodge, I—that is, we—well—uh— Mary said—to ask . . . ."

c. The dash should not be carelessly used as a substitute for other marks of punctuation.

(In general the dash serves as a signal that either the substance or the construction of the material it sets off demands particular attention. In typing, the dash is made by combining two hyphens.)

39. ELLIPSIS (. . .)

Ellipsis is used to indicate the omission of a word or words needed to complete a sentence, or the omission of part of a quotation. The ellipsis consists of three spaced periods.

Four periods instead of three are used in an ellipsis if it comes at the end of a sentence which is closed by a period, or if a period occurs in the material omitted.

I know that I should do it, but . . . .

Newman says that a university education "gives a man a clear conscious view of his own opinions and judgments, . . . an eloquence in expressing them, and a force in urging them."

40. EXCLAMATION POINT (!)

The exclamation point is used after an ejaculation (word, phrase, or entire sentence) to indicate emphatic utterance or strong feeling.

Ouch!   Get out!   And we spent our youth learning grammar!

Overuse of exclamation points can suggest that a writer is gushing or insincere:

> It was her first dance! She was going with Ted! Wonderful Ted! And he had sent her a corsage! A corsage of white roses!
>
> Her husband has bought her a Whiz vacuum cleaner! Now she knows, he loves her! Now housework will be thrilling!

41. HYPHEN (-)   H

The hyphen is used primarily to show close relationships between words or parts of words.

a. The hyphen is used at the end of a line when part of a word is carried over to the next line. (See "Syllabification," page 470.)

b. Hyphens are used in the writing of certain compound expressions.

Rules for the writing of compound words are not completely fixed, and authorities differ about the use of a hyphen in particular cases. Some compounds (especially those that have been long and frequently used) are written as one word *(nevertheless)*, other compounds are hyphenated *(ex-president)*, and still others are written as separate words *(commander in chief)*. Hyphens should always be used when they are necessary for clarity; for example, *a wooden-shoe maker* and *a wooden shoemaker* have different meanings. Although a writer often has an option of using or not using a hyphen, after he has made his choice he should be consistent. The best source of information about hyphens in particular expressions is a good modern dictionary.

Common practice calls for the use of hyphens:

(1) in compound numbers from twenty to one hundred and in the writing of fractions.

> twenty-one, twenty-first [*but*] one hundred and twenty-one and one hundred and twenty-first
> two-thirds, three one-hundredths, forty-two twenty-fifths

(2) between the letters of a spelled word, and to indicate the division of a word into syllables.

> *Already* is spelled a-l-r-e-a-d-y.
> *Athlete* has two syllables: ath-lete.

(3) in most compounds made up of nouns and prepositional phrases.

> hand-to-hand, eyeball-to-eyeball, mother-in-law, man-of-war

(4) between words which function as a single adjective before a substantive (noun or pronoun).

an off-the-face hat [*but*] off the face of the earth
a broken-down car [*but*] The car was broken down.
a hard-drinking man
a will-you-step-outside-with-me look

(5) in a word to differentiate it from another word spelled the same way.

re-cover and recover
re-creation and recreation

(6) in most words compounded with *self* or *ex* as a prefix.

self-conceit, self-reliance, self-pity [*but not in* selfless, selfsame]
ex-president, ex-senator, ex-convict, ex-wife

(7) in most compounds made up of prefixes joined to proper nouns.

anti-American, pro-Communist, pre-Raphaelite

(8) between two or more words that, though separated, modify the same noun.

differences between pre- and post-revolutionary China
using 2- by 6-inch boards

42. ITALICS   Ital, Und

Italics are indicated in manuscript by underlining the word or words to be italicized. Practice varies greatly in the use of italics by newspapers, magazines, and book publishers, and italics (i.e., underlining in manuscript) are more frequently used in formal than in colloquial or familiar writing. The following rules should be followed in formal or high informal writing.

a. Italics are used for titles of books, pamphlets, newspapers, magazines, musical compositions, works of art, plays, movies, and for names of ships and aircraft.

Green Mansions, MLA Style Sheet, Boston Globe (or Boston *Globe*), *Newsweek, Idylls of the King,* U.S.S. *Missouri* (or the *Missouri*)

b. Italics are generally used for foreign words and phrases that have not been absorbed into English.

The ambassador was *persona non grata.*
The detective said, *"Cherchez la femme."*

c. Italics are used to call attention to words as words, letters as letters, figures as figures.

freedom, a word with many meanings
a word spelled with four *s*'s
the 7's that look like 9's

d. Italics are sometimes used for emphasis. (But italics, like other mechanical devices for emphasis—capitalization, use of exclamation points—lose their effect unless they are used sparingly.)

I shall *never* consent. [But not: The baby *was* a *darling* and Jane couldn't *wait* to tell Doris how *cute* he was.]

e. Italics are used for the scientific names of genera, subgenera, species, and subspecies.

the genera *Quercus* and *Liriodendron*

43. PARENTHESES (( ))

Parentheses are used to set off material (definitions, additional information, asides, illustrative detail) which helps to clarify, but is not essential. (Such material is thrown in, as we say, parenthetically.)

She said (but of course we knew better) that she was younger than her husband.
When the boy from Kentucky asked for a *sack* of peanuts in Boston, the clerk was puzzled. (New Englanders use the word *bag*.)
When he first introduces the symbol of the lantern (page 13, paragraph 2) he is describing his boyhood experience.
The dash has the following uses: (1) to . . . , (2) to . . . , and (3) to . . . .
The gear shift (see Diagram A) is different in the 1970 models.

In a composition, the deletion of a word or phrase is indicated by drawing a line through it, *not* by enclosing it in parentheses.

Except in business and legal usage, it is not customary to repeat a sum previously stated in words:

Legal or business usage: I enclose two hundred dollars ($200.00).
General usage: Here is a twenty-dollar check for your birthday.

When parenthetical material is at the end of an introductory clause or phrase that is to be set off by a comma from the rest of the sentence, the parenthetical element is *followed by,* not preceded by, the comma:

After Father had admonished me about driving carefully (as he often did), he delayed me further by asking me about my plans for the evening.
He said (I wondered why), "Do you expect to be going out again tomorrow?"
In the meantime (and it was a long time), the demonstrators had to content themselves with promises.

EXERCISES

I. State the main uses of each of the following marks of punctuation: dash, ellipsis, exclamation point, hyphen, italics, parentheses.

II. What is the difference in use between parentheses and brackets, between parentheses and dashes, between the hyphen and the dash? When are italics (or underlining) used in writing titles and when are quotation marks used? (See "Quotation Marks," page 449.)

III. In the sentences below examine the use of the dash, ellipsis, parentheses, and italics. In each case explain why that mark of punctuation is properly used or why it is misused. When you find a mark improperly used, strike it out and substitute whatever punctuation is necessary.

1. John Gunther's *Roosevelt in Retrospect* (New York: Harper & Brothers, 1950) was . . . or at least most reviewers seemed to think it was . . . a satisfactory treatment of a difficult subject.

2. Mr. Hamilton Basso, who wrote the review entitled *Another Go at F.D.R.* in "The New Yorker," expressed the following opinion: "Mr. Gunther . . . is one of the more uncritical of Roosevelt's admirers. He is in there all the time getting in his licks for his hero."

3. Several of the keys of her typewriter—the *a,* the *i,* the *l,* and the *g*—clearly need cleaning; also I wish that she would learn to spell "separate" properly.

4. Senator Rudland said he was going to his hotel (he pronounced it hó-tel) to get some sleep. Tomorrow he will sail for England on the *Queen Elizabeth.*

5. *Op. cit., loc. cit., passim, supra*—these Latin terms were once more widely used in footnotes than they now are.

IV. Supply hyphens where they are needed:

1. His down to earth statement surprised those who had expected a vague and fumbling answer from the eighty seven year old ex president.

2. His sister in law, a strong willed, self reliant woman, refused to wear high heeled shoes, insisted on continuing to wear her out of style hat, and was entirely satisfied with ankle length skirts.

3. We suspected that his never say die attitude was a pose and that his self confident air was equally misleading.

44. PERIOD (.)

a. A period is used at the end of a sentence, or any expression standing for a sentence, that is neither interrogative nor exclamatory. The placing of a period after an unsatisfactory incomplete sentence produces the blunder known as the Period Fault.

In the following examples the period is properly used:

Ralph was here today. [A complete declarative sentence.]
Go soon. [An imperative sentence; the subject *you* is understood.]
He asked where the fire was. [An indirect question.]
Will you please send me a copy of *Pilgrim's Progress,* cloth edition. [A request politely phrased as a question is often followed by a period.]
So much for the preparations. Now the next step. [In expository writing, transitional expressions which are not complete sentences may be punctuated as sentences.]
No. Can't stay any longer. See you tomorrow. [In the recording of spoken English, words or groups of words that stand for sentences are followed by a period.]
No movement of life in this desert. Only the glaring sun and the simmering waves of heat. [In narrative and descriptive writing, freer use is made of incomplete sentences.]

Ability to distinguish between acceptable and unacceptable incomplete sentences is essential to the proper use of the period. (See "Fragmentary and Incomplete Sentences," page 404.)

b. The period is used to make clear that a letter or a group of letters is an abbreviation of a longer locution. If a sentence ends with an abbreviation followed by a period, a second period is not needed.

U.S.A.   B.C.   Ph.D.   *ibid.*   i.e.   Dr. Holt   A.M. (or a.m.)
She lives in Boston, Mass.

(Certain abbreviations—UNRRA, UN, UNICEF, IOU—are written without periods. For information about particular abbreviations, consult your dictionary.)

c. The period is used to mark a decimal.

She paid $403.50 for the furniture she bought at the auction.
The cost of living has risen 60.42 per cent.

A series of periods, called *ellipsis,* is used to indicate the omission of a word or words necessary to complete a sentence, or the omission of a part of a quotation. (See "Ellipsis," page 442.)

EXERCISES

I. Define (1) complete sentence, (2) incomplete sentence, (3) fragmentary sentence. (If necessary see "Fragmentary and Incomplete Sentences," page 404.)

II. In the passages below (1) point out any fragmentary sentences and revise to eliminate the period fault, (2) point out any acceptable incomplete sentences and explain why you think they are acceptable, (3) point out the subject and the verb of each independent clause or sentence, and (4) add any periods that are needed and strike out any unnecessary periods.

1. He did not know the abbreviation for United States. Which is U.S.

2. We were pleased at the progress our club had made. Only a year, yet twenty-seven members now and $227.40 in our treasury.

3. We told the freshman to ring the chapel bell at two A.M. Which, much to our surprise, he did and woke up Dean Holden.

4. What would be a reasonable sum? Dick did not want to overpay the man, but he wanted to be fair. Perhaps thirty dollars. That seemed too much. Perhaps twenty-five or perhaps even twenty. Yes, twenty would do.

5. Henry was surprised to see Andy walking slowly ahead of him.
"Andy," he shouted, "Is that you, Andy?"
"Yeah." Andy's voice didn't sound friendly.
"Where are you going?"
"Just walking." Andy was waiting for him now under the light. His collar was turned up and he looked cold.
"I thought you were seeing Anne tonight."
"Yeah. I was."
"But it's only—"
"Only nine. That's right, and I'm not with Anne. Funny, isn't it. Well, I'll tell you . . ."

6. She was thinking. Of nothing at all. When suddenly the doorbell rang, she went to answer it.

7. He did very little studying. Although he was a member of the ROTC and needed to maintain a high average.

8. Everything he saw pleased him. The spacious campus. The ivy-covered buildings. The friendly students. He felt sure now that he would like college. Very much.

9. Bright sun. Blue sky. White sand. Mrs. Marlowe looked at the scene in amazement.

10. I received four dollars in tips. Thus making my income for the day $12.75.

45. QUESTION MARK (?)

The question mark is placed at the end of a direct question or is used parenthetically to express doubt.

When are you going? [A direct question.]
He asked when we were going. [An indirect question; no question mark is needed.]
He asked, "When are you going?"
Did he really say, "You will regret this"? [An interrogative sentence that contains a quoted statement.]
Did he actually say, "Why should I pay for food like this?" [A question that contains a quoted question.]

She says—can you believe it?—that she will be prompt.

Arnold promised to come, but can we really expect him? [A sentence beginning with a statement but ending with a question.]

Chaucer, born in 1342(?), anticipated the English Renaissance. [A parenthetical expression of doubt or uncertainty.]

Because punctuation of indirect questions sometimes poses a problem, it is well to emphasize that indirect questions are not followed by a question mark. The following examples are declarative sentences; the indirect questions embedded in the sentences are the objects of the verbs and are properly followed by periods.

I wondered if I should answer.

Neil asked himself what he should study first.

She inquired what the hurry was.

Many people have asked why we should go to Mars.

A question mark used to indicate humor or irony is often better omitted:

My father was glad to see his handsome(?) and intelligent(?) son.

The dancer innocently(?) cast off the sixth veil.

46. QUOTATION MARKS (" ")   Quot

Quotation marks are used to enclose direct quotations and to call attention to locutions used in special ways.[2]

Single quotation marks (') are used within double quotation marks (" ") for a quotation within a quotation.

Quotation marks, whether single or double, are used before and after a locution to set it off. Careless omission of either the "before" or "after" mark is confusing to the reader.

In typed quotations, passages of two lines or more are usually single-spaced and indented from both margins. Quotation marks are then unnecessary. For long quotations which are not single-spaced or indented, a "before" or left-hand mark is placed at the beginning of each paragraph, but the "after" or right-hand mark is used only at the end of the last quoted paragraph, where it serves to indicate the end of the quoted material.

a. Quotation marks are used to enclose direct quotations.

The reporter wrote, "President De Gaulle did not say, 'We have faith in NATO'; he said, 'France must have a bomb of her own.'"

---

[2] Though printers and editors are in agreement about the use of quotation marks to indicate direct quotations, they are not in complete accord about special uses of quotation marks or about the position of other marks when quotation marks are used. The intent of this article and the following article is to indicate what appears to be the best practice for college students.

The first two lines of this poem are: "Thou still unravished bride of quietness,/ Thou foster child of silence and slow time."
Ned wrote home, "I don't much like the food or the discipline of the army."

b. Quotation marks are used to enclose locutions used in special ways:

(1) Titles of short poems, stories, magazine articles, and chapters of books. (Underlining—to indicate italics—is generally used for titles of books, magazines, newspapers, and plays.)

He read aloud parts of "To Autumn" and then gave a lecture on Keats.
He wrote a book report on Hardy's *The Return of the Native*.

(2) Technical terms that might confuse the reader if they were not identified as technical.

In the "lead" the reporter must give certain information.

(3) Expressions that the writer wishes to call attention to as words, sometimes for ironic effect. (In formal writing, such words are usually italicized, but they are commonly put in quotation marks in informal writing.)

"Recession" is a more pleasant word than "depression," and "strategic withdrawal" sounds better than "retreat."

c. Quotation marks should *not* be used to enclose indirect quotations or to excuse inappropriate phrasing:

WRONG: He said "that Tom will come."
POOR: Polonius was deceived because he did not know that Hamlet was "kidding him along."

47. QUOTATION MARKS WITH OTHER MARKS OF PUNCTUATION

a. Periods and commas are conventionally placed inside the close-quotation mark.

"It is difficult," Archibald said, "always to be in the right."
Richard, not understanding the word, was puzzled when his uncle talked about the importance of being a "gentleman."

Sometimes, as in the sentence just above, logic suggests putting a comma or a period outside the quotation mark. We are dealing here, however, not with logic but with convention, in this case a convention designed to make manuscript and printed pages neat and uniform. According to this convention, all commas and periods are put *inside* quotation marks.

b. Other punctuation marks should be placed inside the quotation marks only if they are part of the matter quoted.

"What do you mean?" he asked. [Since the quotation is a question, the question mark is inside the quotation marks.] .

Can we ignore what Carl Becker called "the climate of opinion"? [The quotation is not a question; the question mark is therefore outside the quotation marks.]

"Stop!" she cried. [The quotation is an exclamation; the exclamation point is inside the quotation marks.]

"But I thought—" she began, then recalled her promise. [The dash is part of the quoted matter because it shows the abrupt halt in speech.]

He calls himself a "liberal"; what he means is not clear.

According to the defendant, these are the "facts": he was not in town on the night of the robbery, and he had honestly earned the money found on his person.

Semicolons and colons at the end of quoted material are almost never part of the quotation. These two marks of punctuation are, therefore, nearly always outside the quotation marks.

c. In quotations broken for identification of the speaker or for added detail, choice of other marks of punctuation depends on sentence structure.

"What I wonder," Janice said, "is how it can end." [The speech tag interrupts an unfinished sentence and so is set off by commas.]

"You can feel the air pollution today," Roger said. "It must be well above the safe level." [Here a period follows *said* because Roger's first sentence is complete.]

"What is it?" She looked closely at him. "Has something happened?" [Added detail is a complete sentence between the two quoted questions.]

EXERCISES

Use quotation marks or italics where they are needed in the following sentences. When italics are needed, underline the word which should be italicized. (For the use of italics see page 444.) When quotation marks are needed, be sure to place them properly before or after other marks.

1. Dean Warren said, When I heard that student say ain't got no and this here, I understood why he did not pass his freshman English course.

2. The professor read aloud Browning's My Last Duchess; then he asked his students to give their interpretation of the poem.

3. Was it General MacArthur who said, I shall return?

4. While I waited for Dr. Martin, I read an article in Time entitled Congress and the Russians.

5. The footnote in Arthur G. Kennedy's book English Usage reads as follows: See H. B. Allen, The Standard of Usage in Freshman Textbooks, English Journal, Vol. 24, 1935, pp. 564–571.

6. I am very tired, Alice said emphatically, of hearing him talk about what he calls his sensitivity.

7. Sam's short story was entitled Beyond the Generation Gap. He said that it was publishable; but he added, My teacher has the soul of a proofreader.

8. Can you help me understand, Eleanor said, exactly what Camus means by the absurd?

9. John recited his favorite lines from Macbeth: Methought I heard a voice cry, Sleep no more! Macbeth doth murder sleep!

10. In which poem, the teacher asked, in The Road Not Taken or in Stopping By Woods, do we find the line But I have promises to keep?

48. SEMICOLON (;)   Semi

The semicolon, though actually an easy mark of punctuation to master, is second only to the comma in producing faults in student writing. In general a semicolon indicates a shorter pause and a closer connection than a period, and a longer pause and a less close connection than a comma.

a. The semicolon is used to separate two independent clauses *not* joined by *and, but, for, or,* or *nor.*

They had reached a stalemate; neither would give in.
He was discouraged; life had disappointed him.
He irritates me at times; nevertheless I like him.

NOTE 1.—Failure to follow this rule produces the error known as the run-together sentence. (See "Fused and Run-together Sentences," page 407.)

NOTE 2.—An exception to Rule a above is the punctuation of three or more independent clauses in series: He was tired, he was hungry, and he was very late.

b. The semicolon is used to separate coordinate clauses joined by *and, but, for, or,* or *nor* when one of the coordinate clauses contains commas. (This is always a safe rule; one need not follow it, however, when a comma will give the desired clarity and emphasis.)

The French fought for liberty, equality, fraternity; and peace was a secondary consideration. [Here the semicolon is needed for clarity.]

Charles, Tom, and Elliot came in late, and their father asked them where they had been. [Here the comma is certainly justifiable.]

c. The semicolon is used to separate items in a series when one of the items itself contains a comma. (This rule, too, is dependent on context. Oftentimes a comma will serve the purpose.)

She ordered doughnuts, cookies, and pies from the bakery; ice cream, chocolate sauce, and sherbet from the drugstore; and balloons, horns, and cap pistols from the corner store.

EXERCISES

(Before doing these exercises read the treatment of fused and run-together sentences, page 407, as well as the rules for the use of the semicolon.)

I. State the subject and the verb of each independent clause in the sentences below; then insert or substitute semicolons where they are required by Rules **a, b,** and **c.** As you punctuate each sentence, indicate which rule you are following, and indicate also whether a period or a comma might be used in place of the semicolon.

1. He will go his way, she will go hers.
2. He placed the key in the lock, and then, very cautiously, he opened the door.
3. When he is happy, she is happy, when he suffers, she suffers with him.
4. At first the man seemed friendly, then he became angry and abusive.
5. I know that he will come, what I don't know is how long he will stay.
6. He had talked about a new car and he had dreamed about a new car, now he was going to own one.
7. Some people content themselves with wishes, others turn wishes into actualities.
8. Life is a comedy to those who think, a tragedy to those who feel.
9. Still they came, the old men, the women, the children, and the young lieutenant looked on, full of pity but unable to help.
10. He refused to help, although the food was there and he could easily have spared it.
11. He finished the report, then he went to bed and slept for fourteen hours.
12. It isn't that he means to be cruel, he simply doesn't understand boys of that age.
13. I'm sure that he's coming to the game, in fact I sold him a ticket just an hour ago.
14. Open the door and let him in, he's standing out there in the rain.
15. He was sleepy, he was tired, and he was very cold.

II. Which of the following are run-together sentences?

1. Although he was not cowardly, he valued his life and he was unwilling to risk it unnecessarily.
2. She knows he will be in later, that is all she will say.
3. He was in need of money, therefore he accepted the job eagerly.
4. At first he was conscientious, later he became very lax.
5. Yes, Mercedes told me she had dented my fender naturally I wasn't pleased.

HANDBOOK

Section 5

MECHANICS

Spelling is important because it is so often the first basis on which a writer is judged. Conventional spelling is probably the clearest example of an established procedure to which one must conform, not because nonconformity destroys the sense of the communication (a word is seldom so badly misspelled as to be unrecognizable) but simply because many readers respond unfavorably, with irritation, disrespect, and mistrust, to the writer who cannot spell.

An occasional misspelling, particularly of an uncommon word, is not a serious error. Conspicuously poor spelling is serious, however, because it suggests that the writer is unfamiliar with printed material, or unable to learn what most educated people learn without great difficulty, or both. Such errors as confusing *there* and *their, its* and *it's, quite* and *quiet,* and misspelling words like *receive, believe, tries, beginning,* which are spelled according to established rules, create an impression of illiteracy. To many people, spelling is an index to the writer's education and intelligence. Actually it is not a reliable index, but the fact remains that one is judged by the way he spells.

Good spelling requires attention, memory, and the use of the ear, the eye, and the hand. In learning to spell a word the student should first be sure he knows the meaning and has before him the accepted pronunciation, syllabification, and spelling of the word; a good dictionary supplies this information. Next he should pronounce the word to fix it in his auditory memory, look at it closely to fix it in his visual memory, check his visual memory by looking a second time at the word, and then write it twice to record it in his muscular memory and to see it in his own handwriting. If the word is not yet fixed in his mind, he may find it useful to try other memory (mnemonic) devices: for example, he can write *separate* as *sepArate,* emphasizing the trouble spot with the large A, or he can fix in his mind the fact that there is *a rat* in *separate;* or in learning to spell *receive,* he can note that it follows the *ei-after-c* rule.

The student whose spelling is weak should not take the attitude that poor spelling is an incurable affliction to which he should be stoically—or even worse, cheerfully—resigned. Our experience leads us to believe that any college student (except for the very rare individuals who have special visual or psychological handicaps—perhaps one or two in a thousand) can become an average or better-than-average speller if he is willing to work on the Spelling List (pages 458–464) for five to fifteen hours, and to follow other reasonable and not-very-time-consuming procedures.

Students who wish to improve their spelling in an efficient way should follow these steps:

1. On a sheet of paper write down in brief form the spelling rules given in section **a** and refer to them when they are useful. For the word *beginning,* for example, rule 2 will be useful; for *excitable,* rule 4, etc. If you follow this method, you will not have to memorize the rules mechanically, but will learn them in the process of applying them, as a bridge player learns the rules of bidding.

2. Master the Spelling List (section **b**). When you have learned to spell the words on this list, you will have eliminated half of your spelling errors and will be able to avoid the most glaring and embarrassing blunders. Also you will have developed habits of attention and analysis that will help you in the spelling of words not on the list.

3. Keep a list of words you have misspelled in your writing. Learn this list as you have learned the Spelling List.

4. In revising your writing, look up in the dictionary the spelling of any words you are unsure of. If the word is one you will use frequently, add it to your spelling list.

5. As you read for your college courses, underline new words or terms that are important in your study, and take care to learn their spelling, along with their pronunciation and meaning.

6. Start today to learn the words on the Spelling List and systematically follow the methods suggested as you learn these words and other words.

a. **Spelling rules.**[1] There are exceptions to nearly all spelling rules, but a sure grasp of a few basic rules will eliminate many common misspellings.

(1) Words spelled with *ie* or *ei* are nearly always spelled correctly according to the old rhyme:

> *I* before *e*
> Except after *c,*
> Or when sounded as *a,*
> As in *neighbor* and *weigh.*

Believe, relief, grieve, chief, piece, niece, field are examples of *i* before *e.* The reversal of the letters when they come after *c* is shown in *receive, deceit, perceive, conceive.* (Some exceptions to the rule are *weird, leisure,* and *seize.*)

(2) Words ending with a consonant double that final consonant before a suffix beginning with a vowel when the word has only one syllable, or is accented on the last syllable, and when the final consonant is preceded by a single vowel:

> begin, beginning, beginner
> stop, stopped, stopping, stoppage
> control, controlled, controlling
> occur, occurring, occurrence

The final consonant is not doubled when it is preceded by a double vowel or two vowels, when the word is not accented on the last syllable, or when the suffix begins with a consonant:

> *Preceded by a double vowel:* need, needed, needing
> *Preceded by two vowels:* treat, treated, treating
> *Word not accented on the last syllable:*
> offer, offered, offering
> benefit, benefited, benefiting
> *Suffix beginning with a consonant:* ship, shipped, shipping, [*but*] shipment

(3) Words ending with *y* change the *y* to *i* when a suffix is added, if the *y* is preceded by a consonant:

> lovely, lovelier, loveliest
> mercy, merciful, merciless
> pity, pitiful, pitiless
> copy, copied, copies

An important exception: the *y* is kept before *ing* endings:

> copy, copying
> try, tried, tries, [*but*] trying
> carry, carried, carries, [*but*] carrying

---

[1] Other useful rules are those for the spelling of the possessive case and the plural. See page 366.

The *y* remains *y* when it is preceded by a vowel:

play, played
gay, gayer, gayest
joy, joyous, joyful

Important exceptions are *said, laid, paid* [*not*] sayed, layed, payed.

(4) Words ending in silent *e* drop the *e* when they add a suffix beginning with a vowel, and keep the *e* when they add a suffix beginning with a consonant:

Suffix beginning with a vowel:
love, loving, lovable
guide, guiding, guidance
dine, dining
become, becoming
desire, desirable

Suffix beginning with a consonant:
immediate, immediately
force, forceful
sincere, sincerely

Exceptions to the rule of dropping the *e* before a vowel are *changeable, noticeable, courageous.* (The *e* is kept to preserve the soft sound of *g* and *c.*) Exceptions to the rule of keeping the *e* before a consonant are *argument, truly, awful.*

(5) The addition of the prefixes *dis-, mis-,* or *un-* does not affect the spelling of the basic word:

dis plus *agree—disagree*
mis plus *spell—misspell*
un plus *necessary—unnecessary*

b. Spelling List: Words and Word-Groups Most Commonly Misspelled. The following scientifically compiled list of words and word-groups is the result of a study of the spelling of college students made by Thomas Clark Pollock,[2] Vice President of New York University. Mr. Pollock examined 31,375 instances of misspelling collected by 599 college teachers in fifty-two colleges and universities in twenty-seven states. Although a total of 4,482 different words were misspelled, Mr. Pollock found that 407 words and word-groups were responsible for fifty percent of the more than thirty thousand instances of misspelling. Thus, by mastering the 407 words or word-groups printed below—a feat that most students can accomplish in less than ten hours—a poor speller can eliminate one half of the errors he now makes in spelling.

The words in the list are grouped on the basis of frequency of misspelling in the 31,375 instances studied; trouble spots in the words are indicated by

2 We are grateful to Mr. Pollock for permission to use the list.

the use of boldface italics, and the number at the right of each word or word-group indicates the frequency with which that particular word was misspelled.

The best way to use this list is to have someone read the words to you and put a checkmark by any word that you misspell or feel uncertain about. One method of learning the checked words is to write them on small slips (with the word *separate,* for example, one would write on one side of the slip the word properly spelled and on the other side *sep—rate* with the trouble spot left blank). The advantage of the slips is that they are easy to carry around and can be referred to in odd moments. Some students, when they have particular trouble with a word, find it helps to work out mnemonic devices—"inf*I*nite is spelled like f*I*nite," "He *ran* with persever*ance*"—beneath the proper spelling of the word on the slip.

I. Words and Word-Groups Misspelled 100 Times or More

bel*ieve*		lo*se*		rec*ei*ve	
bel*ief*	200	lo*sing*	184	rec*ei*ving	357
bene*f*it		ne*c*essary		re*ferr*ing	140
bene*f*ited		un*nec*essary	103		
bene*f*icial	144			sep*a*rate	
		o*cc*asion	186	sep*a*ration	216
ch*oo*se					
ch*o*se		o*cc*ur		simil*a*r	109
cho*ice*	116	o*cc*urred			
		o*cc*urring		su*cc*ess	
de*fi*nite		o*cc*urrence	279	su*cc*eed	
de*fi*nitely				su*cc*ession	140
de*fi*nition		*per*form			
de*fi*ne	216	*per*formance	112	*than*	
				then	125
des*cri*ption		person*al*			
des*cri*be	152	person*nel*	126	*their*	
				they're	
envir*on*ment	126	prece*de*	142	*there*	440
ex*i*st		prin*ciple*		*too*	
ex*i*stence		prin*cipal*	123	*two*	
ex*i*stent	305	privi*le*ge	127	*to*	434
its		pro*fessor*		*write*	
it's	130	pro*fession*	104	*writing*	
				writer	161

II. Words and Word-Groups Misspelled 50 to 99 Times

accommodate	51	controlled controlling	99	intelligence intelligent	65
achieve achievement	92	controversy controversial	92	interest	54
acquire	55	criticism criticize	75	interpretation interpret	62
affect affective	86	decision decided	50	led	64
all right³	90	disastrous	56	loneliness lonely	64
among	54	embarrass	69	marriage	57
analyze analysis	87	equipped equipment	87	Negro Negroes	55
apparent	73	excellent excellence	69	noticeable noticing	58
argument arguing	95	experience	50	origin original	54
began begin beginner beginning	99	explanation	62	passed past	56
busy business	55	fascinate	62	possess possession	89
category	71	forty fourth	76	prefer preferred	63
comparative conscience conscientious	50 52	grammar grammatically	68	prejudice	57
conscious	72	height	54	prevalent	66
consistent consistency	67	imagine imaginary imagination	57	probably	58
control		immediate immediately	62	proceed procedure	93

³ Although the spelling *alright* is also accepted by some dictionaries, it is listed as non-standard usage by others. Many college teachers regard *alright* as a misspelling.

prominent	50	rhythm	84	tries	
psychology				tried	82
psychoanalysis		sense	73		
psychopathic				useful	
psychosomatic	88	shining	50	useless	
				using	59
pursue	50	studying	72		
				varies	
realize		surprise	63	various	72
really	65				
				weather	
repetition	68	thorough	60	whether	81

III. Words and Word-Groups Misspelled 40 to 49 Times

accept		characteristic		hero	
acceptance		characterized	42	heroine	
acceptable				heroic	
accepting	44	coming	45	heroes	45
accident		convenience		humor	
accidentally	42	convenient	46	humorist	
				humorous	43
acquaint		difference			
acquaintance	48	different	45	hypocrisy	
				hypocrite	42
across	40	disappoint	40		
				incident	
aggressive	40	discipline		incidentally	48
		disciple	43		
appear				independent	
appearance	46	dominant		independence	44
		predominant	44		
article	40			liveliest	
		effect	47	livelihood	
athlete				liveliness	
athletic	41	exaggerate	48	lives	41
				mere	46
attended		foreign			
attendant		foreigners	44	operate	42
attendance	45				
		fundamental		opinion	46
challenge	41	fundamentally	41		
				opportunity	45
character		government			
		governor	47	paid	45

particular	44	quantity	43	suppose	40
philosophy	41	quiet	45	technique	44
planned	42	recommend	47	transferred	44
pleasant	42	ridicule ridiculous	46	unusual usually	41
possible	46	speech	41		
practical	49	sponsor	41	villain	45
prepare	47	summary summed	46	woman	49

IV. Words and Word-Groups Misspelled 30 to 39 Times

advice advise	30	consider considerably	36	further	32
				happiness	33
approach approaches	31	continuous	36	hindrance	31
author authority authoritative	36	curiosity curious	39	influential influence	30
		dependent	36	knowledge	39
basis basically	36	desirability desire	39	laboratory	32
before	36	efficient efficiency	34	maintenance	35
careless careful	35	entertain	30	ninety	39
carrying carried carries carrier	33	extremely	36	oppose opponent	32
		familiar	37	optimism parallel	38 35
		finally	36	permanent	38
conceive conceivable	36	friendliness friend	34	permit	35
condemn	35	fulfil	34	physical	31

piece	34	satire	36	undoubtedly	39
propaganda propagate	32	significance	30	weird	35
		suppress	37		
relieve	38	temperament	34	where	37
religion	38	therefore	32	whose	37
response	33	together	38	you're	38

V. Words and Word-Groups Misspelled 20 to 29 Times

accompanying accompanies accompanied accompaniment	25	attitude	21	divine	24
		boundary	21	especially	27
accomplish	22	Britain Britannica	28	excitable	28
accustom	23	capitalism	24	exercise	29
actually actuality actual	20	certain capital certainly	24	expense	21
				experiment	20
adolescence adolescent	20	chief	24	fallacy	27
		clothes	21	fantasy fantasies	21
against	20	completely	28	favorite	28
amateur	21	counselor counsel council	24	fictitious	24
amount	27				
appreciate appreciation	20	curriculum	27	field	20
approximate	27	dealt	28	financier financially	27
arouse arousing	22	despair	22	forward	23
		disease	27	guarantee guaranteed	26
attack	21	divide	28		

source	25	suspense	28	thought	20
story		symbol	21	tragedy	20
stories	24	synonymous	22		
straight	22			tremendous	23
		tendency	26		
strength	24			vacuum	23
		themselves			
strict	21	them	22	view	23
		theory			
substantial	26	theories	23	whole	26
subtle	29	those	20	yield	20

c. Spelling Test.[4] The purpose of this test is to let you see how your ability to spell compares with that of a group of other college freshmen. At Tufts University, an entering class of about 700 took this test. The table below records the results:

Rank	Score
Upper 10th	50–46
2nd 10th	45–43
3rd 10th	42–41
4th 10th	40–39
5th 10th	38–37
6th 10th	36
7th 10th	35–34
8th 10th	33–32
9th 10th	31–27
Lowest 10th	26–6

After you have taken the test, check your answers with those supplied at the end of this article, count the number of right answers, and consult the table to see where you stand or sit or lie.

In each of the following lines there will be *either one misspelled word* or *no misspelled word*. If you find a word misspelled, enter the number of the column in which it appears in the blank space to the right of the line; if you find no misspelled word, enter the number 5 (for the appropriate column) in the blank space. DO *NOT* MERELY LEAVE THE BLANK SPACE EMPTY IF THERE IS NO MISSPELLED WORD IN THE LINE.

[4] For this test we are indebted to Harold G. Ridlon, of Tufts University. Professor Ridlon is now chairman of the English Department at Bridgewater State College.

	1	2	3	4	5
(1)	undoubtadly	proceed	equipped	extremely	none _____
(2)	politician	seperate	acquaint	fallacy	none _____
(3)	controversy	sophomore	seize	believe	none _____
(4)	apparent	alright	already	altogether	none _____
(5)	curiosity	similiar	parallel	prominent	none _____
(6)	their	religion	suspense	concievable	none _____
(7)	hinderance	piece	laid	heroes	none _____
(8)	difference	relative	fallacy	sponser	none _____
(9)	disastrous	fourty	accommodate	fulfil	none _____
(10)	benefit	professor	personnel	especially	none _____
(11)	basicly	efficiency	laboratory	opponent	none _____
(12)	environment	analyze	definate	guarantee	none _____
(13)	substantial	influential	grammer	therefore	none _____
(14)	government	exaggerate	height	rhthym	none _____
(15)	wierd	tries	temperament	meant	none _____
(16)	philosophy	indispensible	mathematics	sense	none _____
(17)	definition	approximate	reminicse	completely	none _____
(18)	hypocrisy	acquire	occurrence	achieve	none _____
(19)	theories	catagory	mechanics	necessary	none _____
(20)	tragedy	miniature	prevelant	receive	none _____
(21)	interference	noticable	medicine	maneuver	none _____
(22)	experiment	sacrifice	agressive	adolescence	none _____
(23)	equiptment	affect	ninety	leisurely	none _____
(24)	magazine	desiribility	vacuum	likelihood	none _____
(25)	naturally	capitalism	sentence	transfered	none _____
(26)	lonliness	accompaniment	chief	counselor	none _____
(27)	significance	permanent	optomism	several	none _____
(28)	council	tremendous	despair	consistant	none _____
(29)	criticism	acceptable	begining	challenge	none _____
(30)	morale	accidently	divine	medieval	none _____
(31)	succeed	beneficial	surprise	posession	none _____
(32)	technique	losing	license	persistant	none _____
(33)	occured	fundamentally	comparative	shepherd	none _____
(34)	repetition	explanation	fascinate	humorous	none _____
(35)	primitive	reccommend	narrative	fantasies	none _____
(36)	preferred	controling	conscientious	height	none _____
(37)	irrelevant	expense	excellence	villian	none _____
(38)	embarass	immediately	conscious	attendant	none _____
(39)	boundary	pursue	occassion	fictitious	none _____
(40)	marriage	acheivement	grammatically	laborer	none _____
(41)	criticize	independant	perceive	guidance	none _____
(42)	amateur	synonymous	magnificence	interupt	none _____
(43)	quanity	phase	playwright	ignorance	none _____
(44)	forward	roommate	atheletic	pertain	none _____
(45)	discipline	dominant	incidentally	privilege	none _____

	1	2	3	4	5
(46)	surpress	represent	stories	accustom	none _____
(47)	strength	schedule	tendancy	source	none _____
(48)	performance	controlled	benefitted	psychology	none _____
(49)	writing	authoratative	precede	maintenance	none _____
(50)	considerably	financially	existence	arguement	none _____

Answers:

(1) 1	(11) 1	(21) 2	(31) 4	(41) 2
(2) 2	(12) 3	(22) 3	(32) 4	(42) 4
(3) 5	(13) 3	(23) 1	(33) 1	(43) 1
(4) 2	(14) 4	(24) 2	(34) 5	(44) 3
(5) 2	(15) 1	(25) 4	(35) 2	(45) 5
(6) 4	(16) 2	(26) 1	(36) 2	(46) 1
(7) 1	(17) 3	(27) 3	(37) 4	(47) 3
(8) 4	(18) 5	(28) 4	(38) 1	(48) 3
(9) 2	(19) 2	(29) 3	(39) 3	(49) 2
(10) 5	(20) 3	(30) 2	(40) 2	(50) 4

50. CAPITALIZATION   Cap

Although capitalization is not completely standardized, most capitalization is conveniently prescribed by convention. Capitals are used for two general purposes: to mark beginnings and to indicate proper names and words derived from proper names.

a. A capital is used as the initial letter of:

(1) A sentence or group of words punctuated with an end stop.

Will the Senate ratify the measure? Perhaps. If it does, the President will have gained a victory.

(2) A sentence (or sentence equivalent) directly quoted within another sentence.

He said, "You are right."

(3) Traditionally, each line of poetry.

Each might his several province well command,
Would all but stoop to what they understand.

(4) Sometimes a formally introduced series or an independent statement that follows a colon.

A capital is used as an initial letter in: A sentence or group of words that . . . .
A useful spelling rule is: Words ending with *y* change *y* to *i* when a suffix is added, if the *y* is preceded by a consonant.

b. One or more capital letters are used for:

(1) Proper nouns—nouns that name particular persons, places, institutions, organizations, creeds, nations, races, tribes, things (Mary, Fifth Avenue, the Supreme Court, the United Nations, a Baptist, Italy, a Negro, a Mohawk, the Ohio River).

(2) Derivatives of proper nouns (especially adjective derivatives) used with a "proper meaning" (British, Ciceronian, Miltonic). Some derivatives of proper nouns, after long-continued usage, lose their proper meaning and are sometimes written in lower case (venetian blinds, plaster of paris). Good desk dictionaries indicate whether a particular entry is capitalized.

(3) Names of deity and (often) pronouns referring to deity (God, His will, the Holy Spirit).

(4) Names of sacred books or the equivalent of names (Bible, Koran, Old Testament, the Scripture).

(5) Important words in titles of books, periodicals, articles, literary works. It is customary *not* to capitalize an unemphatic article (a, an, the), preposition, or conjunction unless it appears as the first word of the title (*The Turn of the Screw, The Man Who Came to Dinner*).

(6) A title or designation immediately preceding the name of a person (President Nixon, Secretary of State Rogers, Captain Jones, Father Ryan, Chairman Humphrey, Dean Barker). When the title follows the name as an appositive, usage differs. Some authorities would capitalize such appositives only when the titles indicate preeminence or distinction (Richard M. Nixon, President of the United States, or Victoria, Queen of England). In certain contexts, though, less important titles are capitalized. A college newspaper editor might appropriately capitalize: Richard Manifriends, President of the Student Council, or Mr. Claude Choosey, Director of Admissions.

(7) Many widely used abbreviations for proper names (CORE, WAVE, CARE, UN, N.Y., N.J.).

(8) Academic degrees and their abbreviations (Doctor of Laws, Master of Arts, A. B., Ph.D.).

(9) Days of the week, months of the year, periods of history, holy days and holidays, the abbreviations A.D. and B.C. (Monday, October, the Middle Ages, Good Friday, the Fourth of July, A.D. 307), but *not* autumn or other seasons unless they are personified—"Old Winter with his blustering breath...."

(10) The pronoun *I* and the interjection *O*.

College students ordinarily have little trouble with capitalization. Their only common difficulty comes from failing to distinguish between words used to name a *particular* person, place, or thing (used, that is, as proper nouns), and the same words used in a general way, and therefore not conventionally capitalized. Some illustrations will clarify this distinction.

I told the whole story to Mother. [*Mother* here takes the place of a proper name, and so is capitalized.]

I told the whole story to my mother.

He had an audience with the King. [*King* refers to a particular person.]
He had seen enough of kings and queens. [The words *kings* and *queens* are used generally.]

He went to Elliot High School and then to Oberlin College. [Names of particular institutions]
Since he barely got through high school, he is sure to fail in college.

I used to live on Quincy Street, but now I live on Ashland Boulevard. [Proper names]
They are planning to make this street into a boulevard.

He intends to vote for Mayor Dawson.
Dawson hopes to be elected mayor.

I am taking Mathematics 2 and History 2. [Names of particular courses]
I am taking mathematics and history. [*But*] I am taking French and English. [Names derived from proper nouns]

He comes from the South and does not like the Middle West. [Proper names of sections of the country]
He lives two miles south of town.

EXERCISES

Insert capitals where they are needed in the following sentences.

1. the doctor gave mrs. smith a book entitled *the care of young children* and told her to take it with her on her south american trip.

2. he said that judge black and dr. holmes live on high street near a broad avenue that leads to cherokee park.

3. "the high school i attended was small," mother said. "when i was in college at the university of southern california, i wished i had taken more french and latin; then i could have got my a.b. degree more easily."

4. my father and uncle gerald were freshmen in college together and members of the same fraternity, beta theta pi; later they served together in the united states navy, and both became captains on destroyers before the end of world war ii.

5. mr. martin, my chemistry professor, thinks the republicans are stronger than the democrats in the middle west; professor boyd, who drove west last summer during the months of july and august, says that the negroes and the indians will vote democratic.

51. TITLES

a. Titles of books, magazines, newspapers, and plays are conventionally italicized. This practice should be followed by college students in their writing. Italics are represented in manuscript by underlining.

b. Titles of short pieces—articles, stories, essays, poems, chapters of books—are put in quotation marks. Usage varies on the titles of long poems and essays; usually they are italicized if they are being discussed as separate units, and put in quotation marks if they are regarded as parts of a larger work.

c. Capital letters are used for the first word of a title and for all other words except unemphatic articles, conjunctions, and short prepositions:

The Short Stories of Henry James	*Romeo and Juliet*
The Naked and the Dead	*The Atlantic*
How Green Was My Valley	the New York *Times*

(Note that the name of a city which is part of the title of a newspaper is usually not italicized.)

d. In writing the title of his own theme, the student should center the title on the first line of the first page, and capitalize the first word and all other important words. He should use neither underlining nor quotation marks for this title.

For titles of people see "Capitalization," page 466.

For further information about titles in bibliographies and footnotes see pages 313 and 329.

EXERCISES

Correct the writing of titles in the following sentences:

1. His article entitled where is America going? appeared in Saturday review and was later reprinted in reader's digest.
2. He has written three short stories, love lost, the spider, and the quiet around the pool, and one novel, the sadness in the heart.
3. The article Mars in the Columbia encyclopedia enabled me to understand the chapter called the atmosphere of Mars in that difficult book the universe we live in.
4. This week I read the ladies' home journal, the Yale review, time magazine, the Boston herald, and the Sunday New York times, in addition to Shakespeare's Hamlet and Keats' sonnet Bright Star.

52. SYLLABIFICATION   Div

Sometimes, in manuscript as well as in print, it is necessary to divide a word at the end of a line to make a reasonably even margin. Such division is best avoided as much as possible in typed or handwritten manuscript. Where it seems necessary, the following principles should be kept in mind:

a. **Words of one syllable are never divided, and words of more than one syllable are divided only between syllables.** Often the pronunciation of a word will indicate its syllabification: *re-lief, al-to-geth-er, dis-ad-van-tage.* When pronunciation is not an adequate guide, the dictionary, which shows the syllabification, should be consulted.

b. **Words should not be divided in such a way that a single letter stands at the end of one line or the beginning of the next.**

c. **The hyphen, indicating that the word is divided, is placed at the end of the line, not at the beginning of the next line.**

EXERCISES

Which of the following words can properly be divided at the end of a line? How should the division be made?

alone, school, many, obedience, although, through, elegant, enough, height, hilarious, swimming, drowned, interesting, erase, eradicate, irate, italics, heavy, interpretation, difference, additional

53. NUMBERS   Num

a. **In formal and informal writing, numbers are usually spelled out when the number can be expressed in one or two words:** *two, fifty-three, six hundred, ten thousand, five million.* **They are commonly written as figures when more than two words are needed to express them:** $29.95; 1,571,142; 10:45 A.M.

b. **Figures are used in writing dates, street numbers, page and chapter numbers, and any group of numbers appearing in the same passage.**

May 30, 1964   19 Weston Avenue   Chapter 4, page 215
Take notes on 3 by 5, 4 by 6, or 5 by 8 cards.

c. **Figures are not used, however, in formal invitations and replies.**

Sunday, the twentieth of January, at four o'clock

d. A number is always written out when it occurs at the beginning of a sentence.

Three hundred and sixty people were present.

e. Roman numerals are used for main headings in outlines, usually for chapter headings, for acts and scenes of plays, sometimes for volume numbers in footnotes, and for page numbers in the preliminary pages of books.

A small Roman numeral preceding a larger one is subtracted from it: ix (9), xix (19). The basic Roman numerals from which other numbers are created are: i (1), v (5), x (10), 1 (50), c (100), d (500), m (1000). The following table shows how these basic numerals are combined to make other numbers:

2 ii	19 xix	70 lxx	200 cc
4 iv	30 xxx	80 lxxx	400 cd
7 vii	38 xxxviii	90 xc	600 dc
9 ix	40 xl	99 xcix	900 cm
12 xii	43 xliii	120 cxx	1500 md
15 xv	51 li	150 cl	2000 mm

EXERCISES

What numbers in the following sentences should be written in words?

1. $5000 is not an adequate income in 1971, however adequate it may have been in the 1st years of the 20th century.

2. I live at 2083 Percy Street; I am 62 years old; I have been unemployed for 1 year, since September 22, 1969; and I have no private income aside from $150.00 from investments. You can reach me by calling 617–2236.

3. *Encyclopaedia Britannica*, I, 863.

4. Mr. John Brown accepts with pleasure the kind invitation of Mr. and Mrs. James Albert Smith for Saturday, June 30, at 3:00.

5. In Chapter 3, page 486, the author says that in 1935 pork chops were 19 cents a pound, lettuce was 5 cents a head, a good suit cost $22.50, and a ton of coal was $10.95.

54. ABBREVIATIONS   Ab

In a time of multiplying national and international organizations, projects, and agencies, space-saving abbreviations appear increasingly in print. SALT (strategic-arms-limitation talks), MIRV (multiple independently targetable reentry vehicles), AFVN (Armed Forces Vietnam), LM (lunar module), FAA (Federal Aviation Administration) are some of many examples. Such abbreviations, especially when they are new, may be confusing; if they become well established, they are convenient short cuts.

In general, students will be wise to avoid in formal and in high informal writing all abbreviations except very well-established ones. If, however, the content of a paper requires frequent repetition of a long name for which there is a recognized abbreviation, it is permissible first to write the full name with the abbreviation following it in parentheses, and after that to use the abbreviation alone: National Institute of Mental Health (NIMH).

a. Well-established abbreviations that are conventional even in formal writing are:

(1) Abbreviations of time accompanying the year or hour: B.C., A.D., a.m., p.m. [or] A.M., P.M.

(2) Certain titles used with proper names: Mr., Mrs., Dr. [but] President Nixon, General Marshall, Governor Ford, Senator Fulbright, Professor Brown, the Honorable James Peel, the Reverend Lloyd Bone.

(3) Titles and degrees used after proper names: Sr., Jr., Ph.D., L.L.D., M.D.

(4) In footnotes, certain conventional abbreviations: *op. cit., ibid.*, cf., p., vol., ed.

(5) A few generally accepted abbreviations for technical terms: T.N.T. (or TNT), D.D.T. (or DDT).

(6) Widely accepted abbreviated names of organizations and government agencies: D.A.R., Y.M.C.A., NBC, NASA, NLRB. (Note that periods, the usual sign of an abbreviation, are omitted in some abbreviated names of organizations, and are generally omitted in names of government agencies.)

b. Other abbreviations should usually be avoided in formal and high informal writing, and especially the following abbreviations:

(1) Abbreviations of countries, states, months, days, streets, and proper names.

(2) Abbreviations of titles, even generally accepted abbreviations like Mr., Mrs., and Dr., when they are not used with proper names.

(3) Slang abbreviations like "lab," "ec," "frat," "phys ed."

EXERCISES

Correct the faulty use of abbreviations in the following sentences:

1. I have an appointment with the Dr. next Tues. at 9:45 a.m.
2. I hope to spend the Xmas vacation, from Dec. 20 to Jan. 3, visiting Rev. Jones & family in Madison, Wis.; his son Jr. is my roommate.

3. Prof. Lane discussed with the ec. class the recent AFL–CIO dispute in Paterson, N.J.

4. According to an AP report, unemployment in the U.S. has decreased five % since last Feb.

5. The noted artist Chas. Lee was born in a humble cottage on Elm St. in Springfield, Mass., in the p.m. of November 14, 1920.

55. MANUSCRIPT FORM   Ms

a. A typewritten paper should be double-spaced, on a good grade of standard 8½- by 11-inch paper.

b. A theme in longhand should be written legibly in dark ink, on wide-lined white paper, 8½ by 11 inches.

c. Only one side of the paper should be used.

d. Substantial margins should be left on both sides of each page.

e. The title of the paper should be written, and centered, at the top of the first page.

f. Pages should be numbered with arabic numerals in the upper right-hand corner.

g. The method of endorsement prescribed by the instructor should be carefully followed. The endorsement here recommended is as follows:

Henry C. Walker [Student's name]
English 1C [Course and section number]
October 1, 1971 [Date the paper is due]
Professor J. S. Holt [Instructor]
My Brother and I [Title of the paper]

h. The finished paper should be neat and legible; however, slight revisions may be indicated in the following ways:

(1) The signs, ¶ and "no ¶," in the margin may be used to mark a change in paragraphing.

(2) The deletion of a word or phrase is indicated by drawing a line through it. Words and phrases to be omitted should *not* be put in parentheses.

(3) Insertions are written between the lines and indicated by a caret [∧].

56. OUTLINE FORM   Outl

In Chapter 3 we discuss the kind of outline most useful to students in writing informal themes—the rough outline which is simply an informal jotting down and logical grouping of ideas for the paper. The more formal outline, usually required for longer papers and sometimes for short ones, is a systematic and conventionalized way of representing the content and organization of a piece of writing. In the formal outline, the headings and subheadings are arranged, and numbered or lettered, in such a way that the order and importance of points in the paper and the relationship between those points is shown exactly and clearly. The formal outline is the skeleton of the paper. We say in Chapter 3 that its very formality and inflexibility sometimes bind the writer to an organization not the best for his material. To avoid being so bound, the writer should begin with a rough outline, and let the formal outline evolve from the material itself. This process of building an expanded formal outline from a tentative informal outline is discussed in the section "Building the Outline" in Chapter 14. The virtue of the formal outline is that it enables the writer, as well as the reader, to see at a glance the plan and logic of the whole paper.

Outlines usually follow a conventional system of alternating numbers and letters to show the relationships between sections of the material:

    I. _____
        A. _____
        B. _____
        C. _____
            1. _____
            2. _____
    II. _____
        A. _____
            1. _____
            2. _____
                a. _____
                b. _____
            3. _____
        B. _____
    III. _____
        A. _____
            1. _____
            2. _____
            3. _____
        B. _____
        C. _____
            1. _____
            2. _____
                a. _____
                b. _____
                c. _____
    IV. _____
        A. _____

B. _____
    1. _____
    2. _____
       a. _____
       b. _____
C. _____
D. _____

There are two principal kinds of formal outlines: the *topical outline,* in which the headings are brief phrases or single words; and the more elaborate and less common *sentence outline,* in which the headings are complete sentences. The form adopted should be followed consistently; a complete sentence should not appear unexpectedly in a topical outline, nor should a sentence outline lapse suddenly into phrases or single words in its headings.

Whether the outline is sentence or topical, it should observe three main principles of correct outline form. These three principles are matters not simply of convention and form, but of clear thinking and logical arrangement.

a. Headings and subheadings that are designated by the same kind of number or letter must be of approximately equal importance.

Points I, II, III, and IV must be equally important main divisions of the paper; points A, B, and C under I must be topics of equal weight, all similarly related to I, of which they are subdivisions. (Students should re-examine an outline with more than six major headings. Usually it represents poor division, because the major headings are unequal; some of them could better be made subordinate to a single, more inclusive heading.)

b. Headings of equal importance must be expressed in parallel form. (In the sentence outline, parallel form is maintained as long as each heading is a full sentence.)

This is the familiar principle of parallelism applied to the outline. If A and B are noun phrases, C must be a noun phrase too, since the three of them have the same relationship to I, and a function of the outline is to make such relationships clear.

c. Any heading that has subdivisions must have at least two subdivisions.

This is simply a matter of logic and common sense. A subordinate heading in an outline indicates that a major heading is being divided into parts. Since nothing can be divided into only one part, correct outlines do not have single subheadings.[5]

The outline below violates all three of these principles of good outline form. Its lack of logic may serve to clarify the principles:

[5] The one possible exception to this rule is that one may list by itself an example used to develop a particular heading.

MY TASTES IN READING

I. Westerns and detective stories
    A. Excitement and adventure
    B. Relaxation
    C. Quick and easy reading

 II. Biography
    A. Feel that I am learning something

 III. Lytton Strachey's biographies
    A. *Eminent Victorians*
    B. *Queen Victoria*
    C. *Elizabeth and Essex*

 IV. I most enjoy reading actual history
    A. Journals and personal accounts of the war
    B. Books on Russia
    C. Books on American life
        1. *State of the Nation*
        2. *Inside U.S.A.*
        3. *Segregation*

This outline violates the principles of logical outlining in these ways:

(1) The four main headings are not of equal importance. Heading III, "Lytton Strachey's biographies," is not equal to the other headings, but is logically a subdivision of II, "Biography."

(2) The main headings are not expressed in parallel form. I, II, and III are topical in form; IV is a complete sentence.

(3) Heading II has a single subtopic; that is, the topic "Biography" is illogically divided into only one point. Changing III into B under II, and rephrasing A ("Feel that I am learning something") so that A and B are parallel in form would remedy this defect in logic in the outline.

The following formal, topical outline of a student research paper illustrates correct outline form:

THE BATTLE OF TRAFALGAR

I. Situation in 1805
    A. Napoleon's invasion plans
    B. French and Spanish fleet at Cadiz

II. Nelson's command of the English fleet at Cadiz
    A. His plan for victory
        1. Memorandum
        2. Reaction to plan
    B. Condition of his fleet
        1. Smallness of fleet compared to that of enemy
        2. Loss of ships sent to Gibraltar
        3. Request for additional force

III. Preliminaries to attack
  A. October 19
  B. October 20
  C. Dawn of October 21
IV. The advance to attack
  A. Nelson during advance
    1. Presentiment of death
    2. Prayer for victory
    3. His immortal signal
  B. Arrangement of ships in advance
    1. In leeward division
    2. In windward division
V. The battle
  A. Attack of leeward line
    1. Firing on *Royal Sovereign*
    2. Action against *Santa Anna* and *Fougueux*
  B. Attack of windward line
    1. Firing on *Victory*
    2. Attack on *Bucentaure*
    3. Engagement with *Redoubtable*
      a. Damage to French
      b. Injury to Nelson
    4. Other ships in the fighting
  C. English successes in center and rear
    1. *Redoubtable*
    2. *Fougueux*
    3. *Bucentaure*
    4. *Santissima Trinidad*
    5. *Santa Anna*
    6. *Belleisle*'s action against the enemy
  D. Entrance of enemy van
    1. Defeat of two
    2. Flight of three others
    3. Flight of Dumanoir with remainder
VI. Results of battle
  A. Immediate
    1. Death of Nelson
    2. Ships captured by English
  B. Long-run
    1. English superiority on the sea
    2. Cancellation of Napoleon's invasion plans

    The sentence outline is more complex than the topical outline: it is longer than a topical outline of the same material, and it often requires more careful phrasing; sometimes there is a certain artificiality and repetition involved in stating points in complete sentences. On the other hand, the sentence outline has the advantage of being more detailed and informative, and so of giving a clearer view of the contents of the paper. The following sentence outline of the same material represented by the topical outline above will illustrate:

THE BATTLE OF TRAFALGAR

I. The situation in 1805 was grave for England.
    A. Napoleon planned to invade England with a large army.
    B. The French and Spanish fleet at Cadiz was to gain temporary control of the Channel for the invasion attempt.

II. Nelson was sent to assume command of the English fleet at Cadiz.
    A. Nelson devised a brilliant plan for victory by a double line of attack.
        1. He described the plan in a memorandum to Collingwood, his second in command.
        2. Commanders and captains received the plan with enthusiasm.
    B. Nelson was seriously concerned about his fleet.
        1. He had only twenty-seven ships of the line compared to the thirty-six the enemy was reported to have.
        2. He was forced to detach a squadron of four to Gibraltar.
        3. He sent the Admiralty an urgent request for additional force.

III. The preliminaries to attack began two days before the battle.
    A. On October 19, the Allies unmoored and the English sailed to the Straits of Gibraltar.
    B. On October 20, the English headed back to Cadiz, discovered the Allies, and trailed them through the night.
    C. At dawn on October 21, the fleets sighted each other, and the Allies headed north to form their battle line.

IV. The advance to attack followed Nelson's plan exactly.
    A. During the advance Nelson remained calm.
        1. He had a calm presentiment of death.
        2. He prayed for victory.
        3. He sent the fleet the signal: "England expects that every man will do his duty."
    B. The English approached in two elongated groups.
        1. Collingwood's *Royal Sovereign* led the leeward division.
        2. Nelson's *Victory* led the windward division.

V. The battle was a decisive victory for the English.
    A. The leeward line attacked the rear.
        1. The *Royal Sovereign* was fired on.
        2. She blasted the *Santa Anna* and the *Fougueux*.
    B. The windward line attacked the center.
        1. The *Victory* was fired on.
        2. She cut line and attacked the *Bucentaure*.
        3. She closed with the *Redoubtable*.
            a. The French were driven from their guns.
            b. Nelson was hit by a French marksman.
        4. Other ships entered the fighting.
    C. The English were victorious in center and rear.

        1. One by one the *Redoubtable,* the *Fougueux,* the *Santissima Trinidad,* and the *Santa Anna* were overcome.
        2. The English ship *Belleisle* raised havoc among the enemy.
    D. The enemy van unsuccessfully entered the action.
        1. Two ships were overcome.
        2. Three others fled to the southeast.
        3. Dumanoir fled with the remainder.
VI. The results of the battle of Trafalgar were important.
    A. The immediate results were these:
        1. Nelson died.
        2. The English captured eighteen ships and broke Allied sea power.
    B. The long-run results were these:
        1. English superiority on the seas was assured.
        2. Napoleon's plan to invade England was cancelled forever.

Formal outlines are correct and useful when they accurately reflect the organization of the paper, and when logical subordination and proper parallelism show the relationship between sections of the material.

HANDBOOK

Section 6

USING
THE DICTIONARY

Much of the value of dictionaries is lost by the uninformed use or inadequate use which many people, including some college students, make of these remarkable books. Although students have been, to some extent, familiar with dictionaries for years, they frequently do not know what kinds of information dictionaries contain; and they are frequently incompetent in the most common use of the dictionary—finding the pronunciation or the definition of a word—because they have not familiarized themselves with the methods and symbols by which information is conveyed.

Dictionaries differ, of course, in their size and completeness. The next time the student is in the reference room in the library he should examine such massive unabridged dictionaries as *The Oxford English Dictionary* (ten volumes and supplement); *Webster's Third New International Dictionary of the English Language; The New Standard Dictionary of the English Language; A Dictionary of American English on Historical Principles* (four volumes); and *The Random House Dictionary of the English Language.* Such dictionaries, though invaluable for certain scholarly purposes, are beyond the means of most college students. For ordinary use, a good desk dictionary is entirely satisfactory.

Listed below, in alphabetical order, are six widely-used desk dictionaries:

The American College Dictionary. New York: Random House.

The American Heritage Dictionary of the English Language. Boston: Houghton Mifflin Company.

Funk and Wagnalls Standard College Dictionary, Text Edition. New York: Harcourt, Brace and World.

The Random House Dictionary of the English Language, College Edition. New York: Random House.

Webster's New World Dictionary of the English Language, Second College Edition. Cleveland, Ohio: World Publishing Company.

Webster's Seventh New Collegiate Dictionary. Springfield, Massachusetts: G. and C. Merriam Company.

The way a dictionary presents information about words can best be shown by examining an entry:

fin·ish (fin′ish) *v.t.* **1.** To complete or bring to an end; come to the end of: to *finish* a job; to *finish* a semester. **2.** To use up completely; consume. **3.** To perfect or complete by doing all things requisite or desirable: to *finish* a work of art. **4.** To perfect (a person) in social graces, education, etc. **5.** To give (fabric, wood, etc.) a particular surface quality or effect. **6.** *Informal* To kill, destroy, or defeat. — *v.i.* **7.** To reach or come to an end; stop. — *n.* **1.** The conclusion or last stage of anything; end. **2.** Something that completes or perfects. **3.** Completeness and perfection of detail; smoothness of execution. **4.** Perfection or polish in speech, manners, education, etc. **5.** The surface quality or appearance of textiles, paint, etc.: a rough or glossy *finish*. **6.** Woodwork, such as paneling or doors, used to complete the interior of a building. **7.** A material used in finishing: an oil *finish* on a painting. [< OF *feniss-,* stem of *fenir* to end < L *finire* < *finis* end] — **fin′ish·er** *n.*
— **Syn.** (verb) **1.** conclude, terminate, close. Compare END.

Reprinted by permission from the FUNK & WAGNALLS STANDARD ® COLLEGE DICTIONARY, copyright 1963 by Funk & Wagnalls Company, Inc.

We see that dictionaries give this information about entries: (1) spelling of the word, including the way it is divided into syllables; (2) pronunciation; (3) grammatical function or functions of the word; (4) definitions; (5) etymology or history of the word; (6) sometimes synonyms and antonyms. Dictionaries also supply information about principal parts of irregular verbs, irregular plurals of nouns, case forms of pronouns, capitalization of proper nouns and adjectives derived from proper nouns, idiomatic use of certain words and expressions, and the status of some words and expressions.

The student, to use his dictionary efficiently, should be familiar with the front and back matter; that is, the sections preceding and following the main alphabetical listing of words. He should locate, for easy reference, the table of abbreviations used in the dictionary. Some abbreviations name the grammatical function of a word: *n.* (noun), *v.i.* (intransitive verb); some mark the use of a word in a special field: *Econ.* (Economics), *Geol.* (Geology); some indicate etymology: OF (Old French), Gk. (Greek); still others may be status or stylistic labels: *dial.* (dialectal), *obs.* (obsolete), *illit.* (illiterate), *Brit.* (British rather than American usage). Of particular importance is the section on the plan and use of this dictionary. The owner needs to know, for example, whether to look for biographical names in the general alphabet of the book (as in most dictionaries) or whether to look in a separate listing of biographical names (as in *Webster's Seventh*). Editors of the dictionary describe their policies in arranging several definitions of a word and in giving alternate spellings or pronunciations of a word. Editors also define any restrictive labels they use, such as *colloquial, informal,* or *slang.* Since dictionaries differ somewhat about the meaning of status labels, the owner of a dictionary should be sure that he is interpreting the labels as the editors intended.

In general, the marking of a term as informal, colloquial, dialectal, or slang is not necessarily a condemnation of the term. Though such expressions are out of place in formal writing, the fact that they appear in the dictionary is evidence of their wide use. The writer must judge whether they are appropriate in the context in which he thinks of using them; the dictionary label is not a prohibition but simply an aid to him in judging.

Judgments about usage have been a problem for makers, critics, and users of dictionaries, especially since the publication in 1961 of *Webster's Third New International Dictionary,* on which *Webster's Seventh New Collegiate* is based. In these dictionaries, the Merriam-Webster editors abandoned both the label *colloquial* and the practice of labeling words and phrases that are generally called colloquial. A student using *Webster's Seventh* should be aware that many expressions given without limiting label in that dictionary are marked *colloquial* or *informal* in other dictionaries. The *Standard College Dictionary,* published later, freely uses the label *informal* and also includes full usage notes about a number of troublesome terms. In a recent innovation in dictionary-making, editors of *The American Heritage Dictionary* (1969) submitted some six hundred matters of debatable usage to a panel of more than a hundred experts on language—writers, editors, and public figures who had demonstrated their ability to use English well. Members of this Panel on Usage were by no means unanimous in their judgments; but the Usage Notes following entries in *The American Heritage Dictionary* report the number of panelists who found acceptable or unacceptable the expressions submitted to them. The Usage Notes in this dictionary provide valuable guidance to the student concerned with appropriate usage and style.

In view of disagreements among the panelists of *The American Heritage Dictionary,* it is not surprising that different dictionaries do not always agree about the status of particular words or meanings. For example, *contact* as a verb meaning "to get in touch with" appears without restrictive label or comment in *Webster's Seventh;* it is labeled *informal* and is accompanied by a comment ("This informal usage, regarded with disfavor by some, is widely used") in the *Standard College Dictionary;* and it is found "not appropriate to formal contexts" by sixty-six per cent of *The American Heritage* panel.

When experts do not agree—and even, sometimes, when they do—the writer must rely on his own sense of language. He will develop that sense by reading, listening to, and absorbing the language of educated and able people.

In another way, too, dictionaries cannot take the place of experience with words. Every time a word appears in context it has a meaning at least slightly different from that in other contexts. Dictionary editors note the meaning of the word in a number of contexts and attempt to define it. Sometimes, for further clarification, they distinguish between the meaning of a word and that of other words used as synonyms. For example, here is a part of the entry for the adjective *base* taken from *Webster's New World Dictionary*.

> *SYN.*—**base** implies a putting of one's own interests ahead of one's obligations, as because of greed or cowardice (*base* motives); **mean** suggests a contemptible pettiness of character or conduct (his *mean* attempts to slander her); **ignoble** suggests a lack of high moral or intellectual qualities (to work for an *ignoble* end); **abject**, in careful discrimination, implies debasement and a contemptible lack of self-respect (an *abject* servant); **sordid** connotes the depressing drabness of that which is mean or base (the *sordid* details of their affair); **vile** suggests disgusting foulness or depravity (*vile* epithets); **low** suggests rather generally coarseness, vulgarity, depravity, etc., specifically in reference to taking grossly unfair advantage (so *low* as to kick a cripple's crutch); **degrading** suggests a lowering or corruption of moral standards (the *degrading* aspects of army life). —*ANT.* noble, moral, virtuous.

Page 121
From *Webster's New World Dictionary, College Edition*,
copyright 1964 by The World Publishing Company,
Cleveland, Ohio.

The best that dictionary editors can do, though, is to define the central and common meanings of a word; they cannot communicate the full range of meaning and suggestion that the word may take on as it is used in different contexts. For this reason an English instructor may be justified in objecting to the use of a word in a particular context even though that usage appears to be sanctioned by a good dictionary. For this reason, too, it is generally wise not to use a word that one finds in a dictionary (or in word lists) until one has heard or read the word in contexts which further establish the shades of meaning and suggestion that it may carry.

These limitations, however, are slight in comparison with the varied, valuable and interesting information that dictionaries give. Because the dictionary is the most useful of reference books, a student is seriously handicapped unless he has an up-to-date dictionary of his own and knows how to use it well. Knowing and using his dictionary, on the other hand, can greatly increase the student's vocabulary and stimulate new interest in the fascinating study of words.

EXERCISES

1. On a sheet of paper to be turned in to your instructor, supply the following information about the dictionary that you are using in this course.

(a) the full title

(b) the latest copyright date (to be found on the back of the title page)

(c) the pages in the front matter on which the following are discussed: (1) pronunciation, (2) etymologies, (3) synonyms and antonyms, (4) restrictive labels (also called "functional labels," "levels of usage," or "usage labels")

2. Sometimes your dictionary will list alternative pronunciations or spellings. What do the editors say about the standing (i.e., acceptability) of such alternatives?

3. Before consulting your dictionary, pronounce aloud each of the words listed below, then look up each word, consult the pronunciation chart, and pronounce the word carefully in the way or ways indicated in your dictionary. If there are words that you have mispronounced, note beside them on this page the pronunciation or pronunciations given in your dictionary:

abdomen	detour	government	library
athlete	dictionary	hotel	*pièce de résistance*
Beethoven	economics	interesting	Roosevelt
bottle	either	laissez-faire	stomach
chauffeur	farther	leisure	tomato

4. Read the full entry, paying especial attention to etymology, for each of the following words and consider the ways in which word meanings change and develop. Which word seems most interesting to you and why?

agnostic	gerrymander	metaphysics	harrowing
barbecue	glamour	paragraph	sanguine
divine	humor	period	sophomore

(For a full treatment of the history of these words you would find it interesting to consult in the library the *Oxford English Dictionary*.)

5. Choose three words, any three you wish, and look up each in the *Oxford English Dictionary, Webster's Dictionary of Synonyms,* and *Roget's Thesaurus.* Consider the usefulness for different purposes of these three books.

6. Choose a common word that you know well and write a dictionary entry for it. Make your entry as complete as you can without consulting a dictionary.

7. Consult your dictionary and jot down the principal parts of the following verbs.

break	hang (a person)	
dive	spring	swim

8. Below is a list of words similar in appearance and sometimes confused in meaning. Read the list and then look up in your dictionary any words you are not sure about.

adapt, adopt	continual, continuous	peace, piece
all ready, already	credible, credulous	personal, personnel
allusion, illusion	formally, formerly	principal, principle
berth, birth	human, humane	quiet, quite
censor, censure	imply, infer	right, rite
coarse, course	later, latter	stationary, stationery
conscience, conscious	passed, past	weather, whether

9. According to your dictionary, as what parts of speech are the following words used? Are there some uses not appropriate in formal English?

aggravate	enthuse	like
bust	good	slow
contact	human	sure
due (also *due to*)		

10. Examine the following sets of words derived from the same Greek or Latin root. From the words that you know in each list, determine the meaning of the root, and then try to determine the meaning of any unfamiliar words. Look up in the dictionary words about which you are unsure.

1. telegraph, phonograph, autograph, graphic, graphics, monograph, graphology, diagram, epigram, electrocardiogram.

2. convert, divert, pervert, revert, subvert, convertible, extrovert, introvert, verse, adverse, conversely, advertisement.

3. biology, biography, bioplasm, biogenesis, biotherapy, biochemistry, antibiotic.

4. spectator, spectacles, inspect, prospect, aspect, respect, disrespect, specter, perspective, retrospect, introspective.

5. philanthropy, Philadelphia, philosophy, Anglophile, bibliophile, philharmonic.

6. reduce, deduce, adduce, seduce, produce, productive, deductive, induction, introduce, educate, duchess, ductless, aqueduct.

11. In the lists of words in exercise 10, of how many roots besides the ones in boldface print, and of how many prefixes, can you deduce the meaning? Try to think of other words in which these forms (*tele, phono, epi, mono, con,* etc.) are used.

12. What are the plurals of the following nouns? Consult your dictionary if you are uncertain.

alumnus	deer	index
basis	father-in-law	phenomenon
commander in chief	hanger-on	president-elect
curriculum		

HANDBOOK

Section 7

A GLOSSARY
OF USAGE

The purpose of this glossary is to supply information about a number of expressions and constructions in current American usage. As we have suggested elsewhere, accepted usage is not determined by logic or "rules" of grammar, but by the actual prevailing practice of what linguists call the "prestige group," educated people who occupy positions of respect or leadership in their society. Modern grammarians, dictionary makers, and other authorities on language generally agree that their objective is not to *prescribe* what is correct but to *describe* the actual practice of speakers and writers whose use of language determines the standard.

Although these authorities agree that their function is descriptive rather than prescriptive, they are still faced with the difficult problem of giving an accurate description of a language that varies somewhat in different sections, that changes with time, and that is used by about two hundred and fifty million people. It is not surprising, therefore, that dictionaries and books on grammar and usage sometimes differ in their effort to describe the standing of a particular word or expression.

In preparing this glossary we have examined such books as *The Oxford English Dictionary, Webster's Third International Dictionary,* the six desk dictionaries listed in the section on the dictionary, *A Dictionary of American*

Usage by Margaret Nicholson, *The Perrin-Smith Handbook of Current English,* *A Dictionary of Contemporary Usage* by Bergen Evans and Cornelia Evans, *Current American Usage* by Margaret M. Bryant, *Modern American Usage: A Guide* by Wilson Follett (edited and completed by Jacques Barzun and others), H. W. Fowler's *A Dictionary of Modern English Usage* (second edition), and *The Random House Dictionary of the English Language.*

The student, before he uses this glossary, should be familiar with Chapter 2, in which various terms used here—*standard* and *nonstandard, formal, informal,* and *colloquial*—are discussed and defined.

A, an. *A* is used before words beginning with a consonant sound or a sounded *h*—*a chair, a Yale lock, a house; an* is used before words beginning with a vowel or an unsounded *h*—*an elm, an honor.*

Accept, except. *Accept* is a verb meaning *to receive willingly* or *with approval:* "He accepted the gift"—"He accepted the decision." *Except* may be a verb meaning *to exclude* ("He excepted Tom, but he invited the others"), or it may be a preposition meaning *with the exclusion of:* "Everyone was pleased except the instructor."

Ad. The abbreviated form of *advertisement* is colloquial. The full form is preferable in writing.

Affect, effect. *Affect* is most commonly used as a verb. In one sense it means *to pretend* or *to assume* ("He affected ignorance"); in another sense it means *to influence* or *to move* ("The tragic accident affected him deeply"). Used as a noun, *affect* is a psychological term meaning *feeling* or *emotion.* *Effect* used as a verb means to *bring about* ("to effect the rescue of the trapped miners"); used as a noun, *effect* means *result* or *consequence* ("We were surprised at the effect of his words on his audience").

Aggravate. In formal English *aggravate* means *to make worse* or *more severe.* *Aggravate* in the sense of *to irritate* or *vex* is a colloquial expression appropriate only in very informal writing.

Ain't. A nonstandard contraction of *am not, are not, has not,* and *have not.*

Alibi. In formal usage *alibi* is a noun meaning "the plea or fact that an accused person was elsewhere than at the alleged scene of the offense with which he is charged." The use of *alibi* as a verb or as a vague noun meaning *excuse* or *explanation* is colloquial. "Their *excuse* [rather than *alibi*] was that they had a flat tire."

All right, alright. *All right* is the generally accepted spelling. *Alright* is now regarded as acceptable by some authorities but is labeled nonstandard by others. *The American Heritage Dictionary* calls *alright* "a common misspelling."

All together, altogether. *All together* means *united.* *Altogether* means *entirely.*

> The family will be all together this Christmas.
> The injured man was altogether helpless.

Allusion, illusion. An *allusion* is a reference: "The Commencement speaker made several allusions to our college traditions." An *illusion* is a false mental image or impression.

Almost, most. See *Most.*

Altho, tho, thru. These shortened forms of *although, though,* and *through,* despite some objection, are now accepted variant spellings.

Alumnus, alumni, alumna, alumnae. Latin forms kept in English and applied in strict usage to graduates of a school or college; loosely used, however, to refer to former students of a school or college.

> *Alumnus,* masculine singular; *alumni,* masculine plural.
> *Alumna,* feminine singular; *alumnae,* feminine plural.
> *Alumni* is used as a collective term for men and women graduates or former students.

It seems that there are two reasons for keeping the Latin words instead of using the English word *graduate:* (1) the Latin words carry the suggestion of group unity and loyalty to the institution and (2) they enable one to include all past students, whether or not the students are graduates.

Amount, number. *Amount* refers to mass or quantity—"an amount of money"; *number* refers to countable items—"a number of dollars," "a number of people."

And etc. See *Etc.*

Anyways. Nonstandard for *anyway.*

Anywheres, somewheres. Nonstandard for *anywhere, somewhere.*

As. Frequently used as a connective where *because, for, when, while, since* or some other more exact connective would convey the meaning more clearly.

> I knew that he was there, as I saw him enter the door.
> IMPROVED: I knew that he was there because I saw him enter the door.

As . . . as, so . . . as. In positive comparisons—"Mary is as tall as Helen"— *as . . . as* is the standard usage. In negative comparisons, either *as . . . as* or *so . . . as* is standard usage—"Mary is not so tall as Helen" or "Mary is not as tall as Helen"—and the choice is a matter of taste.

As, that. *As* is not an acceptable substitute for *that* in sentences like: "I don't know *that* [not *as*] he will be able to come."

As to, with respect to. Though these phrases are standard English, they sometimes lead a writer into wordiness or jargon.

> WORDY: He inquired *as to* when I would pay the bill.
> REVISED: He asked *when* . . .

> WORDY: She asked a number of questions *with respect to* his absence.
> REVISED: She asked a number of questions *about*. . .

As to (or *as for*) at the beginning of a sentence can serve to emphasize the noun or pronoun that follows: "*As to* [or *as for*] Harry, he was indifferent or unwilling to act."

Awful, awfully. *Awful* in the sense of "inspiring awe" and *awfully* meaning "in a way to inspire awe" are, of course, standard English. *Awful* in the sense of "bad," "ugly," or "disagreeable" is colloquial, and *awfully* in the sense of "very" or "extremely" is also colloquial. *Awful* used as an adverb ("He came awful close to losing") should be avoided in college writing except to represent speech.

Bad, badly. *Bad* is an adjective and *badly* is an adverb. Choice between the two words is usually easy except when a linking verb is used. Linking verbs (*appear, be, seem, become, feel, look, smell, taste, sound,* etc.) are followed by an adjective instead of an adverb, and hence *bad* and not *badly* is established usage in the sentences below.

> He looks bad.
> He feels bad. (The expression *feels badly* occurs frequently in colloquial usage.)
> The apple tastes bad.

Because. See **Reason is because.**

Being as, being that. Misused for *as, because,* or *since.*

> Because it was a hot day the men took off their coats. [Not—*Being as* it was a hot day]

Between, among. In general, *between* is used with two persons or things and *among* with more than two.

> He sat between the two captains.
> He was not among the winners.

But *between* is sometimes used for more than two:

> The voters found it hard to choose between the three candidates.

Broke. *Broke* in the sense of "lacking funds" is colloquial. *Broke* used as the past participle of *break* is nonstandard. "He has *broken* [not *broke*] his arm."

Bunch. In formal English, *bunch* refers to objects that are growing together or fastened together—"a bunch of grapes." Applied to people—"a bunch of sailors"—*bunch* is colloquial usage.

Can. See **May.**

Can't hardly. *Can't hardly* is colloquial for *can hardly* or *can scarcely:* "He can hardly [not *can't hardly*] speak English." *Can't hardly* frequently occurs in speech but is out of place in formal or informal writing.

Can't help but and **cannot help but.** Both of these expressions—"I can't [or cannot] help but be bored by his dull stories"—are established in American usage but are regarded as slovenly by some writers, who prefer "I can't [or cannot] help being bored."

Can't seem. *Can't seem* for *seem unable to*—"I can't seem to do this problem"—occurs in standard conversational English but is out of place in formal or high informal writing.

Case. *Case* is a much overworked word and is responsible for many wordy expressions. Students should not be afraid to use it, but they should avoid it when it is merely padding or when a more exact word is called for.

> UNSATISFACTORY: In the case of a word that is difficult to spell, students should consult a dictionary to be sure that they have the correct spelling.
> REVISED: To insure correct spelling of difficult words, students should consult the dictionary.

Complected. Although *Webster's Seventh New Collegiate* enters *complected* without restrictive label, other dictionaries describe it as dialectical or colloquial. In formal and high informal English *complexioned* is the accepted expression.

Considerable. Used as an adjective—"He had considerable respect for his employer"—*considerable* is standard English. *Considerable* used as an adverb—"He had considerable [instead of *considerably*] more money than his friend"—is nonstandard English.

Contact. Although *contact* as a verb meaning *get in touch with* is widely used in the language of business and advertising, many people object to it as commercial jargon. The expression is generally out of place in college writing. Sixty-six per cent of the Usage Panel of *The American Heritage Dictionary* found the verb not appropriate to formal contexts.

Contractions. Contractions (*don't, won't, he's, they're,* etc.) are appropriate in conversation and in writing that is personal and informal. In formal, and in most impersonal writing, they are out of place.

Could of. Nonstandard for *could have:* "He could have won." [Not—He *could of* won.]

Couple. Used colloquially in "He ate a couple of oranges." *Couple* in the sense of "married couple" or "young couple" is a usage not limited to colloquial expression.

Data. *Data,* the plural of the Latin *datum,* is used in current English as a collective noun and so may have a singular or a plural verb.

> This data is unconvincing.
> These data are not consistent.

The plural construction is more often used in formal writing.

Definitely. *Definitely* in the sense of *certainly* is a colloquial expression frequently overused by college students.

> Lincoln was *certainly* [in preference to *definitely*] a great president.

Different than. *Different from* ("My book is different from yours") is the more common usage, but *different than* is now regarded as acceptable. *Different to* is British usage.

Disinterested, uninterested. Careful speakers and writers keep the distinction between these two words. *Disinterested* means *impartial, unbiased, objective. Uninterested* means *indifferent, not interested. The American Heritage Dictionary* labels nonstandard the use of *disinterested* to mean *uninterested.*

Don't. *Don't* is properly used as a contraction for *do not:* "I don't, you don't, we don't, they don't." *Don't* used as a contraction for *does not* ("he don't, she don't, it don't") is nonstandard.

Due to. *Due to* in the sense of *because of, owing to,* is avoided by many careful writers. Most authorities on modern usage, however, take the view that though some people object to it, it should be accepted as established usage. *Webster's New World Dictionary* calls the usage colloquial, and says that *due to* is widely used in the sense of *because of* "despite objections by some grammarians."

> Due to the wreck, the train was late. [Debatable usage]
> Because of [or owing to] the wreck, the train was late. [Established formal usage]

Due as an adjective is unquestionably established usage: "The train is due at three o'clock."

Effect. See *Affect.*

Enthuse. This word is described as colloquial or informal in several dictionaries and is entered without restrictive label in *Webster's Seventh New Collegiate.* Although *enthuse* is in wide use, there is objection to it. In college writing it is better to say "He was enthusiastic about [or showed enthusiasm for] the production of *Hamlet*" rather than "He enthused over the production of *Hamlet.*"

Etc. An abbreviation of the Latin *et cetera,* meaning *and so forth. And etc.* is poor usage because the Latin expression already contains the *and. Etc.* is a useful expression when it saves the continued enumeration of the obvious: "Let *A* equal 1, *B* equal 2, *C* equal 3, etc." Sometimes, however, writers use it as a way of avoiding thought. The student who writes, "I came to college to prepare for medical school, to get an education, etc.," has given the reader no definite information by the use of *etc.,* and one suspects that he had nothing definite in mind. It is better to omit *etc.* when the expression is vague or meaningless.

Expect. Expect is colloquial in the sense of *suppose* or *suspect:*

> I expect [suppose] he had reasons for leaving early.
> I expect [suspect] that it was Frank who put the cat in the piano.

Farther, further. In *Current American Usage* Margaret M. Bryant concludes that "the two words are interchangeable in all uses, except that *further* is always used in the sense of 'more' or 'in addition,' as in '. . . as weapons to fight off *further* inquiry' . . . and 'They might be *further* astonished to learn . . . .' "

Fellow. Fellow used in the sense of *young man, boy, suitor* is colloquial usage, and is inappropriate in formal and high informal language.

Fewer, less. In formal English *fewer* refers only to countable things; *less* usually refers to extent, amount, or degree: "If there were fewer children in the neighborhood, there might be less noise."

Field of. The expression *in the field of* is often wordy. "I am majoring in the field of English" is a wordy way of saying "I am majoring in English" or "I am an English major."

Fine. In informal speech *fine* is often a convenient word. It is widely used in the loose sense of *good* or *admirable.* In writing, however, especially in formal writing, it is better to use a more exact word. *Fine* meaning *exact, precise* ("fine distinctions," "fine measurements") is of course appropriate in formal English.

Fix. In the following meanings *fix* is informal or colloquial:

> Repair: He will *fix* the clock.
> Predicament: He was in a peculiar *fix.*
> Arrange: She *fixed* her hair.
> Punish: I will *fix* him for overcharging me.
> Preparing or planning: He was *fixing* to leave early.

Foreign terms. Frequent use of foreign terms in writing or in speech is likely to be regarded as a mark of poor taste and poor manners rather than as a sign of learning. As a general rule it is best to use foreign terms only when there is no English equivalent and when the reader can be expected to understand them.

Get, got. The principal parts of *get* are *get, got, got* or *gotten.* Some people object to the use of *gotten,* but it is clear that both *gotten* and *got* as the past participle are now accepted in American usage.

Get or *got* meaning *to kill,* or *to irritate,* or *to understand,* or *to be obliged to* is colloquial usage, near the level of slang.

Get across as in "to get across an idea" is at best a colloquial expression.

Good, well. *Good* is properly used as an adjective, not an adverb. Expressions in which it is used as an adverb ("He runs good") are at best colloquial. *Well* is an adjective or an adverb.

> The child is good. [*Good* is an adjective.]
> The child is well. [*Well* is an adjective.]
> That apple looks good. [*Good* is an adjective following the linking verb *look.*]
> He runs well. [*Well* is an adverb modifying *runs.*]

Had of. The *of* is superfluous.

> I wish I had [not *had of*] gone.

Had ought, hadn't ought. Inappropriate in written English:

> He *had ought* to go. [*should* or *ought to* go]
> Deborah *hadn't ought* to have done it. [*shouldn't have* or *ought not to have* done it]

Hanged, hung. In formal usage a man is *hanged* and a nonhuman object is *hung:* "He hanged himself with the rope on which his wife had hung the clothes." The principal parts of *hang* in the first sense are *hang, hanged, hanged;* the principal parts of *hang* in the second sense are *hang, hung, hung.* In informal usage, *hang, hung, hung,* is commonly used for any kind of hanging.

Have got. In many uses *got* is superfluous.

FORMAL AND HIGH-LEVEL INFORMAL: I have to be there at five.
COLLOQUIAL: I have got [or, more commonly, I've got] to be there at five.

Healthy, healthful. These two words are now used without fine distinction in informal English. It seems unfortunate, however, to lose the distinction between *healthy*, meaning *in good health*, and *healthful*, meaning *conducive to health*.

Hopefully. *Hopefully* in the sense of *it is to be hoped* or *let us hope* is widely used but is regarded as unacceptable by many authorities. It is better to write *We hope to be home by midnight* rather than "Hopefully, we will be home by midnight."

Human. Human used as a noun ("Humans live longer than dogs") is standard usage. In earlier usage, *human* was an adjective in formal English ("To err is human"), and *human being* was generally used when the noun form was called for.

Imply, infer. To *imply* is to suggest without stating directly; to *infer* is to draw a conclusion, to make an inference, from what someone else has said, or from observed data.

> In talking to his daughter the father implied that she was spending too much money. The daughter inferred from her father's words that he would be opposed to her buying a new evening gown.

There has been some tendency in recent years to blur the useful distinction made by these two words, and to use *infer* to mean both *infer* and *imply*. College students should make the distinction.

In back of. *In back of* is informal; in formal English, *behind* is used.

INFORMAL: The tree *in back of* the house . . . .
FORMAL: The tree *behind* the house . . . .

In regard(s) to. *In regards to* is nonstandard for *in regard to*. The expression *in regard to* is often a wordy substitute for *about* or *concerning*.

WORDY: What have you done *in regard to* the shortage of paper?
IMPROVED: What have you done *about* the shortage of paper?

Irregardless. A nonstandard expression meaning *regardless*.

She will go, *regardless* [not *irregardless*] of the weather.

Its, it's. *Its* is the possessive of *it* ("The tree lost *its* leaves") and is spelled without an apostrophe; *it's* is a contraction of *it is* or *it has*.

It's me. Most authorities on present usage regard *It's me* as an acceptable substitute for the formal and often unnatural *It is I* or *It's I*. *It's him* and *It's her*, however, are not acceptable usage.

Kind, this, these. Formal English requires the use of *this kind, that kind, these kinds, those kinds.* The expressions *these kind* ("I like these kind of oranges") and *those kind* ("He buys those kind of shoes") are colloquial and best avoided in writing, even though good writers do occasionally slip into them.

Kind of, sort of. Colloquial for *somewhat* or *rather:* "I am kind of tired today." *Kind of* and *sort of* in this sense are fairly common in speech, but should be avoided in formal or high informal writing.

Lady, woman. Every lady is a woman, but is every woman a lady? *Landlady, Lady . . .* (the wife of a lord), First *Lady* (the wife of the President) are clearly established usages, and the custom of addressing an audience of women as "ladies," or a mixed audience as "ladies and gentlemen," also is well established. A woman in the professions or the arts is referred to as a *woman* (not *lady*) doctor, lawyer, novelist, painter, etc.

The choice between *woman* and *lady* sometimes calls for tact as well as knowledge of usage, but unless there are special considerations, it seems reasonable to use *woman* as the general term for an adult female and to reserve *lady* for special circumstances and connotations. "Mrs. Roosevelt was an admirable *woman* and a charming *lady.*" This principle would suggest the use of *salesgirl* or *saleswoman* rather than *saleslady,* and *cleaning woman* rather than *cleaning lady.*

Lay, lie. *Lay,* a transitive verb meaning *place,* takes an object: "Lay the book on the table." *Lie,* an intransitive verb, does not take an object: "He likes to lie in the sun." The principal parts of *lie* are *lie, lay, lain.* The principal parts of *lay* are *lay, laid, laid.*

Lead, led. The principal parts of the verb *lead* are *lead, led, led.* Note that the past tense is spelled *led:* "He led the man across the street."

Learn, teach. *Learn* in the sense of *to impart knowledge, to teach,* is nonstandard: "I studied with him for a year, but he never *taught* [not *learned*] me anything." The principal parts of *learn* are *learn; learned* or *learnt; learned* or *learnt.*

Leave, let. The verb *leave* in the sense of *let* or *allow* is nonstandard: "*Let* [not *leave*] him go if he wants to."

Lend, loan. In earlier formal English, *lend* was a verb; *loan* was the noun: One *lends* money or one asks for a *loan.* There is considerable authority now for *loan* as a verb, but many careful writers still prefer *lend. The College Standard Dictionary* says that *loan* as a verb is standard English, especially business English, in the United States but not in England.

Less. See ***Fewer.***

Liable, likely. *Liable* implies exposure or susceptibility to something unpleasant. *Likely* can be used when either favorable or unfavorable consequences are to be expected.

> A child who plays with fire is *liable* to be burned. [*Likely* could also be used here.]
>
> He is *likely* to be his father's heir. [*Liable* would be inappropriate unless being the heir is considered unpleasant.]

Like, as. Although the use of *like* as a substitute for *as* or *as if* is now very common, careful users of English avoid it, especially in formal English.

> Do *as* I do. [Not—Do *like* I do.]
>
> He acted *as if* he wanted to escape. [Not—He acted *like* he wanted to escape.]

The American Heritage Dictionary labels nonstandard the use of *like* as a conjunction in such sentences, and *The Standard College Dictionary* says that in formal American English *like* is not considered acceptable as a conjunction.

Like to, almost. *Like to* in such expressions as "I *liked to* killed myself riding that horse" is a regionalism. In standard English, *almost* or *nearly* should be used.

Line, along the line of. The expression *along the line of* frequently produces wordiness. "Next summer I expect to do work along the line of salesmanship" is a wordy way of saying "I expect to work as a salesman next summer."

Locate, settle. *Locate* is colloquial in the sense of *settle, take up residence.*

> The family *located* [i.e., *settled*] in Iowa.

Loose, lose. *Loose* as an adjective means *unattached;* to *lose* is to *suffer loss.*

> A man with a *loose* belt may *lose* his trousers.

Lots of, a lot of. Colloquial for *many, much, a large amount. A lot* is written as two words.

Mad. Colloquial American usage in the sense of *angry.*

> Dennis knew his family would be *mad* [i.e., *angry*] when they found out he was on probation.

Majority. Properly used in such expressions as: "the majority party," "received a majority of the votes" [i.e., more than half the total], "reached his majority [full legal age] at the age of twenty-one." College students tend to overuse or misuse the word in sentences like:

> The *majority* [*most*] of the campers dislike beans. [*Majority* is a heavy word here.]

A *majority* [*most*] of the lake front has now been sold.

May, can. The important difference between *may* and *can* is that in formal language *may* is used *to request* or *to give permission,* and *can* is used *to express ability to act.*

> May I have this dance?
> Can I find your name in the telephone book?

Mighty. Colloquial as a substitute for *very:* "I am *mighty* [i.e., *very*] sorry I am late."

Most, almost. In colloquial English *most* is sometimes used in the sense of *almost:* "He was ready to drink with *most* [*almost*] anyone." In formal and high informal English, *almost* is the accepted expression.

Muchly. Nonstandard for *much:* "Your *much* [not *muchly*] valued letter arrived today."

Myself. In strict usage *myself* is a reflexive pronoun ("I cut *myself*") or an intensive pronoun ("I *myself* am unable to go, but I shall send a representative"). It is accepted usage to limit *myself* to these two uses in writing. In familiar conversation, however, cultivated people sometimes use *myself* where strict usage would call for *I* or *me:* "The news was quite a shock to Father and Mother and *myself.*"

Nice. In conversation, *nice,* used to indicate general approval, often serves as a convenient expression when a more exact word does not readily come to mind. In writing, when one has time to choose words carefully, more exact words than *nice* are usually preferable. "He is nice" gives less definite information than "He is well mannered" or "He is friendly" or "He is interested in students and easy to talk to." Words like *nice* and *fine* are so general in meaning that they often blur communication.

None. *None* may be either singular or plural.

> None of us is [*or* are] willing to go.

No one. No one is sometimes mistakenly written as a single word, perhaps because it is confused with *none.* It should be written as two words, and it is followed by a singular verb.

Nowhere(s) near. *Nowhere near* is standard English, but *not nearly* is the preferred expression in formal use. *Nowheres near* is nonstandard. "He is *nowhere near* [*or not nearly*] as old as his wife."

Number. See **Amount.**

Of, have. *Of* as a substitute for *have* in such expressions as *could have, would have, might have* is nonstandard usage. "He would *have* [not *of*] come if we had asked him."

Off from, off of. *From* and *of* are superfluous.

> He stepped *off* the platform.

On account of. The use of *on account of* to mean *because* is a regional colloquialism, out of place in standard English. "He was unpopular *because* [not *on account of*] he was stingy."

One. Authorities on usage once insisted that the pronoun *one* should not be followed by *he* or *his* but should be followed by *one*.

> One should choose *one's* [not *his*] words with care.
> When one is asked what *one* [not *he*] thinks, *one* [not *he*] should give an honest answer.

In present-day usage, however, the use of *one . . . he* [or *his*] is in good standing; often the use of *one . . . one* [or *one's*] requires a frequent repetition of *one* and suggests affectation; in such cases it is preferable to use *one . . . he* [or *his*].

Or. When *or* is used to join two or more subjects, the general rule is that the verb is plural if the subjects are plural ("Axes or saws are used to cut the logs") and singular if the subjects are singular ("An axe or a saw is used to cut the logs"). If some of the subjects are plural and some are singular, the verb agrees with the subject nearest it: "A tractor or several horses are used to pull the machine"—"Several horses or a tractor is used to pull the machine."

This last sentence follows the rule, but sounds awkward. It is best to revise such sentences or to rearrange them so that the plural subject is nearest the verb. For a fuller consideration of the use of *or* see "Or" in Margaret Nicholson's *Dictionary of American-English Usage*.

Outside of. Colloquial when used to mean *except for, besides,* or *other than.* "*Except for* [or, colloquial, *outside of*] Gerald, no one in the group knew the words of the song."

Outside of sometimes produces awkward or ambiguous sentences like the following:

> *Outside of* her long nose, her features were good.
> *Outside of* the dirty window, the room looked clean.

Per. Except in technical and commercial writing, *a* or *an* is generally preferable to *per* in such expressions as *per day, per week, per hour.* "His father earned fifteen dollars *a* [rather than *per*] day."

Plenty. *Plenty* used as an adverb meaning *very* (*plenty* cold, *plenty* angry) is colloquial and is often vague in meaning. A reader may wonder whether *plenty tired* means *exhausted,* or *very tired,* or *tired enough to sleep,* or *comfortably tired.*

Preposition at the end of a sentence. There is no recognized rule of usage that forbids placing a preposition at the end of a sentence; in fact, idiomatic and direct English sometimes requires that the preposition come at the end. Students can concentrate on writing clear, emphatic, rhythmical sentences and can let the prepositions fall where they may.

Principal, principle. These two words are frequently confused. *Principal* is most commonly used as an adjective meaning chief, or first in rank ("the principal difficulty"), or as a noun meaning one who has a chief or leading position ("the principal of the school"—"the principals in the play"). *Principle* means a fundamental truth, law, or rule of conduct ("the principle of relativity"—"a man of principle").

Proposition. *Proposition* has many meanings. No one questions its use as a more-or-less technical term in mathematics, logic, and grammar, but *Webster's New World Dictionary* labels the following uses as colloquial: an indecent or immoral proposal; a project, business undertaking; a person, problem, undertaking, etc. to be dealt with. In many of its popular uses, *proposition* is a vague word that can well be replaced by a more specific word such as *proposal, plan, scheme, offer, suggestion, project.*

Provided, providing. Both expressions are standard equivalents to *on the condition that; provided* seems to be more frequently used.

I will go *provided* [or *providing*] you go with me.

Often the use of *if* will produce a less heavy sentence: "I will go *if* you will come too."

Quite a. Colloquial usage in such expressions as *quite a few, quite a number, quite a while.* The equivalent expressions *many, a large number, for a long time* are, of course, established usages.

Quote. *Quote* as a noun for *quotation* or *quotation mark* is informal usage. Eighty-five per cent of the Usage Panel of *The American Heritage Dictionary* found it unacceptable in writing. *Webster's New World Dictionary* marks it colloquial.

Real. In formal and high informal English, *real* used as an adverb in the sense of *very* is not acceptable.

He was very [not *real*] tired.

Reason . . . is because. Margaret M. Bryant (*Current American Usage,* pages 170–171) gives evidence that *the reason . . . is because* is used in formal English, though less frequently than *the reason . . . is that.* College students should know that some people object to *the reason . . . is because,* especially in formal writing, and that there is no similar objection to *the reason . . . is that.* "*The reason* for my failing the course is *that* [or *because*] I spent so much time on my other subjects." Another and shorter way to express the same idea is: "I failed the course because I spent so much time on my other subjects."

Right. Right in the sense of *very*—"That tasted *right* good," "She was *right* tired"—is dialectal or colloquial except in such titles as "The Right Reverend . . ." or "The Right Honorable . . ."

Seem. See *Can't seem.*

Set, sit. *Set* is a transitive verb and so takes an object: "He set the vase on the table." The principal parts of *set* are *set, set, set. Sit* is an intransitive verb and so does not take an object: "He often sits before the fire." The principal parts of *sit* are *sit, sat, sat.* An exception to the rule is the use of *set* in reference to fowls and the hatching of eggs, where *set* is used as an intransitive verb: "The hen is setting." Another exception is the use of *set* in "The sun is setting."

Shall, will. In formal usage, many careful writers still try to preserve some of the distinctions between *shall* and *will,* and *should* and *would.* In informal English there is a growing tendency to use *will* in place of the more formal *shall,* and *would* in place of the more formal *should.* For a fuller discussion, see page 393.

Should, would. See page 393.

Should of. *Should of* is sometimes misused for *should have.*

He should have [not *should of*] answered my letter sooner.

So. Careless or inexperienced writers tend to overuse *so* in joining two independent clauses, and also to use *so* in contexts where *so that* or *and so* is needed to make the meaning immediately clear. *So that* indicates purpose ("He is saving money so that he can marry in the fall"); *and so* indicates result: "He has saved money and so he will be married this fall." The use of *so* as an intensive ("She was so tired" or "She was so angry") is more appropriate in conversation than in writing. Many students can improve their writing by scrutinizing their use of *so* and by substituting a more exact or a more complete expression whenever it is needed. This treatment of *so* is not intended to induce students to avoid the word; it simply recommends discrimination.

Some. In the following sentences *some* is colloquial usage:

He felt *some* [instead of *somewhat*] better after the game.
That was *some* [i.e., *an extraordinarily good* or *bad*] fight!

Somewheres. Nonstandard for *somewhere.*

Sort of. See *Kind of.*

Split infinitive. See page 384.

Sure. In formal and high informal usage, *sure* is an adjective and is not properly used as an adverb.

> He surely [not *sure*] knows what he wants.

Swell. Slang in such expressions as *swell party, swell meal.*

Take and. Nonstandard in such expressions as "I'll *take and* write him [I'll write him] a check" or "He *took and* threw [He threw] the television set out the window."

These kind. See *Kind.*

Teach. See *Learn.*

This here, that there. *This here book* or *that there book* is nonstandard for *this book* or *that book.*

Tho. See *Altho.*

Thru. See *Altho.*

Thusly. Not a standard word; use *thus.*

Too, very. Expressions like "He is not too handsome" and "She isn't too eager to go" are slang and are not appropriate in serious writing. Usually in such expressions *very* should be used in the place of *too,* or the expression should be revised to make the meaning more exact.

Till, until. There is no difference in factual meaning between the connectives *till* and *until,* and both are established as good usage.

Try and. Colloquial usage for *try to,* and more appropriate in speech than in writing: "Try and come to see us this weekend" is colloquial for "Try to come to see us this weekend."

Type, type of. In popular speech, expressions like "That *type* [for *type of*] man is dangerous" and "I need a better *type* [for *type of*] paint" are frequently used; in writing, *type of* is the standard expression.

Unique. *The Standard College Dictionary* notes that *unique* is used loosely to mean *unusual, rare,* or *notable.* Since, however, *unique* in formal usage means "being the only one of its kind," it is better to avoid modifying it with words that express degree or intensity. Examples of undesirable usage are *very unique, rather unique,* and *the most unique.* Words like *unusual, rare,* or *remarkable* often are more exact than *unique* in expressing the writer's meaning.

Used to could. Nonstandard for *used to be able to* or *once could.*

> He *used to be able to* [not *used to could*] shoot better than any of us.
> I wish I could swim as well as I *once could* [not *used to could*].

Used to, use to. In writing, *use to* is a nonstandard variant of *used to;* in speech, the two expressions sound the same. "He *used to* [not *use to*] work in the bank."

Want. *Want* for *had better* or *ought* is colloquial: "You want to [had better] come in before it rains." *Want in* and *want out* are, at best, colloquial for *want to come in* and *want to get out.* "Open the door; I *want to come* [not *want*] *in.*"

Way. *Way* for *away* is colloquial: "way over there among the trees" for "away over there among the trees."

Well. See **Good.**

Where . . . at. In sentences like "He doesn't know *where* he is *at,*" the *at* is redundant and should be omitted.

Who, whom. In formal English, *who* is subjective, *whom* objective: "Who is going?" "Whom shall we ask?" Many students of usage now defend the use of *who* in informal English in a sentence like the last one: "Who shall we ask?"

Whose, who's. *Whose* is the possessive form of *who* ("I don't know whose hat that is"); *who's* is a contracted form of *who is* ("I don't know who's coming tonight").

Will, shall. See **Shall, will,** page 500.

-wise. The suffix *wise* occurs in established English words like *otherwise, clockwise,* and *sidewise.* Indiscriminate use of *wise* to form new compounds should, however, be avoided; *moneywise* and *programwise* and *datewise,* for example, are awkward jargon.

You. *You* is often used in speech and in informal writing as an indefinite pronoun in place of *anyone, one, a person,* but such usage is not appropriate in formal writing. In a sentence like "When you are in prison you are sorry that you broke the law" the use of *you* is incongruous; it is advisable to express the idea in another way.

Your, you're. *Your* is the possessive form of *you; you're* is a contraction of *you are:* "You're going to enjoy your English course in college."

HANDBOOK

Section 8

A NOTE
ON PLAGIARISM

Plagiarism is the dishonest use of the work of others.

Few students in composition courses plagiarize deliberately; that is, few copy, with conscious dishonesty, another student's theme, or a passage from a book or magazine. But a number of students, feeling the pressure of regular writing assignments and actually confused about the legitimate use of materials, may be tempted to "borrow" sentences and patterns of ideas, or to "get help" on a theme, unless the whole concept of plagiarism is clarified for them. It is the purpose of this note to make clear what plagiarism is and how it can be avoided.

Plagiarism means presenting, *as one's own*, the words, the work, or the opinions of someone else. It is dishonest, since the plagiarist offers as his own, for credit, the language, or information, or thought for which he deserves no credit. It is unintelligent, since it defeats the purpose of the course—improvement of the student's own powers of thinking and communication. It is also dangerous, since penalties for plagiarism are severe; they commonly range from failure on the paper to failure in the course; in some institutions the penalty is dismissal from college.

Plagiarism occurs when one uses the exact language of someone else without putting the quoted material in quotation marks and giving its source. (Exceptions are very well-known quotations, from the Bible or Shakespeare, for example.) In formal papers, the source is acknowledged in a footnote; in informal papers, it may be put in parentheses, or made a part of the text: "Norman Cousins says . . . ." This first type of plagiarism, using without acknowledgment the language of someone else, is easy to understand and to avoid: *when a writer uses the exact words of another writer, or speaker, he must put those words in quotation marks and give their source.*

A second type of plagiarism is more complex. It occurs when the writer presents, as his own, *the sequence of ideas, the arrangement of material, the pattern of thought* of someone else, even though he expresses it in his own words. The language may be his, but he is presenting as the work of his brain, and taking credit for, the work of another's brain. He is, therefore, guilty of plagiarism if he fails to give credit to the original author of the pattern of ideas.

This aspect of plagiarism presents difficulties because the line is sometimes unclear between borrowed thinking and thinking that is our own. We all absorb information and ideas from other people. In this way we learn. But in the normal process of learning, new ideas are digested; they enter our minds and are associated and integrated with ideas already there; when they come out again, their original pattern is broken; they are re-formed and re-arranged. We have made them our own. Plagiarism occurs when a sequence of ideas is transferred from a source to a paper without the process of digestion, integration, and reordering in the writer's mind, and without acknowledgment in the paper.

Students writing informal themes, in which they are usually asked to draw on their own experience and information, can guard against plagiarism by a simple test. They should be able honestly to answer *No* to the following questions:

1. Have I read anything in preparation for writing this paper?
2. Am I deliberately recalling any particular source of information as I write this paper?
3. Am I consulting any source as I write this paper?

If the answer to these questions is *No,* the writer need have no fear of using sources dishonestly. The material in his mind, which he will transfer to his written page, is genuinely digested and his own.

The writing of a research paper presents a somewhat different problem, for here the student is expected to gather material from books and articles read for the purpose of writing the paper. In the careful research paper, however (and this is true of term papers in all college courses), credit is given in footnotes for every idea, conclusion, or piece of information which is not the writer's own; and the writer is careful not to follow closely the wording of the sources he has read. If he wishes to quote, he puts the passage in quotation marks and gives credit to the author in a footnote; but he writes the bulk of the paper in his own words and his own style, using footnotes to acknowledge the facts and ideas he has taken from his reading. Fuller information on the use of sources in research papers and other term papers is given in Chapter 14: The Research Paper.

INDEX

Sentence outline, 477–479

Sentences: "and-and," 106; basic patterns of, 99–100; beginning and end of, 146–149; choppy, 106; climax in, 147–149; complete, incomplete, and fragmentary, 404–405; defined, 404; economy in, 116–123; embedded, 102–103; emphasis in, 143–150; faulty relationships of elements of, 413–417; fragmentary, 404–405; functions of words in, 366 ff.; fused, 407–409; incomplete, 405; loose and periodic, 139, 147–149; normal and inverted order, 99–100, 146–147; periodic and loose, 139, 147–149; run-together, 407–409; simple, complex, compound, and compound-complex, 403; structure of, 98 ff.; topic, 165–166; unity in, 428–429; variety in, 137–142

set, sit, 500

Setting, 299; *see also* Description

settle, see *locate, settle,* 496

Shakespeare, William, quoted, 7–8, 118, 160–161

shall and *will,* 393–394, 500

Shifts: *see* Inconsistency, 108–110; in paragraphs, 170

Shoptalk, 60–61

should and *would,* 393–394

should of, 500

Simile, 131, 423

Simple narratives, 301–305

Simple sentence, 403

sit, set, 500

Slang, 60–61

Slanting, 26 ff.; by charged words, 32–33; by emphasis, 28–29; by selection of facts, 29–32; defined, 28

Smathers, Senator, quoted, 47

Smith, F. H., quoted, 185

so (usage), 500

so . . . as, see *as . . . as, so . . . as,* 488

Socrates, quoted, 54

some, 500

somewheres, 500

Sorensen, Theodore C., quoted, 178

sort of, see *kind of, sort of,* 495

Speech, figures of, defined, 422–423; *see also* Figurative language

Spelling, 454–466; lists of commonly misspelled words, 458–464; Pollock report on, 457 ff.; rules, 456–457; test, 464–466

Split infinitive, 384–385

Stafford, Jean, quoted, 299–300

Stagefright in public speaking, 244

Standard College Dictionary, The, quoted, 481

Standard English, 61–67

Statement of purpose, 83–84

Steffens, Lincoln, quoted, 65, 140–141

Steinbeck, John, quoted, 73, 193, 294, 299, 409

Stevenson, Adlai E., quoted, 153–154, 154, 183, 188, 240–241

Stevenson, Robert Louis, "Requiem," 17; quoted, 72–73, 133, 138–139

Structure: of paragraphs, 164–187; of sentences, 98–110

Student writing, samples of: informative themes, 91–97; research paper, 339 ff.

Style, 115 ff., 418–430; *see also* Language, Meaning, Sentences, Tone, Words; adjusting to audience, 259–263; appositives, 104–105, 120, 139; appropriateness, 58–71; balance, 100; climactic arrangement, 147–149; concreteness, 127–137; consistency, 108–110; cutting clauses, 119–121; defined, 115–116; economy and conciseness, 116–123; effective repetition, 149–150; emphasis, 143–150; exact words, 121–127; figurative language, 131–133, 422–423; fogginess or gap in expression, 88–89; formal, 61–65; heavy or incongruous connectives, 401; heavy words, 68; in informative writing, 259–263; in persuasion, 285–287; in public speaking, 240–242; in research papers, 333–335; informal, 62, 65–66; inverted and normal order, 99–100, 146–147; originality, 123–124; overuse of adjectives and adverbs, 397; parallelism, 100–102, 120–121; personal and impersonal, 61, 62, 259–263; subordination, 105–108, 119–121, 143; triteness, 123–124; variety, 137–142

Subject, delayed, 117, 146

Subject card, 316–317

Subjective complement, 381, 396–397

Subjects for student writing, 264–265, 270, 290–291, 300, 307–308; for autobiographies and simple narratives, 302–303; for informal themes, 79–81; for research papers, 312–313; limitation of, 82, 252, 311–312

Subjunctive mood, uses of, 390

Subordinate clause, 402–403

Subordinating conjunctions, 399–400